KERUX COMMENTARIES

LEVITICUS

———

KERUX COMMENTARIES

LEVITICUS

A Commentary for Biblical Preaching and Teaching

MICHAEL A. HARBIN

MARK C. BIEHL

Leviticus: A Commentary for Biblical Preaching and Teaching

© 2024 by Michael A. Harbin and Mark C. Biehl

Published by Kregel Ministry, an imprint of Kregel Publications, 2450 Oak Industrial Dr. NE, Grand Rapids, MI 49505-6020.

All rights reserved. No part of this book may be reproduced, stored in a retrieval system, or transmitted in any form or by any means—electronic, mechanical, photocopy, recording, or otherwise—without written permission of the publisher, except for brief quotations in printed reviews.

Unless otherwise indicated, the translations of the Scripture portions used throughout the commentary are the authors' own English rendering of the original biblical languages.

Scripture quotations marked ESV are taken from The Holy Bible, English Standard Version. Copyright © 2001 by Crossway Bibles, a publishing ministry of Good News Publishers. Used by permission. All rights reserved. May not copy or download more than 500 consecutive verses of the ESV Bible or more than one half of any book of the ESV Bible.

Scripture quotations marked HCSB are from the Holman Christian Standard Bible®. Copyright © 1999, 2000, 2002, 2003 by Holman Bible Publishers. Used by permission.

Scripture quotations marked KJV are from the King James Version.

Scripture quotations marked NASB are taken from the New American Standard Bible® (NASB), copyright © 1960, 1962, 1963, 1968, 1971, 1972, 1973, 1975, 1977, 1995, 2020 by The Lockman Foundation. Used by permission. www.Lockman.org

Scripture quotations marked NEB are from The New English Bible. Copyright © 1961, 1970 Oxford University Press and Cambridge University Press. All rights reserved.

Scripture quotations marked NET are from the NET Bible® copyright ©1996–2006 by Biblical Studies Press, LLC (www.bible.org). Scripture quoted by permission. All rights reserved.

Scripture quotations marked NLT are taken from the *Holy Bible*, New Living Translation, copyright © 1996, 2004, 2015 by Tyndale House Foundation. Used by permission of Tyndale House Publishers, Inc., Carol Stream, Illinois 60188. All rights reserved.

Scripture quotations marked NIV are taken from the Holy Bible, New International Version®, NIV®. Copyright © 1973, 1978, 1984, 2011 by Biblica, Inc.™ Used by permission of Zondervan. All rights reserved worldwide. www.zondervan.com

Scripture quotations marked NJB are from The New Jerusalem Bible. Biblical text copyright © 1985 by Darton, Longman and Todd Ltd and Doubleday, a division of Random House, Inc. All rights reserved.

Scripture quotations marked NRSV are from the New Revised Standard Version Bible, copyright © 1989 by the National Council of the Churches of Christ in the U.S.A. Used by permission. All rights reserved.

Scripture quotations marked RSV are from the Revised Standard Version of the Bible, copyright © 1946, 1952, and 1971 by the National Council of the Churches of Christ in the U.S.A. Used by permission. All rights reserved.

Italics in Scripture quotations indicate emphasis added by the authors.

The Hebrew font, NewJerusalemU, and the Greek font, GraecaU, are available from www.linguistsoftware.com/lgku.htm, +1-425-775-1130.

Unless noted otherwise, all photos and other illustrations are by Michael A. Harbin.

Figure 21: Broad fat tail sheep. By Shi Zhao, Beijing, China, DSC_1845, CC BY-SA 2.0, https://commons.wikimedia.org

Figure 22: Long fat tail sheep. ICAR Central Wool & Sheep Research Institute, Rajasthan, India. http://www.cswri.res.in

Figure 30: High Priest in Robes. Illustrators of the 1890 Holman Bible, Public domain, via Wikimedia Commons.

Figure 34: High Priest Sacrificing a Goat. By illustrator of Henry Davenport Northrop, *Treasures of the Bible*, 1894. Public Domain, https://commons.wikimedia.org

Figure 37: Two Priests Are Destroyed. By James Tissot, Public domain, https://commons.wikimedia.org

Figure 50: White catfish. Photo by Raver Duane, USFWS on Pixnio, public domain.

Figure 52: Humpback whale. https://www.publicdomainpictures.net

Figure 54: Cooked lobster. https://www.publicdomainpictures.net

Figure 55: Fire shrimp. www.aquarium.co.za. Public domain.

Figure 60: New moon. Photo by NASA.

Library of Congress Cataloging-in-Publication Data

Names: Harbin, Michael A., author. | Biehl, Mark C., 1960– author.

Title: Leviticus : a commentary for biblical preaching and teaching /
   Michael A. Harbin, Mark C. Biehl.

Description: First edition. | Grand Rapids, MI : Kregel Ministry, [2024] |
   Series: Kerux commentaries | Includes bibliographical references.

Identifiers: LCCN 2024010813

Subjects: LCSH: Bible. Leviticus—Commentaries.

Classification: LCC BS1255.53 .H369 2024 | DDC 222/.1307—dc23/eng/20240423

LC record available at https://lccn.loc.gov/2024010813

ISBN 978-0-8254-2552-3

Printed in China

24 25 26 27 28 / 5 4 3 2 1

Contents

Publisher's Preface to the Series / 7

Preface to Leviticus / 9

Exegetical Author's Acknowledgments / 10

Preaching Author's Acknowledgments / 12

Overview of All Preaching Passages / 13

Abbreviations / 27

Introduction to Leviticus / 31

PART 1: GUIDELINES FOR PERSONAL AND CORPORATE WORSHIP OF A HOLY GOD (1:1–10:20)

Worshipping a Holy God (1:1–3:17) / 87

Purifying Oneself Before a Holy God (4:1–6:7 [HB 5:26]) / 119

The Role of the Priests (6:8 [HB 6:1]–7:38) / 137

Inauguration of Ancient Israelite Religion (8:1–9:24) / 157

Standing Before a Holy God (10:1–20) / 183

PART 2: GUIDELINES FOR DEVELOPING AND PRESERVING A HOLY NATION (11:1–27:34)

Quality of Worship (11:1–15:33) / 195

The Day of Atonement (16:1–34) / 221

Life and Blood (17:1–16) / 239

Preserving the Social Fabric (18:1–20:27) / 255

A Holy Priesthood for a Holy Nation (21:1–22:33) / 293

Strengthening the Social Fabric (23:1–24:9) / 313

Repairing a Social Snag (24:10–23) / 345

Preventing Social Unraveling, Part 1 (25:1–22) / 359

Preventing Social Unraveling, Part 2 (25:23–55) / 371

Alternative Outcomes for the Community of God (26:1–46) / 387

Vows and Values (27:1–34) / 405

APPENDIXES

Appendix 1: Molech / 421

Appendix 2: Gleaning—A Case Study in Ruth / 423

Appendix 3: *Ḥerem* / 427

Appendix 4: Slaves and Emancipation in Israel / 431

Appendix 5: The Year of Jubilee / 435

Appendix 6: Land Measurement and Crop Value / 441

Appendix 7: Vows and Nazirites / 445

References / 449

PUBLISHER'S PREFACE TO THE SERIES

Since words were first uttered, people have struggled to understand one another and to know the main meaning in any verbal exchange.

The answer to what God is talking about must be understood in every context and generation; that is why Kerux (KAY-rukes) emphasizes text-based truths and bridges from the context of the original hearers and readers to the twenty-first-century world. Kerux values the message of the text, thus its name taken from the Greek *kērux*, a messenger or herald who announced the proclamations of a ruler or magistrate.

Biblical authors trumpeted all kinds of important messages in very specific situations, but a big biblical idea, grasped in its original setting and place, can transcend time. This specific, big biblical idea taken from the biblical passage embodies a single concept that transcends time and bridges the gap between the author's contemporary context and the reader's world. How do the prophets perceive the writings of Moses? How does the writer of Hebrews make sense of the Old Testament? How does Clement in his second epistle, which may be the earliest sermon known outside the New Testament, adapt verses from Isaiah and also ones from the Gospels? Or what about Luther's bold use of Romans 1:17? How does Jonathan Edwards allude to Genesis 19? Who can forget Martin Luther King Jr.'s "I Have a Dream" speech and his appropriation of Amos 5:24: "No, no, we are not satisfied, and we will not be satisfied until 'justice rolls down like waters, and righteousness like a mighty stream'"? How does a preacher in your local church today apply the words of Hosea in a meaningful and life-transforming way?

WHAT IS PRIME IN GOD'S MIND, AND HOW IS THAT EXPRESSED TO A GIVEN GENERATION IN THE UNITS OF THOUGHT THROUGHOUT THE BIBLE?

Answering those questions is what Kerux authors do. Based on the popular "big idea" preaching model, Kerux commentaries uniquely combine the insights of experienced Bible exegetes (trained in interpretation) and homileticians (trained in preaching). Their collaboration provides for every Bible book:

- A detailed introduction and outline
- A summary of all preaching sections with their primary exegetical, theological, and preaching ideas
- Preaching pointers that join the original context with the contemporary one
- Insights from the Hebrew and Greek text
- A thorough exposition of the text
- Sidebars of pertinent information for further background
- Appropriate charts and photographs
- A theological focus to passages

Publisher's Preface to the Series

- A contemporary big idea for every preaching unit
- Present-day meaning, validity, and application of a main idea
- Creative presentations for each primary idea
- Key questions about the text for study groups

Many thanks to Jim Weaver, Kregel's former acquisitions editor, who conceived of this commentary series and further developed it with the team of Jeffrey D. Arthurs, Robert B. Chisholm, David M. Howard Jr., Darrell L. Bock, Roy E. Ciampa, and Michael J. Wilkins. We also recognize with gratitude the significant contributions of Dennis Hillman, Fred Mabie, Paul Hillman, Herbert W. Bateman IV, and Shawn Vander Lugt who have been instrumental in the development of the series. Finally, gratitude is extended to the two authors for each Kerux volume; the outside reviewers, editors, and proofreaders; and Kregel staff who suggested numerous improvements.

—Kregel Publications

PREFACE TO LEVITICUS

Leviticus describes the transition of Israel from that unruly mob that left Egypt to a fledgling nation. After God had extracted a mixed group of slaves (predominantly descendants of Abraham) from Pharaoh's oppression "with a mighty hand" (Deut. 7:8) and brought them to Sinai, he provided the nation's foundational documents that are collected in the OT books of Genesis, Exodus, Leviticus, and the first part of Numbers. These documents became the core of a socioeconomic-judicial-po-litical-religious system designed not only to govern Israel, but to transform it into a kingdom of priests who would mediate between God and the world and set the stage for the coming Messiah, who would reconcile the world to himself.

We tend to think of Leviticus as a book of laws, and it does contain various commands and other directives. But the word *Torah*, the collective term for those foundational documents, which we usually translate as law, really means "teaching." Consequently, the book should be thought of as a book of teaching focusing on relationships. The Levitical paradigm shows how to cultivate and practice good relationships. The first part centers on relationship with God primarily in terms of worship, and the second part develops the idea of good relationships with other people as a consequence. Three intertwining themes tie these together for the nation of Israel: corporate worship, personal and collective holiness, and righteous living as a covenant community.

EXEGETICAL AUTHOR'S ACKNOWLEDGMENTS

I dedicate this to my wife, Esther,
with thanksgiving for her life of prayer
and her encouragement and support.

I further dedicate this study to Eugene Merrill,
my dissertation advisor, who introduced me to the riches of the Torah
and supported me through difficult times.

Regularly over the past seven or eight years, the question has crossed my mind: "Who am I to write a commentary on Leviticus?" I must say that it was not one of my top priority research projects when I completed my graduate training in the OT. In fact, it really wasn't even on my radar. Thus, as I completed this manuscript, I reflected on how it came about. The foundation for this study was laid during a year-long sabbatical at Taylor University in 2009–2010. The seed was a paper that I wrote that year for the annual meeting of the Evangelical Theological Society in which I started exploring what the OT had to say about social justice. I was surprised and intrigued as I realized how much of the OT material on social justice was in Leviticus. The paper was well received, and I then began to address some of the questions that my research had raised. This led to a series of peer-reviewed articles over nuances of the OT justice system including Jubilee, the Sabbath year, the OT concept of *'ebed* (both as slavery and servanthood), and what it means to be holy. All of these areas draw heavily on Leviticus.

I began further work on two major questions. The first question, which was multifaceted, was about the sacrificial system. The OT sacrificial system is described in Leviticus, and the description is both complex and confusing. It presumes that humankind has always known sacrifice, but how the Levitical system is tied to that earlier knowledge is not clear. That was also a question left hanging from my earlier study on the history of religion (see Harbin 1994). There I showed that the biblical view of the origin of religion began with the worship of the one true God and degenerated into idolatry—contrary to the modern idea that religion evolved into monotheism. But I did not address the role of sacrifice, saving it for a future study.

The second question addressed the culture underlying the guidelines set forth for the nation of Israel when they settled the land. I am not a farmer, but I have spent much of my life in the transition zone between urban and rural cultures. Much of my childhood was literally on the edge of a city, often with nothing but fields behind our house and modern suburbia in front. For the past thirty years, I have lived on the edge of a small Midwestern town surrounded by agriculture. As such, as I studied Leviticus, I often found myself questioning interpretations that seemed to reflect our largely urban, modern culture. These questions were heightened as I reflected on the several trips I had made to the Middle East both with the Navy and while leading students.

Exegetical Author's Acknowledgments

So, when Herb Bateman of the Kerux project asked me how I was in Leviticus, I realized that I had already done some significant work on aspects of Leviticus. The question was, could I put the pieces together into a coherent whole? Herb told me that his desire was that the exegesis of this commentary relate to what the text would have meant to the original audience. That has been my focus in the exegetical portion and has demanded a lot of thought regarding what an OT community would have been like. However, as Herb described the series concept, he also noted the desire for solid application to a modern culture in the homiletical portion. My mind immediately went to our pastor at Upland Community Church, who had done two sermon series on Leviticus in the not-too-distant past. Interestingly, the first was on the sacrificial system, and the second was on the last portion of the book, focusing on how individual believers were to image God in their culture. Mark Biehl was gracious enough to agree to write the homiletical portion of this commentary, and I am very thankful for the excellent work he has done.

It has been a seven-year project that stretched into eight—which seems somewhat ironic, although very fitting for the book of Leviticus. I thank Herb, his successor Shawn Vander Lugt, and the entire Kregel team for entrusting me with it and bearing with me as it stretched out. In the process, I have been able to dig deeply into areas where there is significant disagreement, or where commentators have tended to treat the difficult issues rather lightly. There are many others for whom thanks should be given, who encouraged or provided small insights that strengthened the final product. My goal has been to give what I perceive is the best understanding of the Hebrew text. That is not to say that this is the final answer to all of those questions. My hope is that this volume presents the book of Leviticus as a unified whole, describing how God gave to the nation of Israel a cohesive socioeconomic-judicial-political-religious system that would ultimately point to the greater gift of his Son. In that light, my prayer is that this work would help students of his Word regardless of their backgrounds.

—Michael A. Harbin

PREACHING AUTHOR'S ACKNOWLEDGMENTS

To my wife Dianne—for her daily insight, patience, and perseverance in Christ.

For reasons unknown to me, I have always been drawn to the places in Scripture that many others may think of as "fly-over" texts. In time, I realized that mining these less-explored texts often yielded missing components in my theology by connecting many of the central themes running throughout Scripture.

There is no better case in point than Leviticus. Though commonly identified as one of the least favorite (and studied) books of the Bible, Leviticus offers unifying theology for two of the greatest questions before every believer: What does it mean to worship our God? What does it mean to love our neighbor? Any answer to these questions is incomplete apart from a deep dive into Leviticus.

Thus, I am indebted to a lifetime of teachers and mentors who constantly pressed me to dive deeper into the text until it yielded its gems. Also, I am thankful to my elders and congregation at Upland Community Church for faithfully standing with me on our initial journey from animal sacrifice to scapegoats, and later from the Day of Atonement to the making of vows. Together we sat in awe as we prepared to share communion together and reflected on the perfect sacrifice of Christ. Through this process, everything came into focus—from Jesus's sacrifice on the cross to the atonement of our sins. In response to this gift, we are called to love our neighbor as ourselves.

Ultimately, I am grateful to Dr. Michael Harbin, the exegetical author, for his initial invitation, patient coaching, and constant encouragement, without which my homiletical contribution would never have materialized.

—Mark C. Biehl

OVERVIEW OF ALL PREACHING PASSAGES

Leviticus 1:1–3:17

EXEGETICAL IDEA
After the tabernacle was erected, the glory of God filled the Tent of Meeting, and then the Lord directed Moses to convey to the people of Israel why and how they should bring sacrifices in worship.

THEOLOGICAL FOCUS
Access to our all-holy God is initiated by God giving worshippers guidance for bringing voluntary sacrificial offerings before him.

PREACHING IDEA
Worship of (a seemingly inaccessible, holy) God is initiated by God.

PREACHING POINTERS
In the original context, the introductory words of Leviticus 1:1–2 would probably come as a complete shock and even strike a note of terror in the heart of every Israelite. They may have chosen to know the God of glory who filled the Tent of Meeting from a distance. They may have preferred to relate to him as one whom they could summon when they encountered a perceived threat or need. An invitation to come before the throne of the all-powerful warrior who had struck down Pharaoh and his army, the devouring fire who had descended before their eyes onto Mount Sinai, the divine judge who had struck down his chosen people with a plague after they worshipped a false god, would invoke more fear than excitement. Yet, with these words the One who is seemingly (and safely) inaccessible was personally calling those he had set apart to step into his presence and worship. The all-holy God who redeems and judges was inviting them to come with an offering. Could they trust him? Was he safe? A humble attitude of trust was required if they were to enter into worship of the Lord their God.

Today, God may appear equally inaccessible to us, not because of his power and holiness, but because of our rebellious spirits. An autonomous heart is reluctant to respond to an invitation to come in humility before a sovereign God and worship. This passage reminds us that though we may prefer distance, God initiates personal worship. He invites us to bring an offering, step into his presence, and worship. He prescribes the way. He provides the means. But is he safe? Can we entrust our lives to him? A humble attitude of trust remains the foundation of authentic worship of the Lord our God.

Overview of All Preaching Passages

Leviticus 4:1–6:7 (HB 5:26)

EXEGETICAL IDEA
As worshippers receive the Lord's conviction of an error before him or others, they are called to confess the error, bring a cleansing offering, and when necessary offer reparations.

THEOLOGICAL FOCUS
True worship should be preceded by true confession and repentance.

PREACHING IDEA
Correction, confession, and repentance before a holy God are transformational components of authentic worship.

PREACHING POINTERS
These chapters clarify that worshipping the Lord God will not be a tangential component in the life of God's people. If they pictured that they would be marking the calendar, taking their turn to bring an offering, and then returning their focus to living their normal lives (until their number came up again), they were mistaken. The worship of God was designed to transform their heads (how they thought), hearts (how they felt), and hands (what they did). The worship of God would revolutionize who they were as individuals and as a people. It would define how they saw God, themselves, and others!

Why do we come to church? What is our posture as we gather for worship? Are we carrying a private (or communal) you-need-to-do-this list before our God? Are we actually intending to transform the living God (who is transforming us)? Through his Word, God intends to sufficiently soften us to continually receive his correction and humbly proceed to confession and repentance so we may know authentic worship.

Worship, by definition, implies that the worshipper reveres the one being worshipped. If that is so, then we should expect that authentic worship will frequently require us to correct our thoughts, confess our error, and repent of our sin, in order to cleanse us that we may become more like Christ. This is nothing short of a deliberate, progressive metamorphosis.

Leviticus 6:8 (HB 6:1)–7:38

EXEGETICAL IDEA
A life of worship should include both planned and spontaneous events.

THEOLOGICAL FOCUS
The worship of God demonstrates for the worshipper and the community a life that is at peace with who God is and what God is doing.

PREACHING IDEA
Being at peace with God is evident through a worship-filled life.

PREACHING POINTERS

The Israelites were recovering from years of captivity under harsh taskmasters who drove them to fulfill the vain will of a ruthless pharaoh. Under the covenant with the Lord God, the people began to discover that they had not been redeemed from their bondage only to be released into a Promised Land where each clan would fend for themselves and find their own way. Rather, their Redeemer would be their new king as they lived together in community before the priests. They were invited to acknowledge their peace with his permanent lordship over them by bringing specific offerings. This called for more than mindlessly making an extra helping or trimming a crust to send up to the tabernacle. Rather, they were instructed how to confess a critical reality openly yet humbly—that they were dependent on the Lord and his community. Were they "at peace" with their God? His intermediary? His people? The call to bring offerings of peace before the priest was not intended to feed the vanity of their master. It was to arrest the vanity and wayward independence of their own hearts.

Believers are set apart in Christ. We are redeemed from self-worship to the worship of the Lord God. The realities of daily life can distract us, allowing our focus to turn away from the purposes of God and center on our own personal agenda. Left to ourselves, such distraction can escalate into dissatisfaction. The result is that we are no longer at peace with our God, his intermediary, or his people. What will keep our heart loyal to our Redeemer? Hearing and proclaiming openly who God is and how he is actively at work has the power to redirect our gaze fully onto our God.

What is the role of public testimony in your church today? Is it present? Has it been relegated to "how God saved me"? This section reminds Israel that their redemption was only the beginning of the story. It will be his ongoing work in their lives that he is calling them to share with the community. This message encourages us to publicly honor God by proclaiming how we see him at work and how we are finding peace with that work!

Leviticus 8:1–9:24

EXEGETICAL IDEA

God desired deep, covenant fellowship with his chosen people, which required the establishment of holy priestly mediators—men who were chosen by God to be set apart and made holy before God's people.

THEOLOGICAL FOCUS

Our holy God set apart holy priestly mediators to atone for the sins of his people, so that they could be free to come before him in worship.

PREACHING IDEA

God provides a mediator to atone for our sin, so that we may come before him in worship.

PREACHING POINTERS

As Aaron and his sons were led before God, the people may have expected a public execution—an extermination of the line of Aaron. Yet God, again choosing to reveal his

Overview of All Preaching Passages

nature to them, gathered his people that they could witness a public redemption. Through a carefully detailed ritual of cleansing, preparing, and sacrifice, the same Aaron who had fashioned a golden calf was anointed as high priest by God. The one who fashioned an idol and led the people into false worship, saying, "These are your gods" (Exod. 32:4), was now publicly refashioned by the hand of God to lead the same people into true worship. What did this communicate to the people about their God? Having previously been chosen by God, God did not reject Aaron because of his sin against God and the people. Rather, the Lord God had mercy upon him, redeeming him from his sin for his greater purposes. The people looked upon Aaron and saw living evidence of the mercy of God at work. They worshipped a God who publicly redeems, restores, and recognizes his own.

What seems lost to us is not lost! What seems beyond hope is not hopeless when there is a God who is merciful and displays his glory through redemption. Our sinfulness has not permanently disqualified us from serving a holy God who is merciful and gracious, slow to anger, and abounding in steadfast love. It was and it is the Lord God's desire to demonstrate his mercy and forgiveness by redeeming us (publicly) from our sin and bringing us into relationship with him so that the world may see the character of our God.

Leviticus 10:1–20

EXEGETICAL IDEA
The decision of Nadab and Abihu to usurp God's revealed standards and set out on their own in establishing a novel means ("strange fire") to come into his presence predictably led to their public destruction.

THEOLOGICAL FOCUS
Because he is holy, God, not man, establishes the means by which his people are able to safely come before him.

PREACHING IDEA
We are not free to usurp God's standards to design a personalized means of coming into his presence.

PREACHING POINTERS
The minds of God's people were overwhelmed with the joyful knowledge that Aaron, the former law-breaking idol-maker, had been publicly cleansed and refashioned under the authority of God to be their high priest! What an amazing and glorious God they served! Then suddenly, in a flash, they were jolted by the equally public destruction of Aaron's two oldest sons, Nadab and Abihu. The offense? Nadab and Abihu disregarded God's instructions and chose to experiment with their own ideas about how to come into the presence of the Almighty God of creation. The result was their public, personal destruction. A week that had showcased the abundant mercy of God ended with a dramatic exhibition of the unyielding holiness of God.

Finding the sweet spot between freshness and impulsive innovation in worship will often prove to be tricky. Yet, when coming into God's presence becomes too much about us, we may become casual or aloof and carelessly seek novel tools to bring with us into God's presence. When does this desire for individualized worship reveal something to us about us? We should not settle for bland worship, but we should remember that our omniscient God is the one who establishes the means by which we are to come before him safely. What is it that tempts us to carelessly venture outside of God's directives? Are we making worship more about us than about God? To do so is to risk personal destruction. When we so customize worship that it emphasizes us, it quickly becomes unsafe.

Leviticus 11:1–15:33

EXEGETICAL IDEA
God called his people to set themselves apart from the fallen world by being clean, differentiating themselves by adhering to distinct freedoms and limitations in all areas of daily life: diet, male and female hygiene practices, and visible skin and housing concerns.

THEOLOGICAL FOCUS
God calls his people to express their devotion to him through living holistically clean lives that mark those devoted to God from the common uncleanliness of the fallen world.

PREACHING IDEA
We are distinguished as God's people not only by avoiding forbidden practices but by recognizing the need for cleansing from the inherent uncleanliness of this fallen world.

PREACHING POINTERS
Having witnessed first the mercy of God in raising up Aaron and his sons, and then the holiness of God in striking down two of those sons, the children of God had come face to face with a potentially paralyzing problem—how to distinguish between holy and unholy, clean and unclean. Was there a clear standard one could attain (and keep) that would then free him or her to do what seemed right in his or her own mind? It does not appear to be that simple. God presented the priests with meticulous examples of freedoms and limitations extending into all areas of daily life that could make one unclean or even unholy. Holiness would need to always remain in the forefront of their minds if they were to thrive as a nation of priests to the world.

Holiness remains a standard that eludes precise definition. We may prefer a well-defined standard that we can attain and thus be free to move on to the more pressing matters of daily life in this world. Are there more pressing matters in this world? God's desire is that each moment of each day we are aware of the uncleanliness inherent to our lives in this world so that we may grasp our ongoing need to be cleansed and made holy by him. Holiness is reaching far deeper than outward moral purity. God's wants our souls to long for the perfection found in Christ alone.

Overview of All Preaching Passages

Leviticus 16:1–34

EXEGETICAL IDEA
The Lord God established the Day of Atonement as a day when the high priest would offer specific sacrifices to atone for the sins of the nation, reminding them of their individual need to be purified before God.

THEOLOGICAL FOCUS
Knowing the need, God establishes the means by which the sins of his people can be effectively "carried away forever," leaving them holy before him.

PREACHING IDEA
Sin is carried away by a specific atoning work of God on a day set by God, in order that we may be in fellowship with him forever.

PREACHING POINTERS
The people of God were teetering on the edge (possibly trembling in fear) with their expanding understanding of the incendiary nature of sin and their need for personal atonement. There was a growing reality that their ability to live under the standards of holiness would be an enduring obstacle. Some may have thought it impossible to navigate. It was made clear through Nadab and Abihu that God's standard of holiness is more than a suggestion—it is a necessity for all who enter into the presence of the living God. The people could humbly work to avoid (and eliminate) all uncleanness, they could openly confess and make sacrifices for their unintentional sin once they become aware of it . . . yet, what if their judgment of uncleanness missed the mark? What if there was unconfessed sin of which they are ignorant? Would the humble in spirit destined to be struck down by the holy God they serve? May it never be! In his mercy, God established the means by which his people could be made clean from all their sin—even that of which they were unaware!

We have a bad habit of branding God's requirements confusing, unclear, or even unfair. How can one be expected to abide by such divine (subjective?) standards of holiness? Are we not destined to fall short? Yes, but in his mercy, God has established the means by which all who humbly seek him may be personally redeemed from their fall and made holy through the atoning work of Christ. It is a work that reaches far beyond the sin we see, because it is a work sufficient to carry away a lifetime of sin we have yet to see. Being made holy is a process of confession (as God accurately identifies our sin), of mourning (as we grieve over our disobedience), and casting away (as God removes sin from our lives).

Leviticus 17:1–16

EXEGETICAL IDEA
God called his people out of the "open fields," gathering them for lawful worship in a specific place (tabernacle) and instructing them on the lawful handling of blood to safeguard them from being lured and enticed into the worship of false gods.

THEOLOGICAL FOCUS

God distinguishes himself from pagan worship and the false gods that permeate the land and surround his people by establishing where and how they can worship to keep their hearts safely focused on him.

PREACHING IDEA

We worship according to God's revelation, not our own personal disposition.

PREACHING POINTERS

Though the people of God were set free from their former Egyptian taskmasters, private desires, habits, and experiences threatened to lead them to serve new taskmasters. They had walked away from the gods of Egypt to celebrate new life under the Lord God, yet their hearts remained vulnerable. It would have been easy to doubt the Lord God and wander back to the comfort of old practices and beliefs (or even dabble in some new ones they had uncovered in their wilderness wanderings!). Would their worship focus on the Lord God alone, or would he become diluted among a pantheon of gods they recognized and called upon in times of need? Would a craving for meat create an appetite for idolatry, secret sacrifices, and private feasts? Apparently, it would. In the words of Leviticus 17:7, they were in danger of prostituting themselves after other gods—giving their bodies to another in exchange for a payment.

The Lord God is not a "hire for services" god! God not only knows what we, his people, need (and how to provide it for his glory and our good), but how we may foolishly lust after many things that pack the power to become taskmasters that will enslave us. To safeguard us from pursuing the folly of our misguided desires, God calls us in from the unprotected open fields of isolation and privatized worship to gather communally before him. Sustaining steadfast relationships with other believers provides protection and accountability from chasing after other gods. Furthermore, God carefully guards what is central and sacred in worship (redemption) from reckless acts of contempt and scorn. The Giver of Life makes clear that the life/soul of an animal is in the blood. This sets blood apart as the means to make atonement for sin. The life is in the blood. Without the shedding of blood there is no forgiveness of sins (Heb. 9:22). Blood is essential. It is sacred. It begins to unfold the story of the coming redemptive life of Jesus Christ.

Leviticus 18:1–20:27

EXEGETICAL IDEA

God instructed his people in how to grow in holiness by living together in community. He taught them how to recognize, excise, and replace destructive beliefs and practices that may have risen up from inside them or crept in from the culture around them, with God-defined holy living that calls them to love their neighbor by proclaiming God's holiness through all they do.

THEOLOGICAL FOCUS

God defines love for others as humble, intentional, sacrificial intervention to direct each person toward him. This is in stark contrast to the world's current definition of absolute, nonjudgmental, unconditional affirmation that leaves each person to do what is right in his or her own mind.

PREACHING IDEA
We are made holy by God by loving our neighbor, whom we love best by living holy lives before God.

PREACHING POINTERS
God prepared families to establish new holy communities in the Promised Land. Would these communities thrive? What would prove to be the key threats? Their hearts melted at the thought of the spears, swords, and chariots coming at them. But they were told the greater threat was found in the depravities, perversions, and abominations that caused the land to "vomit out" its inhabitants. The people of God could not rest in Israel's history nor Canaanite customs, as both accommodated the inner lusts that defiled them and their neighbors. God called them to vigorously resist the lust that might arise in their hearts and faithfully pursue the covenant love that was revealed through God's instruction—a sacrificial love for others that would build community relationships through loving one's neighbor.

Everyone hungers for meaningful community. Few agree on how to establish it. These chapters point out how freeing our spirits to crash against God's created order quickly tears away at our social fabric by devastating relationships. God alone knows the depths and dangers of our desires and cravings. He alone is able to establish decrees to safeguard our reasoning from being bent by our wayward desires. His appeal is that of a loving father. He calls us to reflect him and love others in all interactions (1) by finding contentment in his created order, words, statutes, and character; and (2) by evading the snare of serving the god of superior happiness. That means that loving our neighbors should look more like humble, sacrificial intervention than free, unconditional affirmation!

Leviticus 21:1–22:33

EXEGETICAL IDEA
To avoid openly profaning his name before the people (and the nations), God required the priests to be held to the highest standard of holiness, specifically regarding their mourning over death, entering into the covenant of marriage, personal physiological limitations and defects, and their administration of the offerings of the people.

THEOLOGICAL FOCUS
The highest standards of holiness are required of the one who is to come into God's presence and serve as his representative to God's people.

PREACHING IDEA
As needy, imperfect intermediaries, we are called to perfectly represent a perfect God as the one who sanctifies.

PREACHING POINTERS

The Lord God had already severely limited the pool of potential priests through restrictive gender and genealogical constraints (a male descendant of Aaron). The number decreased further through binding restrictions on how and for whose death priests might mourn and whom they might and might not choose for a spouse. Would some become reluctant to make this sacrifice? Next, a list of prohibiting physiological constraints (most beyond their control) further diminished the pool of who might still be willing. Was anyone left? Then, Moses detailed God's restrictions on how priests must receive, process, and preserve the offerings of the people with integrity. Could the priesthood possibly maintain these costly and cumbersome relational, social, physiological, and administrative standards? If they failed to do so, they would profane the name of God! Would anyone in the line of Aaron be able to fill this role?

The same dilemma remains before church leaders today: "you are a chosen race, a royal priesthood, a holy nation, a people for his own possession, that you may proclaim the excellencies of him who called you out of darkness into his marvelous light" (1 Peter 2:9 ESV). How do church leaders proclaim the excellencies of God as unholy, imperfect, fallen, and wounded servants? How can a leader accurately image God's holy perfection to the nations? To deny the effect of sin is to profane his name. To rest in our fallenness is to celebrate cheap grace. To lower the standards of holiness to a level that is attainable is to turn everyone's eyes onto us and away from our need for a savior. When Paul outlines the standards for church leaders in 1 Timothy 3 and Titus 1, he is not offering a means to identify those already sanctified. He is calling out leaders who know their need for sanctification. God alone is the One who sanctifies. We are the ones who point to the One who sanctifies through Christ.

Leviticus 23:1–24:9

EXEGETICAL IDEA

God established seven divine, recurring appointments for the people of Israel to meet regularly with him. The purpose of summoning everyone to these community celebrations (and priestly tasks) was to strengthen the social fabric of his people and keep their corporate focus on the worship of God.

THEOLOGICAL FOCUS

God commands corporate celebrations to gather his people before him, so that they may remember and rejoice in him as their Creator, redeemer, and provider.

PREACHING IDEA

We are summoned by God to stop and appear before him to affirm that he is our Creator, redeemer, and provider.

PREACHING POINTERS

Every agrarian community is dependent upon every individual doing an abundance of work. The animals need to be fed. The crops should be weeded. The fruit trees are ready to be pruned. There is so much to do! Will there be time to do it? The Lord God already claimed a day for worship (limiting the Israelites' work week to six days). He then established six annual feasts and daily maintenance tasks in the tabernacle! All of this would require time and expense. Worse yet, the feasts tended to be clumped around the busiest time of their year——when the harvest was coming in! Were these daily, weekly, and annual reminders really necessary? Did God not understand that his people were too busy in this fallen world to stop what they were doing for yet another holy gathering? Did God fail to realize that the work of his people would bring in the harvest so they would be free to continue worshipping him?

Is it our work or is it the blessing of God that will bring in the harvest? How we answer this question will in large part determine what holds our communities together. Do we believe we are blessed primarily through diligent work, wise decisions, and strategic planning, or by the ever-present hand of a gracious God? Our beliefs will determine whether we anticipate the coming celebrations with growing excitement or increasing dread. An easier question may be, which do we tend to minimize or even forget: God's blessing or our hard work? More often, we forget our God more than our own sacrifice. Once again, God knows us, his people. If our churches are to remain focused on worshipping our Creator and redeemer, we will need daily, weekly, and annual celebrations sewn into our social lives, reminding us of the source of our daily provision. Left to ourselves, we will fail to stop. We will quickly forget. We need a summons to recapture our attention.

Leviticus 24:10–23

EXEGETICAL IDEA
God's law had been given to Moses and read before the people, establishing how they as a people were to reflect him through their words and in their actions. When this law was violated, the people were expected to judge publicly and responsibly as directed by his Word in order to redeem the person and the community.

THEOLOGICAL FOCUS
God holds us accountable for both our words that bring spiritual harm (by inaccurately declaring something about his character or profaning his nature) and our actions that bring physical harm to others in the community—native and sojourners.

PREACHING IDEA
As image-bearers, we are responsible before God for all of our words and actions.

PREACHING POINTERS
The Israelites had received volumes of law for how they were to live before God and one another in community. When an unnamed man, in the heat of anger, spoke defaming words against the Lord God, it was a sobering moment for all present. They knew immediately this was a serious violation. His words could not be unheard. How was this man to give account for his careless words? What were the people to do? Who was to judge? How should they judge?

We are guilty of being careless with our words. We may blame our emotions or other people, or say, "That's just how I feel." Does this diminish our responsibility before God for every word that proceeds from our mouth? Are we accountable for the potential damage our words may cause to the souls of others? Jesus is very clear: "I tell you, on the day of judgment people will give account for every careless word they speak, for by your words you will be justified, and by your words you will be condemned" (Matt. 12:36–37 ESV). Words that escape from our mouths reveal deeper thoughts that we hold within our hearts (Matt. 12:34). So, this goes much deeper than a problem with our speech! We need someone to reach into our souls to fix our hearts. God is focused on redemption, not retribution. And it is ultimately our heart, not simply our tongue, that must be redeemed.

Leviticus 25:1–22

EXEGETICAL IDEA
God purposefully wove Sabbath and Jubilee years into the social fabric of his redeemed people so that they may live securely as stewards of the faith in the land that he had entrusted to them.

THEOLOGICAL FOCUS
God instructs his people in how to anchor their lives to him by corporately living out their belief in his faithfulness and imaging his gracious redemption to each other and the world, through their stewardship of his land and labor contracts with one another.

PREACHING IDEA
We declare our relationship to God and to the world through our relationships with others and our possessions.

PREACHING POINTERS
The people received the Sabbath and Jubilee commands from God through Moses when they were completely landless and dependent on daily manna. They were living for a promise that they were redeemed from bondage in Egypt to live one day in a land of milk and honey. But during Sabbath and Jubilee years it sounded like they would remain stewards of what belonged to God, never owners of the land they were preparing to possess. Would their life in the wilderness be more preparatory than temporary? A life of dependence sounded more like a permanent way of life under the Lord God that would continue as they entered the Promised Land. What was the purpose behind such binding laws? (The Scriptures record a consistent failure to observe the Sabbath and Jubilee years.) Why were the people hesitant to embrace these marks of permanent dependence on the Lord God?

It is easy as believers to reason ourselves away from all directives that reflect our dependence on God. God wants us to be fruitful, right? And he wants us to flaunt how he blesses us, right? And if we don't maximize our possessions, profits, and investments, then we will not be free to be generous with others! Through this vortex of unbelief, we effectively deny God his seat as the decisive factor in providence. Furthermore, we assume that seat as we are consumed by work, goals, planning, and prosperity. God draws us away from the toxic belief that we can be self-sustaining in this fallen world. He is repositioning us before him by directing how we are to relate to others and our possessions.

Leviticus 25:23–55

EXEGETICAL IDEA
God established (legislated) moral actions through detailed civil law to create a social reset—to confront the anticipated poverty and inequity that were expected to arise among the stewards of his land.

THEOLOGICAL FOCUS
As stewards, God's people are expected to attend to the social (and spiritual) health of the whole community by imaging his patience, grace, and mercy, in hopes of restoring each individual steward.

PREACHING IDEA
We are called to pursue those who are sinking into hardship and poverty in a redemptive way that images God's restorative patience, grace, and mercy to us.

PREACHING POINTERS
The people received these civil from God through Moses when they were completely landless. They heard that they would enjoy the power and provisions of the One who redeemed them from their bondage to Egypt. In the Promised Land, God would be the owner. He would provide for their needs. He would be their God! They would be his stewards. They would remain under his care. They would be a nation of priests to the world! Why then would there be a need for detailed civil law to confront poverty and inequity? How could it happen? *Why* would it happen? They might be quick to love the ill-fated and unfortunate, but were they expected to love the neighbor who squandered his resources and abused his possessions?

Wait! Are we accountable before God to invest in the lives of family and neighbors who are sinking into hardship and poverty? This is an invasive call to actively love family and neighbor through means that transform the way we live, the way we understand our lives, and the way we pursue our possessions. This call requires an outlay of time, emotion, and resources without a guarantee of return on investment. Will we be owners who amass fame and possessions for our name (and glory), or will we be progressively transformed into stewards who invest in others to glorify God's name?

Leviticus 26:1–46

EXEGETICAL IDEA
After God instructed his redeemed people to image his mercy as a nation by observing Sabbath and Jubilee years, he vowed that they belonged to him forever and were required to continuously walk in his presence under his law, to live in his protection, and to know his blessings (an opportunity to "reverse the curse" of Genesis 3).

THEOLOGICAL FOCUS

God is righteous and merciful. His character is revealed to his people and to the world not through his unconditional affirmation of a disobedient people, but by his sacrificial intervention to renew them from corporate disobedience into life-giving obedience.

PREACHING IDEA

We are loved by God through his sacrificial intervention to rescue us from the curse of following our own voice rather than his life-giving Word.

PREACHING POINTERS

God's people heard the Lord God summarize the legal contract he made between them. This was not new. They heard similar language before. What was unique was that the contract concluded with a detailed list of exciting consequences for walking in God's presence under his law and protection (which sounded like the Promised Land)—along with a more extensive list of horrifying penalties for turning away from his presence toward the idols and ideas of the nations around them! Why were these sevenfold progressive punishments necessary? They seem a bit extreme in light of the fact that the people anticipated leaving temptation behind as they crossed into the Promised Land. And more than that, they already pledged their obedience to God! Had he forgotten?

Sadly, they were the ones who had forgotten. God was preparing his people for the ongoing battle against their own wills. It would be a lifelong war. To remain under his protection, they must deny the voice inside that calls them to craft a law of their own. Would the Creator of the universe be their guiding star as they lived in freedom? Or would they follow another voice and agree to create a new, personalized star they could register as their own?

Their God is our God. Their battle against idolatry is—albeit in different ways—our battle against idolatry. If we elect to step onto the wide path that leads to destruction, what should our loving God do to turn us back?

Leviticus 27:1–34

EXEGETICAL IDEA

After God's people repeatedly witnessed the breadth of his power and goodness, they needed instruction in the foolhardiness of attempting to manipulate the Lord God by declaring rash and reckless personal or corporate vows.

THEOLOGICAL FOCUS

Vows are not a mechanism to manipulate God, but rather a means to humbly convey faithfulness to the Lord God who has been supremely faithful to his people.

PREACHING IDEA

My vow declares my devotion to God only if it is first carefully made and then faithfully kept.

PREACHING POINTERS

God's people gathered to hear a final speech. What more did God need to tell them? They knew they would soon step into the Promised Land. God promised to lead them, bless them, and protect them as he drove out the inhabitants before them. Some may have pondered, "Will God bless us all alike? Do I need to curry his favor to get my share? Are there mechanisms at my disposal to receive a larger share than my neighbor?" It would be easy to imagine gratefully giving to the Lord God when they had nothing—livestock or possessions—to give or withhold. But they speculated: What if the bull they promised to sacrifice matured into a prized bull? Could it be exchanged for one of lesser value? God should not care. One burnt carcass was the same as another, right (Mal. 1:14)? Wrong! Once again, God knew the thoughts and understood the hearts of his people. He warned them of the danger of declaring reckless vows made in haste both in times of hardship and exultation. Affection and gratitude might waver, but the vow must be faithfully kept.

Vows are not to be a declaration of how we feel, nor how we predict we will feel. They are a declaration of what we will do regardless of how we feel. They should not be a byproduct of emotion. They should not be proclaimed to manipulate or exploit. They are a means to harness our will that we will be faithful to a promise made, even if it requires great sacrifice. In our age, careless vows have become such a way of life that they are codified into law. We have no-fault divorce and prenuptial contracts. In many churches, parents take vows as they dedicate (or baptize) their children. Believers take vows when they become members. Why are so many vows so quickly (and thoughtlessly) broken? A vow kept testifies to faithfulness and self-sacrifice. A vow broken often exposes folly and our self-interest over the interests of others. Are our vows rash or reasonable? Is it time to listen more closely to our own words?

ABBREVIATIONS

GENERAL ABBREVIATIONS

A.D.	*anno Domini* (in the year of our Lord)
Akk	Akkadian
ANE	Ancient Near East(ern)
B.C.	Before Christ
HB	Hebrew Bible
LXX	Septuagint
MT	Masoretic Text
NT	New Testament
OT	Old Testament

TECHNICAL ABBREVIATIONS

cf.	compare (*confer*)
s.v.	under the word (*sub verbo*)

BIBLICAL SOURCES

Old Testament

Gen.	Genesis	Prov.	Proverbs
Exod.	Exodus	Eccl.	Ecclesiastes
Lev.	Leviticus	Song	Song of Songs
Num.	Numbers	Isa.	Isaiah
Deut.	Deuteronomy	Jer.	Jeremiah
Josh.	Joshua	Lam.	Lamentations
Judg.	Judges	Ezek.	Ezekiel
Ruth	Ruth	Dan.	Daniel
1 Sam.	1 Samuel	Hos.	Hosea
2 Sam.	2 Samuel	Joel	Joel
1 Kings	1 Kings	Amos	Amos
2 Kings	2 Kings	Obad.	Obadiah
1 Chron.	1 Chronicles	Jonah	Jonah
2 Chron.	2 Chronicles	Micah	Micah
Ezra	Ezra	Nah.	Nahum
Neh.	Nehemiah	Hab.	Habakkuk
Esther	Esther	Zeph.	Zephaniah
Job	Job	Hag.	Haggai
Ps./Pss.	Psalm(s)	Zech.	Zechariah
		Mal.	Malachi

Abbreviations

New Testament

Matt.	Matthew	2 Thess.	2 Thessalonians
Mark	Mark	1 Tim.	1 Timothy
Luke	Luke	2 Tim.	2 Timothy
John	John	Titus	Titus
Acts	Acts	Philem.	Philemon
Rom.	Romans	Heb.	Hebrews
1 Cor.	1 Corinthians	James	James
2 Cor.	2 Corinthians	1 Peter	1 Peter
Gal.	Galatians	2 Peter	2 Peter
Eph.	Ephesians	1 John	1 John
Phil.	Philippians	2 John	2 John
Col.	Colossians	3 John	3 John
1 Thess.	1 Thessalonians	Jude	Jude
		Rev.	Revelation

EXTRABIBLICAL SOURCES

b. ʿArak.	Babylonian Talmud, tractate Arakhin
b. B. Bat.	Babylonian Talmud, tractate Bava Batra
b. Mak.	Babylonian Talmud, tractate Makkot
b. Meg.	Babylonian Talmud, tractate Megillah
b. Sanh.	Babylonian Talmud, tractate Sanhedrin
m. ʾAbot	Mishnah, tractate Avot
m. ʿArak.	Mishnah, tractate Arakhin
m. Git.	Mishnah, tractate Gittin
m. Menaḥ	Mishnah, tractate Menahot
m. Peʾah	Mishnah, tractate Peʾah
m. Roš Haš.	Mishnah, tractate Rosh Hashanah
m. Sukkah	Mishnah, tractate Sukkah
m. Tamid	Mishnah, tractate Tamid
m. Zebaḥ.	Mishnah, tractate Zevahim
Spec. Laws	Philo, *On the Special Laws*

PERIODICALS

BSac	*Bibliotheca Sacra*
CBQ	*Catholic Biblical Quarterly*
CRSQ	*Creation Research Society Quarterly*
Econ Bot	*Economic Botany*
HUCA	*Hebrew Union College Annual*
JAOS	*Journal of the American Oriental Society*
JETS	*Journal of the Evangelical Theological Society*
JQR	*Jewish Quarterly Review*
JSOT	*Journal for the Study of the Old Testament*
PEQ	*Palestine Exploration Quarterly*

Abbreviations

SBET   Scottish Bulletin of Evangelical Theology
TynBul   Tyndale Bulletin
WTJ   Westminster Theological Journal

SERIES

AB   Anchor (Yale) Bible Commentary
AOAT   Alter Orient und Altes Testament
AOTC   Abingdon Old Testament Commentaries
ApOTC   Apollos Old Testament Commentary
BBRSup   Bulletin for Biblical Research Supplement
BJS   Brown Judaic Studies
FAT   Forschungen zum Alten Testament
IB   Interpretation: A Bible Commentary for Teaching and Preaching
JSOTSup   Journal for the Study of the Old Testament Supplement Series
NAC   New American Commentary
NICOT   New International Commentary on the Old Testament
NIVAC   New International Version Application Commentary
OTL   Old Testament Library
PNTC   Pillar New Testament Commentary
SHBC   Smyth & Helwys Bible Commentary
TOTC   Tyndale Old Testament Commentary
WBC   Word Bible Commentary

REFERENCES

ANET   Pritchard, James B., ed. *Ancient Near East Text Relating to the Old Testament.* 3rd ed. Princeton, NJ: Princeton University Press, 1969.
BDB   Brown, Francis, S. R. Driver, and Charles A. Briggs. *The Brown-Driver-Briggs Hebrew and English Lexicon.* Oxford: Clarendon, 1907.
DBL   Swanson, James. 2001. *A Dictionary of Biblical Languages: Hebrew, Old Testament.* 2nd ed. Oak Harbor, WA: Logos Research Systems, Inc.
DCH   Clines, David J. A. *The Dictionary of Classical Hebrew.* 9 vols. Sheffield: Sheffield Academic, 1993–2014.
GHC   Gesenius, Wilhelm. *Gesenius' Hebrew and Chaldee Lexicon to the Old Testament Scriptures.* Translated by Samuel Prideaux Tregelles. London: Bagster, 1846.
GKC   Gesenius, Wilhelm. *Gesenius' Hebrew Grammar.* Edited by Emil Kautzsch. Translated by Arthur E. Cowley. 2nd ed. Oxford: Clarendon, 1910.
ISBE   Orr, James, ed. *International Standard Bible Encyclopedia.* 5 vols. Grand Rapids: Eerdmans, 1939.
JWA-S/HEJW *Jewish Women's Archive: The Shalvi/Hyman Encyclopedia of Jewish Women.* https://jwa.org/encyclopedia.
KB   Köhler, Ludwig, and Walter Baumgartner, eds. *Lexicon in veteris testamenti libros; A Dictionary of the Hebrew Old Testament in English and German; A Dictionary of the Aramaic Parts of the Old Testament.* Leiden: Brill, 1958.

Abbreviations

TDNT	Kittel, Gerhard, and Gerhard Friedrich, eds. *Theological Dictionary of the New Testament.* Translated by Geoffrey W. Bromiley. 10 vols. Grand Rapids: Eerdmans, 1964–1976.
TDOT	Botterweck, G. Johannes, Helmer Ringgren, and Heinz-Josef Fabry, eds. *Theological Dictionary of the Old Testament.* Translated by John T. Willis, et al. 17 vols. Grand Rapids: Eerdmans, 1974–2021.
TWOT	Harris, R. Laird, Gleason L. Archer Jr., and Bruce K. Waltke, eds. *Theological Wordbook of the Old Testament.* 2 vols. Chicago: Moody Press, 1980.
WTNID	*Webster's Third New International Dictionary, Unabridged.* Springfield, MA: Merriam, 1961.
ZIBBCOT	Walton, John H., ed. *Zondervan Illustrated Background Bible Commentary of the Old Testament.* 5 vols. Grand Rapids: Zondervan, 2009.
ZPEB	Tenny, Merrill C., ed. *Zondervan Pictorial Encyclopedia of the Bible.* 5 vols. Grand Rapids: Zondervan, 1975.

BIBLE TRANSLATIONS

ESV	English Standard Version
HCSB	Holman Christian Standard Version
KJV	King James Version
NASB	New American Standard Bible
NEB	New English Bible
NET	New English Translation
NIV	New International Version
NJB	New Jerusalem Bible
NLT	New Living Translation
NRSV	New Revised Standard Version
RSV	Revised Standard Version
TEV	Today's English Version

INTRODUCTION TO LEVITICUS

OVERVIEW OF LEVITICUS

Human Author: Moses

Place of Writing: Mount Sinai

Original Readers: Nation of Israel prior to entering the land

Date: 1445 B.C.

Historical Setting: Newly released Israelites and associated outliers camped at the foot of Mount Sinai following the construction of the tabernacle one year after the exodus.

Occasion for Writing: God instituted tabernacle worship and gave the newly formed nation guidelines for worship and developing and maintaining a God-centered culture.

Genre: Predominantly legal literature, with incidents of historical narrative embedded

Theological Emphasis: Proper worship of God, both as individuals and as a community

---

AUTHORSHIP

The book of Leviticus presents itself primarily as part of a series of revelations that God gave to Moses between the erection of the tabernacle (Exod. 40:1) and the beginning of the trek to the Promised Land (Num. 10:11). They are generally introduced by the statement, "The Lord [YHWH] spoke and said" or something very similar. Almost all of these divine orations represent direct speech from the Lord to Moses, although Leviticus 10:8 is to Aaron and Leviticus 11:1 and 13:1 are addressed to Moses and Aaron together. As a result, orthodox traditions of both Judaism and Christianity have long ascribed the authorship of Leviticus to Moses as part of the Pentateuch or Torah. These traditions are based on specific passages in the larger context that assert that Moses wrote at least part of the Torah.

Mosaic Authorship

Key strands of evidence that support the view that Moses wrote the Pentateuch include specific passages that assert that he wrote at least part of the text, including Exodus 17:14; Numbers 33:1–2; and Deuteronomy 31:22–24. Other passages in the OT refer to a book of the law written by Moses. For example, in Joshua 1:7–8 God tells Joshua to follow the law given by Moses, which is characterized as a "book" (סֵפֶר). Other passages that point to Mosaic authorship include Judges 3:4; 2 Kings 21:8; and Malachi 4:4. In the NT, Jesus cites Moses as the writer of the law (see Matt. 19:8 and John 7:19), as also does Paul (see Rom. 10:5) and Peter (see Acts 3:22). Some passages of the Pentateuch seem to have been added or revised later, such as Deuteronomy 34. Jewish tradition attributes that account of the death of Moses to Joshua (b. B. Bat. 14b).

While Leviticus does not explicitly state it, the text describes itself as a continuation of the book of Exodus, pointing to the conclusion that the author of both was Moses.

God's Revelation to Israel

Exodus 19 presents God giving his first revelation to the nation shortly after their arrival at Sinai, about three months after the Passover and exodus. With the nation camped at the base of Sinai, Moses went up the mountain and received a message from God for the people. That message consisted of two key points. First, they needed to remember what they had seen. That they were eyewitnesses to God's actions was a critical foundation for Israel as a nation, as well as to the canonical report. The first part of the book of Exodus (chs. 1–18) reports events they had experienced, and those thousands of witnesses could verify (or dispute) what Moses recorded. Second, those same witnesses were told to prepare for a momentous event where they would not only see God act, but hear him speak to the entire nation so that they would believe Moses (Exod. 19:9). This speech is recorded in Exodus 19:18–20:17. As Moses climbed the mountain, the people also saw lightning and heard thunder in the cloud. As they stood in wonder and fear, God spoke to Moses and sent him back down to ensure that the people stayed back. While Moses was there, God announced what we call the Ten Commandments *to the nation*. The people backed off from fear and then complained to Moses that God's speaking to them was terrifying. They pled to Moses, "Don't let God speak to us, or we will die." So, Moses went back up the mountain (Exod. 20:21) and became a spokesperson for God.

The Hebrew title for the book is the first word of the book, which is translated literally as "and he called" (וַיִּקְרָא). As shown in the discussion of Leviticus 1:1, this explicitly ties the beginning of Leviticus to the action at the end of Exodus. That does not preclude some annotations within the book from being made at a later date and, in fact, tradition suggests that Joshua and others did make some updates to the text. In terms of the overall Torah, the clearest example of an addition is the final chapter of Deuteronomy.

Could Moses Write?

Our understanding is that Moses lived in the late fifteenth century B.C. and was probably born about 1526 B.C. Writing was invented approximately 3200 B.C. in Sumer, and by about 3000 B.C., the Egyptians had developed writing. Acts 7:22 says that Moses was "educated in all the wisdom of the Egyptians," which would have included Egyptian writing—and probably Akkadian, which was the lingua franca of the day. But what about Hebrew? Kenneth Kitchen observes that an alphabetic script was developed in Canaan in the first half of the second millennium that is found in several forms throughout the region, including simplified cuneiform characters on clay tablets in Ugarit and linear alphabetic writings on pottery, sherds, and presumably papyrus in south Canaan. He concludes, "we should consider a Moses or a Joshua writing on papyrus, skins, or even waxed tablets in alphabetic late Canaanite [a dialect precursor to standard Hebrew]" (Kitchen 2003, 304–7). William Albright and Thomas Lambdin also stress the importance of what they call the Proto-Sinaitic inscriptions dated c. 1500 B.C., "a series of rather crudely inscribed texts discovered at Serabit el-Khadim, an Egyptian turquoise and copper mining site in the Sinai Peninsula" which were presumably etched by the slave miners (Albright and Lambdin 1970, 135–38).

ORIGINAL READERS

In the case of Leviticus, the original readers would have been the audience that first heard Moses declare to the newly formed nation the revelations that God had given him. Historically, even up through the early church period, written documents generally were read aloud, especially before collective audiences. As participants in the exodus, the hearers would have been mostly Israelites who had been enslaved in Egypt, although Exodus 12:38 refers to a "mixed multitude" that left Egypt with the "sons of Israel." The text indicates that this mixed multitude included Egyptians (Lev. 24:10) as well as representatives of various Canaanite tribes (Num. 32:12). Even though the first copy, so to speak, was delivered orally, the biblical evidence suggests that it was in written form at essentially the same time.

As part of the Torah, Leviticus was first written to provide the exodus generation a concrete reminder of God's directions on how they were to both live and worship when they settled in the land to which they were headed. As a written record, it would provide the instruction God gave for future generations that would not have been at Sinai.

PLACE OF WRITING

Since the text of Leviticus flows right out of Exodus, which ends with the shekinah filling the tabernacle, the location of the writing was at the base of Mount Sinai where the nation of Israel was camped, subsequent to the exodus from Egypt. The book begins in the courtyard of the newly erected tabernacle described in Exodus 40. Leviticus consists of some forty pericopes, most of which begin with the statement "the Lord [YHWH] spoke." While given over a period of weeks, the book does not seem to leave that location, although some revelations from God may have been given to Moses atop the mount. Even though it was written at Sinai, much of the book provides guidelines that would not be implemented until the nation was settled in the land; thus, the book applies to Israel in Canaan after the conquest.

Shekinah

The term "shekinah" does not appear in the Bible. It was developed during the postexilic period to describe "the immanent presence and activity of God in the world order" (Drumwright 1985, 388) and especially is used to describe the glory or presence of God in the tabernacle (here) and later in the temple (2 Chron. 7:1–3). It appears to be derived from the root שָׁכַן, which in its verbal form means "to dwell, to settle, to reside, or to be enthroned." The noun translated "tabernacle" is from that same root. While Exodus describes the erection of the tabernacle and the presence of the shekinah, the intermediate step of dedicating the tabernacle actually is described in Numbers 7–9, which culminates with a reiteration of the shekinah filling the tabernacle.

DATE OF WRITING

The book claims to have begun with divine declarations on the day that the tabernacle was dedicated. As demonstrated elsewhere, the probable date of the exodus was spring 1446 B.C. (Harbin 2005, 135–38). According to Exodus 40:2, the tabernacle was set up on the first day of the first month of the following year, which would mean the revelation began in the spring of 1445 B.C., and likely the records of what was revealed were written if not immediately, then very shortly after they were given. Preparations for leaving Sinai began on the first day of the second month (Num. 1:1), and the nation left Sinai on the twentieth day of the second month (Num. 10:11), suggesting that the book was written during that approximately thirty-to-fifty-day period.

OCCASION FOR WRITING

While the covenant between God and Israel was instituted early during that year at Sinai (Exod. 20–24), with the dedication of the tabernacle and its corporate worship system, the nation now needed guidelines on how to live with God as a covenant community. With the establishment of the tabernacle and the organization of a priesthood, Leviticus, along with Exodus 20–40 and Numbers 1–10, provided Israel its first organized religion. While the people were familiar with sacrifices, Leviticus provides a formal *corporate* sacrificial system that instituted regular sacrifices on behalf of the nation. Additionally, the book gives guidelines on how the Israelites should interact with each other as a covenant people, especially with regard to the social structure, including what may be called social outliers.

HISTORICAL SETTING

At Sinai, the Israelites were in a cultural transition. While their ethnic ancestors, the patriarchs in Genesis, had generally been seminomadic, for the previous four hundred years or so the descendants of the patriarchs had been settled in Egypt in the land of Goshen. Evidence suggests that in the process they had become farmers who had flocks and herds, as opposed to being predominantly nomadic shepherds (Exod. 1:14 notes that they labored in the fields, and Num. 11:5 recalls the various crops they grew while in Egypt). The time at Sinai was a brief (year-long) organizational period to prepare Israel to settle in the land of Canaan that had been promised to Abraham. While the interlude between exodus and conquest stretched out to a full generation as a result of the Kadesh-barnea disbelief incident, the goal, as shown in the rest of the Pentateuch and Joshua, never changed: they would settle in Canaan, taking over fully functioning farms (Deut. 6:10–11). In that new land, the agricultural situation would be different from their previous experience. While because of Kadesh-barnea virtually all who were over twenty at the time of the exodus died before going into the land, the new generation of elders would have been teenagers in Egypt and thus have had some agricultural experience. Even so, agriculture in Canaan would be vastly different.

Some crops, such as olives, did not grow well in Egypt and would require new types of horticulture (Borowski 1987, 118). More importantly, Egyptian agriculture depended upon the Nile and its floods. While the annual flood of the Nile marked the start of the agricultural year, the rest of the year required that the farmers irrigate their crops to maintain their growth—a very human dependent process. In Canaan, the source of water would primarily be rain, something over which the people had no control. As such, they would need to live by trust in God throughout the entire year.

THEOLOGICAL THEMES

From our twenty-first-century perspective, we may view the nation of Israel and its worship as a global bridge between the fall and Jesus, the Redeemer of this fallen world. Still, we need to remember that for almost fifteen hundred years, Israel served as God's kingdom of priests, anticipating the coming Anointed One or Messiah. As such, the nation's location at the key land bridge between Egypt and Mesopotamia was crucial to its mission as a theological bridge. Because of their location and their ancestral backgrounds (Abraham was born and raised in Mesopotamia; his descendants spent centuries in Egypt), the Israelites were affected culturally by both regions. Given its mission to be a kingdom of priests, we will see that the rituals and religious practices that God gave to the nation of Israel had some affinity to what Egypt and Mesopotamia already understood. One likely reason for this would be that the pagan worship those regions practiced had derived through the corruption of worship of the true God following Noah. Although corrupted, it still carried traces of the original worship of the one true God who created all humankind (Harbin 1994, 5–44). Consequently, while the Lord directed significant differences from what the Israelites had seen in the worship of their neighbors—such as forbidding idols, which really represented false gods—at the same time there would be aspects

Introduction to Leviticus

that both would be familiar and would convey spiritual truths.

More importantly from our perspective, the rituals and religious practices set forth at Sinai were to anticipate and foreshadow the process of divine redemption and reconciliation executed through the incarnation, crucifixion, and resurrection (Col. 2:17; Heb. 10:1). Designed to serve the nation spiritually for about fifteen hundred years prior to the appearance of Jesus, those rituals and practices would have needed to make sense and provide theological meaning to an Israelite not just in the time of Moses, but in the time of David and beyond. The main portion of this commentary will attempt to understand what the Israelites at Sinai would have understood as to why they were doing what they were doing. This will be followed by bridges to our own culture.

As we work through the book, we will see that it addresses key covenant responsibilities of the common people under the guidance of their religious leaders. This is made evident in the first verses, where Moses is told to speak to the "sons of Israel," that is, the common people, to give them guidelines on to how they (the people) were to worship and maintain ritual purity and carry out their responsibilities toward God. This is the focus of the first third of the book. The remainder explores the implications of living within a community that has a covenant relationship with God. In the process it addresses proper relationships both within and between extended families, giving guidance on how individuals and families were to relate in order to build and maintain a strong society.

The last portion of the book focuses on practices that tend to break society down, culminating with warnings regarding the result to the community as a whole—specifically exile from the land that they were being given. While today we tease out these issues as aspects of what we sometimes call social justice, for the Israelites they simply emphasized proper relationships of the common people with one another

as participants in the national covenant. There we will see how the complex relationships with family and neighbors were to weave an intricate social fabric as a foundation for both cultural and personal well-being, a concept of shalom. Interwoven within those relationships we find the spiritual leaders—the priests (predominantly) and the Levites (more generally) being given responsibilities to help the nation both in its worship and in the practice of its religion within the community. This becomes evident immediately as the book opens and addresses burnt offerings, sacrifices performed by the individuals under the guidance of the priest to demonstrate personal consecration. Before we can explore those concepts, we need to clarify several key terms and theological concepts as they were apparently understood by the Israelites at Sinai.

Sacrifice as Worship

While animal sacrifice is not a part of our modern Western culture, we are not far removed from the practice. Regardless of our cultural or ethnic background, our ancestors at some point practiced animal sacrifice, although today we generally view the practice as barbaric. Perhaps it is because of that perspective that we tend to skip this book with its stress on proper sacrifice, as today these practices are not required for followers of the promised Messiah. And yet, the ubiquitous presence of sacrifices globally throughout history suggests that they represent a profoundly significant role in humankind's relationship with God, which underlies our relationship with that Messiah.

In the ancient world, sacrifices generally seemed to serve two main purposes. Both purposes built on the premise that there were spiritual beings outside of the physical realm that people worshipped. Although they were spiritual beings, they were understood to be somewhat accessible and could intervene in space-time history. Globally the pagan gods were viewed as capricious and their interventions problematic—as likely to be vengeful as helpful. Consequently, on the one hand they were feared. They seemed to be easily offended and demanded that humans provide recompenses intended to placate a god one had somehow offended (Parrinder 1984, 19–20). This may be reflected in that the general response to adversity is an internal seeking, causing one to wonder "What did I do wrong?" In essence, humans have an overwhelming sense of guilt. Historically, the dominant recompense has been an animal sacrifice, although why that specific response was required is not clear (Schwartz 2012, 3–9). While the gods seemed easily offended, and despite the underlying sense of guilt, generally the offenses were not deemed sin so much as personal affronts to the gods. Likewise, there seems to be no place in pagan systems for sacrifices in response to offenses against other humans.

The second main purpose for sacrifices in pagan systems was the hope of enticing the god to intervene on that human's behalf—in essence, a bribe (Noss 1961, 22–23). This is evident in the case of Balaam when he met with Balak. In Numbers 23:1–3, Balaam directed Balak to erect seven altars for burnt offerings, stating, "perhaps the Lord will meet me."

Despite the universality of sacrifice, the reasons are obscure and disputed (Schwartz 2012, 3–6). Moreover, the Bible never specifically delineates the "why" of sacrifice, nor does it explicitly address how the concept of sacrifice was initiated. It does clearly demonstrate that the practice began shortly after Adam and Eve were expelled from the garden. This would suggest a relationship between the fall and the practice of sacrifice (see further discussion under the topic "Atonement," below). If so, then perhaps we can conclude that Adam and Eve carried the practice of sacrifice from the garden as a reminder of how God had clothed them using garments of animal skin (Gen. 3:21). While this background strongly ties the function of sacrifices to the issue of sin, it does not suggest that they performed sacrifices seeking forgiveness for specific sins. Rather, it may be inferred that a key component of the animal sacrifice at this stage (which was prior to the inclusion of meat in the diet after the flood [Gen. 9:3–4]) was to remind Adam, Eve, and their descendants of the general nature of sin as separation from God, and how God had covered them after their awareness of their nakedness resulting from their sin.

However, the OT concept of sacrifice encompassed more than issues of sin. This is evident from the role of what we call in the next section *celebratory offerings*—that is, sacrifices of thanksgiving—which were a very important part of the Israelite system and were perhaps the most frequent purpose of sacrifice in Israel. This suggests that another component of sacrifice from early on would have been thanksgiving for God's provision, as humans were forced to labor for their food (Gen. 3:17–19). This could have been demonstrated by sacrificing a portion of what had been provided. While under the later Israelite system it tended to be an animal offering, which was shared with the community, it often involved what we have called a *gift offering* (מִנְחָה), although the term means much more than that.

TRANSLATION ANALYSIS: OFFERING (מִנְחָה)
While the Hebrew term מִנְחָה primarily means offering, it is often translated as a grain or cereal offering, primarily because of the way it is used in Leviticus 2:1, where it is a type of the larger category of offering (קָרְבָּן), but is associated with grain. It also carries a variety of alternative meanings suggesting "presents" or "gifts," and according to G. Lloyd Carr (1980a, 514–15) is used in both religious and secular contexts "to convey the attitude of homage and submission to that person." In general, we will use the term *gift offering* to show those distinctions. See also the sidebar for Leviticus 2:1.

The first sacrifices *recorded* in the Bible were performed by Cain and Abel, Adam and Eve's oldest sons. Most likely both Cain and Abel, as well as their siblings, had been taught how to sacrifice from their parents, although we are not told how or when. On this occasion, they both brought sacrifices that reflected their occupations: Cain, as a farmer, brought fruit of the ground; and Abel, as a herder, brought from the firstborn (מִבְּכֹרוֹת) of his flock. As is well known, Cain's offering was not "accepted" (שָׁעָה). Scholars have debated the reason. Given the boys' probable ages as adults who had families (see sidebar), it is highly likely that they had previously sacrificed on a number of occasions. Since both sacrifices are called "offerings" (מִנְחָה), a gift of homage, it may be inferred that this particular occasion followed a pattern that they regularly practiced and that their sacrifices on those prior occasions had been accepted by God. But this time something was different. Two hints are suggestive. The first is the observation that Abel brought "from the firstborn," that is, the best. The inference is that Cain did not. Tied to that, the Hebrew term מִנְחָה suggests an "attitude of homage and submission." These would suggest that a likely reason that Cain's offering was not accepted was that he lacked the requisite attitude that the term denotes. This would serve as a warning that appears throughout Scripture.

> ### Adam and Eve's Offspring
> While Genesis 5:4 reports that Adam and Eve had many sons and daughters, only three are named. Genesis 4:1–5 merely mentions the births of the first two, Cain and Abel, then jumps to their adult occupations, noting one occasion when they performed sacrifices. In the process, the text skips over their growing into adulthood and the likelihood that they had a number of siblings as well as their own offspring. When we read the Cain and Abel account, we learn that Cain was married at the time he murdered Abel and likely had children (Gen. 4:17). Further, when God expelled him from his homeland, there were other people spread about (Gen. 4:14–15). That Adam was 130 when Seth, his third-mentioned son who served as a replacement for Abel (Gen. 4:25), was

> born suggests a probability that multiple generations were present at the time of Cain's exile.

Admittedly, there are a number of gaps in our understanding that raise many questions. While most of these questions are unanswerable and outside the scope of this study, in terms of history it would appear that as humankind spread, especially after the diversification of languages at Babel, the worship of the Creator God became corrupted and developed into the increasing polytheisms that are evident through history. In the process humans never lost their sense of guilt, although for a variety of reasons the true God was virtually forgotten, replaced by various substitutes (Harbin 1994, 13–23). As a result, all human cultures have historically understood the need for sacrifice, at least in some sense. So, the practice carried over into the various religions that developed as substitutes for the lost truth. As humans anthropomorphized their understanding of God, the result was a variety of growing pantheons of gods that conceptually were greatly diminished from the true God, but still beyond human beings. In the process, the explanations of the purposes of sacrifice became distorted until, as noted, they came to be seen as either a method by which humans could placate a spiritual being who had been offended or a means of motivating that spiritual being to intervene on their behalf (Teeter 2011, 104–5). In either case, they reflected an innate understanding that a spiritual realm lay behind the scenes and interacted with them.

As far as the Israelites were concerned, Genesis shows that their ancestors sacrificed on an irregular basis. Thus, at Sinai, when God instituted a corporate system for the nation, he formalized and made corporate what formerly had been an ad hoc individual practice. While a strong tie between sin and sacrifice has been inferred, it is interesting that prior to Sinai no direct correlation between sin and sacrifices is indicated. This is demonstrated by the most notable sacrifices mentioned in

Genesis: Noah, who offered a burnt offering after experiencing God's deliverance from the flood (Gen. 8:20); and Abraham, who brought his son Isaac as a burnt offering at God's direction, who then provided a ram in Isaac's place (Gen. 22:2–13). In neither case had the offeror committed sin—but both events demonstrated consecration to God.

The Old Testament Sacrificial System

As presented in Leviticus, the Israelite sacrificial system is complex. While in some regards an individual sacrifice could reflect multiple reasons, the system seemed designed to serve three primary purposes: to demonstrate *consecration* to God, to *confess* sin by demonstrating remorse and repentance, and to *celebrate* God through praise for what he had done (Rainey 1975, 203–9). As described in Leviticus, the OT system divides sacrifices into three main categories that denote those purposes. The following outline points out how the various offerings fit within the overall system, while specifics are addressed in the discussion of the appropriate section of the exegetical study of the text of Leviticus.

Consecratory

Consecratory offerings served to demonstrate the consecration of a person or a thing to God. The issue of the forgiveness of sin might be a correlation of that consecration, that is, the individual may be aware of sin as a barrier and through consecration may be requesting that barriers be removed; but forgiveness of sin does not seem to be the primary purpose. Rather, consecration seems to have been a much more intense expression of the relationship of the offeror to God, with offerings for sin established as a separate category. The main type of consecratory offering was the burnt offering, which is the dominant form of sacrifice offered prior to Sinai, although after Sinai the cereal and the drink offerings were two optional additions.

The Burnt Offering

By definition, the burnt offering (עֹלָה) was an offering in which the sacrifice was totally burned upon the altar (with the exception of the blood and the skin within the Levitical system). In contrast, most Israelite offerings burned just part of the animal and the rest of it was cooked and used as food. As shown in Leviticus 1, Israelites had three options regarding what animals could be used for this offering, depending on the offeror's socioeconomic status.

The primary purpose of the burnt offering was to consecrate or dedicate. As Anson Rainey (1975, 205) describes it, burnt offerings "represented the act of committal that should accompany the repentance expressed by the sin and guilt offerings. They also opened the way to the fellowship of communal sacrifices that could follow." It is significant that when a confessional offering (see below) was included, it necessarily preceded the burnt offering, suggesting that the sin issue needed to be addressed separately before one could be consecrated.

The book of Leviticus begins by describing the process for an individual to present an *optional personal* burnt offering for consecration. As will be seen, this personal offering would represent a special demonstration of piety on behalf of the individual. Later, Leviticus 6 describes how the priests were to represent the nation on a continual basis by offering a *corporate* burnt offering twice daily for national consecration. Whereas personal burnt offerings were optional, after Sinai corporate burnt offerings for consecration were not only mandatory but required to be repeated daily. Subsequent revelation adds specific holy days where special consecration was made. This describes a system where the corporate body was consecrated regularly by a representative (a priest) and the individual participated in that corporate consecration vicariously.

The Gift (or Grain or Cereal) Offering

In the system given at Sinai, the gift (or grain or cereal offering [מִנְחָה]) was predominantly an optional, associated enhancement of the burnt offering. It consisted of a mixture of flour and oil seasoned with salt, with frankincense serving as an optional addition. It could accompany burnt offerings as well as various celebratory offerings. On some occasions, notably firstfruits, it apparently served as an offering in and of itself. Normally part of the gift offerings went to the priests, who ate of it as part of their daily rations. In those cases, the frankincense was removed with the token portion (a handful of the flour and a handful of the oil) that was burned. The exception to this was when the priest brought a gift offering at the time of his dedication.

Drink Offering

The drink offering (נֶסֶךְ) was an offering of wine that accompanied some burnt offerings. It is never described as a separate offering, but was included as part of the ritual procedures on certain occasions, such as the dedication of Aaron as high priest and the annual festivals of Firstfruits and Pentecost. It was poured out on the fire and burned.

Confessional

In the OT system, confessional offerings demonstrated remorse and repentance for violations of the Torah given at Sinai (i.e., sin or transgression). Theologians tend to use the term *expiation* for this category because the term translated as "sin offering" (חַטָּאת) is also the term used for one of the two subcategories translated as "sin offerings" (חַטָּאת) and "guilt offerings" (אָשֵׁם). By their nature, confessional offerings generally were public announcements of guilt by the guilty person with regard to specific issues. Offerings in this category were brought to the priest and the matter was confessed orally. On some occasions, such as Yom Kippur, the confessional offering could reflect a more general recognition of personal (or corporate) sinfulness without a specific issue being named.

After the animal was slaughtered and specific procedures addressed, the blood and certain fatty portions were offered on the altar. If the priest or the whole congregation were confessing, the remainder of the meat was burned in a clean place. Otherwise, the meat was given to the priests.

Purification or Sin Offering

We call the first category of confessional offerings a purification offering (חַטָּאת). It was to atone for a transgression where no restitution was available. This transgression could be either ethical (violation of a moral standard) or ritual (such as touching something unclean). As in the case of the burnt offering, the required animal varied with the socioeconomic status of the offeror.

Reparation or Guilt Offering

The guilt offering or reparation offering (אָשֵׁם) is also called a trespass offering (KJV). This involved a situation where someone had been denied his or her rightful due. It required reparation of the loss followed by public acknowledgment that the offeror had defrauded his or her countryman. The primary transgression involved causing some financial loss to a fellow Israelite (such as through robbery, extortion, or failure to return an item that was found). In this case, the individual admitted his guilt by repaying the loss with a penalty. The penalty was a minimum of a 20 percent fine or penalty (Lev. 5:14), although in Exodus 22:1 it is as much as 500 percent in the case of a stolen ox (five for one). A reparation offering required a ram as the sacrifice. As in the case of a purification offering, the fatty portions were burned, and the meat was given to the priests.

Celebratory

A celebratory offering (שֶׁלֶם) was essentially an offering of thanksgiving and praise. Three subgroups to this category address three different situations as shown below. Deuteronomy 12:10–32 suggests that this category of sacrifice might be offered at places in the land where

Introduction to Leviticus

God had done something special. Again, one of the subcategories is given the same name as the overall category. The key point of the category as a whole was that it expressed gratitude to God for having done something to, or for, the sacrificer.

The Location of Sacrifices

After the nation moved into the land, the tabernacle's role seems to have changed, but the specifics are not clear. While the nation was in the wilderness, the tabernacle was the site of all rituals. Once the nation spread throughout the land where many people required two, three, or more days to walk to the sanctuary, the tabernacle seems to have remained the focus of corporate worship, where the priests served daily representing the nation. For the average Israelites, God's guidelines were that when they got to the land they were to worship at the tabernacle three times a year (Exod. 23:14–17). The Levites, the priestly tribe that was scattered in forty-eight different locations through the land (Josh. 21:1–42), helped serve the people locally.

We are never told what the Levites did once they were dispersed, but Numbers 18:21–32 notes that they would be in charge of managing the tithes once they were settled and growing crops. It also designates them as helps to Aaron and the priest, at least for the time they were in the wilderness (Harbin 2021b, 695–97). Immediately after his first revelation at Sinai, God specifically directed that when they arrived in the land they were to build earthen altars "in every place where I cause my name to be remembered" (Exod. 20:23–26). How God caused his name to be remembered is not specified, but these could be places where he performed significant works or miracles. This passage seems to authorize limited local worship, although idols are expressly and repeatedly prohibited. This could explain situations that we read about in Judges and the Historical Books where offerings were conducted at a number of locations besides the central sanctuary.

Unfortunately, this practice was greatly abused, as the Israelites failed to distinguish worship of the Lord from the natives' gods.

The celebratory offerings are also called communal sacrifices because the meat was eaten by the whole community (or at least by close friends and family). In the process, the fatty portion and offal was burned as an offering to God. The right thigh was given to the priests. But the rest of the meat was eaten by the sacrificer and friends. It is significant that the animal had to be eaten on the day in which it was sacrificed, which would motivate the worshipper to invite as many people as possible to ensure no leftovers. The votive offering was an exception in that leftovers could be eaten the next day, but not on the third. A possible reason for this was that votive sacrifices might tend to be bigger, since they resulted from promises made after God had done something specifically asked for. As noted, Leviticus cites three types of celebratory offerings.

The Shalom Offering

While the term *shalom* (from the same root as שָׁלֵם) is sometimes applied to the entire category of celebratory offerings, it is also a particular celebratory offering. This particular shalom offering is often translated as the peace offering. In this study we will use the term "celebratory" for the larger category, and "shalom" for the particular, although another term used to describe the particular shalom offering is "thanksgiving" or "praise offering" (תּוֹדָה). The shalom celebratory offering was intended to express thanks to God for whatever he had done in the recent past or present. It was not necessarily a result of a request on the part of the observer.

The Votive Offering

Like the shalom offering, the votive (נֶדֶר) offering celebrated a specific work that God had done in direct response to a request or promise to him (a vow, also the Hebrew word נֶדֶר). Once God responded, the vow had to be completed first, and then the votive offering presented before the entire community.

The Freewill Offering

The final category of celebratory offering is called a freewill offering (נְדָבָה). The term derives from a verb that suggests "uncompelled and free movement of the will into divine service or sacrifice" (Coppes 1980d, 2:554–55). No special reason seems to have been given for this last variety of celebratory offering. Rather, it is viewed as a voluntary contribution, hence the term "freewill." It may be that the person just wanted to praise God.

Overall, the celebratory offerings seem to have provided powerful community-building opportunities. As described in the text, each of the three apparently involved a person calling together all of his or her neighbors to have a sacrifice and dinner together. While this may have been done at the central sanctuary as in the case of Hannah's offering in 1 Samuel 1, it is suggested that this could be done locally, where God could be celebrated within the community as in the case of Samuel in 1 Samuel 9:19 (see also Judg. 6:25–26; 1 Sam. 6:15; 7:9). In either case, the process seems to have been that in the process of sacrifice the offeror would recount what God had done that deserved the special praise and the special meal, and perhaps even sing a psalm or two that may have been written for the occasion.

Praise Psalms

As might be expected, praise psalms are simply songs that praise God. We divide praise psalms into two types: descriptive and declarative. Descriptive psalms describe aspects of God's greatness, and as such they are timeless. The classic example of this is Psalm 8. On the other hand, declarative praise psalms recount and thank God for some specific deed he had done. As such, many declarative praise psalms were likely written as follow-ons to a lament. The psalmist was in dire straits. He wrote a song crying out to God asking for deliverance, perhaps making a vow in the process. After God delivered, the psalmist wrote a follow-on song praising God for the answer to prayer.

It seems that many of those praise psalms were sung at a public sacrifice or shalom offering where the Israelite was sharing with his neighbors what God had done. This seems to be especially true in the case of a votive offering, which by its very nature was a sacrifice intended to praise God for his intervention and deliverance in a specific request. For example, David wrote laments about Saul and his men in Psalms 54, 57, and 59. He also wrote Psalm 18, which praised God for his deliverance from Saul, which may have followed any of those laments or on any other number of occasions (Harbin 2005, 236–38). One of the more interesting aspects of the praise psalms is that declarative praise psalms, that is, songs "thanking God for answering [the psalmist's] prayer about a specific instance in the past[,] seem to be unique to Israel" (Hill and Walton 2009, 276).

Sin and Sin (or Confession) Offerings in Leviticus

Sin is generally considered to be an act that violates some religious rule or directive given by God. According to *WTNID* the English word "sin" primarily means "transgression of religious law: an offense against God" or something similar. The popular online resource Wikipedia says essentially the same thing, but adds the popular concept that "each culture has its own interpretation of what it means to commit a sin" (https://en.wikipedia.org/wiki/Sin). However, J. Budziszewski (2011, 19), along with others, argues that there are actually moral absolutes that transcend culture, which we all grasp but try to redefine in order to rationalize our personal behavior. When we look for a biblical understanding of the concept, the original languages use a number of words. Charles Ryrie (1986,

209–12) points out that a number of terms are used in both Testaments that must be studied, including "at least eight basic words for sin in the Old Testament and a dozen in the New." He proposes that a proper definition would require a carefully nuanced integration of all of those terms, which would be lengthy. After some discussion, he cites Augustus Strong's (1907, 549) succinct definition to serve as a starting point: "Sin is lack of conformity to the moral law of God, either in action, disposition, or state." Most importantly, Ryrie argues that "the chief characteristic of sin is that it is directed against God" (1986, 212).

In terms of the OT, four key terms illustrate the scope of meaning of what we call sin: "sin" (חָטָא), a word that can mean "error, failure, miss, miss the way, sin, incur guilt"; "transgressions" (פֶּשַׁע), but with the concepts of "rebel, transgress, revolt"; "iniquity" (עָוֹן), encompassing "iniquity, guilt, punishment"; and "guilt" (אַשְׁמָה) derived from a word meaning "to be guilty or to trespass" (see Daane 1985, 444; Livingston 1980a, 1980b, 1980d; and Schultz 1980a). In other words, Hebrew terminology provides a spectrum of actions that we understand should be labeled as sin, ranging from inadvertent violations of God's standards to overt rebellion or evil acts. All four of the above terms are used in Leviticus, but the most common is the first term חָטָא (ḥaṭaʾ) and its derived forms. It is also the principal word for sin in the overall OT (Livingston 1980b). Additionally, a derivative of ḥaṭaʾ is used as a category of the expiatory offerings. Consequently, this study will focus on that Hebrew term using the transliteration ḥaṭaʾ.

Klaus Koch (1980, 310) observes that the semantic root ḥ/ḥṭʾ is shared by "all the Semitic languages" and it always "designates negative conditions and conduct, especially with reference to human agents in a religious context." A popular understanding is that the term derives from a concept in weapons usage where the individual does not hit the target (i.e., it "misses"). As G. Herbert Livingston

(1980b, 277) puts it, "The verbal forms occur in enough secular contexts to provide a basic picture of the word's meaning. In Judges 20:16, the left-handed slingers of Benjamin are said to have the skill to throw stones at targets and 'not miss.'" To a large extent this seems to be the most common explanation of the word's basic meaning: "to miss the mark." If that is so, then the question one must ask with regard to the context of Leviticus is: What is the mark that has been missed? Based on the English understanding of the term "sin," it seems that the answer is proper obedience to the command or directive of God. However, more recent work has raised serious question with regard to this "'concrete' etymology." Koch (1980, 311) suggests rather that the concrete uses are metaphorical uses of an originally religious term. Similarly, Nobuyoshi Kiuchi (2003, 23–24) argues that ḥaṭaʾ should be understood as an abstract term.

Concrete Etymology

The term refers to the premise that language supposedly developed from concrete (i.e., a reference to physical objects and acts) to abstract (more conceptual understandings). James Barr (1961, 30) states "the idea of the extreme concreteness of the languages of 'primitive' peoples has been much criticized." He suggests two reasons for this. One is confusion between concrete and specific on one hand, and abstract and general on the other. In other words, specificity is often confused for concreteness. The other reason is the struggle that linguists have in validating this pattern. While the standard view of language origin assumes a development from a start where all vocabulary in the original speech was concrete in the sense of being tied to a readily perceptive physical world with abstract usage developing later, the study of language does not seem to support this (Harbin 1982, 53). Rather, there is a historically discerned development of language that shows a pattern of simplification rather than increasing complexity (p. 54).

While René Péter-Contesse and John Ellington (1992, 47) begin with this concrete picture in their discussion of Leviticus 4:2, they then build on it to incorporate relational aspects pertinent to the rest of the book. They state that "the primary meaning of the Hebrew word used for 'sin' here is not a moral one, as if breaking a specific commandment of the Law. Rather, it conveys the idea of breaking a relationship." This would suggest that *ḥaṭa'* was viewed as an act that either by commission or omission failed to develop or maintain a right relationship with another person, especially God.

To clarify, when we think of the OT law, we think of rules, and there is a human tendency to think rules are arbitrary, especially if for some reason we do not want to obey them. While in our fallen world we recognize that some rules are indeed arbitrary and often are intended primarily for the rulemaker's advantage, we also recognize that good social structure demands that rules should articulate specific acts that promote good relationships, although that articulation tends to be done in terms of negatives—that is, defining what good behavior is by giving specifics to demonstrate what it is not. One does not need direct revelation from God to understand that. As Budziszewski expresses it, what philosophers call natural law really contains moral truths "that we all really know—truths which a normal human being is unable *not* to know" (2011, 19, emphasis original).

Defining by Negatives

Defining something by demonstrating what it is not is fairly common, especially with regard to abstract concepts such as infinite (it has no end), or eternal (time has no beginning or ending). Ted Dorman (2001, 47) observes that when we define the incommunicable attributes of God, "much of the language under this heading, including the word incommunicable itself, is negative language which emphasizes what God is not like." When it comes to behavior, the common practice is to define good behavior as avoiding specific bad behaviors—something that is easier to describe. Even there, however, the descriptions are understood to be illustrative, not exhaustive.

Further, "law" translates the Hebrew word *torah* (תּוֹרָה), which actually means *teaching*. While the OT law contains commands and rules, as a whole it is a complex *teaching* on how members of a God-led community may best relate to God and to one another. This teaching in the OT is organized around the Decalogue or the Ten Commandments. While we tend to view them as commandments, the Hebrew labels them "Ten Words" (דְּבָרִים [Deut. 10:4]), and they really articulate principles on which the nation of Israel was to function (Harbin 2005, 142–55, 170–74). Beyond those basic principles, most of the laws are case studies—examples that illustrate how those principles were to be carried out in a God-fearing society.

Old Testament Law

OT law (as all law) consists of two types: apodictic and casuistic. Apodictic law is arbitrary law that is predicated on the authority of the lawgiver. In essence, it might be characterized as "do it because I said so." Casuistic laws are case histories or case studies. The US Constitution is largely apodictic. The authority is "we, the people of the United States." As one reads through the various articles, it is clear that many are just asserted. For example, Article I, Section I reads, "All legislative powers herein granted shall be vested in a Congress of the United States, which shall consist of a Senate and House of Representatives." In contrast, much of our legal system is based on cases, such as *Roe v. Wade* or *Miranda v. the State of Arizona*. In the ANE, most of the laws were actually case studies or examples. For example, Hammurabi's code contains approximately 282 hypothetical cases, such as number 22: "If a free man [*awilum*] committed robbery and has been caught, that free man [*awilum*] shall be put to death" (*ANET*, 167). In the case of the OT, most of the traditional 613 laws (according to the Talmud, b. Mak. 23b) are case studies that illustrate the relatively few apodictic laws, of which the primary example is the Decalogue, although Leviticus 19 also contains a number of apodictic declarations. An example of the distinction is the sixth commandment (Exod. 20:13), which states "You shall not murder"—a flat, arbitrary declaration. Later in the legal material, cases are presented that illustrate when the taking of a life is not considered murder, perhaps because of divine permission (capital punishment) or because it was accidental homicide.

In terms of translation, this suggests that *ḥaṭa'* is a concept much more encompassing than failing to obey some rule. The same may be said for the English word "sin." Thus, while a person who violated one of those rules committed *ḥaṭa'*, a person could commit *ḥaṭa'* without violating one of those rules. Jesus articulated that in his teaching. For example, in Matthew 5:27–28, he points out how looking at a woman with lust is adultery in the heart—that is, sin—even if the man never actually commits the physical act of adultery. As such, it is proposed that the term *ḥaṭa'* denotes an act (physical, verbal, or mental) that damages one's relationship with another person—especially, most frequently, and ultimately with God. This would seem to be especially apropos in the context of the covenant relationship of the nation of Israel.

In the context of Leviticus, the Hebrew term *ḥaṭa'* is especially challenging in that a derivative of the verb, the noun *ḥaṭṭa't* (חַטָּאת), is translated both as "sin" and as "sin offering" (Livingston 1980b, 278). For example, the last part of Leviticus 4:3 could be translated literally as "if the anointed priest sins [חָטָא] . . . let him offer to the Lord [YHWH] . . . a sin [חַטָּאת] for his sin [חַטָּאת] that he has sinned [חָטָא]." It is this relationship that has historically prompted the translation of חַטָּאת into English as "sin offering."

Jacob Milgrom (1991, 253–54) argues that translating *ḥaṭṭa't* as "*sin* offering is inaccurate on all grounds, contextually, morphologically, and etymologically" (emphasis added). He goes on to observe that the "range of the *ḥaṭṭā't* in the cult gainsays the notion of sin." He cites the examples of a woman who recovers from childbirth (Lev. 12), a Nazirite who has completed the Nazirite vow (Num. 6), and the dedication of the new altar (Lev. 8:15), none of which are sins but which all require a *ḥaṭṭa't*. Based on those other uses of the *ḥaṭṭa't*, and on rabbinic sources, he maintains that the purpose of the *ḥaṭṭa't* offering is "ritual purification," and as such the term should be translated as a "purification offering." That is the term we will use.

Milgrom's argument is based on the fact that the noun *ḥaṭṭa't* is derived from the *piel* stem. In this case, the verb would have a "privative connotation" (i.e., the removal of some quality or attribute [GKC §52h]). This is seen in the few cases where the verb shows up in the *piel*, such as Leviticus 8:15 where the NASB and other modern translations translate it as "to purify," or Leviticus 14:49 where they translate it as "to cleanse." While that may explain how the noun can be translated with the idea of "ritual purification," it then raises the question: How can the same noun be used both in reference to an act that the person has done to produce a state, as well as a process to resolve the resulting state? It would seem that what we may actually have here is what grammarians call a "contronym," a word that has opposite meanings depending on the context. For example, the English word "cleave" (noted in the KJV translation of the Genesis 2 account of the creation of Eve) can mean "to cling to," but also it can mean "to divide or separate." In the case of *ḥaṭṭa't*, we may have a situation where two nouns were derived from the two stems and ended up with the same spelling (homonyms), but because of different stem origins they carried opposite meanings (antonyms). It should be noted here, however, that when the word *ḥaṭṭa't* is translated as "sin," it generally is the object of the phrase, "which he has sinned [חָטָא]," thus providing a linguistic indicator of the meaning.

If *hata'* denotes an act (physical, verbal, or mental) that damages one's relationship with another person—especially, most frequently, and ultimately with God—then the *hatta't* offering would reflect the removal of the impediment in the relationship. Ultimately, this is with God. As David points out in Psalm 51:4, although he had committed adultery (a sin against Bathsheba and Uriah, her husband), and murder (a sin against Uriah), not to mention the secondary relationship breakdowns in terms of him and his people, his army, and especially his general who had been tasked to set up the murder, in reality his sin was against God, since it was God's laws that he violated (Ryrie 1986, 212).

However, while *hatta't* appears to have represented purification, nothing inherent in the act itself removes the cause of impurity (or the sin) as if it were a magical formula. Rather, it denotes a public declaration of an internal decision of the will as the person bringing the offering opens his or her heart to the cleansing of the Spirit. In that sense, the *hatta't* purifies the person who brings the offering with the correct attitude and they can leave the altar with a sense of having been forgiven.

Confessional Offerings and Atonement

Perhaps the most important thing that should be stressed is that the act of performing a confessional offering did not produce forgiveness of sins, which is a key reason why the term "sin offering" should probably be avoided. The OT sacrificial system did not provide forgiveness of sin, although the confessional sacrifices seem to suggest that. Key in this regard is the emphasis that the confessional ("expiatory"?) sacrifices were also performed in the case of unintentional acts, or events that were not sins, such as the birth of a baby. That is why David declared that the sacrifices (זֶבַח, a collective term incorporated all categories) God desires are "a broken spirit" and a

---

"broken and crushed heart" (Ps. 51:17 [HB 19]; see also Ps. 40:6, as well as Isa. 1:10–1; Amos 5:21–24; Mic. 6:6–8 7).

As noted above, another use of the *hatta't* offering is in the dedication of the new altar (Lev. 8:15). Clearly an inanimate altar would not have sinned. However, in an analogical sense, the same act can also serve to purify a device such as an altar, which is then used to promote the relationship between a person and God.

Atonement

Atonement is a theological concept that we somewhat intuitively understand, yet find complex and difficult to nail down. Ironically, the English word we use in translation seems clearer than its Hebrew antecedents. Our English word "atonement" exhibits its Middle English root when it is broken down by syllables—"at-one-ment"—where it manifests sharply the idea of bringing together, or reconciliation. Theologically, it is used to describe the bringing together or reconciliation of people and God. But once we get beyond that base, the issue becomes complex.

The basic concept of atonement is bridging the gap between humankind and God, a goal that has historically been the impetus of all religion. However, since the point of separation between humankind and God is the issue of sin, addressing the sin issue is the necessary starting point (see section above, "Sin and Sin (or Confession) Offerings in Leviticus"). From a human perspective, this requires not just recognition of the presence of that gap, but more importantly its implications. These include death, both physical and spiritual; our sin natures, which not only persist in sin (both unintentional and intentional) but drastically distort our perception of the world around us; and our total inability to bridge that gap ourselves. Throughout history, various religions have recognized the first two of these and have attempted to address both issues in various ways. However, it is that last item—our inability to bridge the gap ourselves—where religions all the way back to Adam and Eve have failed. The Genesis account of Adam and Eve relates how, after they had eaten the forbidden fruit, they realized that they were "naked"—that is, they saw the gap. While physical nakedness is clearly part of it, the word used here goes beyond the lack of clothing and implies "awareness of the openness of their guilt to God" (Schultz 1980c, 656).

Naked

Adam and Eve are described as naked both before (Gen. 2:25) and after the fall (Gen. 3:7), but with the major difference that afterward they experienced shame and fear. The two words translated "naked" are spelled differently, and Ronald Allen (1980c) suggests that they may be from different roots. It would appear that "naked" prior to the fall may be from the root עָרָה, suggesting being "uncovered." In contrast, the root of the post-fall term עוּר (Schultz 1980c, 656) suggests being "exposed, or laid bare." It is important to remember that at this point they were the only human beings in the world, and as freshly formed parts of the creation God had pronounced as very good, they would have been physically in their prime, which may be reflected in the statement they were not ashamed (Gen. 2:25). As such, it would then seem that the text uses a wordplay (technically called paronomasia) where the realization of physical nudity/nakedness provides a visible picture of the spiritual issue.

Their immediate reaction was to cover the external manifestation, the physical nakedness. The text tells us that they sewed together fig leaves for that purpose. While fig leaves are large, and as leaves go they are rather tough, they are still easily shredded and are not longlasting. As such, it is significant that when God covered them, it was with animal skins—material that actually toughens as it dries, although it is still temporary. Moreover, once again the Hebrew makes a subtle distinction between the work of Adam and Eve and that of God. They made "coverings" (so the NIV). This term (חֲגֹרֹת) is translated variously as "loin coverings" (NASB) or "loincloths" (ESV) or "girdles" (Yamauchi 1980a, 263). In response, God made "garments" (כָּתְנוֹת), which may have significant theological implications (this word has the idea of tunics—*TWOT* s.v. "כָּתֹנֶת" 1:459). The text does not state what would be obvious to the reader—to get the skin from the animal, it had to die. Thus, from the beginning we see a process whereby an animal had to die to provide a "covering" for fallen people. This substitution seems to provide a visible picture of key issues involved in the reconciliation process. Throughout history, human efforts have attempted to solve the problem of our separation from God, but at best they are fragile, temporary, and thus totally inadequate. Still, we need to keep in mind that this picture of animal sacrifice was something given by God to guide sinful humans in their quest to reconcile themselves with God, although this is but a picture of the vastly more complex spiritual issue.

As we approach the matter from a theological perspective, we note that the English word "atone" translates a variety of Hebrew and Greek words with meanings that do not seem to be as straightforward as the etymological understanding of our English. In the case of the Greek, it is generally various forms of the Greek ἱλάσκομαι, which carries the meanings of "to propitiate" (English synonyms include "to appease, conciliate, or make favorably inclined") as well as "to purge from sin" and "to expiate" (Büchsel 1965). It is the last term, "expiate," that tends to catch our attention in Leviticus, but for our purposes we are concerned about the Hebrew antecedent.

Expiation and Propitiation

These theological terms have subtle differences that emphasize aspects of the process of redemption. Ryrie (1986, 295–97) defines propitiation as "the turning away of wrath by an offering. In relation to soteriology, propitiation means placating or satisfying the wrath of God by the atoning sacrifice of Christ." He differentiates this from expiation, noting that while expiation "has to do with the reparation for a wrong; propitiation carries the added idea of appeasing an offended person and thus brings into the picture the question of why the offended person was offended." In terms of our study in Leviticus, the confessional offerings, specific sacrifices that deal with what we call sin, serve as expiatory sacrifices that address the repairing of relationships.

In the case of the Hebrew, the key term is *kipper* (כִּפֶּר), which is somewhat problematic. The classic Hebrew lexicon, BDB (s.v. "כָּפַר" 497), defines this word in the *piel* stem as "to cover over, pacify, propitiate." BDB's idea of "cover over" largely derives from an Arabic cognate, *kafara*, and given the background of Eden this understanding is very enticing. More recent scholarship, however, has deemed this as problematic for two reasons. First, this connotation of the Arabic cognate is from the Qur'an, and may be an Islamic derivation from a Judeo-Christian background. Moreover, study suggests "an historical relationship between Akk. *kuppuru* [meaning 'purify cultically'] and Heb. *kipper*." Some propose a concept of cultic purification based on this correlation with the Akkadian term *kupபுru*, although the cultic texts do not address any sin offerings or blood sacrifices (Lang 1995, 290).

Second, while there are some places where the Hebrew word does suggest covering in a concrete sense (as in the case of Noah in Genesis 6:14, where he covered the ark with pitch), as the Hebrew term is used in the legal material (including Leviticus) very often the idea of covering even in an abstract sense does not

really seem to apply. For example, in Exodus 29:36, the altar on which atoning sacrifices were to be made is "atoned for" as part of the tabernacle dedication process. Given the variety of uses, some scholars now suggest that the Hebrew term כָּפַר is really at least two homonyms: one suggesting covering as in the case of the ark, the other being a more theological term (Ross 2002, 93).

Even recognizing *kipper* to be a theological term does not address all of the issues arising from the way the term is used in the OT legal material. As we work through Leviticus, we will note that in the majority of the cases where *kipper* is used it is tied to the process of the confessional offerings, that is, offerings traditionally understood to atone for what we call sin—although in the section on "Sin and Sin (or Confessional) Offerings" above, we propose that "purification offering" might be a better understanding than "sin offering." For example, in Leviticus 4:20, the statement is made that when the congregation brings a bull and performs a purification offering (חַטָּאת), "the priest shall make atonement for them, and they will be forgiven." There are several factors that need to be kept in mind here. First, prior to the institution of the sacrificial system being initiated at Sinai, the OT does not record any sacrifices specifically designated to address the issue of sin in the sense of expiation, that is, in making amends for it. While we would suggest that sin is a factor of the pre-Sinaitic sacrifices (the act of self-consecration would derive from recognition of separation and express a desire to alleviate the situation), the examples we see in the patriarchal accounts do not seem to point in that direction. Perhaps the closest would be the case of Job (likely a contemporary of Jacob [Harbin 2005, 115–18]) who performed burnt offerings for his sons in case they had sinned—but the text also states that his sacrifice was "to consecrate them" (Job 1:5). At Sinai, the confessional offerings really were presented as an aspect of the newly established covenant relationship.

A second factor is that for the original audience, the delineation of the Sinai system taken at face value would require an animal sacrifice for every sinful act. Undoubtedly even the original audience would have seen that as a physical impossibility. No one would have enough animals to perform the required sacrifices to address each individual sin. Beyond that, when the text in Leviticus ties purification offerings to sin, it is to *unintentional* sins (Lev. 4:2). No one is really sure of every sinful act he or she has committed unintentionally. Further, the same offering is required in a number of cases where sin is not viewed as an issue, such as a woman who recovers from childbirth (Lev. 12). In addition, the directions are that the person was to bring the sacrifice to the "doorway of the Tent of Meeting" (Lev. 4:4). Even in the wilderness where the nation was camped surrounding the tabernacle, this would have created significant logistical problems. Once they were in the land, where most people lived a multiple days' journey from the central sanctuary, it would have been impossible. It then seems likely that the expectation was that an individual would perform such a sacrifice only in the case of a significant transgression, whether singularly or as an accumulation. As suggested in the "Overview of the Sacrificial System" above, the corporate confessional offerings (especially Yom Kippur) seem to have served to remind the individuals of their needy state, while personal confession addressed the routine sins of daily life for members of the covenant enacted at Sinai. This might be seen in Jesus's parable of the Pharisee and the tax collector (Luke 18:9–14). At a time when the temple still stood and sacrifices were still being offered, Jesus related an account of a Pharisee and a tax collector, both of whom went to *the temple* to pray, with no mention of either performing a sacrifice. The tax collector is portrayed as standing with downcast eyes, beating his breast and crying, "God be merciful to me, the sinner."

Jesus then stated, "this man went to his house justified" (δεδικαιωμένος, "justified, declared righteous"). Since they were at the temple, he may have performed a sacrifice, but based on Jesus's words it is clear that if he had done so, it was not the sacrifice that justified him.

Justify

In his commentary on Luke, Robert Stein (1992, 450–51) observes regarding the tax collector's prayer: "The verb used here (*hilasthēti*) is found elsewhere in the NT only in Hebrews 2:17. It means *to expiate* or *propitiate*. The noun (*hilastērion*) is used in this sense in Romans 3:25 (cf. also 1 John 2:2; 4:10), and in Hebrews 9:5 it designates the place where such expiation/propitiation takes place. The publican in his prayer sought God's mercy in order to have his sins covered and the divine wrath removed from him." Stein goes on to say, with regard to the verb "justified," "This term means more than just being forgiven, for it also involves the gift of a new standing before God. This is evident from 18:9, where the noun is used to describe a 'righteous' standing before God (cf. 16:15). The publican stood before God after his prayer possessing a new relationship (not a moral character) with God. He possessed a righteousness given him by grace (cf. Phil. 3:8)."

In any event, we now understand that the atoning work of Jesus Christ has removed the need for the corporate daily and annual sacrifices. First, Hebrews 10:4 states that "it is impossible for the blood of bulls and goats to take away sins." Subsequently, the writer says that "we are sanctified through the offering of the body of Jesus Christ once for all" (Heb. 10:10), and then "by one offering he has perfected for all time those who are sanctified" (Heb. 10:14).

It would seem that the biggest source of confusion is the tendency to equate atonement with salvation. As Allen Ross puts it, equating atonement with redemption "in the salvific sense . . . is fine if NT doctrine is being discussed. . . . In Israel an atoning sacrifice was not the condition of a relationship to the Lord; rather it was offered as a means of strengthening the relationship that already existed. The existing tie between God and worshiper was renewed and maintained through atonement. Thus atonement in this passage [Lev. 1:4] is closer to the NT doctrine of ongoing sanctification" (2002, 92 n. 17). It is true that the key reason the relationship needed strengthening was sin, which would explain why atonement is generally associated with confessional offerings. But that is not always the case, as noted in Leviticus 1:4, where atonement is given as a result of a burnt offering offered for consecration. Recognizing and confessing sin is not the only way of strengthening a relationship. Relationships also build on expressing appreciation, which would then explain why Paul could continue offering celebratory sacrifices after his missionary journeys even after he had written letters such as Galatians that repudiated adhering to the law (see Acts 21:26).

Today, even ethnic Jews do not live within the covenant community that the nation of Israel did when Leviticus was written. Paul describes the passage of the nation through the sea under the cloud of God's shekinah presence as their baptism. While he cautions that God was not pleased with most of the nation, he does observe that all were "baptized" in the process (1 Cor. 10:1–12). Here he uses baptism as a figure of speech to reflect how those people became a covenant community. This community was formalized when the same people reached Sinai and agreed to abide by the criteria of God's covenant in Exodus 19–20. Even that agreement occurred approximately a year *before* the implementation of the sacrificial system established in Leviticus. As such, it would follow that the sacrificial system was designed for a people who were already members of a community in covenant relationship with God and one another—specifically to provide

them a reminder of who they had once been and what they should now be.

But, we might ask, how does that fit with the declarations in Hebrews 10? It would seem that our first step is to develop a covenant relationship with God through Jesus the Christ. As Peter put it, we "once were not a people, but now [we] are the people of God; [we] had not received mercy, but now [we] have received mercy" (1 Peter 2:10). Earlier he stated that we are to be "a spiritual house for a holy priesthood, to offer up spiritual sacrifices" (1 Peter 2:5). Thus, this covenant relationship is different from the one established for Israel, and we label that new covenant relationship "redemption" or "salvation."

And we use the term "atonement" to describe that step as well, since it was the redeeming act of Jesus that gives us the access to God. Ross (2002, 93 n. 17) goes on to note that "the NT uses 'sanctify' and related words for regeneration, ongoing sanctification, and ultimate glorification, for all have the characteristic of making someone holy" (we address the idea of holiness below, in the section "Holy"). Here the point is that we use the term "sanctify" and even the English word "atone" in multiple senses, and it would seem that the OT does something similar with the word *kipper*.

Regarding the use of the term "atone" with the sacrificial system in the OT law, the sacrifice was to be a visible or physical symbol of a spiritual act for a person who already had a covenant relationship with God. If so, then why do we not offer sacrifices today? Actually, we do, but as Peter noted they are spiritual sacrifices. In terms of a symbol, as participants in the *new* covenant we also have a *new* visible symbol, which we call communion or the Lord's Supper, where we also strengthen the relationship we already have with God and with other believers by recognizing our sins and confessing them. In a sense, our regular observation of communion serves as a virtual sacrifice.

Sacrifice as Symbol

Perhaps an analogous way of understanding the OT sacrifice would be that it, like the subsequent sacrament of communion, served as a physical reminder of the original covering provided by God when he clothed Adam and Eve with the skins of animals rather than immediately taking their lives. As such, an animal sacrifice would serve as a type to point to the yet greater sacrifice at Calvary. Today, that greater sacrifice has been given and we no longer need the type represented by the animal sacrifice. However, we do have a different symbol that draws our attention back to that greater sacrifice.

Addressing the role of the sacrificial system, Geerhardus Vos (1948, 159–61) calls this the symbolic-vicarious theory of its function. As John Feinberg (1981, 67–70) expands the idea, he observes that sacrifices in the OT served four basic functions. There, sacrifice was in essence a *governmental function* recognizing God's role as the ruler of Israel. This function dealt with relational issues within the covenant community. At its heart was a *typological function* that would point to the future work of the Messiah. In many regards, this function would really only become manifest when Jesus demonstrated that he was the Messiah, approximately fifteen hundred years after the function was introduced. A *third function was a role in worship*, especially in the case of the nonexpiatory sacrifices. As developed above, the worship function of the shalom or communal offerings was to praise God for who he is and what he had done. In the case of burnt offerings, the purpose was to demonstrate consecration. While we might include a *soteriological function*, Feinberg expresses great caution. He points out that offering a sacrifice did not provide salvation, even if done with a repentant heart. Rather he suggests that when offered in believing faith, sacrifices evidenced a restoration of fellowship with God. Specifically, he states, "The expiatory sacrifices, then, seem to be primarily involved with the sanctification process," as the believer with a faithful heart obeyed the revealed directions given by God.

In a sense then, both the use of sacrifice under the old covenant and communion under the new covenant serve similar functions with respect to the sin issue noted in Genesis 3. They serve as reminders not only of our nakedness but of the provisions that God has made to allow a restored relationship with him. In effect, they are temporary garments that will be replaced by white robes when Christ returns (see Rev. 7:9). So in this sense, while it is questionable whether the term *kipper* means "to cover," conceptually it is not necessarily wrong, since there is a sense in which we are covered as a result of being atoned for.

It would seem, however, that the idea of *cultic purity* might be a better approach, at least in the context of the OT sacrificial system. It is cultic in the sense that it is tied to the religious ritual presented by God to the nation of Israel for the purpose of worship. Further, as we will see in the last portion of Leviticus, a critical demand God makes on the nation is that it is to be holy, which seems to reflect corporate moral purity. There, aspects of this holiness show up in the way the Israelites were to relate to one another, especially with regard to issues that we would call social justice. The key, however, is that in the OT and Leviticus, the foundation of social justice was a right relationship with God both for the individual and the community.

Holy

When the motley collection of refugees from the plagues of Egypt arrived at Mount Sinai, God gave them a statement of purpose, declaring that they were to be "a kingdom of priests and a *holy* nation" (Exod. 19:6, emphasis added). Throughout their foundational national document, the Torah, God hammered this point home using the term "holy" some two hundred times in the books of Exodus through Deuteronomy—ninety times in Leviticus alone.

Introduction to Leviticus

Seven times in Leviticus, God explained that the reason they were to be holy was because of his holiness (11:44, 45; 19:2; 20:7, 26; 22:2, 32)—they were to emulate him. Given this indication of importance, the question is, what does it mean to be holy? While we tend to somewhat intuitively understand the concept, its "precise significance is elusive" (Wenham 1979, 18).

The Hebrew term we translate as "holy" is *qadosh* (קָדוֹשׁ), or other forms from the root *qdsh* (קדשׁ). Modern lexicons generally translate words built on this root using words or phrases such as "sacred," "consecrated," "dedicated," "sacredness," "a sacred place," "withhold from profane use," and of course, "holy." BDB (s.v. "קדשׁ" 871) suggests that the word possibly goes back to an original root that carried a connotation of "to be set apart." This supposed etymology has distorted much of the study of holiness for the past century or so. For example, Jay Sklar (2014, 39–40) defines holy as "to be set apart as distinct in some way." More examples could be given (Harbin 2018, 18), but overall the conventional understanding of the origin of the concept of holiness is that it primarily denotes a sense of separation or being set apart from the routine (e.g., see Kellogg 1978, 367; KB s.v. "קדשׁ" 825–26; and Wenham 1979, 19).

While enticing, this understanding raises several issues. Perhaps the most significant is that this does not really indicate in what way God is distinct or different from humans. Is it that he is much more powerful? Is it that he is more intelligent? Is it that he exists outside of space-time? All of these are true, and yet these are characteristics that we as humans are not able to emulate, so how could we be holy as God is?

Further, several fallacies underlie this concept of the word's development. Perhaps the key fallacy is the etymological fallacy, which assumes that "the 'etymological meaning' should be a guide to the usage of words, that the words are used 'properly' when they coincide in sense with the sense of the earliest known form from which their derivation can be traced" (Barr 1961, 107–8).

While BDB suggests a concrete origin of the concept, more recent work has suggested that the concept of holiness in general has a more abstract origin. In his classic study *The Idea of the Holy*, Rudolf Otto (1958, 13) argues that "to 'keep a thing holy in the heart' means to mark it off by a feeling of a peculiar dread, not to be mistaken for any ordinary dread, that is, to appraise it by the category of the numinous." Otto coined the term "numinous" to describe this sense of "creature consciousness," which he describes as "the emotion of a creature, submerged and overwhelmed by its own nothingness in contrast to that which is supreme above all creatures . . . a character which cannot be expressed verbally, and can only be suggested indirectly through the tone and content of a man's feeling-response to it" (p. 10). Otto describes this as a complex response, which he terms *mysterium tremendum*—a response to a mystery that "is beyond conception or understanding, extraordinary and unfamiliar" (pp. 12–13). Later he calls this mystery "the wholly other" (p. 26). He suggests that Isaiah 6 seems to demonstrate this, where Isaiah stated that he saw "the Lord sitting on a throne, high and exalted." As he heard the seraphim crying "Holy, Holy, Holy," Isaiah despaired, stating that he was unclean (see the section below, "Clean and Unclean").

This points to one of the strongest advantages of Otto's suggestion: It hints of a reality beyond the physical and concrete. Although there are some positive aspects to Otto's description, one key weakness is that while overall he talks about the holy, as he presents this idea of the numinous, he describes it as something that humans experience in response to the presence of both God and the demons. However, apparently as a result of his understanding of an evolutionary development of religion, he does not explain what caused it. Further, he does not explain why, given this understanding of "numinous," "holy" is a positive term that is applied to

God and not to Satan and that we are to emulate (Otto 1958, 14). Or, in the case of Isaiah, why he should have felt "unclean" as he perceived God on his throne (Isa. 6) and understood his holiness (or as Otto [p. 51] put it, he encountered God's "numinous reality"). To put the question another way, would Isaiah have felt unclean in the presence of a demon?

Isaiah's experience of uncleanness in response to his awareness of God's holiness contrasted the two attributes. That the two attributes contrast is presented more overtly when God directs Aaron and the priests "to make a distinction between the holy and the profane, and between the unclean and the clean" (Lev. 10:10). While many commentators seem to gloss over this verse, it is perhaps one of the more significant verses of the book, in that it gives some insight into the meaning of holiness by means of contrast (see the section "Clean and Unclean," below).

So, what is being contrasted? Milgrom (1991, 731) maintains that "the emulation of God's holiness demands following the ethics associated with his nature." Sklar (2014, 40) says that God is distinct in terms of power and moral purity. He observes that in the context God "commands his people to be morally upright in a number of ways." He concludes: "The idea is straightforward: 'Because I, the Lord, am distinct in terms of my moral purity, you, as my people, must be distinct in terms of your moral purity as well." Likewise, A. Noordtzij (1982, 191) ends up arguing that in reality holiness was dependent on God's character, which is "altogether righteous, faultless, and pure." R. K. Harrison (1980, 31) takes a similar approach when he suggests that God as the essence of holiness involves ethical, moral, and spiritual attributes. Kenneth Mathews (2009, 168) seems to take the same perspective when addressing the Leviticus 19 passage. He states that "the Lord is morally pure. In every way he is inherently pure without sin or corruption."

Based on how the word is used throughout the Pentateuch especially, it would appear that these scholars have caught its essence, and that a basic meaning of the term "holy" must include a concept of moral purity. Cognate usage substantiates that concept in that the various derivatives all seem to carry a concept of purity (Kornfeld 2003, 523–26). However, even that definition raises questions, two of which need to be addressed here.

The first question is: What is meant by "moral"? According to *WTNID* (s.v. "moral") the English term carries a variety of connotations, such as "relating to principles of right or wrong action" or "right behavior." This corresponds with a variety of other sources suggesting that the concept of "moral" combines two aspects: correctness and activity.

Correctness demands a standard. Webster indicated that, although it left open the source or nature of that standard, suggesting it may be personal (i.e., inner conviction), or it may be a broader social network such as society or personal relations. History has demonstrated repeatedly that neither personal convictions nor society provide an adequate moral standard, with the person or culture tending to be drawn consistently into immorality. Rather, a higher standard is needed (Harbin 2018, 26–29).

For the nation of Israel, that higher standard was the Torah, which described how the people of Israel were to relate to God and to each other. Those guidelines to corporate behavior were outlined in the Ten Commandments. Characterized stylistically as apodictic or "absolute commands" (Schnittjer 2006, 250–51), they were arbitrary in that they were given by God without explanation or any rationale. Yet, the theme of Leviticus bases them on the character of God (see Lev. 19:2). In other words, what is right or moral is based on the attributes of the Creator.

This raises the second matter of concern. "Moral" refers to action or behavior. If "moral" defines proper actions between individuals, and God defines what is moral, and there is just one

God, how can God as a single being be moral without the resultant defining characteristics being purely arbitrary?

It could be that this refers to God with respect to his relationships with people. However, that would reflect a relationship that was established at creation. Even if the model is God's prior relationship with angels, the same problem exists, since they also are created beings. The question then is, if holiness denotes moral purity that reflects actions between individuals, how can a single God be holy in and of himself?

An orthodox Christian theological perspective leads to an understanding of a triune being (Reeves 2012, 39–41). That is, holiness is in reality based on how the members of the Trinity—the Father, the Son, and the Holy Spirit—act toward one another. While the Trinity is not specifically mentioned in the OT, that does not prevent the divine author from using the implications of the Trinity to set forth standards for God's people.

In some regards, this is similar to other understandings regarding the relationship of the members of the Trinity. A number of theologians have observed that the concept of love is crucial to the Christian understanding of the Trinity.

The question then is, what is the difference between love and holiness? After all, John indicated that true love is seen in terms of actions or behavior (1 John 3:15–17).

Again, there is the problem of the field of meaning. For the English word "love," Webster gives a variety of meanings that basically build on the concept of "feeling affection for" (*WTNID* s.v. "love"). The Hebrew word generally translated "love" is *ʾahab* (אָהֵב), which BDB (s.v. "אָהֵב" 12) simply defines as "love," although *TWOT* expands it to "love, like, be in love, lovely" (Alden 1980a).

This is evident in the Shema, where Moses declared "You shall love the Lord [YHWH] your God with all your heart and with all your soul and with all your might" (Deut. 6:5). This is the directive that Jesus affirmed as the first commandment (Matt. 22:37; Mark 12:30; Luke 10:27). Robert Bratcher and Howard Hatton (2000, 138) observe, "So love here contains not only the elements of liking and affection but also devotion and commitment to God." But these are aspects of attitude or volition that are illustrated or demonstrated by behavior. As such, then, love is the foundation on which holiness is built.

The proposition is as follows: if love is defined by the relationship of the members of the Trinity so that John could say "God is love" (1 John 4:8); and love is demonstrated by acts, not just verbal declarations; and holiness is to be understood as moral purity, which we have argued characterizes acts; and the holiness of God is presented as the benchmark for holiness, then the basis for defining holiness would be how the members of the Trinity relate to one another in terms of actions.

As such, holiness is really a collective attribute and responsibility, which again is illustrated in Leviticus 19:2 when God used the plural "you" in directing the nation, collectively, to be holy (see also Exod. 19:6; Lev. 11:44, 45; 20:7, 26). In that light, then, it would not be coincidental that this verse introduces the major portion of the book of Leviticus that is often called the Holiness Code (Kiuchi 2007, 17). This section of Leviticus emphasizes morality and lifestyle issues with a focus on social justice, suggesting morality as a corporate concept.

This raises a question regarding God's statement of purpose for Israel with which this study began, that is, that they were to be a "kingdom of priests and a holy nation" (Exod. 19:6). How do those two terms fit together? John Durham (1987, 263) seems close to the point when he observes that "Israel as a 'kingdom of priests' is Israel committed to the extension throughout the world of the ministry of Yahweh's presence." In other words, the focus is not on the nation's position but its function. In that case, as a nation Israel was to mediate between the rest of humanity and God (serving as priests), corporately exhibiting morally pure relationships (being holy).

If this understanding is valid, how does this explain so many uses of the term "holy" that do not address issues of behavior but that really do seem to carry a concept of being set apart for a reason? Here the scope of items that are viewed as holy (קָדוֹשׁ) requires that regardless of how one understands the etymology, some meanings necessarily must be considered derivative. The perspective presented here would then conclude that declaring a space (e.g., the tabernacle [Exod. 29:30], or the ground around the burning bush [Exod. 3:5]) or an item (e.g., the garments of the high priest [Exod. 28:2]) or an occasion (e.g., a holy assembly [Exod. 12:16]) holy would be derivative in a similar sense that Webster suggested for the English word when it stated that something might be termed holy in that it was "venerated because of association with someone or something holy" (*WTNID* s.v. "holy"). This would correlate with Sklar's (2014, 39–40) argument that people or objects are made holy in "dependent holiness," while God's holiness is because of his very nature. Likewise, Peter Gentry (2013, 402) was correct when he observed that the ground of the burning bush was holy not because the mountain was taboo, but because the ground on which Moses stood was associated with the burning bush from which God spoke.

The contention here is that God should be the benchmark rather than humankind. If God is holy because he is separate, humanity is the de facto standard, but this never really defines in what way or how God's separation is good. By recognizing the relationship of the members of the Trinity as the true benchmark, the focus is on God, and it is there one can look for models of true holiness. That would have several ramifications.

First, grounding the concept of holiness in the relationship of the persons of the Trinity gives a dynamic understanding of how God is holy in a very real sense that is coherent apart from the existence of created beings. Further, recognizing absolute moral purity of the members of the Trinity as the defining principle sets a clear standard by which to measure holiness. The process also gives further insight into the nature of God in that it fleshes out the idea of love as the bond between the members of the Trinity in a tangible form that can be demonstrated and evaluated. As such, the term "holy" then makes spiritual sense.

Second, when looking at the case of Isaiah, his response makes sense. Sensing God's perfect holiness or the absolute moral purity between the persons of the Trinity, he suddenly feels impure or unclean. This is illustrated by an episode I (Harbin) experienced at the Naval Academy. The brigade was lined up for evening formation at the end of the weekend. All of the midshipmen were dressed in white uniforms freshly washed and pressed at the academy laundry, and it was an impressive sight as we fell into ranks. Then one individual who had been on weekend liberty came rushing up. While he had been home, he had sent his uniform out to a commercial laundry, and they had used bluing in the washing process. His uniform was a brilliant bluish white, and suddenly the uniforms of the rest of the midshipmen looked yellowish and dirty. Although in fresh white uniforms, we felt somewhat dirty in a physical sense. In Isaiah's case, it was a moral uncleanness. He did not need to be reminded of any specific sin, he just felt dirty inside—very dirty. Hearing the proclamation of the seraphim and sensing the perfect morality of God, he intuitively understood his own moral state to be lacking and worthy of condemnation. He suddenly realized that he was without hope—even the words he spoke were sinful. When one of the seraphim took a coal and purified his lips, he was able to declare that Isaiah's "iniquity [was] removed and [his] sin [was] forgiven," reversing the synecdoche that Isaiah had expressed. Still, given that Isaiah's subsequent mission was to proclaim a message that would serve to harden the hearts of his people, purified lips were imperative.

Finally, and perhaps most importantly, in terms of applying the admonition to be holy to people, whether it is the nation of Israel or the members of the church, this presents a standard of behavior to live up to relationally as a community. John Walton and J. Harvey Walton (2017, 105) express it well when they state, "when the nation or people is identified as holy, it refers to the communal abstraction, not to all of the specific individuals who participate in it." Holiness is then understood not as something that one can do individually, but it is a communal responsibility reflecting how individuals interact with one another. This is probably the most important message that one could derive from this concept today—Christians are to treat each other in morally pure ways. Or, to put it in Southern vernacular, "y'all be holy."

Clean and Unclean

After the deaths of Nadab and Abihu, God strongly admonished Aaron regarding the use of alcohol (Lev. 10:9). It was not prohibited, but the priests were restricted in its use as they ministered. In this admonition, God gave Aaron a vision statement for the priesthood— the priests were to "distinguish between the holy and the common, and between the unclean and the clean" in order that they might properly teach the nation (Lev. 10:10). These distinctions were important so that the nation would be holy (Exod. 20:8; Lev. 11:44). That the alcohol restriction served to support making proper distinctions within two categories suggests some ambiguity in the items being distinguished, thus requiring a clear mind on the part of the priests.

> **Ezekiel and the Profane**
> Ezekiel was a prophet during the exile who severely criticized the priesthood. One particular admonishment states specifically that the priests had both treated God's Torah violently (חָמַס) and defiled (חָלַל) God's holy things because they had not distinguished between the holy and the common (חֹל) or the clean and unclean (Ezek. 22:26).

On one hand, they were to distinguish between the holy (קֹדֶשׁ) and the *ḥol* (חֹל) translated in modern translations as "common" (ESV, HCSB, NIV, NRSV) or "profane" (NASB). We will use the term "common." Based on the need for distinction, at a minimum "common" indicates something that is "not holy" (so KJV). In the previous section, we suggested that term *qadosh* (קָדוֹשׁ), translated "holy," basically denoted moral purity in terms of relationships—primarily with God but also with individuals within one's community. We also noted that a derivative use of the term reflected veneration because of association with someone or something that was holy in itself. Israel understood that someone to be God. Whether in the primary or derivative sense, it would then seem that the first function of the priest was to determine whether or not a given action or item enhanced a person's association with God. If it did not enhance, it was then common. It might not detract from one's relationship with God, thus it was in a sense somewhat neutral in and of itself. Even in that case, since it did not enhance, it was still not holy. Rather, it was common.

As such, daily life was common, a translation of *ḥol* (חֹל). This example would suggest that the first distinction the priests were to make was whether something was appropriately dedicated to God, or just appropriate for ordinary or common use.

TRANSLATION ANALYSIS: חֹל *OR PROFANE*
The primary meaning given חֹל in Hebrew lexicons and dictionaries (BDB, KB, *DCH, TWOT,*

and *TDOT*) is "profane" or "profaneness," derived from the Latin profanus, which basically means "outside of the temple" or "not sacred, ordinary, or common." However, today the English word "profane" carries negative connotations that the Hebrew word חל does not, so most modern translations use the word "common." The Hebrew noun/adjective חל is used six other times in the OT. Four of those times are in Ezekiel, where it shows the same contrast shown here in Leviticus. The other two times are in 1 Samuel 21, where David was at the tabernacle asking for bread. The priest indicated that there was no *hol* (חל) bread available, only "consecrated" bread.

The distinction between "clean" and "unclean" is problematic. Two aspects of this word pair give us problems. First, the standard English use of the terms "clean" and "unclean" seems to suggest the absence or presence of dirt, either as a physical state or at least a metaphorical understanding such as a dirty book or joke. This seems to be the basis of Mary Douglas's (2002, 1–6) take on the idea derived from an anthropologist's perspective. She defines dirt as disorder, which she sees as foundational for all primitive cultures, where it is manifested as taboo or "unclean." It is questionable whether the Hebrew terms carry the same connotations, both in terms of the idea of dirt, and also with respect to a concept of physicality. Second, most scholars perceive the basic issue as regarding a state of ritual purity or cultic purity, which is an abstract concept that really applies to one's spirituality. However, many of the manifestations of uncleanness or impurity are physical. Further, if the issue is really not a matter of hygiene or physical cleanliness, then why does the standard response to the presence of uncleanness typically involve some type of physical cleansing, usually with water?

The word translated "clean" in Leviticus 10:10 is the adjective *tahor* (טָהוֹר), derived from the Hebrew root *taher*. Edwin Yamauchi (1980c)

defines the root as "be pure, clean" and observes that in its various forms it appears some 204 times in the OT, predominantly ninety-four times as a verb and also ninety-four times as an adjective. The term is used both in a physical and nonphysical sense. In a physical sense it refers to items such as gold or silver. For example, it denotes "pure gold" in the description of the ark and other items associated with the tabernacle (Exod. 25:11), indicating that no other metals were mixed with it. Similarly, the phrase "silver . . . refined seven times" in Psalm 12:7 uses a physical concept to illustrate the purity of God's word. This would indicate that even a nonphysical use of טָהוֹר would involve some concept of purity, that is, without contaminants.

In contrast, the word translated "unclean" in Leviticus 10:10 is the adjective *tame'* (טָמֵא). It is derived from the Hebrew root *tame'* (טָמֵא), which Ralph Alexander (1980a) defines as "become unclean" and observes that the verb and its derivatives appear some 279 times in the OT, with the verb being predominant (155 times). While *tahor* is used in a physical sense, *tame'* is not. When used by itself, uncleanness clearly *can be* a result of sin. This is evident in the case of Isaiah who declared in Isaiah 6, when he beheld the Lord on a throne, that he was undone because he was a man of unclean lips. A seraph touched his lips with a burning coal and declared that as a result his iniquity (עָוֹן) was taken away and his sin (חַטָּאת) was forgiven—with neither a reparation offering nor a purification offering. Isaiah reflects a common human reaction to sin as a feeling of being dirty, a reaction noted even today with the concept of "dirty" showing up in a number of modern situations and English expressions, especially pertaining to sexual issues. This is also the case in the last portion of Leviticus where it is translated as "defile" approximately fifteen times, largely in reference to sexual sins such as adultery (Lev. 18:20) and bestiality (Lev. 18:23), but also sins such as consulting spiritists (Lev. 19:31).

Introduction to Leviticus

However, often uncleanness is not a result of sin. This is especially the case in Leviticus 11–15, which lists a number of factors that produce uncleanness, most of which are not matters of sin per se. The list includes inappropriate dietary meat, motherhood, *tsara'at* (צָרַעַת, generally translated as "leprosy"), and normal bodily discharges as items that produce "uncleanness." This is where we run into problems, such as when we read that a new mother is unclean for one to two weeks because she has given birth (Lev. 12:2–7), or that a person who touches the carcass of an animal raised for food shall be unclean until evening (Lev. 11:39). In these cases, there may be no physical manifestation, and the unclean person may not even *feel* unclean. Consequently, commentators tend to stress that it is ceremonial or ritual uncleanness, which would affect how the Israelites were permitted to worship. This might suggest that "clean" or "unclean" are arbitrary, even somewhat artificial, delineations. Certainly, scholars have struggled to explain these concepts. This is somewhat reminiscent of US Supreme Court Justice Potter Stewart, who stated in the 1964 *Jacobellis v. Ohio* obscenity case involving hardcore pornography, "I know it when I see it," although he did not attempt to define it.[1]

As noted, Douglas equates impurity with dirt, which she defines as "essentially disorder" (2002, 2–3). This is a view picked up by a number of commentators, but it does not explain why giving birth made a woman unclean, an issue that she seems to gloss over even in *Reading Leviticus* where she makes no reference to the chapter in Leviticus that addresses uncleanness (1996). Another view associates "unclean" with death. For example, Milgrom (1991, 767) argues that blood is "the archsymbol of life," and thus blood oozing from the body was "the sign of death." However, he doesn't address the issue of why normal discharges rendered a person as unclean, but a wound, even a serious one, did not.

Looking at a broader perspective, Gordon Wenham suggests that the two distinction pairs in Leviticus 10:10 (holy and *ḥol* or common [חֹל], clean and unclean) could be put together as a three-stage single diagram showing stages (holy, clean, and unclean), and processes between them (1979, 19). While Wenham's stages seem to be a helpful start, he seems to muddy the waters a bit, as in essence he uses *ḥol* both as a stage and a process, suggesting that something that has been holy but that is profaned (his term) could then still be considered clean. Sklar also prefers a three-stage overall category, but labels the three stages as holy, pure, and impure. He stresses that these are ritual conditions "because they guide the community in understanding which ritual actions a person may (or may not) do or which ritual places a person may (or may not) go" (2014, 45). One difficulty is that some of the items addressed are not ritual actions or conditions, such as eating meat or having a baby.

Part of the problem is the terminology, especially in translation. Some, like Wenham, use "clean" and "unclean." Others, like Sklar, use "pure" and "impure." While there are other suggestions, all have the same problem. We tend to think of the conditions as binary opposites—that is, something is either one or the other, such as in computer language where the figure is either a one or a zero. At the same time, we realize that uncleanness or impurity is much more complex. Sklar illustrates this when he says, "By nature, Israelites were in a state of purity," but suggests that they may be more or less pure, which he presents as a gradient in his chart—leading to the question of how much "less purity" was allowed before one was impure (p. 46). However, as Ross (2002, 244–45) points out, "anything not *ṭāhôr* is 'impure.'" He goes on to say, "and 'impure'—is not much of an improvement over 'unclean.'" He describes both terms as "freighted with negative connotations."

---

1   Jacobellis v. Ohio, 378 U.S. 184. https://supreme.justia.com/cases/federal/378/184.

Because of this complexity, Ross suggests that expositors should use a series of synonymic contrasting pairs to convey the concept, and lists seven examples.

It seems that a two axis–two stage model might better explain the material, as shown in figure 1. In this model, "common" (חֹל) is viewed as a pole on the holiness axis but as a pivot point or fulcrum for the cleanness axis. On one hand, it was the normal state of everyday life, in contrast to "holiness" or "sacred" as the opposite pole. A person or a thing was normally common, but it became holy upon completion of a specific ritual. However, "common" is not a point. Within daily life, a person or thing that is common may be clean or unclean, which should reflect a spectrum (Sklar 2014, 46). In an analogous physical sense, technically "dry" is totally without moisture, but we will call something dry while it still contains varying amounts of absorbed water.

> **Cleanness Spectrum**
> Trying to develop an appropriate physical model to explain spiritual elements is difficult. In this case the model of humidity is helpful. Relative humidity measures how much water vapor is in the atmosphere compared to how much it could hold at a given temperature, and we talk about whether it is humid or dry outside, but both are relative terms. When I (Harbin) was growing up in Arizona, it was very common to have days in the summer when the relative humidity was in the 5 percent range. We would grouse about how humid it was when the humidity was in the 30–40 percent range. Living now in Indiana, I am amused when meteorologists comment about how dry the atmosphere is when the relative humidity drops into the 40 percent range.

An example might be skin. We talk about dry skin, but absolutely dry skin would be hard and brittle. Likewise, we can think of personal hygiene. A person may cleanse him- or herself with a morning shower. As he or she goes through the day, the degree of cleanliness decreases just through living. For an Israelite, daily showers were luxuries they did not have. Thus they did not begin each day with fresh physical cleanliness (by our standards), and after a bath their cleanness might be viewed as decreasing over a period of days, if not weeks. However, while they might not be considered physically clean because they had not bathed, they were not considered unclean in a spiritual or cultic sense unless they participated in certain acts listed in the teaching of the Torah that the priests taught. The difficulty is understanding exactly how these acts affected a person so that he or she required cleansing.

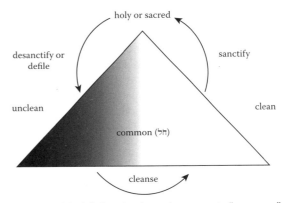

Figure 1. Model showing how the center is "common".

Here, we might consider something that Jesus said recorded in Matthew 15:11 when he talked about the Jewish ritual of washing their hands before eating: "It is not what enters into the mouth that defiles the man, but what proceeds out of the mouth, this defiles the man" (see also the parallel passage in Mark 7:15). In his subsequent explanation to his disciples, Jesus asserted that it is things that come out of the heart that defile a person, indicating that it is intangible. As Wenham puts it, it "was more a matter of the mind than the body" (1979, 225). Another way of expressing this in an OT context might be that the things that produced uncleanness would be things that affected the individual's psyche or heart or perhaps an even better term would be one's spirit (see the section "*Nephesh* [נֶפֶשׁ]: Life and Soul," below) in such a way as to adversely affect that person's perceptions of his or her relationships within the community. Citing Ezekiel, Roy Gane (2004a, 264–65) describes how "blurring ritual distinctions was accompanied by ethical sins" that allowed stronger members of society to prey on the weaker. Putting it another way, one might say that observing the ritual distinctions restrained ethical sins by reminding the individual of proper relationships.

One question that arises is why specific acts might cause those reactions. Two possible reasons come to mind. The first is that they are culturally inculcated. That is, they are things that the culture has deemed impermissible and thus are considered taboo. This is the view that Mary Douglas takes as an anthropologist. In that sense, they can be culturally arbitrary. Projecting those observations onto Leviticus, she concludes that the OT laws are also culturally arbitrary (2002, xii–xvi). The second possibility, which tends to get overlooked, is that the standard might be divinely defined. For the nation of Israel, the text indicates that the actions that produced uncleanness were decreed by the One who knows the human heart (cf. Jer. 17:9–10). In that sense, it would seem that God set forth a series of guidelines designed to mold his people in a specific way based on his knowledge of human nature. This may be indicated by Peter's declaration when he reported to the Jerusalem Council how God had provided the gospel to the Gentiles. Peter declared that "God, who knows the heart, testified to them giving them the Holy Spirit, just as He also did to us; and He made no distinction between us and them, cleansing their hearts by faith" (Acts 15:8 NASB).

According to Leviticus, some things were considered unclean *for the Israelites* by their nature, although it is not clear why. For example, God told Moses and Aaron that "to you" certain animals such as the "swarming things" (שֶׁרֶץ) were deemed unclean (Lev. 11:29, with emphasis indicated by sentence structure). Although those same swarming things were defined as good in the account of their creation in Genesis 1, if an Israelite touched them (when dead), the Israelite would become unclean until evening (Lev. 11:31). Some actions that produced uncleanness seem to reflect innate consequences of the fall. For example, sexual relations or even having a baby, which fulfilled God's design, produced uncleanness, perhaps harking back to Adam and Eve's recognition that they were naked and thus afraid (Kiuchi 2007, 220). Still, in all of these cases, the uncleanness was temporary, although certain ritual cleansings were required. It would be through this act of ritual cleansing that the individual would refresh his or her understanding of the purity and holiness of God. This would suggest that perhaps the emphasis should be on the fact that God provided a means of cleansing for even the mundane affairs of daily life, the common (חל).

Other things became unclean through contagion, a condition that raises a lot of questions. For example, Leviticus 5:2–3 and 7:19–21 warn that a person who touches anything that was unclean, even if he was unaware of it, would become unclean. A number of citations in Leviticus 11 warn that eating something unclean (certain types of meat) would make a person unclean. Leviticus 14 warns that *tsara'at* (צָרַעַת, often translated as leprosy) would make a house unclean, and through contagion any person entering the house as well as anything in the house would be unclean—unless they were removed prior to the priest declaring it as unclean (Lev. 14:36). Likewise, anyone who touches a woman with a discharge would become unclean, but apparently that would not be the case of anything she touched (Lev. 15:19; Kleinig 2003, 320).

In terms of what happens when something is made unclean or clean falls into the category of mystery. The basic question is whether uncleanness is an actual physical state, a psychological state, or perhaps a spiritual state.

Milgrom presents the view that there is an actual physical contamination producing uncleanness, which he calls "an aerial miasma that possessed magnetic attraction for the realm of the sacred" (1991, 257) or "a gaseous substance, a volatile force, a miasma exuded by the source of impurity" (p. 977), or "airborne pollution to the sanctuary" (p. 994). This raises a lot of questions with regard to the nature of that gaseous substance, not the least of which would be how acts performed by people distributed throughout the land might affect the altar at the central sanctuary many miles away.

Gane (2004a, 265) reflects a more intangible perception. He notes how Malcolm Gladwell (2002, 7), drawing on social psychology, maintains that "Ideas and products and messages and behaviors spread just like viruses do." Further, Gladwell premises that "little causes can have big effects" (p. 9). This is very intriguing since Gladwell's present-day examples illustrate how a practice can spread throughout a culture and change its entire direction for good or for bad. One illustration he uses is the relationship between repairing or not repairing broken windows and the crime rate (pp. 140–51). Gane applies those observations to the situation in Leviticus, suggesting that individual acts that produce personal uncleanness can produce a contagion, which would transform into what he calls an epidemic that is out of control. In essence this might explain how the nation of Israel would so quickly abandon the God who had delivered them as individuals and became lax in terms of following God's lifestyle directions that led to personal cleanness. They would individually become personally unclean or impure, influencing others who also lapsed into individual uncleanness. Then, uncleanness would spread like an epidemic (or given current issues, a pandemic) leading to corporate uncleanness.

While Gladwell and Gane suggest psychological contagion, they seem to overlook the spiritual dimension of the issue. It would seem that personal spiritual failure can be contagious within a locale and spread as a contagion throughout an entire nation. Further, as an aspect of the spiritual dimension, this would explain how corporate uncleanness would defile the priesthood and the tabernacle leading to corporate judgment, something that Leviticus 15:31 warns against.

As such, the relationship between cleansing and sanctification is complex, requiring both individual and corporate compliance. Before being sanctified, a person or a thing in the common state might be clean or unclean. This was part of daily life. Normally, it would appear that a person's status would be assumed to be clean unless the person committed a specific act that made him or her unclean (or something happened to an object that rendered it unclean). This would affect his or her relationship with others in a nonphysical manner, which might be either sinful or nonsinful. Generally, the person or thing could be cleansed, often as simply as washing and waiting for evening. For example, handling a corpse did not necessarily produce any physical consequences to the handler, in which case the physical cleansing act could be essentially symbolic. Even then, that person or thing that was cleansed by evening would still be common. While able to consequently participate in routine community activities, the common person or thing would need to be purified before entering a holy or sacred state or location. The more difficult aspect of this system is the corporate awareness required. Commenting on the discharge issues of Leviticus 15, Timothy Willis (2009, 138) observes:

> One other aspect of these regulations is disquieting to some in the modern Western world. This is the apparently public nature of things that Westerners tend to regard as private. These rules assume that a man's emissions and the time of a woman's menstrual flow are known to those around them; otherwise, their associates would not know to take the "necessary precautions."

This would be especially true during the time in the wilderness when the entire nation was camped around the tabernacle. Commenting on the discharge issues of Leviticus 15, Willis goes on to suggest that once settled (after the conquest), most families would not go to the tabernacle on a regular basis, so that "only abnormal emissions would require much, if any, further attention" (p. 138).

Looking at the wide variety of things that produced uncleanness, Sklar (2014, 48) notes two assumptions we need to be careful to avoid. The first assumption is "that there is one overarching rationale to explain ritual states." As we look through Leviticus 11–15, we note different cultural or historical situations. It would seem likely that those five chapters (and other situations cited subsequently that list further matters of uncleanness) serve as illustrations to guide the priests rather than provide an exhaustive list of things that defiled or made unclean. That would explain why the priest needed discernment to distinguish—he would need to properly extrapolate principles underlying the examples and apply them to other situations of various similarities. In that regard, it would appear that this section would be analogous to the covenant stipulations of the law. It is generally accepted that the OT law (both in Exodus–Leviticus, and subsequently in Deuteronomy), followed the format of Hittite suzerain-vassal treaties. As such, it was organized under ten apodictic laws (what we call the Ten Commandments), supplemented by a number of casuistic laws that illustrated how the general principles might be worked out in practice. Those case studies provided precedents from which judgments could be made regarding new situations (Harbin 2005, 170–74).

The second assumption we should avoid is "that the Israelites themselves knew what the rationale was" (Sklar 2014, 48–49). Sklar notes how each culture has practices that few if any are aware of a rationale as to why they practice them. The example he gives is the once common practice in the United States for men to remove their hats when entering a church. In the case of Israel, these are guidelines that God gave to the nation to follow as they became a holy people. It is true that many of the guidelines we see in these chapters and the rest of the Pentateuch do make sense to us today—but many of them do not. To pick one item as an example, we will mention mixing wool and linen in their clothing (Deut. 22:11). No rationale is given as to why a garment of mixed wool and linen was prohibited. Consequently, it would seem that cleanness resulted from obedience rather than the specific acts that they did. From personal experience, I (Harbin) would note that while I was going through the US Naval Academy, there were a number of directives we were required to follow (especially during our freshman year) that did not make sense. As I look back now, I appreciate how they worked together to form the discipline I learned as a result, even though I still do not know the rationale for the specific commands. In terms of Israel, I am convinced that God did have a rationale, but that the planned results were holistic and thus individually more indirect than we would suspect.

Many of the specifics, such as the unclean foods, seem to have been annulled in the NT. Consequently, as we teach this material today we need to exercise care in how we handle the items. As Ross (2002, 246) puts it, "the expositor must be clear here: it was the ritual of the law that came to an end in Christ—not what the law revealed. The regulations were particularly for Israel and were temporary, but the revelation of God's holiness and what it demands remains applicable for all." In this case, it would seem that the main point to get from this material is that our actions should reflect spiritual realities. In the unit "Inauguration of Ancient Israelite Religion" (Lev. 8:1–9:24), we note that the cleansing of the priest is described as a physical process that represented "inner spiritual cleansing" (Kellogg, 1978, 190; see also Kiuchi 2007, 153; Mathews 2009, 75; Rooker 2000, 142; Ross 2002,

Introduction to Leviticus

210; Wenham 1979, 139). We would extend that observation to the cleansing of lay Israelites addressed in Leviticus 11–15. It would thus seem that we could extend to all believers the principle that our lifestyles should differ from the culture from which we come—not in the sense that there are legal requirements that we need to follow, but that they represent spiritual disciplines that draw us closer to God.

Nephesh (נֶפֶשׁ): *Life and Soul*

Leviticus 17:11 is a crucial statement not only with regard to the sacrificial system but with regard to basic issues of life. The crux with regard to the relationship of blood to life is the initial portion translated by the ESV, NASB, and NRSV as "the life of the flesh is in the blood." The meanings of blood and flesh seem obvious in that they were physical items that would have been observed and handled. On the other hand, *nephesh* (נֶפֶשׁ), the Hebrew word translated as "life" in this verse, is ambiguous.

TRANSLATION ANALYSIS∴NEPHESH (נֶפֶשׁ)

For this study, we will use *nephesh* as a loan word to convey the scope of the concept in the OT as will be developed in this section.

According to Horst Seebass, "the concrete primary meaning of *nephesh* is usually assumed to be 'maw, throat, gullet,' as the organ used for eating and breathing" (1998, 504). And yet, that is a rare usage. A Logos Software usage distribution search revealed that it is used that way only five out of 757 times in the Hebrew text. Most frequently it is understood to denote the "inner self" (or "soul," 357 times), and "life" in a person (214 times). Because of their overall dominance and significance, we will focus on these two aspects beginning with "life."

Nephesh (נֶפֶשׁ) and "Throat"

Because *nephesh* (נֶפֶשׁ) can be translated as "throat," the tendency is to see that concrete identification as the original concept, which then abstracted into a nonconcrete concept related to life (Seebass 1998, 504; Wolff 1974, 32–36). As noted elsewhere, the idea that a concrete understanding necessarily lay behind abstract concepts has been criticized (Barr 1961, 30; Harbin 2018, 23–24). In this case, since נֶפֶשׁ is used that way only five out of 757 times, it raises the question as to whether the occasions it is translated as a physical throat might be figurative of a type that E. W. Bullinger calls *descriptio* (1968, 444–58). In other words, early humans may have had an intuitive comprehension of the abstract as hinted at in this case by Seebass (1998, 499–502) in his overview of cognate relationships.

The idea of life has always been mysterious. What is it that changes a collection of inert organic molecules into something that moves, responds to stimulus, and reproduces? Even modern biologists don't really understand what life is. While biologists note that life "consists of cells or is itself a single cell" (Becker, Kleinsmith, and Hardin 2000, 2; see also Mader 2001, 33–76), we will address only multicell life forms of the domain *eukarya* (organisms with a nucleate cell). The two major kingdoms of that domain, plants and animals, can be distinguished by several characteristics including mobility and sentience. Perhaps the most significant distinction is the basic metabolic process utilized by various life-forms within those kingdoms. Plants generally use photosynthesis to combine light, carbon dioxide, and water to produce sugar and oxygen, which are used for nutrition. As a result, plants grow in a variety of ways. Animals, on the other hand, draw nutrition from plants (either directly or indirectly) to transform sugar and other nutrients and oxygen into energy and carbon dioxide. It is the blood, a key distinction between plants and animals and the subject of this verse, that "transports nutrients and oxygen to cells and removes carbon dioxide and other wastes" (Mader 2001, 727). In other words, it gives life to the flesh, something that the Israelites would have understood even without knowing the technical process. Human beings function like the animals in this regard. Overall, these two kingdoms form an extremely complex ecological system perpetuating life on earth (Raven, Evert, and Eichhorn 1999, 2).

The Genesis 1 creation accounts distinguish between those two domains by using different terminology to describe their members. The text in Genesis 1:11–12 states that on the third day God said "Let the earth sprout" (דֶּשֶׁא) three general categories of plants: "vegetation" or grass or green growth (דֶּשֶׁא), "plants [or herbs] yielding seed" (דֶּשֶׁא עֵשֶׂב מַזְרִיעַ), and "fruit trees" (עֵץ פְּרִי)—although actually a longer description is given: "fruit trees producing fruit according to its kind with its seed in it." The text concludes by observing that the earth "brought out" (וַתּוֹצֵא) the three mentioned categories of plants just as God said. Then Genesis 1:20–26 completes the creation process on days 5 and 6 with the creation of several varieties of "living creatures" (1:24, per many translations) or "living beings having a *nephesh*" (נֶפֶשׁ חַיָּה). This included birds and various water creatures on day 5, and cattle, creeping things, and beasts of the earth on day 6. In this manner days 3, 5, and 6 introduce the two main kingdoms of life. Day 6 also includes the creation of humankind, who collectively are given dominion over the various created life forms. According to Genesis 2:7, humans also are "living beings" like the animals although, as will be seen, they have a significant distinction. The key here is that in a general sense, the OT groups of humans and animals differ from the plant kingdom by this mysterious concept of *nephesh*.

While *nephesh* may be translated "life," the English term "life" is a broad category that includes plants, which do not have a *nephesh*. Michael Heiser (2015, 42) suggests that the *nephesh* is a nonphysical aspect that could be understood as "conscious life or animate life," which in the various verses that incorporate the concept seems to set creatures that have *nephesh* in opposition to those that do not, "something like plant life." This distinguishes plants from humans and animals in terms of possessing what we call "life." As Heiser observes, human beings "share a basic consciousness with certain animals, though the nature of that consciousness varies widely." It is for this reason that the term is often translated as "soul" to distinguish animals from plants. However, like the word "life," the English word "soul" has a broad range of meaning including "the immaterial essence or substance, animating principle, or actuating cause of life," which seems to be the dominant meaning (*WTNID* s.v. "soul"). In this sense, soul and life essentially describe the same thing, something that both humans and animals possess. However, according to Webster, the English word "soul" may also denote the "spiritual principle . . . embodied in beings having a rational and spiritual nature" or "the immortal part of man having permanent individual existence." Here, we would distinguish between animals and humans. Further, the OT does not apply the term "spirit" to animals. Given the ambiguity of the dominant terms used to translate it, we will use the Hebrew term *nephesh* in this study, recognizing the overlap between life and soul.

As Leviticus 17:11 ties the *nephesh* to the blood, basically the idea is that both humans and these animals are constituted as possessing both physical (called "flesh" [בָּשָׂר]) and nonphysical (the *nephesh*) aspects. It would appear that it is the integration of these two that makes them "living creatures" (נֶפֶשׁ חַיָּה). It would also appear that there is some sense in which the nonphysical aspect of life is associated with the blood. Here we would suggest two ramifications of that association. First, as noted, the basic role that blood plays in producing life is the more limited sense of animals and humans. The blood and heart system is complex and permeates the physical body (the human blood system incorporates approximately sixty thousand miles of vessels [Mader 2001, 730]). As Sylvia Mader (pp. 3, 100) points out, the blood system transports both oxygen and nutrients to all of the cells in the body where the metabolic processes take place. The red blood cells take the oxygen to the cell from the lungs and remove the carbon dioxide through the lungs. The plasma carries nutrients to the cells and removes wastes following the metabolic processes. This complex transportation system is driven by the heart which, as Mader notes, is one of the first organs to form, and "when it stops, death occurs" (p. 739). So, in this sense clearly the blood is the *life* of the flesh. With the observation that the heart is one of the first organs to form, embryologist Clifford Grobstein observes that for humans, approximately at the fourth week after conception the implanted embryo begins *functional* individuality (genetic individuality begins at conception) with the commencement of its heart beating (cited by Hall 1989, 44, emphasis added). In terms of the *nephesh* as soul, we could think in terms of it being the source of animation. One of the misapprehensions that many scientists labor under is that if one had the capability of arranging the molecules in the right combination, animation (i.e., life) would spontaneously occur (Johnson 1993, 102–12).

> **Spontaneous Generation**
> Even the popular online source Wikipedia notes that "Rejection of spontaneous generation is no longer controversial among biologists. By the middle of the 19th century, experiments by Louis Pasteur and others refuted the traditional theory of spontaneous generation and supported biogenesis [life comes from life]" (https://en.wikipedia.org/w/index.php?title=Spontaneous_generation&oldid=995838287). While rejecting this on a particular level, modern biologists claim that life in general is self-generated, beginning "from *the self-organization of particular categories of matter*" (Denton 2016, 251, emphasis original).

Even though humans and animals begin with a living fertilized egg—that is, a cell—an animation factor is still required. From a biological perspective it is the fertilization of the egg by the sperm that produces the unique genetic structure of the new form. Animation follows as the fertilized egg begins to divide. From a theological perspective, the issue is not quite as clear. Theologians debate as to whether the soul is a special creation of God sometime between conception and birth or whether the soul is derived from its parents (Dorman 2001, 120–21). Regardless, it may be that the animation factor is related to the appearance of the blood system— in essence, the *soul*—although how it is related is a mystery.

To model this in terms of the overall being, I (Harbin) use the diagram in figure 2 to illustrate this idea. This figure is intended to show in a very simplified manner the relationship between the flesh (בָּשָׂר) and the *nephesh*, the nonphysical part of life, within the flesh's physical container. In the illustration, I show the nonphysical portion (shown here with horizontal lines) embedded within the physical (shown with vertical lines). However, the two portions really are integrated with the nonphysical totally

Model of Animals

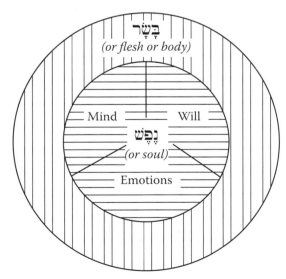

Figure 2. Model of animals.

permeating the physical.[2] It is this consolidated entity that is called a "living being" (Gen. 2:7). Further, this model attempts to illustrate how the nonphysical aspect of these living beings incorporates the intellectual, emotional, and volitional aspects of life (the elements of sentience) that are labeled as the mind, the emotions, and the will.

> **Adam as a Living Being**
> Genesis 2:7 uses the phrase נֶפֶשׁ חַיָּה (literally "a living life or soul") in the case of Adam to indicate that he received life when God "breathed" the "breath of life" into his physical form. The relationship between spirit and soul for humans is problematic and highly debated. J. Barton Payne suggests that part of the issue is the role of the divine image, stating that the spirit (*ruaḥ* [רוּחַ]) "imparts the divine image to man, and constitutes the animating dynamic which results in man's *nepeš* as the subject of personal life. The distinctive personality of the individual inheres in his *nepeš*, the seat of his emotions and desires" (1980, 836–37). If humans have a *nephesh* like animals, and a spirit or *ruaḥ* like God and other spiritual beings, that places them in a unique status in creation, but also leaves a lot that needs to be sorted out.

A weakness of this model is that it suggests that the soul or *nephesh* is embedded in or essentially coincides with the brain. Further, it suggests that the mind, emotions, and will are separate compartments. While I have shown them as separate units for demonstration purposes, they also are really integrated within the individual, and really the matter is even more complex. For example, addressing humans, psychologist Mark Cosgrove (2018, 61–66) relates how psychologists and psychiatrists note two problems. The first is the "binding problem," which derives from the realization that the various parts of the brain (portions of the physical) interact in a unified manner to provide conscious experience (something that is nonphysical). Specifically, they have found that when the person speaks or acts, or even thinks, multiple sections of the brain function simultaneously in a coordinated manner—although these same psychologists and psychiatrists have not been able to identify how these sections coordinate. The second is what psychologists call the "hard problem." That is the term given to the problem of trying to explain consciousness if one assumes a purely physical universe. Cosgrove concludes that accepting a nonphysical aspect is the only solution to both problems.

The "Parts" of Humans

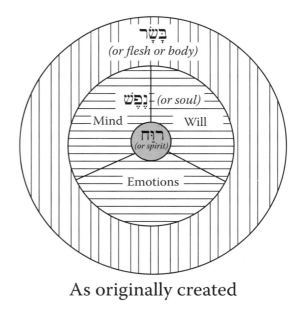

As originally created

Figure 3. Model of humans as originally created.

---

2 For class purposes I use a color slide, portraying the physical portion in blue and the nonphysical in yellow. However, even there a better representation would be if the yellow would totally overlay the blue, producing a green integrated whole.

While animals share to an extent mental, volitional, and emotional traits that humans have, there are distinctions. The most obvious distinctions are in the mental realm. Humans are capable of abstract thought. They are highly creative. They can communicate verbally conveying nonconcrete ideas through abstract symbols. Volitionally, humans are understood to have a free will. In terms of emotions, it would appear that while both have emotions, human emotions are qualitatively different. One more point that must be mentioned is that both men and women share all of the attributes that we suggest make them human as opposed to animals.

Beyond the attributes that humans share with animals and the attributes that quantitatively differentiate them from animals, humans share several attributes with God that qualitatively distinguish them from animals. Dorman (2001, 48–50) includes self-awareness (being personal), having a degree of sovereignty, understanding the concept of holiness and righteousness (whether or not one attempts to live up to them), wisdom, understanding goodness, and the ability to love. As presented in the Bible, however, a key distinction lies in the way humans were originally created. While humans share the trait of having a *nephesh* with animals, the Bible indicates that Adam and Eve were given a spirit or *ruah*, which animals do not possess. It is suggested that since God himself is spirit, it is this element that marks humans as being in the image of God. Figure 3 shows a simple diagram of how this might be represented. Once again, the circle representing the spirit (shown as a circle with horizontal lines) would be better represented as completely overlapping the circle labeled soul in that they are both nonphysical aspects that seem to be integrated and permeate the entire body.[3]

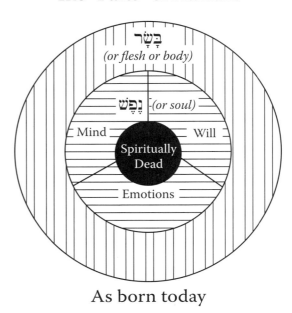

Figure 4. Model of humans after the fall.

The conclusion is that the human race was originally created with its members possessing both physical and nonphysical aspects. In addition, the nonphysical portion consisted of two components—the soul (נֶפֶשׁ), and the spirit (רוּחַ).

> **Soul and Spirit**
> A theological issue is the question of whether humans are dichotomous or trichotomous (having two parts or three parts). The question really is whether there is a distinction between soul and spirit, or whether the terms are interchangeable. I would suggest that this is primarily a translation problem. If *nephesh* is understood as the soul, this is something that animals also possess, although they do not possess a *ruah* or spirit. In this sense, humans are trichotomous. On the other

---

3   Referring back to the model I use for class, I color this portion red. In theory, when all three colors (being primary) totally overlap, the result would be white (recognizing the differences between mixing light and mixing physical colors).

> hand, if the focus of the *nephesh* is on the nontangible aspect, and the awareness that in terms of the *ruah* or spirit humans are dead, then humans, having both physical and nonphysical natures, are dichotomous.

However, as a result of the fall, Adam and Eve are portrayed as dying spiritually (Berkhof 1941, 225–26; Strong 1907, 591–93). Figure 4 shows a simple model that conveys this concept. In this case I show the portion of the diagram representing the human spirit as a black circle analogous to a black hole. In the physical realm, a black hole is a star that has collapsed upon itself to the point that its gravity distorts everything around it, even to the point of bending light. In a similar manner, as fallen human beings, we have an egocentric perception of the world that distorts how we see the world—to use the adage, "it revolves around me."

A physical model that I use to illustrate our spiritual state is the nectar that I make for my hummingbird feeder. It is very simple, consisting of three things: water, sugar, and food coloring. The water gives it physical presence as a liquid. While a solid, the sugar dissolves within that physical presence and is not visible to the viewer, although it permeates the entire contents of the feeder; it gives the mixture flavor. Likewise, the food coloring physically permeates the material and gives it color, although it cannot be tasted. In the feeder, the combination appears to be one substance and I cannot separate the elements unless I evaporate all of the water (a physical demise). However, I have found that if I leave the nectar in the feeder and hummingbirds don't eat it, the dye will fade away. Actually it doesn't really disappear, but it no longer gives any color—in terms of its intended function, it is dead, which might illustrate spiritual death.

While these three diagrams illustrate the world in which we live, I would add one more diagram that illustrates one added feature that is crucial to understand our situation entirely. This last diagram illustrates the situation of a person who has been redeemed in Jesus Christ. One aspect of that is that the Holy Spirit is understood to dwell within that person (John 14:17). Figure 5 suggests this by replacing the dead human spirit with the Holy Spirit, but it is recognized that while we have the Holy Spirit dwelling in us, we still struggle spiritually (Rom. 7:14–25).

The "Parts" of Humans

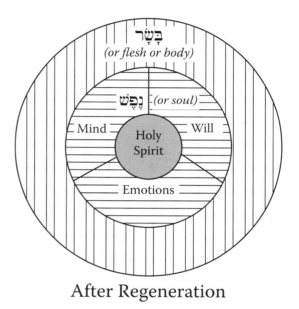

Figure 5. Model of regenerated human beings.

Within the context of Leviticus 17, clearly the ancient Israelites would not have been aware of the complexity of the circulation system and the role that blood plays in providing the elements of life to every cell in the body. Nor would they have been aware of the complexity of the human mind in terms of binding or hard problems. Likewise, they would not have had an understanding of the role of the Holy Spirit in terms of salvation and our relationship with God following the death, burial, resurrection, and ascension of Jesus. However, they did apparently understand that there was a close relationship between blood and life, although not in the sense that "the blood possessed the spiritual life-force of the victim that was released when eaten" (Mathews 2009, 150). Rather, it was in the sense that the loss of blood produces death. Linguistically, this is evident not only in the terminology but also cognates in Ugaritic and Akkadian (Rooker 2000, 236). Further, they would have been aware that there was some relationship between animal sacrifice and one's dedication to God. This seems to be evident in the fact that animal sacrifice seems to have been a key factor in worship in every culture throughout the world. More importantly, biblically it is manifested in the practice of the patriarchs providing burnt offerings at key points in their lives to demonstrate their consecration to God.

As such, we might say that God in his revelation at Sinai used a basic truth of which they were aware to provide a model to illustrate a spiritual truth of which they would have had an inkling from their own cultural background (patriarchal tradition?) and the cultures around them, but that contained such depth and profundity that future generations would be able discover greater nuances. Since blood was viewed as the source of life and represents life (Gen. 9:4, see Rooker 2000, 236), the sacrifice of one's domesticated animal, a key aspect of maintaining one's life in a subsistence culture, was an important demonstration of one's worship, trust in, and desire for a closer relationship with one's god. How that derived from God's response to Adam and Eve's sin (see the section on Atonement above) probably had been handed down through the Israelite ancestral oral tradition prior to Moses so that the accounts recorded in Genesis did not present new concepts to the people. But it seems probable that the accounts we have that were given to Moses at Sinai clarified and expanded the concepts practiced by their ancestors. From Noah to Moses, humans wandered further from God, with the number of gods proliferating in the process (Harbin 1994, 19–43). With Abraham,

God began a process of reconciling humankind, but it was not until Sinai that God provided a formal worship system. As seen in Leviticus, that system clarified standards and processes for worship of God, yet even that was only a prelude and foundation for God's subsequent work at Calvary.

Priests and Levites

The book of Leviticus derives its name from the Levites, and yet they are only mentioned once in the book in chapter 25 and that is with respect to their houses. Instead, the book places a great emphasis on the role of the priesthood, with the term "priest" being used some 194 times in its 154 verses. A good definition of priest is "one who is duly authorized to minister in sacred things, particularly to offer sacrifices at the altar, and who acts as a mediator between men and God" (Moorehead 1939, 2439). One of the key points of Leviticus is the establishment of a functioning priesthood to exercise those functions with regard to the tabernacle and to manage corporate worship for the new nation of Israel.

> *TRANSLATION ANALYSIS: PRIESTS*
> The Hebrew word translated "priest" is כֹּהֵן, which has an unknown etymology. The term shows up in several Western Semitic languages, always with the meaning of "priest" (Dommershausen 1995, 66). While several verbal roots are suggested, the most common seems to be כּוּן, which means "to stand," suggesting that the priest is "he who stands" (Feinberg 1975, 853; so also Dommershausen 1995). *TWOT* and BDB propose different nuances for כּוּן including "to establish or prepare." This might suggest that a priest was one who prepared or made ready for worship. This would certainly fit the various functions of a priest as developed in Leviticus, which centered on performing the sacrifices for the nation.

Prior to the year at Mount Sinai, the Israelites did not have priests. Instead, the head of the

Introduction to Leviticus

extended family filled that role. Noah (Gen. 8:20), Abraham (Gen. 22:13), Job (Job 1:5; 42:8), Isaac (Gen. 26:35), and Jacob (Gen. 33:30) are recorded as having performed sacrifices, considered a priestly function, but are never identified as priests.

Pre-Mosaic Priests

Prior to Sinai, Genesis and Exodus mention just three priests, and none were part of the Israelite ancestry. The first is Melchizedek, who is described as a priest of El Elyon, who seems to be the same God Abraham worshipped; he ruled over the Jebusite city of Salem (later Jerusalem) at the time of Abraham (Gen. 14:18). The second named priest is Potiphera, an Egyptian who presumably served Egyptian gods. He also became the father-in-law of Joseph (Gen. 41:45, 50; 46:30). The last was Jethro, the father-in-law of Moses, a Midianite. Also known as Reuel, "friend of God" (Exod. 2:16–18), Jethro is identified as the priest of Midian (Exod. 3:1). In Exodus 18, Jethro meets Moses and the people of Israel at the "mount of God." While he does observe that YHWH is greater than the other gods (Exod. 18:10) and had delivered Israel, it is not clear whether this is a new faith for him or not. Most likely, Jethro had some understanding of who God was, although it may have been rather vague—which might not be that far from the understanding many people have today.

When the nation arrived at Sinai after leaving Egypt, God told them that they were to be "a kingdom of priests" to him. This seems to mean that they were to serve within the broad concept of priesthood by being a corporate intermediary between the rest of the world and God (Harbin 2005, 144). However, even there, God distinguished a smaller group within that nation of priests who would be *labeled* priests as opposed to the people. Just a few verses later he warned that "even the priests who come near to YHWH must consecrate themselves" and that both the priests and the people must not come up on the mountain (Exod. 19:22–24).

After establishing the covenant between God and the nation, Moses received the directions for building the physical implements of corporate worship in the form of the tabernacle and its furniture (Exod. 25–27). This was followed by the designation of Aaron and his sons as the priests (Exod. 28:1; 30:30). At this point, nothing is said regarding the role of the rest of the tribe of Levi. It is not until the first census that enumerated Israel's fighting forces on the first of the second month of the second year after the exodus that we learn that they were not included as fighters. Subsequently it is revealed that they were to assist Aaron with the maintenance of the tabernacle. As set forth in Numbers 4, their responsibilities primarily were described as setting up and taking down the tabernacle during the continuation of the exodus journey. It is likely that they assumed that their responsibilities after settlement would basically be the same.

Levites and the Israelite Army

The purpose of the first census of Israel was to give the numbers of the men who were to go out to war (Num. 1:2). The men of the tribe of Levi were not included because they were given an alternative assignment of taking care of the tabernacle materials (Num. 3:6–9). This is somewhat ironic since Levi, their ancestor, was told his descendants would be dispersed because of his role in the slaughter of the men of Shechem (Gen. 49:6–7; see Gen. 34). Later the Levites were noted for standing up for God after the golden calf incident (Exod. 32:26).

While all of the Levites were given assignments of ministry at Sinai with respect to the tabernacle, their responsibilities differed depending on which of Levi's sons they descended from (see chart 1). In addition, a portion of Kohath's lineage (the sons of Aaron) filled what are considered "priestly roles" or "the duties of the sanctuary" (Num. 3:38). Specifically, they performed sacrifices in the tabernacle, and consulted God when requested. While all priests were Levites, not all Levites were priests, still, the Levites represented the nation before God (Feinberg 1975, 854). As designated at Sinai, these various Levitical responsibilities clearly served to facilitate setting up and taking down the tabernacle as the nation moved from location to location, although the process is never described.

Family	Ages 1 month and up	Ages 30–50
Gershon	7,500	2,630
Merari	6,200	3,200
Kohath	8,600	2,750

Chart 2. Number of Levites by subtribe when they left Sinai.

Descendants of Gershon	Tabernacle Tent Covering Screen for the doorway Court hangings
Descendants of Merari	Tabernacle frame Bars Pillars Sockets Equipment
Descendants of Kohath	Ark Table Lampstand Altars Utensils Screen

Chart 1. Levite family responsibilities for worship.

The Levite Numbers

According to Numbers 3:39, the total number of Levites was 22,000, but the total number of the subtribes of Levi in Numbers 3:22, 28, and 34 is 22,300. Two solutions have been proposed. L. J. de Regt and Ernst Wendland (2016, 70) cite Rashi and other medieval commentators, who suggest that the discrepancy of three hundred represented firstborn Levites who "could not serve as ransom for another firstborn." R. Alan Cole (2000, 98) and others note that some copies of the LXX have 8,300 for the tribe of Kohath, as opposed to 8,600. They suggest that since the Hebrew writes out the numbers, that in Numbers 3:28, which the MT reads as שְׁמֹנַת אֲלָפִים וְשֵׁשׁ מֵאוֹת, the original number would have been שְׁמֹנַת אֲלָפִים וְשָׁלֹשׁ מֵאוֹת with the middle ל being missed as the result of a copyist's error, changing the 3 to a 6.

According to Numbers 3, when the nation left Sinai, the tribe of Levi from the age of one month old and up numbered 22,000 (Num. 3:39). Chart 2 shows the breakdown by the three subtribes as well as the number of active workers (aged thirty to fifty) after the first census in Numbers 3. Of these, the total number of consecrated priests was five: Aaron and his four sons Nadab, Abihu, Eleazar, and Ithamar. However, we learn in Leviticus 10 that Nadab and Abihu are struck dead on the day the sacrifice is initiated, leaving three consecrated priests noted by name. While it seems likely that others within the subtribe of Kohath served as assistants, we do not have any information in that regard.

As described in Leviticus, this labor distribution was intended for the period between Sinai and the Promised Land. It would seem that an original expectation might have been five to ten years, based on national obedience with regard to the invasion and settlement. Looking back after the fact, we are aware it ended up as forty-five to fifty years as a result of the Kadesh-barnea incident (Num. 14:28–37), with the resulting wandering and five-to-ten-year conquest period. After the nation entered the land and settled, the Levites were given forty-eight cities distributed throughout the nation (Num. 21), where they lived and pastured their cattle, although they did not farm. The Kohathites were settled in the region of Judah, Simeon,

Benjamin, Ephraim, Dan, and the western half of Manasseh (Josh. 21:4–5); the Gershonites were assigned to the region of Issachar, Asher, Naphtali, and the eastern half of Manasseh (Josh. 21:6); and the Merarites ended up in Reuben, Gad, and Zebulun (Josh. 21:7).

What happened to the Levites subsequent to settlement is somewhat of a mystery. The tasks already noted involved transporting the tabernacle. It is clear that after the settlement the tabernacle was moved on occasion, but those moves were rare and there is no discussion of how or why those moves were made. Without that work (which had been vital during the time of wandering), what did the Levites do? Joshua 13:14 states that part of their inheritance was to receive "the offerings by fire to the Lord, the God of Israel." This suggests that the dispersed tribe served priestly functions on a local level, as demonstrated by Samuel (1 Sam. 9:12–13). Numbers 18 adds that the Levites would have a role in tithe distributions once they settled, which may affect some of the social justice details in the last chapters of Leviticus. It would also appear that the way the Levites were distributed throughout the land had implications with regard to teaching and implementing the Torah (perhaps somewhat similar to a modern rabbi), although we have no record regarding how that was to work. The land distribution gave the Levites houses in the Levitical cities and pastureland, indicating they had herds and flocks. What they did not have was fields in which to plant grain. Numbers 18:21–24 indicates that in place of growing their own grain, the Levites were to utilize the grain that the rest of the nation tithed. In terms of actual events, Judges 17–19 show that the Levites were dispersed through the land. Judges 17 suggests that they may have actually served priestly functions, although not in the *corporate* worship of YHWH. Those chapters also suggest that they were as prone to syncretism and theological wandering as the rest of the nation.

> ### Tabernacle Locations
> When the nation crossed the Jordan, the tabernacle initially was set up at Gilgal, an unknown location on the west side of the Jordan River somewhere near Jericho (Josh. 5:10). The OT records it as being located in several other places during the four hundred years of its existence prior to Solomon's temple, including Bethel (Judg. 20:26), Shiloh (1 Sam. 1:3), Gibeon (1 Chron. 16:39), and Jerusalem (Ps. 76:2). In addition, Joshua is reported to have built an altar for corporate worship on Mount Ebal (Josh. 8:30), which Adam Zertal (2018, 225–49) has reported locating.

Samuel may be a model who points to other tasks the nonpriestly Levites did after the conquest. His father Elkanah was pious and went up to worship at Shiloh annually. First Samuel 1:1 labels him an Ephraimite, but 1 Chronicles 6:20–28 seems to show that he was a Levite from the line of Gershom but not a descendant of Aaron. While his city, Ramah, is not listed as a Levitical city, there did not seem to be a requirement that a Levite dwelt in specific Levitical cities (see Deut. 14:29; 16:11–14; 18:1–8). In fact, Judges 17:9 records the testimony of a Levite who came from Bethlehem. After Samuel was raised in the tabernacle by Eli, as an adult we see him performing priestly functions in Ramah (1 Sam. 9:12–13), and then serving as a judge (1 Sam. 7–17), which was one of the responsibilities of the Levites (Deut. 17:9). Later we learn that the Gibeonites, a Canaanite tribe that used subterfuge and lies to avoid being destroyed, were assigned to chop wood and haul water for the tabernacle (Josh. 9:27). In addition, priests had servants or slaves who were allowed special privileges with regard to the priestly foods (Lev. 22:11; 1 Sam. 2:13).

Biblical Family Ties
Families are complex not only in practice but by definition, and recent cultural efforts to change the meanings of various terms

associated with the concept have exacerbated the issue. For the purposes of this study, we will be looking at a biblical perspective and will use various terms in their standard historical meanings. At the outset we must recognize that there is much that we do not know.

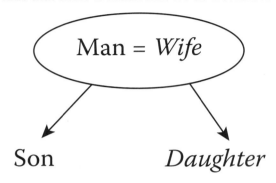

A Basic Nuclear Family

Figure 6. Nuclear family (the number of children will vary).

Historically, there has been a basic differentiation between a nuclear family and an extended family. A nuclear family has generally been understood as a married man and woman who have children (see fig. 6). In essence, we are looking at two generations. In modern western cultures, this differentiation tends to be demonstrated as a child grows up and leaves home to marry a spouse, typically establishing his or her own nuclear family.

Married
While popularly a married couple is viewed as a "family," scholars distinguish between marriage and family with the family concept based on the presence of children in the relationship (Trutza 1975, 92). Marriage has been defined as a rite of passage whereby a man and a woman "are joined in a special kind of social and legal dependence for the purpose of founding and maintaining a family" (WTNID s.v. "marriage"). Given that its purpose was to found a family and the above definition that a family included children, traditionally a marriage has been understood as limited to a legal relationship between a male and a female. Within the OT culture, this did not preclude a man marrying more than one woman, a practice that seemed to have been tolerated although never actually authorized. While most modern cultures see marriage as a legal status providing certain legal benefits and responsibilities, common law marriage is still recognized in a number of states in the United States. Marriage rituals can and historically have varied in degree of complexity, ranging from a simple exchange of vows before witnesses to an extremely elaborate show. The OT gives little discussion of the marriage process, although it typically seems to have been simple. We read in Genesis 29:22–23 that Laban gave a feast, at the end of which he presented Leah to be the wife of Jacob (as a substitute for the agreed-upon Rachel). However, the account of Jacob's father Isaac's marriage to Rebekah is a simple statement that he took her into Sarah's tent and "she became his wife."

Most often the grandparents are then left alone, the stereotyped "empty nesters." In the OT, the differentiation between nuclear and extended families was much more fluid. Typically, the OT family seemed to consist of three generations once the oldest son married: he and his wife moved in with his parents and then had their own children.

Oldest Son
We use the term "oldest son," drawing on our understanding of the inheritance process that the oldest son would receive the birthright, which by custom would include the family name and titles (White 1975, 617). Subsequently he would replace the father upon the father's death, but he may have assumed that position de facto, if through illness, accident, or just age the original father could no longer physically run the farm. In terms of inheritance, Deuteronomy 21:17

specifies that the firstborn would receive a double portion of the father's possessions. What this means for younger sons is not clear. In some cases the evidence suggests that a younger brother would remain in the family compound (sometimes referred to by the Latin name *insula*), producing an extended family living together.

Archaeology suggests that these compounds might include about twenty-five persons (Avner 1990, 132). Another alternative that is not really addressed is that a younger son might actually start his own extended family similar to the situation of Jacob, who received the birthright with the associated family name and titles while his brother Esau headed his own family, which ultimately became a different nation. After Israel arrived in the land and began to settle, it was by families or clans (מִשְׁפָּחָה), which Herman Austel (1980c) concludes "most often refers to a circle of relatives with strong blood ties." The relationship between the two groups, as well as their relative sizes, is not clear and is debated among scholars; it would appear that the two groups are subdivisions of the tribe with the clan (מִשְׁפָּחָה) larger than the house of the father (בֵּית אָבוֹת; Ashley 1993, 58; Harbin 2021a, 485–94). Based on modern evidence from the Middle East, a clan might include a wider scope of descendants of an individual who was no longer alive (Antoun 1972, 37–113). More than one extended family might occupy a village, especially as new extended families developed (Harbin 2016b). On the other hand, since there was still undeveloped land (esp. in the early decades after the conquest), new extended families might initiate their own villages (Josh. 17:15–18; Judg. 18:1–2).

The household was referred to as "house of the father" or "father's household" (בֵּית־אָב). The father would generally be the grandfather or eldest male, who would be referred to as the head of his father's household (רֹאשׁ לְבֵית־אֲבֹתָיו). To differentiate this common three-generation household from our typical Western concept we will use the term *molecular family* (see fig. 7). While the illustration shows both grandparents alive, it appears that a more common structure included just the widowed grandmother.

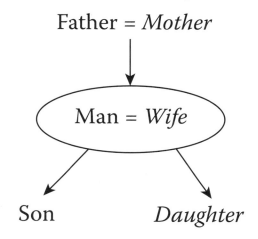

A Basic Molecular Family

Figure 7. Molecular family structure (again, the number of children will vary; the senior generation labeled father and mother likely included just a surviving spouse, more likely the widowed mother).

As they all aged, the current grandparents would pass away, the oldest son would become the "father of the house" and his son (usually the oldest) would marry and they would repeat the cycle. This means that the entire picture was very dynamic, and relationships continually changed. A significant factor for Israelite culture was that through the process, the family would retain the land they farmed and live in the same house. Aspects of this pattern extended beyond Israel, and some are still evident in the Middle East today. I (Harbin) recall that on my first trip to Turkey, our guide related how he was born in the same bedroom that his grandfather had been born in. Although our guide no longer lived on the farm, his family still did.

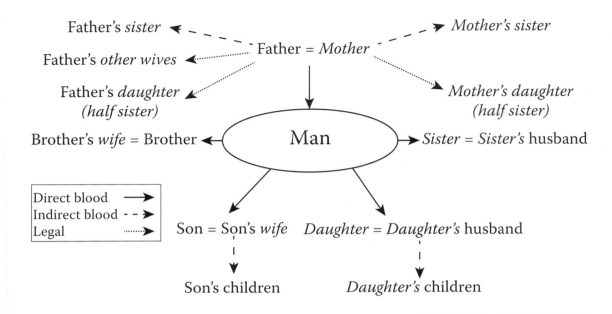

Figure 8. Extended family relationships.

Given the likelihood of multiple siblings, the typical picture would be much more complex as sisters married into other families, and brothers brought in other women as wives. This would produce what is typically called an extended family (see fig. 8).

While this might be the anticipated pattern, there would be a number of variables that would affect outcomes. One variable would be the number of sons. Another might be the early death of the grandparents. Or it might be a premature death of the father without a son for the next generation. The latter portion of Leviticus addresses some of these issues, and we will discuss them there. For our present purposes, the real question is, What are the relationships between a man and various associated women for which sexual relationships (and thus marriages) are forbidden (see fig. 9)?

As we compare figures 8 and 9, it becomes clear that basically a man is forbidden from having sexual relationships, and thus marriage, within what we might call the extended family. However, as one considers the various individuals indicated, it soon becomes clear that some of the figures who are tied to this extended family also have relationships within other extended families. For example, the mother came from another extended family and would serve as a link. If she had a sister, the sister would have married into a third extended family—thus, more links.

We should note that the structures presented in figures 8 and 9 are simplified compared to many of the situations we read about in the OT. First, in many situations as noted, a given man could have several brothers, which meant that there would be multiple sisters-in-law and thus a multidimensional

Introduction to Leviticus

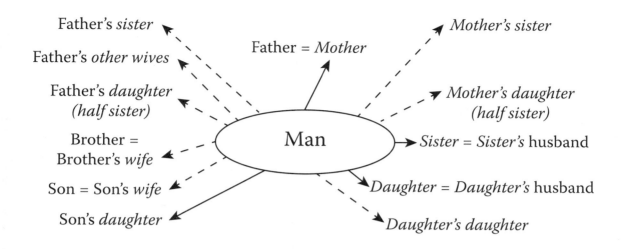

Forbidden sexual relationship (figures in italics) of an individual man. Direct family relationships are solid lines, extended family relationships are dashed lines.

Figure 9. Forbidden sexual relationships.

extended family. It would become even more complex when individuals had multiple wives.

Today, we think of social fabric as denoting a collection of family units, very often not even from the same parts of the world, let alone closely related. For OT Israel settled in the land, most of those relationships would have been either in the same village or other villages in the vicinity. From our perspective, this pattern gives a new emphasis on the concept of "blood relative." Clearly the social fabric of that culture would have been closely knit, producing a situation where a tear in the social fabric would have widespread implications. Expanding the picture beyond this, at some point extended families formulated clans, but where the distinction appeared is not clear.

Given the complexity of this situation I (Harbin) was reminded of a quilt pattern that my mother used to make quilts for all of her grandchildren. The pattern is called wedding ring (see figure 10), and to me, in a somewhat simplified manner, illustrates the overall complexity of intersecting families in a given culture.

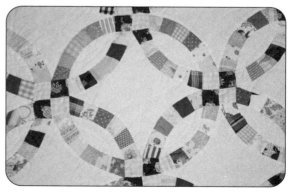

Figure 10. Wedding ring pattern quilt (quilt made by Tressie Palmer and Norma Harbin).

75

In our exegesis of the text, we note that in Leviticus 18, a man's daughter is not mentioned. In our culture, sexual relations outside of marriage are so common that we tend to take as a given the possibility that the text addresses a variety of sexual relationships, with marriage just being one subcategory. However, while the Israelites were aware that sex outside of marriage occurred, there appeared to be stronger social pressure against it, especially where the Torah was followed. Given the strong emphasis on avoiding premarital sex within that culture, the primary focus for this list of prohibited relationships seems more intended to show what *marriage* relationships were permitted, rather than merely guiding the man on whom he must avoid extramarital sexual relations with. As such, the daughter might not be mentioned since it was assumed that a man would not marry his own daughter and that she would be married into another extended family. For other relatives, that might not have been so clear.

Holy Days and Salvation History

Everyone enjoys a holiday—a day intended to allow us to interrupt our routine, especially with regard to work, and enjoy leisure, fun activities, friends and relatives, and often food. At times the concept of holiday seems contradictory because some holidays are rather somber, such as Good Friday. This highlights that the English word "holiday," which is largely seen in a secular sense today, is derived from the term "holy day." This etymology reflects that historically many holidays in most cultures had their origins in religious festivities. But there are many reasons for a culture to establish a holiday. In the United States we have a variety of those, including birthdays of noted individuals (such as George Washington or Dr. Martin Luther King Jr.), significant events in the history of the culture (such as July Fourth, Juneteenth, or Cinco de Mayo), or significant milestones (such as New Year's Day).

While most cultures seem to decide through popular consensus what should be a holiday or holy day, God designated Israel's original holy days when he formed the nation. Specifically, at Mount Sinai God gave Israel the six-event holy day calendar listed in Leviticus 23.

> **God-given Israelite Holy Days**
> For Israel, a complete compilation of holy days should include the Sabbath, the Sabbath year, and Jubilee. The latter two were actually year-long periods incorporating special activities. However, while those periods were given by God for cultural cohesion purposes, their extended length of time removes them from the holiday category.

Leviticus 23:2 calls these six events מוֹעֲדֵי יְהוָה, literally "appointments with YHWH," but we have called them *divine appointments*. They are declared to be "holy convocations" (מִקְרָאֵי קֹדֶשׁ). These terms emphasize that they reflect a time for the people to focus on their relationship with God. As we look at the rationale behind the declaration of the six divine appointments, we find two underlying reasons. According to the OT, it appears that the primary reason for those Israelite holy days was that they remember and commemorate specific interactions between God and his people that produced the nation of Israel.

> **Supplemental Israelite Holy Days**
> Besides the holy days designated by God at Sinai, over the years Judaism has added several other holy days to celebrate other significant interactions between God and his people. The overall collection of interactions "related to divine interventions in Israelite history" are sometimes collectively called "salvation history" (Saggs 1978, 62). Interventions beyond the six denoted at Sinai include Purim, which celebrates God's deliverance of the Jews in exile from the planned genocide in the Persian Empire (Esther 9:21–22); and Hanukkah, which celebrates God's provision of oil for the cleansing of the temple after its defilement

by Antiochus Epiphanes (1 Macc. 4:36–59, referenced in John 10:22–23). Not all Jewish commemorations are celebratory. *Tisha B'av* (the ninth of Av) recalls the destruction of both the first and second temples that reportedly occurred on that day of the Israelite year, although centuries apart. Misnah Taanit 4:6 actually lists five laments for that date, including the declaration that the nation would not enter the land following the spies' report; the destruction of the first temple by Nebuchadnezzar in 586 B.C. (according to the Talmud); the destruction of the second temple by the Romans in A.D. 70; and when the Romans destroyed the city of Betar, crushing the Bar Kohkba revolt in A.D. 135, as well as plowing the site of the temple in Jerusalem in the same year.

Secondarily, in a derivative sense, those holy days served to focus the nation's attention on God's ongoing provision for them, especially in terms of their sustenance as they celebrated harvests. These factors will be discussed in the unit "Strengthening the Social Fabric" (Lev. 23:1–24:9). However, embedded in the instructions for those holy days, we find hints of a bigger picture related to God's purposes for the nation of Israel. Ross (2002, 432) observes, "There seems to be sufficient evidence to affirm that a prophetic element exists in the order of the feasts." Specifically, each of those divine appointments seems to contain various types, that is, physical items or acts that serve as prophetic indicators to collectively delineate in a broad sense salvation history, that is, God's overall program to rectify the brokenness that came about as a result of the fall. This section provides an overview of the surface reasons for each holy day, coupled with evidence that suggests a broader typological significance.

Spring Festivals

As a nation, Israel's first encounter with God occurred while the descendants of Jacob were ensconced in Egypt. This is the very familiar account of how God called Moses and how through him God led the embryo nation out of Egypt to Sinai where God gave the law to Moses, who then announced it to the nation. Moses then recorded it for posterity beginning with the book of the covenant, which through supplementation during the time in the wilderness became what we call the Torah. The heart of the exodus event was the Passover, which is celebrated to this day and is very familiar in a general sense to all Christians and Jews, among others. It is also the first holy day.

The directions given to the nation of Israel required each household to select an unblemished lamb on the tenth of Abib (later called Nisan). They were to keep their lamb until the fourteenth of that month. At twilight the lamb was to be slain. Then the blood of the lamb was to be placed on the doorposts and lintel of the house. That evening the lamb was to be roasted whole and then eaten along with unleavened bread and bitter herbs (Exod. 12:1–13). As is familiar to most, the point was that when the Lord passed through Egypt to strike the firstborn dead, when he saw the blood, he would "pass over" the door and not allow the destroyer to come in (Exod. 12:23). For the Israelites, this was to be a memorial to future generations so that they remembered when God had delivered them (Exod. 12:24–27). While the current study's focus is Leviticus, it seems significant that just a few days after God delineated the various holy days in Leviticus 23 the Israelites celebrated the first anniversary of the Passover by observing the Passover meal on the fourteenth of Abib (Num. 9:1–14).

The NT clearly indicates that there was also a prophetic nuance in this holy day, which is considered to be fulfilled by the crucifixion of Christ as the foundation of Christianity. Jesus celebrated the Passover with his disciples (Matt. 26:18) the night that Judas betrayed him, and then allowed himself to be arrested (Matt. 26:55), tried (John 19:11), condemned, and crucified the next afternoon (John 19:16–17). However, there is more to it than that.

Introduction to Leviticus

After careful consideration, Harold Hoehner (1977, 114) concludes that Jesus was crucified on the afternoon of 14 Nisan, A.D. 33, which would have equated to Friday, 3 April by our calendar. As he evaluated the evidence, he discovered that in the NT times, the Jews were divided in terms of when a day began. The Pharisees and the Galileans (and Jesus and his disciples) began their day at sunrise, while the Sadducees commenced it at sunset (pp. 87–90). Consequently, Jesus and his disciples (along with many others) sacrificed their lamb and celebrated Passover dinner that year on Thursday afternoon and evening at the end of the fourteenth by their calendar. However, the high priest and the other Sadducees performed their sacrifices on Friday afternoon (by NT times "twilight" was viewed as between three and five in the afternoon), which was the fourteenth by *their* calendar. This made the next day, the fifteenth—which was the first day of the Feast of Unleavened Bread, which functioned as a Sabbath—coincide with the actual Sabbath, producing a high Sabbath. With this distinction, following the late Thursday night arrest and the various trials, Jesus was nailed to the cross about 9 a.m. on Friday and died at about 3 p.m., at the same time that in the temple the High Priest, a Sadducee, was beginning the process of sacrificing the Passover lambs for the Judean Passover dinner that evening. Paul alludes to this when he describes Christ as "our Passover" (1 Cor. 5:7).

As directed by Leviticus 23:9–11, on the day following the Sabbath subsequent to the beginning of the Feast of Unleavened Bread, the priest "waved" or "raised up" the first sheaf of the harvest.

Wave Offering
The wave offering is discussed in the section on Leviticus 7:30, where it is concluded that "raised up" would be an appropriate understanding.

In A.D. 33, this would have been the Sunday after the celebration of the Passover—what Christians now refer to as Easter.

Unleavened Bread and Sabbath
There is debate regarding the identity of the Sabbath in the case of the Feast of Unleavened Bread as shown in " Strengthening the Social Fabric," (23:1–24:9). The question is, did the "day after the Sabbath" refer to a regular Sabbath as a Saturday, or as a special day denoted as a Sabbath (see discussion on Lev. 23:6–14)? In the case of A.D. 33, the two different interpretations would have coincided. Thus, in terms of typological interpretation, this would not make a difference.

We note in our exegesis how the stated purpose of the Feast of Unleavened Bread was to remind the Israelites of the time they came out of Egypt (Exod. 23:15). We also note that there was an anticipatory element to it with regard to the upcoming harvest season. While the Feast of Unleavened Bread as a whole does not seem to carry any prophetic significance, it would seem that the signal event of the feast, the raising up of the first sheaf, would have been a type that carried tremendous significance that was not grasped until after the fulfillment event. Paul expressed it when he wrote in 1 Corinthians 15:20 that when Christ was "raised up from the dead," he was the "firstfruits of those who are asleep." On one hand this may be a purely metaphorical description, but given the timing of the resurrection event tied to the festival schedule it seems much more is embedded in that phrase.

Unleavened Bread and Christ
Jewish scholars who see prophetic significance in the festivals essentially ignore the Feast of Unleavened Bread in their discussion, although Sam Nadler (2006, 229) does observe that Paul calls "sincerity and truth" the unleavened bread associated with Christ as our Passover.

The third spring holy day was Pentecost, which was also labeled the "festival of the harvest of the firstfruits of your labor" (Exod. 23:16) or the Festival of Weeks (or of the firstfruits of the wheat harvest; Exod. 34:22). Two points stand out with regard to its relevance to the NT. First, it was one of three pilgrimage festivals where all Israelite males were supposed to gather at the place God designated (Exod. 23:14–15). As such, during the Pentecost celebration following the crucifixion/resurrection/ascension, Jerusalem was crowded with pious worshippers (we use pious because only the pious would undergo the long journey required) and was likely still very much abuzz with the implications of events associated with the earlier pilgrimage festival (Passover/Feast of Unleavened Bread) that spring. It was then no coincidence that the Holy Spirit descended upon the disciples on the day of Pentecost, and as we know it, the church began. Second, as Gane (2004a, 391) notes, this festival had to do with harvest. In spiritual terms, it signified the beginning of the harvest that Jesus alluded to in John 4:35. We might add that the corporate sacrifice on this date specifically included two loaves of *leavened* bread, which may typify the incorporation of gentiles.

Collectively, the spring festivals provide an amazing foreshadowing of God's redemptive process. As a cohesive picture, clearly the elements of the Passover were designed to provide a picture of how God worked with the nation of Israel, not only to provide an annual reminder to the nation of Israel of what God had done, but to serve as an introduction to what he was going to do through Jesus (Fuchs 1985, 15–28; see also Sevener, n.d.; Rubin and Rubin 1998). While perhaps not as overt, the other two festivals in the spring calendar supplement that picture, anticipating both the resurrection and church. As noted, however, these pictures did not become clear until after their fulfillment.

Autumn Festivals

Collectively, the autumn festivals possess several differences from their spring counterparts. In terms of the original audience at Sinai, they were also less clearly tied to both historical events and agricultural milestones. Perhaps the most significant from our perspective is that while the spring festivals are clearly tied to the first coming of Christ, any prophetic ties of the autumn festivals are more inferential and speculative because they are yet future. Still, as Samuel Kellogg (1978, 468) observes, since the "earlier feasts of the year were also prophetic," he maintains, "we may therefore safely infer that these remaining feasts of the seventh month must be typical also." He qualifies this with the caveat that any significance of the last three "must be interpreted in harmony with what has already passed into fulfillment." We might add that since the festivals were given to the nation as national events, it would seem that any typological focus of the festivals would be primarily for the nation of Israel. However, the presence of global implications in the spring festivals suggests global implications for the autumn festivals as well. This derives from the intended purpose of the nation as a kingdom of priests for the rest of the world (Exod. 19:6). In other words, just as guidelines for the Levitical priesthood had implications for the responsibilities and actions of the nation, so then guidelines for the nation had implications for the rest of the world. We note with the spring festivals that the three holy days are designated for the nation of Israel, and the typological fulfillment of them occurs in and for Israel, but the effects of the three antitypes is global.

Pursuing this from a logical rather than chronological sequence, we will begin with the final festival, Sukkoth. Sukkoth is the only autumn festival that had a historical focus, since it reminds Israel of the time in the wilderness. Sukkoth is also the last of the three key pilgrimage festivals announced in Exodus 23. The other two have direct ties with the crucifixion-resurrection-ascension of Jesus and the founding of the church. At this point in history, we lose sight of the fact that the foundation of the church was actually a presentation of Jesus as the nation's Messiah to Israel (Acts 2:15–39).

Joel's Prophecy and Acts

In Acts 2, Peter begins his explanation of what was happening on Pentecost by declaring that what was happening was a fulfillment of Joel's prophecy in Joel 2:28–32. What Acts does not record is Joel's next verse that relates that in those days, God would "restore the fortunes of Judah and Jerusalem."

It then seems interesting that in Exodus this last holy day is called the Feast of Ingathering. It is also described as being at the end of the year (Exod. 23:16), which raises a significant question. When God gave Moses directions for the first Passover, he specified: "This month shall be the beginning of months for you; it is to be the first month of the year to you" (Exod. 12:2). Then, approximately three months later, he declares that the seventh month will be "at the end of the year." Some have taken the description of the first of the seventh month as showing that Israel had an autumnal new year (Lange 1960, 170). But if that were the case, then Sukkoth, beginning on the fifteenth of that month, would be early in the year, not at the end. It would seem that Israel's calendar of holy days operated on a different annual schedule, perhaps something like our modern academic year, which in theory begins in September and ends in May and is thus a nine-month "year." Kellogg (1978, 468) calls the seven-month festival period an "ecclesiastical year."

Israelite New Year

Today the first day of the seventh month is understood to be the Jewish New Year on a civil calendar. There is a caveat to this, since Leviticus 25:8–10 specifies that the Year of Jubilee begins on the tenth day of the seventh month (i.e., on Yom Kippur). This is not in sync with either the civic or the religious year. While it may have a somewhat eschatological significance, that would not be evident until after the fact, which even yet is future.

Leviticus 23:41–43 shows a relationship between Sukkoth and the exodus, since the nation was directed to "live in booths for seven days . . . so that your generations may know that I caused the sons of Israel to dwell in סֻכּוֹת (booths) when I brought them out of Egypt." Based on the terminology of Exodus, Kellogg (1978, 469) argues that "if Pentecost typified the firstfruits of the world's harvest in the ingathering of an election from all nations, the feast of tabernacles must then typify the completion of that harvest in a spiritual ingathering, final and universal" (see also Fuchs 1985, 71). Coulson Shepherd (1974, 76) takes a similar perspective but suggests that it represents "a goal toward which He has been directing all of His marvelous program of redemption." In that light, another item that is interesting is that while a number of festivals were mandated for both native Israelites and resident aliens, 23:42 states that it should be the "native-born in Israel" who were to live in booths. This is very interesting in that Richard Hess (2008, 791), citing Zechariah 14:16–19, points out that Sukkoth is the only feast that will be celebrated in the millennium. However, in this case the participants will include all who are left of the nations "that went against Jerusalem," which suggests that this presently exclusively native Israelite celebration will include all people.

While Michael Norton (2015, 76) cites evidence that suggests that Jesus was actually born during Sukkoth, he does not see that as a prophetic nuance. Rather, he cites Jeremiah and Ezekiel, who look forward to a time when God would "dwell with His people forever," and views Sukkoth as an anticipation of that. He also notes how Sukkoth will be celebrated "every year in the kingdom to celebrate this fact."

Chronologically, the first autumn event is the first day of the seventh month, which is not mentioned until Leviticus 23:24. Biblically, it is not given a name and in Leviticus it is only denoted as a day of rest, when the blowing of the trumpets shall be a memorial, and thus it has commonly been called the Feast of Trumpets.

Rosh Hashanah

While the first of the seventh month is merely called the Feast of Trumpets in Leviticus, later it acquired the name Rosh Hashanah, literally, "the head of the year." Norton (2015, 45) observes that it is also known as *"Yom Teruah* (Day of Awakening Blast or Resurrection); *Yom Hadin* (Day of Judgment); *Yom Zikaron* (Day of Remembrance); and *Yom Hamelech* (Day of Coronation of the King)"—and points out that "all the names allude to the coming of the Messiah." It is not surprising, then, that he understands Paul's reference of the trumpet in 1 Thessalonians 4:16–17 and 1 Corinthians 15:52 to view the Feast of Trumpets as a foreshadowing of the rapture.

Trumpet Blast

Mishnah tractate Roš Haš. 4:9 describes the manner of sounding the trumpet. Norton (2015, 46–47) draws upon Jewish tradition as he describes this as four types of blasts totaling a hundred blasts, "blown with the belief that the gates of heaven will be opened for the home taking."

While the text describes it as a memorial trumpet blast (זִכְרוֹן תְּרוּעָה) or a "reminder" (NASB), the Israelites were not told of what it was to remind them. Consequently, as we note in the unit "Strengthening the Social Fabric" (23:1–24:9), there is a lot of speculation. While it may have been intended to remind the people of the upcoming two holy days, given this vague description one is hesitant to propose possible antitypes that would serve as prophetic fulfillments. Probably, very much like in the case of the first coming, they will be discerned in retrospect. However, one is reminded that Paul twice speaks of a trumpet in association with the return of Christ. First, early in his ministry in 1 Thessalonians 4:16–17, he associates "the trumpet of God" with the resurrection of the dead in Christ coupled with the catching up of those still alive in Christ. Similarly in 1 Corinthians 15:52, he talks of "the last trumpet" where the dead in Christ will be raised, and believers "will be changed." In terms of the holy days for the Israelites, it may be that this trumpet, which signals the return of Christ for believers, might serve as a reminder to any Israelite descendants to return to God through his Messiah.

Between the two autumnal divine appointments we find Yom Kippur. It is on a peculiar date. It is not a key astronomical sign such as a new moon or equinox. There is no mention of any historical event associated with it. It is simply a date arbitrarily mandated by God. In that light, it is interesting that Leviticus 25:9 places this date as the beginning of Jubilee, a celebratory year that came every fifty years (Lange 1960, 177). From a practical perspective this would place the usufruct transition as land was returned to its original family at the beginning of the Jubilee Year, a period during which the land was to rest. Ross (2002, 432) sees the type here in the ritual as "the sacrificial animal that shed its blood to make atonement for sins, and the scapegoat that signified the complete removal of sin from the people." What is interesting in that regard is that the people were not called to assemble but to celebrate a Sabbath rest (שַׁבַּת שַׁבָּתוֹן) in their homes (Lev. 23:31–32) while the priest performed the rituals involved with Yom Kippur, including taking the blood of the sacrificed goat to the mercy seat (see material on Lev. 16:2–28 in "The Day of Atonement") and leading off the scapegoat.

Kellogg (1978, 470) observes that Yom Kippur is "a season marked, on the one hand, by affliction of soul throughout all Israel; on the other, by the complete putting away of the sin of the nation for the whole year." He then concludes that typologically it points to "the great sorrowing of the nation and the great atonement putting away all Israel's sin." Daniel Fuchs (1985, 70) argues that since this was a corporate sacrifice, it therefore addressed forgiveness for the nation rather than the individual Israelite.

This may point to the "sons of Israel" who are sealed and the multitude "who came out of the great tribulation" noted in Revelation 7:4–17, but these are aspects of eschatology that are debated and beyond the scope of the present study.

In somewhat obscure (veiled?) ways then, the festivals appear to be links to the NT and eschatology. They do not seem to be designed to provide what we would call predictive elements, but to show that God has an overall program. The overall picture is one whereby on an annual basis a pious follower of God after Sinai might intuitively develop an expectation of what salvation history might look like. Reflecting back on God's deliverance from Egypt, one might observe God's current provision—and then, as the harvest wrapped up, following the reflection and atonement of Yom Kippur, look at the harvest as an anticipation of God's ultimate victory.

The value then of the festivals as an outline, so to speak, of salvation history really serves to enhance our understanding of the nature of God rather than provide prophecies to look for fulfillment. It would seem highly unlikely that any Israelite prior to the resurrection would have anticipated that Christ was going to be "our Passover" (1 Cor. 5:7) as well as the "firstfruits" (1 Cor. 15:20). And even after the resurrection, Pentecost came as a surprise to the followers of Jesus. Likewise, even if we visualize the fall festivals as emblems of the second coming, it does not really help us in any sense in determining how that might work out. It especially does not indicate when it will occur. As such, we must exercise great care and caution as we look for meanings that might be hidden within.

Still, it would seem that we end up with a picture of a God whose actions and decrees are intentional and as a result carry subliminal meanings. While we laud an extremely skilled playwright who is able to subtly signal important outcomes, we realize that his or her work is somewhat artificial, since the characters are bound to follow the script. Here, we have a picture of a God who allows his "characters" to make their own choices, but who not only knows the future but controls the outcome to such an extent that he could design a series of celebrations centuries in advance that would foreshadow the key points of his redemptive program disguised as regular thanksgivings of his bountiful care. That is an *awesome* God.

PRACTICAL THEOLOGY

The book of Leviticus is challenging and at first glance seems totally alien to us. The first portion of the book primarily addresses animal sacrifices, which we no longer perform. The middle of the book primarily addresses issues of diet that we no longer follow, afflictions of which we are unsure of their exact nature, or matters of hygiene that seem irrelevant to us. The final portion of the book primarily addresses a small village agricultural socioeconomic system from which we are far removed. In addition, aspects of each of the three subject matters appear in each of the other two sections, complicating the sorting out of themes. Still, there are two key underlying principles that a well-planned series of sermons can finesse into practical actions for our modern western culture.

The first and most important principle is that worship of an awesome, holy God requires humility, dedication, and self-denial. We suggested that the worship system for Israel intertwined acts of consecration, confession, and celebration. All three are applicable in today's culture, although manifested differently.

The second principle derives out of the first: a community that worships the awesome, holy Creator God must endeavor to demonstrate corporate moral purity and individual acts of love to develop and maintain a strong social fabric. Again, those will be manifested differently in our primarily urban, postindustrial socioeconomic system, but in many respects they demand the same attitudes of self-denial God demanded of Israel.

Introduction to Leviticus

OUTLINE

Leviticus can be divided into two major sections and preached in sixteen sermons (preaching units).

GUIDELINES FOR PERSONAL AND CORPORATE WORSHIP OF A HOLY GOD (1:1–10:20)

- Worshipping a Holy God (1:1–3:17)
- Purifying Oneself Before a Holy God (4:1–6:7 [HB 5:26])
- The Role of the Priests (6:8 [HB 6:1]–7:38)
- Inauguration of Ancient Israelite Religion (8:1–9:24)
- Standing Before a Holy God (10:1–20)

GUIDELINES FOR DEVELOPING AND PRESERVING A HOLY NATION (11:1–27:34)

- Quality of Worship (11:1–15:33)
- The Day of Atonement (16:1–34)
- Life and Blood (17:1–16)
- Preserving the Social Fabric (18:1–20:27)
- A Holy Priesthood for a Holy Nation (21:1–22:33)
- Strengthening the Social Fabric (23:1–24:9)
- Repairing a Social Snag (24:10–23)
- Preventing Social Unraveling, Part 1 (25:1–22)
- Preventing Social Unraveling, Part 2 (25:23–55)
- Alternative Outcomes for the Community of God (26:1–46)
- Vows and Values (27:1–34)

GUIDELINES FOR PERSONAL AND CORPORATE WORSHIP OF A HOLY GOD (LEVITICUS 1:1–10:20)

This first major section of the book, consisting of Leviticus 1–10, contains five preaching units that address first personal and then corporate worship of a holy God for the newly formed nation of Israel. "Worshipping a Holy God" begins with personal worship, looking at the guidelines that God gave the nation of Israel for voluntary personal worship, including burnt offerings for consecration to God, grain or gift offerings to reflect gratitude for what God has provided, and shalom offerings, a collection of offerings of celebration that praise God and his works within the community (chs. 1–3). While set up as a single preaching unit, it could also be approached as three separate sermons on the three different sacrifices. "Purifying Oneself Before a Holy God" then addresses what is traditionally called expiation, but which we have characterized as confession. This unit looks at the purification and reparation offerings (chs. 4–5). Like the first preaching unit, this unit could be divided into, and in this case delivered as, two separate sermons addressing the two different sacrifices. "The Role of the Priests" addresses the function of the priest as a guide for formal corporate worship for the nation (chs. 6–7). "Inauguration of Ancient Israelite Religion" approaches the commissioning of the priests and the inauguration of the formal corporate worship system as illustrating the importance of rites of passage and symbols with respect to corporate worship (chs. 8–9). "Standing Before a Holy God," the last unit in this section, addresses the need for conformance or obedience to God's teaching as part of honoring God in worship (ch. 10).

Leviticus 1:1–3:17

EXEGETICAL IDEA
After the tabernacle was erected, the glory of God filled the Tent of Meeting, and then the Lord directed Moses to convey to the people of Israel why and how they should bring sacrifices in worship.

THEOLOGICAL FOCUS
Access to our all-holy God is initiated by God giving worshippers guidance for bringing voluntary sacrificial offerings before him.

PREACHING IDEA
Worship of (a seemingly inaccessible, holy) God is initiated by God.

PREACHING POINTERS
In the original context, the introductory words of Leviticus 1:1–2 would probably come as a complete shock and even strike a note of terror in the heart of every Israelite. They may have chosen to know the God of glory who filled the Tent of Meeting from a distance. They may have preferred to relate to him as one whom they could summon when they encountered a perceived threat or need. An invitation to come before the throne of the all-powerful warrior who had struck down Pharaoh and his army, the devouring fire who had descended before their eyes onto Mount Sinai, the divine judge who had struck down his chosen people with a plague after they worshipped a false god, would invoke more fear than excitement. Yet, with these words the One who is seemingly (and safely) inaccessible was personally calling those he had set apart to step into his presence and worship. The all-holy God who redeems and judges was inviting them to come with an offering. Could they trust him? Was he safe? A humble attitude of trust was required if they were to enter into worship of the Lord their God.

Today, God may appear equally inaccessible to us, not because of his power and holiness, but because of our rebellious spirits. An autonomous heart is reluctant to respond to an invitation to come in humility before a sovereign God and worship. This passage reminds us that though we may prefer distance, God initiates personal worship. He invites us to bring an offering, step into his presence, and worship. He prescribes the way. He provides the means. But is he safe? Can we entrust our lives to him? A humble attitude of trust remains the foundation of authentic worship of the Lord our God.

WORSHIPPING A HOLY GOD (1:1–3:17)

LITERARY STRUCTURE AND THEMES (1:1–3:17)

Leviticus 1–3 unites three different individual sacrifices under the general heading of bringing an offering. As such, there are two ways of approaching the material: one may focus on the distinctions between the three sacrifices and address each separately, or one might view the material as a single unit that describes different reasons to bring an offering to God. The first view suggests three or four separate studies or sermons stressing the differences with the risk of overlooking the commonalities and the book structure (specifically how Lev. 1:1–2 ties the three chapters together). The second view emphasizes the commonality of worship through offerings to the Lord. This invites a single sermon, but risks overlooking the distinctions between the three offerings, as well as dulling the contrast of the consecration offerings from the confessional or purification offerings in Leviticus 4–5. While the distinctions in terms of how the sacrifices differed would have been important to the original audience who actually performed the sacrifices, for a modern audience a better focus might be on the basic concept of our attitude when we approach God.

As such, homiletically, we unite the three chapters as a single topic. However, in the exegesis, we will address how the text demonstrates different reasons to worship God through an offering, as we try to clarify the details that reflect a different culture with different expressions of worship. Our goal is to demonstrate how the three different sacrifices really support one theme—sincere worship of an almighty God. For purposes of a more in-depth study showing the distinctions between the three offerings in this section, we would refer to the material on the "Old Testament Sacrificial System" in the introduction.

- ***The Lord Tells Israel How to Worship (1:1–2)***
- ***The Lord Tells Israel How to Bring an Offering of Consecration (1:3–17)***
- ***The Lord Tells Israel How to Bring a Gift Offering (2:1–16)***
- ***The Lord Tells Israel How to Bring a Shalom Offering (3:1–17)***

EXPOSITION (1:1–3:17)

While the first two verses serve to introduce the entire book, perhaps more importantly they provide an umbrella for the rest of the first three chapters, which then serve as three subunits. The overall theme of this unit is to guide the nation of Israel with regard to individuals bringing voluntary offerings of worship to God by giving directions as to what that offering might consist of and how it was to be presented.

The Lord Tells Israel How to Worship (1:1–2)

The book of Leviticus begins rather abruptly with the statement, "And he called to Moses," followed by a message that Moses was to deliver to the nation.

TRANSLATION ANALYSIS: וַיִּקְרָא

"And he called" would be a literal translation of the Hebrew phrase וַיִּקְרָא, which is both the first word of the book and its title in the Hebrew Bible. However, the book begins with the Hebrew all-purpose conjunction *waw* (וֹ). As noted by Carl Philip Weber (1980a, 229), this conjunction may be translated by "*and, so, then, when, now, or, but, that*, and many others." Here it is translated as "and" in the KJV, but as

Worshipping a Holy God (1:1–3:17)

"then" in the HCSB and NASB. It is ignored in the ESV, NIV, NLT, and NRSV. With the imperfect of the verb, this form is called a "*waw* consecutive," a connector that ties the action of the verb with the preceding sequence, which in this case would be the phrase "he erected" (וַיָּקֶם) in Exod. 40:33 and "the cloud covered" (וַיְכַס הֶעָנָן) in Exodus 40:34 (GKC §49). Omitting the term obscures the sequential relationship. While "and" would seem to reflect the continuity, "then" more strongly reflects the sequence and should be preferred.

1:1. Leviticus really continues the text of Exodus. The Hebrew begins "then he said," referring back to Exodus 40:34. Because our modern Bibles divide the text here between Exodus and Leviticus, translators add "the Lord" for clarification. Exodus 40 describes the erection of the tabernacle, which is also called the Tent of Meeting (Exod. 40:29, see the sections on the "Place of Writing" and "Occasion of Writing" in the introduction). When Moses completed the construction of the tabernacle, the shekinah glory of God filled the Tent of Meeting or tabernacle (Exod. 40:34). Turning the page to Leviticus we read how God in that moment spoke to Moses from the Tent of Meeting, which would be the inner portion of the tabernacle containing the Holy Place and the Holy of Holies—the center of worship just completed. The shekinah would have settled on the Holy of Holies where the ark of the covenant was deposited, hovering between the two cherubim attached to the lid of the ark, which was called the "place of mercy" (כַּפֹּרֶת), which is usually translated "mercy seat" (so ESV, HCSB, KJV, NASB, and NRSV).

"Then He Said"
Throughout the book, this phrase introduces individual speeches through which God gave revelation to Moses (and on occasion, to Aaron) to provide information intended for the nation. Overall, the phrase shows that individual portions of the material (generally specific directions)

---

were directly from God and should be understood as being God's revelation to his people. Unless specifically noted otherwise, the structure would suggest that the specific revelation following was given on the heels of the preceding directions or event. In this case, that would suggest that the first portion of Leviticus was given immediately after the cloud filled the newly erected tabernacle. This would mean that the last verses of Exodus (Exod. 40:35–38) are an excursus that relates to the reader how the tabernacle could be moved if the glory of the Lord filled the Tent of Meeting.

Since Moses was unable to enter the Tent of Meeting (Exod. 40:35) he likely was in the courtyard of the tabernacle. There God gave him a message that he was to pass on to the nation of Israel. That initial message is the first part of Leviticus. Given the relationship between the dedication of the tabernacle and the glory of God filling it, the fact that this declaration immediately followed would make it one of prime importance. As such, the subsequent directions have an emphasis we tend to miss. Specifically, the first instruction details how an individual Israelite was to bring a voluntary offering to the Lord.

1:2. Leviticus 1:2 summarizes the message that Moses was to deliver to the people of Israel. Three elements to this message need to be highlighted. First, the expectation of Leviticus 1:2 is that individual Israelites in the future would bring a variety of voluntary offerings to God.

TRANSLATION ANALYSIS: כִּי *AND* אִם
The Hebrew particles כִּי and אִם both can be translated "if" or "when." GKC §159.l indicates that they may be used interchangeably to introduce conditional sentences. That seems to be the case in this section of Leviticus. Consequently, a somewhat colloquial translation of the Hebrew phrase אָדָם כִּי־יַקְרִיב מִכֶּם קָרְבָּן might be "when or if anyone

Worshipping a Holy God (1:1–3:17)

of you-all brings an offering." The introductory כִּי seems to point to an expectation it would be done, but was not necessarily required.

As we will see in the second unit, Leviticus also introduces offerings for the issue of sin, but they will be a separate category. The three voluntary offerings listed in this first declaration from God include one that we would place under the consecratory category (burnt), various preparations of gift offerings (grain), and one that encompasses the various celebratory (shalom or peace) offerings (see the section "The Old Testament Sacrificial System" in the introduction). Overall, the voluntary offering served to draw the attention of the offeror and his or her companions to God in worship, demonstrated by the expectation in 1:2 that these will be brought "to the Lord [YHWH]." As such, the circumstances of the offering provided narrative to the faith of the people involved, whether in celebration of God's actions or the issue of the forgiveness of sin (as we will see later). The fact that many of the offerings involved multiple members of the community also promoted national unity as servants of the Living God.

Second, 1:2 twice addresses an offering (קָרְבָּן) as a concept. This summary of the entire unit (the first three chapters) emphasizes the act of offering, rather than the type of offering. The term קָרְבָּן is generic, referring to offerings in general (Coppes 1980k, 813). As we look at the three specific types of offerings (3:1–17), we will see that each is considered nonexpiatory—that is, they are not in response to sin, although their purposes differ. The phrase "the Lord [YHWH] spoke to Moses, saying" in Leviticus 4 indicates a new unit that introduces what we call confessional offerings to address issues of sin (see "Sin and Sin [or Confession] Offerings in Leviticus" in the introduction). The present unit will focus on the initial triad compositely.

The third element, and what would have caught the attention of the people, is that these instructions are addressed to "the sons of Israel," a generic phrase meaning "anyone who is an Israelite," rather than to the priests, although a priesthood was being set up for the first time (the account of the establishment of the priesthood begins in Leviticus 8).

TRANSLATION ANALYSIS: THE SONS OF ISRAEL
Biblical Hebrew, like most languages that have grammatical gender, uses the masculine gender as an inclusive concept both in terms of pronouns and certain nouns. In this study we will attempt to show the inclusiveness that the author intended and that the original audience understood, but will also try to remain true to the terminology used in the Hebrew and the way the various translations we will be using read. For example, the Hebrew term translated "sons" as used here is a term that not only includes both sons and daughters (males and females), but also grandchildren and subsequent generations.

As discussed in the introduction under the topic of sacrifices, the ancestors of the people gathered at Sinai had used a rather informal form of worship with sacrifices performed on plain stone altars erected for the occasion. But now, God had directed the erection of a permanent (although portable) altar that would be located within a facility specifically designed as a center for worship. Moreover, it had already been hinted that there would be a professional priesthood. What did this mean for the people? As we will see later, the priests would have a significant role representing the people corporately before God and representing God before the people. Further, the sacrificial system about to be implemented seems to have been designed to initially supplement and modify, not to totally replace, the impromptu sacrifices that the ancestors of the Israelites had done for centuries, although this new system would soon receive most of the attention.

As such, it would have been important for the Israelites to hear that they were being

89

given directions on how they, as individuals, were to sacrifice, rather than how an institutional system would formalize worship in their place. What we will see is that under the new system the priests would assist the worshippers not only in worship but also in their relationships with one another. While a portion of each sacrifice would go to the priests, most of each animal would either be burned (consecratory offerings) or given to the worshipper and associates (celebratory or communal offerings). Further, the sacrifices of this first unit are voluntary, not obligatory. Later we will see that in other sacrifices the priests would have a greater role, but it is still greatly diminished compared to the elaborate systems of Egypt and Mesopotamia. In addition to being collectively denoted by the term "offering" and being considered optional for individuals, there is an emphasis on how the portion that is burned on the altar (whether the entire animal in the case of the burnt offering or a "memorial portion" in the other two) produces a "soothing aroma to the Lord" (Rainey 1975, 201). The fact that this is the first item addressed after the construction of the tabernacle as a center for worship suggests an emphasis on voluntary acts of worship to show honor to God.

The Ancient Near Eastern Context

Since Abraham had come from Mesopotamia, and Hebrew is related to the Mesopotamian languages, it would not be surprising if Mesopotamian cultures had affected Israel. However, one would expect that four hundred years in Egypt would also have had a significant effect on Abraham's descendants. When we look at those two regions, we note that what is being presented as the Israelite worship system has several significant differences.

In both Mesopotamia and Egypt, sacrificial ritual at this time was a very elaborate process of providing daily *meals* for the gods (Oppenheim 1977, 183–94; Teeter 2011, 46–53). Both cases required

a vast support system involving dedicated farms, storage facilities, food preparers, and servers. We label many of those individuals priests, but a royal entourage probably gives a better picture. While there were some differences in ritual content between Mesopotamia and Egypt, in both cases the sacrifice consisted of a full meal that was prepared for the god, including beverages, fruit and vegetables, specific cuts of meat, breads, sweets, and even "finger-bowls." Twice a day in Mesopotamia and three times a day in Egypt, this meal would be brought into the local temple and placed on a table in appropriate dishes before the god's image. In some cases, flowers and music would accompany the food. Following a period of time during which the god was presumed to "eat," these items would have been removed, and the physical remains would be provided to the king or his substitute as the god's representative and the local priestly entourage. Given the number of gods and temples, it is readily apparent that the process of serving the gods was a major aspect of each culture and economy. It was also a lucrative business for the priests. As such, the sacrificial systems of both background cultures focused more on providing for the gods and thus (perhaps not just coincidentally) supporting a priestly class (although in Egypt, many of the priests were actually part time) than providing spiritual benefits for the people.

Several points would have stood out for the Israelites as God delineated the new system. First, this was not intended to be a meal for God. This would possibly have been evident in the historical pattern of the Israelite ancestors, where the burnt offerings were totally consumed as contrasted with the pattern they saw in Egypt. Yes, following Sinai, in Israel a given sacrificial ritual might consist of meat and bread, but it was never an elaborate meal as they saw in Egypt. Yes, as we will discuss later, there was a sense in which the sacrifice produced what is called a "soothing aroma" or רֵיחַ נִיחֹחַ, but it would appear this was figurative language pointing to a spiritual truth,

Worshipping a Holy God (1:1–3:17)

not portraying a meal for God. Second, these sacrifices were not intended to be sublimated by the priests (although this would be abused later; see 1 Sam. 2:12–17). Within the sacrificial system presented in Leviticus there was a portion of the sacrifices designated for the priests—but as we will see, this was limited both in terms of which sacrifices they participated in as well as how much of the sacrifice they received and how they received it. Further, there were certain sacrifices (likely the most frequently observed) that were specifically intended for the use of the worshipper and family and friends. Against the ANE background, Leviticus and the sacrificial system of Israel stand in sharp contrast, being primarily aimed to the benefit of the people.

There is a key translation difficulty in 1:2 that is subtle but important. The text literally reads "from the beasts, from the herd, or from the flock you will bring your offering" (מִן־הַבְּהֵמָה מִן־הַבָּקָר וּמִן־הַצֹּאן תַּקְרִיבוּ אֶת־קָרְבַּנְכֶם). Some translations such as the NIV ("bring as your offering an animal from either the herd or the flock") seem to suggest that for an "offering," an animal sacrifice is mandatory (so also the KJV). Others, such as the NASB ("bring your offering of animals from the herd or the flock"), provide a broader understanding that makes an animal sacrifice one variation of offering, but then concludes that *if* the offering is an animal sacrifice, it must be from the herd or flock (so also ESV, HCSB, or NRSV). Given the overall structure of the unit, the use of the term "offering" (קָרְבָּן) and the fact that the very next sacrifice discussed as part of the same pericope in Leviticus 2 is the gift offering (specifically "choice flour"), the latter seems the better translation. In that case, the verse is understood to say that while the offering might be animal or grain, if one brings an animal offering, it needed to be a domesticated animal from one's possession (as will be shown below, this includes pigeons or turtledoves)—wild game was not acceptable. The rationale seems to be that an offering, whatever

its purpose, must cost something. With this, the text turns to describing how these various sacrifices are to be performed, beginning with the burnt offering.

TRANSLATION ANALYSIS: ANIMALS FOR SACRIFICE
Three terms for animals are listed in Leviticus 1:2: "beasts" (בְּהֵמָה), followed by those from the "herd" (בָּקָר), and those from the "flock" (צֹאן). This first category of beasts is a more generic category indicating domesticated animals. The other two are actually subcategories denoting first large animals or cattle, which is generally translated here in the collective sense "herd," and then smaller animals or sheep and goats (Botterweck 1975, 9). The latter term is generally translated here in the collective sense of *flocks*. While burnt offerings may also be from domesticated birds, they are not included in this verse. When they are addressed in 1:14, the Hebrew uses a similar triad: the generic term "birds" (עוֹף), followed by just two varieties that may be used: turtledoves or young pigeons. English may address collections of sheep and goats as either herds or flocks, but it also uses "flock" to describe a collection of birds (*WTNID* s.v. "flock").

The Lord Tells Israel How to Bring an Offering of Consecration (1:3–17)

The rest of Leviticus 1 addresses the first of the three offerings, the burnt offering (עֹלָה). In some regards, this is our stereotypical concept of an OT sacrifice, since the key characteristic of this offering is that the entire sacrifice is burned on the altar. Actually, everything was burned except for the animal's skin, which was given to the priest. Still, the basic concept was totality, a factor pointing toward dedication or consecration.

TRANSLATION ANALYSIS: עֹלָה
"Burnt offering" seems to be the consistent translation of the Hebrew word עֹלָה, although some commentators (especially older ones)

use the term "holocaust." The Hebrew noun seems to be derived from the verb עָלָה, which G. Lloyd Carr (1980b, 666) defines as "go up, climb, ascend." Stephen Sherwood (2002, 54) argues that it "connotes a sacrifice that goes up—an example of spatial symbolism" and observes that our English term is taken from the Septuagint. In the case of the burnt offering the entire animal was burned, except for the skin. The rationale for preserving the skin is not given, although some speculation points to the value of the animal skin. This may point back both to the Cain and Abel account in Genesis as well as the use of the animal skin to cover the nakedness of Adam and Eve. If so, it might suggest that one purpose of the burnt offering under the Sinai system would be to remind the people of the need for God to cover their nakedness. However, we need to exercise caution here because *kipper* (כִּפֶּר), meaning "to cover" or "to atone," is not used in the Genesis account (see the section "Atonement" in the introduction).

A burnt offering showed consecration by offering an animal that was completely consumed by the fire on the altar. In other words, the offeror received no tangible benefits from the offering. This required complete trust on the part of the offeror that God would accept his offering on the one hand, and that God would provide the resources that he needed to live on the other.

The value of the offering system of the OT derived from the covenant relationship the nation and its people had with God. Israel's national covenant had been established earlier in Exodus 19:5–8 when the people standing at the foot of Mount Sinai collectively responded to God's offer of a covenant, "All that the Lord [YHWH] has spoken, we will do!" Thus, when God gave Moses and the people the offering system from the Tent of Meeting a year later, it was to a group of people who had already established a covenant relationship with him. They, like their ancestor Abraham, had to enter that

relationship through faith—just as God's people subsequent to the sacrifice of Jesus have had to do. In the Torah, especially in Leviticus, God teaches the nation a variety of actions by which the people could express their worship of God and strengthen their relationship with him and with one another. While those worship actions would center on the tabernacle, Leviticus shows that they were designed to permeate Israel's entire culture, as will be seen especially in the last third of the book.

As we explore this sacrifice, we will see different levels of burnt offerings denoted by the size of the animal. The level one chose depended primarily on one's economic situation, although the degree of piety likely was an important factor. While externally the sacrifice of a bull was showier than that of a young pigeon, in terms of acceptance by God each level was equally valid based on the heart attitude.

1:3–9. Three different options for burnt offerings are provided, depending on the type of animal. The first type of burnt offering a worshipper might bring is a male animal from the herd of cattle, that is, a bull.

TRANSLATION ANALYSIS: בָּקָר
The term בָּקָר is generally translated "herd" or "cattle". The term is used both for draught animals (oxen) and bulls, cows, heifers, and calves in distinction to smaller domesticated animals such as sheep and goats (Martens 1980b). While the English word "oxen" can just denote animals trained to work, it more properly refers to castrated bulls that were easier to control, which can create confusion when used in this context. Cattle were domesticated very early in the ANE, and Abraham is recorded as possessing cattle (Gen. 12:16). Israelites generally used cows for milk and its by-products, and oxen for work animals. They tended not to use cattle for meat (King and Stager 2001, 119). While a bull need not be castrated to be used as a draft animal, castration made the

animal easier to control, although it is not clear whether Israelites castrated cattle. If they did, it is clear that the sacrificial animal must be "without defect" (תָּמִים; see also Lev. 22:24), which would also have meant that it could not have been a castrated working ox.

This would have been the largest animal and also the most expensive. The process for this sacrifice is given in Leviticus 1:3–9. The key characteristic of this sacrifice (as was the case of most sacrifices) was that it was to be a male animal that was without "defect" (תָּמִים). The animal was then brought to the "doorway of the Tent of Meeting." Given that the altar is also described as being in the "doorway of the Tent of Meeting" (1:5; פֶּתַח אֹהֶל מוֹעֵד), this seems to be a general description of the courtyard in front of the tent denoted the Holy Place. The directions for the three levels of burnt offering suggests that there were different locations for each animal in the courtyard, although there does not seem to be any significance to the difference. There the animal would be examined by the priest to verify that it was indeed without blemish, "that he [the offeror] may be accepted before the Lord" (Milgrom 1991, 149). This is the first point where priests enter the picture as part of the ritual. For the Israelite bringing his offering, this would likely have served to assure him that what he had brought measured up to God's standards and was effectively presented to God as the priest later collected the blood of the sacrifice and sprinkled it on the altar. Once approved, the worshipper would "lay his hand" on the head of the animal.

TRANSLATION ANALYSIS: "LAY HIS HAND"

The phrase "lay his hand" (סָמַךְ יָדוֹ) at the beginning of 1:4 uses the singular "hand." Some sacrifices required both hands (e.g., Yom Kippur in Lev. 16:21), while others, such as the burnt offering here, required just one. Other sacrifices, such as the reparation offering, do not specifically direct either, although most scholars seem to assume that laying on at least one hand was a practice for all. In either case, the word used for "lay" (סָמַךְ) implies pressure (see Judges 16:29, where it describes how Samson "braced himself" on the two pillars to bring down the Philistine temple). Since the term implies putting pressure on the item, *TWOT* gives a primary translation of "lean upon" (Patterson 1980b).

The significance of laying the hands on the head is debated. While there may have been multiple values to this symbolic act, the phrase "to make atonement on *his* behalf" (לְכַפֵּר עָלָיו) in the last part of 1:4 suggests that idea of identification or substitution is at least the most important.

TRANSLATION ANALYSIS: ATONEMENT

The meaning of 1:4 is not clear. Generally, the verse is translated that the burnt offering might "make atonement on his behalf." The meaning of the Hebrew word כִּפֶּר is strongly debated among scholars, but it is worth noting that this is the only time this term is used in these three chapters on voluntary offerings, while it appears about a dozen times in the following three chapters addressing various confessional offerings. In our analysis of this term in the introduction, we concluded that a sacrifice in the Old Testament law was to be a visible or physical symbol of a spiritual act for a person who already had a covenant relationship with God, which could suggest a sense of reassurance of one's status before God.

As such, the laying of the hand on the head of the animal indicates that the worshipper is saying that just as the bull is being totally given, so he (the worshipper) is giving himself totally. As Kiuchi (2007, 56) expresses it, "at the very least, then, the gesture expresses the idea of identification: to say, 'This is myself.'"

Laying the Hand on the Head

Scholars debate the significance of this step in the ritual but have not reached a conclusion. There are four general categories of explanation.

One of the oldest explanations is that it represents a declaration. Philo, in his discussion of the burnt offering, asserts that the laying of hands on the head of the animal is a "symbol of irreproachable actions." In other words, they declare the innocence of the worshipper (Philo 1993, 553). Akin to this, more recent commentators suggest that it allows the worshipper to declare the purpose of the sacrifice. This can be viewed as nonverbal (Willis 2009, 6), or as a precursor to an oral declaration (Harrison 1980, 45; Wenham 1979, 53).

A second explanation is that it symbolizes transference. This could be transferring the sin of the worshipper to the animal so that when the animal was sacrificed, it would carry the sin away with it (Gerstenberger 1996, 30; Wenham 1979, 62). This explanation assumes that all sacrifices are for the purpose of atoning for sin, which, given our understanding of the sacrificial system, is problematic. Alternatively, it has been viewed as transferring the ownership of the animal to God for the purpose intended (Levine 1989, 6).

A third explanation is that placing the hand on the head demonstrates ownership. This position argues that it ensures that the value of the sacrifice goes to the person who is bringing the animal (Gane 2004b, 82; Kleinig 2003, 53; Milgrom 1991, 152).

The fourth explanation is identification or substitution. That is, the worshipper then identifies with the animal as it is sacrificed, so that the sacrifice of the animal takes the place of the worshipper (Gerstenberger 1996, 30; Mathews 2009, 29; Rooker 2000, 87; Ross 2002, 91; Wenham 1979, 62). There are different ways of understanding this. One perspective argues that the soul of the worshipper then penetrates the animal. Another is that when the animal turns into smoke, it brings the worshipper closer to God as the smoke ascends (Milgrom 1991, 151). Or, as preferred, it could simply be a symbolic representation of identification (Mathews 2009, 30).

At this point, the bull was slaughtered. While the text does not spell out the method, rabbinic sources "indicate the animal was killed in the swiftest and most painless way possible, by cutting horizontally across the throat in an uninterrupted movement" (Hamilton 1980m, 915). According to kosher standards today, this means cutting the jugular vein, the carotid artery, the esophagus, and trachea in a "swift, smooth cut of a sharp knife whose blade is free of any dent or imperfection" (Appel 2016). Ben Wolfson (1998) reports that when done in this manner, there is "little or no reaction to the cut."

Humane Animal Slaughter

Observations from a veterinarian (Biehl): Before you begin, it will be essential to gauge how your hearers will react to the idea of animal sacrifice. You may need to navigate the obstacles of the twenty-first-century mind: "How could a loving God prescribe animal cruelty?" It will be helpful to review articles on the humane slaughter of animals that evaluate the kosher method of animal slaughter. When done properly, kosher slaughter has been found to be humane by objective research. Animal welfare expert Temple Grandin concludes the following, "I have observed that when kosher slaughter of cattle is done well, there is almost no reaction from the animal when the throat is cut. Flicking my hand near the animal's face caused a bigger reaction" (https://forward.com/opinion/137318/maximizing-animal-welfare-in-kosher-slaughter/).

In some circumstances, it may be beneficial to limit the details of animal sacrifice and immediately substitute a sacrifice that would be more tangible to the hearer. This will not be easy. The burnt offering captures four of the five senses:

Worshipping a Holy God (1:1–3:17)

sight, sound, smell, and touch. It is centered on sacrificing a prized possession to demonstrate how much you value a relationship. It could be compared to donating a kidney to a loved one, giving your college scholarship to a beloved friend, or donating the car you invested years restoring to a worthy charity.

While the animal was slaughtered, the priests collected the blood and brought it to the altar where they sprinkled it around the altar. The text does not specify what was done with the remaining blood, but based on the Second Temple practice according to the Mishnah, it was then likely they poured it at the base of the altar (m. Tamid 4.1). The purpose of the sprinkling of the blood is not stated, but Leviticus 17:11 notes the relationship between life and blood and the role of blood in atonement (see the section "*Nephesh* [נֶפֶשׁ]: Life and Soul" in the introduction). This will be addressed further in the chapter on Leviticus 17, but we would note here the biblical premise that placed a strong relationship between the blood and the life. In that regard, perhaps John Hartley's (1992, 21) comment sums it up best: "The blood rite signifies that the animal's life is poured out to Yahweh."

TRANSLATION ANALYSIS: SPRINKLE

The verb זָרַק is translated "sprinkle" in a number of translations. Lexicons present it as carrying a stronger connotation, suggesting "to toss, throw, or scatter abundantly" (BDB s.v. "זָרַק" 284). Some translations then take this to mean that the priest would throw (ESV) or splash (NIV) the contents of the bowl on the sides of the altar. Either understanding raises questions. If the priest threw the contents on the altar, what was done with regard to the eventual accumulations of dried blood? If the contents were just sprinkled, what was done with the remainder in the bowl? While not addressed in this case, later directions for the confessional offerings dictate that the remaining blood was poured out at the base of the altar, but there the verb נָזָה ("sprinkle") is

used (see material on Lev. 4:6). Alfred Edersheim (1994, 83–84) indicates that during the Second Temple period, the same process applied to the burnt offering.

Following this, the worshipper skinned the bull down to the knees (Milgrom 1991, 157). The burnt offering is the only sacrifice that specifies that the animal was skinned. As noted above, this alludes to the taking of animal skins to cover Adam and Eve in the garden in Genesis 3, with the worshipper claiming a symbolic garment in his consecration. In this case, however, the skin is given to the priests. After the animal was butchered, the priests placed the pieces on the altar along with wood and coals for burning. Later, Moses will be given directions that the fire on the altar is to be a perpetual fire that does not go out (Lev. 6:9, 13), and it would seem that these coals would have been taken from that fire with fresh wood added. Prior to their placement, the worshipper washed the entrails and the legs of the bull with water (presumably from the bronze "sea"). These would have been the portions that would be defiled by fecal material and dirt, and thus need to be cleansed. After they were cleansed, the priest then arranged them on the altar to be part of the burnt offering.

On the altar with the coals and wood, the sacrificed animal was "turned into smoke" (הִקְטִיר). This process is described first as a fire offering (אִשֶּׁה), which has generally been understood as an offering by fire (Levine 1989, 7), although now it is commonly viewed as a gift, or more technically, a "food gift."

TRANSLATION ANALYSIS: "FIRE OFFERING"

The word אִשֶּׁה has traditionally been understood as being derived from אֵשׁ ("fire") and has been translated as "fire offering" (HCSB, KJV, NASB, NRSV). More recent work has highlighted that understanding as questionable, as indicated by how the word is used elsewhere (e.g., Lev. 24:9). It has been suggested that the word is related to the Ugaritic *itt*, which means "gift." Milgrom ties

Worshipping a Holy God (1:1–3:17)

this to the extended לֶחֶם אִשֶּׁה seen in 3:11 and translates it as "food gift" (1991, 163). ESV and NIV use "food offering." We will use the traditional idea of "fire offering."

The result was that the sacrifice would be received as a "soothing aroma" (רֵיחַ נִיחֹחַ) by the Lord. This phrase is problematic for a couple of reasons. First, the smell of burning flesh is not generally deemed aromatic (Levine 1989, 8). Second, the idea that the smoke was a pleasing aroma seems suggestive of the perceptions in other ANE cultures that viewed their gods as actually deriving sustenance from the sacrifices (see discussion above). Psalm 50 quotes God as telling the nation that he did not need their sacrifices: "If I were hungry, I would not tell you; for the world is Mine, and all it contains" (Ps. 50:12 NASB). It then appears that the phrase "soothing aroma" is an anthropomorphic figure of speech that expresses approval and acceptance of the sacrifice (Noordtzij 1982, 38; Sklar 2014, 92; Willis 2009, 9). This is suggested later in Psalm 50 as the author continues to quote God as saying "a sacrifice of praise [זֹבֵחַ תּוֹדָה] honors me" (Ps. 50:23).

TRANSLATION ANALYSIS: "SOOTHING AROMA" (רֵיחַ נִיחֹחַ)

The phrase translated "soothing aroma," רֵיחַ נִיחֹחַ, with or without the definite article, is used forty-three times in the Old Testament, all but four of which are in the Pentateuch. There the phrase describes God's response to sacrifices. The word רֵיחַ is derived from רוּחַ, meaning "wind, spirit, or breath" (Payne 1980). The word נִיחֹחַ, translated "soothing," seems to come from the verb נוּחַ, which means "to rest" (Coppes 1980f). There are some indications that the word pair was an archaic expression that had become a figure of speech describing satisfaction (Rooker 2000, 89–90). Thus, while the phrase literally describes the smoke of the sacrifice as a fragrance or aroma that is soothing or pleasing, in the biblical context it should be understood to indicate

a sense of pleasure—not in a physical sense but a spiritual one, recognizing and approving of the heart attitude of the worshipper.

1:9–13. The second type of burnt offering is an animal from the flock (Lev. 1:10), specifically of the sheep or goats. While not as expensive or extravagant as the sacrifice of a bull, this would still have been a significant sacrifice for the average Israelite. We tend to think of the Israelites of this period based on the model of the nineteenth-century Bedouins, seminomadic herders with very large flocks. In that case, the sacrifice of a single sheep or goat would have been a relatively minor matter. That does seem to have been true for Israel's patriarchal ancestors, but it would appear that four hundred years of settlement in Egypt had made them more sedentary, which would have had the effect of reducing the sizes of the flocks. The sacrifice of a sheep or a goat would then have been significant.

Israelites, Flock, and Herds

Although the Israelites still had herds and flocks in Egypt (Exod. 10:9), at the end of that period they were living in houses (Exod. 12:7). While they had to revert to a nomadic lifestyle for the forty years of wandering (Num. 14:22), that had not been the intent at the time of the exodus. The expectation was that when they left Sinai a year after leaving Egypt, they would go directly into the Promised Land, where they were to conquer and then live in houses that they did not build (Num. 10–14 compared with Deut. 6:10–11). That, of course, did not come about until the next generation, which did conquer the land (Josh. 24:13). In this more agrarian society, while the size of the flocks might have been reduced, the use of draught animals would have been increased. Thus, the Torah as we have it was written with the ultimate goal in mind, but at the same time with one eye on the situation at hand (Num. 15 and following).

Worshipping a Holy God (1:1–3:17)

This offering was done in the same manner as was the case of the bull, although there are some differences in the description. The same criteria for selecting the animal apply. It must be a male without defects. While not specifically stated, it may be presumed that it was brought to the "doorway of the Tent of Meeting" as was the case of the bull, and then we are told that the place of slaying is on the "north side of the altar, before the Lord." This more specific location would require that the sheep or goat had to be taken through the same region where the bull was offered (1:3). As presented in the text, it would appear that the distinction between the more general location for the slaying of the bull, as opposed to the specific location for the slaying of the flock animal, was a matter of practicality (Milgrom 1991, 164).

Likewise, it may be presumed that the worshipper laid his hand on the head of the animal as in the case of the bull, although again that step is not repeated. Further, as in the case of the bull, the priest sprinkled (the same verb, זָרַק) the blood of the sacrifice around the altar. As was the case of the bull, the worshipper butchered the animal and the priests placed the pieces on the altar in the same manner. One step omitted in the description is the flaying of the animal and giving the skin to the priest, although it seems likely that this followed the process for the bull. The entrails and legs must be washed, and as in the case of the bull it was offered as a fire offering (אִשֶּׁה) and received as a "soothing aroma" (רֵיחַ נִיחֹחַ) by the Lord.

1:14–17. The final category of burnt offering is that of a bird. As noted above, the three different categories of burnt offering seem to give access to all socioeconomic levels. While a bull was very extravagant, at the other end of the spectrum even a poor Israelite could bring a bird. The text specifically mentions "turtledoves" (תֹּרִים) and "young pigeons" (בְּנֵי הַיּוֹנָה). The phrase "young pigeons" may also

reflect an option of several varieties. Both turtledoves and pigeons were domesticated early, as shown both by textual and archaeological evidence (King and Stager 2001, 119), and it would appear that anyone, regardless of socioeconomic status, would have access to one of these for the purpose of a burnt offering. While the Hebrew uses the plural in both cases, the structure suggests that a single bird would be permissible (Péter-Contesse and Ellington 1992, 21).

While one of these birds would be an acceptable burnt offering, there are several distinctions in the process from the other burnt offerings. First, the worshipper would bring the bird to the tabernacle, but then he would give it to the priest. Given the size of the animal and the method of slaying, he would not be required to lay his hand on the head. The priest would take the bird to the altar, where he would slay it by "wring[ing] off" or "pinch[ing] off" its head. While the head would be separated, they were careful not to detach it. The priest would drain its blood at the base of the altar.

TRANSLATION ANALYSIS: "WRING"
The verb מָלַק is defined as "to nip or nip off" (BDB s.v. "מָלַק" 577; *TWOT* s.v. "מָלַק" 2:511), although most translations use the word "wring." According to the Mishnah, the priest would "pinch its head at the border of the neck, but he did not sever it, and he sprinkled from its blood upon the side of the *Altar*, [and] the remainder of the blood was drained away at the *base* [of the *Altar*]" (m. Zebaḥ. 6:4–5; Danby 1933, emphasis original).

Prior to placing the carcass of the bird on the fire on the altar were two more steps. The priest would remove the crop (מֻרְאָה) and associated material (נוֹצָה). Translators have taken the latter term two ways. The ancient Greek and Latin have understood it as feathers, as do the HCSB, KJV, NASB, NET, NIV, NLT, and RSV. The Targumim and Syriac understand it as referring to the contents of the crop, as do the ESV, NEB, NJB, NRSV, and TEV (Péter-Contesse and Ellington 1992, 23). Milgrom (1991, 170–71) suggests that the entire package should be understood as the intestines and tail feathers, which would seem to correlate with the cleansing of the entrails of the larger animals. The part that is removed is thrown on the east side of the altar "in the place of the ashes." Finally, the priest splits but did not separate the remaining carcass, which seems to correlate with the butchering of the larger animal.

At this point the carcass was placed on the altar, where it was burned. Like the larger animals in the first part of the chapter, it was viewed as a burnt offering (עֹלָה), a fire offering (אִשֶּׁה) and a soothing aroma (רֵיחַ נִיחֹחַ).

The Lord Tells Israel How to Bring a Gift Offering (2:1–16)

While structurally part of the same subject unit, Levitcus 2 addresses a different category of voluntary offering, which we termed the "gift offering" (מִנְחָה).

> *TRANSLATION ANALYSIS: WAW*
>
> As we began this study, we noted how Leviticus is connected to the end of Exodus by a simple *waw* that can be translated in a variety of ways. That same connector ties this section to the previous one. It is generally ignored in the translations, although the NASB translates it as "now." Structurally, the gift offering is introduced by the conjunction כִּי, which we noted earlier can be translated "if" or "when." In this case, it seems to set up a new subcategory under the broader topic of קָרְבָּן ("offering").

In Leviticus this term is generally translated as grain offering because of the specified content. The word itself basically means "gift" (Carr 1980a; Fabry 1997, 412–20) and can be used in a variety of contexts.

The Use of מִנְחָה

The scope of the word מִנְחָה (which we translate here as "gift offering") is illustrated in Genesis when both Cain and Abel are said to have brought a מִנְחָה to God (Gen. 4:3–5). While Cain brought "fruit of the ground," likely grain, Abel's מִנְחָה was "firstlings of his flock." Throughout the rest of Genesis, the term מִנְחָה is used only in secular contexts to describe gifts intended to win favor with various people. For example, Genesis 32:13 (HB 14) records that on his return from Haran Jacob sent a large number of his livestock as a מִנְחָה, (generally translated as *present* or *gift*) to Esau fearing that his brother might seek revenge. Similarly, Genesis 43:11–15 notes that Jacob had his sons carry a מִנְחָה (likewise translated as "present" or "gift") of various agricultural items including spices, honey, and nuts, to Pharaoh's representative (who actually was Joseph) on their second trip to Egypt to procure food, in order that the man might have compassion and release their brother.

After the Cain and Abel episode, the term מִנְחָה is not used again in a religious sense until the ordination directions for the priests given in Exodus 29. The ordination process required a variety of sacrifices over a seven-day period. As described in Exodus 29:39–42, the מִנְחָה was the unleavened bread that accompanied the sacrificed ram for both morning and evening offerings (Stuart 2006, 629–30).

As described in the Torah, the מִנְחָה often served to complement an animal sacrifice (generally the burnt offering) but it could also serve as an independent offering (Milgrom 1991, 198). It seems likely that even prior to the exodus the Israelites were familiar with the idea of bringing a מִנְחָה to God, although they did not have a corporate worship system. However, we have no details on how or if any Israelites actually did it.

A Gift for God

While we do not know if Israelites performed gift offerings while they were in Egypt, they were probably very aware of the concept, given the elaborate daily sacrifices the Egyptians performed. It is equally likely that the Israelite perception of the purpose of a מִנְחָה was distorted by the elaborate sacrificial meals the Egyptians provided their gods. As such, the directions that God gives in this chapter may have been designed to demonstrate that the purpose of the מִנְחָה was not to provide a meal for God but to help clarify God's expectations for true worship. If so, it was a lesson that future generations still struggled to absorb (see Ps. 50:12–13).

While the Cain and Abel account uses the term for both animal and vegetable gifts, the sacrificial system developed in Leviticus uses the term "gift offering" (מִנְחָה) solely for nonanimal sacrifices, specifically gift offerings. The overall OT worship system incorporates the gift offering of grain either as a supplement to other offerings (specifically the burnt or shalom offerings), or as a stand-alone sacrifice. As a stand-alone offering, rabbinic tradition claimed that it served as a substitute for the burnt offering for the very poor, a conclusion probably deduced from its textual location immediately following the burnt offering (Milgrom 1991, 195). However, the way it was offered (esp. since the bulk of the gift offering was given to the priest) makes this unlikely (Wenham 1979, 67). Like the burnt offering, the gift offering was considered voluntary for individuals, although some rituals required the inclusion of a gift offering, especially within corporate worship, which we will address later.

Despite this diversity of uses, the text does not give a specific reason for a gift offering, but rather, as in the case of the burnt offering, it begins with the premise that an Israelite would bring such an offering (whether in conjunction with a blood offering, or independently). It then gives directions on how it should be done. The purpose must then be deduced, and modern scholars have proposed a variety of purposes. These include a "gift" (Harrison 1980, 52), "a

present made to secure or retain good will" (Milgrom 1991, 196), "dedication" (Ross 2002, 108), "to confirm and renew the covenantal relationship" (Kiuchi 2007), or "a kind of tribute from the faithful worshipper to his divine overlord" (Wenham 1979, 69).

All of these options seem appropriate to the occasional and voluntary nature of the gift offering. Given the prior description of the burnt offering in Leviticus 1 and recalling that the original text did not have chapter divisions, the last couple of proposals are rather suggestive. But, it seems that the required ingredients provide another perspective. The gift offering described here consisted of flour, oil, and salt, with the spice frankincense added on some occasions. The three basic ingredients were not only common household items, but key aspects of the daily diet of the Israelite—one might say, they were the main parts of their daily "bread." (As an aside, these are the original ingredients of the popular modern cracker called Triscuit.) As such, it would seem that every gift offering would reflect recognition that God was the source of the basics of life, regardless of the socioeconomic level of the individual (Kellogg 1978, 69).

In essence then, the worshipper brought a gift offering to God to show that he understood that the food he ate was from God, and by bringing a portion of that provision he expressed his gratitude. Mark Rooker (2000, 99) expresses it well when he states that the offeror "honored [God] as the source of life and the fertility of the land." As we will see below, the ritual process would highlight that idea of gratitude when the worshipper offered up its "memorial portion." While those ingredients that would be present in every household were all that was required, frankincense, an expensive spice, could be included to show even greater appreciation. By doing so, the worshipper essentially incorporated nuances of each of the various meanings that have been suggested for the act.

> **Frankincense**
> Frankincense is the aromatic resin of several trees in the genus *Boswellia* that are native to the region around the horn of Africa. When the tree is wounded, the resin oozes out and hardens. The hardened sap or resin is harvested and used for incense, perfume, and in some regions as a medicine.

Figure 11. Frankincense.

The fact that the preponderance of the offering is not burned suggests a secondary purpose. As we will see, while a fraction of the gift offering was burned, most of it went to feed the priests—those who labored in coordinating the nation's worship. Prior to Sinai, Israel did not have priests. When Aaron and his sons were anointed as priests, they assumed the special role of intermediaries between God and the people. They were given specific tasks that were performed on a regular basis to symbolically represent the relationship of the nation with God, although how the various aspects of the ritual symbolized that relationship is not always clear. The meaning of a symbol is generally arbitrary, and any understanding of that meaning is sure only when the one who provides the symbol defines the meaning it carries. When that definition is not provided, a meaning might be inferred, but caution must be exhibited, especially when working across cultures (Womack 2005, 5–6). Regardless of the symbolism, when the offeror shared his or her individual gift offering with the priest, the two became partners in worship, which served to strengthen the community of faith in a very real sense.

As discussed in the overview "The Old Testament Sacrificial System" in the introduction, aspects of the gift offering as presented in Leviticus are difficult to understand in terms of their actual practice, no matter how one views the composition of the text. If one takes the modern understanding that the text was written after the exile with the goal of centralizing the cult, the idea that all Israelites would be expected to take a several-day journey to bring their gift offerings to the central sanctuary might suggest that an individual Israelite rarely performed this sacrifice. Further, this would limit Levitical participation to just the priests working at the central sanctuary, although according to Joshua 21 the Levites were originally distributed into forty-eight different cities throughout the land (which did not apply after the exile). Another difficulty derives from the fact that the text suggests that the offering may have been prepared at home prior to its being carried to the priest at the altar. Some was cooked, but some was not (Lev. 2:2), and given a multiday journey to the tabernacle (or later, to the temple) uncooked dough would risk fermenting and cooked items might get stale.

On the other hand, the traditional view of the text that these instructions were given at Mount Sinai where the nation was rather closely camped together, with the tabernacle being built in its midst, simplifies the logistics. As such, it would be no great import to take one's gift offering to the tabernacle to be offered on the altar, with the main portion given to the priests. However, at this time, they were not farming and their primary daily provision was the manna that God provided supernaturally.

> **Manna**
>
> As described in Numbers 11:7–9, manna was grain-like both in appearance and function. In form, it looked like coriander seed.
>
> In function, it could be ground like wheat, suggesting it was hard. It could be boiled, or made into cakes which tasted like "goods [לְשָׁד] baked with oil," which reflects one variety of cooked gift offerings (Lev. 2:4). Even so, there is no indication that manna was ever used as a gift offering,
>
>
>
> Figure 12. Coriander seed.
>
> and given that the offerings were intended to reflect effort on the part of the worshipper, it does not seem that such a use would have been appropriate.

We need to keep in mind that while in retrospect that period in the wilderness subsisting on manna lasted for forty years, the original intent was that the nation would leave Sinai and go directly to settle in the land, which would have put them there within a few years after this system was set up. It was only because of the people's disbelief at Kadesh-barnea that the forty-year period between leaving Egypt and entering the land of Canaan ensued.

> **Subsistence in the Wilderness**
>
> A couple of caveats must be considered with respect to the time in the wilderness. While we tend to think of this period as a time of wandering in the wilderness, according to Numbers 33 they basically camped at nineteen locations over a thirty-eight-year period (Harbin 2005, 169), or an average of two years per spot. Although this would provide adequate periods to do supplemental gardening to provide fresh produce, we have no direct indication that the people did so. Likewise, while they left Egypt with their herds and flocks (Exod. 12:38), we have no indications that they used them for meat during that period, although we do see some livestock being used for sacrifices when the tabernacle was set up. While periods of gardening or farming might have been possible, it seems that the gift offering was really designed to be a future option so that the people could regularly remember and give thanks for their physical sustenance once they were in the land and had begun growing field crops, and were less *directly* dependent on God's care. Given that Israel is recorded as leaving Sinai less than two months after the tabernacle was set up (cf. Exod. 40:17 and Num. 10:11), it seems that the design was that under obedience Israel would have entered the land prior to the subsequent planting season. Still, the theoretical earliest they could provide a מִנְחָה from their own crops would have been a year later. Instead, the overall text of the Torah stresses that the Israelite adults who had experienced God's supernatural deliverance from Egypt were made to wander for forty years because of their lack of faith at Kadesh-barnea (Num. 14:33), an event that is presented as taking place just a few months after the tabernacle was set up and these directions had been given (see Num. 13:25). As a result, that generation had to spend the rest of their days harvesting the manna by faith on a daily basis, rather than immediately entering the land after leaving Mount Sinai.

This still raises the issue of practicality noted above if, after the nation was in the land, all of the gift offerings were required to be presented at the tabernacle once the tribes had dispersed. This is one reason that in the section of the introduction discussing the sacrificial system, we suggest the possibility that the gift offering was one of the sacrifices that could be performed at various ad hoc altars in the land, as suggested by Exodus 20:24–26. Even so, that still presents another problem, in that the portion given to the priest was considered "a thing most holy," which will be discussed below.

As we look at the directions, we will note that two basic kinds of gift offerings are described in this chapter—uncooked and cooked. Further, four different options were provided for the cooked gift offerings. A special version of the gift offering, called "firstfruits," is added at the end of the chapter. This chapter covers the process by which gift offerings were given when they were given as stand-alone offerings. While there were occasions when they supplemented animal sacrifices, we will cover those as they arise in the text.

2:1–3. An individual gift offering (מִנְחָה) could be brought by any person in the nation of Israel.

> *TRANSLATION ANALYSIS: 2:1 PERSON*
> Here the Hebrew denotes the person bringing the offering with the term נֶפֶשׁ, often translated as "soul" as opposed to אָדָם used in Leviticus 1, which is more specifically translated as "man." In this case, both are deemed to reflect anyone, although some suggest that the word used in this case more clearly includes women (Hartley 1992, 30).

The stand-alone gift offering is described as consisting of "choice flour" (סֹלֶת), oil, and frankincense. This last item seems to distinguish the stand-alone gift offering (מִנְחָה) from a complementary gift offering. Later, 2:13 clarifies that all gift offerings were to include salt.

> *TRANSLATION ANALYSIS: CHOICE FLOUR*
> The first use of the word solet (סֹלֶת) in the description of the sacrificial system in Exodus 29:2 specifies that it is wheat flour. Beyond that, the meaning is not clear. TWOT (Patterson 1980a) defines *solet* as "a finely ground flour." In comparison, it defines *qemaḥ* (קֶמַח) as a coarser grind

(Coppes 1980j). This seems to make sense when one recalls that in that culture grain was hand-ground within each household, using a mortar (figs. 13 and 14).

Figure 13. Mortar from display in the Israel Museum.

Figure 14. Mortar from display in the Israel Museum.

Since the key difference would have been how long the individual worked to produce a finer consistency, one might suspect that one would do one's best work for a sacrifice, making finer flour. Consequently, a number of translations and commentators follow suit. However, the Mishnah distinguishes between flour that passes through a sieve from *solet*, which doesn't (m. 'Abot 5:15). This would make the *solet* the coarser of the two. This would appear to be why other commentators (Levine 1989, 10; Milgrom 1991, 1790) use the term "semolina," which is defined as "a coarse flour made from durum wheat, a hard type of wheat" (Zamarripa 2019). While "semolina" may be the best translation, it is a term likely to be unfamiliar with many. Baruch Levine (1989, 10) argues that while the wheat may have been fine ground, the point of the verse is the substance of the offering and not its preparation and suggests that a better translation would be "choice flour." This seems the best option.

The amount of flour included in a gift offering is unspecified, suggesting that it is open to the individual, although rabbinic tradition fixed it at one-tenth of an ephah (a little over two liters) based on Lev. 6:13; Num. 5:11, 15 (King and Stager 2001, 200).

TRANSLATION ANALYSIS: "HANDFUL"

The priest is directed to "take from it his handful [singular] of its choice flour and of its oil" (וְקָמַץ מִשָּׁם קֻמְצוֹ מִסָּלְתָּהּ וּמִשַּׁמְנָהּ). This could be a handful of each, or a portion of the mixed dough. Leviticus 7:10 describes gift offerings as being either "mixed with oil or dry," which could suggest that the worshipper brought the raw materials. However, Leviticus 2:1 specifies that the oil is poured on the flour, which seems to indicate that the presentation is in the dough form.

The directions require the worshipper to pour olive oil (the standard cooking oil) on it and, based on 2:13, add salt. The worshipper could bring the ingredients to the tabernacle and mix it there. However, the description seems to allow the worshipper to mix the flour, oil, and salt into a dough prior to presenting them, and then bring the mixture to the priest. In either case, if frankincense was included, it was not mixed in but placed on top of the dough or raw materials. The priest would take a "handful" of the offering, along with all of the frankincense, and place it on the altar. This portion was then burned, being turned to smoke like the burnt offering. Like the burnt offering, the result is described as an "offering by fire of a soothing aroma" (אִשֶּׁה and רֵיחַ נִיחֹחַ; see burnt offering, above, for discussion).

The burnt portion is termed the memorial or token portion (אַזְכָּרָה). The memorial portion would be burned on the altar but the remainder would be given to the priests, a marked contrast to the disposition of the burnt offering. Both aspects contain difficulties.

TRANSLATION ANALYSIS: "MEMORIAL PORTION"

The term אַזְכָּרָתָהּ is really the noun אַזְכָּרָה with the pronominal suffix (his or its). Several meanings have been suggested for the word. In addition to "memorial," the following three might be noted: "the burnt portion," drawing on Psalm 20:4; "the fragrant portion," based on Hosea 14:8 and Isaiah 66:3; or the "the invocation portion," where the verb זָכַר ("to remember") in the *hiphil* stem is understood to mean "pronounce," thus calling on the name of God (Milgrom 1991, 181–82). While each raises questions, Milgrom and others suggest viewing the memorial portion as a token is best. Given the disposition of the rest of the dough, that is probably correct.

First, the purpose of the memorial portion is not clear. The word אַזְכָּרָה is a noun apparently derived from the verb זָכַר, which primarily means "to think about" or "to remember" (Bowling 1980a, 243). If so, then the question is, in what sense is this portion a memorial? Commentators disagree. Suggestions include that it was intended to remind God of the piety of the worshipper, or more widely to remind the worshipper of God's provision (see Hartley 1992, 30; Rooker 2000, 95; Willis 2009, 13). The directions regarding the remainder of the gift offering may be helpful. The bulk of each gift offering was given to the priest (Aaron and his sons). It is not until Leviticus 6–7 that we learn that the purpose was that they might eat of it. Here it is merely described as "a thing most holy." So, a second difficulty is understanding why the portion of the sacrifice that is given to the priests is described as most holy rather than the part that was "an offering by fire . . . to the Lord [YHWH]."

The phrase "Holy of Holies" is a literal translation of the Hebrew קֹדֶשׁ קָדָשִׁים. It is a standard Hebrew idiom showing it to be a superlative, hence most translations render it as "most holy." As developed in the discussion on "Holy" in the introduction, the primary meaning would be a concept of moral purity as demonstrated by actions with other persons. However, a derived meaning would be to describe something devoted to the worship of God. With respect to the portion of the gift offering given to the priest, it was most holy in the sense that the gift offering was used in conjunction with the community worship of the One who is holy.

This would suggest that by sharing a portion of their daily bread with the priests who served as intermediaries between the nation and God, the offerors were virtually joining the priests in their service to God, and by partaking of the bread that was offered to God, the priests were virtually joining the offerors in their expression of gratitude and appreciation. All this should serve to integrate the people, both priest and laity, together in their worship of God.

2:4–10. While the first three verses suggest offering uncooked flour or dough, gift offerings could also be cooked prior to the offering. Four options were provided. Two are specified as baked in an oven: "unleavened loaves" (חַלּוֹת מַצֹּת) or "unleavened wafers" (רְקִיקֵי מַצֹּת), which are cooked in an oven. The other two are described as cooked either on a griddle (מַחֲבַת) or in a pan (מַרְחֶשֶׁת), which may be described as "fried." For further discussion on these utensils, see the excursus "Cooking and Cooking Apparatuses."

Cooking and Cooking Apparatuses

Cooking is a basic aspect of life for everyone, whether we personally cook or have someone else cook for us. M. H. Heicksen (1975, 956) maintains that the "numerous Bible references to the preparation of various kinds of food . . . afford a fairly complete knowledge of this daily task in the Biblical period." However, this is true only in terms of basic generalities. As Philip King and Lawrence Stager (2001, 64) observe, the Bible "provides little detail about cooking techniques." This is evident in this section of Leviticus, which addresses preparing of sacrifices and uses a number of terms regarding cooking utensils and types of preparation for which the meanings are only vaguely understood.

Raw foods can be divided into five basic categories: meats, cereals, vegetables, fruits, and dairy products. In terms of cooking, we generally think in terms of the first three, but with respect to the sacrificial system, we really only address the first two: cooking meats and cereals.

The most significant is the cooking of meat. God's directions for Passover required that they roast the lamb with fire. The text emphasized this, stating twice in two verses that it was to be roasted with fire (צְלִי-אֵשׁ), with the addition that it was not to be boiled with water (Exod. 12:8–9). These appear to be the two basic methods of cooking meat during the OT period. Roasting was likely done on a spit, either over an open fire or burning coals (King and Stager 2001, 64–65). Later, Leviticus 6:28 (HB 21) directs that the meat given to the priest was to be boiled.

First Samuel 2:13–14 indicates boiling was the standard practice for meat from sacrifices at the end of the time of Judges. That passage mentions four different vessels that were used to boil the meat. As translated by the NASB, they were a pan (כִּיּוֹר), kettle (דּוּד), caldron (קַלַּחַת), or a pot (פָּרוּר) for cooking. Distinguishing these is difficult, although the distinctions seem to relate to the size of the vessel or its mouth and the shape of the vessel (see fig. 15).

The various ceramic cooking vessels shown in figure 15 would seem to have been used both for cooking (the larger vessels) and for eating (the smaller vessels in front). Vessels might be made from ceramic or metal, although most households likely used ceramic. As described in the OT, metal vessels were most often used for the tabernacle.

Figure 15. Various ceramic cooking utensils on exhibit in the Israel Museum.

Figure 16. Cooking pot with stand on display in the Israel Museum.

As described by King and Stager (2001, 65), the vessel in figure 16 would likely have been a cooking pot for meats and stews. The stand likely held the vessel above coals while the food cooked.

Given the sacrificial method, meat was raw when received by the priest. In the case of grain, there seemed to be three options. Raw grain might be given (esp. in the case of firstfruits) or the grain might be processed into flour. When offered as flour, it might also be cooked. If the worshipper cooked his or her gift of grain prior to presentation, the ingredients were mixed and the dough was well kneaded. It would then be rolled out to disk form (either round or oval) and cooked. Cooking basically followed one of two methods: baking in an oven (מַאֲפֵה תַנּוּר) or cooking on a "griddle" (הַמַּחֲבַת) or in a "pan" (מַרְחֶשֶׁת). The latter would be done in a liquid, either water (boiled) or oil (fried). The most common method of preparation was likely baking (Lev. 2:4).

Ovens in the ancient world came in a variety of forms. The most basic, and likely used during the time in the wilderness, was just a hearth, a flat stone, or a ceramic utensil that might be set on top of hot coals (Exod. 12:39). This seems to be what is mentioned in 1 Kings 19:6, where the phrase "cake" or something similar (עֻגַת רְצָפִים) refers to bread that Elijah ate. The phrase used there is literally "bread cake of hot or glowing stone." Figure 17 shows two trays described as baking trays, dating from the eleventh to eighth century B.C., which may have served as early "ovens."

A more typical form seems to have been beehive-shaped, called a *tannur* (תַּנּוּר). According to King and Stager (2001, 67), they might come in several variations. Apparently, the flat bread would actually be cooked attached to the inside of the oven, as seen in figure 18. When cooked this way, the dough was cooked from both sides simultaneously.

Archaeology suggests that during the OT period these ovens were located in a courtyard of the house, in which case it was partially buried. Figure 19 shows one in a later kitchen in the town of Katzrin, Israel, that has been partially reconstructed to a first-century A.D. style. Beside the oven in this picture are a number of kitchen utensils, including what may be a pan for "frying" bread or cakes.

Figure 17. Ceramic "baking trays" on exhibit in the Israel Museum.

Figure 18. Modernized (gas heat) traditional oven, Amman, Jordan.

A second option of preparing bread (Lev. 2:5) was to use a "griddle" (הַמַּחֲבַת), which appears to have been a ceramic or metal sheet placed immediately above the coals on which the bread was baked. In this case, the dough was cooked only from one side. Figure 20 shows this type of baking in operation in a traditional restaurant.

The third option seems to have been frying the bread in a pan. The process seems obscure, but Milgrom (1991, 185) notes the difference between a griddle and a pan as one of depth, stating, "the depth of the two cooking vessels is emphasized by their respective prepositions: the dough is placed *al'* 'on' the griddle but *be* 'in' the oiled pan." It would seem that this process would be similar to modern deep frying.

Figure 19. Oven and kitchen in reconstructed town of Katzrin.

Figure 20. Baking bread, Sirence, Turkey.

One last item that should be mentioned is that while several translations use the phrase "unleavened cakes" to translate the phrase חַלּוֹת מַצּוֹת in Leviticus 2:4, the term "loaves" is preferred. As discussed by Gane (2009, 291–93), a variety of baked items could include various fillings or sweeteners such as honey or figs. These items seem to be more properly viewed as "cakes" (עֻגָה), and these items are specifically forbidden in the gift offerings. Further, these cakes could be made in terra-cotta molds, thus providing various shapes. King and Stager (2001, 66) note a Cypriot example of a mold that apparently portrayed Aphrodite-Astarte, suggesting pagan ritual purposes.

The oven is specified as a very primitive oven called a *tannur* (תַּנּוּר). Commentators and tradition distinguish the two baked products primarily by thickness and texture. The first type is called חַלּוֹת and is translated either as "cakes" (HCSB, KJV, NASB, NLT, NRSV) or "loaves" (ESV, NIV). Because the root *ḥll* is associated with the verb חָלַל meaning "to pierce," it has been suggested that they were either ring-shaped or pierced (Milgrom 1991, 184). These loaves would have been rather thick and probably lumpy (Levine 1989, 11). In contrast, the "wafers" would have been thin. One other distinction is that the wafers were to be spread with oil, apparently after cooking. In either case the dough was to be "unleavened" (מַצּוֹת).

In addition to the two types of gift offerings baked in an oven, the offeror had the option of cooking his or her offering on a griddle (מַחֲבַת, 2:5) or in a pan (מַרְחֶשֶׁת, 2:7). The difference appears to be not only the nature of the utensil but the actual cooking medium. The griddle is basically a flat disk that could cook unleavened bread. In contrast, a pan would cook by heating a liquid, either water or oil, and placing the dough in the liquid to be cooked. These vessels could be made from fired clay or metal (bronze, or later, iron).

TRANSLATION ANALYSIS: "GRIDDLE" AND "PAN"

The griddle (מַחֲבַת) is described as a flat plate (BDB s.v. "מַחֲבַת" 290; *TWOT* s.v. "מַחֲבַת" 1:261). It could be ceramic (fired clay) or metal (Ezekiel describes one of iron). Dough cooked on a griddle likely was something like a pancake. In contrast the pan (מַרְחֶשֶׁת) had sides and could hold a liquid. Some sources suggest that it specifically included a lid (*DCH* s.v. "מַרְחֶשֶׁת" 5:485; *DBL* s.v. "מַרְחֶשֶׁת" 5306). If water was used, the result would be something like a dumpling. If the liquid was hot oil, the result would be deep-fried, something like a doughnut.

While the text states explicitly that the first three cooked gift offerings were to be unleavened, for some reason it does not address that requirement in the case of the fourth. However, the next section specifically commands that leavening was not allowed in any offering that was burned, which will be discussed below.

In the case of the cooked offering, the finished product would be broken into pieces, and oil would be poured on it, and then it would be presented to the priest who would take it to the altar. There, as in the case of the uncooked gift offering, the memorial portion would be removed and then offered up on the altar, presumably with the frankincense if it was included. Again, this portion was burned, being turned to smoke like the burnt offering, and like the burnt offering the result is described as an "offering by fire of a soothing aroma" (an אִשֶּׁה and a רֵיחַ נִיחֹחַ; see burnt offering, above, for discussion).

After addressing the memorial portion, attention is turned to the remainder of the gift offering (מִנְחָה). Here the text just tells us that the remainder of the offering was given to "Aaron and his sons," that is, to the priests. Here we are not told what the priests were to do with it, likely since this portion of the text gives guidelines to the offeror. The priests' responsibility is saved for Leviticus 6:8–7:38 where the Lord gives Moses guidelines for the priests. In 6:16, we learn that the priests were to eat it "as unleavened cakes" in the court of the Tent of Meeting. Other guidelines for the eating of this offering will be covered in the section on Leviticus 6 and 7.

2:10–13. After describing the two general varieties of gift offering, this section briefly gives the Israelites specific admonitions for their presentation of gift offerings. Leviticus 2:11 provides the general admonition that a gift offering was to be unleavened, although no reason is given for this. Several suggestions have been given. One suggestion has been that "yeast is a living organism and only dead things could be burned on the altar in sacrifice" (Wenham 1979, 71). Building on this, another suggestion is that both leaven and honey are "materially associated with *life* not *death*" (Balentine 2002, 32, emphasis original). However, most commentators maintain that leaven is viewed as a corrupting agent, which is why it is forbidden (e.g., Keil and Delitzsch 1956, 518; Milgrom 1991, 188; and Ross 2002, 103). Kiuchi (2007, 70–71), who generally accepts this symbolic meaning, sees a tie-in to the use of unleavened bread in the Passover. In the original Passover the directions were that there should be no leaven in the bread because the Israelites were to "eat in haste," prepared to leave Egypt (Exod. 12:11). This is a very enticing connection in that it provides clear historical anchor for the ritual, especially since the Passover was a clear act of God that the entire nation at the time experienced (Harbin 1994, 219–20). But there is nothing that explicitly ties the use of unleavened bread in the Passover to the various offerings covered in Leviticus.

Given the strong support of both Jewish and Christian tradition, the issue of corruption seems to be the best understanding and certainly has strong appeal, but there are some concerns. We do need to remember that it is an inference, not an explicit symbolic correlation and must be approached with caution. Further, some sacrifices (e.g., at the Feast of Pentecost, Lev. 23:17) were specifically directed to incorporate leaven. Scholars who address this issue generally argue that this "grain offering of early ripened things" is not burned but "placed before the Lord," although this seems a rather fine distinction (Levine 1989, 14). Harrison points out that leaven "enhances and improves the flavor, texture, and digestibility of the baked product rather than causing it to deteriorate." As such, he argues that it is morally neutral in terms of symbolism with a focus on its "permeating effect" (1980, 55). Also, wine (fermented grape juice) served as a drink offering. In response to this observation, Ross (2002, 103) states that the wine is poured out at the base of the altar, but Numbers 15:10 describes the drink offering (wine) as "an offering by fire, as a soothing aroma to the Lord," suggesting that it too was poured on the altar.

The second prohibited item was honey. Regardless of whether the product is fruit syrup or bee honey, like leaven it is not to be included as part of an offering by fire. Again, we are given no reason for it. Harrison (1980, 54) and others suggest that it was because honey was used in sacrifices to idols in the region; that is, it was viewed as the food of gods. However, that raises problems, since the same pagan nations also used flour, incense, oil, and salt (Milgrom 1991, 190). Further, 2:12 states that they might be brought "to the Lord" as part of the firstfruits offering, but not offered up on the altar. While it is claimed that these sweet items are subject to fermentation leading to corruption (Ross 2002, 105) that same process produces wine, which is the substance of the drink offering. Lacking explicit explanations for the prohibition, perhaps the best process is to accept these prohibitions as God-given standards intended to distinguish the nation of Israel from its neighbors.

TRANSLATION ANALYSIS: "HONEY"
The word translated as "honey" is דְּבַשׁ. Scholars debate as to whether the intended meaning is bee honey, or syrup from fruit, usually understood as dates. Apparently it can be used for both products (Caquot 1978, 128). The latter product seems indicated in a number of locations where the subject is agricultural produce, such as the 2 Chronicles 31:5 description of the gathering of "first-processed fruits" during the reign of Hezekiah (Milgrom 1991, 189). On the other hand, both the case of Jonathan's discovery of honey in the woods (1 Sam. 14:26–29) and Samson's encounter of both bees and honey in the lion carcass (Judg. 14:8) clearly point to the former. Other passages that seem to tie honey to a honeycomb

include Psalm 19:10; Proverbs 16:24; and Song of Solomon 5:1. Recent archaeological evidence from Tel Rehov has demonstrated domestic beekeeping dates at least as early as 1000 B.C. (the time of David).

In contrast to the prohibitions, 2:13 specifically ties salt into a representation of the covenant, and consequently every gift offering was to include salt. The origins of the idea of a covenant of salt are not recorded in the OT and are lost to history, but the OT text uses the phrase as if the people would have been familiar with it. Ross (2002, 105) suggests that the idea derives from how salt was used as a preservative and therefore the phrase represented the preservation of the covenant—in Numbers 18:19, forever. This seems likely.

2:14–16. The last section describes a special gift offering that consists of the first of the new crop. As developed in Leviticus 23, it is tied into firstfruits, a holy day that was to be celebrated in the land once they got there. Firstfruits included a burnt offering in addition to the gift offering (מִנְחָה). As a holy day, we will discuss it later. Here, we just note the directions for the gift offering portion. It is to consist of the grain heads of the new crop, which have been roasted in fire. As with a regular gift offering, the grain is to be ground (literally "crushed" [גֶּרֶשׂ]) and mixed with oil and salt, with incense laid on top. In essence, it is a gift offering given on a particular occasion for a special purpose—to show trust and praise to God for the upcoming crop. As we will see in Leviticus 23, there are some differences with respect to the entire holy day, but the process of the gift offering is basically the same.

The Lord Tells Israel How to Bring a Shalom Offering (3:1–17)
Leviticus 3 addresses the third voluntary category. English translations generally call it a "peace offering" (the traditional translation) or "fellowship offering," although the vowels differ

from the word for "peace" (שָׁלֵם as opposed to שָׁלוֹם). Carr (1980c: 2:930) suggests that the complex of terms associated with the *š-l-m* consonantal root carry a general concept of "completion and fulfillment—of entering into a state of wholeness and unity, a restored relationship." Given this broad scope of meaning and how the concept of shalom has been assimilated into English, we will use the term "shalom offering." Here the text just gives directions for all shalom offerings. Later we will see that this broader category might be used for a variety of purposes. Leviticus 7 lists three: thanksgiving (7:12), votive, and freewill (both in 7:16). Likewise, Leviticus 7 gives specifics on how the meat was to be distributed and eaten, and those steps will be discussed in that context. In terms of the basic process of bringing the animal to sacrifice, the procedures are the same for all three, and those general procedures are given here up to the point where the portions dedicated to the Lord are burned on the altar.

TRANSLATION ANALYSIS: "SHALOM OFFERING"

The Hebrew phrase (זֶבַח שְׁלָמִים) is a construct phrase, which suggests that this is a sacrifice of the "shalom offerings" variety. The exact meaning of the initial word, זֶבַח, is debated among scholars, but it seems likely that BDB is correct when it describes it as a "most ancient sacrifice, whose essential rite was eating the flesh of the victim at a feast" (BDB s.v. "זָרַק" 257). The first use of the word in the OT in Genesis 31:54 illustrates this

when it states, "Jacob offered a sacrifice on the mountain, and called his kinsmen to the meal; and they ate the meal." The second word of the phrase is a plural, which may serve to reflect intensity (so Ross 2002, 114). Or, it may indicate that there are multiple kinds of this type of sacrifice. For example, Leviticus 7:11–16 will list three varieties of זֶבַח שְׁלָמִים: thanksgiving (תּוֹדָה), votive (נֶדֶר), and freewill (נְדָבָה).

The operative phrase here is literally a "sacrifice of shalom offerings" (זֶבַח שְׁלָמִים), a construct phrase. Milgrom (1991, 218) concludes that in the OT, sacrifice (זֶבַח) always means a "slain offering whose meat is eaten by the worshipper," which seems to be the best understanding. This presents what may be the most significant characteristic of the shalom offering—unlike the other two examples of offering (קָרְבָּן) cited in this unit, the burnt and gift offerings: the person bringing the offering actually ate some of the meat and was expected to share the meat with his or her neighbors. As we will see later, this corporate meal highlighted the purpose of the sacrifice, which was to give thanks to God for something he had done. By sharing the meal with the community, the offeror was able to praise God before his or her contemporaries, which would serve to focus the attention of the community on God and his deeds, as well as draw the community closer together. It seems likely that on at least some occasions this praise would be in the form of a praise or thanksgiving psalm.

Praise Psalms

The book of Psalms is really the collection of lyrics of songs of worship that the people of Israel sang, but for which we no longer have the tunes. As scholars have studied them they have realized that in terms of content, the psalms may be categorized into several categories by purpose. Here, we would just note that the most basic categorization might be to distinguish between laments or praises.

Laments are expressions of grief or sorrow. Lament psalms are addressed to God with the expectation that God is the only one who can help, and thus are really cries for help. An example might be Psalm 3, which is described by the heading as having been written by David when he fled from his son Absalom (2 Sam. 15:13–16:14). David's passion is seen in 3:7 where he pleads for God to hit his enemies in the jaw and knock out all of their teeth (Harbin 2005, 235).

Praise psalms, as might be expected, are simply songs praising God. They may be divided into two types: descriptive and declarative. Descriptive praise psalms describe aspects of God's greatness, and as such they are timeless. The classic example of this is Psalm 8. On the other hand, declarative praise psalms essentially thank God for some specific deed he has done. As such, many declarative praise psalms were likely written as follow-ons to laments. The psalmist was in dire straits. He wrote a song crying out to God asking for deliverance. After God delivered, the psalmist wrote a follow-on psalm praising God for the answer to prayer.

It seems that many of those praise psalms may have originally been sung at a public sacrifice or shalom offering where the Israelite was sharing with his neighbors what God had done. This seems to be especially true in the case of a votive offering, which by its very nature was a sacrifice intended to praise God for his intervention and deliverance. For example, David wrote laments about Saul and his men in Psalms 54, 57, and 59. He also wrote Psalm 18, which praised God for his deliverance from Saul, which may have followed any of those laments or on any other number of occasions (Harbin 2005, 236–38). One of the more interesting aspects of the praise psalms is that declarative praise psalms "thanking God for answering [the psalmist's] prayer about a specific instance in the past seem to be unique to Israel" (Hill and Walton 2009, 276).

The practice of giving praise to God for what he had done would have been a powerful testimony to the community when shared around a celebratory sacrifice that then turned into a community meal. This would be especially the case when the celebration included a song praising God. The fact that some of those songs have been preserved for more than three thousand years testifies to the power of praise songs.

3:1–5. Leviticus 3 begins somewhat awkwardly with a double "if" clause. The first "if" ties the entire chapter back to Leviticus 1:2, which we noted introduces a unit presenting three different optional or voluntary sacrifices an Israelite might bring to God. The second "if" differentiates the type of animal that might be offered. Three are listed in the chapter: a bull (or cow), a sheep, and a goat. Unlike the burnt offering, regardless of the animal, either a male or female may be offered.

TRANSLATION ANALYSIS: "IF"
The Hebrew text uses "if" four times in this verse. It begins with a conjunction that means "and if" (וְאִם). This ties this section back to Leviticus 1:2

showing Leviticus 3 to be one of the types of voluntary "offering" (קָרְבָּן) that an Israelite might bring to God (Milgrom 1991, 203). The second use of the same conjunction coupled with the third-person singular masculine pronoun sets up qualifications for that voluntary offering, specifically one from the herd. Finally, the text uses it twice more: once for the male, once for the female. But those are better translated as "whether." Thus this initial portion of the verse might be literally translated, "And if a sacrifice of shalom is his *qorban*, if it is from the herd, whether male or female." Subsequently, other options are mentioned including from the flock (3:6, whether lamb in 3:7 or goat in 3:12).

As was the case with the burnt offering, the animal was to be without defect. The procedure was very similar to the burnt offering: the animal was offered "before the Lord [YHWH]" and was slain at "the doorway of the Tent of Meeting," although Anson Rainey (1975, 207) places it at the "entrance to the outer court." Then the priest sprinkled the blood around the altar. After the animal was slaughtered, it was cut up with part of the animal being burned on the altar, part given to the priest, and then the remaining portion cooked and eaten (with limits on how long they could retain leftovers).

> ### Cooking the Sacrifice
> The text does not indicate how the meat was to be cooked. Numbers 6:20 specifies that in the case of the ram shalom offering subsequent to the completion of a Nazirite vow, the thigh of the ram is given to the Nazirite after it has been boiled. Many commentators view this as applicable to the priest's portion. In 1 Samuel 2:15–17, Eli's sons are viewed as out of line when they demand nonboiled meat for roasting, but the admonition given by the offeror is that he should burn the fat first (i.e., give the Lord his portion first), and then the priest might have as much as he pleases. Deuteronomy 18:3 states that the portion for members of entire tribe of Levi would be the shoulder, two cheeks, and stomach of any sacrifice.

A portion of the bull or cow was then burned on the altar. First, the text lists the fat (חֵלֶב) that covered the entrails. Milgrom (1991, 205) translates this as "suet" and explains that it is the "layers of fat beneath the surface of the animal's skin and around its organs, which can be peeled off, in contrast to the fat that is inextricably entwined in the musculature called šûmān in rabbinic Hebrew." The significance of this is debated. Sklar (2014, 103) states, "Apparently, it represented the best part of the meat—the filet mignon—and was thus the most worthy to be given to the Lord," a conclusion Willis (2009, 24) supports, calling it "the most logical interpretation." In contrast Ross (2002, 117) and Milgrom (1991, 207) assert that the fat was inedible, although today suet is used in a large number of recipes and may be purchased at many grocery stores, even processed and prepackaged. However, 3:16 asserts that "all fat is the Lord's" and 3:17 gives a "perpetual statute" that the Israelites were not to eat either fat or blood. Still, while the reason is deemed "shrouded in mystery" (Milgrom 1991, 207), or "elusive" (Kiuchi 2007, 79), the use of the term elsewhere as a metaphor for the best (e.g., in Deut. 32:14 the phrase "finest of the wheat" literally is "the fat of the kidney of the wheat"; see also Num. 18:12; Pss. 81:16; 147:14) suggests that it points to giving of the best to God.

Second, the two kidneys (הַכְּלָיוֹת) are listed along with the fat that covers them. While most translations use the term "loins" for the phrase עַל-הַכְּסָלִים, it better understood as "sinews" (so NET), suggesting that these are the bovine support ligaments. Again, the significance of offering up the kidneys is debated, although it is generally accepted that the kidneys are "associated with the heart as the seat of thoughts, emotions and life" (Milgrom 1991, 207) as shown by a number of passages including Psalms 7:10; 16:7; 139:13; Jeremiah 11:20; 17:10; 20:12.

Third, the lobe or protuberance of the liver (הַיֹּתֶרֶת עַל-הַכָּבֵד) was to be removed with the kidneys and was to be burned. Milgrom (1991, 208) identifies this lobe with the *lobus caudatus*, a "fingerlike projection from the liver close to the right kidney." Commentators generally see this as a prohibition on using the liver for hepatoscopy. Erhard Gerstenberger (1996, 48) notes, "Among the Babylonians, the liver and liver lobes of sacrificed animals served as the basis for divining the future." However, one might question why the entire liver is not included. Given the proximity to the kidney, one reason may have been a matter of practicality.

The general consensus seems to be that collectively these portions of the animal reflect the inner being (Kiuchi 2007, 79). As Wenham (1979, 81) expresses it, drawing on the use of the two terms elsewhere, it is "possible that offering the kidneys and internal fat symbolizes the dedication of the worshipper's best and deepest emotions to God." While that seems to leave the liver as an outlier, it does seem the most reasonable explanation.

Once these parts were removed, the priests placed them on the altar where the daily burnt offerings were burning. They then served as a "soothing aroma" (רֵיחַ נִיחֹחַ) to the Lord. The disposition of the remainder of the animal is given later in Leviticus 7.

3:6–11. The text immediately then switches to the *ovis* option. Here, in distinction to the burnt offering, which included both sheep and goats as one type, the text now distinguishes between sheep and goats. Perhaps the key reason is that the sheep used in that culture was characterized by a fat tail (*Ovis laticaudata*), which made a significant difference in terms of what should be sacrificed. In addition to the fat, kidneys, and liver lobe, the fat tail was also to be removed and burned (3:9).

Fat-tailed Sheep

This tail was noted as early as Uruk II documents, which have been dated to approximately 3000 B.C. (Muigai and Hanotte 2013, 41). Sources indicate two varieties of fat-tailed sheep. Broad fat-tails have fat deposits on both sides of the tail, which makes it appear as an enlarged rump. Long fat-tails have the fat deposits on the tail it-

Figure 21. Broad fat-tailed sheep.

self. This produces an elongated tail that can actually drag on the ground. The tail could weigh up to ten pounds (about 4.5 kg), although other sources suggest even greater weights for the broad

Figure 22. Long fat-tailed (Dumba) sheep.

fat-tails (Sklar 2014, 104). In addition to sacrifices, the fat of the tail could be used for burning in lamps (Clutton-Brock 2012, 64).

While the burning is described as food in 3:11, that should not be construed that God "ate" it. Psalm 50:12–14 indicates that God does not get hungry—and if he did, he owns the entire world. Sklar (2014, 104) expresses it well when he states that "sharing a meal often functioned to confirm a covenant relationship." In this manner, in essence God, the priests, and the offeror and guests all partook, strengthening their relationship. Given the description of the ritual as a shalom offering, emphasized by passages such as Psalm 50:14, the thrust of the sacrifice was to recognize God not only for who he is but what he has done.

3:12–16. The third category of a shalom offering is that of a goat, which is essentially the same as for the bovine and the sheep (with the exception of the fat tail). As noted in the previous section, the directive distinguishes between sheep and goat to give three options, but does not include an option of birds. A number of reasons have been suggested. Milgrom (1991, 222) suggests that all birds were considered wild game. Ross (2002, 116) maintains that the birds had too little blood or fat. It would seem rather that since the primary focus of the offering is a community meal to praise God, then the lack of meat was the explanation for their omission. Birds did not provide enough meat for a communal feast of celebration (so Wenham 1979, 89).

3:17. Leviticus 3 does not finish the directions for the shalom offering. Regardless of the animal, the procedure was the same for all three. The first portion was given to God symbolically through incineration on the altar, in the same manner as the burnt and gift offerings. In the case of the shalom offering, as will be presented in Leviticus 7, after the animal was sacrificed, a portion was given to the priests, and the remainder cooked and eaten as a communal meal to celebrate God.

THEOLOGICAL FOCUS

The key theological theme of this unit is that God initiates worship and provides a variety of ways it may be expressed. In this section, God provided the nation of Israel means of voluntary personal worship that included worship totally focused on God (the burnt offering), worship that incorporated God's ministers (the gift offering, which was shared with the priests), and worship where the individual included others in his or her celebration (the shalom offering, which was shared with the priests as well as the entire gathering).

Exodus ends with the glory of God descending into the tabernacle, identifying it as the Lord God's new dwelling place. An obligatory "veil of separation" hangs between a holy God and his set-apart, yet still unholy, people. Even Moses is no longer able to enter into the Tent of Meeting. So now what? How close can they come? It appears that God will not "lead them from afar," but rather positions himself in the very physical center of their existence. Now from inside this protective veil, the Lord God initiates a personal relationship with his people.

The key theological point is clear: God is the initiator of worship. God desires the heart of the worshipper. While his holy all-powerful presence within the Tent of Meeting is duly intimidating, hope remains because God's personal invitation to come before him is simple and clear. The worshipper is being asked to trust God. This is evidenced further through the establishment of the three initial (burnt, gift, and shalom) worship offerings. These offerings are not to be brought as a direct response to sin, but instead are established to deepen the personal bond of trust between the Lord God and the worshipper.

In every age, true worship is initiated and defined by God. A proper response requires a humble heart that recognizes and trusts in the call of God to come, bring an offering, and worship. To hear and receive his invitation, every worshipper will need to decisively separate him- or herself from feelings of doubt and self-sufficiency, as well as from the steady counsel of the world that is in continual rebellion against God.

PREACHING AND TEACHING STRATEGIES

Exegetical and Theological Synthesis

God redeemed the Israelites from a life of bondage in Egypt, rescuing them from enslavement to a king who was harsh, treacherous, and cruel. In Egypt, an invitation into the throne

Worshipping a Holy God (1:1–3:17)

room of Pharaoh would only come to a select few, and then it would be received with apprehension and dread because he could not be trusted. It is no surprise, then, that the people might expect to maintain a safe distance between themselves and their new king. Their fear makes them reluctant to trust the very hand that rescued them from their taskmasters. Yet God does not abandon them to their ignorance and fear. He enters into their presence and calls them to simply come, bring an offering, and worship him. He is initiating a personal relationship of trust with each worshipper that he has redeemed from slavery. For this bond to deepen, they will need to regularly come before him in worship.

Whether in a desert, on the beach, or on a mountaintop, we are fallen creatures. And as such, we lack the will and the ability to initiate worship with the only One who can save and sustain us. Fallen hearts are not in a posture to seek nor in a condition to trust God. All humankind has turned aside. The Lord looks down from heaven on the children of man, to see if there are any who understand, who seek after God. "They have all turned aside; together they have become corrupt; there is none who does good, not even one" (Ps. 14:2–3 ESV). Our nature leaves us slow to trust and quick to fear, slow to confess and quick to blame. God knows this about us, so he is the one who initiates our worship of him.

Today, our bondage is different, yet our need is the same. We no longer bring regular sacrifices to remind us of who God is. All believers who "live by faith" have entered into a trust relationship with God and have access to him through the person and work of Jesus Christ. Thus, we come to the Lord's Table to remind us of the fulfillment of that model that came through the sacrifice of Christ. "For as often as you eat this bread and drink this cup, you proclaim the Lord's death until he comes" (1 Cor. 11:26 ESV).

Preaching Idea

Worship of a seemingly inaccessible, holy God is initiated by God.

Contemporary Connections

What does it mean?

What did the Israelites hear in these words at Mount Sinai? The Lord God is calling them to come before him in personal worship. Their relationship to God will not be random, distant, and impersonal. They serve a God who is intentional, near, and personal.

This means that hope remains, even when his people stumble and fall! God will not abandon his people to their ignorance and fear. He will not become inaccessible, because worship will not be dependent upon human initiation. Though they may respond to his perfection and call for holiness by ignoring, denying, and dismissing his truth, that will not be the end of the matter. He will be present, initiating a relationship and calling his people to come, bring an offering, and worship.

Is it true?

Is it true that God initiates personal worship (even when his people have strayed)? He initiated it in the garden of Eden after Adam and Eve fell. He initiated it with Abraham after he gave away Sarah (twice). He initiated it with the Israelites after they worshipped the golden calf. He initiated it with David (through Nathan) after David's sin with Bathsheba. This model of gracious, merciful initiation of worship continues through Christ as the resurrected Jesus approaches Peter (and all the disciples) after he had abandoned him.

If God did not initiate worship, there would be no hope. Our faith would be in vain. Believers would be bound to a life of pride and folly. Yet God does initiate. No matter how far we may stray, we cannot go beyond his voice or venture outside his reach. Hope remains alive and well because God is intentional, near, and personal!

It is not the will of the straying sinner but the mercy of our faithful God that is the foundation of true worship!

Now what?

People are seeking someone or something trustworthy to follow. We may turn to pundits, sports figures, and politicians in search of somebody to lead us. This generally fails to satisfy because of the distance—and if we *do* get close, there is disappointment. Yet Leviticus opens with an invitation from the God of the universe, an invitation that comes with an implied RSVP. Will we open or discard the invitation? Will we reply or ignore the call? Will our minds become clouded by the self-protective belief that God is inaccessible, unapproachable, and unloving? Will we wait for a new audible, personalized call from God?

God spoke the invitation to Moses, and Moses conveyed God's words to the people. We hear the invitation as it was recorded so that we can be assured that the God we worship is intentional, near, and personal. Responding to this invitation will transform our hearts and change our lives.

Creativity in Presentation

Structuring messages from Leviticus presents many challenges. In skimming through Leviticus, we read of a God who seems distant and perplexing, even unapproachable and inaccessible. This opening message in Leviticus 1–3 is the perfect opportunity to set the minds of your congregation on a new track. They need to see you presenting the Lord God as he presents himself: intentional, near, and personal. The biggest challenge for you will be to do so without diminishing or dismissing God's perfect holiness. Can this be done?

In our age, people generally expect God to come to them (not vice versa) and to do so on their terms. Our sin is not seen as real barrier and it rarely provokes any measure of personal wrath. We are who we are. God made us this way. It is no wonder people are generally more comfortable with either keeping the Lord God at a distance or creating a personalized (false) god that they are comfortable bringing close. Neither will result in true worship.

The Israelites are being asked to reconcile two truths that are not reconcilable in their minds: (1) God is holy, a devouring fire; and (2) he is asking them, as his unholy people, to come into his presence for personal worship. How can these two things be true? Either God will become unclean or they will become "barbeque." Is it best to remain at a safe distance? Can I swim and not get wet? Can I walk on fire and not get burned? If the focus is on "I," then the answer will be no. But once the focus shifts from "I" to the Lord God, the answer changes.

God is inviting, so it must be possible. He is not a magician, nor is he a deceiver. He is God. He has a plan and a purpose to draw his people into his presence so that they may see their own sin and that he may cleanse them. This is all beyond their comprehension. The invitation is not a call to understand but to trust the ways of God. As you lead them through the five sacrifices listed in Leviticus, your people will see again and again that it is the Lord God who will shoulder the burden. He is inviting. He is pursuing his people. He will complete the work. He will pierce the barrier. And we live in the age where we can see that his work was completed. In Matthew 27:51, we read that the very moment Christ died on the cross, the curtain of the temple was torn in two from top to bottom. The veil of separation that been in place from Exodus 40, hanging as a protection between God and his people, was now torn open from the top. God initiated. God completed. We respond in worship.

It may work best to cover the burnt and gift (grain) offerings in this opening message and hold the peace offerings for the third message. In some circles, it may be beneficial to limit the details of animal sacrifice and immediately substitute a sacrifice that would be more tangible to the hearer. This will not be easy. The voluntary sacrifices capture four of the five senses: sight, sound, smell, and touch. The animal sacrifices call for one to part with a prized possession to demonstrate how much they value a relationship. It could be compared to donating a kidney to a loved one, giving your full-ride college scholarship to a beloved friend, or donating the car you invested years restoring to a worthy charity. In each case, a costly sacrifice is made that validates your commitment to another.

In other circles, it may be beneficial to dramatically walk your hearers through the entire scene of a sacrifice so they can appreciate how personal and costly this sacrifice would be. The intent is to fully engage the senses. For instance, the worshipper walks among the animals he has hand-raised to select the best. He publicly leads his choice by hand to the entrance to the Tent of Meeting to be examined and approved by the priest. He firmly lays his hand upon the animal's head to symbolically identify with the sacrifice before he then slays with his own hand—seeing, hearing, and feeling the life leave the animal before the altar of the Lord. Now he begins to dress out the animal, placing the clean parts on the altar, and smelling the "pleasing aroma" begin to rise. Returning home, all that is left in his hand is the animal lead or bird coop. But in his heart, he holds the memory of personally validating his faith through a costly personal sacrifice. He is "all in." His relationship is not simply one of words. It has been confirmed through action.

These three chapters can be preached as one unit or, as I chose to do, in three distinct messages: Worship of a seemingly inaccessible, holy God is initiated by God.

- The unique details of each offering (burnt, grain, peace)
  - ◦ The personal sacrifice required of the one who brings it
  - ◦ The unique details of the sacrifice

- The focus of each offering
  - ◦ What this offering reveals about worshipping a holy God
  - ◦ How this offering specifically prepares us for the sacrifice of Christ
- What did it mean to them then? What does it mean always? What do we do now?
  - ◦ Then: What did it mean to the people in Sinai and the Promised Land?
  - ◦ Always: What does it reveal to us about the nature of God and man?
  - ◦ Now: Should this sacrifice inform our worship today?

DISCUSSION QUESTIONS

1. Why might God have initiated animal sacrifices? How might we translate that concept into today's culture?

2. We suggested that the three types of burnt offerings provided opportunities for different socioeconomic levels. Why might God have selected those three types? What parallels might we see for today's culture?

3. We noted that the gift offering (מִנְחָה) partially went to the priest. Do we see any analogies for today's culture?

4. Is the idea of the shalom offering perhaps suggestive of ideas of how we might worship God today?

Leviticus 4:1–6:7 (HB 5:26)

EXEGETICAL IDEA
As worshippers receive the Lord's conviction of an error before him or others, they are called to confess the error, bring a cleansing offering, and when necessary offer reparations.

THEOLOGICAL FOCUS
True worship should be preceded by true confession and repentance.

PREACHING IDEA
Correction, confession, and repentance before a holy God are transformational components of authentic worship.

PREACHING POINTERS
These chapters clarify that worshipping the Lord God will not be a tangential component in the life of God's people. If they pictured that they would be marking the calendar, taking their turn to bring an offering, and then returning their focus to living their normal lives (until their number came up again), they were mistaken. The worship of God was designed to transform their heads (how they thought), hearts (how they felt), and hands (what they did). The worship of God would revolutionize who they were as individuals and as a people. It would define how they saw God, themselves, and others!

Why do we come to church? What is our posture as we gather for worship? Are we carrying a private (or communal) you-need-to-do-this list before our God? Are we actually intending to transform the living God (who is transforming us)? Through his Word, God intends to sufficiently soften us to continually receive his correction and humbly proceed to confession and repentance so we may know authentic worship.

Worship, by definition, implies that the worshipper reveres the one being worshipped. If that is so, then we should expect that authentic worship will frequently require us to correct our thoughts, confess our error, and repent of our sin, in order to cleanse us that we may become more like Christ. This is nothing short of a deliberate, progressive metamorphosis.

PURIFYING ONESELF BEFORE A HOLY GOD
(4:1–6:7 [HB 5:26])

LITERARY STRUCTURE
AND THEMES (4:1–6:7 [HB 5:26])

Like the first unit, the second unit includes more than a single chapter. However, the section structure is not as clear. In terms of subject matter, the unit ends with Leviticus 6:7 (in the English—the Hebrew includes 6:1–7 as part of ch. 5). However, unlike the first unit, which contained just one speech from the Lord that was clearly divided into three different sacrifices, as shown by our chapter divisions, this second unit contains three speeches from the Lord that address two different sacrifices, and neither the speeches nor our chapter divisions clearly differentiate the sections.

Collectively the three speeches address two different sacrifices that address situations resulting from human failures. Many commentators use the collective term *expiatory* for the two. Given our understanding of their function, we have called them confessional offerings. Traditionally, English translations of the two sacrifices have used the term "sin offering" (חַטָּאת—covered in 4:1–5:13), and "guilt offering" (אָשָׁם—covered in 5:14–6:7), although there seems to be some overlap, especially in 5:1–13. While most Bible translations still use those terms, many commentators now prefer to use terms that more clearly differentiate between the two sacrifices and more precisely define what is being done. Consequently, many scholars use the term "purification offering" instead of sin offering for חַטָּאת and "reparation offering" instead of guilt for the אָשָׁם. This study will use those terms.

TRANSLATION ANALYSIS: "SIN"

The sacrifice described in Leviticus 4 and most of 5 is called חַטָּאת, which is a noun derived from the root חטא. As discussed in the introduction ("Sin and Sin [or Confession] Offerings in Leviticus"), in the *qal* stem it reflects the failure to adhere to God's standards in terms of relationship. However, in the *piel* stem the connotation of the verb suggests a cleansing or purification where the sin or its effect is removed. For example, the first time the *piel* is used in conjunction with the sacrificial system given at Sinai is in Exodus 29:36 regarding the daily bull offering (פַּר חַטָּאת), which is intended to "purify the altar" (וְחִטֵּאתָ עַל־הַמִּזְבֵּחַ). In Leviticus, beyond issues of sin, this offering provides purification in situations of uncleanness, which exemplifies the need to describe this as a purification offering.

TRANSLATION ANALYSIS: "GUILT"

The second term used in Leviticus 5 and 6:1–7 is אָשָׁם. Milgrom (1991, 339–45) observes that it "is universally accepted that the root 'šm is associated with the concept of legal culpability or guilt, specifically that the noun 'āšām means 'guilt' and the verb 'āšam means 'is guilty.'" However, in terms of cultic material, he sees a consequential meaning, specifically the punishment for the behavior described by the act. The אָשָׁם offering normally addresses situations that require reparation or restitution of property that was damaged, primarily property belonging to the Lord, but also property belonging to the Lord's people, as will be discussed below. For this reason, modern scholars place the emphasis on the act of reparation as opposed to the guilt felt by the individual who had sinned in this regard.

As was the case of Leviticus 1:1, the unit begins with the statement "The Lord [YHWH] spoke to Moses, saying." This phrase is repeated in Leviticus 5:14 where the confessional sacrifice changes from a purification to a reparation, and again in 6:1 (HB 5:20) where the focus of the reparation offering changes from a violation solely against YHWH to one that involves members of the covenant community.

Again, there are two ways of approaching the material: one may focus on the distinctions between the two sacrifices and address each separately, or one might view the material as one unit that describes different reasons to bring an expression of confession to God. The first approach would produce two separate sermons stressing the different needs involved. A focus on the distinction between purification and reparation showing categories that require purification whether or not one sinned inadvertently, or experienced guilt even without any specific sin, could be fruitful in terms of exploring what it means to be unholy. However, it could also be excessively negative and obscure the common feature that all are in need of repentance. While the original audience would have been keenly aware of the distinctions, since they necessitated subtly different sacrifices and approaches, a modern audience might better address the need to repent and confess sin, regardless of the details. Consequently, we will unite the material from 4:1–6:7 as a single topic homiletically. In our exegesis we will address the specifics of the text, emphasizing how that culture addressed the issue of confession of sin. Should one desire to do a more in-depth study showing the distinctions between the two offerings in this section, some guidelines are given in the introduction on distinguishing the offerings.

- ***The Lord Tells Israel How to Bring an Offering of Purification (4:1–5:13)***
- ***The Lord Tells Israel How to Bring an Offering of Reparation (5:14–6:7 [HB 5:26])***

EXPOSITION (4:1–6:7 [HB 5:26])

Because of the fall, all humans are unholy and impure. A worshipper needs to be pure to approach a holy God. While purity is an internal state, Israel was given a physical process to visibly demonstrate that internal process.

The Lord Tells Israel How to Bring an Offering of Purification (4:1–5:13)

Purification offerings were introduced to the nation of Israel at Mount Sinai in Exodus 29 as the Lord gave directions for the future consecration of Aaron and his sons as priests. Before describing the actual consecration, Exodus finishes with the tabernacle being erected and God displaying his presence in it. With God present in the tabernacle, the narrative continues into Leviticus with three chapters relating how Israelites should express personal worship by bringing various offerings. Now God addresses a new issue: What if, in the process of bringing one of those sacrifices to worship God, a person becomes convicted of some issue in his or her life that affects his or her relationship either with God or with one of God's people? Before worship can take place, that issue must be resolved, and in this unit God gives guidelines on how to purify that relationship so that a person can worship properly. While we tend to think of this as an issue of sin, the Hebrew terminology is somewhat more nuanced, as shown in the introductory discussion. Given the fact that translations still translate the root חָטָא as "sin" we will use the term *sin* in our discussion of the reason for the offering. However, we will follow the more recent descriptions of the *offerings* (in this case a purification offering) in order to reinforce the idea that this sacrifice did not seem to be intended to provide propitiation.

4:1–2. Leviticus 4:1 and 2 introduce this section in two ways. First, 4:1 clearly marks a content transition by introducing a new speech: "Then the Lord [YHWH] spoke to Moses." Second, the

Purifying Oneself Before a Holy God (4:1–6:7 [HB 5:26])

Lord tells Moses to inform the nation that there will be situations when the Israelites will unintentionally violate the various commands that God had given. The subsequent material delineates steps that the Israelites would be expected to follow when that happened. These steps are distinguished among four specific groups based on their social status: the priests (4:3), the whole congregation of Israel (4:13), leaders of the nation (4:22), and the common people (4:27). All four groups required a purification offering, with the differences being what animal was presented and how the ritual should proceed.

While Leviticus 4:1 is generally translated the same as 1:1, two subtle differences bear noting. In Leviticus 1:1 the subject was actually "he," referring to God, which served to tie the chapter (and book) to the preceding material in Exodus 40. Here, the text specifically identifies the speaker as the Lord. Since the entire material in Leviticus 1–3 was a single speech of the Lord, this indicates that we are beginning a new topic. This is further indicated by the change in the verb from "call" or "call out" (קְרָא) to "speak" or "declare" (דִּבֶּר). This seems to indicate a person continuing one's conversation to another as opposed to initiating a conversation.

The grammatical transition to 4:1 is the normal *waw*, which basically means "and," but in this context suggests the idea of "then." Here, the *waw* likely indicates that this speech immediately follows the preceding material; that is, it continues the declaration of the Lord that began on the date that the tabernacle was sanctified (Exod. 40:34). But, including the phrase shows a new topic.

As was the case in Leviticus 1, God gives the material to Moses to promulgate to the people of Israel for implementation. The prior material addressed worship; now the issue is impediments to worship, specifically the unintentional commission of an act that served to harm or break a relationship (Péter-Contesse and Ellington 1992, 47). This would suggest that the emphasis is on how the action (or failure

to act) affected the other person, whether that other person was God or another member of the covenant community, rather than the violation of a rule. Second, the stress is that the action was inadvertent or unintentional (בִּשְׁגָגָה) as a result of either negligence or ignorance (Kiuchi 2003, 6–7). Third, the term *nephesh* (נֶפֶשׁ) that is translated either as "anyone" or "person" refers back to the "sons of Israel," indicating it applied to any individual who was a member of that covenant community—regardless of his or her status. However, the consequences would vary depending upon one's status or role within the community. We will discuss this material by the four different groups that are listed.

TRANSLATION ANALYSIS: "INADVERTENT SIN"

Victor Hamilton (1980k) defines the noun שְׁגָגָה to mean "sin (of inadvertence)," derived from the verb שָׁגַג meaning "to go astray or err." Kiuchi (2003, 9) suggests that a more nuanced understanding might be "to go astray inadvertently." Thus, whether one understands the term חָטָא (used here in the *qal* stem) to denote sin as traditionally understood, or "hide oneself" as Kiuchi suggests, the phrase used here (כִּי־תֶחֱטָא בִשְׁגָגָה נֶפֶשׁ) literally says, "a person, if he *ḥāṭā'* inadvertently." How that might happen has traditionally been understood to have two possible reasons. It could be that the person may not have understood what the law said, or, it could be that the person did not realize that a specific act violated a law (Levine 1989, 19).

4:3–12. The first group addressed is that of the priesthood or, since the text specifies the anointed priest, perhaps just the high priest (Levine 1989, 20). The issue is that the anointed priest has "sinned," which brought "guilt on the people." There are two ways of understanding this. On one hand, it could be that the priest caused the congregation to corporately commit an act that violated the law, either out of his own lack of understanding or through providing an interpretation of the law that was in fact erroneous (Milgrom 1991, 242; Sklar 2014, 110–11). The alternative is that a personal sin on the part of the priest jeopardized the entire congregation (Hartley 1992, 59; Lange 1960, 43; Rooker; 2000, 110). Kiuchi (2007, 92) is probably correct when he notes that "since *ḥāṭā'* refers to his whole existence, this question becomes irrelevant." In either case, the priest was to bring a bull without defect as his purification offering. The fact that such an expensive sacrifice was required demonstrates the heavy responsibility incurred by spiritual leaders.

The Anointed Priest

The role of the priest is somewhat ambiguous. At Sinai, God declared that the entire nation was to be a kingdom of priests to the nations (Exod. 19:6). While the way that was supposed to work is not clearly expressed, Douglas Stuart (2006, 423) proposes that "it surely was to take place in four ways." In summary, he suggests Israel was to (1) be an example to other nations, (2) proclaim the truth of God, (3) intercede for the rest of the world, and (4) preserve God's promises. Within this larger role, although not all Levites were designated as priests, the tribe of Levi as a whole had a special function of performing priestly duties for Aaron (the first priest), for the tabernacle, and for the entire nation under the direction of Aaron and his sons (Num. 3:1–13) as discussed in the section "Priests and Levites" in the introduction. While apparently the dispersed tribe served priestly functions for the people where they lived (1 Sam. 9:12–13), within the tribe of Levi, Aaron and his sons were to be anointed priests (Num. 3:3), essentially to serve as priests to the priests. After Nadab and Abihu died, Eleazar and Ithamar remained in that role during the life of Aaron. When Aaron was anointed, his sons were anointed with him (so Exod. 29:29; Lev. 8:30), so some scholars conclude that all priests were anointed (Kiuchi 2007, 92). On the other hand, a traditional understanding is that the anointed priest is synonymous with the term "high priest"

as shown in Leviticus 21:10, which specifically identifies the high priest as the one anointed and consecrated (Kleinig 2003, 100; Levine 1989, 20). If this section refers only to the high priest, then it would seem that the rest of the priests would be included in the third group, the group of leaders.

The actual process of the sacrifice was to begin in a very similar manner to what we have noted in the burnt offering presented in Leviticus 1. The priest brought the bull to the entrance of the Tent of Meeting (which is specified as being "before the Lord"), laid his hand on the head of the bull, and it was slain. It is presumed that the priest explained why the bull was being sacrificed, although the text does not specifically relate that (Wenham 1979, 90). Some of the blood was collected by the anointed priest. In the case of the earlier sacrifices, the blood was sprinkled on the altar. Likely the remainder was then poured out at the base of the altar. In this case, however, the priest collected some of the blood and took it to the Tent of Meeting, where he "sprinkled" (נָזָה) some of the blood "in front of the veil of the sanctuary" seven times.

TRANSLATION ANALYSIS: "SPRINKLE"

This verse uses the verb נָזָה for the process of sprinkling the blood as opposed to זָרַק, which was used with the sacrifices in Leviticus 1 and 3. While both can be sprinkled, it is suggested that זָרַק denotes a heavier dispersion using the full hand instead of the fingers. However there does not seem to be any significant difference between the two in terms of purpose (cf. André 1980, 162; Milgrom, Wright, and Fabry 1998, 300).

He then put blood on the horns of the incense altar (which was inside the outer room of the Tent of Meeting; see excursus in "Strengthening the Social Fabric" [23:1–24:9], below). Next, the priest took the remaining blood out to the altar of the burnt offering and poured it out at the base of that altar.

Figure 23. Stone horned altar at Beersheba.

Following this ceremony, the priest processed the bull. This procedure was similar to that noted in the case of the shalom offering (3:3–4). The fat was removed, as described in that section, and burned on the altar of the burnt offering. But in this case, the priest was not allowed to eat of the meat, and he did not keep the hide. It is generally considered that the priest was not to receive any tangible benefit from any sacrifice for his own sin. The remainder of the bull (the hide, the flesh, the head, and the entrails and refuse) was to be taken outside the camp to a place that was designated as clean (see discussion "Clean and Unclean" in the introduction), which was where the ashes were poured out. There it was to be burned.

One of the difficulties for modern readers is that given the detailed instructions, it seems clear that the various steps in the rituals contain significant symbolism; however, the text does not explicate specific symbolic representations. Thoughtful inferences can provide plausible explanations, although care must be taken to remind the listener that these are somewhat conjectural. In general, the process served to maintain the purity of the tabernacle where God met with the priests as representatives of the nation (Mathews 2009, 44).

4:13–21. The second section involves corporate sin, although the exact nature is not clear. First, there is a question of terminology. The section starts in 4:13 with the if clause regarding how the entire *congregation* (עֵדָה) might go astray. Then in 4:14, the *assembly* (קָהָל) is to bring a sacrifice. As used here, the terms *congregation* and *assembly* seem to be somewhat interchangeable since the *congregation* sins and the *assembly* brings the sacrifice. The leaders (elders of the congregation [עֵדָה]) are the ones who place their hands on the head of the bull when it is presented to the priest (4:15). Given the number of elders (whether in the nation as a whole or just the seventy noted in the sidebar), and the constricted space around the bull, and the fact that the term "elders" does not include a definite article, it would appear that while the entire assembly was involved, a representative group of elders laid their hands on the bull.

> **Congregation and Assembly**
> According to Wenham (1979, 98), Jewish commentators differentiated between the two terms, attributing "assembly" (קָהָל) to the entire nation, and "congregation" (עֵדָה) to the leadership, that is, the Sanhedrin. However, Milgrom (1991, 241) claims that congregation (עֵדָה) is used variously. While more than a hundred times it refers to the entire nation, on other occasions the reference is just the adult males, and on some occasions just tribal leaders. Wenham (1979, 98) also notes that as used in the OT, "congregation" can vary and may include the entire nation, and then observes that consequently most Christian commentators have historically suggested that the terms are interchangeable. He sees the congregation as an intermediary group, "a sort of parliament with representative and judicial functions," which apparently was made up of some of the elders. This is an intriguing thought when we note that God specially spoke to the seventy elders (selected from the larger group of elders) on the mountain (Exod. 24:9) and that the Spirit of the Lord rested on that same seventy later (Num. 11:23).

However, there is no indication that they became a formal body that continued through the generations, nor are any specific representative functions given to them. Throughout the OT, there does seem to be a distinction between the people and the elders, but that distinction predated the exodus event. Overall, it would appear that the legal functions of the elders applied to the entire group of elders.

A second uncertainty is the nature of the error. While the violation was corporate, was it an error of judgment such as when the nation made a covenant with Gibeon in Joshua 9 without consulting God? Or, was the error a case where some ceremonial regulation had been violated, such as the high priest declaring the new moon on the wrong day, causing any festivals of that month to be observed on the wrong day (Milgrom 1991, 242)?

The Covenant with Gibeon

When the Gibeonite envoy met with Joshua, the nation made a mutual defense pact with them without consulting God. Wenham (1979, 99) notes that this covenant was made by the leaders and thus concludes that the congregation was not the "whole people"; however, that is not clear. Joshua 9:6–7 relates how the Gibeonites came to Joshua and the "men of Israel." The Hebrew here uses the singular noun ("man of Israel"), but David Howard (1998, 224) explains that this term is frequently a collective term and suggests that to be the case here, which is evident from the use of the plural in 9:14 to refer to the same group. Still, when the covenant between Israel and the Gibeonites was cut (9:15), it was sworn to by the "leaders of the congregation" (עֵדָה). Subsequently, when the deceit was discovered, the "sons of Israel," which seems to denote that the entire congregation was the nation as a whole, disputed with the leaders; but they do accept the situation (9:18–21).

In either case, the point is that the error is unintentional and it "escapes the attention of" (literally, "is hidden from the eyes of") the entire community, but it is still a violation. The net result is a broken relationship between the community as a whole and God, and they "become guilty" or "suffer the consequences of guilt."

TRANSLATION ANALYSIS: "HIDDEN"
The phrase used here is יִשְׁגּוּ וְנֶעְלַם. The first verb שָׁגָה essentially means the same as שָׁגַג (see translation analysis on Lev. 4:3). It is joined with the verb עָלַם, which means "to be hidden, concealed or secret" (Harris 1980e, 671). This might suggest an attempted cover-up. However, since עָלַם is used in the *niphal* stem as a passive, and the two are coupled, it would seem to indicate rather that the act was done in ignorance.

TRANSLATION ANALYSIS: "GUILTY"
The verb אָשֵׁם can be translated "to be desolate, be guilty, to offend, to acknowledge offense, to trespass," although the primary meaning centers on guilt (Livingston 1980a, 180). Milgrom (1991, 243) proposes that this is a stative form of the verb, which would denote a feeling of guilt. Kiuchi (2007, 95) suggests a concept of realizing guilt, while Levine (1989, 22) prefers "and thereby incur guilt." James Greenberg (2019, 25) chooses "they are compelled by guilt." As the entire congregation, it seems likely that this addresses a corporate awareness of actual guilt.

The text leaves open how the act that precipitates the guilt became known. Sklar argues that the word suggests that the guilty person "suffers guilt's consequences," which would suggest adverse circumstances. He cites the example of David in 1 Samuel 21:1 (2014, 113). Kiuchi (2003, 95) proposes that it might accompany either physical or spiritual suffering. Mathews (2009, 46–47) suggests awareness might come about as a result of reading "the book of the law" as in the case of Josiah. Whether they sense the relationship is broken, or events indicate it, the community perceives a sense of guilt. In any event, the result is that corporately "they are prompted either to think back over what they have done wrong or to seek the Lord directly" (Sklar 2014, 13). Once the community has become aware of the transgression, the requirement then is that the community would corporately offer a bull as a purification offering.

> ### David and the Gibeonites
>
> In 1 Samuel 21, we read that the nation suffered a famine for three years, and David inquired of God and received the answer that it was because Saul had put the Gibeonites to death. On the one hand this seems to be a good illustration, in that a leader (Saul) had made a decision that the nation had concurred in. However, there are two problems with using this as a model today. First, David was able to ask the Lord directly (although one wonders why he waited three years) and got a clear answer that would not have been intuitive, since the issue was an act of the previous administration. Second, Job also asked of God but did not get an answer, and actually had done nothing for which to feel guilt. Although Job was not part of the nation of Israel, we do see here the very real possibility of false guilt in the face of adverse circumstances in a fallen world.

The offering process was generally the same as the purification offering for the anointed priest. However, in this case, the "assembly" brought the offering to the Tent of Meeting and they were led by elders. The elders, representing the community, then laid their hands on the head of the bull, which was then sacrificed. The priest then processed the blood in the same manner as the previous sacrifice, sprinkling it seven times in front of the veil, then placing some of the blood on the horns of the burnt offering altar, and finally pouring out the remainder of the blood at the base of the same altar.

The fat was then removed and burned on the altar, as was done in the case of the purification offering for the priest. At this point the text declares, "So the priest shall make atonement" for the community, and the community will be forgiven, a statement that was not made in the case of the anointed priest. The conjunction starting this statement is once again the versatile *waw*, but it seems likely that the NIV catches the proper nuance when it translates this phrase as "In this the priest will make atonement." Afterward, the remainder of the bull was disposed of in the clean space outside of the camp, as was the case of the bull offered for the purification offering of the priest.

> ### Atonement
>
> In the section "Atonement" in the introduction we do a detailed analysis of the Hebrew term *kipper* (כִּפֶּר). There we concluded that a sacrifice under the Torah was to be a visible or physical symbol of a spiritual act for a person who already had a covenant relationship with God. It would appear that while the priest could pronounce forgiveness to the congregation, he was not allowed to pronounce that for himself, but would have to trust that his act demonstrated the actuality.

4:22–26. The third section involves personal inadvertent sin on the part of a community leader. One point that is easily overlooked is the subtle change of the conjunction. Throughout this unit, typically a case is presented with the word "if" (אִם), but in the case of a leader the term is "when" (אֲשֶׁר). Milgrom (1991, 246) suggests that it signifies a difference in the way the priest handled the sacrifice. In the first two cases of purification offerings, the blood was sprinkled inside the tent and the meat was all burned. Beginning with this case, the blood was put on the horns of the burnt offering altar, and the meat was consumed by the priests (see 6:26 [HB 6:22]). Although many commentators seem to view the two terms as interchangeable, the use of "when" could be understood to suggest that it was expected that leaders would make errors.

In this situation, the person bringing the purification offering was a "leader" (נָשִׂיא) of the community—a term that seems deliberately ambiguous.

> ### TRANSLATION ANALYSIS: "LEADER"
> The term נָשִׂיא could reflect a wide range of non-priest leaders in the community. Often it reflects the "head of the families," and perhaps clans (Josh. 22:21; see also Num. 3:24). In Numbers 16, during the rebellion of Korah, 250 "leaders" are presented as being part of the rebellion, which is only a portion of the overall number. At the other end of the scale, the term is applied to Solomon as the single leader (1 Kings 11:34).

As in the case of the first two sections, this leader inadvertently violated one of the directions that God had given to the nation of things that they were not to do. When the fact that the act was a violation became known (the text does not explain how that might be), the leader was then to bring a purification offering, but in this case, it was to be a male goat. The procedures given are similar to those described previously, although the blood is not sprinkled in front of the veil, and the priest daubs some of the blood on the horns of the burnt offering altar instead of the incense altar. Again, the remaining blood is poured out at the base of the burnt offering altar, but then the appropriate portions are burned as in the case of the shalom offering; and as will be shown later (Lev. 6:26), a portion will be eaten by the priest.

4:27–35. The last section covers the case of a "common person," literally, "a person, one of the people of the land," an individual who is not an anointed priest or a leader. The situation is the same. The person had violated one of God's directives inadvertently. The violation became known. In this case, the person was to bring either a female goat or a female lamb without defect. It is not clear why a female would be specified, although Harrison (1980, 67) suggests that this would be within the means of an average family. In either case, the procedure was the same as followed in the case of a leader, although a slightly different outcome is noted between the two. In the case of the goat, the result is described as a "soothing aroma" (רֵיחַ נִיחֹחַ) to the Lord (4:31)—the first time that phrase appears in the purification offerings. In contrast, in the case of the sheep, the result is viewed as an "offering by fire" or "offered up in smoke" (אִשֶּׁה) in 4:35. Both terms are used to reflect the result of the three worship sacrifices in Leviticus 1–3. In general, their use here is overlooked by commentators. Kiuchi (2007, 98) is probably correct that their presence in the preceding offerings is "self-evident," although his contention that the explicit mention suggests that this is a "less serious nature than the preceding ones" does not seem to follow. More likely their mention would be an affirmation that God offers grace and acceptance to even the least of the people. Both variations of the purification offering for the common person end with a declaration similar to that given to the leader; that is, this process provides atonement and the person is forgiven.

5:1–13. The last portion of this section lists four different situations that would impede the relationship between the person and God, thus requiring purification, but that do not seem to involve sin, at least of the type listed so far. Kellogg (1978, 135) suggests that this list really should be taken as illustrative since "an exhaustive list would be impossible." The situations listed are generally viewed as an appendix to Leviticus 4 (Balentine 2002, 45; Hartley 1992, 54; Milgrom 1991, 309–10), although Ross (2002, 138–39) argues that it is a new topic, seeing several key distinctions. The most obvious distinction is that the categories listed in Leviticus 4 are based on the socioreligious status of the person who has committed the transgression and is bringing the sacrifice, while in 5:1–13 the sacrifice varies (or is graduated) according to the offender's economic means (Milgrom 1991, 307). A second distinction is the terminology:

Purifying Oneself Before a Holy God (4:1–6:7 [HB 5:26])

Leviticus 4 stresses the inadvertent nature of the sins, while the term "inadvertent" or "unintentional" is not used in 5:1–13 (it is used in the last part of the chapter). Rather, the issue is "guilt" (אָשֵׁם), which requires confession. Further, while the situations in Leviticus 4 require a purification offering, the offerings in this section are more difficult in that they are characterized not only as reparation offerings (אָשָׁם or אַשְׁמָה, often translated as "guilt offering"), but also as purification offerings (חַטָּאת). Specifically, 5:6, which summarizes all four situations, states, "He shall also bring his reparation offering [אֲשָׁמוֹ] . . . as a purification offering [לְחַטָּאת]."

The first situation is a failure to testify as a witness. To be clear, this is not viewed as a case of giving false witness (contra Kiuchi 2007, 99). Rather, it seems to be a situation where the witness has not come forward to relate what he or she knows. John Kleinig (2003, 119) reminds that this was a culture that had no police force. As such, voluntary testimony was crucial to provide justice. In a close-knit society, this might run into the temptation to cover up for relatives or get back at enemies by not reporting something one had observed or had other knowledge of. However, even this does not seem to be the problem. Rather, it is a refusal to speak when given a "public adjuration" (אָלָה) to speak up, usually understood in terms of a legal case. This adjuration really "pronounced a curse over anyone who failed to uphold the law" (Levine 1989, 26). The case of Micah the Ephraimite in Judges 17, who admitted his guilt after his mother "uttered a curse" (אָלָה), is viewed by some as an example, as is the case of Jesus before the high priest in Matthew 26:63 who stated "I adjure you by the living God" (Harrison 1980, 69).

The second and third situations are where a person has touched "any unclean thing." This could be the carcass of different categories of unclean animals (5:2), or human uncleanness (see the section in the introduction on "Clean and Unclean"). This concept of ritual impurity was not necessarily a result of sin, and often was really a result of something to celebrate, such as a woman giving birth to a child.

The final situation in this section involves a "thoughtless" oath. According to Milgrom, in Israel there were two types of oath. The first type was assertatory, where the person swore that he or she was innocent of a charge (see Exod. 22:10–11). The second type was promissory, where the person placed an obligation upon him- or herself (see Num. 30:14). This would seem to be an oath that is expressed verbally ("with his lips") rather than a mere thought (Harrison 1980, 69).

The phrase "to do evil or to do good" is a merism, a figure of speech that indicates totality, which is emphasized by the phrase "in whatever manner." The key is that the person "swore" or "made an oath" (שָׁבַע), which carries the connotation "to bind oneself by an oath" (*TWOT* s.v. "שָׁבַע" 2:900). While an oath might not always have been made in the name of God, it often was, and some propose that the Lord's name was implicitly invoked. As such, not keeping an oath "profaned the Lord's name (Lev. 19:12), since it was tantamount to saying that the Lord was unable to judge effectively" (Sklar 2014, 116). The supposition seems to be that since the oath was made rashly—in the heat of battle, so to speak—subsequently it might be forgotten, or perhaps the person might try to rationalize it away (see Eccl. 5:1–5).

Whatever the specific situation, the obligation was that the person who had committed one of these errors first needed to confess it. How the confession was made is not clear. The *hithpael* form suggests that it must be verbal, although whether it must be done prior to beginning the sacrificial process (Gane 2004a, 124–25) or to the priest during the sacrifice is not clear (Kleinig 2003, 120).

In addition, the person must bring a reparation offering (אָשָׁם) as a purification offering. The sacrifice is specified as a female lamb or goat. However, if the person could not afford a lamb or kid, two turtledoves or young pigeons would suffice. If the person could not afford that, he or she would bring one tenth of an ephah of fine flour.

TRANSLATION ANALYSIS: "REPARATION" AS PURIFICATION OFFERING

In this case, the offering that is brought is an אָשָׁם, which we have translated as a "reparation offering." But here it is offered for purification (חִטֵּאת). To amplify our previous translation analysis, both the noun אָשָׁם and the verb אָשֵׁם are rather broad in their use. According to Livingston, "The primary meaning of the word אָשָׁם seems to center on guilt, but moves from the act which brings guilt to the condition of guilt to the act of punishment. In any particular passage it is often difficult to determine which thrust the word has" (1980a, 78). To complicate matters, its etymology is uncertain, with a cognate appearing only in Arabic, and perhaps in Ugaritic. Diether Kellerman (1974, 429–32) suggests that there is such a close relationship between אָשָׁם and חִטֵּאת that by the time of Philo and Josephus the distinction was no longer clear. In the context of this part of Leviticus, the term refers to the punishment, which is a sacrifice required in the case of מַעַל, which Hamilton (1980c, 775) translates as "to transgress, commit a trespass, act unfaithfully." Milgrom (1991, 320) notes that this term is never defined in the Bible, but traditionally was understood as sacrilege. While that fits the situation in Leviticus 5, the use in Leviticus 6 also suggests acts of fraud. Sklar seems to bring these two together when he states that it addresses sin "which betrays covenant loyalty" (2014, 119). In this section, the verb is regularly used with the noun as a cognate accusative (וּמָעֲלָה מַעַל), a combination that is also characterized as a "sin" (חָטָא).

If the offeror brought a sheep or goat, the process would follow that for a sheep or goat purification offering seen in Leviticus 4 above. It would make atonement for his sin (חִטֵּאת). If instead he or she brought two turtledoves or pigeons, one of the birds would serve as a purification offering. The steps for this portion are similar to those seen in the burnt offering (Lev. 1:14–17), although it appears that some of the blood was sprinkled on the side of the altar (not the horns), before the rest was drained at the base. Since it is called a purification offering, the remains of the bird were likely disposed of outside of the camp, as in the case of any other purification offering. The second bird would be offered as a burnt offering, in the same manner seen in Leviticus 1:14–17.

If the person brought flour as the purification offering, then the process followed that of the gift (grain) offering (Lev. 2). The priest would take a handful of the flour (without oil or incense) and burn it on the altar as a purification offering, and the person was forgiven. As was the case of the gift offering, what remained would go to the priest, like a sin offering.

The Lord Tells Israel How to Bring an Offering of Reparation (5:14–6:7 [HB 5:26])

The text now turns to situations that involve material damages. These required restitution prior to a sacrifice.

5:14–6:7 (HB 5:26). Leviticus 5:14 interrupts the text with another transition statement: "Then the Lord [YHWH] spoke to Moses." This begins a section on the second type of offering, the reparation offering, which addresses a different sin issue. Content-wise, the reparation material runs to Leviticus 6:7 in the English, but the Hebrew places it all in Leviticus 5. The probable reason for this difference is that the Hebrew follows the subject matter, but the English chapter 6:1 follows another "Then the Lord [YHWH] spoke to Moses" declaration, which suggests a transition. What we will see is that these two segments of the reparation material differ only in the nature of the "trespass" or "unfaithful act" (מַעַל) that requires the offering, specifically in terms of the person hurt by the unfaithful act—that is, whether it is the Lord or one of the Lord's people. In either case, reparation is required before the reparation offering can be performed.

While the declaration that the Lord spoke to Moses (5:14) introduces a new category of confessional (or expiatory) offerings, this time there is no direction for Moses to speak to the nation, suggesting that this is really a continuation of the previous speech introduced by 4:1. The same declaration shows up again in 6:1 (HB 5:20), but in this case it denotes a separate portion of the same category. There is commonality in terms of the nature of the act for both portions, and the offering is the same—in both cases it is called a reparation offering (אָשָׁם). The difference between the two is in the nature of the damages. The first addresses an act against "the Lord's [YHWH's] holy things," and the second involves false declarations to the Lord's people (which are also viewed as unfaithful acts against God). Because the resolution in both cases is very similar, we will first address what was done wrong in each case, and then look at the resolution.

The first issue begins when a person acts unfaithfully (מָעֲלָה מַעַל), and unintentionally sins "against the Lord's [YHWH's] holy things." Since the concept of acting unfaithfully suggests a relationship that would expect faithfulness, Willis (2009, 51) suggests that "infidelity" or "breach of contract" is closer to the meaning. Again, we are looking at inadvertent sin or violation of God's directives. The key question is what is meant by "the Lord's [YHWH's] holy things." Levine (1989, 30) argues that the legal terms suggest actual loss of property, specifically sanctuary property, not priestly allocations or tithes. In contrast, John Peter Lange (1960, 51) defines this as "the first fruits, the tithes, or gifts of any kind connected with the service of the sanctuary or the support of its priests, by

the withholding of which the Lord is said to suffer loss." Sklar (2104, 120) agrees with this, noting that "the word *qodāšîm* refers elsewhere to various food items that had been given to the Lord and were therefore *holy* (see at 22:2)." Milgrom (1991, 322) essentially agrees with this assessment, although he cites the rabbis who take it as "embracing all sancta, offerable and nonofferable alike." It would seem that this is a broader term that includes all of the above.

The second issue is similar except that the person acts unfaithfully "against the Lord [YHWH]" through an act against "his companion," that is, any fellow Israelite. These unfaithful acts could include misappropriation of money or property entrusted to him or her, theft, extortion, or lying about a found item. This could be done through "crafty deception" (Bailey 2005, 78). A false oath in this situation would involve responding to an accusation by falsely swearing one's innocence similarly to the "thoughtless oath" noted in the previous section (Kleinig 2003, 128; Sklar 2014, 123).

In either case, when the individual who has committed this act realizes what he has done, there are several steps to follow, although the text as we understand it today does not seem completely clear. The most straightforward explanation is as follows. The one who committed the transgression brings a ram without defect (אַיִל תָּמִים), which is the reparation offering. Apparently, the ram is an arbitrary physical representation for a nonphysical loss. If the violation involves material goods that had monetary values, the person must restore whatever had been wrongfully procured, as well as including a penalty of 20 percent (i.e., make reparations, hence the name of the offering; Hartley 1992, 81). One of the difficulties in understanding this section is that as presented in the text, these directives were given prior to the development of a monetary system.

Shekel

It is generally accepted that coins were developed in Sardis, the capital of the kingdom of Lydia shortly before 600 B.C. The Izmir Museum in Turkey suggests that the earliest coins were early Lydian gold and silver, as shown in figure 24.

Figure 24. Gold and electrum coins from Lydia in the Izmir Museum, seventh century B.C.

Figure 25. Scale for precious metals (used for buying and selling), Ephesus Museum.

These, like all coins prior to the middle of the twentieth century, contained a certain weight of precious metal (gold, electrum, silver, or bronze). After forming, they were stamped on both sides with an inscription and image. Early on, coins were minted by a city. The main side (called obverse) usually received the image of some symbol of the city, such as its main god or a political leader. Prior to this, trade was done through barter or through the medium of precious metal, usually gold or silver. This was done through a set of balance scales (fig. 25), with weights to weigh out the amount of silver or gold exchanged.

Archaeology has discovered a number of stone weights. According to the website Jewish Virtual Library, as of 2020 only three weights clearly marked "shekel" (or a portion of a shekel) have been found, and

Figure 26. Official weights, Israel Museum.

they vary from 9.56 to 10.52 grams, which shows some uncertainty (https://www.jewish-virtuallibrary.org/weights-measures-and-coins-of-the-biblical-and-talmudic-periods). In 2018, a weight marked *beka* (a half shekel) was found, which would equate to a shekel of 11.33 grams (https://www.timesofisrael.com/straight-from-the-bible-tiny-first-temple-stone-weight-un-earthed-in-jerusalem). According to Exodus 38:26, the *beka* was "half a shekel according to the shekel of the sanctuary," which was the contribution required during the census (see Exod. 30:13, 15). Other archeological evidence suggests that a shekel might be between 11 and 13 grams (Wells 2009, 258). Figure 26 shows a series of weights found at Lachish described as ranging from 2 *gerahs* to 400 shekels.

Figure 27. Silver hoard, seventh century B.C., Israel Museum.

The precious metal (usually silver) was kept in a purse and weighed out as necessary. Today, when archaeologists find such a collection, it is usually in a ceramic container, often buried, and is called a *hoard*. Hoards also often contain other valuables such as semiprecious stones or faience as shown in figure 27, which was found at Ekron.

Very early in Israel, as part of its ANE culture, the standard weight used for commerce was a shekel, as seen in Abraham's purchase of the field of Machpelah in Genesis 23, although as noted, the actual weight of a shekel varied not only within a culture, but from culture to culture. While Abraham's purchase was conducted according to the commercial standard (Gen. 23:16), the standard in Leviticus was the shekel of the sanctuary, which was considered a "heavy" shekel (Hartley 1992, 81).

Consequently, a question that arises here is regarding the relationship between the ram and its valuation in silver (Lev. 5:15). One view maintains that this allows for providing an alternative amount of silver in place of the actual ram in terms of compensation (Harrison 1980, 71; Wenham 1979, 107). A second view is that there was a minimum required value for the ram, which, however, is not given. Because the term is plural, it was assumed by the rabbis as two shekels, although it may have varied from time to time (Hartley 1992, 81). Another view is that there was a financial penalty instead of sacrifice, which amounted to the value of the ram, plus the value of what had been misappropriated with the addition of one fifth of its value (Kleinig 2003, 126). Since there is no figure given for the valuation, it is probable that the intention is that the phrase "according to your valuation" is an idiomatic expression conveying that the ram is to be valuable in the person's eyes.

TRANSLATION ANALYSIS: "VALUATION"
The term translated "according to your valuation" (בְּעֶרְכְּךָ) consists of the noun עֵרֶךְ meaning "value" with the preposition בְּ and the

second-person masculine singular pronoun. Péter-Contesse and Ellington (1992, 72) suggest that this phrase had become an expression that simply conveyed the idea of "value." As such, the בְּ and ךָ could be omitted in translation, suggesting that the ram was to be a valuable one.

This would be in accord with the earlier guidelines on restitution given in Exodus 22 where the loss does not result from fraud but from carelessness, and the evaluation is that "he shall make restitution from the best of his own field and the best of his own vineyard" (Exod. 22:5). As such, the combination of requiring a sacrifice of high value, restitution of what was taken in the process of fraud, and adding 20 percent to the restitution would indicate that this was viewed as a serious offense.

Restitution and Reparation

The idea of restitution is an important aspect of the Hebrew concept of jurisprudence. As we will see in the last portion of the book, several factors weigh in on this concept, mostly aspects of the socioeconomic system. Once the nation settled in the land, most of the Israelites would live in communities where all of the houses were clustered in the center of an agricultural area where "everybody knew everybody" (Harbin 2021a, 476–85). In this situation, restitution would be important to help restore relationships within the community. The additional requirement of a penalty would also serve to discourage the improper behavior (although given fallen human nature, not eliminate it). Further, the restitution seemed to be graduated. In this case, which seems to reflect relatively small amounts, the amount to be returned was 120 percent. The earlier guidelines in Exodus 22 required a much greater reparation. If the animal was still alive, it must be returned with a second animal of the same kind (200 percent). However, if the animal had been slaughtered or sold, the mandated reparation was 400 percent in the case of a sheep, and 500 percent in the case of an ox. Given a basically subsistence lifestyle, a sheep or an ox would have been a much greater loss. The idea seems to be that the purpose was primarily deterrence rather than retribution, and thus the larger animal would merit a more significant deterrence.

Later we will see that this act of restitution needed to be done before the ram was sacrificed. Here, there are no guidelines given regarding the process (Hartley 1992, 75). However, we will see in Leviticus 7 that the guidelines are given for the priest and that the procedures are the same as for the purification offering. And the conclusion in both cases is that "the priests shall make atonement for him" and he will be forgiven.

THEOLOGICAL FOCUS

In our first unit (Lev. 1–3), we noted the clear key theological point that God is the initiator of worship. Here, the point is that God desires to cleanse the conscience of the worshipper so that true worship may continue.

God's holy, all-powerful, enduring presence within the Tent of Meeting continues to be very intimidating. He is perfect. He resides at the center of the gathered community. From there, he calls his people to reflect his perfection. Failure is inevitable, yet hope remains strong. Amid their repeated failures, the Lord God's personal invitation to come before him does not end with their shortcomings and sin. The worshippers are asked to trust God, not themselves, in thought, word, and deed. They are to hear and receive his correction so that their heads, hearts, and hands may be cleansed of wrongdoing and redirected toward him.

PREACHING AND TEACHING STRATEGIES

Exegetical and Theological Synthesis
Keep in mind that it will initially seem astonishing to most twenty-first-century minds that unintentional sins and inadvertent actions would call for such drastic measures. Isn't God

being a bit extreme? Isn't he too severe? Hasn't he set the bar too high? As fallen creatures, every generation finds a new way to place ourselves—our thoughts, plans, pursuits, and so on—at the center of our world. The center is reserved for God alone. For that reason, he is in the business of faithfully turning us away from our incessant temptation toward the destructive realities of self-worship. Because by nature we default to pursuing a life where we expect God to support us in realizing our personal goals and private agendas (and, shouldn't he divinely introduce other people into our lives that we may use them in that pursuit as well?), he must repeatedly call us back to him to purify our hearts and reestablish our priorities.

In this text, God is directing his people to prioritize him and others before themselves. They are called to actively ponder if they may be unintentionally impeding their worship of God and/or harming one created in God's image through an action or a failure to complete an action. This is a call to live the sacrificial life that demonstrates and develops one's commitment to a covenant relationship with God as well as his people. There is an expectation that worshippers of the Lord God will be willing to release their own thoughts, feelings, and actions when the Spirit brings an offense to mind. Brokenness is to be expressed through humble confession. Material goods are to be sacrificed to transform the mind and cultivate the heart. This is how worshippers nurture authentic relationship, both vertical and horizontal relationships!

Preaching Idea
Correction, confession, and repentance before a holy God are transformational components of authentic worship.

Contemporary Connections

What does it mean?
God is telling his people through his servant Moses that he will provide the means to preserve authentic worship. For this reason, hope remains viable. Whether it is a corporate or individual failure, when his people stumble and fall, when they (inadvertently) become overly consumed in themselves and go astray, when their priorities demand a divine reset, God will not abandon them to themselves. Nor will he become permanently inaccessible as a result of their ignorance or pride. For the humble spirit, there is a path back to the Lord God that corrects the mind, reprioritizes the heart, and frees the hands from clinging to the material over the relational components of life in this me-first world. He will protect them by bringing their fault to mind, that they may hear, receive, and confess their sin, and turn from their ways to sacrificially pursue God's ways. In short, they will not be forever marked by their sin. They will be marked by his purification of them from their sin. This is what makes them his own.

Is it true?
Is it true that God requires purification (correction, confession, and repentance) to preserve his people for authentic worship? We see this repeatedly throughout the Scriptures as God preserves Adam and Eve, Abraham, the Israelites, and David, among others. The pattern is that his people sin. He first brings the sin to mind, then offers correction and calls for confession and repentance. This may be direct as in the case of Adam and Eve or Abraham, or indirectly through a prophet like Nathan to David.

In Matthew 5:23–24, Jesus stresses the necessity of a pure heart in true worship: "If you are offering your gift at the altar and there remember that your brother has something against you, leave your gift there before the altar and go. First, be reconciled to your brother, then come offer your gift" (ESV). Reconciliation to God and others precedes authentic worship. To come with anger, bitterness, or defiance in one's heart is to enter into false worship.

If God did not preserve worship, where would we find hope? Believers would be left bound to a life of pride and folly, battling with one another over whose idea is best. Yet the Spirit of God is positioning us to transform our minds, hearts, and hands. No matter how far we may stray, we cannot go beyond his voice or venture outside his reach. Hope remains alive and well because God is intentional! It is not the will of the straying sinner but the mercy of our faithful God that preserves authentic worship!

Now what?

Using words to express our love of God and others is important. Our words may be true, yet at times words can be cheap when not supported by action. This passage directs the worshippers to real (material?) sacrifice as evidence of repentance.

When God calls us to deny our thoughts to embrace his words, will we respond outwardly in a way that evidences inward change? When it is brought to our attention that we have inadvertently or carelessly harmed another, are we prepared to swallow our personal pride and for the sake of another (and to glorify God) seek forgiveness?

Too often we proclaim that a lack of intent to harm, ignorance of circumstances, or competing interests frees us from guilt toward others. In many instances, that may be the law of the land, but it is not the way of God. God calls those who worship him to sacrificially put the interests of others before themselves. And today, we can see that he is not calling us to do more than he has done through the atoning death of Christ.

Creativity in Presentation

How to structure

This unit addresses both purification (sin) offerings and the reparation (guilt) offerings. By combining them in a single message, it may not be necessary to invest time differentiating between the two. Instead, devote your time to fully developing the idea that one is guilty before God or

another, though they may be unaware of their fault. For many, this will be a novel, possibly even offensive, thought. Emphasize the repeated phrases, "once one realizes their guilt" or "the sin is made known to them, they shall . . ." The focus is not on justifying one's actions. Instead of dismissing, overlooking, minimizing, or even overruling what the Lord God brings to one's mind either directly or through the thoughts of others, the true worshipper is called to be willing to change direction and move toward repentance.

Once again, God provides Leviticus 4–6 as an opportunity to set the minds of your congregation on a new track. We live in a world where we are encouraged to put ourselves first—even before God! Many are expecting God to come to them on their terms. Though sin against others may be considered wrong, in the minds of most it is believed to be justifiable and only becomes a barrier to worship in the most heinous of cases. How is God at work through the theme of this passage, redirecting the focal point of our desires back outward and upward after they begin to bend inward?

Visual and oral creativity

How can everyone feel a measure of the selfless, other-centered sacrifice to which God is calling his people? Today, in our society, many regularly enter a variety of "covenant relationships." Many workers sign a noncompete covenant as a part of an employment contract, which in effect places the objectives of the business above the pursuits of the employee. New homeowners are commonly bound by a neighborhood covenant, which places the purposes of the entire neighborhood above the interests of the individual homeowner. In a Christian marriage, both husband and wife take vows that join them in a covenantal relationship, placing the honor of God and the needs of one another above their own personal interests.

In each example, we are free to graciously assume that individuals have the best intentions when they enter the agreement. What happens if one inadvertently violates the covenant? Or worse yet, what if they determine that it is in their best interest to break the covenant? One's commitment to a covenant relationship becomes apparent when personal sacrifice is called for. Will we forsake our own interest to protect the interest of another? If a new job offer arises that will double our salary yet violate the noncompete agreement, will we abide by our word or seek to circumvent the covenant? If we determine that contentment is not possible without the construction of a new privacy fence that is in violation of the neighborhood covenant, will we follow our heart or sacrifice our desire for others? If our eye wanders and feelings grow for someone other than our spouse, will we follow our feelings or deny them to honor our promise to cleave to our spouse?

Authentic worship is worship that is being purified of our selfishness so that it may be fully directed toward God alone. God provides regular opportunities in each of our lives that we may sacrifice our interests for the sake of another. It may be immediately apparent. He may bring it to our attention later through his Word or through a friend. Either way, it will reveal to us if our commitment to deny ourselves to become more like Christ is active or if it is in need of refreshment and renewal.

These two chapters can be preached as one unit or, as I chose to do, in two distinct messages:

Correction, confession, and repentance before a holy God are transformational components of authentic worship.

- The uniqueness of this specific offering (sin, guilt)
  - The personal sacrifice required of the one who brings it
  - The unique details of this specific sacrifice

- The focus of this offering
  - What this offering reveals about how one comes before a holy God
  - How this offering specifically prepares us for the sacrifice of Christ
- What did it mean then? What does it mean always? What do we do now?
  - Then: What did it mean to the people in Sinai and the Promised Land?
  - Always: What does it reveal to us about the nature of God and man?
  - Now: How should it inform our worship today?

DISCUSSION QUESTIONS

1. How might the concept of sin discussed in this unit affect the way one might approach applying this material? For example, how might it affect the idea of "victimless crimes"?

2. What is the significance of the idea of corporate sin? Is it applicable to modern culture? If not, why not? Is so, how might that issue be approached today?

3. How might the realization that a sin against one's neighbor is ultimately a sin against God affect one's behavior?

4. How might the concept of restitution promote healing within the community?

Leviticus 6:8 (HB 6:1)–7:38

EXEGETICAL IDEA
A life of worship should include both planned and spontaneous events.

THEOLOGICAL FOCUS
The worship of God demonstrates for the worshipper and the community a life that is at peace with who God is and what God is doing.

PREACHING IDEA
Being at peace with God is evident through a worship-filled life.

PREACHING POINTERS
The Israelites were recovering from years of captivity under harsh taskmasters who drove them to fulfill the vain will of a ruthless pharaoh. Under the covenant with the Lord God, the people began to discover that they had not been redeemed from their bondage only to be released into a Promised Land where each clan would fend for themselves and find their own way. Rather, their Redeemer would be their new king as they lived together in community before the priests. They were invited to acknowledge their peace with his permanent lordship over them by bringing specific offerings. This called for more than mindlessly making an extra helping or trimming a crust to send up to the tabernacle. Rather, they were instructed how to confess a critical reality openly yet humbly—that they were dependent on the Lord and his community. Were they "at peace" with their God? His intermediary? His people? The call to bring offerings of peace before the priest was not intended to feed the vanity of their master. It was to arrest the vanity and wayward independence of their own hearts.

Believers are set apart in Christ. We are redeemed from self-worship to the worship of the Lord God. The realities of daily life can distract us, allowing our focus to turn away from the purposes of God and center on our own personal agenda. Left to ourselves, such distraction can escalate into dissatisfaction. The result is that we are no longer at peace with our God, his intermediary, or his people. What will keep our heart loyal to our Redeemer? Hearing and proclaiming openly who God is and how he is actively at work has the power to redirect our gaze fully onto our God.

What is the role of public testimony in your church today? Is it present? Has it been relegated to "how God saved me"? This section reminds Israel that their redemption was only the beginning of the story. It will be his ongoing work in their lives that he is calling them to share with the community. This message encourages us to publicly honor God by proclaiming how we see him at work and how we are finding peace with that work!

THE ROLE OF THE PRIESTS (6:8 [HB 6:1]–7:38)

LITERARY STRUCTURE AND THEMES (6:8 [HB 6:1]–7:38)

Again, this unit contains more than a single chapter, but the structure is more complex than the previous two units. First, the Hebrew text includes the first seven verses of the English chapter 6 with its chapter 5. So, while our present unit in the English begins at 6:8 and includes chapter 7, in the Hebrew the present unit is Leviticus 6 and 7. Further, the material included in this unit contains five speeches from the Lord. The first three are directed to Aaron and his sons (6:8–18 [HB 6:1–11]; 6:19–6:23 [HB 6:12–16]; and 6:24 [HB 6:17]–7:21), the last two are directed to the entire nation (7:22–27 and 28–38). Even so, we view this as one unit because the focus of the five speeches collectively changes from how the people are to worship spontaneously and individually through offering various sacrifices to the role that the priests will play in guiding corporate worship. As such, although there is some repetition in terms of subject matter, it is written from a different perspective, providing amplifying details for the priestly function. Given the continued sequences of the declaration "then the Lord [YHWH] spoke to Moses," it seems that the entire unit continues the declaration that God gave on the day that the tabernacle had been completed as he gave the Israelites guidelines on how the tabernacle was to be used.

TRANSLATION ANALYSIS: "THEN THE LORD [YHWH] SPOKE"
"Then the Lord [YHWH] spoke to Moses" begins with the all-purpose conjunction *waw*. As used here, it serves to characterize the material as historical narrative, that is, relating the material from an historical perspective. While the KJV tends to translate the *waw* conjunction generally as "and," in a situation like this that seems to have a strong chronological sequence, "then" is preferable.

Building on the previous material that was for the entire nation, God now clarifies the responsibilities of "Aaron and his sons," the family that had already been designated to assume the responsibility of serving as priests for the developing nation (Exod. 28:1). Specifically, it conveys instructions for their role in making the tabernacle a focal point for the nation's worship of God. Consequently, although the last two speeches in this section are directed to the entire nation, as we will see, their purpose is to explain to the people the significant role that the priests would play in the shalom offerings.

- ***The Lord Gives Guidelines for the Priests and Corporate Offerings (6:8–23 [HB 6:10–16])***
- ***The Lord Gives Directions to the Priests for Purification and Reparation Offerings (6:24 [HB 6:17]–7:10)***
- ***The Lord Gives Directions to the Priests for Shalom Offerings (7:11–36)***
- ***The Lord Concludes the Teaching on the Giving of Sacrifices (7:37–38)***

EXPOSITION (6:8 [HB 6:1]–7:38)

The first unit of the book explained how the people were to present personal burnt offerings, gift offerings, and shalom offerings. The next, "Purifying Oneself Before a Holy God," followed up with purification offerings and reparation offerings (which we collectively labeled *confessional offerings*). All of those were generally personal offerings, although there is recognition that the people as a whole might need purification. This third section takes more of a corporate approach. It begins with an overview of the key responsibility the priests carried with respect to maintaining the national perpetual fire atop the burnt offering altar. An explanation of how the priest was to handle the gift offerings of the people follows, showing how the gift offerings that the priests were responsible to give on behalf of the nation differed from personal gift offerings.

However, at this point the sequence of offerings deviates from that of the first two major sections, as the text explains how the priests were to administer the two confessional offerings. This may be because portions of both offerings provided the bulk of the priests' personal livelihoods. Finally, although not set apart as a separate speech, the text picks up the shalom offerings, which are personal offerings that have a corporate perspective. At this point three types of shalom offerings are distinguished: offerings of thanksgiving, offerings upon completion of a vow to God, and free-will offerings. These three have in common that while an individual makes the sacrifice, the community participates as an audience. In the process, the offeror explains to the community why God is being honored in this way, and after a portion of the animal is burned and a portion is given to the priest for his services, the remainder is cooked and eaten by the participating community as a communal celebration. The last two speeches wrap up several details with regard to the priestly role. The last two verses of this section really sum up the first seven chapters of the book and indicate that the speeches to this point were given on the same day, and set the stage for the next unit, which is the actual consecration of the priesthood.

The Lord Gives Guidelines for the Priests and Corporate Offerings (6:8–23 [HB 6:10–16])

Following the expiatory offering guidelines for the people, God delivers information for Moses to convey to his brother Aaron, who had been previously designated to become the first priest of the nation. This message is both a command (the verb צָוָה in the imperative) and instruction (תּוֹרָה a noun translated "law" but more appropriately denoting instruction or directions).

First Priest of the Nation

The exodus event marks a significant transition in what is sometimes called salvation history: the process through which God worked in history to reconcile sinful humankind to himself, culminating in the crucifixion-resurrection-ascension event but eventually consummating in the return of Christ and the new heavens and earth (see the section "Holy Days and Salvation History" in the introduction). Following the fall, worship seemed to be an individual or family process from the fall through the flood and then up to Abraham. Beginning with Abraham up to the exodus event, God worked through the promise, the blessing, and the covenant given to Abraham and his lineage. Initially this covenant passed by blessing to one heir in each generation. Subsequent to Jacob the blessing incorporated all descendants of Jacob's twelve sons (Harbin 2005, 114–15). During the centuries in Egypt, this people group grew until it was brought to Sinai, where it was formed into a rudimentary nation, which is the process we see in Leviticus. Key to the new organization was the first formal system of corporate worship God provided humankind. Prior to Moses, worship seems very impromptu and was apparently handled by individual families with each patriarch supervising his own clan. At Sinai, God formalized worship into a corporate system centered on a covenant community, although it included provisions for impromptu and personal worship. This new system would require priests to guide the people and serve as their representatives.

It seems ironic that the group chosen to serve in that priestly role was descended from one of Jacob's sons whose personal blessing was somewhat tenuous. When Jacob blessed his sons, two of the brothers, Simeon and Levi, were told that their future within the nation was that their descendants would be dispersed and scattered (Gen. 49:7). Yet God in his mercy seems to have turned that judgment into an actual blessing. Following the conquest, when the land was divided among the twelve tribes, Simeon ended up with a portion that was "in the midst of the inheritance of the sons of Judah" (Josh. 19:1, 9). Historically, the tribe of Simeon seems to have been absorbed by the tribe of Judah so that when the nation split, while not mentioned by name, Simeon was part of the preserved remnant. Levi, on the other hand, received the priesthood. While never absorbed, during the conquest the Levites were dispersed into forty-eight cities throughout the other tribes (Josh. 21:41), from which they were to minister to the nation as a whole (Deut. 18:1–8). A portion of that tribe then served as the nation's priesthood (Num. 18:1–7). The specific individual picked to head that new priesthood was Moses's older brother Aaron, although Aaron's four sons were selected with him, as we will see below.

6:8–13 (HB 6:1–6). The priestly instruction first expands the guidelines on how the priests were to manage the first offering cited in Leviticus—the burnt offering—by introducing a perpetual corporate rite. The burnt offering presented in Leviticus 1 was an optional offering that an individual might bring to God as an act of worship. In that case, the priest was to assist the individual for proper performance. Here, however, the priests are given the additional responsibility of performing a corporate or national burnt offering to guide national worship by daily consecrating the nation to God. Earlier, Moses and the people had been told that after the tabernacle and priesthood were established, the national burnt offering was to be a perpetual offering of consecration offered twice a day (Exod. 29:38–46). There we learn that daily the Aaronic priesthood would sacrifice two one-year-old lambs, one in the morning and the other "at twilight." Now, they are given details on how this offering was to be maintained. Specifically, the priest would be responsible for ensuring that the fire that consumed the burnt offering was to be a perpetual fire—that is, it was to burn both day and night.

TRANSLATION ANALYSIS: "TWILIGHT"
The phrase translated as "twilight" in Exodus is literally "between the evenings" (בֵּין הָעַרְבָּיִם). Properly, "twilight" translates the word *neshep* (נֶשֶׁף), which is the approximately hour-long period between sunset and total darkness (Joy 1939, 3028). Carl Friedrich Keil and Franz Delitzsch (1956, 12) note that the phrase "between the two evenings" has long been debated. While some have argued for a true sense of twilight, most expositors seem to have accepted the view that it was the time between "when the sun began to descend, viz., from 3 to 5 o'clock" and sunset. Thus, the time of the evening sacrifice would be approximately between 3 and 6 p.m.

Apparently, the reason for a perpetual fire was that the fire was ignited by the Lord himself, after the anointing and consecration of Aaron and his sons to the priesthood in Leviticus 9:24, and thus it would serve as a reminder of God's work and role (Ross 2002, 159; Milgrom 1991, 389).

Fire from the Lord

While many scholars tie the idea of perpetual fire on the burnt offering altar to this fire from the Lord, some disagree. Lange argues that the fire on the altar "had been burning several days before that fire came forth" (1960, 57). It is true that Leviticus 8 indicates that Moses offered several sacrifices during the seven days prior to the fire from the Lord cited in Leviticus 9, but we are not told how that fire was started, so one would assume it would have been through normal procedures.

However, that initial week-long series of sacrifices had the specific purpose of consecrating Aaron and his sons into their role as priests. Leviticus 9 then sets forth another series of sacrifices that Aaron offers on behalf of himself and for the people. It was these sacrifices that the fire from the Lord came out and consumed. As Milgrom expresses it, this fire inaugurated the "public cult" and that it was "*this* fire which is not allowed to die out so that all subsequent sacrifices might claim divine acceptance" (emphasis original, Milgrom 1991, 389). If that was the case, it may have a lot to say regarding the issue of the sin of Nadab and Abihu. In addition, one might note an analogy to the NT day of Pentecost with the appearance of flames of fire over the heads of the disciples (Acts 2:3).

To keep the fire burning, the priests had two responsibilities. First, the priest was to ensure that the fire burned through the night. This began with the evening sacrifice, where the fire would be fed with wood and the evening sacrifice offered on it.

Wood for the Altar

Throughout the time that the nation had the central sanctuary—first in the tabernacle, and then in the temple—a concern was that adequate wood be available to keep the fire going. During the temple period, wood was gathered and stored in a room on the south side of the Temple Mount. Normally wood was cut and brought to the temple nine times a year, generally during the month of Ab (July–August), which culminated in a feast of wood offering on the fifteenth of Ab (Hartley 1992, 97). Milgrom notes that all wood was acceptable except grapevines and olive wood. According to the Midrash this was out of respect for the fruits those plants produced that were used for libations on the altar. However, he observes that the Talmud suggests that those two did not burn well and produced too much smoke (Milgrom 1991, 387–88). The current writer (Harbin) notes that when he lived in Spain, his family heated their house with olive wood in a fireplace, and that it burned well and did not produce any smoke problems.

The fire then likely was allowed to burn down to embers, and preserved through the night following traditional methods.

Banking a Fire

A common practice when houses were heated by fireplaces was banking a fire overnight. Basically, this involved allowing the fire to burn down to coals, then piling the coals and any still-burning wood to the center. The key was to surround the burning coals with ashes and then gently cover the coals with the ashes. In the morning, the ashes would be removed. Kindling laid on the hot coals would catch fire, and soon new wood could be added to rebuild the fire. Although not addressed, apparently this method was effective even in the event of rain (Migrom 1991, 389). A similar process could be used to transport coals in ceramic pots called *fire pots* as the tabernacle moved from place to place. In that regard, some modern translations (including ESV and HCSB) and apparently older editions of the KJV use the term "fire pot" in the case of Abraham's vision in Genesis 15:7. This may have interesting implications in terms of symbolism of a yet future fulfillment of the covenants being conveyed.

In the morning, the priest was to don his linen robe and undergarments and clean the ashes off the altar, placing them beside the altar temporarily. The exact sequence is not clear, but likely at this point the priest would put fresh wood on the fire and perform the morning sacrifice.

Linen Clothes and Undergarments

Ezekiel 44:18 maintains that priests were to wear linen and not wool when serving in the temple for purity: "they shall not gird themselves with anything that makes them sweat." Similarly, according to Exodus 28:41, the requirement for "linen breeches" served to "cover their bare flesh" (a euphemism for genitals). Ross (2002, 158) expands on this, suggesting that the clothing had both functional value and symbolic meaning. He proposes that "the symbolic meaning associated with the priestly garb is that pure linen garments represented holiness as the priest ministered in the sanctuary." He also cites Revelation 19:8 to support this premise. Linen clothing was worn only when officiating at the altar and in the Holy Place. While Lloyd Bailey (2005, 84) argues that this text necessarily came from when Israel was settled in the land and was able to grow flax, the use of linen in Egypt long predated Israel's sojourn there. In fact, the Smithsonian Institute asserts that linen had been used for centuries prior to this time, both in Mesopotamia and especially in Egypt (www.si.edu/spotlight/ancient-egypt/mummies). While the Israelites would not have had access to flax in the wilderness to make linen, linen is included as a resource present in the camp during the construction of the tabernacle, apparently carried out of Egypt when they fled (Exod. 25:1–7).

After the altar was cleaned, the priest then removed his priestly garments, put on other garments, and carried the ashes outside of the camp to a "clean place." After the ashes had been removed, the priest would return, put his priestly robes back on, and then through the day offer other sacrifices, placing them on top of the burnt offering still on the fire until it was time for the evening offering.

A Clean Place

The clean place (see the section "Clean and Unclean" in the introduction) would be the site mentioned in Lev. 4:12 where ashes were poured out and the portions of the sacrificial animals that were not burned on the altar were incinerated and thus disposed of. The idea is that there was no "cultic contamination," even though it was not considered a "holy place" (Noordtzij 1982, 75).

Several points stand out with regard to this corporate burnt offering. First, the idea of a perpetual fire serves as a powerful symbol, which is used even today in a variety of contexts. The fire that came from the Lord demonstrated his presence in the camp, and the idea of perpetuity would be an encouragement (Kleinig 2003, 147). Second, if the burnt offering was an offering of consecration, this would suggest that corporate consecration was to be a daily process—both morning and night. As such, this corporate offering would serve as a model to the people of personal consecration. Third, it seems significant that one of the responsibilities of the officiating priest was to remove the ashes from the altar and transport them to the clean place. As Harrison (1980, 75) puts it, "even in so apparently menial a task as the removal of ashes from the altar, it was the officiating priest, and not a deputy, who performed it."

Removing the Ashes

Lange (1960, 57) cites two Jewish traditions related to this observation. First, it is maintained that the carrying out ashes "might be done by any of the priestly family who were excluded from officiating at the altar by reason of some bodily defect." It would appear that this would affect only the removal of the ashes from the tabernacle itself, not removing them from the altar,

Figure 28. Incense shovel from Dan, Israel Museum. While labeled as an incense shovel, it likely also served to remove ashes.

which would need to be done by the priest while properly attired. Tradition also maintains "that it was only required each day to carry forth a small quantity of the ashes—a shovel-full—allowing the rest to remain until the hollow of the altar below the grating was filled up, when all must be emptied and carried away." This might raise the possibility that the priest did a daily token removal, but another member of the priestly family finished the job when required.

6:14–18 (HB 6:7–11). Leviticus 2 discusses the voluntary gift offering (מִנְחָה) on the behalf of an individual, with detailed instructions on how the individual was to present it. Now, in Leviticus 6, the text turns to the role of the priest. This short section is not introduced with a "then the Lord [YHWH] spoke to Moses" statement, which suggests it is tied to the previous instructions to Aaron and his family.

After the introduction in 6:14 (HB 6:7), 6:15–16a (HB 6:8–9a) essentially repeats the priest's responsibility presented in Leviticus 2:2–3a. Leviticus 2:3b–15 then informs the offeror on how to prepare the offering—in other words, all of the steps leading up to the presentation, which are summarized in 2:17. Now the text expands on that verse. First, there is a how-to for the priest in 6:15 (HB 6:8) with a reminder in Leviticus 6:17a (HB 6:10a) that the cooked offering may not contain leaven. Overall, Leviticus 6:16–18 (HB 6:9–11) explains how after the presentation and the placing of the memorial portion upon the altar, the rest of the gift offering is for the priests.

The heart of this material lies in 6:16b (HB 9b), which relates where the gift offering may be eaten, and 6:18 (HB 11), which relates who may eat of the priests' portion. These are the easy issues. The gift offering is to be eaten in a "holy place," which is defined as the "court of the Tent of Meeting." In terms of the tabernacle, this would be anywhere inside the outer screens. Participants included any male who is descended from Aaron, that is, any male member of the priestly family.

The difficult portion of this section is the last sentence in 6:18 (HB 11), which reads in the NASB: "Whoever touches them [the offerings by fire to the Lord] will become consecrated." Most modern translations seem to translate this verse similarly. While that seems to be the surface meaning of the text, it does present problems in that it suggests that someone could become holy by "touching" or "eating" the holy bread. However, an alternative reading would require that the person who eats the bread needed to be holy.

TRANSLATION ANALYSIS: "CONSECRATED"

In this case, a word-for-word literal translation of the last portion of this verse would be "all who touch in them will be holy" (with the Hebrew verb *qadash* [קָדַשׁ] in the *qal* stem). There are two translation questions. First, should the relative pronoun *asher* (אֲשֶׁר) be translated "who" or "which"? The second question is how is the verb *qadash* used? Thomas McComiskey (1980e, 787) suggests that the verb form "is used most frequently to describe the state of consecration effected by Levitical ritual." The question then is whether an item (in this case, the bread of the grain offering) that has been placed in a state of consecration would in and of itself place anyone who or anything which touches it into the same state. If the answer is yes, the follow-on question here would be, To what purpose? That there is no further elucidation seems to suggest that the rationale of the statement is a warning against inappropriate eating of the holy bread—that is, the person who does so must be holy.

Lange (1960, 58) succinctly delineates the choices: "Two senses are possible: (a) nothing shall be allowed to touch them which is not holy; (b) whatever does touch them shall thereby become holy." Commentators disagree on how this statement should be understood. Samuel Balentine (2002, 67) takes the second understanding, contending that God "is able to bestow holiness on and in the world." Milgrom (1991, 443–51) and Kiuchi (2007, 125) agree, suggesting a concept of

The Role of the Priests (6:8 [HB 6:1]–7:38)

"holy contagion." Noordtzij (1982, 76) argues "ritual holiness could be communicated as readily as ritual uncleanness; like something tangible or material." On the other hand, others including Levine (1989, 37), Hartley (1992, 97), and Sklar (2014, 129) argue that the statement is an admonition that any person who eats of the holy bread must be holy himself. Haggai 2:11–13 seems helpful with respect to this issue. There, Haggai proposes two questions to the priests. The first is whether "holy meat" in the fold of a garment could make bread or other food holy, and the response is "No."[1] The second question is whether one who has become unclean by touching a corpse and then touches bread or some other food would make it unclean, and the response is "Yes." A basic question underlying the issue is the nature of holiness. Is it something tangible that one can "catch," a status that might be conferred, or a state that reflects an aspect of identity? As suggested in the "Holy" section in the introduction, when referring to humans, holiness is a state; however, inanimate objects might have a holy status conferred upon them.

6:19–23 (HB 6:12–16). The next short section addresses a special gift offering given on behalf of the priest, which is introduced with a "then the Lord [YHWH] spoke to Moses" statement. Here it would seem that the intent is to distinguish this priestly gift offering from the personal one just discussed. While the description is brief, there are some points that require clarification.

The material in Leviticus 2 on gift offerings did not specify the amount of grain. At least in terms of the daily corporate offering, the priest is told here (6:20) that it should be one "tenth of an ephah of fine flour" (סֹלֶת).

> **Gift-Offering Ingredients**
> The text here specifies one-tenth of an ephah, which is estimated to be about three-eighths to two-thirds of a bushel. Numbers 28:5 expands on the ingredients, noting that it should be mixed with a fourth of a hin of beaten olive oil, which is approximately five and half quarts (5.7 l). Despite the uncertainty of the modern equivalents, it would appear that this roughly approximates the modern rule of thumb that "almost any bread will follow the ratio of 5 parts flour to 3 parts liquid" (https://www.myrecipes.com/how-to/important-cooking-ratios).

This sacrifice is split, with half offered in the morning and half in the evening along with the regular corporate burnt offerings. Further, while the individual gift offerings described in Leviticus 2:4–10 may be offered in a variety of forms, the daily corporate gift offerings are described very specifically. They are to be well kneaded, cooked on a griddle, and then offered in pieces. Significantly, there is no memorial portion, but the entire offering is burned, since the priest is not to benefit from his own sacrifice, or from a national sacrifice that would include him (Levine 1989, 39).

TRANSLATION ANALYSIS: "GRIDDLE"
Leviticus 6:21 (HB 14) is rather awkward to translate. In the Hebrew, it begins with the phrase עַל־מַחֲבַת, "upon a griddle" (see excursus "Cooking Apparatuses," and translation analysis for Lev. 2:5). In our discussion of Leviticus 2:5, we described this procedure as "fried." The position of the phrase "upon a griddle" at the beginning suggests emphasis. It is followed by the phrase "in oil it will be made" (בַּשֶּׁמֶן תֵּעָשֶׂה), and then, "well-kneaded" (מֻרְבֶּכֶת), a *hophal* participle (essentially denoting a passive state [GKC §§53h, s, and 107d]). This term is used

---

1   Rooker (2000, 130 n. 234) suggests that the Haggai passage is not relevant since "in Haggai offerings that are קָדְשֵׁי קָדָשִׁים ('most holy') are not under discussion." However, it would seem that the argument from the lesser to the greater would indicate that it is relevant.

three times in the OT (Lev. 6:21; 7:12; 1 Chron. 23:29). It is understood to mean "well-mixed," "well-kneaded," or "well-stirred." Then, following the main verb clause "you will bring it," there is a very difficult word, *tupini* (תֻּפִינֵי), a *hapax legomenon* that is thought to indicate slices or pieces (Levine 1989, 39). The rough understanding then is: "On a griddle it will be fried in oil after it is well-kneaded, and then you will bring it as cooked slices or pieces."

The text describes this offering as one that Aaron and his sons were to present "on the day when he is anointed." It is generally understood that this refers both to Aaron and to the high priests who followed him. However, the same verse also describes it as a regular gift offering, literally "grain offering continually" (תָּמִיד). Hartley (1992, 97) observes that "many delete one term or the other depending on whether they read the passage as a specific regulation for a single day or as a general regulation." Noordtzij (1982, 77) suggests that it be viewed as a regular ritual for each new high priest when he was anointed. However, Levine (1989, 38) notes that during the Second Temple period the high priest performed this rite as a daily practice. Milgrom (1991, 397) argues that because of the term "continually," the usual translation of "on the day" cannot be valid. Rather he claims that the phrase could mean "from the day." In that regard, Harris observes that the preposition בְּ has been recognized as having a wider range of meaning than previously understood, including, based on Ugaritic evidence, "from" (Harris 1980a). Given the description of the daily offerings in Numbers 28:4–5, it would seem that the intent is that beginning on the day of his anointing, Aaron and his subsequently anointed descendants were to offer this gift offering on a daily basis.

Another key point is that if the priest brings a gift offering, he may not eat from it, but rather it must be burned in its entirety.

The general consensus is that, as Hartley (1992, 58) puts it, "cultic laws prevent the priests from benefiting from either their own sins or the sins of the covenant community." While the meat from animals that the priests were not permitted to eat was to be burned outside of the camp (Lev. 4:12), it appears that the gift offering was all burned on the altar.

The Lord Gives Directions to the Priests for Purification and Reparation Offerings (6:24 [HB 6:17]–7:10)

6:24 (HB 17)–7:5. Following another introductory "then the Lord [YHWH] spoke to Moses" statement, the priests are given guidelines on the handling of the purification and reparation offerings. The conclusion of this section (in 7:7) tells the priests that the reparation offering is like the purification offering—"there is one law for them"—so the directions for both may be discussed here.

We noted above that Leviticus 4 and 5 delineate guidelines for purification offerings that can be either individual or corporate. In either case, they generally are offered on an as-needed basis. While the current material mandates daily burnt and gift offerings for the nation, there are no provisions for daily purification offerings. Rather, regular purification offerings for the nation were to be given at the beginning of each month and then at the three great holidays where Israelites were instructed to go to the central sanctuary (at the time, the tabernacle)—specifically Passover, the Festival of Weeks, and then the fifteenth day of the seventh month. This suggests that most of the purification offerings that the priest would see would be personal purification offerings in conjunction with the situations described in Leviticus 4. Similarly, as covered in Leviticus 5, reparation offerings are individual offerings *only* done on a case-by-case basis and that require personal restitution prior to the sacrifice.

The Role of the Priests (6:8 [HB 6:1]–7:38)

> ### New Moon Offerings
>
> Under a lunar calendar, the first of the month is the new moon, which is when the waxing moon first appears behind the setting sun. John Lilley (1975, 417) notes that the new moon is a "minor festival" that is "linked with the sabbath" in 2 Kings 4:2 and other passages. See the discussion with regard to appointed times in Leviticus 23:24–25.

With respect to the process, the text directs that both purification and reparation offerings are to be slain in the same place where the burnt offering is slain, "before the Lord," which would be at the doorway of the Tent of Meeting (Lev. 1:3; 4:4, 14). Interestingly, the text does not describe the steps involved in the purification offering, but it does so for the reparation offering (7:1–6). It is key that after the proper process of sacrificing the animal and then burning the requisite portions, the priest is to eat of the sacrifice (with exceptions noted below). Since bovine purification offerings were burned outside the camp (Lev. 4:12, 20), this limits the meat to that of the sheep or goat (animals from the flock), and the reparation offering is limited even further to a ram. The meal is to take place in the court of the Tent of Meeting, "a holy place." Subsequently (in 6:29 [HB 6:22] and 7:6), clarification is added that not only should the priest handling the offering eat of the sacrifice, but also any male among the priests. However, the eating must be in the court of the Tent of Meeting.

> ### Priests Eat the Purification Offering
>
> Milgrom (1991, 407) suggests that there is an apparent conflict between this statement that the priest shall eat it and 6:29 (HB 22), which says that every male among the priests may eat of it. However, as Hartley (1992, 98) points out, this verse does not say that only the officiating priest may eat of it. As noted, the only purification offering that the priest would eat from would be from the flock, which precludes the priest from eating from any purification offering brought by

> the priest, or by the congregation as a whole. It is generally understood that the rationale is that the priest should not benefit from his own sacrifice.

Once again, we run into that problematic statement that the NASB translates as "who touches its flesh will become consecrated." As noted in our discussion of 6:18 (HB 11), the best understanding of this is that the person who eats of the purification offering must be holy. The directions given here with regard to handling the blood of this offering seem to support this understanding. As is always the case, the blood of the sacrifice needs to be captured in a utensil, and depending on the type of sacrifice it is sprinkled on the altar, poured out at the base of the altar, applied to the horns of altar (either burnt offering altar or altar of fragrant incense) by the priest's finger, or sprinkled "in front of the veil." Now, two specific cautions are expressed with regard to the sacrifice. First, if any of the blood splashes on a garment, then the garment must be washed. Milgrom (1991, 403) makes a telling observation:

> the garment does not become holy by coming into contact with the blood of the purification offering. Instead of being confiscated by the sanctuary, as would any object that is rendered holy, it is restored to its former status by having its so-called holiness effaced through washing. Thus the garment is actually treated as if it were impure, for it is impure clothing that always requires laundering (e.g., 11:25, 28, 40; 15:5–8, 10–11).

It is significant that this laundering must be done in "a holy place," that is, in the same court of the Tent of Meeting where the priests were to eat their portion of these offerings. This would suggest that the issue is that the blood that had been part of the sacrifice should not leave the Holy Place where it had been sacrificed.

The Role of the Priests (6:8 [HB 6:1]–7:38)

But blood was not the only concern. The portion of the meat that was to be given to the priests was to be boiled. No information is given on where this was to take place, but since the product is most holy, it would seem to be located in the courtyard of the tabernacle. Although the utensil could be either ceramic or bronze, the vessel needed to be pure. If an earthenware vessel is used, it must be broken afterward. While the reason is not given, scholars generally agree that the concern is particular residue from the cooked meat might lodge in pores of the earthenware, which was not a problem with a metal vessel (Levine 1989, 40). A bronze vessel, however, must be scoured and rinsed with water (m. Zebaḥ. 11:6, 7).

One other caution is indicated in 6:30 (HB 23), which specifies that purification offerings from which the blood had been brought into the Tent of Meeting were not to be eaten but burned. This would apply to the purification offerings of the anointed priest and the congregation, both of which were bulls whose carcasses were directed to be burned. Later, we will see that it also applied to the offerings of Yom Kippur (Lev. 16).

7:7–10. While technically not addressing either the purification or reparation offerings, the last portion of this section stresses a couple of points with regard to the portions the priests received from the sacrificial system. First, while not mentioned in Leviticus 1, in the case of a burnt offering, the priest who served to present the offering would receive the skin.

Animal Skins

The animal skins were valuable commodities, which could be tanned to produce leather that would be used for a wide variety of products. They also provided the priests with a trade good that they could use to procure other items that they might not be able to make. According to the Mishnah, (m. Zebaḥ. 12:3), the skins of the "most holy offerings" went to the priests, while the skins of other offerings returned to the offeror.

Additionally, as mentioned in Leviticus 2, the bulk of gift offerings went to the priests. This direction seems to differentiate between cooked and raw gift offerings. Cooked offerings would need to be eaten quickly, and thus direction is given that the priest who has handled the sacrifice takes it. In the case that the food was uncooked, the food was shared among all of the descendants of Aaron (i.e., the priests). It would appear that this food could be stored for future use; thus, a secondary use of the sacrificial system was the support of the priests (Lange 1960, 60).

The Lord Gives Directions to the Priests for Shalom Offerings (7:11–36)

The final section of the directions for the priests covers the shalom offerings. Leviticus 3 gives the guidelines for Israelites who bring shalom offerings. In our first unit, "Worshipping a Holy God" (1:1–3:17), we noted how the particular animal the offeror brought could vary depending on the ability of the offeror, and perhaps on the degree of gratitude he or she desired to express. There we noted that the text simply noted the broad category of shalom, but now we see that three different varieties of shalom offerings are described, which we denoted as *thanksgiving*, *votive*, and *freewill*. In terms of structure, this section is complicated, and the best way to approach the material is thematically. It begins with the declaration that the following material provides teaching on the "sacrifice of peace offerings that shall be presented to the Lord" (Lev. 7:11). However, subsequently two "then the Lord [YHWH] spoke to Moses" statements divide the material at Leviticus 7:22 and 7:28. Both serve to change the intended recipients from the priests (Lev. 6:24 [HB 17]) to the people as a whole. The first "the Lord [YHWH] spoke" section, 7:22–27, seems to serve to remind the people that God's guidelines with respect to fat and blood apply regardless of where the animal is eaten ("in any of your dwellings").

The second "the Lord [YHWH] spoke" section, 7:28–36, returns to the subject at hand and describes the ritual that must be followed.

7:11–36. The first purpose of a shalom offering mentioned is thanksgiving. Thanksgiving is a standard translation of the Hebrew term תּוֹדָה, a noun derived from the verb יָדָה, which means "to confess, praise, or give thanks." Alexander (1980d, 364) explains that it was "predominatly [sic] employed to express one's public proclamation or declaration (confession) of God's attributes and his works. This concept is at the heart of the meaning of praise. Praise is a confession or declaration of who God is and what he does."

A second purpose of a shalom offering would be a votive offering, which was offered in fulfillment of a "vow" (נֶדֶר). This offering served to recount to the company at hand how God had fulfilled the offeror's request, and thus to give praise (תּוֹדָה) to God. Perhaps the best example of a fulfilled vow is the case of Hannah (1 Sam. 1–2). Childless, Hannah vowed that if God gave her a son, she would devote him to God for life and he would be a lifelong Nazirite. When God gave Hannah a son (Samuel), she brought him to the tabernacle, where she performed a votive offering including a bull, flour, and wine (1 Sam. 1:24). This account demonstrates the expected pattern of a votive offering (fulfill the vow first and then give the offering).

Vow and Votive Offering

Interestingly, the term נֶדֶר is used both for the vow and the offering (Coppes 1980e, 557–58). A votive offering was intended to thank God in response to a quid pro quo request, that is, one that had been made with promise such as "if God . . . then I . . ." The promise could be very broad (Rainey 1975, 208). Jacob vowed that *if* God preserved him and he returned to Canaan, he would serve God (Gen. 28:20–21, emphasis added). Hannah's promise was much more specific: *if* God gave her a son, she would give him to the Lord for all the days of his life (1 Sam. 1:11, emphasis added).

Passages such as Deuteronomy 23:21–23 and Ecclesiastes 5:4–5 suggest that fulfilling one's vow may have been a problem within the OT period. It seems likely that this is the same type of promise that Jephthah made (Judg. 11:18). In his case the vow seems to have included alternative responses, since that flexible *waw* can be (and in this case should be) translated as "or" rather than "and." In that case, Jephthah promised that "whatever comes out of the doors of my house . . . it shall be the Lord's *or* I will offer it up as a burnt offering" (emphasis added, see appendix 7, "Vows and Nazirites").

The "freewill" offering is the translation of the Hebrew נְדָבָה. While the word suggests something "offered voluntarily" (Coppes 1980d, 554), there seems to be a contrast to both the thanksgiving (תּוֹדָה) and the votive (נֶדֶר) offering where the offeror, while offering voluntarily, was responding to something specific God had done. Apparently in the case of the freewill offering, it was a spontaneous celebration of who God is.

After the warning on eating blood or fat, the how-to of the shalom offering is presented. In all three cases, the priest would guide the offeror in performing the sacrifice in accordance with the directions provided in Leviticus 2 and now amplified in 7:29–36. As the animal was brought to the priest, the offeror actively participated, presenting the animal with his or her own hands. As the animal is sacrificed, the portions that are to be burned (the fat and other portions as listed in Lev. 3:3–4) are presented to the priest for incineration. In addition, the offeror was to bring two pieces of meat from the animal, which became the portion given to the priest. The first is the breast. Leviticus 7:30 describes it as a "wave" (תְּנוּפָה) offering.

The Breast

While *WTNID* defines the brisket as "breast of a quadruped animal" (see fig. 29), as used today, there is a distinction between the two. The Food

Network Kitchen specifies that the brisket is half of the breast, and thus the cow has two, one on each side, "just above the front shanks and below the chuck" (https://www.foodnetwork.com/how-to/packages/food-network-essentials/what-is-brisket). As described in Leviticus, it appears that the priest would receive the entire breast as a piece of meat. Modern butchers cut each brisket (or half of the breast) into two pieces: a pointed, fattier, portion called the point; and a leaner portion called the flat. The former is typically used in barbecue, while the latter has traditionally been

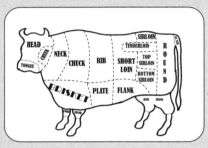

Figure 29. The location of the beef brisket.

prepared on Jewish holidays. In either case, the breast is considered a "tough cut of meat that needs to be cooked low and slow."

TRANSLATION ANALYSIS: "WAVE OFFERING"
The Hebrew word translated "wave offering" is תְּנוּפָה, which is derived from the verb נוּף. According to *TWOT*, there are three possible roots of the verb, which denote a variety of motions (cf. Bowling 1980d, 1980e; and *TWOT* s.v. "נוּף III" 2:565). Traditionally it has been understood to indicate a side-to-side movement of the item being presented, which in addition to the breast of the shalom offering may refer to a variety of items that are presented as a sacrifice, including gold (Exod. 35:22), the two loaves on Pentecost (Lev. 23:17), and the male lamb when cleansing lepers (Lev. 14:12). Collectively they suggest that the verb נוּף when used in the *hiphil* stem (which is the stem used in this text) serves "both as a general verb for such ideas as lifting, waving, etc., and as a cultic term for presenting the 'wave offering.'" It would then seem that "raised up" would be an appropriate understanding and many commentators now suggest that the actual action was a lifting of the sacrifice as an act of dedication (see, e.g., Kiuchi 2007, 136; Rooker 2000, 136–3; Wenham 1979, 126 7).

The other portion is the right thigh. Leviticus 7:32 specifies this is given to the priest as a "contribution," although some translations call it a "heave offering" as an alternative translation of the Hebrew תְּרוּמָה.

TRANSLATION ANALYSIS: "CONTRIBUTION"
The word translated "contribution" or "heave offering" is תְּרוּמָה, which is derived from the verb רוּם, which means "to be high, lofty; rise up" (Bowling 1980f, 838–39). Based on that derivation, it has been suggested that originally the offering was raised up before the Lord, although no uses of the term in the Bible clearly indicate that. Now it is generally accepted that the term simply means "gift" or "contribution." In the shalom offerings, not only is the thigh considered a תְּרוּמָה but the offeror must provide a portion of the three varieties of unleavened bread as well as the leavened bread to the priest, which is also called a *teruma* (תְּרוּמָה).

It would likely have been expected that the offeror would share with his or her guests the reason for the shalom offering.

Shalom Offerings and Praise Songs
As noted in the unit "Worshipping a Holy God" (1:1–3:17), it seems likely that a number of the praise psalms were actually first sung in conjunction with a shalom offering. The example of Hannah provides a good picture of how a shalom offering proceeded. As described in 1 Samuel 1–2, Hannah brought Samuel to the tabernacle, where they sacrificed the bull (this would suggest that her husband was fairly well off). She shared with Eli how she had prayed to God, and how

> God answered her petition, and that she was now fulfilling her vow. Then, 1 Samuel 2 records a praise song Hannah sang.

After the priestly portions are given, the rest of the animal is cooked (apparently by boiling) and shared with the company at hand. Interspersed, three cautions are expressed with regard to the meal. First, anyone who participates in this ritual must be ritually clean (7:20–21). The warning is that anyone who participates in this meal who is unclean will be cut off from his people, a warning that is repeated twice.

TRANSLATION ANALYSIS: "PEOPLE"
The Hebrew word עַם carries many of the same ambiguities as the English word "people," which is its usual translation. According to Gerard Van Groningen (1980c, 676), "'am is predominantly used to express two basic characteristics of men considered as a grouping: 1) relationships sustained within or to the group and 2) the unity of the group." As used in Leviticus, "people" is used predominantly in reference to two groups. The first is the entire nation of Israel, which is generally indicated by a definite article (הָעָם, translated as "the people"). The second is indicated by a possessive pronoun indicating closer relationship, generally translated as "his people" (e.g., בְּעַמָּיו, "among his people"). With regard to the present context, see also the sidebar "Cut Off from His People" below. Commonly it seems to reflect either one's extended family, although at times it may reflect an entire tribe, such as the tribe of Levi.

We are never told specifically what "cut off" means. Most modern scholars suggest that this was a community judgment that led to excommunication or death of the person who violated this act. In contrast, a more traditional view seems to suggest premature death, although often with an addition such as extirpation of offspring, or separation

from God after death. Milgrom (1991, 457–58) lists nineteen different categories of offenses for which being "cut off" (כָּרַת) is warned, from eating suet to certain types of illicit sex, to neglecting certain purification rituals, to working on the Sabbath, to the worship of Molech. Further, as Rooker (2000, 135) notes, the punishment was "the result of a direct judgment of God." This strongly suggests that the traditional view of premature death would seem to be an aspect, but not necessarily the complete story.

> ### Cut Off from His People
> Milgrom explores the additional possibility that the punishment is carried out after physical death—that is, the individual may not join his ancestors in the afterlife. In this light, he notes that in Leviticus 20:2–3, the warning is that if someone "gives any of his offspring to Molech . . . the people of the land shall stone him with stones . . . [and I] will cut him off from among his people." Here he suggests that instead of the usual understanding that if the people don't execute him God will, both will occur—the "*karat* awaits the criminal" after the death. If that is the case, we would also note that the Hebrew phrase translated in the NASB and many modern translations as "cut off from his people" in both 7:21 and 22 adds the term *nephesh* ("his soul"; וְנִכְרְתָה הַנֶּפֶשׁ הַהִוא מֵעַמֶּיהָ). In both cases the phrase translated "from his people" (מֵעַמֶּיהָ) ends with a third-person singular feminine pronoun. However, this is because *nephesh* is a feminine noun; that is, the soul is cut off. As already noted, the term *nephesh* seems to denote any person. However, it is possible that its use here may be suggestive to point to what survives physical death (see the section "*Nephesh* (נֶפֶשׁ): Life or Soul" in the introduction).

Second, the meat must not touch anything unclean (7:19). Should it do so, it becomes unclean, and then it should be burned with fire.

The Role of the Priests (6:8 [HB 6:1]–7:38)

Third, there is a caution with regard to leftovers. In the case of the thanksgiving offering, anything left over at the end of the day in which the animal was sacrificed must be burned. In contrast, in the case of the votive or freewill offerings, leftovers may be eaten on the second day, but anything remaining at the end of the second day must be burned. Mathews (2009, 68) suggests that the purpose is to avoid spoiling. Given the climate and the lack of refrigeration, this clearly could be a factor. However, no reason for the difference in the number of days is given. In any event, the text states that anything left to the third day will be פִּגּוּל, which both BDB and *TWOT* define as "foul thing, refuse" (BDB s.v. "פִּגּוּל" 803; *TWOT* s.v. "פִּגּוּל" 2:714). Further, eating of the sacrifice beyond the requisite time nullifies the value of the sacrifice (7:18). This would serve to emphasize the role of inviting neighbors to the celebration that was intended to magnify God and to promote community.

This section ends with the reminder in 7:34–36 that the breast and the thigh belong to Aaron and his sons. While the NASB uses the phrase "that which was consecrated to," many modern translations use "portion." In the Hebrew there is a wordplay. The term used is *moshḥa* (מָשְׁחָה) which, while derived from a verb meaning "to anoint," is understood to mean *portion* (Hamilton 1980d, 532). In the next verse, we read that Aaron and his sons were anointed, using the infinitive of the homonym *mashaḥ* (מָשַׁח "to anoint") with the possessive pronoun. In other words, it was anointed to them because of their anointing. The use of the wordplay might serve to make the requirement stand out in the Israelite mind.

The Lord Concludes the Teaching on the Giving of Sacrifices (7:37–38)

7:37–38. It has been suggested that the last two verses serve as a colophon that sums up the first seven chapters. Gerstenberger (1996, 83) argues that the use of the singular Torah here emphasizes that the material is a unit. While the last

verse could be translated that the teaching was given "in" or "on" Mount Sinai, the preposition בְּ could also be translated as "at," which is the way most translators understand it. The tabernacle and the encamped nation were in the wilderness of Sinai, located at Mount Sinai.

With this summary, the text now prepares us for the next step in the development of the national worship. The tabernacle has been completed. The shekinah has descended on it, and Moses has received an extensive Torah on how to worship. In our next unit, we will see how God initiates the priesthood to direct that worship.

THEOLOGICAL FOCUS

This entire section addresses the importance of corporate worship. At Sinai, the people group of Israel was in the process of being developed into a nation that had a corporate priestly function of serving as intermediaries between God and the world. Ultimately the goal was to produce a redeemer or messiah to reconcile that fallen world to God. In the interim, the nation of Israel was to model worship of the true God. One aspect of that role would be through a formal system of worship that would represent God to the nation and through them to the world. It would also provide ritual that would serve to focus worship on the true God.

Historically, humankind had recognized the need for sacrifices to demonstrate a repentant heart and a desire for consecration. Up to this point, that process had been personal, local, and short-term. This is still true in the first two sections of Leviticus. Now we see the beginning of a transition that would ultimately lead to a corporate, global, and eternal resolution to the problem of the fall.

The first step would be a provision for corporate sacrifices that would serve the entire nation. These sacrifices would be done daily (morning and evening) on an altar ordained by God that was built on a heavenly model (Exod. 25:9). They would be burned on a fire that God sent down, and that burned perpetually. While the fire from God burned perpetually, the consecration represented by those sacrifices needed to be renewed daily, morning and night.

Because of the purpose of the sacrifices, the offerings and all of the materials associated with them needed to be treated with reverence and respect. This required moral purity both internally and in relationship with others. To assist in this regard, God provided religious leaders who had a special responsibility of guiding the rest of the people in the matter of worship. A significant point of consideration is that the leaders were not chosen because they were any better than the rest of the people. They too needed to purify themselves regularly as a model to the rest of the people, and we will see later that in some respects they had higher standards to live up to.

Finally, this section ends with a provision for sacrifices where individuals could celebrate with their families and neighbors the things that God had done. One of the emphases of these shalom offerings is people sharing with others how God had worked in their lives. This might be recognition of a specific act of favor, an answer to a prayer when the person was in trouble and had made a promise to God as he or she asked for help, or just a spontaneous declaration of God's love, grace, and mercy. Overall, this would serve to remind the nation that God was active in the world in which they lived. Thus, this call to celebrate is a call to publicly proclaim how they are "at peace" with their God, his intermediary (priest), and his people (those with whom they share the meal).

PREACHING AND TEACHING STRATEGIES

Exegetical and Theological Synthesis
In the previous section, we saw the role of sacrificial offerings in the confession of sin emphasized. Now we see the emphasis shift to the ongoing dynamic role of planned and spontaneous sacrificial offerings in a worship-filled

life. God providing for the cleansing of their sin is only the beginning. He is instructing them how, through shalom offerings, they are to live a life of worship! This process will include a priest to serve as an intermediary and an ongoing connection to a community of believers with which to share. (If you invite enough people, you will not have to discard leftovers!)

In structuring these messages, it is important to note that there is content overlap between what is covered in this third unit and what we have already covered in the first unit (1:1–3:17). As stated previously, we highlighted the burnt and gift offering before, so now we will use this as our opportunity to highlight aspects of the shalom offering.

God knows the heart. Those who worship him need a reminder lest they forget who he is, what he has done, and how he has set apart his people to live in community. Since Eden, those created in God's image have been prone to entertain thoughts of independence—thoughts that lead them away from the one who loves and protects them. These shalom offerings are far from perfunctory. They are intended to proclaim the significance of the Lord God as the source of life. Bringing the best of what we have and sharing it with others testifies to a humble heart, bowing down to publicly confess our ongoing dependence on the Lord God.

Knowing that the heart is deceitful (who can trust it?), God graciously provides a means to protect worshippers from their own hearts and to hold them accountable to the truth. To be accepted, like all offerings, this gift is to be examined by the priest, who will identify whether it meets the prescribed standard. If presented as divinely instructed by God, the gift will be accepted by God's chosen intermediary and the distinct fragrance of humble obedience will soon arise as it burns to be recognized by much of the surrounding community.

Unlike the burnt offering and gift offering, the shalom offering calls for a noteworthy sacrifice *and* provides an immediate tangible

The Role of the Priests (6:8 [HB 6:1]–7:38)

return. The priest will be delighted in what he receives, and the worshipper will return home to satisfy his stomach and those of his friends as he shares what God has done in his life. Through this offering, God provides the means to combat the constant lie that though made in God's image, we can break free and find a greater happiness by going it alone. The shalom offering signifies our ongoing need for our Creator, his intermediary, and a community of believers.

Preaching Idea
Being at peace with God is evident through a worship-filled life.

Contemporary Connections

What does it mean?
A life dreaming of independence from God and others promises a false peace. True peace is found through a life of dependence upon our Creator, his intermediary, and our community of believers. The people of God are being directed in how to establish their lives through daily worship. Whether an offering of thanksgiving for what God has done, an offering for the completion of a vow for how God has protected, or simply a freewill offering reminding everyone of the greatness of the Lord God, each sacrifice provides a testimony that secures the people to the foundation of the enduring faithfulness of the true God.

Because this offering is a public rather than a private act, the extended family and community see and likely participate. They may ask questions: "Why do we do this?" "Who is God?" "What did God do?" In addition, the community of priests receive their portion, reminding them how (without land) they will remain dependent on God and his people. The expanding community of faith smells the aroma of humble obedience, possibly reminding them that it is time for them to bring an offering of their own to testify to the goodness of God.

Apart from such a public gift (and the accountability of the community), people are left to rely on the vacillation of their own feelings about God. They may begin to deny the need for God. They may neglect testifying of God's work to the next generation. They may neglect the priests, leaving them to sell their services. They may fail to jog the memories of others in the community. A proper gift refreshes the bonds of dependence and demonstrates the joy of a worship-filled life.

Is it true?
One who is at peace with God will desire that others know this peace—that others know who God is, what he has done, and how he is at work in this world. This peace is made evident through a worship-filled life. Our love of God can be demonstrated when we share freely of our time and resources with little or no expectation of a return. A gift with an expectation of return is not a real gift. There is no real sacrifice. It is more of an investment (or even a gamble). Yet if one brings a gift that visibly demonstrates an investment of thought, time, and effort without an expectation of receiving a gift in return, one is proclaiming his or her love for the receiver.

Consider for a moment all the various gifts you are called to offer. Many are simply offered out of a felt (or real) obligation. You may be expected to come to a birthday party or a wedding shower with a gift. The gift you select may speak about the pressure you feel to impress the recipient or other attendees. Or it may be an attempt to avoid embarrassment by violating perceived social standards. How can the one bringing a gift best communicate their commitment to the relationship they have with the recipient? This happens when they offer a gift that represents a personal sacrifice of time and resources. An Amazon order says something different than a handmade scrapbook. The former is easily purchased. The latter is painstakingly created. A gift that requires an investment of time and effort will freshen the memory of the giver as to what the receiver means to them. It will serve as a tribute to how central this relationship is. It will quietly proclaim a bond of love for all who share in the act.

Now what?

Being at peace with God is proclaimed through a worship-filled life. What does that look like? We must start by asking, are we at peace with God? If not, then why not? Are we seeking a false peace through independence? Are we worshipping something other than the Lord God? If we are at peace, how might God be calling us to express that "peace of dependence," first to ourselves and then humbly to those around us through tangible forms of worship? A worship-filled life is a life centered on who God is and what he is doing. Are we seeing what God is doing? If we become too entangled in ourselves and focused on our needs, we will begin to mispresent who he is and distort what he is doing.

What is our means to first recall to ourselves and then to share with others God's ongoing work? This could be done verbally over the dinner table, in small groups, or even in a chat room. It could be a part of a worship service or any larger public gathering. This could also take the form of a gift of service or assets. Whatever the form, to be authentic worship, motivation is important. God, not the worshipper, needs to be at the center—the protagonist of every story we share, the reason for every deed we do.

Creativity in Presentation

The challenge of Leviticus will be to remain true to the theme without becoming bogged down in the details. Cultures change; God does not. The preaching idea is relevant in any age. It should immediately capture the mind of everyone present because all present desire to be at peace, though they may not see being at peace with God as the pathway to being at peace. Your job is to turn their focus from a never-ending list of what "they need God to do" to be at peace

to what they can begin to share with others as they deny themselves and come to be at peace with God.

Consider asking them to list all the things they now have that they were confident that once they received, they would be at peace—content with their life. They may be thinking of material items, educational degrees, better jobs, more exotic vacations, a marriage, children, and so on. Then ask if these things generated a lasting contentment. You should provide one significant personal example.

Now, turn their minds to a current (or sadly for some an imagined) relationship they have that they highly value—one that brings deep satisfaction and joy. What can they do to demonstrate to that individual and everyone in their community the value of this relationship in their life? It is common for a husband or wife to publicly celebrate their spouse on their anniversary. That would be a planned celebration. But in addition, something deeper is said when a spontaneous eruption of thanksgiving occurs—an unplanned, sacrificial offering that proclaims how important this individual is in your life.

That is the culture God is creating for his people, so that they may not chase after all that will never satisfy but look more deeply into the one who is worthy and share all they find with others.

Being at peace with God is evident through a worship-filled life.

- Planned and spontaneous offerings to God
  - ◦ An offering of thanksgiving to God
  - ◦ Fulfilling a vow to God
  - ◦ An unexpected blessing from God
- The uniqueness of a peace offering
  - ◦ The personal sacrifice required of the one who brings it
  - ◦ The unique details of this specific sacrifice
  - ◦ The immediate blessing

- The unique focus of the peace offering
  - What this offering reveals about how one comes before a holy God
  - How this offering specifically prepares us for the sacrifice of Christ
- Valuing our relationships
  - At peace with God
  - At peace with neighbors

DISCUSSION QUESTIONS

1. What might be some of the advantages or disadvantages of having a formal priesthood?

2. What is the value of corporate worship?

3. What is the significance of purification? How might purification be practiced today?

Leviticus 8:1–9:24

EXEGETICAL IDEA
God desired deep, covenant fellowship with his chosen people, which required the establishment of holy priestly mediators—men who were chosen by God to be set apart and made holy before God's people.

THEOLOGICAL FOCUS
Our holy God set apart holy priestly mediators to atone for the sins of his people, so that they could be free to come before him in worship.

PREACHING IDEA
God provides a mediator to atone for our sin, so that we may come before him in worship.

PREACHING POINTERS
As Aaron and his sons were led before God, the people may have expected a public execution—an extermination of the line of Aaron. Yet God, again choosing to reveal his nature to them, gathered his people that they could witness a public redemption. Through a carefully detailed ritual of cleansing, preparing, and sacrifice, the same Aaron who had fashioned a golden calf was anointed as high priest by God. The one who fashioned an idol and led the people into false worship, saying, "These are your gods" (Exod. 32:4), was now publicly refashioned by the hand of God to lead the same people into true worship. What did this communicate to the people about their God? Having previously been chosen by God, God did not reject Aaron because of his sin against God and the people. Rather, the Lord God had mercy upon him, redeeming him from his sin for his greater purposes. The people looked upon Aaron and saw living evidence of the mercy of God at work. They worshipped a God who publicly redeems, restores, and recognizes his own.

What seems lost to us is not lost! What seems beyond hope is not hopeless when there is a God who is merciful and displays his glory through redemption. Our sinfulness has not permanently disqualified us from serving a holy God who is merciful and gracious, slow to anger, and abounding in steadfast love. It was and it is the Lord God's desire to demonstrate his mercy and forgiveness by redeeming us (publicly) from our sin and bringing us into relationship with him so that the world may see the character of our God.

INAUGURATION OF ANCIENT ISRAELITE RELIGION (8:1–9:24)

LITERARY STRUCTURE AND THEMES (8:1–9:24)

Leviticus 8–10 records three phases of a single week-long event in the form of an extended historical narrative, the longest narrative section in the book. The background is Exodus 28 and 29 where God revealed to Moses details regarding the soon-to-be-established priesthood. That earlier revelation had occurred shortly after the nation had arrived at Mount Sinai following the exodus (see chart 3 showing the chronology of the time at Sinai).

1446 B.C.	14 Nisan*	God "passed over" the firstborn of the Israelites.[1]
1446 B.C.	15 Nisan	The people of Israel left Egypt.
1446 B.C.	Fifteenth of fourth month	The people arrived at Sinai.[2]
1446 B.C.	Fifteenth of fourth month	Moses climbed Mt. Sinai; met with God (Exod. 19:3).
1446 B.C.	Eighteenth of fourth month	"On the third day" God spoke to the people of Israel as a group, with Moses standing with them at the foot of Sinai. God gave the Ten Commandments (Exod. 19:11).
1446 B.C.	Eighteenth of fourth month	People demanded that Moses represent them before God—they were scared (Exod. 20:18–20).
1446 B.C.	Eighteenth of fourth month	Moses climbed Mt. Sinai; received specifics of the covenant (Exod. 20:21–23:33).
1446 B.C.	Fourth month	Moses wrote down the book of the covenant (Exod. 24:4).
1446 B.C.	Fourth month	The nation affirmed the covenant as written with burnt and shalom offerings (Exod. 24:3–8).
1446 B.C.	Fourth month	Moses, Aaron, Nadab, Abihu, and seventy elders returned to the mountain (Exod. 24:9).
1446 B.C.	Seven days later, fourth–sixth months (forty days)	Moses alone climbed to the top of the mountain; remained for forty days. Received rest of covenant and details of tabernacle and priestly garments (Exod. 24:16–18).

---

1   Nisan is the first month of the Hebrew year, which begins with the first new moon after the spring equinox—thus during late March or early April.

2   "Three months to the day" after leaving Egypt (Stuart 2006, 420).

Inauguration of Ancient Israelite Religion (8:1–9:24)

1446 B.C.	Sixth month	Golden calf incident; broken tablets (Exod. 32:1:19)
1446 B.C.	Sixth month	God's judgment; replacement of tablets (Exod. 34:1)
1446–45 B.C.	Sixth–twelfth months	Construction of tabernacle (Exod. 36:2–39:32)
1445 B.C.	1 Nisan	Completed tabernacle, inaugurated (Exod. 40:2); Leviticus 1–7 given; consecration of priests directed (Lev. 8:1)
1445 B.C.	2–8 Nisan	Priesthood consecrated
1445 B.C.	8 Nisan	Nadab and Abihu struck down
1445 B.C.	9–12 Nisan	Rest of Leviticus written; leaders bring dedicatory offerings; tabernacle dedicated (Num. 7:1)
1445 B.C.	14 Nisan	First anniversary of Passover celebrated (Num. 9)
1445 B.C.	20 Nisan	Cloud lifted and nation leaves Sinai (Num. 10–11)
1445 B.C.	Tenth of seventh month	First celebration of Yom Kippur

Chart 3. Chronology of time at Sinai.

After the nation affirmed their covenant with God, Moses wrote the book of the covenant and then spent forty days with God on Sinai. During that conference, God gave Moses many of the details of the priesthood and the sacrifices the nation would now be required to offer. In the process, God showed Moses the heavenly prototypes of the tabernacle and the priestly garments. Exodus describes those items; Leviticus merely repeats enough material that one who is familiar with the descriptions in Exodus can follow the sequence of events at the time of implementation. While Leviticus 8–10 records one event that lasted eight days, the text really only describes days 1 (Lev. 8) and 8 (Lev. 9–10). The activities of days 2–7 apparently repeat those of day 1, and thus are subsumed within the first day description. While Leviticus 10 is part of day 8, the events are so starkly different, for homiletical purposes we will address the last portion separately. Thus, we divide this eight-day-long event into two units, which may be labeled dedication and desecration.

In this unit we read about two complementary rituals: consecration (Lev. 8), and inauguration (Lev. 9). Leviticus 8 relates how God guided Moses through the first day of his consecration of Aaron and his sons as a class of priests to supervise corporate worship. Skipping over days 2–7, Leviticus 9 finishes the consecration process on day 8 as Aaron and his sons inaugurate that worship system, performing their first sacrifices for the nation in their roles as consecrated priests. God spectacularly confirmed their status by sending divine fire to consume the sacrifices.

The text presents the material as having been written during or shortly after the events it describes. For the Israelites, the text would serve as a sharp reminder, not only to the first generation that experienced the inauguration but to future generations, that in terms of corporate worship God had specific guidelines regarding who might lead the nation in worship, and how they were to be designated by specific, God-ordained rituals. A number of scholars describe this text as the rite of passage by which the Aaronic

158

Inauguration of Ancient Israelite Religion (8:1–9:24)

priesthood was established. This ritual authorized Aaron and his family to preside over the national worship system and, as we will see subsequently, gave them the responsibility to ensure that worship was done properly. Further, that ritual was intended to serve as an anchor point for the future delineation of valid worship—although as seen in subsequent material, such as the book of Numbers, even within that generation opposition to God's program would arise through individuals who had their own agendas.

- *Moses Consecrates Aaron and His Sons (8:1–36)*
- *Aaron Inaugurates Corporate Worship in the Tabernacle (9:1–24)*

EXPOSITION (8:1–9:24)

Leviticus 8 and 9 serve as a critical pivot point for the nation of Israel. We have already noted how the first seven chapters present a transition from personal offerings to corporate offerings. While personal worship was still encouraged and expected, for Israel to serve as a nation of priests in a fallen world the nation would need a system that illustrated perpetual worship of the God who had redeemed them out of Egypt. Thus, the Lord established for the first time a God-ordained system of corporate worship. In these two chapters, we see the consecration of this new class of priests, followed by their initial round of sacrifices.

Moses Consecrates Aaron and His Sons (8:1–36)

The consecration of Aaron and his sons followed a divinely directed ritual that lasted seven days and involved purifying them and the tabernacle and dressing them as priests.

8:1–5. Leviticus 8 begins with another "then the Lord [YHWH] spoke to Moses" statement. Up to this point, the Lord's communications in Leviticus had been instructional for the long-term, giving directions on how certain activities

were to be done in the future. Now, however, the Lord directed Moses to do something at this time: He was to gather Aaron, his sons, the previously prepared priestly paraphernalia, and the entire congregation "at the doorway of the Tent of Meeting." While the specific time of this direction is not given, it would appear to have been immediately subsequent to directions on how to do personal sacrifices. Likely it occurred at the end of the first-day directions given in Leviticus 1–7, suggesting that the eighth-day event set forth here began on the day following the setting-up of the tabernacle in Exodus 40.

Two points stand out as we begin this section. First, this ordination process was public; the people observed it and, based on the spectacular conclusion of Leviticus 9, at the end of the process they expressed their acceptance of God's organization. Second, the process was intended to show that Aaron and his sons "as sinners . . . needed atonement, as common men they had to be consecrated and set aside, as ordinary men they had to be endowed" (Mays 1963, 40–41). While not stated specifically, it would appear that this took place on the same day that the earlier declarations from God in Leviticus were made.

The Priestly Line

The ancestor of the priestly tribe was Levi, one of Jacob's twelve sons. When Jacob blessed his sons at the end of his life (Gen. 49) he lambasted Levi and his brother Simeon for what they did to the city of Shechem after their sister was raped (Gen. 34). Despite this, God designated the descendants of Levi as the priestly tribe. Levi had three sons, Gershon: Kohath, and Merari (1 Chron. 6:1; see the section "Priests and Levites" in the introduction). Moses and Aaron were descendants of Kohath. At this point in Leviticus, Aaron has four sons who are ordained with him: Nadab, Abihu, Eleazar, and Ithamar (1 Chron. 6:3). As we will see, the oldest two, Nadab and Abihu, are struck dead (without sons), leaving Eleazar and Ithamar to head up the genealogy of priests. Both seemed

---

159

to have notable priests among their descendants, although Eleazar's descendants significantly outnumbered Ithamar's (1 Chron. 24:2–3). Zadok, descended from Eleazar, anointed Solomon (1 Kings 1:34). Ahimelech from Ithamar's line was serving in the tabernacle when David fled Saul and was killed by Doeg the Edomite (1 Sam. 22:9). His son Abiathar anointed Adonijah, Solomon's older brother, as king in Adonijah's attempt to usurp the throne. He was removed from the priestly role by Solomon, which removed Eli's house from the priestly line (1 Kings 2:26–27).

After telling Moses to take Aaron and his sons, the Lord told Moses to take "the garments" with them. The definite article in front of "garments" refers to the specific priestly garments described in Exodus 28. The text lists the items for Aaron in the next section, as Moses dresses him for the first time (see chart 4, "Priestly garments for Israelite priests"). These garments seem to have served several purposes. First, the garments publicly showed the office of the priests (some have described it as a uniform). Second, the make-up of the garments "symbolically communicated important spiritual lessons" (Mathews 2009, 74). Third, the wearing of specific garments served to represent specific priestly acts, such as cleaning the ashes off the altar (see Lev. 6:10–11). Fourth, certain portions of the garments served very practical functions as part of the priestly role, such as the Urim and Thummim, which were used when the priest was seeking divine guidance for the nation.

The Priestly Garments for the High Priest (Listed in Exodus 28:4)				
Item	Significance or practical purpose	Material		Additional data
Breastpiece (Exod. 28:15–30)	Judgment (names of tribes over heart of priest as memorial) Hold Urim and Thummim	Gold, blue, purple, and scarlet material Fine twisted linen Breastplate chains, cordage and gold Two rings of gold Blue cord to attach	Precious stones[3] Chains and rings attach to ephod	Square, folded double, 9 in x 9 in Twelve stones mounted in four rows engraved with names of tribes
Ephod (Exod. 28:6–14; 29:6)	Hold the breastpiece Gird robe	Gold, blue, purple, and scarlet material Fine twisted linen Two shoulder pieces Woven Band (same materials as ephod) Two chains of gold	Onyx stones (set in gold on the shoulder pieces)	Engraved names of tribes, six on each onyx stone (a memorial)

---

3   The precious stones are for each tribe four rows of three; the exact stones are debated. NASB translates as
      Row 1: ruby, topaz, and emerald;
      Row 2: turquoise, sapphire, and diamond;
      Row 3: jacinth, agate, and amethyst;
      Row 4: beryl, onyx, jasper.

Inauguration of Ancient Israelite Religion (8:1–9:24)

The Priestly Garments for the High Priest (Listed in Exodus 28:4)			
Item	**Significance or practical purpose**	**Material**	**Additional data**
Robe (Exod. 28:31–35)	Hold the ephod Tinkling of bells to protect priest	Open at the top (to fit over the head)	Binding around opening On hem, pomegranates of blue, purple, and scarlet and gold bells, alternating
Tunic (Exod. 28:39)	Basic garment	Checkered work of fine linen	
Turban (Exod. 28:39)	Head covering, holds the crown	Fine linen	Distinguishes high priest (see "caps" below)
Gold plate or holy crown (Exod. 28:36–38; 29:6)	Allow acceptance of consecrated things	Fastened to turban with blue cord	Engraved with "Holy to the Lord"
Sash (Exod. 28:39)		Work of weaver	
Urim and Thummim (Exod. 28:30)	Judgment		
Linen breeches (Exod. 28:42–43)	Cover bare flesh		Cover from loins to thighs

Priestly Garments for Other Priests				
Item	Significance or practical purpose	Material	Additional data	
Tunic (Exod. 28:40)	Basic garment Glory and beauty*			
Sash (Exod. 28:40)	Glory and beauty*			
Caps (Exod. 28:40)	Cover head Glory and beauty*			Covered head of all priests but the high priest
Linen breeches (Exod. 28:42–43)	Cover bare flesh			Cover from loins to thighs

*While Exodus 28:2 states that all of the garments were for glory and beauty, 28:40 specifies that purpose for the tunic, sash, and cap.

Chart 4. The priestly garments for the Israelite priest.

The second material Moses brought was the anointing oil (see Exod. 30:23–25, where the Lord gave Moses the recipe for the anointing oil). This specially formulated oil would be used to consecrate not only Aaron and his sons but also the tabernacle and its furnishings.

Figure 30. Artist's representation of high priest in priestly robes.

Anointing Oil

According to Exodus 30, the recipe for the anointing oil was 500 shekels of flowing myrrh, 250 shekels of fragrant cinnamon, 250 shekels of fragrant cane, 500 shekels of cassia, and a hin of olive oil. There are three areas of uncertainty for today's reader. First, there are questions regarding the measurements. At the time of the exodus, an Old Testament shekel was a unit of weight that was used for precious metals as well as other materials, and historically commentators have differed with their estimates regarding a modern equivalence. Milgrom (1991, 498) follows Norman Snaith who concluded that the result is a combination of fifty-four pounds of dry spices and a pint of oil, although it is not clear how the "liquid myrrh" is twenty-one pounds of dry spice. More recently, actual inscribed weights have been found, which help (see excursus "The Shekel," above). These would suggest that the combined weight of the spices was about twenty-three pounds. The other part of the mixture was a hin of olive oil. It seems generally accepted that a hin would have been approximately 3.667 liters or about 0.9686 gallons (https://www.convert-me.com/en/convert/history_volume/). Given these proportions, it would seem that regardless of how the liquid or flowing myrrh was understood, the anointing oil would have been rather thick.

Second, there are questions regarding make-up. It is not clear how the "liquid myrrh" is accounted (Milgrom 1991, 498). Keil and Delitzsch (1956, 215) follow rabbinic tradition that glosses over the liquid myrrh. They suggest that the three dry spices were soaked in water and boiled to extract their essence. This extract was mixed in the oil and liquid myrrh, and boiled again until the water evaporated.

Third, there are varying degrees of uncertainty regarding the identity of the spices. The first spice is flowing or liquid myrrh. Myrrh is generally accepted as the solidified resin of the *Commiphora myrrha* tree, which is native to the southern Red Sea region. The term "flowing myrrh" is less certain. Suggestions include a liquid exuded naturally prior to the resinous flow, an oil extract of the spice, or possibly resin from a different tree (Tucker 1986, 429; Van Beek 1958, 141–44; Van Beek 1960, 71–75, 84–86). The second spice is fragrant cinnamon, generally regarded to be the bark of *Cinnamomum zeylanicum*, which was found in India. The third spice is cassia. It is believed to have been the inner bark of the *Cinnamomum cassia* tree, which was found in Southeast Asia (Parry 1955, 193). The fourth spice, קְנֵה-בֹשֶׂם, is fragrant cane, translated as "calamus" in the KJV. It is generally considered to be *Acorus calamus* or sweet cane, although Maimonides and some Jewish scholars suggest *Cymbopogon* or ginger grass. Either grow in Palestine (https://www.templesinairi.org/biblical-garden-blog/the-mystery-ingredient). While some of these spices came from long distances, trade between Egypt and the spice sources predates the exodus event. For example, Hatshepsut, the female pharaoh who may have been the daughter of the pharaoh who raised Moses, is recorded to have sent ships east to bring back spices, most notably cinnamon, cassia, and myrrh (see figs. 31 and 32; Parry 1955, 194); so it seems likely that in the exodus, the Israelites carried the requisite spices out of Egypt with them.

Figure 31. Temple of Hatshepsut, Luxor, Egypt.

The third requirement was the sacrificial elements, specifically a bull for a purification offering, two rams, one for a burnt offering, and one for an ordination offering, and a basket of unleavened bread. Later (in 8:26) the text will clarify that the basket of unleavened bread included three types of bread.

Finally, the congregation was "assembled at the doorway of the Tent of Meeting." Given the small stage on which the ordination was to take

Inauguration of Ancient Israelite Religion (8:1–9:24)

place, there is debate as to who actually gathered. Today's audience might have two points of concern. The first concern would be the size of the crowd. The term used that is translated "congregation" (עֵדָה) is the same term used in Leviticus 4. Milgrom (1991, 499) argues that this term has flexibility. Here, given the significance of the event, it likely refers to the entire nation, or at least to all of the adult males. If indeed this was the same day that the tabernacle was dedicated, which included the shekinah descending onto the Holy of Holies, one might expect that everyone who could be at the tabernacle, would.

Figure 33. St. Catherine's Monastery, encampment plain, and surrounding hills.

Figure 32. Locations of exotic tree remains in front of the Temple of Hatshepsut.

If that is the case, the next concern might be how would it have been possible to for such a large group to gather in such a small space? Ephraim Radner (2008, 89–90) seems to picture a scenario where most of the crowd was outside the tent walls looking on, and thus viewed the scene at a distance. An analogy that comes to mind is Woodstock, where a crowd estimated at some 400,000 crowded around a small stage. If the location is the traditional site at Jebel Musa, it seems likely that many of the crowd could have been located on various hills that surround St. Catherine's monastery, looking down on the events at the entrance to the newly constructed tabernacle (see fig. 33).

Moses did "just as the Lord [YHWH] commanded him." This phrase will be repeated approximately eight times in these two chapters, showing the reader that Moses and Aaron carefully followed directions. With the congregation assembled, Moses set the stage for the nation by pointing out to them that the consecration process they were about to follow was at God's direction. This would show that there was divine sanction behind the actions being taken, which would be significant when questions arose regarding the basis on which Aaron or his successor acted. It would also be a ceremony that Aaron and his sons could later reflect upon to remind them of their consecrated status.

8:6–9. The actual consecration was a multistage process. The first stage was washing Aaron and his sons.

TRANSLATION ANALYSIS: "WASH"
The term רָחַץ is generally translated "wash," with the idea that it refers to "ritual washing" (see White 1980b), although BDB (s.v. "רָחַץ" 934) adds "wash off, away, or bathe." This is to be contrasted with כָּבַס which is used in Leviticus 11–15 to refer to laundering clothes in the case of uncleanness, or with שָׁטַף which is used in Leviticus 15 to refer to rinsing of hands or a bowl. In Leviticus, רָחַץ is

Inauguration of Ancient Israelite Religion (8:1–9:24)

used to refer to washing sacrificial animals as well as the flesh of the person.

It seems a general consensus that the washing of Aaron and his sons reflected a physical process that represented "inner spiritual cleansing" (Kellogg 1978, 190; Kiuchi 2007, 153; Mathews 2009, 75; Rooker 2000, 142; Ross 2002, 210; Wenham 1979, 139). At the same time, there is debate as to whether this required washing the entire body or just the hands and feet. Several factors are involved. First, Exodus 30:19 directs that prior to entering the Tent of Meeting the priest must wash his hands and feet. In contrast, directions for the Day of Atonement state that the priest needed to "bathe his body." Using the Day of Atonement as an analogy, Milgrom (1991, 501) argues for full immersion. Levine (1989, 50), on the other hand, notes a distinction in the wording and argues that when the word "to wash" (רָחַץ) is used alone, it applies only to the hands and feet analogous to the Exodus 30 directions. To complicate matters, the directions for the Day of Atonement in Leviticus 16:4 seem to show a sequence of dressing prior to the bathing, although the sequence is merely indicated by the ambiguous *waw* (which could mean "and" or it could mean "then"). Hartley (1992, 111) favors the concept of immersion, but notes that there are no directions regarding how and where the washing was done. He suggests "perhaps some type of a pool or a bath for immersion was set up in the courtyard of the tabernacle and screened off with a curtain." In contrast, the Exodus passage specifically mandates that the normal washing process (which directs washing just the hands and feet) is to be done in the laver, which in the tabernacle was set up between the Tent of Meeting and the altar (Exod. 30:18).

The Bronze Laver

The description of the tabernacle in Exodus 30:18 mandates a single bronze laver for washing. The description of Solomon's temple in 2 Chronicles describes a large "bronze sea" (יָם), but in addition, Solomon also made ten "basins," which is the same word translated as "laver" (כִּיּוֹר) in Exodus. While the priest was to wash in the laver or basin in Exodus, in the case of the temple the priests were to wash in the "sea"—the purpose of the basins was to wash the sacrifices (2 Chron. 4:6). We do not have any information regarding the size of the bronze laver in Exodus, but would note that it was to be portable. In contrast, 2 Chronicles describes the bronze sea as a large fixture measuring ten cubits from brim to brim (about fifteen feet across) and five cubits (about seven and a half feet) tall but was also on twelve oxen stands. According to 2 Chronicles, the sea would hold about three thousand baths of water (which would be more than seventeen thousand US gallons or about sixty-six thousand liters). The walls were a "handbreadth thick," (about three and a half inches or nine centimeters). Clearly this was not an item that could be transported easily, especially during the time in the wilderness. In addition to the fact that the laver had to be carried, another interesting tidbit suggesting its relatively small size is the statement that it was made "from the mirrors of the serving women who served at the doorway of the Tent of Meeting" (Exod. 38:8). Another point that should be noted is that while Solomon added the ten basins for the temple, the 2 Chronicles account also adds ten tables in the courtyard (2 Chron. 4:8).

While the practice of immersion seems to better portray the idea of overall spiritual cleansing, and one might expect that the ritual for the consecration of the priest should be on a par with the ritual for the critical important ceremony for the atonement of the nation, it would seem that the ritual for the consecration of Aaron as chief priest would follow the directions that had been given to this point. Assuming that the material of Sinai is generally chronologically sequenced, at the time of the consecration of the priests the only guidelines that had been given the priests were those in Exodus 30, which directed that they wash their hands and feet. It therefore seems likely that that would have been what Aaron and his sons did on this occasion. We should note that the directions for the Day of Atonement were given on the same day the events in Leviticus 8 occurred but subsequent to those events (i.e., after the consecration was complete) as shown by Leviticus 16.

After all were washed, for the second stage Moses dressed Aaron with the priestly garments that had been described in Exodus 28, consisting of a tunic, sash, robe, ephod, breastpiece containing the Urim and the Thummim, and a turban. Exodus gives a detailed description of the priestly garments, beginning with the external items. The actual consecration event covered here just mentions them by name, listing them in the order in which they were donned. Here we will just give a summary with a few salient observations. The last item listed in Exodus is linen breeches, "to cover their bare flesh." The text goes on to say they were to reach "from the loins even to the thighs" (Exod. 28:42). Leviticus does not mention them, which leads Levine (1989, 50) to assume that at the beginning, the priests were wearing their linen breeches. Balentine (2002, 73) suggests that it may mean that they were not sacred priestly garments, although that seems unlikely. Whether they already were dressed in the breeches may be a factor in the discussion of whether they washed their hands and feet, or bathed.

The Urim and Thummim

These two items are very obscure. The meaning of the names is speculative, which is why the names are left untranslated. Levine (1989, 50) looks at proposed etymologies and suggests that Urim indicates "curse," and deduces then that Thummim indicates "innocent." Rabbinic tradition suggests they mean "lights" and "perfection" although the LXX and Vulgate translate them as "teaching and truth" (Hartley 1992, 112). Outside of the citations in Exodus and Leviticus indicating that they were part of the high priest's clothing, they are mentioned by name only three other times in the Bible. Two of those are Ezra 2:63 and Nehemiah 7:65, which merely note that they were no longer present (both passages defer judgment on the issue of eating most holy things until such a time a priest arises who has the Urim and Thummim). The little we know about them essentially derives from Exodus 28. There they are noted with the definite article, suggesting that they were already in existence, but there is no explanation of their origin (Lange 1960, 72). That description shows that they were small, since they fit into the breastpiece of judgment, which was a one-span-by-one-span square pouch (approximately nine inches or twenty-three centimeters square) worn by the priest, but we are given no description. Their function seemed to be to provide information from God in response to inquiries by the high priest, but we are not told how. Many scholars suggest they are essentially two sacred lots, although how they were used is speculative. One view is that when there was an inquiry, the priest pulled out one stone which was either yes or no (Baker 1996, 58–59). Another view is that each was two-toned. If both were one color, the answer was yes, but if both were the other color, it was no. Two different colors indicated no response (Kleinig 2003, 189).

Other suggestions are similar. While most scholars seem to accept some concept of lots, there are problems with this. As Milgrom points out, "It is also clear that the Urim and Thummim had to be capable of answering more than merely yes or no because citations show they selected a tribe . . . and a city . . . indicated the hiding place of Saul . . . and detailed a complex military stratagem" (1991, 508). For example, in 1 Samuel 10, while Samuel apparently initially used "lots" (so most translations of the verb לְכַד, literally "to take") to identify the new king, when Saul was not present, further inquiry revealed "he is hiding himself by the baggage," not only showing Saul's location but the reason for it. Consequently, some scholars look beyond somewhat naturalistic explanations. For example, in his extensive study of the items, Cornelius Van Dam (1997, 224) suggests that the Urim and Thummim would illuminate (with "true" or "perfect" light) when removed from the ephod to verify the divine source of a declaration given by the high priest. In other words, they provided the people a supernatural validation of revelations that the high priest received from God. There is no reference to the use of the Urim and Thummim subsequent to David. Several scholars see an association between the disappearance of the Urim and Thummim and the rise of the office of prophet, perhaps as a consequence of priestly unfaithfulness. It is worth noting that if the function of the Urim and Thummim was essentially that of lots, conceivably they could have readily been replaced; and in fact, even in the NT, we see the use of lots to determine God's will, as in the case of the apostles in Acts 1:26.

The first item that Moses actually places on Aaron is the tunic (Exod. 28:39), which is made of "fine linen."

TRANSLATION ANALYSIS: "TUNIC"
The tunic (כָּתֹנֶת) was the basic garment of all priests. *TWOT* (1:459) describes it as a "long shirt-like garment." The word is related to the Akkadian *kitinnu*, which was a "linen garment made from *kitū* linen [*sic*]." It is interesting that this is the word used to describe the garment that God made for Adam after the fall, although that one was made from the skins of animals (see "Atonement" in the introduction). The word translated "fine linen" (שֵׁשׁ) is an Egyptian loan word (*sš*), which Austel (1980f, 959) describes as "white linen of exceptional quality imported from Egypt." Historically, linen seems to have been one of the first fibers used for textiles. The earliest Sumerians made linen garments for their priests (Kramer 1963, 104). Likewise, it was a common material in predynastic Egypt (Wilson 1956, 22, 24). Tanis, located near Goshen in Egypt, was a major center for linen manufacture (Baumann 1960, 100). Given the amount of time the nation had spent in Egypt, it is very likely that they were familiar with linen, and when they fled Egypt as refugees, may have taken an adequate amount of linen cloth with them.

While it may have been white, it also might have been multicolored, consisting of blue, purple, and scarlet threads, with gold threads interwoven.

Blue, Purple, and Scarlet

Exodus states that the priests' tunics all were to be woven. According to *TWOT* (2:901), the term שָׁבַץ describes the particular weaving pattern that is called "checkered" or "plaited." Milgrom (1991, 502) notes that the LXX translates it as "fringed," but the targumim suggest "checkered." Checkered weaving is a pattern that alternates strips of different colors in both directions. This could mean that the tunics were not white, but perhaps as Stuart (2006, 584) suggests, the material consisted of multicolored threads dyed "blue, purple, and scarlet." In addition, gold threads were also part of the weave, although how that was done is not clear (Rooker 2000, 142). While the ephod, band, and breastpiece are specifically delineated as being "blue, purple, and scarlet" (Exod. 28:6, 8, 15), the robe is specifically died blue, although it is also "checkered work" (Exod. 28:31, 4), and the tunic, turban, and sash have no color noted (Exod. 28:39).

The three colors blue, purple, and scarlet are the most common translations of the Hebrew phrase תְּכֵלֶת וְאַרְגָּמָן וְתֹלַעַת, which consistently appear together in the materials on the tabernacle and the clothing of the priests. All three colors used organic dyes, and modern analysis has discovered some of the sources. Blue or indigo came from a variety of plants. Purple was derived from several different Mediterranean shellfish. Scarlet (or red) dyes were taken from parasitic insects, or roots of plants belonging to the madder family (Melo 2009, 6, 10–11, 14). Milgrom (1991, 549) argues that "in ancient times only wool could successfully be dyed" and therefore claims that these three terms really refer to yarn of those colors. There is question regarding that conclusion since Eliso Kvavadze and colleagues (2009, 1359) note archaeological evidence of flax fibers (i.e., linen) from the Upper Paleolithic that were dyed. Further, if the three terms designated threads of wool, that would mean that the garment was a mixture of linen and wool, which raises questions with regard to Deuteronomy 22:11, which directs that the Israelites were not to wear "a material mixed of wool and linen together." In colonial America, this mixture with a linen warp and a woolen weft was known as "linsey-woolsey," which "combines the properties of strong linen with spongy wool" (https://www.eatonhilltextiles.com/woolens). In terms of Israel, Milgrom (1991, 501) argues that this mixture was considered holy, hence this directive that it was to be avoided by the people. Itamar Singer (2008, 30) notes that in the ancient world, red, blue, and purple were symbolic as the colors of gods and kings, which may have been a factor in the directive. While no reason is stated, it seems likely that the blend of those colors, not only in the garments of the priests but in the curtains of the tabernacle, served to present testimony to the God whom they served, although it is not clear how it was done.

As Mathews (2009, 76) states, it "communicated the holiness and majesty of God." Moses then girded Aaron with the sash (Exod. 28:39). The sash was essentially a belt used to tie the tunic around the waist. It, like the curtains of the tabernacle, was blue, purple, and scarlet (Exod. 26:36; 27:17), and is to be the work of a "weaver."

Inauguration of Ancient Israelite Religion (8:1–9:24)

> ### "Weaver"
> In the Exodus passage, the sash was described as the work of a רֹקֵם. This is a participle that is translated variously as "weaver," "embroiderer," or "needlework." The NASB translates it as "weaver" in Exodus 28:39 but adds a note suggesting that it literally means "variegator" (*TWOT* s.v. "רָקַם" 2:861). Embroidery would suggest sewing a raised thread design upon a fabric, such as making pomegranates on the hem of the blue robe (Exod. 28:31–34). Given that the items this term describes are the items made from the blue, purple, and scarlet materials, "weaver" is the better translation.

The third item of dress that Moses placed on Aaron was the robe (Exod. 28:31–34). As described in Exodus 28, it was a single piece of material that had a hole in the middle through which the priest could place his head. As such, it would fall down his chest and back, hanging on his shoulders—overall somewhat similar to some serapes seen in various westerns. The head slot was to be finished so that it did not unravel. The text does not specify the material, but it does indicate that it is to be all blue, and thus contrast with the tunic underneath it. Likewise, the size of the robe is not given. In addition, the robe was to have pomegranates placed around the hem. These may have been embroidered, or be pomegranate-shaped tassels made from the blue, purple, and scarlet material (Stuart 2006, 613). Between the pomegranates, the robe was to have gold bells that would tinkle as the priest entered and left the Holy Place—so that the priest would not die (Exod. 28:35).

The next item of clothing was the ephod (Exod. 28:6–13), which was apparently a "torso garment, that is, a piece of clothing that covers the body from thigh to shoulder, normally without covering either arms or legs" (Stuart 2006, 606). While often just white linen, in this case it is described as consisting of gold, blue, purple, scarlet, and fine twisted linen, the same composition as the rest of Aaron's garments. The front and back pieces were joined by two shoulder pieces by which it rested on the shoulders. Each shoulder piece also held an onyx stone mounted in gold filigree settings. The names of the twelve tribes were engraved on the onyx stones, six on each stone. As the text says, "Aaron shall bear their names before the Lord [YHWH] on his two shoulders for a memorial" (Exod. 28:12). A woven band served to secure the front and back pieces around the waist. In addition to the onyx stones on the shoulders, the priest also wore a breastpiece (Exod. 28:26–30), which basically was a pouch made from the same materials as the rest of the garments. The breastpiece was attached to the filigree settings of the onyx stones by two gold chains. On the breastpiece were four rows of precious stones, with the name of a different tribe engraved on each stone (see Exod. 28:17–20). Inside the breastpiece were the Urim and the Thummim (Exod. 28:30).

> ## The Breastpiece
> The Exodus passage directs that the breastpiece contain four rows of three precious or semiprecious stones each. While the text specifies what stones go in each row, translators disagree on what the modern terminology should be. Three popular translations are shown in chart 5.

While each tribe's name is engraved on a stone, we are not given a sequence, nor any indication of any particular value or relationship between any tribe and its stone. As Stuart (2006, 610) says, "they were all valuable gems, indicating how precious the Israelites were to Yahweh."

NASB		
Ruby	Topaz	Emerald
Turquoise	Sapphire	Diamond
Jacinth	Agate	Amethyst
Beryl	Onyx	Jasper

ESV		
Sardius	Topaz	Carbuncle
Emerald	Sapphire	Diamond
Jacinth	Agate	Amethyst
Beryl	Onyx	Jasper

NIV		
Carnelian	Chrysolite	Beryl
Turquoise	Lapis Lazuli	Emerald
Jacinth	Agate	Amethyst
Topas	Onyx	Jasper

Chart 5. Different understandings of the stones on the high priest's breastpiece.

The final item of clothing was the turban (Exod. 28:39), which was made of fine linen. Like the tunic, it is not clear if it was white, or blue, purple, and scarlet. The turban also set Aaron off from his sons—Leviticus 8:13 states that they were clothed with "caps" or "headbands." More importantly, it contained a "golden plate" on which was engraved the phrase "Holy to the Lord [YHWH]" (Exod. 28:36–38).

The Turban

As noted in Exodus, the dress of the high priest concluded with a "turban" (מִצְנֶפֶת), which Charles Feinberg (1980a) describes as "a sign of royalty." In contrast, the ordinary priests wore a "cap" (מִגְבָּעוֹת). The turban was further distinguished by a golden plate inscribed "Holy to the Lord [YHWH]," which here is given the further denomination of "holy crown." However, as Umberto

Cassuto (1987, 384) notes, it differs from a crown in that it really is placed only on the forehead and held in place by a blue cord. The word translated "plate" (צִיץ) can also mean flower or blossom. According to Hartley (1980a), it is derived from a verb that might refer to the growth of plants or the gleam of a crown. As such, it is possible that the item had the shape of a blossom (see also Hartley 1992, 107).

8:10–12. Following the dressing of Aaron, and before Moses dressed Aaron's sons, he anointed the tabernacle and Aaron, which is stage three. Using oil to anoint people and things was a practice seen throughout the OT. Ross (2002, 211) and others note that the overall evidence of Scripture is that the oil represents the Spirit of God. The purpose of anointing was to consecrate persons or things so that they were "set apart or made distinct for the service of the Lord." Aaron was the first person anointed in the OT, and his position was that of priest. While oil alone could serve to anoint in ordinary circumstances, for the tabernacle and priesthood, God prescribed a special blend of anointing oil that was not allowed to be replicated for other purposes.

Anointed

While the first position to be anointed was that of priest, when the nation began asking for a king, God sent Samuel to anoint Saul as king. Given the suggested definition, this would indicate that the role of king for Israel was a unique position "for the service of God." Building on this, the OT use of messiah (anointed one) would carry a double significance of both priest and king, which for the nation of Israel was a syncretism that was not possible.

Lange (1960, 72) has suggested that as Moses went through the tabernacle and anointed "all that was in it," it would seem that he necessarily entered the Holy of Holies. However, that may not be the case, since the purpose was to consecrate each item for the service of God. This, of course, would have included all of the furniture and utensils that the priests would use. However, the only thing that would have been in the Holy of Holies would have been the ark of the covenant, upon which had already descended the shekinah, and the ark was not really an item that the priests utilized as part of their service. While the admonition to Aaron not to enter the Holy of Holies except on Yom Kippur would not occur until Leviticus 16, given the evidence of Exodus 40 of how the glory of the Lord (the shekinah) filled the tabernacle, it seems unlikely that Moses would have been able to enter at this time.

It would seem that the normal practice would have been that Moses would have dipped his finger into the oil, and then sprinkled with one stroke for each item (Milgrom 1991, 518). It is interesting that the text clearly states that the altar is anointed seven times. This would be indicative of a special status of the altar. Kleinig (2003, 190) notes that the closest parallel is the case of a leper in Leviticus 14:27 who would be sprinkled with the blood of the sacrificed bird seven times and then pronounced clean.

Following the anointing of the tabernacle and all of its furnishings, Moses then anointed Aaron. However, instead of sprinkling, Moses poured some of the oil on Aaron's head to anoint him. Compared to the normal process of anointing, this was clearly extravagant. As such, David uses it as a figure of speech in Psalm 133:2.

8:13. Very briefly the text relates how Moses then dressed Aaron's four sons in a manner similar to how he dressed their father. They too were clothed in tunics that were tied up with sashes. Exodus 28:4 indicates that these items were identical to those made for their father. Overall, however, there were several key differences. First, as noted already, instead of turbans they received caps. The remaining differences really are items that they did not receive. They did not receive an ephod, nor did they receive a breastpiece. Likewise, they did not receive the golden plate or "holy crown" on their foreheads. Lastly, whereas Aaron was anointed with the special oil, the text never states that the sons were anointed. This, however, is a debated issue. Gane (2004a, 164) seems to see only the high priest as anointed, and as a consequence he is called the "the anointed priest" in passages like Leviticus 6:22. The statement in 7:30 that Moses sprinkled the anointing oil and blood mixture on Aaron and his sons, following by the statement in Leviticus 10:7 that after the Nadab and Abihu incident "the oil of anointing is still on you," strongly indicates that they had been anointed along with Aaron. However, it is also evident that when the oil was poured on Aaron's head (Lev. 8:12) as opposed to the later sprinkling, it showed an elevated status for Aaron (Hartley 1992, 112).

8:14–29. With all the priests properly attired, the next step was a series of sacrifices that represent the consecration and atonement for the priests so that they might preside over the sacrificial rituals for the nation. The process that was followed was very similar to the daily sacrifice routine.

First, they brought the required bull of the purification offering (Lev. 4:3–12). In this case, Aaron and all of his sons followed the requisite procedure and laid their hands on the bull. Moses served as the priest and took some of the blood. Instead of sprinkling it before the Lord as in the normal purification offering, Moses put it on the horns of the altar, a step that is only otherwise done on the Day of Atonement. The purpose of this step was to purify the altar. Moses then poured out the remaining blood at the base of the altar to consecrate it. The net result is that the altar was now prepared for atonement.

TRANSLATION ANALYSIS: "PURIFY," "CONSECRATE," "ATONE"
Leviticus 8:15 combines three theological terms that we tend to struggle with. First, the blood "purifies" the altar. This uses the *piel* stem of the verb חטא, which we indicated in the unit "Purifying Oneself Before a Holy God" (4:1–6:7 [HB 5:26]) serves to indicate that the "sin" or its effect is removed (see the translation analysis for 4:2). The question that arises is, what is being removed? Hartley (1992, 113) concludes that what is removed is "any uncleanness that is present from either the altar or the priests before they are consecrated as holy." However, Mathews (2009, 78) correctly observes that "the blood does not literally cleanse; rather it symbolizes the spiritual cleansing that can only be accomplished by the spilling of blood, that is, at the cost of a life." This is further indicated by the noted result—with the combined daubing and pouring out of the blood, the altar was now "consecrated." As noted in the discussion of "Holy" in the introduction, this would be a derivative meaning of קדֹשׁ, which signified a specific function with respect of drawing sinful humans closer to God. As such, "atonement" was not made for the altar itself. The issue is the last word in the Hebrew, עָלָיו. This is the preposition על with the third-person masculine singular suffix. The preposition is better translated "upon" rather than "for." As the HCSB translation puts it, "that atonement can be made on it."

With the altar prepared following the blood manipulation, Moses processed the bull's carcass following the Lord's directions. He took the required fat and entrails and burned them on the altar. The guidelines in Leviticus 6:9–13 direct that the fire on the altar is to be perpetual, but it appears that that perpetuity would start after the inaugural service in Leviticus 9:24. While the ongoing services had not yet started, during the inaugural week, sacrifices were being made, including morning burnt offerings (Lev. 9:17). However, it would seem that each offering during the inaugural week was burned with "ordinary fire" (Lange 1960, 83). Based on Leviticus 6:30, the priest would have eaten a portion of the purification offering; however, Moses was not a priest. Consequently, he continued on and burned the remains, including its hide and flesh, at the fire outside the camp.

Moses next presented the ram of the burnt offering, an offering of consecration. Again, Aaron and his sons laid their hands on the animal. After sprinkling the blood around the altar, Moses then burned the sacrifice in accordance with previous directions.

The sacrifice of the second ram is very similar to the shalom offering, but there are some significant differences in the ritual. First, instead of sprinkling the blood against the altar after slaughtering the ram, Moses took some of the blood and placed it on the right ear lobe, the right thumb, and the big toe of the right foot, first of Aaron and then of his sons. The significance of these three daubs is not given in the text, but two explanations are suggested. First, it might be viewed as a visual figure of speech—the parts represent the whole. It is generally agreed that in that culture, the right side was preferred, but that only explains part of the matter. Why were just those three parts picked? For that reason, most scholars seem to understand it as indicating some correlation between the particular parts and various activities of life. Noordtzij (1982, 99) succinctly describes it as the "organs of hearing, doing, and walking were in this manner consecrated to the service of the Lord." This seems the most likely explanation.

A second difference is that in the case of the shalom offering, the breast and the right thigh were given to the priest as his portion (Lev. 7:32). In this case, Moses received the breast as his portion, but the right thigh was burned, probably because Moses was not a priest. After Moses daubed the blood on the five men, he took the right thigh along with the portions of the animal normally burned, and with one each of the three types of bread in the basket, placed them on the

hands of Aaron and his sons. They lifted the items they held to the Lord as a "wave offering" (תְּנוּפָה). Moses then retook the items and burned them as a fire offering (אִשֶּׁה). They became a "soothing aroma" (רֵיחַ נִיחֹחַ), showing that the sacrifice was acceptable (see the translation analysis on Lev. 1:9). Overall, these items were termed an "ordination offering" (מִלֻּא).

TRANSLATION ANALYSIS: "ORDINATION OFFERING"

The term translated "ordination offering" is a noun defined by Walter Kaiser (1980f) as "installation." It is derived from the verb מָלֵא, which means "to be full or to fill" (Kaiser 1980f). In this case, it seems the hands of the priests are literally filled with the assigned portions of the sacrifice, although in return the priests give it back to God. As Levine (1989, 53) describes it, "the priests surrender their own portion to God."

After burning the ordination offering, Moses presented the breast as a wave offering to God, in essence acknowledging that God was the source of this provision. The text does not mention it, but it would appear that the remainder of the ram would have been cooked and given to Aaron and his sons in accordance with the normal procedure for the shalom offerings—the offeror receives the meat. This would be the meat that Aaron and his sons cook and eat in 8:31. Once again, the text notes that Moses had done "just as the Lord [YHWH] had commanded." However, there was still more to be done.

8:30–36. After the sacrifices were completed, Moses took some of the blood from the altar and mixed it with some of the anointing oil and sprinkled Aaron and his sons and all of their garments. This seems to be the only time that the blood would be mixed with the oil, suggesting a relationship between the consecration of the altar (8:11) with that of the priests (Kleinig 2003, 193). Levine (1989, 54) suggests that this sprinkling completed the ordination. However, there does seem to have been two more steps, which were related to Aaron and his sons by Moses.

First, they boiled the meat and ate it along with bread from the basket that had been brought earlier. By direction, the cooking and the eating were to be done at the doorway of the Tent of Meeting. After they had eaten, they were to burn any remainders in the fire, which fits the pattern of the shalom offering, which required that nothing could be left until the next day (Lev. 7:15).

Finally, the newly consecrated priests were to remain in the doorway of the Tent of Meeting for seven days. We are not told what happened during those seven days, but several things are clear. Leviticus 8:33 emphasizes that the ordination process is a seven-day process, and would not be complete until that week was finished. Second, that entire process is again viewed as an atonement process. Third, this is a life-and-death matter—if they violated God's directives, they would die.

TRANSLATION ANALYSIS: "KEEP THE CHARGE"

The phrase translated "keep the charge of the Lord [YHWH]" in several translations is an interesting phrase that contains a bit of a word-play. The main verb, "keep," is a second-person plural, *qal* perfect of the verb שָׁמַר, which means "to keep, guard, observe or give heed" (Austel 1980b, 939). The basic idea is "to exercise great care over." The word translated "charge" (מִשְׁמֶרֶת) is a noun meaning "obligation or service" derived from the same verb (Austel 1980b, 940). As such, a plausible translation might be "exercise great care of the things of YHWH that need great care."

Exactly how this directive to remain in the doorway of the tent worked is not clear. If the ordination process concluded with the sprinkling in 8:30, one wonders what the new priests did for the next week. Was that to be a time of prayer and fasting? There is nothing that points in that direction. The traditional view is that they repeated the entire sequence seven times. While this fits well with other "important transitions in human life" (Baker 1996, 61), it still leaves a lot of practical questions. Does 8:35 literally mean they were to be there twenty-four seven? What else did they do besides repeat the sequence? What did they eat? Where did they sleep? What about toiletry issues? Milgrom (1991, 535) sees the Festival of Booths as an analogy, where they might be allowed to leave the courtyard for bodily needs. However, he also sees the possibility of a space within the courtyard "reserved for toilet facilities." While ideally the idea of a week praying and fasting is attractive, without specific directions in that regard it seems best to follow the traditional view that they repeated the rituals of the first day, which would not preclude time of prayer and fasting. In any regard, the chapter ends with another statement that they did everything that God commanded.

Aaron Inaugurates Corporate Worship in the Tabernacle (9:1–24)

With the tabernacle complete and consecrated, and with the priests now dressed and ordained, the new priests initiated corporate worship using the newly commissioned sacrificial system.

9:1–4. Leviticus 9 jumps a week to the conclusion of the ordination of Aaron and his sons. At this point Moses directed Aaron, his sons, and the leaders of the nation to begin Israel's corporate worship system that they had been preparing for over the previous several months. The book of Leviticus began the day that the tabernacle was erected. On that day, the newly constructed altar had been anointed and initiated as Moses performed sacrifices on behalf of the priests. Now, for the first time, the priests will perform sacrifices on behalf of the nation. The timing is significant since the nation was approaching the one-year anniversary of the exodus, and in a week would celebrate the first commemoration of Passover.

Moses told Aaron that the inaugural service was to consist of two parts. First, Aaron would offer a male calf for a purification offering and a ram for a burnt (or consecration) offering for himself. The requirement for another purification carries a subtle but extremely significant message here, since Aaron and his sons have just spent a week in the tabernacle where at least once (and if our supposition is correct, daily) they had performed a purification offering. And during that week, Aaron apparently never left the Holy Place. This would seem to indicate that even after being "purified" he was not pure, which should signal to all the challenge of approaching a holy God. It is somewhat ironic that in this case, Aaron was told specifically that his purification offering was to be a calf. A week earlier, in his instructions the Lord told Moses that "if the anointed priest sins" (and Aaron is now the anointed priest), his purification offering was to be a bull. The fact that Moses directed Aaron to sacrifice a calf instantly would bring to mind the earlier issue of the golden calf idol (Exod. 32:4), a fact that was picked up by early Jewish targumim (Hartley 1992, 122).

> *TRANSLATION ANALYSIS: "CALF"*
> The term used in both cases is עֵגֶל, which could be a calf as old as two years (Milgrom 1991, 572). Here, the descriptor "son of the herd" is added (עֵגֶל בֶּן־בָּקָר), from which most modern translations add "bull," indicating a male.

While several options were provided for burnt offerings, Aaron is also directed to provide a ram. The reason a ram was directed is not clear, but Sklar (2014, 151) suggests that the reason both a calf and a ram were directed is that it would have been an offering "especially fit for a king," which may indicate something regarding the role of the high priest in the theocratic nation.

Figure 34. High priest offering a sacrifice of a goat.

The second portion of that inaugural worship was a corporate sacrifice for the nation. The leaders were to provide a male goat for a corporate purification offering. There are two points of interest regarding this offering that are unique. First, in the case of unintentional sin requiring corporate purification, the required sacrifice was a bull (Lev. 4:14). A goat was the required sacrifice for individual unintentional sin for "anyone of the common people"; however, in that case it would be a female goat (Lev. 4:27–28). A male goat for a purification offering was the required sacrifice for an individual leader (Lev. 4:23), but the text is clear that this offering is for the purification of the people (Lev. 9:15). That a male goat is required here for a corporate offering may hint at individual responsibility even within a corporate setting. Key for this case is that the congregation has no specific sin but still needs purification. The purification offering is followed by a calf and a lamb for a burnt offering for consecration, an ox and a ram for shalom offerings, and a gift (grain) offering mixed with oil. His directions end with a clause asserting that "the Lord [YHWH] will appear to you."

Inauguration of Ancient Israelite Religion (8:1–9:24)

TRANSLATION ANALYSIS: "THE LORD [YHWH] WILL APPEAR"

This relative clause is introduced with the conjunction (כִּי), which may be translated two ways, either as "because," showing that the appearance is certain and they need to be prepared (Rooker 2000, 151), or as "that," suggesting that the appearance is conditional (Bailey 2005, 110; Wenham 1979, 148). Given the subsequent explanation in the final clause of 9:6, which is introduced with a *waw*, it would seem that the latter should be preferred. The verb in this clause, רָאָה, "to see," is in the *niphal*, a passive form. In essence, the Lord will allow himself to be seen, a reminder that his presence is not always visible. This is amplified in 9:6 with the emphasis on the "glory of the Lord [YHWH]."

9:5–22. Having received those instructions, Aaron and his sons brought what Moses had commanded to the front of the Tent of Meeting, and the congregation gathered outside. Basically, the focal point is now the altar. At this point, Moses has turned the worship process over to Aaron, and he and his sons perform the entire ceremony. While the text traces that process, it parallels previous passages. It might be described briefly as following the directions that have been given "just as Moses had commanded." It is significant that Aaron's first sacrifice is his own purification offering.

After he finished the sacrifices, Aaron lifted his hands and blessed the people. Tradition suggests that he pronounced the "priestly blessing" that is in Numbers 6:22–27, although that is not specified here. Ross (2002, 224) observes that it was common for Israelites to use the phrase "the Lord bless you" (see Ruth 2:4) as a greeting. However, he suggests that as the "theocratic leader," Aaron's blessing was much more; it was "a word from God." If Aaron's blessing was something like the passage in Numbers, it would be an assurance that God was with the worshipper and as a result would empower the worshipper following his worship.

> **Blessing**
>
> Like its English equivalent ("bless"), the verb *barak* (בָּרַךְ) is somewhat vague. While we think of good things when we hear the term, in the OT some of the blessings are a mixed bag. For example, when Jacob blessed his twelve sons in Genesis 49, at the conclusion the text says, "He blessed them, everyone with the blessing appropriate to him" (Gen. 49:28). And yet, Reuben's blessing was that he would lose preeminence (49:3); and with regard to Simeon and Levi, Jacob declared "Cursed be their anger, for it is fierce; and their wrath, for it is cruel. I will disperse them in Jacob and scatter them in Israel" (49:7). Overall, as used in the OT, the term seems to reflect God's "guarantee that they will achieve the [God's] desired objective" (Harbin 2005, 92). In essence it would seem that the blessing would be an interweaving of God's sovereign work with human endeavors. Here it would derive out of a sincere desire on the part of the individual or group to truly worship God, which means that they would be subsuming their desires to his, and that he would sustain them in the process.

It is not clear where Aaron made this declaration. According to Exodus 27, this altar was approximately seven and a half feet square, and four and a half feet high. This would suggest that some type of platform was next to the altar for the priest to stand on. Exodus 20:26 warns against having steps, which leads to a conclusion that an earthen ramp may have been constructed (Milgrom 1991, 587).

After blessing the nation, Aaron descended, and he and Moses went into the tent of the meeting. We are not told what happened there. Levine (1989, 57) suggests it was to pray for the anticipated appearance of God. Gane (2004a, 178–79) suggests they prayed that "God would accept the sanctuary, its priesthood, and their sacrifices." Lange (1960, 78) suggests that Moses entered to complete the initiation of Aaron. Within that context, it seems a likely aspect might be that Moses took Aaron into the Tent of Meeting where he then "officially" (before God) passed the responsibility of the sacrificial worship on to Aaron. Whatever passed between the three (Moses, Aaron, and God) when Moses and Aaron came out from the Tent of Meeting, they blessed the people and the "glory of the Lord [YHWH] appeared to all the people." Kleinig (2003, 210) points out that this was the first and only time in the history of Israel that the glory of the Lord, unveiled, appeared to the whole congregation. It is not clear what that might have been like, but Sklar (2014, 154) suggests the idea of a fiery cloud with fire coming out. At a minimum it would seem to have involved extremely brilliant light.

However the glory manifested itself, the episode concludes with fire that "came out from before the Lord [YHWH], and consumed everything that was on the altar." While the sacrificial portions on the altar would have been burning gradually, now they were suddenly and totally consumed. Hartley (1992, 121) understands that this total consumption of the already burning sacrifices is "characteristic of the synergistic nature of biblical faith, that is, God and man working together. God accepts and enhances what people have begun in obedience to his instructions." Perhaps that is why the resulting embers on the altar became the perpetual fire (Lev. 6:9, 12) that tradition maintains kept burning until the temple was built, and once rekindled there, burned until the reign of Manasseh (Lange 1960, 79).

The response of the people was to shout and fall upon their faces. Sklar suggests that the shout was one of joy in response to the activity of the Lord (2014, 154). As such, this event would seem to stand in stark contrast to the same people's response several months earlier when God spoke to them shortly after they arrived at Mount Sinai where they backed away in fear (Exod. 20:18).

> *TRANSLATION ANALYSIS: "SHOUT"*
> Most translations seem to translate רָנַן as "shout." William White (1980d, 851) adds the idea of "shout for joy." He goes on to point out that the term is used throughout the OT "to describe the joy of Israel at God's saving acts."

Their physical response to fall on their faces before this revelation of God in his power would have been one that demonstrated profound worship and awe. In essence, this was a third portion of the inaugural service, which was performed by the Lord and concluded the inauguration of the nation's corporate worship system.

THEOLOGICAL FOCUS

Israel was brought out of Egypt to be a kingdom of priests. The idea of a kingdom demands organization and a king. The king was to be God. The priesthood of all Israelites required a structure. As we have already noted, one of the functions of the time at Sinai was to develop and begin a system of corporate worship for God's people, that kingdom of priests that would proclaim the glories of the Lord God. Priests will not be sinless. They will know their sin and their God who forgives, cleanses, and restores. This will be the message they will be called to proclaim as a kingdom of priests to the nations.

PREACHING AND TEACHING STRATEGIES

Exegetical and Theological Synthesis

The selection of the Levites as a tribe of priests for the kingdom and the selection of Aaron as the original high priest would have been surprising to any outside observer. Levi was a tribe that would not possess a territory in the kingdom because of a mistake its ancestor had made. And yet, God in his mercy would give the tribe a greater position. Aaron was an abject failure whom God chose specifically to portray his redeeming grace.

In this unit, we see Aaron chosen and set apart by God for service through a series of rituals that provide symbolic representations of spiritual truth. Aaron's brokenness before God is evidenced through his obedience to every detail that the Lord commanded. God intends for Aaron to be identified by his new covering and position (high priest), not by his former sin and trade (idol maker). Those symbolic representations are discussed in some detail in Exodus. Here they merely provide the foundation on which the ordination of Aaron and his sons is built. We should not get so deeply involved in trying to understand those details that we miss the overall picture.

The unit wraps up with Aaron assuming his responsibilities as the high priest for the nation and performing the first of what would be continuing daily responsibilities. That he was effective in fulfilling the role God gave him is evident in the last verse, where God emphatically endorses his position and service with fire that consumes the sacrifices. It is significant that Aaron is the only high priest who is ordained and inaugurated through such a spectacular sign. When it came time for Aaron to die, he was taken to Mount Hor along with his son Eleazar. There, Moses stripped Aaron of his priestly robes and dressed Eleazar with them. In this rather subdued and somber manner, the high priesthood would pass to the next generation. This would be perpetual, in preparation for the one true High Priest.

Preaching Idea
God provides a way to atone for your sin, so that you may come before him in worship.

Contemporary Connections

What does it mean?
What does it mean that God must atone for sin if we are to worship him? Leviticus is the unfolding story of how a holy God creates the means for his unholy people to worship him.

They were created by him and redeemed from bondage for this purpose. Yet, none is worthy to come before him. All are unclean, unholy. Divine cleansing (God's prescribed atoning work) is the means by which God prepares us to enter into relationship with him. By selecting Aaron as high priest from the tribe of Levi, the Lord God places both the need for and the effectiveness of atonement at the forefront of the thoughts of his people. They see that worship is founded upon atonement.

This decision by God imbeds two other truths into their lives. First, the priest is not the focus of worship, but God's chosen means by which they may be led to worship. This abolishes the dangerous practice of placing one's faith in the ongoing sanctity of a priest. Second, their past sin does not hold sufficient power over them to prevent them from going before the Lord God in worship. It is God's desire and character to display his mercy by cleansing and restoring those who humbly return to him.

Is it true?
Is it true that God provides a way to atone for our sin so we can worship him? This is the gospel story. God has chosen to prepare us for this truth by displaying his glory through the remarkable practice of drawing unworthy, fallen sinners to the altar, only to send them out into the world as forgiven witnesses of his grace and mercy. Consider Abraham giving away Sarah, or Moses murdering a man. Think of David the adulterer, Jehoshaphat the ally of Ahab, Peter the denier, or Paul the persecutor of Christ. God demonstrates his steadfast love and mercy by forgiving those who have sinned against him and sending these fallen individuals out into the world cleansed and restored, so that other sinners may know that their past sin may be forgiven, and they can be free to worship their Creator.

We see this practice throughout personal redemptive history. Our story will primarily be a story of how God has forgiven us rather than a story of our sinlessness. This is the story God gives to us, to draw others who are burdened by their sin to humbly come before him.

Now what?

There are many in our world who are weakened by past sins and heavy with the burdens of life who do not see God as either relevant or approachable. How does a holy God call those he has redeemed and restored to draw others to lay their broken lives before him? He provides those who come before him with a new identity—cleansing us of the old self, setting us apart, and dressing us as a new creation in Christ. If God is doing the work, who cannot be made clean? Who will not be restored? No one lies outside the reach of his almighty hand!

As one who is humbled and burdened understands who another believer once was and experiences who they now are under Christ, they should see an example of the hand of God at work before them. There is great release in knowing that God knows us not by the old covering (who we were) but the new (who we now are). Being a child of God is coming to a joyful understanding of the centrality God's atoning work in your life.

Creativity in Presentation

Everyone in the congregation is aware of examples of ugly duckling stories, where what something or someone once was is eclipsed because of what they have now become. Here is a short list you could draw from:

1. Extreme makeover: you could use an example of a house or a person if appropriate
2. Cinderella: one everyone despised becomes someone truly treasured
3. Example of a current sports figure on a new team with a breakout season because of a new coach or trainer
4. A fresh Navy recruit going into training, and then coming out at graduation

These are all pictures of visible transformation made possible in large part by the work of someone else. Encourage them to focus on the before and after. What has changed? Is the change real or only a facade? How would they know? What evidence would they have that this was real? Will they know the person/object by the way it was or the way it now is? What would be necessary for them to submit themselves to such a makeover?

Another idea may be to appeal to the love of a parent. Parents see their children in both their worst and in their best circumstances. Ask them to remember a particular behavior or character flaw that they have invested much time, effort, and prayer in leading their child through. Now, as they see their child, do they see them as they once were (steeped in immaturity and selfishness) or as they now are (humbled and growing in obedience)? How does God see us? How does he desire that we see other believers?

God provides a way to atone for your sin so that you may come before him in worship.

- Aaron, a high priest?
  ◦ Fit for execution (golden calf), but chosen for the priesthood
  ◦ Not the focus of their worship, but the one who will lead them into worship
  ◦ A visual reminder that past sin does not prevent them from humbly going before the Lord
- Being made holy: an extreme makeover
  ◦ Cleansing inside and out
  ◦ Ready to worship
- What did it mean to them then? What does it mean always? What do we do now?
  ◦ The need for a holy intermediary
  ◦ The ongoing need for a holy intermediary
  ◦ Seeing the role of Christ now for eternity

DISCUSSION QUESTIONS

1. What is the value of rituals as part of the consecration of spiritual leaders?

2. Why might the selection of Aaron to be high priest be both a concern to the nation of Israel as well as an encouragement?

3. God designed special clothing for his priests to wear when they served, a practice that seems to have been abrogated in the early church. What might be the advantages of each?

Leviticus 10:1–20

EXEGETICAL IDEA
The decision of Nadab and Abihu to usurp God's revealed standards and set out on their own in establishing a novel means ("strange fire") to come into his presence predictably led to their public destruction.

THEOLOGICAL FOCUS
Because he is holy, God, not man, establishes the means by which his people are able to safely come before him.

PREACHING IDEA
We are not free to usurp God's standards to design a personalized means of coming into his presence.

PREACHING POINTERS
The minds of God's people were overwhelmed with the joyful knowledge that Aaron, the former law-breaking idol-maker, had been publicly cleansed and re-fashioned under the authority of God to be their high priest! What an amazing and glorious God they served! Then suddenly, in a flash, they were jolted by the equally public destruction of Aaron's two oldest sons, Nadab and Abihu. The offense? Nadab and Abihu disregarded God's instructions and chose to experiment with their own ideas about how to come into the presence of the Almighty God of creation. The result was their public, personal destruction. A week that had showcased the abundant mercy of God ended with a dramatic exhibition of the unyielding holiness of God.

Finding the sweet spot between freshness and impulsive innovation in worship will often prove to be tricky. Yet, when coming into God's presence becomes too much about us, we may become casual or aloof and carelessly seek novel tools to bring with us into God's presence. When does this desire for individualized worship reveal something to us about us? We should not settle for bland worship, but we should remember that our omniscient God is the one who establishes the means by which we are to come before him safely. What is it that tempts us to carelessly venture outside of God's directives? Are we making worship more about us than about God? To do so is to risk personal destruction. When we so customize worship that it emphasizes us, it quickly becomes unsafe.

STANDING BEFORE A HOLY GOD (10:1–20)

LITERARY STRUCTURE AND THEMES (10:1–20)

In our last unit, we noted that Leviticus 8–10 constitutes an extended historical narrative that records three phases of a single week-long event. We included the first two phases as a single unit where God directed the implementation of the priesthood and the priest-led corporate sacrificial system. The second phase began a week after the first phase began. In the first phase, in Leviticus 8, Moses prepared the priests, clothed them in their priestly robes, and then ordained them, a process that lasted a week. At the end of that week (on the eighth day), in Leviticus 9, the newly ordained priests inaugurated the corporate sacrificial system, which God validated by sending fire to the altar to consume the freshly prepared sacrifices. Apparently, Leviticus 10 took place on that same day, in which case the disobedience of Nadab and Abihu transformed the day of pious celebration into a somber tragedy.

Indications That Leviticus 9 and 10 Were on the Same Day

The events in Leviticus 10 clearly follow the ordination of Aaron and his sons as priests and their inaugural sacrifice, although the text does not relate how soon. While in a different chapter in our modern Bibles, in the Hebrew it is connected to the preceding events simply by the standard historical narrative sequence indicator, a *waw*. Textually, the Nadab and Abihu incident appears immediately after the fire that "came out from before the Lord [YHWH] and consumed the burnt offering." In 10:7, Moses tells Aaron and his other two sons that they need to remain in the tabernacle "for the Lord's anointing oil is upon you." While this may just mean that they were

---

now anointed, more likely it suggests that the oil is still present from the earlier ritual. Additionally, the last portion of Leviticus 10 that addresses the priestly eating of sacrifices seems to refer to the sacrifices just offered in Leviticus 9. The final step of the priests eating the meat had not taken place, but that food was not allowed to remain until the next day. Also, in 10:19, Aaron responds to Moses and refers to the sin and burnt offerings Nadab and Abihu offered "this very day," which seems to refer to the sacrifices described in Leviticus 9. The description of the sacrifices in Leviticus 9 suggests that the inaugural events took place early on the eighth day, that is, the communal offerings in Leviticus 9:15–22 seem to set the normal sequence for the daily sacrifices the priests followed subsequent to this event (Rainey 1975, 203). As such, the goat of the sin offering that Aaron did not eat would have been the people's sin offering presented in 9:15.

Key themes in this chapter are that God will judge disobedience, even in the case of his chosen priests; and that disobeying God's express directions, even with the best of intentions, can have devastating consequences.

- *Nadab and Abihu Disobey God (10:1–2)*
- *Responses to Nadab's and Abihu's Deaths (10:3–20)*

EXPOSITION (10:1–20)

Following God's validation of the new priesthood, Aaron's sons Nadab and Abihu prepared to offer incense. If Leviticus 9 and 10 took place on the same day, then the action

Standing Before a Holy God (10:1–20)

of Nadab and Abihu in 10:1 would proably have been intended to be part of the evening burning of incense as laid out in Exodus 30:8. However, they did something wrong and were immediately struck dead. Moses hastened to ensure that further mistakes were not made and that the inaugural corporate worship service finished appropriately, even if in a flawed manner.

Nadab and Abihu Disobey God (10:1–2)

10:1–2. The problem related in 10:1 is that Nadab and Abihu offered "strange fire before the Lord [YHWH]" and, as a result, in 10:2, they died.

> *TRANSLATION ANALYSIS: "STRANGE FIRE"*
> The phrase translated "strange fire" is אֵשׁ זָרָה. The word אֵשׁ simply means "fire," but could denote the coals or "burning embers" placed within the firepan that would gradually burn the incense (Levine 1989, 58). Levine goes on to note that the meaning of the word זָרָה is "elusive." Before one determines how it was strange, one must decide what is strange—the coals, or the incense? It seems more likely that it was the coals they used that were strange.

Exactly what they did is unclear, and as a result, various speculations have been offered. Possibilities as to their offense include that the incense was impure, that it was made from the wrong mixture, that they used coals from a wrong source, that they were adding an incense offering that God had not directed, or that they went too far into the sanctuary (drawing on a nuance in the verb קרב meaning "to come near," or in the *hiphil* stem, "to bring near or offer"). Given that the fire that consumed the offering was reported in the previous verse (in 9:24), it seems likely that the problem was that they did not draw from the now-to-be-perpetual fire on the burnt-offering altar to take embers for the incense.

> **Burning Incense**
> The process of burning incense normally involves placing the incense on top of live coals.
>
>
>
> Figure 35. Ninth-century B.C. limestone incense altar, Megiddo, Israel Museum.
>
> According to Exodus 30, the incense altar was in front of the veil "near the ark of the testimony" (Exod. 30:6). Figure 35 shows an example of an incense altar.
>
> Exodus directs Aaron (and subsequently, his successor) to burn incense on that altar twice a day: in the morning and the evening when he "trimmed the lamps." The actual word is יָטַב in the *hiphil*, which might better be translated "to make good." We use the expression "trim the lamps" based on more modern oil lamps with adjustable wicks that require trimming, but for these early oil lamps the action probably included replacing the wick and adding fresh oil. Figure 36 shows an oil lamp of the general type that was used throughout the history of Israel. It consists of

a terra-cotta dish that would hold the oil and a wick that would stick out above the edge of the lamp and could be lit.

While the daily procedures are not described, Leviticus 16:12 addresses specifics for the Day of Atonement, which likely were sim-

Figure 36. Oil lamp of the type used in ancient Israel.

ilar. If so, the incense process required that the priest take two handfuls of incense (which Nadab and Abihu likely did), a "firepan full of coals" (which Nadab and Abihu did), and to take them "from the altar," which is generally understood to be the altar of the burnt offering (which Nadab and Abihu apparently did not do). This material would then be taken into the holy place and placed on the incense altar that was in front of the veil (Exod. 30:6, see fig. 63). There it would smolder, producing an aromatic smoke. The smoke from the incense is generally considered to represent the prayers of the nation (Mathews 2009, 94; see also Ps. 141:2). While Israel was likely familiar with incense from its time in Egypt, this appears to be the first time it was incorporated into Israelite worship.

The result was that "fire came out from before YHWH and consumed them, and they died before YHWH." The wording suggests that both fires were from the same source. As Levine observes, God's fire was a "blessing to those who pleased God, but destructive to those who angered Him" (1989, 58).

Figure 37. Artist's representation of the death of Nadab and Abihu.

The most direct translation of the verb here (אָכַל) seems to be "consumed." While commonly understood in a figurative sense, the English term does tend to convey a nuance that can be problematic in that it may suggest a total annihilation of the physical body. This raises questions in subsequent verses where the bodies are carried away in their clothing—if they were consumed, would not their clothing also be consumed? A better take might be to translate it as "destroyed," indicating that their physical lives were extinguished. The emphasis seems to be that they died immediately.

TRANSLATION ANALYSIS: "CONSUMED"
The Hebrew verb אָכַל is defined as "to eat, consume, devour, burn up, feed" (Scott 1980c, 39). It is used in a variety of ways to indicate the destruction of an object, both literally and figuratively. However, the Hebrew term does not necessarily indicate the total disappearance of the item consumed.

Responses to Nadab's and Abihu's Deaths (10:3–20)

10:3–7. To the reader, the impact of the event is shocking. To the original audience, it was extremely shocking. While a few hours might have passed following the sacrifices just described, it seems likely that most of the congregation was still present. Then, in the middle of that celebration of the worship of God, two of the newly commissioned priests were struck dead by fire from the very God they were attempting to worship. In response, Moses declared that it was "what the Lord [YHWH] spoke." At first glance from our perspective, this response to Aaron seems to be rather harsh and callous, perhaps similar to the way Job's counselors came across as they tried to console him. Since the Bible does not record the statement that Moses quotes, we really don't know when the Lord spoke those words. It is possible that this was directly revealed to Moses at this point to provide an explanation for what had just happened (Baker 1996, 69). It seems more probable that Moses cites an earlier revelation that had been given to him, and perhaps even to Aaron and his sons, as a warning that had not been recorded in the growing Torah. If so, it likely was revealed during that week of consecration, suggesting that God may have used that time for instruction.

Aaron remained silent (וַיִּדֹּם), which seems to indicate that he was aware of the Lord's mandate. Milgrom notes that the Septuagint translated the verb as "'was stupefied' . . . implying that Aaron was paralyzed, rather than resigned." He rejects that idea, stating "Aaron, on his own initiative, did not mourn" (1991, 604). However, one must reckon that the suddenness of the situation would have been a shock, and an immediate response of temporary paralysis would not be unexpected. In any case, Aaron seems to have recognized that his sons had committed a grave error. Later, we will see that while Aaron did mourn, it was a quiet personal mourning, not the loud lamentation one would expect in that culture at the sudden death of two sons. Rather, it was as if Aaron had recognized at the time that something was wrong with the situation, although he may not have pinpointed exactly what it was in order to prevent it.

Beyond explaining what had happened, Moses's statement also pointed to the future:

that what had happened was a lesson to be learned. Sklar (2014, 157–58) puts it this way: "The Lord is therefore issuing a very strong warning to the entire priestly family: if you do not set me apart by your actions as the God worthy of reverence, I will use your death as an opportunity to remind all the people that I am the God who is to be revered above all." As such, this seems to hint at other aspects of the event that the Lord would address shortly. In the interim, there was a very practical matter that needed to be dealt with. It was grossly inappropriate to leave the two dead bodies lying in the courtyard, but it was equally inappropriate that any of the remaining priests remove them. Moses then directed Aaron's cousins, Mishael and Elzaphan, to remove the bodies.

> ### Cousins of Aaron
> Mishael and Elzaphan were sons of Aaron's uncle Uzziel, which incidentally would make him Moses's uncle also. While members of the tribe of Levi, they could not be priests, since that office was reserved for the descendants of Aaron. Still, as Levites who supported religious services, it is plausible that they were on duty, especially since this was a special day of services.

Several things should be noted here. First, normally, the closest relatives of the deceased would be responsible for funerary duties, but that would have been Aaron's other sons, Eleazar and Ithamar. As Moses notes, they have just been anointed and have greater responsibilities (10:7). Second, as Levites, Mishael and Elzaphan were probably close at hand in the courtyard of the tabernacle. Third, given the location of the bodies, Nadab and Abihu apparently died in front of the sanctuary, thus outside of the location of the incense altar, suggesting the preemptory nature of the death. Fourth, Nadab and Abihu were carried out by their tunics, which indicates that while the fire killed them it did not consume them, a strong indication of the

Standing Before a Holy God (10:1–20)

supernatural quality of the judgment. Fifth, they were buried outside of the camp.

At this point, Moses warns Aaron, Eleazar, and Ithamar not to go through ritualistic public mourning. As Kiuchi (2007, 186) points out, there is both inward and outward mourning. Outward mourning generally follows cultural guidelines, such as wearing black in the modern Western world. In the case of ancient Israel, it included tearing one's clothes (an extremely powerful indication of mourning in a culture where, generally speaking, wardrobe changes were few) and either uncovering their heads or disheveling their hair.

TRANSLATION ANALYSIS: "DISHEVEL"
The verb in 10:6 that the NASB and KJV translate as "uncover" is פָּרַע, which is understood to have a basic meaning of "to let loose." Levine (1989, 60) prefers "dishevel," while noting that one must uncover his head to dishevel the hair. Hamilton (1980h) suggests that here it is used in a sense of "cutting" hair. Given its later use in Leviticus 21:10 with regard to the high priest in mourning that seems to parallel the prohibition against "making baldness" for the regular priest (Lev. 21:5), it would seem that the concept is more of a prohibition against cutting or shaving one's head in mourning in this context, although "dishevel" might be a good ambiguous term to use.

Inward mourning is less obvious, although it may still be apparent. For example, we might note how Nehemiah's inward sorrow was evident to the king in Nehemiah 2:2. Anticipating subsequent actions, it would appear that Aaron's inward mourning was partially responsible for his not following the guidelines for eating the sin offering (10:19). As anointed priests, external mourning would have indicated sympathy for the sinners and represented a conflict of interest (Gane 2004a, 191).

However, beyond the family of Nadab and Abihu, the rest of the Levites and in fact the entire house of Israel were not only given permission to mourn, but directed to do so—not for the death of Nadab and Abihu, rather "for the burning." While this might be a figure of speech where the cause of the death is substituted for the actual death, it seems that the emphasis is on the fact that the Lord had been dishonored resulting in the fire, which indicated a rift between the people and God as a result (Willis 2009, 96).

Finally, Moses reminded Aaron and his sons that they were still undergoing the inauguration of the worship system as well as their consecration, and thus they needed to stay within the courtyard. Sometimes duty for individuals in leadership positions overrules personal responses to tragedy, even if the tragedy has corporate implications. It is not clear how much of that inauguration ritual remained to be conducted, but it seems likely that it would not be complete until the evening sacrifice was completed, which is what Moses seems to address in 10:12 and following. Once again, we are told that Aaron and his remaining sons "did according to the word of Moses."

10:8–11. Before Moses continued, however, the Lord spoke directly to Aaron—the only occasion in the book of Leviticus where the Lord speaks directly to Aaron alone.

God Speaks to Aaron

Most of the Lord's communications to the people were through Moses. There are several occasions at Sinai where the Lord spoke to Moses and Aaron (Lev. 11:1; 13:1; 14:33; 15:1; Num. 2:1; 4:1; 17). On two occasions, he spoke directly to Aaron alone. Here, which is the only case in Leviticus, and three times in Numbers 18 (vv. 1, 8, and 20) following Korah's rebellion. In both cases, God's speech to Aaron alone follows a situation where God took someone's life for wrong actions with regard to worship and addressed the duties and responsibilities of the Levites, especially the priests.

Standing Before a Holy God (10:1–20)

Given the context, it seems that there is a correlation between the command that Aaron and his sons were not to drink wine or strong drink when they went into the Tent of Meeting and what happened to Nadab and Abihu.

> ### TRANSLATION ANALYSIS: "WINE OR STRONG DRINK"
> The phrase translated "do not drink wine or strong drink" is יַיִן וְשֵׁכָר אַל־תֵּשְׁתְּ. The verb is a jussive or directive. The word order emphasizes the "wine and strong drink." "Wine" is straightforward. "Strong drink" (שֵׁכָר) is a noun derived from the verb שָׁכַר, which means "to be drunk or intoxicated." However, since it tends to appear in conjunction with wine, the pair carries the idea of "wine or anything that makes one drunk." The most common other item in that culture would have been beer. While often translated "strong drink," this English phrase suggests distilled liquors, which were not developed until long after biblical times (including NT), but certainly they would be included by extension.

The warning that violation could lead to death is very suggestive of the situation of Nadab and Abihu. While suggestive, the text does not specifically say that they were intoxicated, and it does not appear that they had actually entered the tabernacle, which would make this a preemptive judgment (Gane 2004a, 183). Given the subsequent rationale, the text seems to be broadly inclusive as a warning against anything that detracted from the solemnity of the task at hand. The rationale lists three tasks assigned to the priests: distinguish between the holy and the profane, distinguish between unclean and clean, and teach the Torah ("all the statutes") that the Lord had provided through Moses. It would appear that the two areas of distinction provide significant parameters for understanding the book of Leviticus overall. The next section of Leviticus ("Quality of Worship" [11:1–15:33]) provides guidance for the priest and examples of areas where the priests would need to be able

to make those distinctions. In connection with that material, this directive is explored in more detail in the section "Clean and Unclean" in the introduction.

10:12–20. After the Lord finished his guidance, Moses reminded Aaron and his sons that they needed to finish the day's sacrifices. The final steps required the priests to properly follow directions regarding the disposition of the portions of the sacrifices that were assigned to them. Three are listed.

The first is the priests' portion of the gift (grain) offering of the people (see 9:17). The portion that was left over from burning was to be eaten beside the altar, that is, in a holy place. As presented in 2:3, 10; 6:16; and 7:10, after the memorial portion of the gift offering was burned, the rest of the gift offering belonged to Aaron and his sons. While the directions relate to the priests eating their portion, this step seems to be important to the efficacy of the ritual (Balentine 2002, 88), although it is not clear why it was mandatory, outside of the fact that it was considered "most holy."

The second is the breast of the wave offering (תְּנוּפָה) and the lifted-up thigh (9:21). As noted in Leviticus 7:34–36, these are the portions of the shalom offerings that belonged to the priest.

> ### Wave and Uplifted Offerings
> Here the text distinguishes between the offering of the breast as a wave offering and the right thigh as the "lifted up" or "heave" offering as seen in Leviticus 7. In Leviticus 9:21, where the two offerings are described in this situation, both seem to be described as a wave offering. However, the Hebrew does not specifically give the title תְּנוּפָה ("wave offering") to them, but uses the verb from which it is derived, נוּף, which may be translated as "lift or wave" (Bowling 1980e).
>
> Unlike the gift offering, these pieces may be eaten in a clean place, which indicates that it would be outside of the courtyard. While Leviticus 7 states

Standing Before a Holy God (10:1–20)

that this portion was given to Aaron and his sons, the text here clarifies that by specifying both sons and daughters. This inclusion suggests that the location might be the domicile of the priest (Milgrom 1991, 619).

TRANSLATION ANALYSIS: "DAUGHTERS"
The addition of daughters here along with sons (אַתָּה וּבָנֶיךָ וּבְנֹתֶיךָ אִתָּךְ) can raise questions. In Leviticus 7 these portions are assigned to Aaron the priest and to his sons (בָּנָיו) as their dues, which seems to omit daughters. The fact that it is a shalom offering, where most of the meat was eaten by the offeror and his guests, may be a factor that implied that the daughters could also eat of the priests' portion. However, the Hebrew term "sons" can include daughters and thus Leviticus 7 *may* reflect all offspring. The rabbinic tradition is that Leviticus 7 designates sons as those who have a *right* to this portion, while this passage includes the daughters "by sufferance" (Milgrom 1991, 621). Leviticus 22 later seems to support this when it amplifies the inclusion of the daughters by showing that not all daughters are permitted to participate—just those who are not married to laymen (unless widowed or divorced without children), and it will also add certain servants of the priest. The wives of the priests are not addressed.

The third and apparently final step is the eating of the priests' portion of the goat of the purification (חַטָּאת) offering (10:16). The sequence suggests a follow-up on the procedures, reminding the priests of what needs to be done. In the process, he does not see the goat of the purification offering that had been offered for the people (9:15). The structure of 10:16 places the emphasis on the goat of the purification offering.

TRANSLATION ANALYSIS: "GOAT OF THE PURIFICATION OFFERING"
There are two points of interest in translating the first sentence of 10:16. To begin with, the object,

"the goat of the purification offering" (חַטָּאת) is placed first showing emphasis. This suggests that the generic *waw* should be translated as "but" showing contrast. Second, the verb דָּרַשׁ, which means "to search carefully" (Coppes 1980b) is intensified using an infinitive absolute along with the *qal* perfect verb form.

Since this was a corporate offering for the people where the blood was not brought into the Tent of Meeting (Lev. 6:26–30), the priest was required to eat the meat. As Moses looked, he did not find it, but learned that it had been burned. Apparently Aaron's sons were the ones who actually burned the goat, since Moses was angry with them because it was "most holy" and was an important part of the ritual.

> **Aaron's Sons and the Missing Goat**
> Several aspects of this interaction are not clear. First, the high priest was responsible for the sacrificial procedures, which would have been Aaron. It is not clear as to why Moses was angry with Eleazar and Ithamar. Second, if the gift offering, the wave offering, and the lifted-up thigh had not yet been eaten, why was the purification offering already burned instead of being eaten? A third unclear point is how the priest's eating of the sacrifice contributed to the efficacy of the sacrifice—the text simply states, "He gave it to you to bear away the guilt of the congregation, to make atonement for them before the Lord [YHWH]." Baker (1996, 172) sums up the issue as follows:
>
> > This can be interpreted in several ways. It may indicate that: (1) The priests received the meat in exchange for performing the sin-offering ritual for the people (6:26; 9:15; Milgrom 1991:623). Moses's anger would necessitate that the regulation of 6:26 would be violated if the sacrifice were burnt rather than eaten. (2) The purpose of giving the meat to the priest was to remove the people's guilt and by not eating it, the guilt had not been removed.

Standing Before a Holy God (10:1–20)

> (3) The meat of the sin offering was seen as actually absorbing the guilt, which would have passed on to the priest, being borne by him, when he ate it (Kiuchi 1987:47; Milgrom 1991:624–625). But assuming guilt by eating is not known elsewhere in the Bible or in the ancient Near East. Also, the offering was "most holy" (6:25; 10:17; cf. 10:12), arguing against its being tainted by guilt. Though the Hebrew is difficult, the context of 10:18 would argue for the first interpretation.

> Gane (2004a, 196), after observing that the eating was part of the ritual, sees an analogy of bearing culpability like Yom Kippur and Azazel's goat (Lev. 16:21). In a more pragmatic sense, it is not clear where the goat was actually burned—whether on the altar or outside of the camp like the purification offering for Aaron (Lev. 9:11).

However, it was Aaron who replied to Moses, and his response seems to link his actions to the earlier events of the day—although the rationale is not completely clear and has prompted different responses. One view is that Aaron was concerned that their death suggested that Nadab and Abihu were invalid as priests, and as such, the sacrifice was invalid. Some suggest that Aaron refrained because he was not permitted to (Milgrom 1991, 639), or at least was unsure whether he was permitted to (Noortzij 1982, 115). A large part of the discussion seems to focus on the intent of the sacrifice. While it was presented as a corporate purification offering, the death of Nadab and Abihu may have raised the question as to whether the sacrifice also applied to Aaron and his sons, in which case, the requirement was that it should be burned (Sklar 2014, 161). However, that raises another question in that if the sacrifice included the priests, then the blood should have been sprinkled on the veil (Lev. 4:6–7).

It is interesting that Moses challenged Aaron's decision, and not the Lord. This would suggest that he was "carrying out the mandate to 'make a distinction between the holy and the profane, and between the unclean and the clean' (10:10)" (Rooker 2000, 163). As such, it would appear that while he was not expressing mourning overtly, he was doing so in a quiet, personal, manner. As Rooker expresses it, "Even though Aaron's sorrow was based on the just judgment of wickedness, God is sympathetic. The Lord comforts those who have lost loved ones even when death comes as a consequence of their own sinfulness." Moses also came to understand that, and the text says, "it seemed good in his sight."

THEOLOGICAL FOCUS

The key theological issue of this passage is the importance of obedience to God's revelation. While offering incense as part of the daily worship seems to be an innovation for the nation of Israel, it was directed by God, and apparently God had given the new priests careful directions on how they were to do that. Since this text recounts events that took place on the day the system was set into operation, following directions as a model for future reference would have been especially important. In this context, Nadab and Abihu disobeyed the directions that God had given, although we are not told specifically what they did. A NT corollary to this might be Paul's admonition in 1 Corinthians 14:40, "But all things must be done properly and in an orderly manner."

The suddenness of this event brings a sobering shock to Moses and Aaron, the Israelites, and all who would later hear (and read) Leviticus. The negligence of Nadab and Abihu provides all of God's people with a vivid, permanent juxtaposition between God's lavish mercy and uncompromising holiness. All are free to come into his presence in worship . . . through the means that he established. All other means fall under the category of humankind's reckless experimentation of how to flatter an anonymous god.

God has not changed. He remains merciful. He remains holy. His holiness cannot be veiled by His mercy. His mercy will not be overruled by his holiness. He revealed who he is and how his people could safely come into his presence. Aaron's sons either declined to believe (understand) his words or believed so strongly in themselves that they elected to forge a novel pathway into God's presence. They publicly failed as leaders of the people of God and will forever be remembered for it.

Should this now become a day of mourning? No, Aaron and his remaining anointed sons needed to complete the work for which they had been set apart (though they were likely inwardly mourning over the consequences of disobedience). Their cousins were called to attend to the burial as they attended to the Lord's work. They were not to "tear their clothes" to signal this as a day of mourning for those whom the Lord had struck down, but rather to focus on work the Lord had entrusted to them.

PREACHING AND TEACHING STRATEGIES

Exegetical and Theological Synthesis

God provides the means of grace by which his fallen people can safely come into his presence. The prescribed means has been revealed to the Israelites—there will be an established priesthood chosen and sanctified by God that will lead his people before him into worship. Deviation from God's prescribed means of coming into his presence will lead his people into peril.

Apart from God's means of grace, those who come before him will die. Seeking a novel variant of God's grace may lead to death. God is a consuming fire. He is the fire that consumes the burnt offerings and sin offerings that are brought to serve as substitutes for our disobedience. And he is the fire that will destroy us in our willful disobedience.

This passage is a vivid illustration of the narrow pathway of life between God's mercy and holiness. God's people are to savor his mercy without diminishing his holiness. The only way one can safely do that is to adhere to his prescribed methods for entering into his presence.

Preaching Idea

We are not free to ignore God's standards to design a personalized means of coming into his presence.

Contemporary Connections

What does it mean?

The Creator is not drawn to nor awed by our novelty, ingenuity, or creativity. He is moved by our worship. Once again, we see that obedience is superior to sacrifice (1 Sam. 15:22). In our made-to-order, self-indulgent world, this biblical directive may appear counterintuitive. Yet, with some honest self-reflection, we can see how easy it is to be taken in by enthusiasm over our own ideas, methods, and means of worship instead of being struck by the holiness and majesty of the one whom we worship. In its worst form, such a desire for "strange fire" can redirect worship and awe from the Lord God onto our own methods and means.

Is it true?

God established a safe means for the children of Israel to come into his presence. Venturing outside those means proved hazardous. Today, God has clearly established Christ as the sole means for coming into his presence. There is salvation found in no one else (Acts 4:12). "I am the way, the truth, and the life. No one comes to the Father except through me" (John 14:6). To seek any means of coming into the Father's presence outside of Christ will prove hazardous.

Now what?

Worship is not to be dull or rote. It is to be fresh. How do seasoned believers bring variety, originality, and crispness into worship without violating God's established means of coming into his presence? Our worship must turn the focus onto Christ. All leaders are called upon to humbly ask: Who is in the spotlight as I teach, lead, sing, and the rest? Are people seeing me or Christ through me? Will people remember the means and methods I use, or will they remember the God I am leading them to worship? Is this a high standard? Yes. And it is the standard God has established for all who serve him.

Creativity in Presentation

Everyone recognizes branding. Whether you are marketing a product, experience, or even a church, it is recommended that you develop your brand. As a pastor, you can identify brands that would be especially important to your local economy. Companies invest enormous amounts of time and effort in creating a brand that accurately reflects who they are (or at least who they want people to think they are). Once that brand is precisely established, every detail is copyrighted. No one is free to steal it, alter it, or modify it even slightly.

What happens if an employee elects to adjust (or revolutionize) the brand? What if a local KFC franchise amends the recipe? Or a neighborhood Starbucks dials up a slightly different brew? Or the distillery allows the whiskey to age a bit less? Even if their intentions are good, such a reckless undertaking is breaking the law and insulting the creators of the brand. Employees are not asked to reinvent the product. Their role is to promote the recipe of the creators, not to experiment with their own novel ideas. To do otherwise would be to exploit the goodwill of the company they serve.

And what if the brand is not simply an item of taste, but a matter of life and death? What if a medical intern at his/her own discretion revises a trusted surgery technique or reworks a medical procedure? What if a local manufacturer of insulin decides it is time to experiment with a customized formula? In the end, the result will be introducing "strange fire" with the potential to harm others.

We are not free to ignore God's standards to design a personalized means of coming into his presence.

- God establishes and reveals how his people can safely come into his presence.
  - God is merciful; God is holy.
  - Arrogant deviation from God's revealed standard proves deadly.
    - An individualized, unauthorized (unholy) fire before God
    - An immediate response by a holy God
    - Not a time to mourn man's folly before God
- What did it mean to them then? What does it mean always? What do we do now?
  - God's holiness cannot be veiled by his mercy.
  - God's mercy cannot be overruled by his holiness.
  - God alone sets the means by which he may be safely approached— seeking any means other than Christ will prove deadly.
  - Worship may be fresh and novel, yet it must be fully focused on God to be safe.

DISCUSSION QUESTIONS

1. While the NT does not give such explicit instructions on how to worship, what might be some of the guidelines that are provided on how to worship?

2. What are some of the ways we might profane the worship of God in an effort to either take a shortcut or a new approach?

3. Why is following God's directions with regard to worship important?

GUIDELINES FOR DEVELOPING AND PRESERVING A HOLY NATION
(LEVITICUS 11:1–27:34)

The second major section of the book, which consists of Leviticus 11–27, contains eleven preaching units. While the first section focused on worship, the second section addresses how relationships affect the shalom, or well-being, of the nation. The second section is further divided into two portions connected by a hinge chapter. Leviticus 11–15, "Quality of Worship," develops the nation's relationship with God further by stressing how personal cleanliness is crucial to the well-being of the nation. This preaching unit shows what a clean life might look like. "The Day of Atonement," Leviticus 16, then describes how the people might become clean. Leviticus 17, "Life and Blood," serves as a hinge, transitioning from the components of a culture of shalom, one that has life, to the overall structure of culture, which we call the social fabric, building on the concept of blood as the source of physical life. Leviticus 18–20:27, "Strengthening the Social Fabric," addresses issues of a strong social fabric. However, the text is interrupted in the middle of Leviticus 24 by an incident that threatens to unravel that fabric. That incident and the God-directed response provide "Repairing a Social Snag." Coming off of that snag, "Preventing Social Unraveling, Parts 1 and 2" (Lev. 25) provide guidance on how to keep the social fabric from unraveling by addressing needs sometimes regarded as social justice. Drawing on that guidance, "Alternative Outcomes for the Community of God" (Lev. 26) projects what the social fabric would look like should the nation not follow God's guidance, but ends with a promise that even if the fabric seemed to rot away, God would restore it at the end. Finally, Leviticus 27, "Vows and Values," circles back to the role of the individual—where the book began in "Worshipping a Holy God," Leviticus 1–3.

Leviticus 11:1–15:33

EXEGETICAL IDEA
God called his people to set themselves apart from the fallen world by being clean, differentiating themselves by adhering to distinct freedoms and limitations in all areas of daily life: diet, male and female hygiene practices, and visible skin and housing concerns.

THEOLOGICAL FOCUS
God calls his people to express their devotion to him through living holistically clean lives that mark those devoted to God from the common uncleanliness of the fallen world.

PREACHING IDEA
We are distinguished as God's people not only by avoiding forbidden practices but by recognizing the need for cleansing from the inherent uncleanliness of this fallen world.

PREACHING POINTERS
Having witnessed first the mercy of God in raising up Aaron and his sons, and then the holiness of God in striking down two of those sons, the children of God had come face to face with a potentially paralyzing problem—how to distinguish between holy and unholy, clean and unclean. Was there a clear standard one could attain (and keep) that would then free him or her to do what seemed right in his or her own mind? It does not appear to be that simple. God presented the priests with meticulous examples of freedoms and limitations extending into all areas of daily life that could make one unclean or even unholy. Holiness would need to always remain in the forefront of their minds if they were to thrive as a nation of priests to the world.

Holiness remains a standard that eludes precise definition. We may prefer a well-defined standard that we can attain and thus be free to move on to the more pressing matters of daily life in this world. Are there more pressing matters in this world? God's desire is that each moment of each day we are aware of the uncleanliness inherent to our lives in this world so that we may grasp our ongoing need to be cleansed and made holy by him. Holiness is reaching far deeper than outward moral purity. God's wants our souls to long for the perfection found in Christ alone.

QUALITY OF WORSHIP (11:1–15:33)

LITERARY STRUCTURE AND THEMES (11:1–15:33)

The next five chapters probably constitute the most difficult section of Leviticus. In terms of genre, it is legal material—that is, it presents rules that the Israelites were to obey. And yet, it is not a comprehensive legal code. It addresses in depth just a few issues of life that would defile the nation's relationship with God. The material is very technical. It is long, and it is detailed. From our perspective, the section seems arbitrarily thrown into the book. And, because it addresses issues that under NT revelation we no longer address—specifically, the issues of distinguishing between things that are ritually clean and those that are unclean (cf. Mark 7:19; Rom. 14:14)—we tend to gloss over it.

For the original audience, this section was very important in that it gave examples and how-to's for the priests with regard to the mission statement that God had given Aaron, when he declared in Leviticus 10:10–11 that they (Aaron and his sons, i.e., the priests) must be able to "make a distinction between the holy and the profane and between the unclean and the clean" and to teach the Torah ("all the statutes"). This directive is crucial for understanding the intent of these five chapters.

While the topics of the five chapters are diverse—including issues of diet, sex, health and hygiene, and housing—they have a common theme of elucidating what it means to be holy and clean as God admonished Aaron in Leviticus 10:10–11. Consequently, we combine these five chapters as one unit for homiletical purposes. We will explore the exegesis of the entire unit by subsections in the chapters, but even there we will not make a detailed analysis, although we plan to address salient issues. Our goal is to extract an overall principle with which one might work in terms of developing a sermon from this unit appropriate for today's culture. In terms of the many details of the text, we would refer the reader to other sources for that material with the caveat that there are many questions for which we do not have clear answers, such as the identities of all the unclean birds, or what exactly was meant by leprosy on houses. The key theme of this section is distinguishing between *clean* and *unclean*, and we would encourage that one read the section "Clean and Unclean" in the introduction prior to working through the text to see how we understand this material to fit together.

- *Diet Affects One's Ability to Worship (11:1–47)*
- *Motherhood Affects a Woman's Ability to Worship (12:1–8)*
- *Physical Afflictions Affect Worship (13:1–14:57)*
- *Sexual Issues Affect One's Ability to Worship (15:1–33)*

EXPOSITION (11:1–15:33)

Despite a major initial misstep, the tabernacle was now functioning. God's next step following that inauguration was to provide the nation with ceremonies and directions to guide its corporate development as God's representative, starting with the Day of Atonement in Leviticus 16. But first, the Lord would give the nation, through the priests, some guidelines to clarify the priesthood mission statement that he gave in 10:10–11. That clarification is recorded in a series of six speeches—four are given to Moses and Aaron jointly, the other two just to Moses. While only three (the first two and the last) were specifically directed to be repeated to the people, their content suggests that all were intended to inform the nation.

> ### TRANSLATION ANALYSIS: "THE LORD [YHWH] SPOKE"
> As noted before, the statement "Then the Lord [YHWH] spoke to Moses and to Aaron" begins with the all-purpose conjunction *waw*. In this section it is best translated as "then." The declaration "and the Lord [YHWH] spoke" shows up in 11:1; 12:1; 13:1; 14:1, 33; and 15:1. It would appear that this sequence follows the Nadab and Abihu incident, and precedes the next section beginning in 16:1, but likely not on the same day.

Leviticus now focuses on aspects of everyday life. While the first ten chapters of the book covered proper worship, the book now turns to relate how that worship should prepare one for the daily business of living at home in a community of faith. At the same time, one's life at home and in the community prepares one for worship. The overall thrust of this five-chapter section is that because the nation of Israel has been chosen for a specific mission, the lifestyle of the people was to differ from the nations around them. As such, these five chapters should be viewed as a holistic unit, even though they address different aspects of life that we might categorize as areas of diet, sex and family, physical afflictions, and health. Overall, these aspects are categorized with the terms *tahor* (טָהוֹר), translated as "clean" or "pure," reflecting conditions or practices that they should aspire for; and *tame'* (טָמֵא), translated as "unclean" or "impure," regarding aspects of life to be avoided in order to prepare for proper worship of God. For the purposes of this work, we will generally use the more familiar terms of "clean" and "unclean."

Diet Affects One's Ability to Worship (11:1–47)

This long chapter limits what meat the Israelites might eat and historically has probably been the most prominent in terms of Israelite and Jewish lifestyle. The section addresses three categories of animals based on the environments generally associated with the animals: land, water, and air. This division hints at a connection with the creation of animals on days 5 and 6 shown in Genesis 1:20–31. Three times in that section God states that his creation was good, and the final declaration emphasizes that the entire creation was "very good" (וְהִנֵּה־טוֹב מְאֹד). Consequently, one is surprised to now read thirty-two times in Leviticus that some of the animals were unclean and would make Israelites "unclean" (various forms of טָמֵא), or ten times that they were "detestable" or "abhorrent" (various translations of שֶׁקֶץ).

> ### What About Plants?
> It is interesting that throughout this chapter no mention is made of plants. Levine (1989, 63) claims, "All that grows in the soil of the earth may be eaten," at least according to the Torah. However, this is not to say that there are not plants humans should not eat. Most people are aware that certain berries or plant parts are toxic. For example, 2 Kings 4:38–41 relates an account where Elisha had to detoxify (the terminology used is that he removed evil from) a stew that contained poisonous gourds. However, since no plants are viewed as producing uncleanness, this would suggest that several of the proposals as to why certain animals are viewed as producing uncleanness are invalid (e.g., they are loathsome, or the hygiene hypothesis). This might tend to support the arbitrary direction rationale. As Bailey (2005, 148) expresses it, "God does not call upon us to 'be reasonable': God calls upon us to obey."

Scholars have long struggled to provide general categories that would explain why specific animals were considered clean or unclean. Historically, several different explanations have been proposed as rationale for the distinction. The dominant reasons have been characterized as the hygienic, cultic, moral-symbolic, aesthetic, and anthropological reasons (Houston 1993, 69–78; Sklar 2014, 166–67).

Hygienic: This view uses a rationale of good health, proposing that the prohibited meat can cause disease when eaten. The primary example of this is pork, which can cause trichinosis if undercooked. There are several concerns regarding this explanation. First, it is not clear that all of the animals specifically mentioned potentially transmit disease, and some of the clean animals can cause disease if not properly prepared (e.g., undercooked beef can transmit salmonella). Another consideration is that if the concern was a healthy diet, then why would the guidelines not cover plants, since some plants can also have unhealthy consequences if eaten? Perhaps more importantly, in the NT God declares all meats clean. This raises a question as to whether God would now specifically authorize his people to eat something that caused physical harm (Sklar 2014, 166).

Aesthetic: Somewhat similar to the hygienic argument is the aesthetic, which is not widely held today. Walter Houston (1993, 71) proposes that it derives from the principle "the law enjoins the removal of the sight of loathsome objects." He notes how it does not explain why a particular culture might find a specific animal repulsive and for that reason dismisses it as a possible explanation. It also doesn't explain how loathsome plants might be acceptable.

Cultic: This explanation looks at Israel in its broader cultural context and proposes that the unclean animals were used by neighboring peoples in their worship or represented their gods. The idea is that God's people were not to use animals that other cultures worshipped. The problem is that it does not explain why cattle, sheep, and goats were considered clean even though they also were used as sacrificial animals in those other cultures (Houston 1993, 72–73).

Moral-symbolic: This view argues that some animal behaviors or characteristics could symbolically represent either good (pure) or evil (impure) actions. Because no symbolism is delineated in the text, Wenham (1979, 168–69) cautions against this approach as subjective, citing various attempts as "interesting and imaginative," but also "at best partial, . . . and at worst whimsical and capricious."

> **Moral-symbolic Interpretation**
> This view is one of the oldest and dates back to the second century B.C. in a pseudepigraphical work called The Letter of Aristeas that is quoted extensively by Josephus. Aristeas claims, for example, that "Everything pertaining to conduct permitted us toward these creatures and toward beast has been set out symbolically" (line 150). For example, he cites the cloven hoof as a sign of distinguishing actions for good (lines 151–53) and maintains that chewing the cud (or rumination) serves to remind us to remember God by meditating on the law (lines 154–58; Shutt 1985, 22–23). This interpretation still has some advocates, such as Kiuchi (2007, 207–10). A key concern is that different characteristics might be drawn from the same animal and a specific characteristic might be viewed positively for one culture but negatively for another (McNutt 1990, 216–27).

Anthropological: This view largely draws on the work of Douglas (1993, 3) who focuses on a comprehensive understanding of the law from an anthropological position. In some respects this theory can be deemed a variation on the moral-symbolic, which ties the Levitical distinctions to cultural taboos throughout

Quality of Worship (11:1–15:33)

the world. As presented by Douglas, this view suggests that everything needs to correspond to its order. If it does, then it is pure and whole. If it does not, it is impure, blemished, or mixed (Douglas 2002, 69–70).

Anthropological Interpretation
Drawing on the threefold classification of animals in Genesis 1, Douglas (2002, 69–70) suggests that the locomotion for the environment is a key category for differentiation: winged fowls with two legs fly in the air, scaly fish swim with fins through the waters, and four-legged animals "hop, jump, or walk" on land. So, for example, four-legged creatures that fly do not move in accordance with their order (land), and thus are unclean. She also argues that in the case of the swarming creatures, their means of locomotion is indeterminate and thus they are unclean.

In general, two weaknesses are noted of these various proposals. First, the presentations of the various proposals seem to claim exclusivity for that proposal in terms of rationale for all fauna, but in the text different specific statements of prohibition seem to reflect different rationales, or even multiple rationales. Second, the dietary laws are a portion of a five-chapter discussion of cleanness in multiple areas, a precursor to holiness that is the real goal not only of Leviticus but the entire Torah. As such, as Sklar (2014, 48–49) notes, we should not expect a single overarching rationale. Consequently, there is a sense in which specifics may appear to be somewhat arbitrary, at least from a human perspective.

Make the Nation Holy
The term "holy" appears in the Exodus-Leviticus material that addresses giving of the Torah and its contents 199 times. While it addresses a number of factors such as the tabernacle, certain days, and the role of the priests, at least seven times God tells the people that they are to be holy (Exod. 19:6; 22:31; Lev. 11:44, 45; 19:2; 20:7, 26).

While the text does not state that doing all of the various commands would make them holy, the inference is that those guidelines reflect aspects of life that would be manifest in a holy person. For further discussion see the sections "Holy" and "Clean and Unclean" in the introduction.

11:1–8. Animals of the land that the Israelites may eat. The first category of animals that God addressed is land animals, specifically "the animals that are upon the earth" (הַבְּהֵמָה אֲשֶׁר עַל־הָאָרֶץ). While it reflects Genesis 1:24–25, this text only addresses one of the three categories of land animals noted here, translated as "cattle" (בְּהֵמָה).

TRANSLATION ANALYSIS: "ANIMALS THAT ARE ON THE EARTH"
Genesis 1:24 lists three categories of animals on the earth: "cattle [בְּהֵמָה] and creeping things [רֶמֶשׂ] and beasts of the earth [חַיְתוֹ־אֶרֶץ]." Leviticus 11 does not address "creeping things," but later in the chapter it discusses "teeming" or "swarming things" (שֶׁרֶץ), which *TWOT* (Austel 1980e, 956) suggests is "to some extent synonymous and used interchangeably" with "creeping things." The Hebrew word in the phrase "animals that are on the earth" in Leviticus 11:2 is בְּהֵמָה, which is translated "cattle" in Genesis. This term בְּהֵמָה is used approximately 189 times in the OT. The NASB translates it as "beast" or "beasts" seventy-five times, "animal" or "animals" sixty times, and "cattle" fifty-two times. The noun חַיָּה is used ninety-six times, and translated as "beast" or "beasts" sixty-nine times, and as "something living" seventeen times. The remaining uses of חַיָּה seem best represented by terms such as "beasts of the herd" or "wild beasts." Further, both are used in the terms translated with "of the field" and "of the earth" and both seem to denote both domestic and wild beasts. As such, while the focus is on domesticated animals, the term is broad enough to include wild beasts that meet the same physical criteria.

Quality of Worship (11:1–15:33)

The point of the passage is that only one category of meat is permissible for Israelites to eat—animals that have cloven hooves and chew their cud. This category includes cattle, sheep, and goats among the domestic animals the Israelites kept, and wild animals that met the same criteria (see Clean and Unclean Land Animals excursus). For the priests, the hooves and cud criteria would be adequate for them to evaluate any wild animal that an Israelite procured in hunting when they arrived in Canaan, where this generation had never been. Four specific animals that might *appear* to fit that category are specifically forbidden because they only have one apparent trait: the camel, the shaphan, the rabbit, and the pig (see "Clean and Unclean Land Animals" excursus). For the nation of Israel, they are designated as unclean.

Clean and Unclean Land Animals

Leviticus 11 provides criteria for land animals that are clean, which means that the Israelites could eat their meat. There are two criteria: they have a split hoof and chew the cud. For the Israelites, these included three they primarily domesticated, specifically cattle, sheep, and goats.

Figure 38. Cow grazing.

Figure 39. Sheep in pasture.

Figure 40. Goat.

Figure 41. Whitetail deer.

Figure 42. Pronghorn antelope.

But given the criteria, other nondomesticated animals would be included, some of which are noted in other texts, such as deer and antelope.

However, this would include some surprising animals, including American bison and giraffes (https://defendmyfaith.org/2020/05/17/clean-and-unclean-animal-list-and-unclean-ingredients-list/).

Figure 43. American bison.

Figure 44. Giraffe.

The Leviticus text also lists four animals that meet one criterion but fail on the other. These are the camel, the shaphan, and the rabbit, which appear to chew the cud but do not have divided hooves, and pigs, which have divided hooves but do not chew a cud.

Figure 45. Camels.

Figure 46. Shaphan or hyrax.

Figure 47. Rabbit.

Figure 48. Pigs.

11:9–12. Animals of the water that the Israelites may eat. The Israelites who were at Sinai receiving this message had eaten fish when they lived in Egypt that they would have caught from the Nile (Num. 11:5). The OT does not seem to record Israelite fishing as a contemporary practice, although we are very aware that at a later time several of the apostles were fishermen who fished predominantly in the Sea of Galilee. The OT does not record whether anyone fished in the Jordan River. We do have record that when Nehemiah supervised the building of the walls of Jerusalem, one of the gates was called the fish gate, likely because it was the gate through which fishermen brought fish. Nehemiah also records that people of Tyre imported fish, likely from the Mediterranean, which they sold to the Israelites (Neh. 13:15). The guidelines for water animals that might be eaten were that they have fins and scales, clear criteria that would make it easy for the priest to evaluate whether the creature was permissible for food. Catfish, whales, and eels would be forbidden because they did not have scales. Shellfish and crustaceans would be forbidden because they had neither.

Unclean Water Animals

Leviticus 11 provides criteria for water animals that are clean, which means that the Israelites could eat their meat. There are two criteria: they have fins and scales. This would include most fish such as trout.

But it would exclude an American favorite, catfish, which at first glance looks very similar but does not have scales. The same is true of sharks.

Figure 49. Cutthroat trout.

Figure 50. White catfish.

Figure 51. Sand shark.

This would also exclude marine mammals which also possess swimming fins, such as whales and seals.

It would also exclude favorites such as lobster and shrimp, which lack scales but also do not have fins.

Figure 52. Humpback whale.

Figure 53. Seal.

Figure 54. Cooked lobster.

Figure 55. Fire shrimp.

A broader list that gives more specific examples may be found on the "Defend My Faith" website (https://defendmyfaith.org/2020/05/17/clean-and-unclean-animal-list-and-unclean-ingredients-list/).

While these criteria are the key items the priest would look for, in this section the Hebrew uses an interesting term to describe a broader category, שֶׁרֶץ, which may be translated as "swarming things."

TRANSLATION ANALYSIS: "TEEMING" OR "SWARMING THINGS"

As noted in the translation analysis of animals that are on the earth, the Hebrew uses the term שֶׁרֶץ in this chapter, which seems synonymous to "creeping things" (רֶמֶשׂ) in Genesis 1. Modern English Bibles translate this noun as "teeming creatures" or "swarms." While the verbal root שָׁרַץ primarily suggests movement, the noun seems to suggest collective movement of a group, thus leading to the translation of "teeming" or "swarming things." Leviticus 11 uses this term with respect to all three categories of animals. In 11:10, it refers to all the teeming things of the water that do not have fins and scales and is generally translated as "swarming creatures" or something similar. In 11:20–23, which describes animals of the air, it is generally translated "winged insects." In 11:29 and following, it refers to small land animals and is often translated "swarming things" or "creatures that swarm." Wenham (1979, 175) sums it up: "They are small creatures that often occur in swarms and move to and fro in haphazard fashion."

In terms of sea creatures this may include animals such as shrimp and jellyfish. While these criteria might seem to include small fish with

Quality of Worship (11:1–15:33)

fins and scales that swim in schools, it may be that the distinction is the issue of swarming. While schools of fish move erratically, the fish themselves seem to align in terms of movement. In contrast, the "swarming things" tend to be more cloud-like, with each individual moving more or less erratically within that group.

Interestingly, in this section, the forbidden marine animals are not indicated as unclean (טָמֵא), but as detestable or abhorrent (שֶׁקֶץ). Kiuchi (2007, 196) suggests that this term is stronger than unclean, and elsewhere shows contempt. Perhaps one distinction might be that unlike the unclean animals, the carcass of the detestable marine creature would not make the person who touched it (such as the fisherman taking it out of his net) unclean (Lev. 11:24).

11:13–23. Animals of the air that the Israelites may eat. The third category of animals includes animals that move through the air. This category is more complicated because, while many translations render the term as "birds" (עוֹף), the word really means a winged or flying creature.

TRANSLATION ANALYSIS: "BIRDS"
Two Hebrew words are translated bird: עוֹף, which *TWOT* translates as "flying creatures" (Schultz 1980b) and צִפּוֹר which *TWOT* translates as "bird" (Hartley 1980c). The former, עוֹף, is a broader term, which is used with respect to birds, insects, and flying mammals in this chapter, and elsewhere is applied even to angelic beings (Exod. 37:9; Isa. 6:2, 6). As such, when the text uses עוֹף the context determines which winged creatures are addressed. While the word צִפּוֹר seems to be limited to the equivalent of the English word "birds," translations do not always make a distinction. For example, in Deuteronomy 14, in the second list of unclean birds, the list of birds cited as unclean is both preceded and followed by the statement in the NASB: "You may eat any clean bird." However, in 14:11 the text uses צִפּוֹר, while in 14:20 it uses עוֹף.

As listed, this includes birds, flying mammals (bats), and insects, which the text carefully differentiates. The section is divided into two sections. The first addresses detestable birds/flying mammals, and the second detestable insects. The text does not give characteristics by which the priest would evaluate a given bird, but lists twenty winged creatures (nineteen birds and bats as a group) that are specifically identified as impermissible for food—they are detestable (שֶׁקֶץ) like the forbidden aquatic animals. It has been suggested that one thing that the birds listed here have in common is that they are carnivorous, but that would depend on the proper identification of the birds listed and would not explain the inclusion of bats (Harrison 1980, 13–20). As Kiuchi (2007, 197) observes, most of that list of twenty "birds" cannot be identified. For a list of possible identifications see the sidebar "Forbidden Winged Creatures," with chart 6 showing differing suggestions. Leviticus does not indicate that the listed birds are unclean, but describes them as abhorrent or detestable. However, the parallel passage in Deuteronomy 14 does indicate that these are unclean birds. As such, this would suggest that those listed were the only unclean birds, and indeed Deuteronomy 14:11 and 20 suggest that the Israelites were permitted to eat any bird not specifically named as unclean. However, only pigeons or doves were acceptable for a sacrifice (Lange 1960, 92).

Forbidden Winged Creatures

When Noah took the animals aboard the ark centuries before Moses, he was directed to take the clean animals by sevens (understood to be seven pairs ["a male and his female"]) and every unclean animal by a pair (a male and his female). This suggests that the idea of clean and unclean animals preceded Sinai. If so, the distinction likely had been articulated by God very early in the history of humankind. Still, it appears that at Sinai, the directions that the Israelites received were specific to them, apparently as a mark of distinction from other cultures. When God spoke to Noah, in Genesis 7:2 he directed that the birds of the sky (מֵעוֹף הַשָּׁמַיִם) were to be taken by sevens, which would seem to suggest that they were considered clean. While in Genesis 8:20, after the flood, when Noah sacrificed a burnt offering on the altar of "every clean animal and of every clean bird," there does not seem to be any birds that are specifically listed as unclean. However, in Leviticus 11, the forbidden winged creatures, regardless of type, like the forbidden teeming marine animals are deemed detestable or abhorrent.

As noted, specific birds are listed as abhorrent or detestable and thus are not to be eaten in Leviticus 11. In Deuteronomy 14, they are labeled unclean. There is no real category such as we see in the land and water animals. Rather, a specific list of twenty birds is given. For the most part their identity today is debated, and it seems every translation and commentator has a somewhat different list. The one thing that does stand out is that there is somewhat of a consensus that carnivores and carrion eaters are the focus of the prohibition. This may be an indication of the broader Noahic grasp of what constituted unclean animals.

If the issue is that unclean birds are carnivores, this raises questions regarding birds such as ducks that eat fish. Daniel Weiss argues that the issue is whether they eat "any animals with blood." He states that "the Torah does not classify these latter [fish and insects] as blood-containing animals," which we would understand to mean red blood (www.thetorah.com/article/predators-are-prohibited-why-are-ducks-kosher).

The following brief chart is basically derived from Godfrey Driver's (1955a, 1955b) two articles on birds in the OT, which is then coupled with four English translations. Driver states that his interpretation is based on extensive evaluation of the philology of the Hebrew name, ancient translations, and any description of each bird's habitat and habits. His conclusion is that the text to a large extent lists *raptores* (with the exception of the last two) that have dirty habits.

	Hebrew Name	Driver's Suggestion	KJV	NASB	NIV	ESV
1	הַנֶּשֶׁר	Griffon-vulture	Eagle	Eagle	Eagle	Eagle
2	הַפֶּרֶס	Black vulture	Ossifrage	Vulture	Vulture	Bearded vulture
3	הָעָזְנִיָּה	Ossifrage or bearded vulture	Ospray	Buzzard	Black vulture	Black vulture
4	הַדָּאָה	Black kite	Vulture	Kite	Red kite	Kite
5	הָאַיָּה	Any large falcon	Kite	Falcon	Black kite	Falcon
6	עֹרֵב	Raven	Raven	Raven	Raven	Raven
7	בַּת הַיַּעֲנָה	Eagle-owl	Owl	Ostrich	Horned owl	Ostrich
8	הַתַּחְמָס	Medium-sized owl	Night hawk	Owl	Screech owl	Nighthawk
9	הַשָּׁחַף	Long-eared owl	Cuckow	Sea gull	Gull	Sea gull

Quality of Worship (11:1–15:33)

	Hebrew Name	Driver's Suggestion	KJV	NASB	NIV	ESV
10	הַנֵּץ	Small hawk	Hawk	Hawk	Hawk	Hawk
11	הַכּוֹס	Tawny owl	Little owl	Little owl	Little owl	Little owl
12	הַשָּׁלָךְ	Fisher-owl	Cormorant	Cormorant	Cormorant	Cormorant
13	הַיַּנְשׁוּף	Screech owl	Great owl	Great owl	Great owl	Short-eared owl
14	הַתִּנְשֶׁמֶת	Little owl	Swan	White-owl	White owl	Barn owl
15	הַקָּאָת	Scops-owl	Pelican	Pelican	Desert owl	Tawny owl
16	הָרָחָם	Osprey	Gier eagle	Carrion vulture	Osprey	Carrion vulture
17	הַחֲסִידָה	Stork and heron	Stork	Stork	Stork	Stork
18	הָאֲנָפָה	Cormorant	Heron	Heron	Heron	Heron
19	הַדּוּכִיפַת	Hoopoe	Lapwing	Hoopoe	Hoopoe	Hoopoe
20	הָעֲטַלֵּף	Bat	Bat	Bat	Bat	Bat

Chart 6. Differing understandings of forbidden winged creatures.

As can be seen from the four popular translations, there is little agreement regarding the exact creature involved. While a number of Driver's conclusions may be questioned, his two articles do extract key characteristics of the various winged creatures.

The other group of winged creatures is that of insects, which are described as swarming things of the air.

TRANSLATION ANALYSIS: INSECTS
Literally, the expression is "שֶׁרֶץ of the air that walk upon fours." We recognize that insects actually have six legs, but this appears to be an idiomatic expression. As Sklar (2014, 169) describes it, "since the Israelites ate certain insects (and thus would have known how many legs they had), it is likely that the phrase *to walk on all fours* is simply a general expression for 'walking'" (emphasis original).

In contrast to the larger flying creatures that have specific varieties labeled as detestable or unclean, insects are generally forbidden for food with just one group permitted. That exception is the locust, cricket, and grasshopper categories. These are defined as having "jointed legs with which to jump on the earth."

11:24–25. Ways that animals made Israelites unclean. Leviticus 11:24–25 serves as somewhat of a hinge. On the one hand it sums up the previous section on winged insects. But at the same time, the verses point toward ways that other animals can make unclean. Notably, they could also defile various aspects of an Israelite abode.

11:26–28. Carcasses that defile. The first way that a person might become unclean from these animals is touching or handling certain carcasses. The carcass of any of the land animals that did not both have a split hoof and chew its cud (11:26) made anyone who touched it unclean. Perhaps for emphasis, the text specifies the category of animals who walk on "paws."

205

TRANSLATION ANALYSIS: "WALK ON PAWS"
The word used here is כַּף, which means the "hand" or the "palm of the hand," or in this case, the "sole of the foot." Since it specifies walking on all fours, the text is talking about quadrupeds that did not have chitinous feet, such as dogs, lions, and bears (Gerstenberger 1996, 142).

In both cases, the one who touches the carcass is unclean until evening. Based on the overall text of this section, it is generally agreed that in all of these cases, the individual needs to wash his or her clothes (11:28), and although the text does not say so, the traditional understanding is the person must also bathe.

11:29–38. How swarmers defile. Swarming things defile in a variety of ways. The text lists eight specific rodents and reptiles that are considered problematic with respect to homes and food storage areas. Once again, the terms are difficult to understand, but in general it seems the text talks about small mammals and lizards that could easily slip into a dwelling (Sklar 2014, 170). The problem was, because of the damage they caused, they needed to be removed whether they were found alive or dead. In either case, they not only defiled the person removing them but also the container or surface on which they were found. If the material was washable (i.e., wood, clothing, or skin), it was to be placed in water until evening, and then it would be considered cleansed and thus usable once more. Anything that was made of earthenware had to be broken, whether a vessel (11:33) or a stove (11:35). Likewise, any food or liquid contained in the vessel would become unclean.

TRANSLATION ANALYSIS: "LIZARD"
In these verses, several terms seem to address varieties of lizards, which are translated a variety of ways. Two seem most problematic. The first is the term that NASB translates "great lizard" in 11:29. The Hebrew term is צָב, which *TWOT*

(2:751) defines as "lizard." *DBL* (s.v. "צָב" 7730) defines this it as "reptile" of the order *Lacertilia*, of which "more than forty species are found in Bible lands, and it could be any one of them." The second is the term that the NASB translates as "crocodile" in 11:30. The Hebrew term is כֹּחַ which *TWOT* (1:436) defines as "a small reptile, lizard" and *DBL* (s.v. "כֹּחַ" 3947) defines as a "reptile," noting that in various translations it has been interpreted as "monitor lizard," "chameleon," "crocodile," "land-crocodile," or "sand gecko." Given that it is a possible source of uncleanness if it falls into an earthenware vessel, this suggests it should be understood as a small reptile that could invade the storage area.

In contrast, a spring or cistern that gathers water remained clean, while the one who removed the swarmer carcass became unclean (11:36). Commentators struggle with this. For example, Willis (2009, 111) argues that because running water (from a spring) is called living water, the "life" in the water negates the "death" that claimed the animal. However, he does not address the case of a cistern that is a storage tank where the water is not running. It would seem that the difference would be the mass of water as opposed to size of the animal, although this is not clear.

Another situation that seems confusing is the situation where a swarmer falls on seed. If the seed is to be sown, the seed remains clean. However, if water has been placed on the seed, and the swarmer falls on it, it is then unclean. While commentators differ on this, it would seem that Wenham (1979, 180) is correct that the water indicates that the seed is being prepared for cooking. In the case of sowing, the seed goes into the ground and in essence dies as the new plant sprouts.

11:39–40. Unclean food. Here the question is about animals that normally would be used for food, but die as opposed to being slaughtered. Apparently, the case is that the blood was not drained. In this situation, one who touches the

Quality of Worship (11:1–15:33)

carcass or who eats from the carcass (no distinction is made between inadvertently or of necessity) will be unclean until evening and must undergo cleansing. It is interesting that neither touching the carcass nor eating it are labeled as sin, but both produce a situation of uncleanness (although this meat is forbidden to priests [Lev. 17:15; see Mathews 2009, 110]).

11:41–47. Admonition to be clean. Summing up this section, the text reminds the reader that swarmers are detestable, and if eaten, the one who eats it becomes detestable. The warning is to avoid making oneself detestable or unclean. The rationale for the entire chapter seems to lie in 11:44–45: they were to be holy for which a precursor of cleanness was required (see the sections on "Holy" and "Clean and Unclean" in the introduction). Finally, in the last two verses, the text reminds the reader that what had been given as the Torah (i.e., the teaching) was for the priests to understand how they were to make distinctions between clean and unclean on all living creatures, both as to whether they were clean or unclean, and whether they were permissible for food or not.

Motherhood Affects a Woman's Ability to Worship (12:1–8)

In a new speech, the Lord spoke to Moses delineating a second factor that affected worship: the birth of children. With respect to what should be done, this short section is clear and concise.

12:1–2a. The first clause sets forth the situation: "if" (the word here is כִּי, which may also be translated "when") a woman gives birth to a child, she is unclean. The rest of the chapter traces the process for addressing that uncleanness, giving specific time frames and procedures. However, there are several aspects of the situation that we find troublesome. First, if having children is a desirable thing, why does childbirth make the mother unclean? Then, there is the question: Why is the time frame of purification split into

two unequal periods? This immediately brings up the follow-on question: Why do the unclean periods differ based on whether the child is male or female?

12:2b–3. Why mothers are unclean. The most difficult part of this is the issue of motherhood producing uncleanness. Having children is part of the first command that God gave humankind in Genesis 1:28: "Be fruitful and multiply." Moreover, in Israelite culture having children was considered a blessing and a lack of children was viewed as disastrous. Why then was a new mother unclean? As discussed in the "Clean and Unclean" section of the introduction, the word used here is טָמֵא, which does not denote sin but seems to reflect a response of the psyche that affected one's relationship with others. In the case of motherhood, scholars throughout the centuries have attempted to determine why the mother was placed in this category.

The Bible never explains why this is the case. Scholars have noted some similarities in the views on birth rituals throughout the world (Milgrom 1991, 763), and in general they attempt to universalize the concept (Balentine 2002, 102; Noordtzij 1982, 131). One of the most dominant historically has been the idea that menstrual blood and the blood associated with birth were viewed as "the repository of demonic forces." Milgrom (1991, 766) observes that "Israel's monotheism had exorcised the demons." While one might argue that many if not most Israelites seemed to follow folk religion that incorporated many external influences, that would not explain the official guidelines given in Scripture as direct revelation from God. Another popular view ties life to blood (Lev. 17:11), which might suggest that the issue is the loss of blood that weakens the person (Bailey 2005, 156; Mathews 2009, 114; Willis 2009, 120). However, bleeding from a wound that may be more life-threatening does not render one impure (Gane 2004a, 225).

Quality of Worship (11:1–15:33)

Bailey's (2005, 157) comment is probably pertinent when he states, "Study of the 'why' is a modern scholarly question; for piety, there was merely the matter of obedience." In this light, two connections with Leviticus 15 are helpful, although they will be addressed more fully when we reach that chapter. Leviticus 15:19–24 shows a correlation for a woman with the normal menstrual cycle. She was considered unclean for the period of discharge. Afterward, she was to bathe in water and then provide two turtledoves or pigeons as offering, and she was considered clean. Similar guidelines are given in 15:2–15 for bodily discharges for men, suggesting that the issue is genital discharges rather than blood. Hartley (1992, 169) then may be on the right track when he looks for a theological explanation rather than physical. He states:

> In giving birth the woman challenges the penalty of death on mankind for sinning against God in the Garden of Eden (Gen. 2:16–17), for each birth insures the continuation of the race. Symbolically each birth strikes a blow on the head of the paradisiacal serpent, the champion of death (Gen. 3:15). Giving birth was a momentous act of victory. But the regulations of ritual purity did not allow a new mother to exalt herself as divine in her great accomplishment. These regulations relegated her triumph to the sphere of this earth without diminishing her great joy in bringing forth new life.

This might suggest that the purpose of the entire ritual was to allow the woman to contemplate the significance of the event with isolation from the sanctuary intended to emphasize the need for God and for a redeemer.

TRANSLATION ANALYSIS: "WHEN A WOMAN GIVES BIRTH"

Literally, the opening of the sentence might be translated as "A woman, when she produces seed," which is an unusual use of the word זָרַע, used here in the hiphil, or causative stem. Normally it refers to male semen in the sense of pregnancy and birth. Here it brings to mind the curse on the serpent in Genesis 3:15, which announces perpetual conflict between the serpent's descendants and Eve's. While in that case it is a collective, the next sentence indicates also a future individual who would fatally wound the serpent.

12:4–5. The period of purification. Interrelated with the above are two follow-on questions. The period of uncleanness is defined as one week if the child is a male, and two weeks if the child is a female. Subsequently, she "remains in the blood of her purification" for thirty-three days if the child is male and sixty-six days if female. During that period, she is restricted from entering the sanctuary, but is not viewed as unclean. First, why is this purification period divided between a week of uncleanness, and then a following period where she is able to do all of the normal activities of life (defined in the introduction as "common")? Second, why is this period doubled for a female? Again, we are not told why in either case; and again, scholars speculate. Many of the suggestions regarding the first question center on the idea that this is a period when the mother was more vulnerable, and that the declaration of impurity attempted to protect her, whether from physical debilitations or demonic (Levine 1989, 249). One thing that should be observed is that except for the sacrifice at the end, the guidelines for the seven- (or fourteen-) day period are the same for the menstrual period in Leviticus 15, which would suggest that the nature of the impurity is the same and the purpose is theological, although not explained.

With regard to the question of the double purification time for mothers with female babies, again we have no answer. Many suggestions have been made but all seem rather speculative. Some are based on assumptions of bias against women on the part of the culture

Quality of Worship (11:1–15:33)

or human writers. Milgrom (1991, 750) suggests just the opposite based on the Mishnah, which points out that Scripture produces uncleanness in the hands of those who handle it, as opposed to regular writings. That might suggest that the birth of a female provided another link in the continuation and growth of the human race, which was to be celebrated. But again, we really have no answer.

12:6–8. The purification offering. The last guideline is that when the purification period is complete, the woman is to bring to the priest a lamb for a burnt offering and a young pigeon or turtledove for a purification offering. In the case of poverty, a second turtledove or pigeon may substitute for the lamb. The process is the same as set forth later for purification in the case of certain diseases and fulfilling a Nazirite vow. While the order is reversed, with the burnt offering listed first here, this may be the distinction between the administrative listing and the procedural listing. In any case, upon completion of the offering at the end of the requisite period, the text states, "she will be clean."

Physical Afflictions Affect Worship (13:1–14:57)

This extremely long section essentially consists of two parts that are very detailed, technical, and obscure. Both chapters address the issue of ṣāraʿat (צָרַעַת), which has historically been understood as leprosy.

TRANSLATION ANALYSIS: "LEPROSY"
Until recent years, the Hebrew word צָרַעַת has been translated as "leprosy," primarily based on the Septuagint translation of the word as lepra (λέπρα) and the NT use of the same Greek term. This has produced the impression that it referred to the modern disease called leprosy. The disease known today as leprosy is sometimes called Hansen's disease after the doctor who identified its bacterial cause in 1874. Because of the negative connotations of uncleanness,

the use of the term "leprosy" as a translation is problematic, although an appropriate term has not been agreed on. A number of scholars use awkward phrases such as those suggested by E. V. Hulse (1975, 103): "a repulsive scaly skin disease"; in the case of houses, "an objectionable scaling condition"; or in the case of garments, "an objectionable powdery condition."

Because of the confusion associated with the term "leprosy," we will use the Hebrew term ṣāraʿat for clarity. We will mention two confusion factors. First, the characteristics listed as signs of ṣāraʿat do not match the modern disease of leprosy.

Leprosy

Leprosy as we know it apparently originated in India and was introduced to the Graeco-Roman world after the time of Alexander the Great (Hulse 1975, 88). In his medical analysis of the biblical description of ṣāraʿat, Hulse concludes that what is being described is a condition that on humans produced "fine white, almost powdery, scales being loosened from the affected area," which might be described as "falling 'like snow'" as opposed to "white as snow" (p. 93). This flakey surface sloughing off could explain the inclusion of ṣāraʿat of garments and houses. Most scholars see the ṣāraʿat of houses and garments as some type of fungal (mold or mildew) infection, which also produced flaking. Medically, Hulse suggests that in terms of the skin disease the following would be modern candidates for a diagnosis of ṣāraʿat: psoriasis, seborrhoeic dermatitis, fungus infections of the skin particularly favus, patchy eczema, and pityriasis rosea (p. 96). He concludes that psoriasis and favus would be the primary candidates (p. 99), but cautions that ṣāraʿa more probably denoted "a conglomeration of a number of diseases" with similar appearances. He suggests that since these diseases are not considered contagious, aesthetic reasons with regard to the loose scales may have been a factor in defining cultic uncleanness (p. 103).

Second, the same term is applied to afflictions that could affect clothing and houses. In those cases, the description seems to better fit a fungus (mold or mildew). As noted in the translation analysis, this term probably referred to a number of different maladies that presented similar appearances that specifically affected human skin or the surfaces of clothing or houses. As such, it is not really clear today what the actual physical problems were. The key is that all of the manifestations produced uncleanness (diagnosed for skin and clothing in Lev. 13 but for houses in Lev. 14), and the rituals were intended to restore cleanness after the malady was cured (described in Lev. 14). In addition to the question of the specific problem, the text never explains why a person with these symptoms was unclean. Further, while provisions are given for the determination of healing, no method of healing is provided—rather, guidelines for reinstituting cleanness are provided for when such healing takes place. As part of the bigger picture of cleanness and uncleanness, we will simply survey the basic issues involved with regard to the diagnosis and the cleansing steps.

13:1–46. *Ṣāraʿat* of the skin. Somewhat surprisingly, this section does not associate the issue of *ṣāraʿat* with any sin or act that the individual had done. Rather, it presents a situation where an individual realized that he (or she, and so throughout this unit) had one of the three diagnostic indicators on his (or her, and so throughout this passage) skin (13:2).

TRANSLATION ANALYSIS: 13:2 DIAGNOSTIC INDICATORS שְׂאֵת אוֹ־סַפַּחַת אוֹ בַהֶרֶת
These three terms reflect something that the individual or priest could clearly determine as to whether it was *ṣāraʿat* or not. Scholars disagree as to whether the first term (שְׂאֵת) is a swelling or discoloration. Kaiser (1980g, 2:600) suggests swelling, from the root נָשָׂא meaning "to lift," but the next verse, 13:3, suggests it is deeper.

Rabbinic tradition proposes discoloration, specifically different shades of white (Milgrom 1991, 773). Translations and commentators are in general agreement with regard to the second and third terms. The second term (סַפַּחַת) seems to be a scab or flaking (*TWOT* s.v. "סַפַּחַת" 2:631). The third term (בַהֶרֶת) suggests a bright spot (Milgrom 1991, 774).

In this case the person was brought to the priest, who examined the "mark."

TRANSLATION ANALYSIS: "MARK"
The word translated "mark" is derived from the verb נָגַע, which means "to touch or strike" (Coppes 1980c, 551). This term is used twice in the case of a person (13:3 and 6), but twelve times in the case of a garment, and ten times in the case of a house. While one may think of a person or garment as having a mark, in the case of the *ṣāraʿat* of a house, Leviticus 14:34 quotes God telling Moses and Aaron that when they got into the land, that there "[he would] place a mark of *ṣāraʿat* on a house." This could suggest the infestation was punishment, but there is no mention either of sin or forgiveness in this section. Sklar (2014, 196) suggests that it is "the Lord's affirmation that such events happen under his sovereign control which would suggest purpose, perhaps as testing."

There were three possible diagnoses: it was obviously *ṣāraʿat*, and the individual was unclean; it was obviously not *ṣāraʿat*, and the individual was pronounced clean; or it was not clear, in which case the priest quarantined the person for a week and examined him again. The options for the second exam were the same. After a second quarantine, if the indicator had significantly faded the individual was clean, otherwise he was unclean. In the subsequent appearances before the priest, it would seem that the whiteness or redness of the flesh indicated either new healing skin (white) or raw flesh (red; Levine 1989, 78).

Quality of Worship (11:1–15:33)

If it was determined that the person had *ṣāra'at* and was diagnosed as unclean, he was required to live outside of the camp. He must also show signs of mourning (torn garments, uncovered hair, and "covered mustache" [13:45]), and proclaim "unclean."

> ### TRANSLATION ANALYSIS: "COVERED MUSTACHE"
> The word שָׂפָם is normally translated "mustache," which would only be the case of a male. Since females also could contract *ṣāra'at*, "upper lip" may be a better translation (Kiuchi 2007, 237).

It is interesting that the text states specifically that this is the case "all the days during which he has the infection," which suggests that the *ṣāra'at* was expected to heal. If that is the case, it is very possible that the *ṣāra'at* presented in Leviticus was a disease that is no longer present or that has modified so that it is no longer an issue.

13:47–59. *Ṣāra'at* of the clothing. The text turns immediately to the case where a garment had a "mark" of *ṣāra'at*. Three materials are noted: wool, linen, and leather. The first two were woven, as indicated by the "warp and woof" terminology. Regardless of material, the item must be shown to a priest. The priest examined the item and followed similar procedures as in the case of a person. If the mark was determined to be *ṣāra'at*, the item was to be burned. If after quarantine the mark had not spread, it was to be quarantined again and washed. This time, if the mark had faded but was still present, it was to be "torn out." Apparently, the garment was then repaired, but if the mark returned, it was burned. If the washing had removed the mark, then the item was washed again and it was pronounced as clean.

14:1–32. Cleansing of victims of *ṣāra'at*. The cleansing of a victim of *ṣāra'at* could only take place after the person had been healed. One of the most difficult parts of this section is following the complex interplay of physical objects involved in the cleansing and the purification sacrifices. In essence the rituals provided an external affirmation that the malady had been cured, and the victim's community relationships could resume. This ritual involved three stages over a period of a week, which have parallels with both the purification of the priests (see Lev. 8) and the Day of Atonement (see Lev. 16). The first stage was done outside of the camp, where the priest went to the person who had been declared unclean and was living in isolation. After examination and ascertaining that the person was indeed healed, the priest now pronounced that the person was clean, and the stage one initial ceremony would be performed.

> ### *Ṣāra'at* Purification, Stage 1
> The stage one ceremony began after the priest had examined the now-healed person and determined him or her as healed. It would seem that the items specified provided symbolism in the ritual, but the specifics are not spelled out, so any suggestion is largely speculation. The priest would have two live clean birds, cedar wood, a scarlet string, and hyssop brought. One bird was slain in an earthenware vessel over "living" water. The remaining bird, the cedar wood, the scarlet string, and the hyssop were taken together and dipped in the blood of the slain bird. After the person who was being cleansed was sprinkled seven times, he was pronounced clean and the live bird was released—a process that seems to emulate what will be later performed nationally on the Day of Atonement. The person now washed his clothes, shaved off his hair, and bathed. He was now allowed to return to the camp, but must remain outside of his tent for a week.

At this point, he was allowed to reenter the camp, but was not allowed to enter his tent. The second stage was performed a week later. On the seventh day, he shaved his head (including hair, beard, and eyebrows), washed his clothes again, and bathed again. Apparently at this point he could reenter his tent.

Ṣāraʿat Purification, Stage 2

The second stage of purification was at the end of the week, when he entered the camp. While the rationale is not clear, the presence of the person in front of his tent would announce to the community that he had been healed. On the seventh day, he would again shave off all of his hair including his head, beard, and eyebrows. He was then to wash his clothes and "wash his flesh" (וְרָחַץ אֶת־בְּשָׂרוֹ, i.e., bathe his entire body).

The third stage took place on the next day (the eighth day); he performed a second purification ritual before the doorway of the Tent of Meeting. At this point he would be deemed clean and could now worship.

Ṣāraʿat Purification, Stage 3

The third stage took place the next day. On the eighth day he was to take purification sacrifices, which included two male lambs, a female yearling ewe, three-tenths of an ephah (about six and a half liters.) of flour, and a log (about a pint) of oil to the Tent of Meeting. The priest who had pronounced him clean before the Lord would present him at the doorway of the Tent of Meeting. The ceremony would begin with the sacrifice of one male lamb as a reparation offering. We noted in Leviticus 5:14–6:7 (HB 5:26) that normally a reparation (אָשָׁם) offering followed inadvertent sin and required restitution prior to presentation; however, ṣāraʿat does not necessarily involve sin, so perhaps what is being signaled here is an inadvertent breakdown of the person's community relationship as a result of the ṣāraʿat. The log of oil was presented with the lamb. The priest took from the blood of the lamb and placed it on the lobe of the right ear, right thumb, and right big toe of the person being purified. The priest now poured some of the oil into his left hand, and then sprinkled some of the oil seven times before the Lord.

Then he put some of the oil on the same appendages he had previously anointed with the blood, and then placed the remaining oil in his hand on the person's head. Subsequently the priest sacrificed a second lamb as a purification offering (חַטָּאת). Finally, the last lamb was sacrificed as a burnt offering (for consecration) along with flour as a voluntary gift offering (מִנְחָה). The final verses of this section provide substitutes and decreased amounts for individuals who might not have the means for the standard offerings.

14:33–57. Cleansing of ṣāraʿat houses. The final portion of this section is challenging for several reasons. First, the material up to this point has very pointedly addressed the Israelites camped at the foot of Mount Sinai who had just erected the tabernacle. Any Israelite who contracted ṣāraʿat was removed from the camp (Lev. 13:46), and when healed the priest went to him "outside of the camp" (Lev. 14:3). When healed he might enter the camp, but could not enter his *tent* for seven days (Lev. 14:8). Now, in a new declaration to Moses and Aaron, the scene changes to a yet future time after the nation entered the Promised Land, and the people were dwelling in *houses* (בַּיִת), instead of tents (אֹהֶל). Second, although Moses and Aaron would not go into the land and thus would never experience this, at this point they would not have been aware of that coming judgment, so the information was still relevant and the record would be important for the generation that did go into the land. Third, the term ṣāraʿat, which described uncleanness on people's skin or garments, is now used to describe an affliction on the houses they would occupy in the future. It would have been expected that the houses would be built of inorganic material; that is, they would have a stone foundation/footer with either stone or mud-brick walls above them, which were then plastered. Apparently, it was on those walls that the infection would have developed (Milgrom

1991, 871). Fourth, while the infection would render the house *unclean*, that designation would not be given until the priest examined it. Interestingly, anything removed from the house before the priest got there would not be considered unclean, although if it was still there when the priest made his pronouncement it would now be unclean. Fifth, as already noted, the direction from God is that the "mark" of *ṣāraʿat* would have been placed there by him (see translation analysis of "mark").

The *ṣāraʿat* problem for the house seems to have been a form of mildew (Milgrom 1991, 870). The process of addressing the issue was similar to that of the garment. It began when the homeowner noticed the problem. The family moved everything out and then called the priest, who came and diagnosed the problem. If potentially unclean, the priest would quarantine the house for seven days to see if the mark spread. If the mark had spread on the seventh day, the family was required to scrape off the plaster and remove the affected section and then take it outside of the city. The wall was to be repaired, and the family (and if appropriate—if the house shared the wall with the neighbor—working with the affected neighbor) would repair the wall. At this point, the process is not clear. The text states that the priest would come back and reinspect the house, but it does not define when. On the one hand, there seems to have been a period of time to see if the mark reemerged. On the other hand, the house has not yet been pronounced clean and yet the people seem to have moved back in. When the priest did come back for the inspection, if the mark had spread, the house was pronounced unclean and destroyed with the materials moved out of the city. If the priest pronounced it clean, the ritual for cleansing was very similar to that for the individual who was pronounced clean from *ṣāraʿat* (see "*Ṣāraʿat* Purification, Stage 1" sidebar).

Mildew

As previously noted, *ṣāraʿat* seems to be a general term that addresses a variety of afflictions. In the case of houses, Solomon noted when he prayed at the dedication of the temple in Jerusalem that a possible future problem for the nation would be "blight or mildew" (2 Chron. 6:28). "Mildew" is the translation of the Hebrew word יֵרָקוֹן, which derives from a root that denotes greenness or paleness (*TWOT* s.v. "יֵרָקוֹן" 1:409). The word translated *blight* is שִׁדָּפוֹן, which BDB (s.v. "שִׁדָּפוֹן" 995) translates as "smut." Conversely more recent sources define blight as the "effect produced by the dry hot wind," which withers grass and other vegetation in a day (the type of wind described in Jonah 4:8–10; KB s.v. "שְׁדֵפָה" 950; Hamilton 1980l, 908).

Sexual Issues Affect One's Ability to Worship (15:1–33)

The last chapter in this section covers several bodily discharges that render a person unclean. The Hebrew word translated "body" is בָּשָׂר, which is often translated as "flesh." While it can mean the entire body, here it is understood to refer to the genital organs (both male and female). Thus, while the topic is physical discharges, it seems that it is only discharges from the sexual organs that render a person unclean. The first part of the chapter addresses male discharges, while the second discusses female. While both sections address normal and abnormal discharges, the order is reversed in the second section.

The Structure of Leviticus 15

This chapter is structured as a chiasm, which "emphasizes formal equivalence in the ritual status of men and women" (Kleinig 2003, 317):
A—Abnormal male discharges (15:2b–15)
B—Normal male discharges (15:16–18)
B'—Normal female discharges (15:19–24)
A'—Abnormal female discharges (15:25–30)

> However, 15:18 serves as a hinge, since it addresses uncleanness as a result of sexual intercourse, which renders both the male and female as unclean simultaneously. Interestingly while the focus is the male discharge, the female is mentioned first, producing an "inverted hinge" that is seen as tying the two together.

15:1–15. Abnormal male discharges. The text describes this as a discharge (זוֹב) that either flows (רִיר) from or obstructs (חָתַם) the genital-urinary tract. In either case, he is considered unclean. It is understood that in this state he would be unable to participate in corporate worship but would be allowed to remain in the camp and his tent with the caveat that his seat or bed or various other items would become unclean if they touched him. The same applied to people if he touched them without rinsing his hands.

TRANSLATION ANALYSIS: "DISCHARGE"
The basic term "discharge" (זוֹב), used here as a *qal* participle in 15:2 but as a noun in 15:3, describes liquid movement. According to *TWOT* (Wood 1980a), the word suggests the flow of a liquid. In this chapter it refers to a flow from the genital organs for both women and men. In the case of the male, it denotes an abnormal discharge that either רִיר, "flows (like slime)" (*TWOT* s.v. "רִיר" 2:846), or חָתַם, obstructs or seals up the urethra (Lewis 1980b). The latter case likely describes a situation where urination is painful and difficult (Hartley 1992, 209). Historically, the most frequent diagnosis has been gonorrhea, primarily because of the LXX translation. However, the modern disease termed gonorrhea was not documented prior to the fifteenth century (Milgrom 1991, 907). While specific symptoms of modern gonorrhea have been described in ancient Greece (although not before the third century B.C.), they are not described together. As Rebecca Flemming (2019) describes it, "while *gonorrhoia* [sic] became, and persisted as, a well-established disease in classical medical discourse, it was not modern gonorrhea, either in concept or actuality." She does note, however, that "diseases are often historically unstable entities." Given the limited description of symptoms, the exact nature of the affliction in Leviticus is not clear. Further, there is no indication of sin, which might be expected for a sexually transmitted disease.

While a seminal discharge (שִׁכְבַת־זֶרַע, 15:16–18) also produces uncleanness, it is considered a normal discharge.

In the case of a female, the term "discharge" describes a blood flow (דָּם), both as a normal menstrual discharge as well as a prolonged period (in the case of the woman healed by Jesus, she had experienced this for twelve years [Matt. 9:20; Mark 5:23; Luke 8:43]).

Secondary uncleanness would develop when someone else touched something that he had made unclean. Interestingly there is no process provided for healing, but an understanding that apparently the discharge would heal on its own. When that occurred, the person would be responsible for bringing an offering of two turtledoves or pigeons to the priest at the Tent of Meeting and go through a cleansing ritual.

15:16–18. Normal male discharges. A normal discharge is defined as a seminal emission (שִׁכְבַת־זֶרַע) whether or not it was the result of sexual intercourse (Wenham 1979, 219). In either case, the man was unclean until evening and needed to undergo an abbreviated cleansing ritual of bathing. If this was during sexual intercourse, the result was that both partners were considered unclean until evening and needed to bathe. The primary effect this would have on the Israelites would be for the priests who were expected to enter the tabernacle regularly. Beyond that, marital sexual relations were clearly within the common area of life (as explained the section

Quality of Worship (11:1–15:33)

"Clean and Unclean" in the introduction) and carried no stigma, as shown by the fact that normal discharges (for both male and female) did not require a sacrifice for cleansing, just a bath and waiting until evening. In a literary sense, the inclusion of the woman in 15:18 makes that a hinge verse, as the text now turns to discharges in the case of women. For the original audience this also had a practical effect of invalidating sexual fertility rites, whether in the sanctuary or any pagan shrine (Hartley 1992, 210).

15:19–24. Normal female discharges. For women, the normal discharge was her menses. As a result, she was considered unclean for seven days. As in the case of a male, she would be allowed to remain in the camp and her tent with the caveat that her seat or bed or various items, including people, would become unclean. Interestingly, commentators note that no statement is made regarding anything she touched becoming unclean, as opposed to the case of the man for whom that was true only if he had not rinsed his hands. As such, they suggest that she is still able to do her normal household routine.

Touch of Uncleanness

This traditional understanding might suggest that in the case of the woman with the blood flow that Jesus healed (Matt. 9:20; Mark 5:23; Luke 8:43), the fact that she touched the hem of his garment might not have transmitted uncleanness. The text does not indicate that Jesus himself touched her, but stated as he looked at her that she was healed by her faith. Even if this is the case, the incident takes place as Jesus is en route to the house of Jairus, a synagogue official. Jairus's daughter had died, and when Jesus arrived, he took the dead child by the hand and raised her, which according to a later revelation would cause the one who touched the corpse to be unclean. As such, it is still clear that the overall situation shows Jesus in a situation where according to the law, he would theoretically have become

unclean. However, in both cases, it would seem that the healing would override the issue of uncleanness, and the main point of each incident was that Jesus has power over the most dreadful aspects of life.

However, secondary uncleanness for others would develop when they touched something that she had made unclean by sitting or lying and, as in the case anything made unclean by a male, that person was unclean until evening. The exception would be should the man lie with her while she was unclean, then he also is unclean for the same seven days. Most commentators suggest that would be a situation where the flow started during intercourse.

Menstruation and Uncleanness

Later passages warn Israelites not to have sex during the time of the menstrual flow, with severe repercussions should they do so (Lev. 18:19; 20:28). Hartley (1992, 212) states: "The best way to account for this apparent discrepancy in severity of the consequences is to hold that these texts address different situations. In this text it is assumed that a man surprisingly and unwittingly discovers that he has come into contact with menses, probably from intercourse at the inception of the woman's menstrual period, while in the other law a man brazenly breaks the decree by knowingly lying with a woman during her period."

15:25–30. Abnormal female discharges. An abnormal discharge would be one that lasted "many days," or at a time other than normal, which might suggest a miscarriage. During the time of the discharge the issue was handled just like the normal menstrual period. The difference would be after the flow stopped. After the healing she would count seven days and bring two turtledoves or pigeons for an abbreviated purification ceremony.

Quality of Worship (11:1–15:33)

15:31–33. Separation from uncleanness. The last three verses serve two purposes. As at the end of other divine revelations, 15:32–33 summarize the material on discharges (see 11:46; 13:59; 14:2, 32, and 54). However, 15:31 also seems to be a summary. Even though they appear to be reversed from our perspective, 15:31 likely summarizes the entire section of Leviticus 11–15, showing how aspects of the common life (חל) can cause uncleanness (טָהוֹר) by giving illustrative cases. The challenge for the reader is that the people are to be "separated" from their uncleanness. The reason is that if they remain in uncleanness they will die in it and make the tabernacle unclean, although that term is translated "defile."

> ### "Separate"
>
> The priestly mission statement in Leviticus 10:10 uses a common word for "separate," בָּדַל, although the concept of that term lies more in the sense of "distinguish" or "divide." Here the word used is נָזַר, which is defined as "to separate, consecrate" (McComiskey 1980d, 567). This is the root behind "Nazirite," a consecrated person (usually for a period of time). While most versions use a "keep separate" sense of translation, as used here in the *hiphil* stem with the מִן preposition ("from") it would seem to carry the connotation of causing the separation rather than maintaining it.

> ### "Defile"
>
> As noted in the introduction, the word translated "defile" is the verb form of the noun that is translated twice in this verse as "unclean." The English word "defile" denotes a greater degree of degradation than to make unclean, as shown by Webster's primary definition of "to make filthy" (*WTNID* s.v. "defile"). It would seem from this context that the defilement at this juncture is a corporate concept. In other words, the warning seems to be for each individual to maintain his or her own cleanness by performing the requisite ritual cleansing as needed, in order that the nation

> as a whole does not become unclean—pointing out how individual and corporate responsibilities intertwine.

THEOLOGICAL FOCUS

Following the death of Nadab and Abihu but prior to describing the Day of Atonement, God gave Moses and Aaron guidelines covering aspects of ordinary life that required the Israelites to carefully monitor their everyday lifestyles. This unit seems to highlight how aspects of everyday life can be problematic with respect to our relationship to God. In these six messages God uses the term "unclean" approximately forty-five times, but not once does he use word "sin" outside of the English translation of "sin offering" for חַטָּאת, which we suggested is better translated "purification offering," used throughout this section to make something described as unclean into cleanness. It is clear that even when we do not sin, our need for cleansing remains. More significantly, as Mathews (2009, 130–32) points out, there is no separation between one's religious and one's secular life; that is, there is nothing in our daily lives that God's Word does not impact. Drawing on Colossians 1:19–23, he goes on to state that "holy living is at its most fundamental level the *relationship* we have with God" (emphasis original). We have noted how routine aspects of human life such as normal physical discharges or eating meat, or even having children, produce uncleanness that affects both our relationship with God and our relationship within the community.

Beyond that we observed that we might encounter afflictions such as long-term discharges, or *ṣāra'at*, which God indicates that he sends. And yet there is no indication that the individual has done anything to deserve these, and there is no condemnation for the person who has received them. Even so, they affect how one might worship. In the OT, this was an actual barrier preventing access to the tabernacle. In the post-NT period, these barriers are often more psychological. In any case, the real focus

Quality of Worship (11:1–15:33)

of this section seems to be on how cleansing is possible and thus there is hope. In terms of teaching, an emphasis on Christian compassion by focusing on how ceremonial cleansing (perhaps in terms of NT teaching, anointing with oil, per James 5:14) might be relevant.

These chapters emphasize the need for our hope to remain focused on God alone. He reminds us of our daily need for him and his ongoing work in us and among us. We may often confess our need for his grace to remove the sin that rises up inside us and to recognize the common grace of sunshine and fresh breezes that surrounds us. Through these cleanliness laws, God is helping his people humble themselves before him as they grasp their need for divine grace to remove the uncleanliness that is coming at them in this fallen world.

While addressed to the nation corporately, all of the examples given in this section really are individual issues, specifically related to when an individual eats the wrong meats, when a particular woman gives birth to a child, when an individual or family encounters ṣāraʿat, or when an individual has sexual issues. In contrast, the next unit will address a broader concept: what to do in terms of purification of the nation as a whole, especially with regard to small issues that may not have been noticed but that have accumulated nationally. This is the purpose of the holy day Yom Kippur.

PREACHING AND TEACHING STRATEGIES

Exegetical and Theological Synthesis

Does the consumption of food or drink actually make one created in God's image unclean? Can touching what is dead or consuming blood truly render one defiled? Will mold in one's house or discharge from the body really cause a person to be unholy? Are these questions for God's people to answer? Or are they questions that reveal a heart that is prone to wander?

The Scriptures convey how in our fallen state, humankind has historically been overconfident in its ability to foresee, appraise, and overcome the inherent dangers in our world that seriously imperil our souls. It short, we have shown ourselves to be more than foolish. We can be utterly haughty in our foolishness. By discounting what God classifies as dangerous, we become reckless with our own lives and the lives of those around us. In the spirit of Nadab and Abihu, we believe that if we could only understand the basic standard of holiness, we would keep it, abide by it, and if need be amend it to enhance what God has divinely established.

Once again, the heart is wickedly deceitful. Who can know it (Jer. 17:9)? In his mercy, God is working to protect us from deeper dangers that we do not see (and may never understand) and often insist are not present. He is developing the believer's ability to be prudent as they explore their surroundings and to be wary of all that may harm them, in order to cultivate a posture of holiness marked by God's words. The result is a life set apart from the standards of this world—a life distinguished both by the freedoms and limitations of living a godly life in a fallen world.

Preaching Idea

We are distinguished as God's people by avoiding forbidden practices and recognizing the need for cleansing from the inherent uncleanliness of this fallen world.

Contemporary Connections

What does it mean?

How will God differentiate those who are to be "priests to the world" from the surrounding humanity? It will involve more than simple adherence to an ever-evolving list of dos and don'ts. It will require their willingness to humbly yield to God's commands concerning (1) what one is able to pursue, (2) what one should specifically avoid, and (3) how one who becomes unclean (whether from natural acts or disobedience) can be made clean again.

With both wholesome and toxic choices within our reach, God did not leave us oblivious, releasing us to discover for ourselves the poisonous consequences of chasing after the perilous or embracing what would eventually prove to be deadly. He categorized many things surrounding us (which appear desirable) as forbidden, thus alleviating the necessity of experiencing the painful realities of living a life based upon trial and error.

In addition, God provides the means for cleansing those who trust in him from the natural effects of daily living in an unclean world. All humanity is well aware that this world is not a perfect place. It is populated by imperfect people—a population to which we each add. No, we cannot avoid all the effects of the world in which we live. We will need daily cleansing to counter all we see, experience, and do. Seeing and confessing this need, and growing in our willingness to yield in obedience to God's commands, is progressive sanctification.

Is it true?
God is calling those who trust him to be distinguished by avoiding what he has labeled forbidden and confessing our need to be cleansed from the uncleanliness inherent to life in this broken world. One will find little argument that the world and all who occupy it have become "unclean." The debate begins once we consider how such uncleanliness occurs, who is responsible, and how (or whether) one may be made clean again.

Humanity generally considers the majority of God's standards both random (Why does this actually matter?) and invasive (Why must I change who I am?). Yet, as we all see the need to identify and maintain a standard, by avoiding particular practices and adhering to others, we are at a minimum proclaiming that some standard must exist. Everyone cannot be free to simply resort to what they feel in the moment to be best. From where will this standard come? Culture? Parents? Majority vote? God?

If the lives of God's people are visibly distinct first by action (what we determine to pursue and avoid) and second by attitude (how we humbly approach our failures to maintain our own standards), then we will serve as witnesses to the world of God's holiness and grace. We humbly confess there is a standard, we are falling short of that standard, and we need ongoing forgiveness and cleansing before God and one another.

Now what?
Holiness is not a collective creation of the minds of God's people. Holiness originates in God himself. Thus, we can cease setting our own standards based on exploring ourselves or one another. Gazing inward cannot lead us to discover a divine standard. For that, we must gaze upward to embrace the standard for holiness God has set for us.

We are free to explore a garden filled with delightful fruit, but it will prove perilous if we overrule God's commands on what to pursue and what to avoid. Foolishly experimenting with what is categorized as dangerous puts us on the road to spiritual death. Confessing our need to yield to the wisdom of God's word puts us on the road to new life. Ultimately, God has provided the means for fully sanctifying all who have defiled themselves through disobedience.

Creativity in Presentation
Going into this message, expect resistance. Begin by admitting that the careless application of standards and rules can advance into legalism. Yet, living apart from any standards and rules will progress into chaos. The goal is to help everyone see (1) the necessity for standards both personally and in community, (2) that we may not be the best ones to set and measure our own standards, and (3) that we need to trust God even when we don't understand why.

Quality of Worship (11:1–15:33)

Demonstrate the necessity of standards

Offer the scenario of establishing a new group—a new class of students, a business startup, a shipwreck of strangers on an island, or some other situation. Choose what best engages your context. If your group is interactive, let them answer questions. If not, pose them and answer them yourself. What will they allow? What will they forbid? What do they pursue? What do they avoid? Will their decisions prove helpful or harmful? Foolish or wise? Then provide the opportunity to describe one person (not in the group) who would be most helpful in guiding them to what is helpful and wise. Clearly, they want someone with experience—someone who has had the class, started a similar business, lived on the island before, or similar. Will they (can they) trust this recognized expert, or will they follow their own instincts?

Explain how we are not equipped to set and evaluate the standard for ourselves

Ask if anyone has ever worked in a unique smelly job. From personal experience I (Biehl) can give a lot of personal testimony here! After working on a dairy farm, pig farm, slaughterhouse, and many factories, one realizes that one quickly takes on the odor of one's work. And in a short time, we will soon become desensitized to even the most obnoxious odors. Furthermore, we will carry those odors home on our clothes, skin, and hair until eventually our entire home boasts the same obnoxious odor as our work . . . and we are not even aware of it!

How can we be made clean again? If we are desensitized, we are rendered incapable of judging our own cleanliness. How can we be made aware of what "clean" is? It will require the help of another nose—maybe not a divine nose, but the nose of one who is not deeply involved in our work. If we humble ourselves before the nose of another, we can know if we and our home are actually clean.

We are distinguished as God's people by avoiding forbidden practices and recognizing the need for cleansing from the inherent uncleanliness of this fallen world.

- Living in an "unclean" world
  - Food: a need to separate the clean from the unclean
  - Childbirth: a need to purify from what grew from within
  - Disease: a need to purify from what came at us
    - Skin diseases
    - Environmental contamination
    - Discharges
- What did it mean to them then? What does it mean always? What do we do now?
  - Avoiding forbidden practices and foods will not keep them clean
  - There is inherent uncleanliness from living in a fallen world
  - The people of God should recognize their need for cleansing from:
    - the uncleanliness and sin that arises from within us.
    - the uncleanliness and sin that comes at us.

DISCUSSION QUESTIONS

1. Perhaps one of the most common understandings of Judaism is the restrictions they have regarding what meats they may or may not eat. Is it important that one understand why those restrictions exist? Why or why not?

2. Why might the concept of uncleanness be important to Christians?

3. How does recognizing that something that was unclean was not necessarily sin affect how we view some of the restrictions we might encounter in life?

Leviticus 16:1–34

EXEGETICAL IDEA
The Lord God established the Day of Atonement as a day when the high priest would offer specific sacrifices to atone for the sins of the nation, reminding them of their individual need to be purified before God.

THEOLOGICAL FOCUS
Knowing the need, God establishes the means by which the sins of his people can be effectively "carried away forever," leaving them holy before him.

PREACHING IDEA
Sin is carried away by a specific atoning work of God on a day set by God, in order that we may be in fellowship with him forever.

PREACHING POINTERS
The people of God were teetering on the edge (possibly trembling in fear) with their expanding understanding of the incendiary nature of sin and their need for personal atonement. There was a growing reality that their ability to live under the standards of holiness would be an enduring obstacle. Some may have thought it impossible to navigate. It was made clear through Nadab and Abihu that God's standard of holiness is more than a suggestion—it is a necessity for all who enter into the presence of the living God. The people could humbly work to avoid (and eliminate) all uncleanness, they could openly confess and make sacrifices for their unintentional sin once they become aware of it . . . yet, what if their judgment of uncleanness missed the mark? What if there was unconfessed sin of which they are ignorant? Would the humble in spirit destined to be struck down by the holy God they serve? May it never be! In his mercy, God established the means by which his people could be made clean from all their sin—even that of which they were unaware!

We have a bad habit of branding God's requirements confusing, unclear, or even unfair. How can one be expected to abide by such divine (subjective?) standards of holiness? Are we not destined to fall short? Yes, but in his mercy, God has established the means by which all who humbly seek him may be personally redeemed from their fall and made holy through the atoning work of Christ. It is a work that reaches far beyond the sin we see, because it is a work sufficient to carry away a lifetime of sin we have yet to see. Being made holy is a process of confession (as God accurately identifies our sin), of mourning (as we grieve over our disobedience), and casting away (as God removes sin from our lives).

THE DAY OF ATONEMENT (16:1–34)

LITERARY STRUCTURE AND THEMES (16:1–34)

After the five-chapter interlude illustrating matters of everyday life (חֹל) that would produce uncleanness or impurity for Israelites, Leviticus 16 picks up where Leviticus 10 left off. Throughout those five chapters individual cleansing for individual impurities was provided. The text now turns to the matter of corporate cleansing. The basic focus of this chapter is an annual process to purify the nation as a whole. This process is a God-directed and God-focused one-day ritual of corporate repentance for atonement that would take place during the autumn. As presented here in Leviticus, the first performance of that ceremony would have been several months in the future. As we will see in Leviticus 23 when we look at national holidays, the Day of Atonement would become a second liturgical anchor for the fledgling nation. It and the Passover would provide semiannual reminders of the purpose of the nation's founding and existence. In the spring, Passover focused on God's grace and mercy, demonstrated by his deliverance in the exodus. In the fall, the Day of Atonement focused on God's grace and mercy, demonstrated through an annual spiritual cleansing of the nation. While the efficacy of the atonement ritual depended on a corporate awareness of the nation's shortcomings, the intended outcome was a purification of the altar, the tabernacle, and the nation as a whole.

- ***Revelation to Be Given to Aaron (16:1–2a)***
- ***Guidelines for the Day of Atonement (16:2b–28)***
- ***Directions for the Occasion of the Day of Atonement (16:29–34)***

EXPOSITION (16:1–34)

In Leviticus 10 we saw that in the midst of the spiritual high of the priesthood inauguration by the ordination of Aaron and his sons, tragedy struck. Nadab and Abihu were struck down by the God they thought to honor in the very sanctuary they were dedicating. At the end, Aaron lamented that they had died as "they presented their purification offering [חַטָּאת] and their consecration offering [עֹלָה] before the Lord [YHWH]" (Lev. 10:19). Aaron's unspoken question seems to have been "How are we supposed to serve this God who strikes down his servants while they strive to serve him?" That question was left hanging as God provided information that clarified the priestly mission to distinguish "between the holy [הַקֹּדֶשׁ] and the common [הַחֹל], and between the unclean [הַטָּמֵא] and the clean [הַטָּהוֹר]" (Lev. 10:10), beginning with the latter. Five chapters illustrated how even amid normal life individual uncleanness was inevitable—but individual cleansing was possible. The variety of items that produced uncleanness demonstrated that on any given day a portion of the nation would be unclean, and often a significant portion. It was in that somber situation that God provided new revelation to Moses to pass on to Aaron that addressed the conundrum of how a nation that included unclean individuals could serve a holy God who demanded cleanness. While the event described here is called the "Day of Atonement," that name is not given until Leviticus 23:28, where it is actually called "a day of atonements" using the plural indicating that the one act done by a solitary priest in isolation atoned for the entire nation.

The Day of Atonement (16:1–34)

Revelation to Be Given to Aaron (16:1–2a)

Leviticus 16 is unique in that it has a double introduction. Leviticus 16:2 begins with the typical "the Lord [YHWH] said to Moses" seen in previous pericopes of instruction, the most recent of which would have been the five-chapter section illustrating uncleanness covered in the unit "Quality of Worship" above. Preceding that typical introduction, 16:1 anchors the new material chronologically to Leviticus 10. While it begins with the versatile *waw*, the structure suggests that the coming material was not only subsequent revelation, but consequent.

> *TRANSLATION ANALYSIS: WAW*
>
> The *waw* serves to show sequence and can be important. In this case, many translations omit the *waw* since the phrase "after the death of the two sons of Aaron" also shows the connection.

While closely tied to the events of Leviticus 10, given all that had occurred on the day that Nadab and Abihu died, it seems probable that the material in Leviticus 11–16 had not been given on the same day (see chart 3, the "Sequence of Events at Sinai," above). If not, it came very shortly afterward. Likewise, as shown below, it appears that while God gave the ritual guidelines for the Day of Atonement at this time (shortly after the dedication of the tabernacle), those guidelines merely anticipated the actual first celebration that would take place approximately six months later. In a similar manner, the Exodus 28 description of the ordination of the priests had preceded the actual event by several months. While the process of revelation here seems designed to provide information about the Day of Atonement so the nation could anticipate and prepare for the date, it also served to answer Aaron's unspoken question following the Nadab and Abihu incident (see above). In any case, the first observance of the Day of Atonement is not recorded in the OT—nor is any subsequent observance, which is

somewhat surprising given the fact that by the Second Temple period, the ceremony was important enough that it became known simply as "The Day."

> ### The Day
>
> While the ceremony is not named here, it is given the name יוֹם הַכִּפֻּרִים (the Day of Atonements [plural]) in Leviticus 23:27—the only place it is named, although the ceremony is also addressed in Numbers 29:7–11. Philip Blackman, in his introduction to the Mishnah tractate Yoma, notes that it was also known as "The Great Day," which was shortened to "The Day" (1963, 271). It is mentioned once in the NT as "the fast" in Acts 27:9, where Paul observes that sailing was now dangerous because "the fast was already over." Hartley (1992, 220) observes that after the destruction of the Second Temple with the resulting termination of sacrifices, this day became even more important in Judaism, although the focus now was entirely on the self-abasement directed in 16:29.

Later it was given a full tractate in the Mishnah. In terms of the original audience, the first observance apparently took place after the rebuke at Kadesh-barnea (Num. 14) but before the death of Miriam (Num. 20:1). If that is the case, God giving the decree at this time may also anticipate the *national* act of malfeasance that would take place several months later at Kadesh-barnea, by formulating a requisite response in advance.

Guidelines for the Day of Atonement (16:2b–28)

Now that the nation had a functioning system of worship centered on the tabernacle enclosing the ark where God would meet with the national representative (indicated by a singular pronoun in Exod. 30:6), they were to exercise great caution with respect to that location because of those meetings. Those meetings would take place in front of the כַּפֹּרֶת. This term, often translated as "the mercy seat," referred to a

222

The Day of Atonement (16:1–34)

space above the ark in the Holy of Holies. Only the high priest would be allowed entrance to that room and then only once a year. The timing and nature of God's directions suggest that the Nadab and Abihu incident may have involved an attempt on their part to enter the Holy of Holies. God begins his message to Aaron with the warning that he (and by extension, any subsequent high priest) was not allowed to enter that Most Holy Place at will, perhaps distinguishing future access from the apparently unrestricted access to God that Moses had had up to this point at the Tent of Meeting (Exod. 33:8–9). Rather, while the high priest would have the authority to enter on a designated date, he must do so only by strictly following the proper protocol coupled with appropriate national preparation. The descent of the shekinah in the cloud over the mercy seat may have necessitated the new guidelines. Or it may have been that the freedom given to Moses was unique. Whatever the case, the rest of the message outlines the priest's role and responsibility for his limited periodic access. As such, the emphasis is on the process, not the occasion on which it was done. In fact, that occasion is not even indicated until the end of the directive.

16:2b–5. God began by warning Moses (and thus Aaron) that entry into the Holy of Holies was generally forbidden, even for the high priest.

TRANSLATION ANALYSIS: "SHALL NOT ENTER"

The phrase וְאַל־יָבֹא בְכָל־עֵת אֶל־הַקֹּדֶשׁ literally says, "and he will not come at all times to the holy [place]." The idea is that entrance is restricted (i.e., only when permitted, not whenever he wanted to), not that it was totally forbidden. Here, "holy [place]" (see translation analysis for הַקֹּדֶשׁ, below) refers to what is more often referred to as the Holy of Holies, or the most holy place, or the inner shrine, which was separated from the outer holy place by a "veil" (Exod. 26:33–34; see fig. 63 in 23:1–24:9). Although

this chapter is the only place the phrase is used this way, the location is clearly demonstrated by the phrase "inside the veil" as well as "before the mercy seat" (Milgrom 1991, 1013). Likely the reason for this is to indicate that inside the veil the holiness was much greater than outside, since the priest was supposed to enter the space outside the veil at least twice daily to burn incense (Exod. 30:7–8).

The reason given for this is that the mercy seat was located inside the veil that divided the Holy Place. That was where the nation's representative would meet with God. God stated that he would appear "in the cloud" above the mercy seat, and for that reason no one was allowed to enter the Holy of Holies without special provision for protection.

TRANSLATION ANALYSIS: "MERCY SEAT"

The term *kapporet* is used in Exodus 25:17–22 to denote the top of the ark of the covenant. There it is described as "pure gold, two and a half cubits long and one and a half cubits wide" and was placed on top of the ark. At each end of the *kapporet* was a cherub made of hammered gold. The two faced toward the center of the *kapporet*, with their wings spread above the *kapporet*. As described in Exodus, God would meet with the nation's representative in front of that spot. Leviticus 16:2 indicates that God's presence would be within a cloud apparently poised above the wings of the cherubim.

It has been suggested that the English term "mercy seat" derives from two sources. First, the concept of a seat derives from Psalm 99:1. There God is described as "enthroned *on* or *above* the cherubim" (literally "sitting" [יֹשֵׁב], a participle without a preposition to connect with the cherubim). While the psalm may more likely reflect something like what Ezekiel saw in his initial vision (Ezek. 1:22–28), the cherubim atop the *kapporet* is suggestive of this as a location of enthronement. Then, the idea of "mercy"

The Day of Atonement (16:1–34)

likely comes from the LXX translation of the root *kipper* as *hilasterion*, which means "propitiation" (Harrison 1980, 171). Some modern translators prefer a term like "lid" or "cover" for *kapporet* since there is no description of a lid in Exodus (Kiuchi 2007, 290), or "slab" given the basic description in Exodus, which indicates that the ark was closed (Kleinig 2003, 329). While the *kapporet* does seem to cover the top of the ark, the idea that it was merely a "slab" of gold does not seem to fit the statement that the *kapporet* and the cherubim were one unit. The idea of a lid also suggests something that could be opened, whereas if the *kapporet* was even a mere eighth of an inch thick, it would weigh more than sixty pounds, not counting the two cherubim.

demonstrate that. In Leviticus 16:2, the actual phrase is "the holy room" (הַקֹּדֶשׁ מִבֵּית, literally "holy house") inside the veil. Subsequent cases omit the word "room" but they suggest that the term "holy [place]" refers to this location. A second point of confusion here is the term "Tent of Meeting" (אֹהֶל מוֹעֵד). While Moses utilized a Tent of Meeting with the Lord prior to the construction of the tabernacle following the construction of the tabernacle, this term, which is really a function descriptor, seems to have been transferred to the tent within the tabernacle courtyard that contained two rooms, which we call the Holy Place and the Most Holy Place. Thus, when Aaron presented the animals here (16:7), it was in front of the tent holding those two rooms.

As described here, the Day of Atonement process would begin by Aaron bringing a bull for a purification offering (חַטָּאת, see see comments on Lev. 4), and a ram for a consecration or burnt offering (עֹלָה, see comments on Lev. 1). While Leviticus 16:3 states that he was to enter the holy [place] with sacrifices, the action actually would begin outside of the Tent of Meeting (see 16:7) with several stages performed in the tabernacle courtyard. These first sacrifices were to be for his personal and household purification and consecration that were necessary before he could intercede for the nation. It is interesting that while the personal purification sacrifice would precede that of the congregation, both consecration sacrifices were to be done concurrently.

In addition to bringing the sacrifices, Aaron would need to be dressed appropriately. Instead of the normal high priestly attire including the magnificent breastpiece, ephod, and robe, he would be dressed just in the linen undergarments and tunic, along with the linen sash and the linen turban. Except for the turban, these would have been essentially the same garments that the other priests would have worn. Characterized merely as "linen" as opposed to the checkered work and the colored materials noted in Exodus 28, these garments are generally understood as being plain white, which a number of commentators have noted could suggest purity, righteousness, or humility based on comparisons with later biblical descriptions of saints or angels (Balentine 2002, 127; Ross 2002, 318; Wenham 1979, 230; Willis 2009, 143). Characterized as holy garments, the high priest would don these after he had washed (see comments on Lev. 8).

TRANSLATION ANALYSIS: הַקֹּדֶשׁ

The term translated "holy place" is really just the noun "holy" with the definite article (הַקֹּדֶשׁ); the idea of place is inferred. As used in this chapter (and only in this chapter), that term seems to refer to what Exodus 26:33 refers to as "the Holy of Holies" (קֹדֶשׁ הַקֳּדָשִׁים; Milgrom 1991, 1013). The phrase "inside the veil" as well as the observation that this is the location of the mercy seat

Holy Garments

These garments are discussed in regard to the dressing of Aaron for the ordination in Leviticus 8 (see comments there). Exodus 28:39 describes

The Day of Atonement (16:1–34)

the garments the high priest wore as a tunic of "checkered work of fine linen, a turban of fine linen, and a sash the work of a weaver." In contrast, the garments for the Day of Atonement are all described as merely linen—the same description given to the garments of the other priests, except that they had caps as opposed to a turban. Here, the only description of the material is that it is linen, but the Mishnah specifies that the garments were white (m. Yoma 3:6). Rooker's (2000, 214–15) observation that these "garments indicated a contrite, reflective approach to the Most Holy Place" is pertinent.

Dressed in the appropriate clothing, the high priest then would receive from the congregation of the sons of Israel a corporate offering: two male goats for purification and one ram for consecration. While not stated, they were likely brought to the tabernacle by national leaders. Prior to settling in the land, with the nation camped around the tabernacle, many people probably gathered there to witness the sacrifices. However, as will be seen later, the Day of Atonement was not one of the days when all men were to gather at the central sanctuary. Rather, it was to be a day when the people focused on personal contrition, and once settled they would likely be within their hometowns while national leaders brought the sacrifices to give to the priest.

16:6–10. As presented in the text, it would seem that the purification processes of the priest and the nation (esp. within this section) were intertwined, which might suggest that while the priest represented the nation before God, at the same time he was clearly part of the nation he represented and subject to the same imperfections. As the priest, he would present his personal purification offering (חַטָּאת) following the directions delineated in Leviticus 4. While some translations suggest that 16:6 specifies the actual sacrifice of his personal purification offering, the text says literally that he would "bring near [וְהִקְרִיב]" the bull of the purification offering that was for him.

While listed following his purification offering, before he would actually sacrifice his bull, he would take the two goats of the congregational purification offering and present *both* of them at the doorway of the tent of the meeting "before the Lord [YHWH]." There, they would be differentiated by "lots."

Lots Cast

The idea of the casting of lots has caused much speculation. While the concept is familiar in the abstract, the exact process used by the Israelites is not clear. Some argue that this involved using the Urim and Thummim (Harrison 1980, 172–73). However, the description here does not fit the criteria for the Urim and Thummim (see sidebar "Urim and Thummim" within the unit "Inauguration of Ancient Israelite Religion," 8:1–9:24). While the term "lots" (גּוֹרָלוֹת) is used, it seems likely that the term was used in a more generic sense such as the English phrase "draw straws." While technically this refers to a specific process whereby two or more straws are held with one being of a different length, it also is often used as a generic term to refer to any process that allows random differentiation. According to the Mishnah, during the Second Temple period an actual casting of lots sorted out job assignments with the process not specified (m. Yoma 2:2–4). In contrast, when determining the scapegoat the Mishnah describes a specific process that was used. A wooden box held two "lots" that were ebony. On one was written "to YHWH" (לַיהוָה; the Mishnah states לשם, that is, "to the Name"), and on the other was written "to Azazel" (לַעֲזָאזֵל; usually translated as "scapegoat"). The high priest would reach into the box, and take one in each hand, and set them on the head of the respective left and right goats. A strip of crimson wool was placed on the head of the scapegoat (the לַעֲזָאזֵל goat), and another crimson strip around the throat of the goat to be sacrificed (m. Yoma 3:9–4:2). Kleinig (2003, 330) argues that the text

The Day of Atonement (16:1–34)

should not be translated as "cast lots" since it is misleading in terms of process. He argues that the verb used here (נָתַן) would mean "cast" if it was in the *hiphil* stem. However, as used here in the *qal* stem, it should be understood as "placing to distinguish," thus denoting attaching tags. This would seem to fit the process as presented in the Mishnah.

One goat would be designated as "for YHWH" (לַיהוָה) and the other "for Azazel" (לַעֲזָאזֵל) often translated as the "scapegoat."

"For Azazel"

The term translated "scapegoat" is problematic. The Hebrew term is לַעֲזָאזֵל, a term that is only used in this passage, and scholars debate both its meaning and its etymology. All agree that in essence the term contains the word עֲזָאזֵל (Azazel) with the לְ preposition (meaning "to") as a prefix. One view understands the term "Azazel" as an abstract noun that means "total removal," seeing a relationship with an Arabic word meaning "vanish." Subsequent to the LXX, the Jewish tradition took the view that the term referred to the goat's destination. This view understands the term עֲזָאזֵל to derive from a root עזז meaning "to be strong or fierce," thus abstractly denoting the wilderness to which it was driven. A more recent view takes the term to refer to a "goat demon." Based on a parallel with the other goat, which is designated לַיהוָה, it is viewed as a proper name and thus the goat is designated for a second being. This view sees the second being as a demonic ruler of the wilderness, thus providing a correlation to a reference to goat demons in 17:7 and the much later passage in 1 Enoch 10:4–5 where Raphael is commanded to "bind Azaz'el [Milgrom (1991, 1020) cites as 'Azel] hand and foot" and to cast him into "the desert which was in Duda'el." While most modern scholars take the last view, it really is the weakest for several reasons. This view seems to have developed during the Second Temple period after 1 Enoch was written, with no prior references to Azazel

as a demonic being. The term is not found outside this chapter, including ANE texts. The traditional view as presented in the LXX and the Vulgate seems to combine the function of the goat and understanding that the word is derived from a root meaning "go away" (אזל). Combining that with a term for "goat" (עז), it thus describes it as "the goat that goes away." Since it is clear that the scapegoat is not an offering and thus not appeasing another god, this is the most likely explanation.

Although the two goats are differentiated with one to be sacrificed and the other to be sent off into the wilderness, the main thing to keep in mind here is that *the two goats together constituted the purification offering* for the congregation. Again, while the text seems to suggest that he immediately sacrificed the goat designated for the Lord, the next section returns to Aaron's personal purification offering, with the two goats designated for their function still standing in the courtyard in front of the Tent of Meeting.

TRANSLATION ANALYSIS: "TWO MALE GOATS"

Leviticus 16:5 states that Aaron was to take from the congregation "two male goats for a purification offering" (שְׁנֵי־שְׂעִירֵי עִזִּים לְחַטָּאת), which would indicate that the purification came about through one goat dying and the other living but leaving. Later the two aspects are differentiated in 16:9, which indicates that the goat that is killed is a purification offering, while 16:10 observes that the other goat is sent into the wilderness "to make atonement."

16:11–14. With the goats for the congregation's purification offering now presented, the priest was to sacrifice the bull for himself and his household in accordance with the purification offering directions given in Leviticus 4, although there are some differences. The text here does not specify that he should lay his hand upon the head of the bull (as in Lev. 4:4), but the

The Day of Atonement (16:1–34)

Mishnah does, as it specifies that he should lay both hands on the head of the bull and pray the following prayer:

> I pray, O Eternal! I have done wrong, I have transgressed, I have sinned before Thee, both I and my house; I pray, O Eternal! Forgive, I pray, the iniquities, and the transgressions, and the sins, which I have wrongly committed, and which I have transgressed, and which I have sinned before Thee, both I and my house, as it is written in the Law of Moses, Thy servant, *"For on this day shall atonement be made for you to cleanse you from all your sins, before the Eternal shall ye be clean."* (m. Yoma 3:8, emphasis original)

In addition, in contrast to the normal purification offering where he would sprinkle the blood in front of the veil (Lev. 4:6) on this occasion he would sprinkle it within the veil on the mercy seat.

At this point he would slaughter the bull but would not place it on the altar. Rather, he would collect some of the blood in a basin, a firepan full of coals of fire from the altar, and two handfuls of incense. With these three items, he would go inside the veil. The text emphatically states that he must take the incense with him "lest he die," but it is not clear how the incense shielded the priest. Most commentators suggest that the incense provided a cloud that hid the ark from the eyes of the priest so that he did not actually see it, but the way the ark was carried about during the time of the judges and the united kingdom raises questions in that regard (see, e.g., 1 Sam. 4–7). One might also note that the issue addressed here is not the ark per se, but the mercy seat (16:2). Also, since the purpose of incense in general was aromatic as opposed to visual, it would seem to make the function of the incense more ceremonial and spiritual than a physical protection.

The Cloud of Incense

Exodus 30:34 gives the recipe for the incense: "spices, stacte and onycha and galbanum, spices with pure frankincense; there shall be an equal part of each" (NASB), which is generally understood to denote four specific spices. However, Milgrom (1991, 1026–31) cites an experiment by one of his students based on this recipe that suggested that the smoke produced by this mixture would be inadequate to provide a visual screen before the priest. He then observes that the rabbis specifically describe the incense used in the Herodian temple as consisting of eleven different spices. Milgrom concludes that these extra materials served to provide adequate smoke so that the high priest would not see the ark and die. However, this presumes that the sense of covering is visual, that is, it hides the ark from the vision of the high priest.

The verb used here is כָּסָה, which is defined as "to cover, conceal, hide" (Harris 1980d, 448). While generally this seems to make reference of visibility, it does not seem to necessarily have a primary purpose of describing something as not visible. For example, Genesis 7:19–20 uses the same verb to observe that during the flood the waters rose to the point that the hills were "covered," which primarily describes the depth of the water, not the obscuring of the hills. In this light, Levine (1989, 164) notes that incense was "widely used as an apotropaic substance, or means of protection" and cites Numbers 16:46–48 (HB 17:11–13) as an example in the case of Moses and Aaron. Hartley (1992, 226) finds it "curious" that עָנָן, "cloud," is used differently in its two occurrences in this chapter. Further, he comments that the only other place it is used for a cloud of incense is Ezekiel 8:11. There it specifically refers to the fragrance of the incense as opposed to visibility, which may suggest hiding the stench of sin.

Logistically, according to the Mishnah, with the incense burning inside the veil the high priest would set the fire pan down, step out

The Day of Atonement (16:1–34)

from beyond the veil where he would get the basin of blood, and then return to the Holy of Holies. There he would sprinkle the blood of the bull on the mercy seat, once on the east side with an upward motion, and then seven times with a downward motion (m. Yoma 5:1–3), after which he would again go outside the veil.

16:15–19. Having returned to the courtyard where the two goats were being held, the high priest would now sacrifice the goat that has been designated for the Lord. This sacrifice was characterized as a purification offering for the people of the nation. While the Day of Atonement purification offering for the priest was a bull—the same as a personal purification offering for a priest—for the congregation the purification offering was a goat, instead of the bull as directed in Leviticus 4:14. However, we need to remember that in essence the congregational purification offering on the Day of Atonement was two goats—one of which was killed, and the other cast out. While it may be inferred that this dual function was the reason for the goats for the congregation instead of a bull, it is not stated. The process for the goat that was killed, the one designated for the Lord, was the same as had been done for the priest's bull. It was slaughtered and the blood was collected in a basin. The high priest took the blood into the Holy of Holies before the mercy seat and sprinkled in the same manner as he did the bull. While the text does not mention the incense here, the directions in 16:13–14 clearly indicate that it was used.

The remainder of this section is somewhat vague, primarily because of language difficulties in 16:16 and 18, notably the use of the verb "atone," and the use of prepositions. The first phrase of 16:16, וְכִפֶּר עַל־הַקֹּדֶשׁ, reads literally "and he will atone on the holy [place]." Then in 16:18 the high priest would go out to the altar, and using the same preposition, the text reads literally "he will atone on it." Most translations

and commentators take the preposition עַל to indicate that the Holy Place or the altar is the object of the atonement and they use the English word "for."

TRANSLATION ANALYSIS: עַל־
The Hebrew preposition עַל is defined as "on" (*DCH* s.v. "עַל-I" 6:385) or "above" (Carr 1980b, 666). *DCH* does add that it is translated over thirty different ways, "the most common being above, against, beside, concerning, on, over, upon." The common translations of Leviticus 16:16 and 18 use the word "for," suggesting that the Holy Place and altar are the recipients of the atoning action. While unusual, it seems that it could be an allowable understanding (GKC §119). It would seem that the driving factor is the summary statement in 16:20, which shows the Holy Place, the Tent of the Meeting, and the altar all as the objects of אֶת; the Hebrew direct object marker would make them the objects of the verb "atone" in this verse.

While that seems appropriate in this case, it raises an issue regarding the verb "atone." As discussed in the section "Atonement" in the introduction, as a theological concept the Hebrew word כִּפֶּר would describe a ritual that served as a visible symbol of a spiritual act for a person—or in this case, the community—who already had a covenant relationship with God. In what sense then would either the Holy Place or altar, both physical objects, be atoned? The best solution seems to lie in how the text uses two other verbs in 16:19, specifically "cleanse" (טָהֵר) and "consecrate" (קָדַשׁ). That statement seemingly uses the three verbs interchangeably to relate that in some manner the sprinkled blood of the bull and the goat provide cleansing. Essentially, just as in the case of the verb *qadosh* (קָדַשׁ; see the section "Holy" in the introduction, where we noted a derivative sense for nonliving objects), the verb *kipper* (כִּפֶּר) would be used here in a derivative sense that would carry a connotation somewhere within a context of

The Day of Atonement (16:1–34)

"consecrate" and "cleanse." However, even this does not resolve all of the issues. As Hartley (1992, 228) observes, this is a surprising shift from "expiating the people's sins to cleansing the sanctuary from the impurities released by the people's and priests' sins."

Even so, we are still left with the difficulty of understanding why nonliving objects need to be atoned for, even if understood as cleansed or purified. A common explanation seems to be that either in the routine practice of the rituals or in the routine matters of living, the Holy Place and altar would become polluted. Wenham (1979, 233) explains it as "The uncleanness that affects every man and woman to a greater or lesser degree (see Lev. 11–15) pollutes the sanctuary." Or, as Ross (2002, 320) expresses it, "the result of Israel's sin is impurity, which attaches to the sanctuary and pollutes it." Since this is a nonphysical process, we used the term "cultic purity" in the atonement discussion, that is, that the ritual would serve as a means of assurance to the congregation that God did and would cleanse spiritually. Thus it was a means of corporate worship of God designed to lead to greater moral purity or corporate holiness for the entire congregation.

That still leaves one more area of difficulty. For the nation of Israel, this portion of the ceremony addressed three key areas of concern—national impurity, national transgressions, and national sins. National impurities (מִטֻּמְאֹת בְּנֵי יִשְׂרָאֵל) are mentioned first, likely to mirror the preceding five chapters, which had focused on individual impurities. The next term, national transgressions (פֶּשַׁע), describes acts of rebellion (Livingston 1980d). Rooker (2000, 218–19) describes this term as "the most grievous word for sin in the OT. The term refers to sin in its grossest manifestation. It indicates a breach of relationship between two parties." As such, impurities and transgressions together would represent the spectrum of everything that disrupted relationship—from acts that affected one's spirit that blurred one's perception of one's relationship within the community even though they might not be sin (see the discussion on "Clean and Unclean" in the introduction) to outright rebellion that threatened to destroy the community.

The third term is difficult. In the introductory section on sin we concluded that the term *ḥāṭā'* (חָטָא) is probably best understood as anything "that damages one's relationship with another person, especially, most frequently, and ultimately with God." "Sin" is probably the best shorthand term for this, although that English word carries a lot of extra baggage. Here, rather than just another category of wrongdoing, the phrase "all their sins" seems to emphasize the inclusiveness of the other two terms, bringing the categories together as a whole.

TRANSLATION ANALYSIS: "FROM" (מִן) AND "TO" (לְ)

The structure of the clause "because of the impurities of the sons of Israel and because of their transgressions in regard to all their sins" (מִטֻּמְאֹת בְּנֵי יִשְׂרָאֵל וּמִפִּשְׁעֵיהֶם לְכָל־חַטֹּאתָם) suggests that the three terms are not presented as three categories of wrongdoing. The first two items have the מִן preposition ("from") attached, so both would be viewed as denoting areas that the Holy Place was atoned "from." This likely suggests that they represent two extremes denoting everything in between. The difficulty then is, how does the לְ preposition ("to") on the last item fit? It would seem that the addition of the term כָּל to the לְ (literally reading "to all their sins") might suggest that the last phrase serves as a collective, stressing the totality of atonement. This then produces a statement that might be translated, albeit somewhat awkwardly, as "he will atone the Holy Place from the impurities of the sons of Israel, from their rebellions, that is, all of the ways they have damaged their relationships with each other and with God."

For this process, the high priest was required to act alone—no one was allowed to be in the

The Day of Atonement (16:1–34)

Tent of Meeting while he made atonement. It was a hidden act that required the nation of Israel to exhibit faith. First, the people had to trust that their representative would truly represent them. Then they had to trust that he would survive meeting with God on the back side of the veil. Then they had to trust that when he returned, atonement had been made for whatever issues they had that damaged relationships, whether they were personal issues of impurity or corporate issues of rebellion.

But the actions of the high priest inside the Holy of Holies were only part of the ceremony. The second step required that the high priest, after he had sprinkled on the *kapporet* the blood of the goat sacrificed for the people, would exit the Tent of Meeting and put some of the blood of both the bull (his personal purification offering) and the goat (the congregational purification offering) on the horns of the altar in the courtyard where consecratory offerings are offered. The fact that the blood of the two purification sacrifices were to be mixed (the only time that was to be done) seems to emphasize the unity of the high priest and the people as needing purification before God.

Then, he was to sprinkle some of the blood on the altar seven times just as he had done twice on the mercy seat (once for himself and once for the congregation). The text says that in this process, he would cleanse (טָהֵר) that altar and consecrate (קָדֵשׁ) it "from the impurities of the sons of Israel." The juxtaposition of those two terms is unique, pointing to not just a cleansing, but a rededication of the altar (Kiuchi 2007, 302).

16:20–22. The third step involved the second goat, the one that had been left alive. The high priest now was to go to that goat, lay both hands on its head, and "confess over it all the iniquities of the sons of Israel and all their transgressions in regard to all their sins."

> ### The High Priest's National Confession over the Scapegoat
> According to the Mishnah, the high priest would say for the nation:
>
> I pray, O Eternal! Thy people, the house of Israel, have done wrong, they have transgressed, they have sinned before Thee. I pray, by Thy Name! Pardon, I pray, the iniquities, the transgressions, and the sins, which Thy people, the house of Israel, have wrongly committed, and which they have transgressed, and which they have sinned before Thee, as it is written in the Law of Moses, Thy servant, *"For on This day shall atonement be made for you to cleanse you from all your sins, before the Eternal shall ye be clean."* (m. Yoma 6:2, emphasis orginal)

It is interesting that just as in the case of the sacrificed goat, three issues are involved. However, in this case, it is the national "iniquities" (so KJV, NASB, NRSV [עָוֹן]) that are cited instead of national impurities (טָמֵא) along with the national transgressions (פֶּשַׁע) and national sin (חָטָא). The term translated "iniquity" (עָוֹן) may also be translated "guilt," and as noted in the analysis, likely is a better understanding.

TRANSLATION ANALYSIS: "GUILT" (עָוֹן)
A common noun (used about 231 times), עָוֹן appears to be derived from a rather rare verb (used seventeen times) that means "to bend, twist, or distort." The noun is generally defined as "iniquity" or "guilt." However, those two English words carry different connotations. According to *WTNID* (s.v "iniquity"), iniquity connotes "gross injustice or wickedness," which characterizes the nature of the act. Guilt characterizes the consequences of the act, and the English word carries both an objective and subjective weight. As *WTNID* (s.v. "guilt") describes it, objective guilt reflects actual culpability for having committed an offense (which can be moral or legal), while subjective guilt is a feeling or self-reproach resulting from having committed

The Day of Atonement (16:1–34)

an offense (whether actual or perceived). While *DCH* notes that the distinction between the two concepts is not always clear in the Hebrew term (s.v. "עָוֹן I" 6:308), it would seem that the Hebrew term focuses on the consequences rather than the deed, although it would appear that "in the thought of the OT sin and its penalty are not radically separate notions" (Schultz 1980a, 651). Drawing on Leviticus 5:17, Koch describes the process as a logical sequence: "sin (*ḥaṭā*ʾ)— incur guilt (*ʾāšēm*)—bear [guilt] (*ʾāwōn*)" (1999, 552–60). Rather, עָוֹן seems to be a consequence that one bears or carries, which is suggestive of a concept of guilt.

Substituting עָוֹן for טָמֵא in this context may reflect that the high priest was making confession, as opposed to the earlier situation where the text was noting the scope of atonement. While impurities did not need confession, iniquities did, and yet since both affected relationships, both were included in the atonement ritual. Thus, the scope of the confession is an admission of guilt (both objective and subjective) as well as transgressions and sin.

The purpose of the scapegoat was to carry all of עָוֹן, the areas of guilt, away from the nation—as repeated twice, into the wilderness (מִדְבָּר).[1] To amplify this, the matters of guilt are described as being carried into a land that is גְּזֵרָה, a word translated "solitary" in the NASB but translated a number of ways in other English translations, including "remote," "desolate," "not inhabited," "inaccessible," and "barren." All are attempts to show how remote and isolated the place was from the Israelite culture.

To make sure that the scapegoat followed its assignment, the text notes that after the national iniquities, transgressions, and sin are laid on the head of the scapegoat, it was to be sent away "by the hand of a man who stands in readiness." This would be an individual who had been selected beforehand to drive the goat away from the tabernacle, and the camp while the nation was wandering.

> ### The Scapegoat
> According to the Mishnah, during the Second Temple period, after the high priest had made confession upon the scapegoat, he delivered it to the person who was to drive it away. The goat was driven out into the wilderness area a distance of about twelve miles. There, at a precipice, the goat was pushed over the precipice in order to ensure that it did not find its way back to the temple (m. Yoma 6:3–8).

16:23–25. Following the dismissal of the scapegoat, Aaron (or the future high priest) would come back into the Tent of Meeting and remove the linen garments he had worn up to this point. At this point he was to "bathe" and then put on his standard high priestly garments. This verse introduces an anomaly in our understanding, since it seems to suggest either that he bathed inside the Holy Place (whether that is understood as the Most Holy Place, or even the holy anteroom of the Tent of Meeting), or that he went naked into the courtyard where he bathed. Either would have been scandalous, if not blasphemous. As noted earlier (Lev. 8), it would appear that this would be a ritual washing. The Mishnah indicates that he did strip and immerse himself (m. Yoma 7:4), although Levine (1989, 107–8) points out that text describes actions in the temple, not the tabernacle, and suggests a screened off area within the temple courtyard. Now the high priest would perform the burnt

---

1 As I (Harbin) grew up in Arizona, the idea of wilderness usually denoted an area of wild growth filled with wild animals with no roads. My first deer hunt was just above the Sycamore Canyon Wilderness Area, a large canyon filled with a thick Ponderosa pine forest with access limited to the means of horseback or on foot. For the Israelites, wilderness really reflected a place of barrenness, without life, without water—in essence, desolation as shown in fig. 56, a photo of the Judean wilderness.

offerings—that is, offerings of consecration—both for himself and for the congregation. He also would at this point actually burn the fat from the two purification offerings.

16:26–28. The last item of business for the day involved two other individuals who had assisted indirectly in the ritual. The first was the individual who drove the scapegoat into the wilderness.

Figure 56. Judean wilderness.

Upon his return, he would be required to wash his clothes and bathe, the standard ritual for cleansing that we noted in Leviticus 11–15. The second individual disposed the remains of the two purification offerings, the bull of the high priest and the goat for the congregation. Those remains were to be burned outside of the camp in their entirety. Afterward, the person who burned them also would be required to wash his clothes and bathe.

Directions for the Occasion of the Day of Atonement (16:29–34)

16:29–31. Up to this point, the material in this chapter has consisted of directions regarding the process of the Day of Atonement without any discussion of when it would be celebrated. The final portion of the chapter addresses the actual event, setting it into the liturgical calendar to join the events that had originally been set forth in Exodus 23. That initial calendar description specified three key festivals that were to be celebrated by all men appearing before the Lord God (Exod. 23:17): Unleavened Bread, the Harvest of the Firstfruits, and Ingathering. This pronouncement sets up a fourth holy day that would be commemorated specifically on the tenth day of the seventh month based on the calendar established in Exodus 12:2 with the announcement of the Passover. We will address the two calendars (the liturgical and the agricultural) in comments on Leviticus 23, where the entire liturgical calendar is set forth.

> **The Date of Yom Kippur**
> Twice before (Exod. 23:15–19; 34:18–23) God directed that the nation was to celebrate three primary festivals: Unleavened Bread or Passover, Harvest or Weeks or Pentecost, and Ingathering or Succoth (Stuart 2006, 536). For those three all men were to appear before the Lord. Those directions were to be fleshed out later, as we will see in Leviticus 23. Additional information included when the festivals would be held. Passover would be the fourteenth of Nisan (March–April time frame) with the fourteenth of the second month as a fallback for those unable to observe on the requisite date. Unleavened Bread would be observed the seven following days. Pentecost would be fifty days after Passover, which would put it early in the third month. Ingathering or Succoth would be "at the turn of the year," which is generally understood as the end of the agricultural year, which would be in the September–October time frame. This would coincide with the end of the sixth month on the newly developed liturgical calendar, with the liturgical seventh month being the agricultural first month.

In addition to when the ritual was to be performed, the text now sets forth the guidelines for the people. To this point, the instructions have covered the ceremony that the high priest was to perform on behalf of the nation, incorporating other actions required to help him. Now, guidelines for the people are given, and they are disarmingly simple.

First, it should be noted what is *not* required. Surprisingly, given the theological significance of the Day of Atonement, it was not one of the three days on the liturgical calendar where they were to gather at the central sanctuary. This suggests that participation of most Israelites would be in their own homes and communities.

Second, the people were to afflict themselves. The verb עָנָה is defined as "to afflict, oppress, humble" (Coppes 1980g, 682). Leonard Coppes goes on to suggest that the primary meaning is "to force" or "to try to force submission." In this context, it is suggested that it should be a time of fasting and contrition, although fasting (צוּם) is not specifically enjoined.

Third, the people were not to work. Not only were they not to work, the phrase here is שַׁבַּת שַׁבָּתוֹן, literally, "a Sabbath of rest" (for further discussion, see the translation analysis of "Sabbath" at Lev. 23:3). As Kleinig (2003, 334) notes, "this would be a superlative form." The admonition for not working is the only part of the observance that includes other than ethnic Israelites. It also applied to the resident aliens (who will be addressed when we cover Leviticus 25). That the people were to rest suggests that beyond physical rest, they were to experience spiritual rest as atonement was being made for them and they were being cleansed—they were to rest in solemn understanding of what being done on their behalf.

16:32–34a. This short section merely emphasizes that the high priest is the one who would be expected to perform the ceremonies just discussed. It was a ceremony that was required to be performed annually. Yet there is no record of its observance anywhere in the OT.

16:34b. The last sentence presents two issues. The first is the question of to whom "he" refers. Some understand this to refer to Aaron—that is, everything that God told Moses, Aaron

did. This underlies the thought that the ceremony was performed immediately following, thus rededicating the tabernacle almost immediately after the Nadab and Abihu incident (Kiuchi 2007, 292; Willis 2009, 142). The alternative is that the "he" refers to Moses. This leads to the subsequent question regarding the scope of the compliance in this statement. Some see it indicative of a major change in the source of the material; specifically they view this statement as a bracket for the material in Leviticus 17–26, which is called the Holiness Code (Hartley 1992, 240). Often the Holiness Code is viewed as a separate document or source underlying the composition of Leviticus. In that case, the scope of the compliance would seem to be the entire book up to this point. Grammatically, it seems more likely that it refers to Moses, with reference to the directive given in 16:2: he did what he was told to do, which was relate the information to Aaron (Sherwood 2002, 72). Further, other compliance statements appear in other places in the book suggesting a progressive compliance, as we will see in subsequent material.

THEOLOGICAL FOCUS

While the thrust of this chapter is to describe work that the Israelite high priest would do on a holy day, which does not seem to have carried over into messianic fulfillment like Passover or Pentecost, two key theological themes seem to stand out. The first is that on an annual basis, the nation should stop its work and each individual was to humbly review his or her life for the past year and confess his or her shortcomings. This would serve as a solemn expression of the ongoing danger of personal sin. Perhaps one of the most thought-provoking aspects of this is the fact that this was not a day that the people were to gather at the central sanctuary, which was the focus of corporate worship. Rather, it was to be a time when they would remain in their local communities and dare we suggest remain at home with their families. Rather than a time of celebration and feasting, it was to be a time of contrition and fasting.

The second theme is that at that same time, the high priest individually would represent the nation as it confessed its failures before God in the Holy Place before the mercy seat. The people were to trust in the priest to faithfully carry out the Lord's directions. Here it would seem that, as shown in the book of Hebrews, there was a carryover into messianic fulfillment. As Harrison (1980, 175) expresses it, "in the same sense Christ was also uniquely alone when he was atoning for the sins of the world." While one should exercise care when explaining possible symbolism when the symbol referent is not specified, one also might see in retrospect a messianic anticipation of the two goats that are presented as a unit as a corporate purification offering. As Rooker (2000, 221) describes it, while the first goat "pictures the means for atonement, the shedding of blood in the sacrificial death," the second goat "pictures the effect of atonement, the removal of guilt." If so, then the picture of the scapegoat perhaps symbolically portrays what the psalmist declares in Psalm 103:12: "As far as the east is from the west, that far he has removed our transgressions from us." Regardless, even for an Israelite who would not at this point be able to make a messianic association, the picture of the scapegoat scampering out across the wilderness would have been a fantastic image of God removing the national guilt following its confession.

PREACHING AND TEACHING STRATEGIES

Exegetical and Theological Analysis
Once again, God confirms that hope abounds because of the breadth of his mercy and grace! By any honest gauge, even the humblest of God's people will soon fall short of the standard of true holiness and purity. And what is unclean (especially in ignorance) is effectively incapable of self-cleansing. Left to ourselves we, like Nadab and Abihu, may falsely assert that we are sufficiently holy to enter directly into God's presence. Having measured ourselves by ourselves, we conclude that we have met the standard (we have personally set). So, we are ready to step forward and meet our maker! Such reckless assertions are life-threatening because they follow the reasoning of a fallen mind.

God has not left us to ourselves! He has provided the means by which we humbly approach him with willing hearts, afflicting (denying) ourselves, and receiving atonement for sins that we may not yet understand, sins he will carry away as far as the east is from west (Ps. 103:12). This Day of Atonement is perpetual because the need will not go away in this life. It is integral because it effectively changes how believers evaluate themselves and understand their obedience before God. And it is communal because, though it may be practiced individually, it is a day set aside for the entire community of believers.

What is remarkable about this unique passage is how the Day of Atonement is fully a sovereign work of God while it calls for personal action by every believer. It is God's plan. And it requires a sinless priest to stand in the gap between God and his people, one who is set apart as worthy to cleanse the dirt from all that is holy before God. Before the eyes of the people, their sins are atoned for then symbolically carried away, vanishing to never return again. Such imagery creates a beautiful portrait of how God is establishing the means for the humble of heart to be permanently cleansed.

Preaching Idea
Our sin is carried away forever by an atoning work of God on a day set by God, in order that we may be in fellowship with him forever.

The Day of Atonement (16:1–34)

Contemporary Connections

What does it mean?

How does one address "unidentified" sin? We could decide to ignore or overlook sin by minimizing or even denying its effect on us. Or we could agonize daily, growing increasingly anxious as to whether we have fully confessed every wrong. Either error mistakenly places us in the role of casting away our own sin. God has lifted that burden from his people and placed it on their intermediary priest.

Thus, there is not a level of righteousness we must first attain to step forward. Nor are we dependent on perfect confessions to remain. We are reliant upon God to fulfill his promise. He has done the work sufficient to atone for all our sin and he will carry it away forever from those who trust in him.

Is it true?

Can God make our sin vanish forever? Scripture plainly tells us, yes. As the one true God, the author of holiness, he alone knows what sin-free is for one he has created and for a community he has established. By the atoning death of the sinless Son of God, the sin of believers, past, present, and future, has been paid for, not to be catalogued for future use against believers, but to be destroyed forever.

Good Friday marks this definitive day of atonement. Christ, our great high priest completed the perfect once-for-all sacrifice. Like with the Israelites, the work is done by the high priest. Christ has perfected for all time those who are being sanctified (Heb 10:14). Believers can now draw near in full assurance. There is no other sacrifice for sin (Heb 10:26).

Now what?

This central truth holds the power to change our lives. As one grows humble in spirit, it is easy to become burdened by the weight of one's own sin. Some will say, "Reflect on sin less. God wants you to simply enjoy the salvation he brings!" Others will counsel, "Reflect on sin more. God wants you to confess all sin to be free of its burden!" The Day of Atonement directs God's people to lift up their heads and reflect first upon him—his holiness and how he has established the means to effectively cast away all our sin. So, reflect on his work more to see the breadth and completeness of his forgiveness. Then reflect on your sin to see how his work is sufficient to "carry away forever" the worst that we find in ourselves!

Creativity in Presentation

Rarely are we given such a clear and colorful picture as a ready scapegoat! The list of potential illustrations is long. You could tell the familiar story of Tom Sawyer taking the punishment for Becky Thatcher's wrong. Or you might detail the rising role of paid "sin-eaters" in seventeenth-century history described by John Aubrey. Or you might refer to the old TV show *Branded* (Chuck Connors), or maybe *Tale of Two Cities*. Or you can select one of the countless historical examples where someone willingly steps in to receive the punishment due another. Though exciting, that is only the beginning of the story.

Once the punishment due another is intentionally taken on, it is taken away forever, vanishing completely! There is no fear that one day the truth will come out—Tom may rat out Becky if they have a falling-out, the "sin-eater" will reject his pay and walk out before the friends and relatives of the deceased, or Chuck Connors will finally become fed up with being falsely labeled as a coward. There is no such worry with the Levitical scapegoat. The work is completed forever.

Don't get too excited! It must be repeated annually! Like our own physical bodies, cars, or finances, they get out of balance with use and must return for regular inspection and repair. This will require us to humble ourselves, confess that things may not be as they should be, and step forward regularly to reaffirm our dependence on the scapegoat!

On a more serious note, this may be a great time to challenge your body on the importance of intentionally scheduling time to "soul cleanse." This may be completed in part through the regular celebration of communion. In addition, by setting aside a time for willing reflection and personal affliction, a body of believers may find great blessing as they reflect on the breadth and completeness of Christ's forgiveness, readied to concede sin before God that he may carry it away forever! Finally, you may want to consider a responsive reading from a passage like Psalm 32, to direct the congregation in how to meditate on the glorious freedom that forgiveness brings!

Our sin is carried away forever by an atoning work of God, on a day set by God, that we may be in fellowship with him forever.

- What is the Day of Atonement?
  - A day of rest to reorder life and priorities
  - A day of affliction to reorder worship and cravings
  - A day of reflection to concede and cast away sin
- What did it mean to them then? What does it mean always? What do we do now?
  - An annual day introduced to be perpetual, integral, and communal
  - What the Day reveals about who God is and who we are before him
  - Good Friday as the annual Day of Atonement
    - A day set by God for all to see the need and celebrate the work of atonement
    - A day created by God that we may remain in fellowship forever

DISCUSSION QUESTIONS

1. First John 4:20 says, "If anyone says, 'I love God,' and hates his brother, he is a liar." How does Leviticus's command for all who belong to God to love their neighbor provide the foundation for John's teaching?

2. How does loving our neighbor make us holy? How does practicing holiness become a means of loving our neighbor?

3. The Day of Atonement called for solemn rest, affliction, and reflection to remind God's people of his holiness. What is your current practice of solemn rest, affliction, and reflection?

4. Do you think it was a surprise to the people of God that their sin would be an ongoing obstacle to them? Is it a surprise to you?

5. Read Hebrews 10:19–31. How can we stir one another up to love and good works as we see the day drawing near?

Leviticus 17:1–16

EXEGETICAL IDEA
God called his people out of the "open fields," gathering them for lawful worship in a specific place (tabernacle) and instructing them on the lawful handling of blood to safeguard them from being lured and enticed into the worship of false gods.

THEOLOGICAL FOCUS
God distinguishes himself from pagan worship and the false gods that permeate the land and surround his people by establishing where and how they can worship to keep their hearts safely focused on him.

PREACHING IDEA
We worship according to God's revelation, not our own personal disposition.

PREACHING POINTERS
Though the people of God were set free from their former Egyptian taskmasters, private desires, habits, and experiences threatened to lead them to serve new taskmasters. They had walked away from the gods of Egypt to celebrate new life under the Lord God, yet their hearts remained vulnerable. It would have been easy to doubt the Lord God and wander back to the comfort of old practices and beliefs (or even dabble in some new ones they had uncovered in their wilderness wanderings!). Would their worship focus on the Lord God alone, or would he become diluted among a pantheon of gods they recognized and called upon in times of need? Would a craving for meat create an appetite for idolatry, secret sacrifices, and private feasts? Apparently, it would. In the words of Leviticus 17:7, they were in danger of prostituting themselves after other gods—giving their bodies to another in exchange for a payment.

The Lord God is not a "hire for services" god! God not only knows what we, his people, need (and how to provide it for his glory and our good), but how we may foolishly lust after many things that pack the power to become taskmasters that will enslave us. To safeguard us from pursuing the folly of our misguided desires, God calls us in from the unprotected open fields of isolation and privatized worship to gather communally before him. Sustaining steadfast relationships with other believers provides protection and accountability from chasing after other gods. Furthermore, God carefully guards what is central and sacred in worship (redemption) from reckless acts of contempt and scorn. The Giver of Life makes clear that the life/soul of an animal is in the blood. This sets blood apart as the means to make atonement for sin. The life is in the blood. Without the shedding of blood there is no forgiveness of sins (Heb. 9:22). Blood is essential. It is sacred. It begins to unfold the story of the coming redemptive life of Jesus Christ.

LIFE AND BLOOD (17:1–16)

LITERARY STRUCTURE AND THEMES (17:1–16)

Leviticus 17 contains further revelation from God to Moses as part of the tabernacle dedication at Mount Sinai a year after the exodus to expand on the issue of atonement. While given to Moses, he was directed to disseminate it to Aaron, his sons, and the entire population of Israel. Many of the problems regarding this chapter result from overlooking or denying that historical context of the tabernacle dedication.

Literarily, the chapter serves as a hinge for this section, marking a transition in focus. Leviticus 11–16 focuses on Israel's proper relationship with God—concentrating on purity, both individual and corporate, as a means of worshipping God. Leviticus 18–27 then provides guidance to the people of Israel, showing how they were to relate properly with one another. Because of this emphasis on lifestyle derived from the nation's relationship with God, this section is often called the "Holiness Code." Leviticus 17 shows affinity to both sections. Clearly its emphasis on proper sacrifice and worship builds on the material in the first portion of the book. Still, the internal structure of the chapter, showing five basic laws explicating a social function of those sacrifices, anticipates the latter portion. Interestingly, Leviticus 17 names just two sacrifices, each of which has both worship and communal aspects. The burnt offering, which represented consecration to God, showed a communal aspect in its public performance. The shalom (or peace) offering, while noted as a communal sacrificial meal with family and friends, showed worship as it celebrated God either for who he is or what he had done.

The Holiness Code

For the past century or so, modern scholars have suggested that the book of Leviticus derived from two sources, both of which are presumed to have originated after the exile. Because most of the book addresses ritual, it has been deemed as derived from the hypothetical "Priestly" source. However, the last portion of the book has been viewed as coming from an alternative source called the Holiness Code because of "its demand on holiness on the part of the Israelites" (Rooker 2000, 231). Other factors involved in this division include the focus regarding sacrifice in the first portion of the book coupled with sparse mention of that ritual in the last portion, along with the rather extensive use of "I am the Lord [YHWH] your God" in Leviticus 18–27 (twenty-three times as opposed to once in the first seventeen chapters).

The role of Leviticus 17 is debated. Most commentators see the second section beginning with Leviticus 17 (Hartley 1992, 249; Rooker 2000, 231; Ross 2002, 330), while others see it as an appendix to the first section (Harrison 1980, 177; Wenham 1979, 240). We have suggested that the division point of the book should be the institution of the sacrificial system and the subsequent disaster in Leviticus 10. The material subsequent to that event really addresses social cohesion around the worship of God. Leviticus 17 then serves as a hinge between an emphasis on the divine foundation of society in Leviticus 11–16 and how that foundation should be built on within the human culture. As a hinge, Leviticus 17 has ties to both aspects (Gane 2004a, 301; Sklar 2014, 217).

Two key themes stand out in this chapter, although they are interrelated. The first theme is a strong directive regarding the proper slaughter of animals suitable for sacrifice, most notably for the two offerings specified. There are two aspects to this directive. Within the context of the nation at Sinai and subsequently during its time in the wilderness, these sacrifices were to be performed at the tabernacle, without exception. The operative terms are "in the camp" (בַּמַּחֲנֶה) as opposed to the "open field" (עַל־פְּנֵי הַשָּׂדֶה). The second aspect addresses how to handle the blood of the animal, whether it was a domesticated animal that was sacrificed or a clean game animal taken while hunting. The second theme develops the relationship between the blood and sacrifices, and atonement.

- ***The Lord Gives Directions Regarding the Slaughter of Cattle, Sheep, and Goats (17:1–9)***
- ***The Lord Gives Directions Regarding the Handling of Blood (17:10–16)***

EXPOSITION (17:1–16)

Following the directions for the Day of Atonement in chapter 16, Leviticus 17 elucidates the issue of animal blood that was so critical to the sacrificial system but was forbidden to the Israelites for human consumption. In conjunction with this directive, specific guidelines were given with regard to the slaughter of the three domesticated animals permitted for food in Leviticus 11: cattle, sheep, or goat. In addition, God also gave directions on properly disposing of the blood of wild game.

TRANSLATION ANALYSIS: "SHEEP"
Lexicons differ on whether the Hebrew word כֶּבֶשׂ should be translated "lamb" (BDB s.v. "כֶּבֶשׂ" 461) or "sheep" (*DCH* s.v. "כֶּבֶשׂ" 4:468). In the vast majority of cases (100 out of 106) the term is used in a sacrificial context (*TWOT* s.v. "כֶּבֶשׂ" 1:429). Although *TWOT* lists both

English words as alternative equivalents, most modern translations use "lamb," likely because of association with the Passover lamb where a lamb (שֶׂה, technically a small sheep, but specifically cited as a year old [Exod. 12:5]) was required. We have chosen "sheep" here because of the broader context of animals permitted for sacrifice.

The Lord Gives Directions Regarding the Slaughter of Cattle, Sheep, and Goats (17:1–9)

The first set of guidelines addresses the slaughter of clean domesticated animals permitted for sacrifice. It requires that the animal must be brought to the doorway of the tent of the meeting and presented to the Lord as an offering, whether the animal was slaughtered in the camp or outside of the camp. Anyone who did not adhere to this would be subject to dire consequences.

17:1–2. The guidelines begin with the statement that the direction came from God and was to be conveyed not only to Aaron and his sons, but to the nation, here referred to as "all the sons of Israel." It begins with the requisite *waw*, which basically means "and," but should be translated as "then" in this narrative where it shows a sequence. In this case, the sequence would be revelation provided subsequent to the directions for the Day of Atonement presented in the previous chapter. The material itself is designated as a command.

TRANSLATION ANALYSIS: "SONS OF ISRAEL"
Three different phrases are used in this chapter to denote the recipients of these directions beyond Aaron and his sons. First, the chapter is addressed to "all the sons of Israel" (כָּל־בְּנֵי יִשְׂרָאֵל) in 17:2, which is understood to mean the people gathered at Sinai as a whole (Levine 1989, 112). Then in 17:3, the phrase אִישׁ אִישׁ מִבֵּית יִשְׂרָאֵל is used, which would literally be "a man, a man, from the house of Israel." The אִישׁ אִישׁ is understood as an idiom

Life and Blood (17:1–16)

meaning "any man" (Milgrom 2000, 1452). However, the house of Israel here would seem to denote the physical descendants of Jacob, as indicated by 17:8 and 10 where the same phrase is coupled with the additional phrase וּמִן־הַגֵּר אֲשֶׁר־יָגוּר בְּתוֹכָם, which adds literally "and from the sojourner who sojourns in your midst." This distinction suggests that while the overall chapter applied to both groups, the sojourners were not subject to the initial directive requiring presenting a slaughtered animal before the tabernacle. This would seem to allow the sojourners to perform secular slaughters in the field as long as they followed the subsequent directive regarding the draining of the blood. While we do not know how many nonphysical descendants of Jacob left Egypt with the Israelites, Exodus 12:38 states that it was a "mixed multitude," which might suggest more than a few. In that context, apparently addressing the actual exodus event, the phrase "sons of Israel" was used collectively for the entire group (see Exod. 14:2 as an example).

17:3–4. The first aspect of the command addresses the slaughtering of the three clean animals—ox, sheep, or goat—that were allowed to be used for sacrifice. The text specifies that whenever an Israelite slaughtered one of those animals, he or she was required to present it as an offering before the tabernacle. This mandate has raised a number of questions and is highly debated in several regards. Because these questions are somewhat intertwined, resulting in a variety of proposals, we will first list the issues that we see from our perspective and then provide what seems to be the overall intent of the passage.

To begin, the Hebrew word שָׁחַט can mean "slaughter" or "kill," and in terms of animals may indicate that either a sacrifice or a meal was intended. The question that arises from the use here is whether this directive required every animal killed for meat to be presented

as an offering (the broad view) or only animals slaughtered for a sacrifice (the narrow view).

TRANSLATION ANALYSIS: "SLAUGHTER"
While lexicons agree that the word שָׁחַט may mean either "kill" or "slaughter" (Hamilton 1980m, 915), the significance of the term is debated. Hamilton suggests that it is used "most often in a ritual sacrifice," although it may also be used to denote killing another person (e.g., 2 Kings 25:7) or an animal (e.g., Gen. 37:31). The context here is clearly that of a clean animal, so the question is whether the intent here is only for a ritual sacrifice or any animal desired for meat. The Wellhausen school claims that all slaughter was intended for ritual sacrifice. While some conservatives accept this view, they tend to limit it to the time in the wilderness (Hartley 1992, 270).

Tied to that question: What does 17:3 mean by the phrase "in the camp"? If this material was a contemporary record of what happened while the nation was at Sinai, the intent was clear. Prior to the dedication of the tabernacle a few days earlier, if an Israelite had slaughtered an animal, likely he would have just gone outside of the camp. Now, although still camped in the wilderness, the animal was to be brought to the tent of meeting (or tabernacle), the location of the newly dedicated altar. However, the question for future generations would be, what did that mean after the nation settled in the land? Does the camp serve as a "prototype of the city," thus denoting the location of the tabernacle (Milgrom 2000, 1454)?

The follow-up question is with regard to the application of the statement in 17:7b: "this shall be a permanent statute to them throughout their generations." Does the statute include all of the material leading up to the statement (17:3–7a), or just the first half of 17:7 forbidding sacrificing to the "goat demons"? In other words, would the expectation for the original audience be that once they were settled in the land they would still need to present the animals intended for slaughter (as defined by how one understood the term "slaughter," and whether it reflected the broad or narrow view) at the central sanctuary as an offering, regardless of the distance?

Given the above issues, other questions derive from the use of sojourner in 17:8 and 10. If the passage applies to the time of the settlement, would that mean that Canaanites who remained in the land following the settlement would be expected to comply with these guidelines? Or, would that only apply to sojourners who moved into land subsequent to Israelite control? In either case, what about animals slaughtered just for meat? Conversely, if it only applied to the nation while it was in the wilderness, who were the sojourners?

TRANSLATION ANALYSIS: "SOJOURNER"
The phrase in both verses uses the Hebrew term גֵּר, which is often translated as "sojourner," as both a noun and a verb: literally, "a sojourner who sojourns." The word may also be understood as "alien" or "stranger," so translators use a variety of expression so as to not repeat the noun and verb. The concept is that the term refers to a person who is not a native Israelite but has settled in the land and seems to have at least begun to adopt the Israelite culture, for which reason *TWOT* (Stigers 1980) describes him or her as a proselyte, which would be one who is also adopting the Israelite religion. We will discuss the sojourners more in later units, where they are the focus of specific guidance.

It would seem that the best understanding of the text is that the requirements presented here were intended for the nation while it was in the wilderness—a view that now seems to be the consensus of scholars, even those who claim this material was written after the exile. As presented in the text, during the wilderness period the nation would have camped around the tabernacle in their tents, thus all were a short distance from the altar (see excursus "Israel in the Wilderness").

Israel in the Wilderness

We have difficulty visualizing the camping logistics of a nation of the size given in the text. Two key aspects are relevant here. The first is the size of the camp. The second is the layout, incorporating the flocks and herds. It is suggested that mentally one needs to visualize a nucleus of all of the tents clustered around the tabernacle surrounded by the flocks and herds. As will be seen later, this basic pattern of a cluster of housing surrounded by agricultural pursuits typified permanent settlements in the Middle East even up to the twenty-first century. The difficulty here is whether even a temporary community of the size and compactness demanded by the numbers given in the text is possible. There are two aspects to consider. The first is the camp layout, which is described in Numbers 2–3.

There are a multitude of charts showing the general layout of the camp. For our purposes, we have chosen to include the diagram generously provided by Ralph Wilson (https://www.jesuswalk.com/moses/7_tabernacle.htm) rather than add to the multitude. The text specifically delineates which tribes camped on which sides of the tabernacle, but there is discussion of the arrangement of the four sides.

Life and Blood (17:1–16)

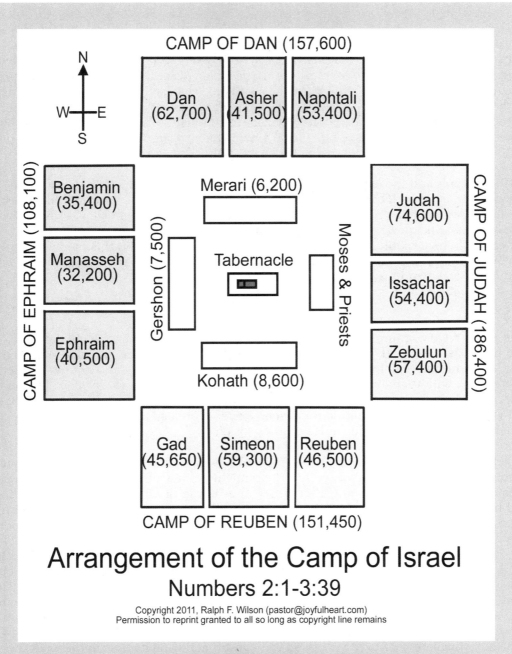

Chart 7. Israel in the wilderness, camp arrangement.

The second aspect is the most difficult. This is the question as to whether the numbers are even feasible. In that light, in 2002 the *Saudi Aramco World* magazine reported on the 2002 Hajj to Mecca. This article included aerial photos of the 2002 tent encampment, along with a full-page chart entitled "Hajj by the Numbers" describing that event. According to Saleem Bukhari, during the event 2,371,468 pilgrims were recorded as visiting Mecca, with 1,596,525 from outside Saudi Arabia. Further, he records that 1,728,000 stayed in 43,200 tents. which covered a space of 618 acres or about 2.5 km^2 or about 0.95 sq. mi. (Bukhari 2002, 27).

The pictures and the data they illustrate give pause, although they leave many unanswered questions. Clearly the accommodations are much more crowded than most of us today would be comfortable with. Moreover, while this might show a somewhat comparable parallel in a short-term situation, could it be maintained for multiple years? There are multiple logistic and sanitation issues. And yet, this modern event conducted without divine support does provide a degree of theoretical plausibility to the biblical situation.

In the open fields around the camp, they would have pastured their "flocks and herds, a very large number of livestock" that the Israelites took with them out of Egypt (Exod. 12:38). As a reminder, according to the traditional view, at this point the nation had been at Sinai for a year, and would be leaving it in a couple of months (Num. 10:11). When they left Sinai the nation was projected to enter the Promised Land directly. The subsequent period of wandering that produced much of the material in Numbers and Deuteronomy was a result of a lack of faith at Kadesh-barnea.

The Time of Wandering

While characterized as a period of wandering (Num. 32:13), apparently this city that moved spent most of its time in relatively few locations. The summary of their campsites in Numbers 33 suggests that over the period of thirty-eight years they camped at nineteen sites, or an average of two years per location. Numbers 9:16–23 relates how the nation moved in conjunction with the lifting and settling of the cloud. On some occasions the cloud settled just for a day or two, reflecting a more extended journey segment. On other occasions, they would camp for years (although often translated as "a year," the Hebrew word is plural).

Following that observation, another question might be how often would Israelites (whether the "house of Israel" or the broader "sons of Israel") have actually used meat? The common assumption is that "not much animal food was used in the wilderness, as is evidenced by the various murmurings of the people" (Lange 1960, 134). While it is true that the bulk of their provision was the manna, Exodus notes that they took with them a very large number of livestock. A very straightforward understanding of this chapter would strongly suggest that during its time in the wilderness, the nation's primary diet of manna essentially replaced their bread and grain, since they were not able to farm.

Manna

The issue of the manna is challenging. As we look at it, we again run into the issue of presuppositions. The text tells us that when God provided the manna, the Israelites looked at it and asked, "What is it?" and that became the name. Today, we ask the same question: What is it?

There are a number of attempts to explain what manna is that begin with naturalistic presuppositions. Part of the problem is that some of the descriptions don't seem to mesh, at least in our English translations. The first reference is Exodus 16:14, which relates that dew would evaporate, and a residue would be left behind. Both the NASB and the ESV translate the description (דַּק מְחֻסְפָּס דַּק כַּכְּפֹר עַל־הָאָרֶץ) as "a fine flake-like thing, fine as the frost on the ground." The driving force seems to be that the term דַּק is used twice, which is understood to be flake-like. Cole (1973, 138–39) observes that while early versions proposed "scales" as the meaning, the "early Jewish commentators understood the word as meaning 'globule,' something circular." He also suggests that the term "frost" only addresses the color.

This description is amplified in Numbers 11:7–9, which must be included. That text describes the appearance of manna like coriander seed. As seen in figure 57, this is a medium-sized seed, about one-eighth to one-quarter of an inch in diameter, which would seem to fit alternative suggestions regarding the meaning of דַּק such as "fine" (Wolf 1980b, 194).

Figure 57. Coriander seed.

Figure 58. Portable mortar for grain, from Israel Museum.

These are hard seeds, and the text indicates that the manna would be ground in a mortar similar to wheat or barley. This would produce flour that could be baked into bread. The taste of the bread was described as that of a cake baked with oil.

Additionally, the text observes that the manna could be boiled, again similar to the qualities of wheat or barley. Despite this explicit description, the most common explanation heard today argues that manna was the secretion of the tamarisk tree

Life and Blood (17:1–16)

(Wenham 1981, 121–22). These trees are found throughout the Middle East today, as well as parts of the American Southwest (see fig. 59). The argument is that the resin is somewhat wax-like and melts when the morning sun hits it. It is also predominantly sugar. Growing up in Arizona (Harbin), we called the trees "salt cedars" because their thin needle-like leaves exuded salt. Wenham notes that other suggestions include a variety of lichens and some insects. Overall, these explanations do not fit the characteristics that the text gives such as grinding and boiling. It is interesting that even the popular Wikipedia has made the following comment: "Manna is from heaven according to the Bible, but the various identifications of manna are naturalistic" (https://en.wikipedia.org/wiki/Manna)—an observation borne out by multiple online and academic searches.

Figure 59. Tamarisk trees in Goshen, Egypt.

Even if during an extended stay at some locations some gardening took place, it likely would have been for vegetables, not the grain that was the main part of their diet (King and Stager 2001, 93). Even that would not have been sufficient to sustain the entire population for extended periods of time. Two specific supplements to the manna are noted, where quail were provided. The first was shortly after they left Egypt (Exod. 16), and the second was shortly after they left Sinai (Num. 11). Even so, the directions here suggest that they did slaughter some of their livestock over the next thirty-eight years. Given the guidelines of Leviticus, that would definitely be the case for sacrifices. Since those guidelines included celebratory or communal offerings, it would appear that on occasion, they also slaughtered for meat.

Did the Israelites Eat Meat?
If the people did slaughter some of their livestock for meat, the question immediately arises, why did they weep and beg, "Who will give us meat to eat?," complaining that they had "nothing to look at except this manna" (Num. 11:4–6)? This likely is one of those imponderable questions regarding human nature, but it may be that they expected God to give them so much more despite all that they had. It also may explain why they were described as "those who complain of adversity" (Num. 11:1).

If the guidelines in Leviticus 17:3–4 were intended for the period in the wilderness, when did they change? Many scholars see that the national guidelines were changed by Deuteronomy 12:15–16, 20–27. Given the traditional location and date of Deuteronomy, that would have been just prior to their actual entering the land and would explain the widespread offering of sacrifices in a variety of locations throughout the entire period of the judges and early monarchy.

Local versus Central Worship
The main difficulty with this passage lies in the tension inherent in a situation where once they were settled in the land, the nation's worship was to focus on the altar and the tabernacle, while the people were dispersed throughout the entire

Life and Blood (17:1–16)

land with most of the people two or more days of travel away from the tabernacle. As suggested in the discussion of the sacrificial system in the introduction, burnt offerings and communal offerings seem to have been permitted on temporary altars wherever God had caused his name to be remembered, as specified in Exodus 20:24, which may suggest places where God had acted. However, even those local sacrifices were apparently to be administered by priests or Levites who were dispersed throughout the land (e.g., Samuel in 1 Sam. 9:12–14). If that was the case, then the issue of the high places where the people worshipped might have been illicit altars where the people took it upon themselves to do personal sacrifice, succumbing to the enticement of other gods (perhaps reflected in the situation in Judg. 17:5). While that may have been the case, *corporate* worship supervised by the high priest would still have taken place only at the tabernacle, which moved periodically throughout the land prior to David. It was then anchored in Jerusalem by Solomon with the building of the temple (see 2 Chron. 6:1). The subsequent history of the monarchy is one of tension between central worship at the temple and local worship at various high places, where the tendency was to turn to other gods. This does not seem to have been resolved until the exile and the destruction of the temple. With the return from exile, it would appear that local worship morphed into local synagogues replacing local altars, and that the local slaughter was solely for meat with the one requirement that the blood be drained properly.

With respect to the question of who was required to follow this procedure, based on the translation analysis of "sojourners," the use of "the house of Israel" here would seem to refer to the descendants of Jacob as opposed to the non-Israelites or sojourners who left Egypt with the Israelites. In other words, worshippers of the Lord God were expected to use their periodic meat procurements as times of solidifying community faith through communal offerings.

If so, then it would seem sojourners who left Egypt with the house of Jacob could perform secular slaughter in the open fields. That would also seem to leave open the possibility that these outliers might surreptitiously perform pagan sacrifices out in the fields—an issue addressed in the next section that refers to "the sons of Israel," that is, the entire group.

> ### Sojourners from Egypt
> The mixed company who came out of Egypt likely included individuals who fled Egypt for a variety of reasons and may not have immediately bought into the worship of Israel's God. Given the signs presented during the exodus and time at Sinai, it could be expected that some non-Israelites, both Egyptians and other non-Egyptians residing in Egypt, would have decided to throw their lot in with Israel, even if they were not ready to worship God. Despite the various signs and revelations, it could also be anticipated that they might have varying reactions: some might balk at worshipping God; others might just want to add him to their personal pantheon of gods. The understanding presented here regarding the slaughter in the fields could then be viewed as an accommodation to these last two groups, who would not be forced to worship the God of Israel but at the same time would not be allowed to practice the worship of other gods. The tension here recognizes that people cannot be forced to worship God, which reflects a heart attitude, but at the same time mandates that if they were going to travel with Israel, they needed to at least recognize that in Israel, only worship of the Lord God would be allowed.

The final item in this section is the warning that an Israelite who failed to bring the animal as an offering faced a charge of bloodguiltiness, with the consequence that the person would be "cut off from among his people." These phrases are debated. "Bloodguiltiness" is our understanding of the Hebrew phrase דָּם יֵחָשֵׁב, which, as used here, essentially equates the violation to murder.

Life and Blood (17:1–16)

TRANSLATION ANALYSIS:
"BLOODGUILTINESS" (דָּם יֵחָשֵׁב)
Translated literally, the phrase might mean "credit or considered (as) blood" (*DCH* s.v. "חָשַׁב" 3:326). The reason is that the phrase דָּם שָׁפַךְ, which means to "pour out or shed blood" (*DCH* s.v. "שָׁפַךְ" 8:538), is usually used in reference to homicide (Levine 1989, 113). This latter phrase is first introduced in Genesis 9:6, where it applies to all mankind.

Several suggestions have been made for the meaning of the phrase "cut off from among his people," including human trial with death penalty, banishment, or that it might be judgment in the life to come (i.e., he would not "sleep with the fathers"). The use of the passive (*niphal*) suggests that the act would be one that was done to the person from God, rather than something the corporate body was to do to the person. In that sense, the best understanding seems to be, as Balentine (2002, 145) puts it, that "the offender will have no descendants in this world and perhaps no possibility of being gathered with his ancestors in life after death."

17:5–9. As already noted, the text indicates that prior to this point some of the Israelites had slaughtered their animals out in the open field, likely just for meat but perhaps also as personal sacrifices to God. While this may have been a carryover from the time in Egypt, in terms of the newly established covenant there were several consequences. Without the guidance of the newly commissioned priests, they were not considered shalom offerings, and consequently the connection of praise and thanksgiving to God for who he was and what he had done was missed. At a minimum they lost opportunities to build the faith of the community by sharing the way God was working for them. If our understanding of the occasion of this declaration is correct, then this also set the stage such that some Israelites might violate the newly given guidelines for the shalom offerings either by

eating portions that were now forbidden (Lev. 3) or failing to give the priest his portion (Lev. 7:11–34). More seriously, apparently some of the Israelites offering sacrifices in the open field had drifted into considering them sacrifices to "goat demons" (שְׂעִירִם). While it is not clear what they were offering sacrifices to, clearly by offering sacrifices they were treating them as gods, and the command was that they no longer do so. Leviticus 7:8 specifically notes the burnt offering (עֹלָה), which indicated consecration, but then uses "sacrifice" (זֶבַח), a term that addresses sacrifices in general. Some take the phrase "whole offering and sacrifice" as a merism denoting all sacrifices (Hartley 1992, 265). Based on 7:5, which mandates them to be זִבְחֵי שְׁלָמִים (literally, "sacrifices of shalom"), the alternative is that this refers solely to the shalom offerings (Milgrom 2000, 1467). In that case, this directive required that nonconfessional sacrifices be presented to the priest, which at least during the wandering, meant they were to be brought before the tent of meeting.

> ### Goat Demon
> Translated "goat demons," שְׂעִירִם is the plural form of שָׂעִיר, which literally means "male goat" (*DCH* s.v. "שָׂעִיר I" 8:172). The reference here is very obscure. Based on the context that these figures were being offered sacrifices in the open fields, the conclusion is that they were false gods. Jeroboam I is recorded as setting up high places for them (2 Chron. 11:15), although that is the only other place in the OT they are mentioned. While Milgrom (2000, 1462) states that the rabbis were aware of a "demonic aspect of goat worship," there are no clear analogies either elsewhere in the OT or in contemporary cultures. Given that the nation had just emerged from Egypt, one might expect an Egyptian connection, but there does not seem to be any evidence of the Egyptians worshipping goats. Lange (1960, 135) refers to a goat worshiped in Egypt at Mendes, but his sources (Josephus, Herodotus, Diodorus Siculus, and Strabo) are all much later, from the

Hellenistic and rabbinic period. As a result, Lange questioned whether it existed as early as Moses. Hartley (1992, 272) seems to connect the reference here with satyrs, citing Isaiah 13:21 and 34:14. But those passages really include שְׂעִירִם in lists that refer to a variety of desert creatures dwelling in ruined cities along with hyenas and jackels, so they may just refer to wild goats. It is interesting that at the end of the wandering, the Song of Moses (Deut. 32:17) refers to a worship of "demons," but uses the word שֵׁדִים. Eugene Merrill (1994, 301) observes that those demons "were technically not deities but spirits that served especially to guard persons and places from harm."

The use of the term "sons of Israel" in this command could indicate that everyone camped at Sinai was expected to follow this guideline, but the text goes on to make this explicit. Leviticus 17:8 clarifies who is subject to this guideline by naming two groups: "the house of Israel" and the "resident aliens [or sojourners] who sojourn among them." In other words, anyone who is part of the Israelite camp was expected to comply with this. Again, the consequences are significant: failure to comply would result that the guilty one would "be cut off from his people."

The Lord Gives Directions Regarding the Handling of Blood (17:10–16)

17:10–12. At this point the text shifts to address another issue. Thus far in the book, much attention has been paid to the role of blood in the sacrificial system. Now the text explains why that is the case, but it does so in an interesting way—by warning against eating blood. Four times in these three verses the point is made that no one in the nation, whether descendants of Jacob or resident aliens, may "eat blood." The verb אָכַל may be translated "consume," and given the nature of blood might seem to suggest "drink." However, given the context, which discusses the eating of meat, it seems clear that the intent is a warning not to eat the blood within the meat (Hartley 1992, 273).

As discussed, the relationship between the blood and the sacrifices on the altar derives from the relationship between blood and life (see the section "*Nephesh* (נֶפֶשׁ): Life and Soul" in the introduction). Given that connection, God reminded the Israelites that blood was not to be disrespected for two reasons. First, while it was crucial to life, it did not possess any magical qualities in and of itself that one might acquire by consuming it. Rather it was to be respected because it had a special role in terms of mankind's relationship with God. Specifically, it was given on the altar to "provide atonement." And yet, as Hartley (1992, 273) notes, "blood in itself does not effect expiation, only blood from an animal sacrificed before Yahweh according to prescribed rituals," which would imply that proper handling of it was crucial. Even there, the ritual itself was not efficacious (p. 276), but as the prophets carefully pointed out over the decades, it was the heart attitude that trusted in God—one that brought the sacrifice out of a sense of love, fear, and obedience, but not with the expectation that merely killing a sheep or goat solved the problem (something like a child saying "I'm sorry" through gritted teeth).

17:13–14. With that warning not to eat blood, the next section addresses the issue of hunting. Wild game, although clean, was not sacrificed, and thus would not go through the rituals described thus far. In fact, it would be likely that the hunter was some distance away from home. Given that, the question would be how to handle the animal so that they did not eat the blood. Here the directions were intended to show the requisite respect for the blood by draining and burying the blood from the animal that had been caught. This would show respect by preventing it from being eaten or used for other illicit purposes (Sklar 2014, 222).

17:15–16. The final direction with regard to blood has to do with animals that died naturally or had been killed by wild beasts. Two basic situations are presented where the blood could not be properly drained, both of which are partially addressed by previous laws. Exodus 22:31 (HB 30) forbids eating any "flesh torn to pieces in the field." Leviticus 11:39–40 allows the eating of an animal designated for food (a clean, domesticated animal) that died naturally, although the eating of the animal produces uncleanness "until evening." While both situations would result in uncleanness until evening as clarified in Deuteronomy 14:21, the first situation would apply only to resident aliens (Sklar 2014, 222).

Dead Animals

At first glance, this passage seems to allow Israelites to eat the meat of an animal that has been "torn" or mauled (and presumably has died as a result), contrary to the guidelines in the Exodus and Deuteronomy passages. However, the Hebrew uses two different words for carcasses, which seem to reflect the way of death: נְבֵלָה used in Leviticus 11:40 and 17:15 is defined just as "corpse" or "carcass," but seems to denote "an animal that died of natural causes or accidentally" (Hartley 1992, 277). The passage in Exodus uses the term טְרֵפָה, which is derived from a root that has a connotation of tearing the flesh (Alexander 1980b). Thus, it would be "an animal that had been mauled by another wild animal" (Hartley 1992, 277). While the entire sentence addresses both "a native or an alien," the native has already been excluded from eating the meat of the טְרֵפָה. Most Leviticus commentaries do not seem to address the relationship of this passage with the Deuteronomy passage that was given subsequently as the nation prepared to enter the land, where Israelites were now told that they were not to eat נְבֵלָה, animals that died naturally. Lange (1960, 132) suggests that this change is "a concession to the enlarged relations in Canaan." Specifically, it gives to the resident alien a general permission for the practice, while initiating a higher standard for the Israelites. This may be an indication that at least some of the dietary laws were given for specific purposes at specific times,

and thus set the stage for the subsequent revelation given to Peter in Acts 10:10–16.

Thus, three different scenarios are presented. The first would be for a native Israelite in the case of an animal that died naturally. The second would be for a resident alien in the case of an animal that died naturally. The third would apply to a resident alien in the case of an animal that had died "torn by wild beasts." While in all three cases the designated person might eat the meat, whoever did would be unclean (which, as we have noted, was not in itself sinful), and he or she would be required to perform the ritual for cleansing as set forth in Leviticus 11:39–40. Any person who failed to do so had to bear his "guilt" or "iniquity" (עָוֹן; see translation analysis for Lev. 16:20).

THEOLOGICAL FOCUS

This chapter essentially reiterates the guidelines that God gave Noah after the ark opened following the subsiding of the flood. There, while God allowed the descendants of Noah and his family to eat meat, he placed a high value on animal life by prohibiting eating the blood with the meat, noting that the blood was the *nephesh* of the animal (Gen. 9:4). Here, after providing the nation of Israel more specific directions on how to properly handle the blood of the animals that they would eat, God expands the identification of the *nephesh* with the blood by declaring that the blood is provided upon the altar for atonement because of the *nephesh* that is within the blood.

Because of that, all blood must be handled in accordance with the very life it represents. For one to disregard this command was to cast blood guilt upon oneself. Passages such as Exodus 20:23–26 allow for praising God in locations where he would cause his name "to be remembered," which seems to have allowed for consecration and celebration. But because of the close relationship between the blood and the altar, two caveats needed to be observed.

Even those demonstrations of praise required designated supervision and guidance. In terms of confession and atonement, for the nation of Israel there was but a single altar, which was before the opening to the tent of meeting. Otherwise, one risked worshipping goat demons.

PREACHING AND TEACHING STRATEGIES

Exegetical and Theological Synthesis

As God's people stepped out of Egypt into the wilderness away from their old taskmasters, they carried within their spirits what was old and familiar (Egyptian gods). As they wandered, they stepped into the prospect of being overcome by all that was novel and intriguing (Canaanite practices), making them potential prey for deception by new taskmasters.

They were not well positioned to discern by themselves what was safe from what was deadly. Fear, hunger, uncertainty, and lust each held the power to draw their naïve hearts away from the One who redeemed them from their bondage. What was true in the wilderness remains true today. God, not our private disposition, reveals to us how we can safely worship.

Our ability to distinguish what is safe from what is potentially deadly to the soul is not as dependable as we may want to believe it is. We can lust irresponsibly after the freshness of what is new and intriguing, or cling stubbornly to the comfort of what is old and familiar. Is our personal discernment sufficiently reliable to safeguard us? Or should we admit our need to understand God's revealed boundaries? In this passage, God establishes a means to safeguard worship and preserve the purpose of sacrifice.

As they wandered in the wilderness, the worship was centralized at the tabernacle. They may have preferred the privacy of the open field, where their sacrifices could be more self-directed, spontaneous. Yet, such a place would leave them vulnerable to venturing into the practices of the Canaanites, worshipping goat demons and fertility or rain gods. It may not be blatant, but in isolation, the likelihood of straying into danger grows dramatically. In the absence of an ordained altar before which to present the blood or burn the fat, will they construct their own from their own imagination? What or who will guide them? Will the purpose of worship be tweaked? Modified? Forgotten? Is everyone in a position to judge what is right in their own mind? Should each believer choose how to worship based on personal disposition rather than divine revelation?

False worship is never presented as neutral. We are either worshipping the Lord God or we are worshipping Satan, who will take the form of every idol we can imagine. How can one test their own heart? By pursuing the established purpose and preserving the central tenets of worship as God reveals it to us through his Word. When left to our own, it is too easy to prostitute ourselves before the "god of the hunt"—allowing a need or fear to draw us into worship practices that are driven to satisfy a need or eliminate a fear. We are fashioning a "payment for services" god from the metal of our own mind.

Preaching Idea

We worship according to God's revelation, not our own personal disposition.

Contemporary Connections

What does it mean?

In general, we tend to naïvely exaggerate our ability to discern what is good and true from what is evil and errant. This is dangerous, as it is a form of self-worship that can elevate our private disposition or feelings over God's divine revelation. Temperament and mood are poor guides for worship. The heart is desperately wicked; who can know it (Jer. 17:9–10)? How does one keep the focal point of worship on God rather than (carelessly) shifting the focus onto oneself? Fresh methods and familiar forms each carry the power to taint the purity of our worship. "Fresh" does not ensure it is from God. "Familiar" does not secure its safety. Like the Israelites, we may be tempted by convenience or intrigued through curiosity to pursue new opportunities to head out to the privacy of the open fields. One must appreciate the inherent danger. Stepping away from established gatherings or boldly setting aside central tenets of worship increases the risk of inadvertently transferring the focus of our worship from recognized sacrifice to private exploration.

Furthermore, private exploration may even require the question: Are we attempting to appease God, or expecting to propel him into a specific action? Worship can devolve into sacrificing before a "payment for services rendered" god! This is not the God we worship. He has established by the revelation of himself through his Word who he is, who we are, and how he is fully worthy of our worship. We do not direct him to our desires. He directs us away from desire back to him.

Is it true?
We possess an insatiable desire to explore beyond the boundaries. We can easily become enslaved by the taskmasters of our private desires. Praise be to God! He knows this about us, even if we don't know it about ourselves! How does one harness desire? Desire can lead the faithful through open doors to new fields of harvest. It can unlock new forms of worship and found new ministries that proclaim the glories of God. Yet left unchecked, desire can lead to unfaithfulness, cultic beliefs, and apostasy. In his mercy, God reveals boundaries to protect us from ourselves, protect us from others . . . and protect others from us!

We can drift toward false worship when we feel a need and see (or imagine) an opportunity. In time, the focal point of worship can veer from the glory of God to recenter on the particularity of a felt need. God has established the church to protect believers from this natural drift. Sustained, reliable relationships can help us safely evaluate desires. Are my desires driven by the prospect of glorifying God or by the potential of spotlighting the self? Are they elevating or diminishing the foundational sacrifice of Christ?

Consider the ordinance of communion. How will we celebrate? The symbolism is central, but it is messy (body and blood). God has established that we are to gather as a body of believers to remember that the blood of Christ was given for us so that we may be spared eternal judgment. There is no alternative sacrifice. There is no other means by which we can regularly remember. If we are worshipping the Lord God, we are proclaiming the death of Christ until he comes.

Now what?
The warning in this passage is severe—bloodguilt! We are not free to escape to the comfort of the open fields in search of a privatized, more convenient means for worship. We risk the bondage of new taskmasters. Worship is, first of all, God-centered and Christ-exalting. It may not always be convenient. It will demand sacrifice. But that is intentional. It changes who we are—and we are what we worship (Ps. 115). There is no other means by which we can be saved (Heb. 9:14). New life is from the blood of Christ (Matt. 26:28).

Creativity in Presentation
As with many other sections of Leviticus, you will have to judge your own congregation. What will be illuminating to some may prove repulsive to others. The call to worship at one location and never consume (and always bury) blood can be brought to life by illustrating the importance of these two principles. In 2020, COVID-19 sent all of us into the "open fields" of our living rooms, to privately worship on our own. How did we do? What dangers did we discover? How were we tempted during our secret worship? Did we cease singing, fast-forward through prayers, scroll through social media during the sermon? It may be a great exercise to

ask everyone what they personally lost during the isolation of worship in the pandemic. Even when it was deemed safe, some did not return to gathered worship. They enjoyed the freedom of being out of the presence of others. If all the discomfort or perceived hardship is removed from worship, if I only do what I want and resist the calls to accommodate others, who is now the center of my worship?

The second principle of not diminishing or even spurning what God has set apart as sacred has many contemporary comparisons. For avid sports fans, you can recall a story of how stomping on the image of a mascot in the center of a field or court led to passionate retaliation! A mascot is symbolic, but its sacredness must be preserved in the minds by all who "worship" the team. Similarly, desecrating the flag of a country before some can become a life-threatening act. For the married, one's wedding ring may only be a band of metal, but it represents a sacred bond between husband and wife. Symbols are not idols, but they can devolve into idols. They are meant to be reminders of the importance of what they represent.

Finally, you can demonstrate that we can all become vulnerable, especially in times of great need or fear, to begin to treat God as a "payment for services" god—God through the image of a slot machine. What may begin as entertainment can grow into an obsession. How long will one keep putting in quarters in the vain hope that eventually God will provide a big payout? It is a game of chance, not true worship. It is a vain hope, not an act of faith.

- We worship according to God's revelation, not our own personal disposition.
- Are we "prostituting" ourselves (giving oneself in exchange for payment) before other gods?
  ◦ What tempts us?
  ◦ What will prevent us?
- How God safeguards our worship of him

  ◦ Persons and place: God establishes where it is safe to worship.
  ◦ Provisions and purpose: God establishes a sacred role for blood.
- What did it mean to them then? What does it mean always? What do we do now?
  ◦ All life belongs to God.
  ◦ Our desires may lure us into the open fields to worship.
  ◦ God establishes boundaries to protect his people from their desires.
  ◦ Am I approaching God as a "payment for services" god?

DISCUSSION QUESTIONS

1. How can one determine if worship is centered on God alone?

2. Why are believers commonly lured and enticed to mysterious and fresh experiences of worship?

3. When might we tend to think of (and treat) the Lord God as a "payment for services" god?

4. Why is it good that God is jealous? How does his jealousy protect us from peril?

5. If someone has bloodguilt it means that no person can excuse or save the offender—only God. When might we be attempting to excuse another's bloodguilt? Why is this a wayward attempt at loving our neighbor?

6. Blood holds the power of life. Jesus held up the cup and told his disciples to drink it: "This is my blood of the covenant, which is poured out for many for the forgiveness of sins" (Matt. 26:28). Why would the disciples hesitate to drink the cup? What is Jesus telling them?

Leviticus 18:1–20:27

EXEGETICAL IDEA

God instructed his people in how to grow in holiness by living together in community. He taught them how to recognize, excise, and replace destructive beliefs and practices that may have risen up from inside them or crept in from the culture around them, with God-defined holy living that calls them to love their neighbor by proclaiming God's holiness through all they do.

THEOLOGICAL FOCUS

God defines love for others as humble, intentional, sacrificial intervention to direct each person toward him. This is in stark contrast to the world's current definition of absolute, nonjudgmental, unconditional affirmation that leaves each person to do what is right in his or her own mind.

PREACHING IDEA

We are made holy by God by loving our neighbor, whom we love best by living holy lives before God.

PREACHING POINTERS

God prepared families to establish new holy communities in the Promised Land. Would these communities thrive? What would prove to be the key threats? Their hearts melted at the thought of the spears, swords, and chariots coming at them. But they were told the greater threat was found in the depravities, perversions, and abominations that caused the land to "vomit out" its inhabitants. The people of God could not rest in Israel's history nor Canaanite customs, as both accommodated the inner lusts that defiled them and their neighbors. God called them to vigorously resist the lust that might arise in their hearts and faithfully pursue the covenant love that was revealed through God's instruction—a sacrificial love for others that would build community relationships through loving one's neighbor.

Everyone hungers for meaningful community. Few agree on how to establish it. These chapters point out how freeing our spirits to crash against God's created order quickly tears away at our social fabric by devastating relationships. God alone knows the depths and dangers of our desires and cravings. He alone is able to establish decrees to safeguard our reasoning from being bent by our wayward desires. His appeal is that of a loving father. He calls us to reflect him and love others in all interactions (1) by finding contentment in his created order, words, statutes, and character; and (2) by evading the snare of serving the god of superior happiness. That means that loving our neighbors should look more like humble, sacrificial intervention than free, unconditional affirmation!

PRESERVING THE SOCIAL FABRIC (18:1–20:27)

LITERARY STRUCTURE AND THEMES (18:1–20:27)

We presented Leviticus 17 as a hinge, marking a change in focus, and suggested that the rest of the book would have less emphasis on the nation's relationship to God while providing guidance for proper human relationships. Still, there continues to be a strong stress on right worship, since the foundation for proper human relationships is a solid relationship with God. We understand this unit to consist of three chapters that address the well-being of the community and ultimately the nation. Leviticus 18 and 20 are clearly tied together by their common focus on avoiding sexual immorality and idolatry. Seemingly separating them, Leviticus 19 contains a variety of commandments, several of which amplify some of the Ten Commandments, but others that seem somewhat random. Still, the section presents a sense of cohesiveness (Balentine 2002, 167; Willis 2009, 172). We would suggest that this sense of cohesiveness derives from the corporate atonement presented in Leviticus 16, adhering to different aspects of the importance of blood. Leviticus 17 addresses the proper respect for the blood of the animals they slaughtered for food or for sacrifice. In contrast, Leviticus 18 promotes the proper respect for human blood *relationships* in terms of family by prohibiting improper sexual relations. Leviticus 19 then looks to the broader relationships of the community in the sense of a national social fabric. In the process, it reiterates portions of the Decalogue, amplifying some of them in terms of how even somewhat small transgressions may snag the fabric of social justice by impairing relationships. Leviticus 20 emphasizes social responses to patch the damage done by violations of the guidelines.

Given those interweavings, these three chapters form another unit that may be preached as a single topic (esp. Lev. 18 and 20), although they may be divided into several sermons should one desire to focus on specific items of interpersonal dynamics. The integrating feature of these three chapters seems to be a concern for maintaining the integrity of the social fabric produced by key relationships that hold society together. For Israel, those key relationships were familial. While primarily derived from their common ancestry (i.e., blood relationship) as descendants of Jacob, they were cemented by their common participation in the Abrahamic covenant (a spiritual and cultural relationship). God gave this covenant initially to Abraham and then passed it down individually first to Abraham's son Isaac and then to his grandson Jacob. From Jacob, who was renamed Israel, it passed collectively to all twelve of his sons, who became the twelve tribes of Israel. Through the Passover-exodus event, this national covenant was not limited to a closed group, but open to all who would willingly serve Israel's God and adhere to the Torah that was being given at Sinai.

> ### Jacob's Wives
> Technically Jacob had two wives and two concubines, but at times the concubines are described as wives (see Gen. 37:2). More importantly, the sons of all four women were treated as legitimate heirs of the Abrahamic covenant (Gen. 49).

- ***The Lord Defines the Social Fabric of Israel by Limiting Sexual Relationships (18:1–23)***
- ***The Lord Warns That Violating the Previous Guidelines Would Tear the***

Social Structure by Defiling the People and the Land, and Result in Expulsion (18:24–30)

- ***The Lord Warns of Other Covenant Violations That Would Also Defile the Nation (19:1–18)***
- ***The Lord Provides Other Statutes That Define Israel as a Whole as God's People (19:19–37)***
- ***The Lord Provides Patches for Tears in the Social Fabric Produced by Specific Violations of the Covenant (20:1–27)***

EXPOSITION (18:1–20:27)

As a unit, these three chapters give general guidelines on how members of the community were to live together. It is then likely that they were given to Israel at the same time. Simplistically, the material may be defined as follows. Leviticus 18 limits sexual relationships, primarily addressing and thus defining the extended family. Leviticus 19 expands some of the most pertinent commands of the Decalogue that affect relationships. While many observe that it seems to touch on all of the Decalogue (Hartley 1992, 309–10; Rooker 2000, 251–52; Ross 2002, 355), others note that it "is more exemplary than exhaustive" (Willis 2009, 171). Either way, Leviticus 20 then contains corrective provisions, showing how the community should respond to violations of the above directives and prohibitions.

The Lord Defines the Social Fabric of Israel by Limiting Sexual Relationships (18:1–23)

Leviticus 18 bans certain sexual relations. Those forbidden relationships essentially describe the extended family unit, which was to be the heart of the social structure. The interweaving of extended families provided parameters for the national structure and established the basics for social interactions and justice (see the section "Biblical Family Ties" in the introduction). Within the Israelite culture, this extended family was critical for several

reasons. Throughout history, the family has been the foundation of culture, which derives from the marriage mandate in Genesis 2:24; but for the Israelites, as for much of the ancient world, that idea was more than just the so-called nuclear family of parents and children we tend to recognize today. Rather, the integration of multiple nuclear families into a cultural whole provided a social infrastructure designed to meet most social needs through the extended family and subsequent links that then knit the entire culture together, which we have called the social fabric.

18:1–2. Once again, the section begins with a *waw*, which should be translated as "then" in this narrative, showing the continued sequence of revelation. But while sequential, we do not know how long after the previous section (Lev. 17) this subsequent oration was given. Since Leviticus concludes with the statement that these were various commandments given at Sinai, it seems likely that this section soon followed the previous material—although it is also likely that it was not the same day, given the amount of material that had been given previously and the amount included now. Again, Moses was directed to share the following material with "the sons of Israel."

To emphasize the importance of what follows, Moses was told to begin this teaching with the declaration "I am YHWH your God." This statement is more than just a reminder of who is speaking. Rather, it emphasizes their relationship that had been established when they arrived at Sinai (Exod. 20) as a result of his delivering them. Since he was their God, there were certain obligations they were required to adhere to. This declaration emphasizes that what is coming is one of those nonnegotiables. This phrase or its shorter version "I am YHWH" will be a point of emphasis for the rest of the book. Used just twice in the first seventeen chapters (Lev. 11:44 and 45), it will be repeated approximately forty-seven

Preserving the Social Fabric (18:1–20:27)

times in the remainder of the book, stressing that their relationships with each other derived from their united position of having been chosen by God as his people.

18:3–5. The unit begins with the declaration that Israel's relationship with God was to be distinct. They were to avoid doing what they had observed while living in Egypt, and perhaps more critically they were not to pick up habits from the Canaanites whose land they were being given. The final exhortation in this chapter will emphasize this latter point, noting those habits were a factor as to why the Canaanites were to be evicted from the land. Yes, a basic reason for the eviction was because the land had been promised to Abraham's descendants. That same promise had contained a deferral clause: Abraham's descendants would not receive the land until the current occupants came under judgment, that is, when the "iniquity of the Amorites" (a collective term for the ten different people groups listed) was complete (Gen. 16:16). In this declaration, God served notice that while that time had come and the Israelites were about to receive the land, they were also to take caution and view the Canaanite eviction as a warning for themselves.

Not only were they warned to avoid the evils of Egypt and Canaan, they were exhorted to observe positive guidelines that God was giving them, which are expressed as "judgments" and "statutes." While the two terms are sometimes perceived as synonymous, the statutes would reflect specific laws that were given by God, while the judgments would reflect legal decisions that were to be based on the given directives. The phrase "walk in" is a common Hebrew idiom that reflects routine actions, that is, a lifestyle. But theirs was to be a thoughtfully cultivated lifestyle in that they were to be careful to "keep" them, a term derived from the verb שָׁמַר. While שָׁמַר may be translated as "keep, observe, or give heed" (*TWOT* s.v. "שָׁמַר" 2:939–40), it carries a stronger connotation of "to guard," indicating that the people were to exercise due diligence to make sure they remembered and preserved his guidelines.

TRANSLATION ANALYSIS: "STATUTES" AND "JUDGMENTS"

"Statutes" translates the term חֹק, which is derived from a verb meaning "to engrave" or "inscribe" (Lewis 1980a, 317). This vividly brings to mind the Decalogue that the nation had just recently received inscribed on the two stone tablets. The same term is used to denote the *customs* of the Canaanites that the Israelites were to avoid (Lev. 18:30; 20:23), setting up a sharp contrast between the cultures. "Judgments," which is translated from מִשְׁפָּט, technically denotes decisions made in the process of government (Culver 1980, 948–49). Later, when Israel had a monarchy, judgments could reflect the decisions of the king, but even those decisions were to be derived from the Torah (Deut. 17:18–20). When given at Sinai, the term seems to anticipate the decisions that the elders made as they sat in the gates of their cities, addressing cases as they arose. However, even there, their judgments were expected to be based on a correct understanding of the intentions of the statutes, which they were to guard. Milgrom (2001, 1521) notes that the term also could be applied to oracular decisions, for which he prefers the term "jurisprudence."

Overall, the rationale given is that "a man may live if he does them." This phrase was later taken by some of the targumim and some early Jewish commentators as a promise of eternal life (Levine 1989, 119). Most commentators feel that reads too much into the phrase (Harrison 1980, 188; Sklar 2014, 229). The way the sixth commandment in the Decalogue qualifies honoring one's parents suggests that this phrase implies passing on a family heritage as part of the national heritage, thus giving an indication of the intent

Preserving the Social Fabric (18:1–20:27)

of the command—that is, that children would honor their parents by upholding their values and preserving their God-given culture. Just as the evil lifestyles of the Canaanites were going to result in their eviction, following God's directions would prolong the Israelites' days *in the land* that God was giving them. A negative expression of the same concept is seen in Deuteronomy 4:26, where the nation was warned that if it disobeyed, it "shall not live long on it, but will be utterly destroyed." As such, the perspective of this exhortation that "a man may live" relates to physical life specifically in the context of dwelling in the land that had been promised. As Hartley (1992, 293) explains, "it means that Israel will have a secure, healthy life with sufficient goods in the promised land as God's people."

18:6–18. The bulk of the chapter is a sequence of specific sexual relationships that were not permitted for Israelites. While providing moral guidelines, the list also seems to describe the structure of what we might call the extended family as discussed in the "Biblical Family Ties" portion of the introduction. In summation, this section centers the Israelite extended family on the male head of the father's house and then delineates the extended family by specifying the female members that the male was forbidden to have sexual relations with. As shown in the material on the biblical family, the various women served as links to other extended families and through this developed the overall social fabric. For example, the wife of the head of the family would be the daughter of the head of another father's house, linking those two families. She would likely have siblings in other extended families, providing other links.

> **Father's House**
>
> The phrase "father's house" (בֵּית־אָב) is defined as "a multiple-family household consisting of blood relatives as well as the women connected though marriage." It is viewed as the basic unit of Israelite society (King and Stager 2001, 39). The phrase appears in the OT approximately forty-seven times, although the concept is used more often. While only used once in the book of Leviticus (22:13, where it refers to the family of a priest's daughter who become a widow or divorcee), the idea is evident here where the phrase "blood relative" that introduces the section seems to refer to that concept. As a point of comparison, in modern bedouin society the "father's house" is considered to consist of three to five generations: the householder and his brothers, the two preceding generations and the two following generations (Matthews and Benjamin 1993, 7).

The section starts with the interesting phrase: אִישׁ אִישׁ, literally "a man, a man," which is best translated as "any man." However, throughout the section, that man is addressed in the second-person singular pronoun, which "has the effect of making the restrictions upon behavior direct and personal" (Bailey 2005, 220). The opening statement provides a general summary statement that a man is not allowed to "approach any blood relative of his to uncover nakedness."

> *TRANSLATION ANALYSIS: "UNCOVER NAKEDNESS"*
>
> The term translated "nakedness" is עֶרְוָה, which after Genesis 3:7 became a "symbol of human shame" (Allen 1980c). The verb is גָּלָה, which means "to uncover" (Waltke 1980b, 160) or "to reveal" (*DCH* s.v. "גלה" 2:348). Thus, literally, the concept is to expose one's genitals, but it often suggests sexual relations.

While it may denote an exposure of shame, "uncovering nakedness" more generally serves as a Hebrew idiom for illicit sexual relations (Sklar 2014, 231). In this case it involves any "blood

258

Preserving the Social Fabric (18:1–20:27)

relative" (שְׁאֵר בְּשָׂרוֹ), which might be literally translated "relation of the flesh," in essence a physical relation.

TRANSLATION ANALYSIS: "BLOOD RELATIVE"
The phrase "blood relative" (שְׁאֵר בְּשָׂרוֹ) literally is "flesh of his flesh." The first word, שְׁאֵר, can mean "flesh, food, body, or near kin" (Cohen 1980c, 895; Ringgren 2004, 270–71), which is coupled with בָּשָׂר, which means "flesh" (Oswalt 1980a, 136). Thus, this is not the same expression used by Adam in Genesis 2:23. When Adam called Eve "flesh of my flesh" (בָּשָׂר מִבְּשָׂרִי), he repeated the noun בָּשָׂר. The difference between the two words for flesh is not clear, although BDB suggests that שְׁאֵר might denote "the inner flesh" or the "flesh next to the bones" as opposed to בָּשָׂר, which denoted the "flesh next to the skin" (BDB s.v. "שְׁאֵר" 984). The word שְׁאֵר is used by itself in 18:12 and 13 to denote the blood relative of the father and mother.

The specific female relatives mentioned are the man's mother, any other wife of the man's father, the man's sister (full or half), the man's granddaughter, the man's aunt (either father or mother's side), the man's daughter-in-law, and the man's sister-in-law (while the brother is alive).

TRANSLATION ANALYSIS: "SISTER"
The text in 18:9 reads literally: "your sister [אָחוֹת], the daughter of your father or the daughter of your mother, born at home or born outside." As such it may be understood as referring to two types of sister (the daughter of a person's mother, or of a person's father), both of which are half-sisters; or three types, a full sister and two types of half-sisters. It probably reflects a full sister, as well as a half-sister (i.e., a sister born either to the father or mother outside of the current marriage; Milgrom 2000, 1539). The phrase translated "born outside" has been understood as referring to an illegitimate daughter (Harrison 1980, 189), but probably refers to a daughter born prior to the present marriage (Hartley 1992, 295).

In addition, the man is not allowed to have sexual relations with a woman and her daughter or granddaughter, nor marry sisters. In both of these latter cases, the reference suggests that the prohibition addressed the time both women were still living (Milgrom 2000, 1546). The last item contains the warning that the sisters would be rivals. One anomaly of this list is that while the man's granddaughter is mentioned specifically, his daughter is not. Some argue that the issue was economic, since that would affect the "bride price" (Ross 2002, 345). Most commentators see an implicit inclusion of the daughter, although they disagree regarding in which way. One view subsumes the daughter under the phrase "blood relative" in 18:6, which seems to summarize the entire section (Kiuchi 2007, 331; Kleinig 2003, 385). Another view sees the daughter as implied by the granddaughter in 18:11 (Keil and Delitzsch 1956, 596; Sklar 2014, 233), which seems the most reasonable explanation.

A point to ponder is that various ancestors of the Israelites at Sinai had violated many of the prohibited relationships. Some view this as evidence that the material was written late and that "regulations have changed and developed over the years" (Bailey 2005, 220). This does not follow. It is true that those ancestors had preceded the law given at Sinai and thus could not be viewed as violating that law, but that does not demonstrate an evolving legal structure as opposed to one given at Sinai after those individuals had lived. One may suppose that the various relationships cited represented innate taboos built into the human psyche, and in some cases that might be so. At the same time, the classic conundrum of where Cain got his wife is very relevant. If the Genesis creation account that all humans are descendants of the original couple is historically valid, and, as is traditionally understood, Cain married a sister, it then seems likely that a number of such sibling relationships would have been manifested in the early history of humankind (and perhaps repeated after the flood genetic "bottleneck") as a matter of necessity. As developed in the introduction, it is suggested that at Sinai God formatted a new social fabric, and the concept of an extended family was to be a major building block of that structure. Here he defines that basic building block.

As such, this foundational document presents new criteria intended primarily to build a stronger social structure. A key point relevant to the function of the passage is that the last prohibition uses a different term for the action. Throughout this section, the operative phrase has been "uncover her nakedness," which we noted reflects sexual relations. However, in the case of the sisters, the text uses "marry" (. . . אִשָּׁה לֹא תִקָּח, literally, "a wife he will not take"). While this stresses the illicit nature of the various relationships, it allows for some of the situations to be "time-bound prohibitions" such as the case of the brother's wife (18:16) or a woman and her sister (18:18). Once the brother or the woman was deceased, marriage to the survivor would not have violated this direction, which would remove an apparent obstacle to levirate marriage (Milgrom 2000, 1550).

Additionally, the examples of the ancestors showed the value of this social structure. Presuming that Genesis was written by Moses, it is likely that it was read to the Israelites at Sinai. As they listened to the book, they would have been struck by how their ancestors served as pertinent examples of why those restrictions were being given. For example, they would have been very aware of the stresses generated by conflict between Leah and Rachel, the sisters who were the wives of Jacob, the father of the twelve tribes.

18:19–23. The next section cites five other relevant actions that would tear the social fabric.

Some of these are not as clear with regard to how they affected the extended family foundation that we have been addressing. That is especially the case of items that are also addressed elsewhere, such as the first item in this list.

18:19. The first direction is that a man is not to have sexual relations with a woman during the period of menstrual impurity. Two things stand out about this direction. First, this prohibition seems to contradict the guidelines in Leviticus 15:24 where the direction is that if a man has sexual relations with a woman during this time, he is unclean for seven days and then must undergo ritual cleansing. As noted in our discussion of that passage, that seems to address a situation where the flow started during intercourse. Here the issue seems to be a deliberate violation and thus rebellion (Ross 2002, 346). This is indicated by the verb structure that describes the process of approaching the woman for sexual relations during this time frame. Although the effect of violating this on the social fabric is not clear, Noordtzij (1982, 186) suggests that the prohibition was a requirement to "sanctify the intimacy of their conjugal life to the Lord," a crucial aspect of the foundational husband-wife relationship.

18:20. The text does not specify it, but the assumption is that the neighbor (i.e., someone who is known, not necessarily just one who lives in close proximity) is still alive, which would make this another "time-bound prohibition." Here the act is just listed as one that would tear the social fabric and is thus forbidden. Moreover, if the neighbor was still alive, violating this would be adultery, which would be defiling, and in Leviticus 20:10 the consequences are presented as requiring the stoning of both members of the adulterous relationship.

18:21. The statement in 18:21 forbidding the "giving of your offspring" to Molech seems straightforward, but there are a number of issues. The most pertinent one in this context is that offering one's child to Molech seems anomalous to the series of prohibited sexual relationships in the rest of the chapter. Most of the various studies of this issue focus on the identification of the figure called Molech and the traditional understanding that what was involved was child sacrifice through burning, although some argue that it involved giving the child to Molech as a living servant. As shown in appendix 1 on Molech, the key factor in this directive is that the man is turning over a child of his, either to death or to pagan service to a pagan god instead of YHWH (Noordtzij 1982, 187). Obviously if the child is sacrificed (i.e., the child is the object of sacred killing), whether by fire or any other means, an invaluable human asset is removed from the Israelite culture. Further, the death of the child would affect both the parents individually as well as their relationship. The alternative view of devoting the child to the service of a pagan god not only would be a loss to the Israelites, but a child trained to serve idolatry would be a disruption to the culture later. While in either case, this act would demonstrate that the parents were idolatrous, a horrendous rent in the social fabric, a number of related passages suggest that the practice being addressed here is the actual sacrifice of a child (e.g., see Deut. 18:10; 2 Kings 23:10; Ezek. 23:37–39; Mic. 6:6–7).

18:22. The fourth prohibition in this section is homosexual relations. Since this entire section is addressed to the male head of the house, it specifically forbids him from "lying with a male as one lies with a female," in other words, a homosexual act. While a logical inference would extend this prohibition to relations between two women (Sklar 2014, 237–38), one must remember that the person addressed is the male head of the father's house. Here, a rationale is provided—this is "an abomination" (תּוֹעֵבָה).

TRANSLATION ANALYSIS: ABOMINATION
The idea of abomination is significant since the term תּוֹעֵבָה appears approximately 117 times and characterizes either an act or a thing that is abhorred by either God or humans for physical, ritual, or ethical reasons (Youngblood 1980). The basic idea is that an act might be "aesthetically and morally repulsive." For humans the repulsion might be innate or it might be culturally inculcated, as in the case of Egyptians considering eating bread with Hebrews (Gen. 43:32) as "loathsome" (תּוֹעֵבָה). In the case of something being an abomination to God, the appraisal would derive from his character and as such be universal.

Several reasons have been suggested for this strong demarcation and command. Harrison suggests that "sacro-homosexual practices" were part of Canaanite idolatry; thus, there is a religious aspect (1980, 194; so also Ross 2002, 346). Kleinig (2003, 380) views it a matter of defiling both the participant and the environment, although he does not specify why. Another reason, derived from God's design of a male-female marital relationship as the basis of society (Gen. 2:24), sees a homosexual relationship as a perversion of God's design (Hartley 1992, 283). While all of the above seem true, it would seem that the critical factor for including the command in this context might be that the practice is destructive of the social fabric, since it violates the premise that the family is the basic unit for the social structure. By their nature homosexual relations are sterile and cannot build a family unit, which biblically is the purpose of marriage. Additionally, it would seem that if the female was the link to other extended families as noted above, a male-male relationship (or by extension a female-female relationship) would be a rip in the social fabric.

18:23. The final item in this section is bestiality. In this case, the issue goes beyond the head

Preserving the Social Fabric (18:1–20:27)

of the family. While still in the second-person plural, the addition of "any woman" as initiating the action shows the directive includes any human. The final declaration that "it is a perversion" emphasizes the earlier statement that it defiles the human involved. There is some evidence that these practices were practiced both in Canaan and Egypt (Hartley 1992, 297–98). Again, perverted sexual activity defiles the persons involved and breaks down social relationships, weakening the overall social fabric.

The Lord Warns That Violating the Previous Guidelines Would Tear the Social Structure by Defiling the People and the Land, and Result in Expulsion (18:24–30)

The last portion of the chapter summarizes how the various specific issues listed might affect not only the overall nation but the land in which it would dwell—both would be defiled. In terms of the nation, the warning was that the social fabric needed to be treated with care. Careless violations of various relationships would destroy the social fabric of the community and the nation as a whole.

Additionally, at this point, the land they were going to occupy is personified as someone who has ingested something injurious. They were warned that these violations would result in the land vomiting the occupants out, a phrase that might denote removal from the land either by exile or death (Ross 2002, 348). The nation is advised that the land was about to do that to the Canaanites.

TRANSLATION ANALYSIS: "THE LAND HAS VOMITED OUT ITS INHABITANTS"
The Hebrew uses the perfect tense here, which denotes completed action. While some see this as a "linguistic slip" suggesting a writer from a much later date (Bailey 2005, 217), it is better understood that it "expresses facts which are undoubtedly imminent, and, therefore, in the imagination of the speaker, already accomplished" (GKC §106n).

In their case, Israel might be viewed as the purgative agent that would cleanse the land from uncleanness. On the other hand, the nation is warned that just as the land was about to vomit out the Canaanites, should Israel follow their pattern, the same would occur to them. As such, this section incorporates a point of irony in that the pagan fertility cults that purported to make the land more fruitful actually polluted the land (Hartley 1992, 298). Overall, this section shows that "The measure of Israel's obedience to God is not only the *purity of its rituals*; it is also the *morality of its everyday conduct*" (Balentine 2002, 153, emphasis original). This section closes with another emphatic reminder that this directive is from YHWH, who is their God.

The Lord Warns of Other Covenant Violations That Would Also Defile the Nation (19:1–18)

While Leviticus 19 is a single speech that God gave to Moses to promulgate to the entire nation of Israel, it can be divided into two parts. The first part addresses other aspects of the covenant relationships that necessitated care. The previous speech (Lev. 18) focused on the extended family as a block within the overall social fabric of Israel and it addressed how tears within that block affected all of society. The exhortations in this section extend beyond that block to the overall fabric, indicating ways that the connections between the extended family blocks could be damaged. Commentators note that the directives given here are diverse and there is no clear structure, although they do seem to address aspects of relationship demonstrating faithfulness, love, respect, and justice (Hartley 1992, 308). The declarations in this chapter are largely apodictic in nature, being based solely on God's demands, emphasized through God's declaration "I am the Lord [YHWH]," a phrase repeated fifteen times in the chapter. The repetition of this phrase seems to serve as a textual divider, especially in the first half of the

262

chapter, where they seem to indicate conceptual couplets. The phrases are almost evenly split between using the phrase by itself (eight times), stressing God's authority as God, and including the delineation "your God" (seven times), emphasizing God's relationship to the nation.

19:1–2. This speech begins with the standard *waw*, showing a continued sequence. God informs Moses that the following is a speech that he was to give to the entire nation, showing that everyone was responsible for carrying out the directions. The contents of the chapter are summarized by the declaration that they (here the address shifts to a plural pronoun that might be translated as "you all") were to be holy, because God was holy. As shown in the introduction, holiness seems to have a corporate focus, which here would reflect how the people of Israel were to relate to one another in moral purity. That suggests a stress in this section on personal relationships.

19:3. Leviticus 19:3 contains two distinct commands united as one statement that has an unusual structure. Both commands derive directly from the Decalogue, specifically the fourth ("remember the sabbath day") and the fifth commands ("honor your father and your mother") as listed in Exodus 20:8 and 12, although they are reversed and contain several subtle grammatical differences.

TRANSLATION ANALYSIS: LEVITICUS 19:3
Grammatically, Leviticus 19:3 contains several interesting features that merit explanation. The verse is one sentence that begins with an indefinite noun as the subject, "a man" (אִישׁ), combined with a plural imperfect form of the verb used as an imperative. This combination emphasizes that the command applies to every individual (Levine 1989, 125; Peter-Contesse and Ellington 1992, 283). Further, the verb-direct object order is reversed, emphasizing the

direct object. Additionally, while the verse is derived from the Decalogue (which Moses had received a year earlier), the direct object order of mother, then father, reverses the order given in the Decalogue. While commentators have made a number of speculations regarding the rationale of placing the mother first, the most plausible would be Milgrom's suggestion that this reversal along with the verb-object reversal is just structural, which provides a chiastic effect with the declaration in Exod. 20:12 (Milgrom 2000, 1608–9). This portion of the sentence is then joined to a reiteration of the fourth command regarding the Sabbath by a *waw*, which has the effect of equating the two directives as one basic social admonition. The verb used here is the verb "to keep or to guard" (שָׁמַר), as opposed to "remember" (זָכַר) in Exodus 20:8. Further, although translated as an imperative, the verb form is an imperfect, which may take an imperative force (GKC §107n), especially in coordination with the first verb in a sentence as seen here.

Two other verbal changes also seem significant. Here the parents are to be feared (יָרֵא), while in the Decalogue they are to be honored (כָּבֵד). The concept, however, is not fear as an emotion but analogous to the frequent use of fear with respect to God in the sense of "revere," although a true understanding of who God is certainly promotes an emotional aspect (Bowling 1980b). The other change is the use of "Sabbaths" in the plural, as opposed to the Decalogue designation specifically of the "Sabbath day." This would seem to include specific holidays that are also specifically designated as Sabbaths, including Yom Kippur (Lev. 23:32) and the Sabbath year (Lev. 25:2–4). One might also include times that, while not called Sabbaths, call for rest, such as Firstfruits (Num. 28:26) and Jubilee (Lev. 25:11).

While both commands essentially convey the same ideas as in their earlier iterations, uniting the two as a single statement at this

Preserving the Social Fabric (18:1–20:27)

point seems to provide a crucial cornerstone for a strong spiritual foundation for the society as a whole. This is especially evident here where the command seems directed to the children, not the parents (Hess 2008, 748). While the responsibility for the fear or honor of the parents is on the children, there is a flip-side requirement on the part of the parents that they would have modeled a God-honoring lifestyle and teaching that the now-adult children have picked up and now practice (Mathews 2009, 170). In that light, coupling this command with keeping the Sabbath is neither random nor coincidental. It highlights the fact that habitual observation of the Sabbath as the basic ritual of the Israelite religion (as it is of Judaism today) was the responsibility of the family and served as a crucial matrix for passing their spiritual heritage from generation to generation. The consistent following of this spiritual heritage would be what would preserve the nation in the future—and the failure to do so would bring about the defilement noted in the preceding section.

National Preservation

The Israelite at Sinai might have recalled the first promulgation of this command a year earlier as recorded in Exodus 20:12, where the purpose of this declaration was, "Honor your father and your mother that your days may be prolonged *in the land* that the Lord [YHWH] your God gives you" (emphasis added). When Moses repeated the Decalogue in Deuteronomy 5 approximately forty years later, he stated it slightly differently: "Honor your father and your mother, as the Lord [YHWH] your God has commanded you, that your days may be prolonged and that it may go well with you upon the land that the Lord [YHWH] your God gives you" (Deut. 5:16). Here the phrase "upon the land" seems to reflect both "days may be prolonged" and "it may go well with you." Deuteronomy adds the phrase "as the Lord [YHWH] your God has commanded you," which would refer both to the Exodus declaration

and the repeat here in Leviticus. Paul notes this promise when he cites the verse from Deuteronomy in Ephesians 6:2–3. There he uses the Greek word γῆς, which may be translated as "earth" as well as "land." With this ambiguity and his omission of the final phrase, "which the Lord [YHWH] your God gives you," it seems that Paul is expanding the concept to be inclusive of Gentiles. However, that does not indicate that he is suggesting that the promise is a long life, that is, "being on the earth a long time," as is sometimes understood by commentators who overlook the OT background (Hendriksen 1995, 260).

19:4. While Leviticus 19:3 denotes positive things that the Israelites were to do to promote holiness and produce a spiritual foundation for subsequent generations, 19:4 sets forth a negative. They were to avoid turning to "idols" (הָאֱלִילִים) and "molten gods" (וֵאלֹהֵי מַסֵּכָה).

TRANSLATION ANALYSIS: "IDOLS"

Translated as "idols," the word הָאֱלִילִים seems to derive from a root meaning "to be weak, deficient" and suggests "something worthless" (Scott 1980d, 146). As such, it does not specifically refer to an idol as we tend to think of it, but anything physical that is intended to serve as a representation or substitute for the Lord God.

The former denotes any substitute for God, while the latter specifically addresses metal images, perhaps subtly warning against a repeat of the golden calf incident (Exod. 32:4). At first, it seems strange that while the first and second commands in the Decalogue warn against going after other gods or making idols, here these warnings show up as third. And yet, one might sense a sequence where one dishonors the teachings of one's parents, and abandons (or forgets) the heritage of the nation, and then looks for other gods. Here is the emphatic reminder that for Israel, the only God was the Lord.

19:5–8. In contrast to seeking other gods, this section stresses the value of the shalom offering and warns against its misuse or abuse. It seems significant that God only addresses one of the various offerings directed earlier, and even then, only one aspect of that offering. Earlier, Leviticus 3 merely introduced the concept of the shalom offering, explaining the process (see section "The Lord Tells Israel How to Bring a Shalom Offering" [3:1–17]). Subsequently Leviticus 7 differentiated the shalom offering into three categories—thanksgiving, votive, and freewill—giving more details on the process, specifically addressing the portions of the meat that were burned and that were given to the priest, as well as describing how the remainder of the meat was to be cooked and provided to the offeror and his or her companions (see section "The Lord Gives Directions to the Priests for Shalom Offerings" [7:11–36]). In both cases, the shalom offering is just part of the overall sacrificial system, but here it stands by itself.

Beyond the question of why this is the only sacrifice that is included, there is the question of "What is this unit doing here?" Milgrom claims this is the primary question with regard to this material and complains that commentators do not address the issue (2000, 1615). When commentators do mention the matter, their approach tends to be variations of the idea that this is the only sacrifice handled by lay persons and they associate it with the idea of holiness.

The fact that the material here essentially cautions the Israelites to be sure that the offering is done properly so that the person and the offering would be accepted suggests that the shalom offering is important for maintaining the social fabric. Based on our discussion of sacrifices in the introduction, we would suggest that an integral key to understanding this is the recollection that the shalom offerings (all three types) were celebratory offerings that promoted corporate worship of God by reminding each other of the works he had performed. As discussed there, while it seems likely that the average Israelite ate meat much less frequently than modern diets, that does not necessarily suggest that the only time they ate meat was following sacrifices. Rather, the celebratory offerings were special meals intended for the entire community, or at least for family and friends, to give honor to God in various ways.

As such, a properly observed shalom offering reflected another step in solidifying the nation as God's people, and as Noordtzij (1982, 194) observes, "There was always a danger that, in this meal, the eating of the meat could become the primary matter." In that case, it would desecrate the sacrifice. Emphasizing the two-day limit encouraged a broader invitation list to ensure that the animal was eaten in the requisite time. As Milgrom (2000, 1615) questions, "How much of a whole animal can a family consume in two days?"

> **Limit on Eating Sacrifices**
>
> In our discussion of shalom offerings earlier (under Lev. 7:11–36), we observed that the time frame for eating the shalom sacrifices varied. For the thanksgiving offering, intended to express one's public proclamation of God's attributes and works, the meat was required to be eaten on the day of the sacrifice and anything left over was to be burned. In the case of votive and freewill offerings, the meat could be eaten the second day, but anything left over must be burned by the third day. It would seem that the latter two might reflect situations that were more personal; thus one might expect smaller, more intimate gatherings, and thus suggesting a longer time frame to eat the meat. In contrast, when proclaiming what God had done, the impetus would to be to access as wide of an audience as possible, and one way of doing that was to limit how long any leftovers might be kept.

Our premise that our current three-chapter section addresses issues that would rend the social fabric provides a plausible explanation for including just the shalom offering in

Preserving the Social Fabric (18:1–20:27)

this section. Violating the guidelines for the various shalom offerings would most likely involve selfishly hoarding the meat just for the family, overlooking members of the community. This would produce a greater temptation to keep the meat beyond the two-day limit, but more importantly would miss the point of celebrating what God had done and the strengthening of community bonds.

19:9–10. Leviticus 19:9–10 introduces a new topic that will play a significant role in the rest of the book: provision for the poor and the resident aliens, once the Israelites have settled in the land.

TRANSLATION ANALYSIS: "SOJOURNER"
In English translations, the Hebrew word גֵּר is translated variously as "stranger" (KJV), "sojourner" (ESV, RSV), or "alien" (NASB, NIV). At Sinai, the concept might have been alien or foreigner as opposed to a descendant of Jacob. However, it might be expected that those non-Israelites who had come out of Egypt with the Israelites would have been largely absorbed by the time the second generation finally entered the land since they apparently participated in the initial land distribution after the conquest. Non-Israelites who dwelt in the land prior to the conquest and were not driven out seemed to remain on the land they had historically possessed. Thus, within the context of this law, a foreigner would seem to have been someone who entered the land at some time after the conquest. A גֵּר, however, should be distinguished from a "foreigner" (נְכָרִי or נֵכָר), in that he or she would have taken up residence in the land as opposed to just visiting it; hence, the term "resident alien" is preferable. As such, resident aliens had privileges and responsibilities beyond those of foreigners, but fewer than those of the natives. At this point where the idea of life in the settlement is just being introduced, the idea of a stranger might be appropriate, but from our perspective it misses

the anticipated context of Israel being settled in the land and farming their own farms.

At first glance, it appears to be a sharp departure from the previous section that focused on the proper handling of the shalom offering, which we understand served as an act of worship. However, it really marks a significant implication of the shalom offering, which centered on giving thanks to God for his provision. As Ross (2002, 359–60) indicates, to express gratitude to God without showing generosity was "a hollow claim." Ross goes on to suggest that it also promoted corporate unity by giving even the poor provision for which they could offer praise. Moreover, as Radner (2008, 221) suggests, this served as "an important instance of receiving the providential love of God as a community."

As expressed here, the command merely anticipates a broader social justice system, which will be described in more detail in the last chapters of the book. At this point, the following observations may be noted. Once the Israelites were settled and farming, they were to be circumspect as they harvested, leaving a portion of their crops for the needy to glean (see appendix 2, "Gleaning: A Case Study in Ruth"). Likewise, as they brought the crops in, anything that fell to the ground was also to be left for the needy. The implications of this practice will be discussed in more detail in our discussion of Leviticus 23, "Strengthening the Social Fabric," as a means by which the Israelites could give opportunity for the needy. It should be noted that it was expected that the needy who took advantage of this opportunity had to expend the labor to gather the materials.

19:11–12. While the shalom offering and the gleaning rules guided positive actions that would help strengthen the social fabric, they are followed by a series of actions prohibited because they would rend it. The first section begins with a prohibition against theft and fraud, both actions that misappropriate property. This is followed by a prohibition against lying and falsely swearing by the Lord's name. This section has been understood two ways. One is that it warns against theft followed by lying and deceit to try to cover up (Sklar 2014, 245). The other sees the deception and false oaths as the means to wrongfully acquire the property (Hartley 1992, 315). Since the basic issue is honesty in word and deed, both nuances should be understood.

> ### False Swearing
> The warning here is against not just falsely swearing, but against using God's name as the foundation of the oath. Levine (1989, 127) points out that both the Mishnah and Sifra (the halakic midrash to Leviticus) see this as related to the third commandment, "You shall not take the name of the Lord [YHWH] your God in vain." While Exodus uses the verb שָׁוְא, meaning "emptiness" or "vanity," Leviticus uses שֶׁקֶר, meaning "to lie," which helps clarify the issue involved. The point is that through this deceit God's name is profaned, and as Exodus points out "the Lord [YHWH] will not leave him unpunished."

19:13–14. While the preceding verse couplet stresses honesty between essentially equals, the stress here is a prohibition against exploiting those who are unable to defend themselves. Three general situations are presented as principles of actions to avoid. The initial warning is against oppression (עָשַׁק) or robbery (גָּזַל). Both terms suggest a use of force or at least a threat of it to achieve one's intentions (Hartley 1992, 315). The second admonition is against withholding the wages of a hired man. In that culture, a hired person was often paid on a daily basis, a practice illustrated in Matthew 20:8. Here the concern is failing to give a person his or her just due,

when due. The third admonition is against cursing a deaf person or placing a stumbling block before a blind person. While these specific cases are noted, Levine (1989, 128) observes that the phrase "treating lightly" (עָוֶה) views the situation as one of "taking unfair advantage of another's disabilities." Kiuchi (2007, 351) sums up the section as "both a verbal and non-verbal act of despising."

> ### Hireling's Wages
> While given at Sinai, this provision anticipated the period after the nation settled in the land. Although it was expected that everyone who entered the land would be given land to work, it was also expected that at some point there would be some who would work for others as hired help for a variety of reasons. The indications are that there were two types. The first might be the hireling who was generally paid by the day (see also Deut. 24:15). In this case, payment was to be made at the end of the day's work. The second type would be one who was hired "year by year" (Lev. 25:53), although it is possible that this includes indentured servants (Lev. 25:50–52) who sold themselves into servanthood for a period of years. It would seem that in this case payment would be made at the end of the year or the period of servitude (which may be relevant to the situation of Jacob working for Laban for seven years prior to receiving his "pay," which was actually Laban's daughter Rachel [Gen. 29:20–21]).

19:15–16. As a couplet, these two verses stress fairness in judgment. Commentators generally agree that legal cases are involved in 19:15, but disagree on whether 19:16 continues to focus on legal situations (Sklar 2014, 246) or if it addresses regular activities within the community (Rooker 2000, 258).

TRANSLATION ANALYSIS: "JUDGMENT"
The noun מִשְׁפָּט, translated "judgment," is derived from the verb שָׁפַט, which means "to judge or govern" (Culver 1980, 947). Based

on cognate usage it is generally assumed that the root has the connotation of "an act of ruling or the exercise of authority" (Niehr 2006, 415). Robert Culver (1980, 947) picks up on this root and states that its primary sense is "to exercise the processes of government," but he then continues to note that because of cultural differences "the common translation, 'to judge,' misleads us." Perhaps the largest issue involved is the perception that a formal governmental structure, and thus also a legal system, necessarily underlie "judgment." Regardless of one's understanding of human origins and development, it seems that the idea of evaluating right or wrong or fairness is an intuitive act. Within the biblical context, judging right and wrong is understood to derive from the nature of God. The word is used both in terms of God's character and in human actions in the life of Abraham (see Gen. 15:14; 16:5; 18:25; 19:9), as well as with subsequent patriarchs, centuries before the events at Sinai. However, the concept of judgment shows up in the life of Cain (Gen. 4:13–15) as well as his descendant Lamech (Gen. 4:23–24), where it carries an understanding of vengeance. As such, it seems that the foundational concept of מִשְׁפָּט in the OT would be evaluating an act as right or wrong, and in terms of persons, evaluating their actions as right or wrong.

Given the legal structure at that time in Israel, it seems likely that both aspects are involved for both verses. As Culver (1980) points out, translation of this noun as "judgment" (מִשְׁפָּט), along with the verb "judge" (שָׁפַט) from which it is derived, is often misleading due to the way that we view the concept of judging. Rather than a formal legal system, jurisprudence for Israel prior to the monarchy consisted of ad hoc "juries" of local leaders or elders who gathered in the city gate to evaluate a situation. No lawyers were involved, and every adult male could participate in the judgment process, as shown in Ruth 4.

> ### Israelite Jurisprudence
> Ruth 4 gives us a case history of the judicial process for Israel during the time of the judges. Boaz, a citizen, goes up to the gate, where he finds the other relative involved in the situation. Boaz and the other relative sit down, and as various elders of the city pass by, ten are asked to sit down for the case. Boaz presents his case, and the other relative responds. In this case, there is no question regarding the outcome, since the other relative agrees with the situation and defers to Boaz with regard to Ruth. The ten elders then serve as witnesses to the resolution the two men reached. In cases of disagreement, it would appear that the elders or witnesses would then serve as arbitrators, either singly or as a group, to provide a just outcome (Exod. 21:22; Num. 35:25–28; Judg. 20:6). Beginning with the exodus, Moses served as a higher judge when the other judges could not reach a conclusion (Exod. 18). In Deuteronomy 16–17 Moses indicates that after the Israelites settled in the land they should appoint judges (Deut. 16:18–19), who would apparently replace Moses with respect to appeals, although the Levitical priest also was designated in that regard (Deut. 17:9). Early on, the high priest could use the Urim and Thummim to inquire of God regarding more difficult questions (Num. 27:21). Following Samuel, the people asked for and got a king, who provided that appellate role. It then seems that by setting up kingship they let the king take the place of the high priest and the Urim and Thummim (1 Sam. 8:6, 20). It is interesting that there is no reference to the presence of the Urim and Thummim as part of the high priest's apparatus subsequent to David.

There are two points to the present couplet. The first relates to matters where the actions (or inactions) of a person harmed another, whether intentionally or not. This would be the legal aspect requiring both an evaluation of the issue, as well as proper resolution in terms of whether recompense was merited and if so, in what manner. The second, which seems to be

Preserving the Social Fabric (18:1–20:27)

the focus of 19:16, is the issue of slander, which relates to making false assessments of the character of another person.

TRANSLATION ANALYSIS: "SLANDER"
The Hebrew word רָכִיל is a noun meaning "slander." Here it could denote the person performing the action, with the verb הָלַךְ meaning "to walk or go," thus providing the translation "go about as a slanderer" (White 1980c, 848). It has also been understood as the purpose of the action, thus "go about (for) slander" (*DCH* s.v. "רָכִיל" 7:492). In either case it suggests an individual who is making malicious accusations or characterizations of his or her neighbor.

While clearly regarding testimony in legal situations, as used with the verb "to go about," this verse also seems to address gossip as one talks about another within the community (Bailey 2005, 230). The Talmud adds another nuance when it maintains that the last phrase "you are not to act [lit. stand] against the life of your neighbor" requires a witness not to remain silent "when you could offer testimony in someone's behalf" (b. Sanh. 73a).

19:17–18. Leviticus 19:17–18 seems to directly follow the admonitions in the preceding two verses to avoid injustice and not to slander, as it begins by warning the Israelites not to hate their fellow Israelites, a heart attitude. Concluding with the admonition to love one's neighbor, this couplet seems to summarize the previous sections of this chapter, which address community relationships. That concluding admonition is very familiar to New Testament readers, since it is cited several times, especially by both Jesus and Paul: "you shall love your neighbor as yourself."

> ### Love Your Neighbor
> While the phrase "love your neighbor as yourself" is perhaps most noted as the response of Jesus to the question of what was the greatest commandment, it actually shows up in the NT nine times: Matt. 5:43; 19:19; 22:39; Mark 12:31, 33; Luke 10:27; Rom. 13:9, 10; and James 2:8. In addition, there are a number of allusions to the concept.

Sandwiched within the verses of the couplet are three amplifications. In 19:17, while a fellow countryman should not be hated, he should be reproved in the event that he does something wrong.

TRANSLATION ANALYSIS: "REBUKE"
The verb יָכַח basically means "to decide, judge, prove, rebuke, or correct" (Gilchrist 1980a, 376). It carries a concept of a reasoned argument to show that something that someone had done was wrong (e.g., note Jacob's protestation against Laban in Gen. 31:36–42). While it may reflect emotions, the key is that it should consist of evidential data. Here it is used as a complex term consisting of a *hiphil* imperfect in the second-person singular coupled with a *hiphil* infinitive absolute, carrying the sense of an obligation.

The reason for the reproof is so that the person reproving "shall not incur sin." This has been understood two ways. Some understand the alternative as either taking vengeance or bearing a grudge, both of which are sins (Sklar 2014, 246). Others suggest that the issue is that if he continues to sin, the one who fails to reprove shares the guilt with him (Kellogg 1978, 401–2; Lange 1960, 150). This is likely one of those cases where the ambiguity deliberately carries both connotations.

Overall, this last couplet seems to serve as a summary of the preceding couplets. In general, they have been understood in two ways. Some see this section as actions that serve as alternatives to going to court (Wenham 1979, 268). Others focus on the command to love and see this as a basic principle for holiness (Noordtzij 1982, 160; Ross 2002, 362).

Preserving the Social Fabric (18:1–20:27)

It is interesting that these two verses use four different terms to denote community relationships: brother (אָח), associate (עָמִית), son of your people (בְּנֵי עַמֶּךָ), and neighbor (רֵעֶה), suggesting that the entire scope of society is included in this admonishment.

The Lord Provides Other Statutes That Define Israel as a Whole as God's People (19:19–37)

While part of the same speech, the last portion of the chapter seems less directly dependent on the guidelines in the Decalogue. Rather, it presents areas where the nation should show itself distinct from the surrounding cultures. Corporate responses to violations of the directions in Leviticus 18–19 are presented in Leviticus 20, but many of the items in this section seem much more free-standing, and in some regards, non sequiturs. However, their relevance to the nation is underlined with the opening and closing declarations that Israel was to keep God's statutes.

19:19. Leviticus 19:19 contains three directives that address the mixing of kinds (כִּלְאַיִם). The first prohibits breeding two kinds of "cattle" (בְּהֵמָה).

> *TRANSLATION ANALYSIS: MIXING "KINDS"*
> The word כִּלְאַיִם is the dual form of a noun that appears only in that form and is used but four times in the OT, three here and once in Deuteronomy 22:9 in a similar legal context. The dual form emphasizes that it is two items that are being mixed, which the Deuteronomy passage spells out giving specific cases. The idea of "kind" here contrasts the concept in Genesis 1 where various animals reproduce after their "kind"; Genesis 6–7, where Noah took animals after their "kind"; and even in Leviticus 11 where various birds are listed according to their "kind," all of which use the word מִין. The difference between the two is not clear.

The second disallows sowing two kinds of seed in a field. The third forbids wearing a garment made of two kinds of material (שַׁעַטְנֵז). No reason is given, and the exact intent of this passage is not understood and highly debated. The following observations relate to the issue. In the first case, while the word בְּהֵמָה is often translated "cattle," the basic meaning is "beast," for which reason several translations translate it more broadly as "animal" (e.g., NIV, NRSV) or livestock (HSCB). It is generally assumed that the warning is against hybridization or crossbreeding. While the science of genetics was a long time in the future, it would appear that the ancients did have a basic understanding of breeding, as evidenced by Jacob as he used chicanery and basic breeding practices to appropriate Laban's flocks (Gen. 30:31–33). While the case against beasts seems to be interbreeding, the issue of the seed is sowing two different kinds of seed in the same field—or in Deuteronomy 22:9, in the same vineyard. However, wheat and grapes "sown" together would not hybridize. Although each would produce its particular fruit, such a mixture would present other problems, such as one kind choking out the other or killing grape vines while harvesting wheat.

In the third case, the historical understanding of the garment material is that it was a prohibition against using two different types of yarn to weave the cloth. This translation is based on the understanding of the word שַׁעַטְנֵז that dates from the time of Josephus. This is a rare word used only here and in Deuteronomy 22:11, and *TWOT* suggests it to be a loan word, although it does not suggest a source (s.v. "שַׁעַטְנֵז" 2:945). A key problem with understanding this as a general statement regarding mixtures is that the parallel passage in Deuteronomy specifically identifies שַׁעַטְנֵז as a mixture of wool and linen, and tradition has it that the priest would wear garments that are understood to have had that specific mixture. However, as discussed in the unit "Inauguration of Ancient Israelite Religion" (8:1–9:24), this is a supposition drawn

270

Preserving the Social Fabric (18:1–20:27)

from Jewish tradition, based on the understanding that the term "scarlet" in Exodus 28:5 is used for woolen material that has been died scarlet, rather than just indicating color (Lange 1960, 151).

Crossbreeding

The Hebrew רָבַע is translated as "breed together" (NASB) or "crossbreed" (HCSB) or something similar in modern translations. The basic idea of the three items in this verse seems to be to "not to mix the things which are separated in the creation of God" (Keil and Delitzsch 1956, 601). However, there are questions in this regard. First, while the three items cited are all matters of mixture, the mixing processes of the three differ drastically. Second, in two of the three cases, there seemed to be exceptions. On a number of occasions, the OT notes mules, a cross between a donkey and a horse, as a means of transportation (see 2 Sam. 13:29; 18:9; 1 Kings 1:33). While 1 Kings 10:25 notes that Solomon imported mules, using imported products they were forbidden to produce does not legitimatize the result. While the mixed seed and material admonitions are repeated in the parallel passage of Deuteronomy 22:10, this one is not, but in its place they are told not to "plow with an ox and a donkey together." Perhaps for this reason, some have suggested that the verb רָבַע has an interchange between ע and צ, and has a meaning of "lie down" (*GHC* s.v. "רָבַע I" 755), and thus might be better understood here as making the animals kneel in order to yoke them (see also Hess 2008, 753). If that were the case, then this would reconcile this passage with Deuteronomy.

While there is a lot of debate regarding the issue and a number of suppositions, the bottom line is that no rationale is given outside of the introductory statement, "You are to keep my statutes." Since the only thing the three prohibitions share is mixing of unlike items, it seems that rather than stretching for a reason, the best approach might be to follow Jewish exegesis, which viewed these declarations as three specific statutes (חֻקּוֹת) that were "to be treated as 'decrees of the king;' to be obeyed simply because they come from God" (Radner 2008, 213). As such, this would limit these admonitions to specifics of the national covenant with the nation of Israel, intended primarily to differentiate the nation and its culture from its surrounding cultures. In essence, obedience would provide unique cultural aspects that served as threads binding the social fabric of God's people, the nation of Israel, as opposed to their neighbors.

19:20–22. This section is ambiguous and debated for several reasons, including the vagueness of the description, the use of rare words, and its presence at this place in the text. The basic situation involves a man who has sex with a woman whose status is a "slave" (שִׁפְחָה).

TRANSLATION ANALYSIS: "FEMALE SLAVE"
The word שִׁפְחָה is generally translated as "slave," but seems to be distinct from the alternative term for "female slave or "maidservant," אָמָה, although the relationship between the two terms is "problematic" (Reuter 2006, 406). At times both terms are used for the same person. E. Reuter senses a distinction in the patriarchal narratives in the relationship between the שִׁפְחָה and the matriarch. But he also notes that a significant feature of the שִׁפְחָה was as a surrogate mother. For example, in Genesis 30:3–4, Rachel tells Jacob, "Here is my אָמָה, Bilhah, go in to her that she may bear on my knees. . . . So she gave him her שִׁפְחָה, as a wife" (Reuter 2006, 407–9). If Reuter's distinction is valid, then it would seem that the real issue is the relationship with the patriarch, that is, was the woman to serve as a concubine, especially to provide children? If so, that may explain the use of the concept of "acquired" (see the excursus, "Sex with a Betrothed Female Slave") rather than "betrothed." It still would leave a question regarding the issue of her being redeemed or given her freedom.

Because of her status, they are not put to death, but are punished. Further, the *man* must bring a reparation (or "guilt") offering to the Lord. For a deeper discussion of the details regarding the vagueness of the description and its use of rare words, see the excursus "Sex with a Betrothed Female Slave." The bottom line is that in the situation given here there would be punishment—which is not specified, but it would not be capital punishment for the pair, which would be the punishment if the act were adultery. The man who presumably seduced the woman would be required to bring a reparation offering, following the directions given in Leviticus 5–6. While reparations are not noted, Ross does suggest that reparations "appropriate to the loss of value would be incurred" (2002, 363).

Sex with a Betrothed Female Slave

The title of this excursus uses the terminology that most commentators use; however, there are a number of uncertainties. First, as discussed in the translation analysis, the woman is described as a slave, using the word שִׁפְחָה, which is the same word used for Hagar (Gen. 16:1), as well as Zilpah (Gen. 29:24) and Bilhah (Gen. 29:29). According to Austel (1980c, 947), while the OT uses the term "in the sense of 'female slave' generally, those who are mentioned individually in the Old Testament are personal maids-in-waiting to a married woman." *TWOT* states that the term is apparently "indistinguishable and in several passages interchangeable with *'āmâ* "translated as 'maid servant, female slave'" (Scott 1980e, 49). However, אָמָה seems to be the female equivalent of עֶבֶד, which is translated as "slave" or "servant" (Kaiser 1980h, 639–40). As suggested in the translation analysis, it would seem that the role of a שִׁפְחָה was that of a concubine or secondary wife, with a specific emphasis on providing a child.

TRANSLATION ANALYSIS: "SLAVE" (עֶבֶד)
As Sklar (2014, 307–8) points out, the use of the English word "slave" to translate עֶבֶד can be misleading since it describes both "morally illegitimate forms of servitude" as well as at least four forms of legitimate servitude including: God's servant, a king's servant, an indentured servant, and a permanent servant. The last two are the most misleading, since what we understand as slavery today (or in the Greco-Roman world), which views the person as legal property, was forbidden to the Israelites (see also Chirichigno 1993, 225; Harbin 2012, 54–57). See further appendix 4, "Slaves and Emancipation in Israel."

Second, most commentators view the woman as being betrothed, but that is not clear from the text. The word for betrothed is אָרַשׂ, which is used in Exodus 22:15 in the case of a betrothed woman who is seduced. The verb used here is חָרַף. BDB (s.v. "חָרַף" 357–58) gives four entries for the term with the following meanings: "I: a verb meaning 'reproach'; II: a noun denoting harvest-time; III: a denominative verb meaning 'remain in harvest-time'; and IV: a verb meaning 'to acquire.'" The last case occurs only once, in this passage, as a *niphal* participle. *DCH* (s.v. "חרף III" 3:320) gives a similar distribution, although for this case it suggests the meaning as "to designate."

As such, it would appear that the woman had been acquired or designated for another man (perhaps promised like Michal had been to David by Saul [2 Sam. 3:14]). In this case, it may be that because of her status as a שִׁפְחָה she or her master have not yet been given a betrothal gift, which would redeem her and that would make the betrothal official (while in David's case Michal was not a שִׁפְחָה, the betrothal did not become official until he produced the dowry [1 Sam. 18:25]; Sklar 2014, 248–49). Or, it may be that because of her designation as a שִׁפְחָה, the verb חָרַף merely indicates that the intention was that she should go with another man.

Third, a number of commentators assume that she was forced—that is, it is a case of rape (Gerstenberger 1996, 274). It is true that her lack of freedom might suggest that she had no say in the matter, but force is not necessarily a factor here. In fact, the statement that "*they* shall not die" might suggest mutual responsibility (Bailey 2005, 233, emphasis added).

Fourth, since it would seem that the woman acquiesced, whether or not seduction was involved, many commentators treat the issue as a case of adultery (Wenham 1979, 270). Since she was not betrothed, whatever the circumstances, she was not legally united with another man. Therefore, under Israelite law it would not be adultery and consequently a death penalty would not be in store. Rather, it would be a case of premarital sex, and the expectation would be that they would marry (Deut. 22:28–29). If so, that raises another problem, in that it would appear that the person who "acquired" her (i.e., arranged the relationship) would have made an oath to the Lord (e.g., Gen. 24:3, 9). Then, according to Sklar (2014, 249), if the man who actually slept with her did marry her, that would violate the oath of the "master," explaining the need for a reparation offering.

Finally, in the situation where there would be no death penalty, we are told that there would still be obligation or punishment (בִּקֹּרֶת), which is another term used only in this place. Elmer Martens (1980d, 125) defines it as "compensation," based on an Akkadian cognate. There are several different views taken of the word. Some tie the term to בָּקָר, which means "cattle" or "ox," and assume that what is involved is scourging. This seems to be a traditional rabbinic understanding (Noordtzij 1982, 201). More recent scholars see a variety of options, including indemnity to compensate the master who has promised the woman, but now found her value diminished (Mathews 2009, 171), or an inquest or inquiry into the situation (Milgrom 2000, 1671). Given the complexity of the situation, Gane (2004a, 339) amplifies Milgrom's suggestion and sees the בִּקֹּרֶת as an inquiry that would sort out the details of the woman's exact status, and who would receive compensation, which may be the best understanding.

In terms of context, we would suggest that this situation is placed here as another factor that could damage the social fabric of the nation. Since the sexual liaison is not with a relative, and the situation is that she is labeled a "female slave" (as noted in the excursus), the situation is not included with the material in Leviticus 18, which we suggested addresses extended families. Rather, as Gane (2004a, 339) suggests, this section combines themes of ethical holiness, concerns for the socially disadvantaged, and issues of sexual relationships that can affect the strength of the social structure.

19:23–25. Commentators have struggled to explain the rationale for this section. The directive itself states that this would be something that they would need to address only after they entered the land, and then only after they planted fruit trees. While seemingly straightforward in content, the question remains: Why include it here? Suggestions have included "a test of obedience" (Ross 2002, 363), or to "reinforce to the Israelites that the land is the Lord's and that he is giving it to them as a gift" (Rooker 2000, 260), or "The inclusion of a few agricultural laws is to communicate that every area of Israel's life is governed by the call to holy living" (Hartley 1992, 319). The dominant view is that it addresses an agricultural practice the Israelites were to follow once they settled in the land (Wenham 1979, 271). But that practice appeared to be one that was common to the ANE. For example, Hammurabi's Code directs a practice of not using the produce of a fruit tree until the fifth year (*ANET*, 169). If that was a common practice, and perhaps one that had been long employed by the Israelites, why include it here? The effort to explain this has produced some rather strained explanations. A common argument is that the fruit was not very good the first three years, and the fourth year was "the best" so should be given as a thanks offering (Ross 2002, 363). Others argue that it is just a

reworking of "older customs" to adopt to worship of God (Gerstenberger 1996, 275).

An alternative perspective proposed by several scholars is that the first three years are the first three years of settlement, which meant that Israelites would not eat of any of the trees that were already planted by the Canaanites. The fourth year would be a year of purging, and then after five years they would be able to eat the fruit (Rooker 2000, 260). This is problematic for two reasons. Most importantly, the text specifies that these would be trees that the Israelites planted (נָטַע) after they settled. Practically, that would have meant that although the manna had stopped, they would still not be able to use much of the produce of the land, which they were told to do (Josh. 10:12). While clearly this is an agricultural guideline, it would appear that the guideline is really just the background to clarify the real purpose—honoring God with firstfruits—as shown by a careful analysis of the terminology.

While modern translations have consistently translated the verse as saying that for the first three years the fruit is "forbidden," the KJV uses "uncircumcised," a literal translation of the Hebrew עָרֵל. Later rabbinic law took a literal view and understood the phrase to mean that the fruit for those first three years needed to be removed (i.e., treated like a foreskin) before it matured, so that the tree grew stronger (Levine 1989, 132). However, the concept of circumcision is often used metaphorically in the OT. For example, Deuteronomy 10:16 admonishes the Israelites to "circumcise your heart" (Rooker 2000, 260). While one might wonder what it meant for the fruit to be considered as "uncircumcised," the idea that it is viewed as unclean and thus not to be used would justify using the term "forbidden."

It would seem that the heart of this section really is 19:24. If the practice was to not harvest fruit during the first three years, then the designation that in the fourth year the fruit was to be considered "holy" and brought as "an offering of praise" to the Lord essentially designates the presentation of the fourth-year produce from a newly planted fruit tree as firstfruits (Keil and Delitzsch 1956, 602). In the context of the new legal paradigm with the apparent introduction of firstfruits, a natural question for Israelites under the new religious guidelines being given might be: When did one bring firstfruits for fruit trees if the tree produced fruit for several years before it was usable? In that case, the primary focus of the passage would be to designate the occasion of firstfruits for a product that took years to produce a viable product. While that question would likely not have been an item that by itself would rip the social fabric, it would be one over which there could be disagreement. As such, this clarification, while relatively minor, would serve to help promote social harmony.

Regarding location, Rooker (2000, 261) seems to suggest that this could be included with the next section, which addresses conduct in the land after they occupied it. However, that section seems to focus on issues of idolatry. In that case, could this particular practice reflect an idolatrous practice? Levine (1989, 132) hints that might be the case, as he evaluates the noun הִלּוּלִים, which many translations render as "offering of praise." He notes that the only other use of that term is with regard to the Shechem festival in Judges 9:27, where it "connotes a pagan rite."

Shechem Festival

The festival noted in Judges 9:27 is described as being done by the men of Shechem. Shechem was originally a Canaanite city where the sons of Jacob, Simeon and Levi, "killed every male" (Gen. 34:25). The location is mentioned later in Genesis as the place where Jacob collected the foreign gods within his household and buried them under an oak (or terebinth) tree (Gen. 35:4). It was also the location where Joseph was sent to check on his brothers (Gen. 37:12–14). There is no mention as to whether the city had been re-populated after the slaughter of Simeon and Levi, and if so, by whom. Joshua 24:32 notes that Joseph's bones were buried in Shechem. At the time of the settlement, one of the descendants of Manasseh was named Shechem, and Joshua 17:2–7 indicates that his descendants settled in a location called Shechem, presumably the same city (see also Josh. 21:21; 24:1, 25). In the time of the Judges, Gideon (also named Jerubbaal [Judg. 7:1]) had a concubine in Shechem who bore a son named Abimelech (Judg. 8:31). The focus of the story is that Abimelech moved to Shechem, "to his mother's relatives" (Judg. 9:1). While one may presume that the inhabitants of Shechem at this time were Israelite, there is a good chance that there had been intermarriage with Canaanites, so it is not clear whether Abimelech's relatives were Israelite or not. The key for present purposes is that at this point, the men of Shechem worshipped a pagan god, apparently Baal-berith (Judg. 9:4, 26–27).

TRANSLATION ANALYSIS: "OFFERING OF PRAISE"

The word הִלּוּלִים is derived from the root הָלַל, which means "to praise." Here the term is combined with two qualifiers: "holy" and "offering of praise." The term הִלּוּלִים is used only one other time in the OT, in Judges 9:27, where it is translated "festival" during the grape harvest, presumably to a pagan god (see sidebar "Shechem Festival"). Interestingly, here the KJV is perhaps the most literal translation: "the fruit thereof shall be holy; praise to the Lord withal." Most modern translations add the idea of "offering," which logically fits the idea of it being considered holy. While the Festival of Firstfruits seems to have specifically directly corresponded with the grain harvest (Exod. 34:22), the concept did carry over into other areas, as shown in Deuteronomy 18:4 and 2 Chronicles 31:5. The latter source clearly directs that firstfruits include "all the produce of the land."

However, Levine (1989, 132) suggests that since the basic meaning of the root *hillel* is

Preserving the Social Fabric (18:1–20:27)

"to praise," here the text "obviously enjoins the Israelites to rejoice before the Lord." Thus, while we have addressed this section separately in the exegesis, it is possible that it would fit within the context of the subsequent verses warning against idolatry, and for homiletical purposes there does not seem to be a need to produce a separate sermon.

19:26–32. The next section contains a number of issues that we have integrated as aspects of the issue of idolatry. Some are overtly so, but the others not as clearly so, especially from our modern cultural perspective. The unifying issue seems to be that the Israelites were to avoid different methods intended to control or even to know the future. This effort would primarily involve consulting spirits, a summary term that could include pagan gods, demons, or deceased ancestors, in other words, any being that is in the spiritual realm—behind the scenes.

Spiritual Realm

The Israelites lived in a world where there were a variety of spiritual beings (Kleinig 2003, 415). These would include gods, which would be localized divinities—that is, spiritual beings with certain powers but limited to specific locations, demons, and spirits of dead ancestors. The perspective of many groups was that after the ancestors died, their spirits remained in the area. Because of their greater age, and the fact that they were beyond the physical realm, it was felt they had a better perspective on issues and thus could be consulted for counsel.

Divination (נָחַשׁ) is premised on the idea that there is "an impersonal force, sometimes called necessity or fate, that determines the destiny of all things" (Hartley 1992, 320). Soothsaying (עָנַן) was another form of occultism, although the specific form is not clear (*TWOT* s.v. "עָנַן II" 2:685). Sometimes this would be done through personal acts; other times they would be done through intermediaries such as mediums or spiritists.

Mediums and Spiritists

The terms "mediums" (הָאֹבֹת) and "spiritists" (הַיִּדְּעֹנִים) reflect two ways that individuals in the ancient world sought counsel and advice; however, we don't really grasp the significance of what might be involved. As Gerstenberger (1996, 293) put it, the punishment does not seem to fit "what in our opinion is the relatively harmless act of seeking clarification from a soothsayer concerning one's future." Clearly in the minds of the ancient Israelites, the practice was thought to actually provide contact with nonphysical beings, and a biblical perspective would affirm that to be the case. However, from their perspective, those nonphysical beings might have been departed ancestors, gods, or familiar spirits, while from our perspective we might see them as demons. There is no consensus on the meaning of the term translated "mediums" (הָאֹבֹת). Milgrom concludes that the word אוֹב originally meant "spirit," but it could also be used to denote the one who conjured up the spirit, as is evident in 1 Samuel 28 (Milgrom (2000, 1969). The term יִדְּעֹנִי translated "spiritist" is derived from the root יָדַע, which means "to know." Because הָאֹבֹת is feminine, and הַיִּדְּעֹנִים is masculine, and the two always appear together, it would appear that they represent the different genders of the individuals who provide the service (like witch and wizard in English).

The first warning is normally understood as forbidding the eating of meat with the blood in it, which sounds very much like the prohibitions in Leviticus 17. This translation raises questions regarding repeating that command here. However, the use of the preposition עַל, which means "above" (Carr 1980b, 666) suggests a different practice, as does the combination with the prohibition against divination and soothsaying. Lange (1960, 151) cites Maimonides, who referred to "a heathen custom of eating flesh over the blood of the animal from which it was taken as a means of communion with demons who were supposed to feast upon the blood itself." Structurally, 19:26 consists of two staccato-like

Preserving the Social Fabric (18:1–20:27)

declarations, and as such may be understood as, "Don't eat above the blood; that is, don't practice divination or soothsaying."

The cutting of one's body is shown elsewhere to be associated with pagan worship (1 Kings 18:28), suggesting illicit spiritual rituals (see Isa. 15:2). Likewise, cutting off locks of hair could carry occult connotations. Noortzij (1982, 204) notes that "offerings of hair were presented both in the Astarte-Tammuz religion of Syria and among various Arabian tribes." Likewise, Bailey (2005, 234) mentions an Egyptian practice involving hair in the worship of Osiris, as well as references in Homer (*Odyssey* 4.197) and Herodotus (*Histories* 9.24). The phrase וּכְתֹבֶת קַעֲקַע, which is translated "tattoo marks," appears only here and is debated. It may have had connection with mourning or with religious worship, for which reason it was prohibited (Sklar 2014, 250).

Scholars also debate whether 19:29 refers to cultic prostitution (Wenham 1989, 272) or a more general practice (Harrison 1980, 204). Some who take the broader view argue that there is no written reference to religious prostitution in the ANE law codes. Hess (2008, 756) points out that does not demonstrate that it did not exist. Moreover, Yamauchi (1973, 213–22) shows a number of references that do point to its existence, although after significant evaluation of ANE data Budin (2008, 47) flatly concludes, "There were no sacred prostitutes in the Ancient Near East." Still, while general prostitution might be a result of poverty (or greed), cultic prostitution might reflect a false sense of piety, an aspect of idolatry. In either case, the prohibition here points out two areas where the practice was harmful: to the woman (who would be degraded, the same word as seen in 19:8 where it is translated "profaned"), and to the land.

In contrast to actions that profane, in the middle of this section is a warning to show reverence both for the Sabbath and for God's sanctuary. Hartley (1992, 321) suggests that this positive reverence would help guard against importing pagan culture into the temple and sees a connection with Ezekiel 8. This is reinforced with the warning against consulting "mediums or spiritists," which brings us back to the warning in 19:26 against divination and soothsaying. Here the warning is against mediums (אֹבֹת [Alden 1980b]) and spiritists or familiar spirits (יִדְּעֹנִים [Lewis 1980c, 367]). Based on the gender of the two words, the former were likely women and the latter men, which may explain why the two terms often appear together (Alden 1980b). Characterized as necromancy, these would have represented attempts to gain contact with the spirits of the deceased to gain knowledge. Understood as warnings to avoid inappropriate efforts to access spiritual beings, this verse then seems to flow naturally into the next verse with its admonition to honor the aged (19:32). In essence, it would have been recognition that living elders were better sources for wisdom than efforts to contact dead ancestors (Kleinig 2003, 416). Because of their knowledge and wisdom, Israelites should show deference or respect to them, and one way of doing that was to stand in their presence.

Deference

While it is suggested that the way the idea of showing deference to the aged is used here likely reflected looking to them for wisdom instead of to other sources such as mediums or spiritists, the idea of deference to the aged in general was a significant aspect of the Israelite culture. For example, Job 12:12 states, "With the aged is wisdom, and many days, understanding." Bailey (2005, 239) observes three assumptions that Israel made with regard to the aged: (1) "The longer one lives, the more opportunity there is to understand the workings of the world"; (2) older people "would know the sacred traditions and rites of the community"; and (3) "long life may be considered a sign of divine blessing." He then observes that "There were a number of instances in the history of Israel where the advice of the young led to catastrophe." Levine (1989, 134) adds a practical sense by observing that later rabbinic law expanded the idea of deference of the elderly as including caring for them.

Given these various admonitions, this section would warn that properly seeking wisdom required not going to other spiritual beings that would create cultural division through spiritual division, as different individuals ended up serving different gods. While different allegiances were bad enough, it would be compounded by the actions of deceiving spirits (1 Kings 22:21). Rather, the nation needed to collectively serve and honor the God who had called them—a reminder repeated four times in this section alone.

19:33–36. One of the difficult aspects of the Torah from our perspective is that it was primarily written to a largely monoethnic people group who were in the process of becoming a monocultic nation, while incorporating outliers.

Monoethnic Israel

The typical description of the nation of Israel is that it consisted of twelve tribes who were descended from the twelve sons of Jacob who was renamed Israel. Examination shows a somewhat more nuanced picture. While Jacob, as well as his father Isaac, married relatives of their ancestor Abraham (although the mothers of four of Jacob's sons were not from that family), the same cannot be said of Jacob's sons. It would appear that the wives of the twelve sons were from the various tribes that had settled in the land before Abraham arrived there from Haran. Judah's wife was Canaanite (Gen. 38:2), although after she died he inadvertently fathered two sons with Tamar, the widow of his sons Er and Onan. Tamar's ethnic background is not mentioned. Joseph's wife was Egyptian (Gen. 41:45). The ethnic identity of the other sons' wives is unknown, but like Judah they likely married woman from local tribes. Centuries later, when the Israelites left Egypt, it was

described as a mixed group (Exod. 12:35). From Leviticus 24, we know that it included Egyptians, but it likely included other individuals, some of whom may also have been enslaved by the Egyptians. Still, in terms of family identity that was established through the father's line, the vast majority (both male and female) of the embryo nation at Sinai were physical descendants of Jacob. It would appear that after Sinai, the outliers from other ethnic backgrounds who joined the Israelites were essentially absorbed. Given that background, worship prior to Sinai likely included a number of permutations and variations even among the physical descendants of Jacob, who may have attempted to adhere to the worship of their ancestors. Exodus and Leviticus present God at Sinai unifying these diverse elements into a new nation and formal religion through the revelations he provided over that year.

While some of the individuals had different ancestors, in terms of identity, they seem to be included with the Israelites. One example seems to have been Caleb, who appears to have had Kenizzite ancestry but is listed as part of the tribe of Judah (Josh. 14:6).

Caleb the Kenizzite

Joshua makes a special reference to Caleb as the son of Jephunneh the Kenizzite. This would suggest that his father was the actual Kenizzite, although his mother's ethnic identity is unknown. According to Genesis 15:19, the Kenizzites were a Canaanite tribe that occupied the land that God promised to Abraham. After Israel left Sinai, Caleb represented the tribe of Judah as part of the advance reconnaissance party that searched out the land (Num. 13:6), and received special honor for his faith in YHWH so that he was one of the two of that generation that entered the land forty years later, and was given a special inheritance in the land (Josh. 14–15).

So, while predominantly descendants of Jacob, the population at Sinai had somewhat mixed ethnic backgrounds. To this mixed group, God provided a new socioeconomic-judicial-political-religious system that would incorporate everyone present, regardless of their ancestry (Harbin 2005, 144–46). When this system was presented to those present at Sinai as God's covenant, they *all* opted in, speaking not only for themselves but for future generations (Exod. 24:3, 7). The glue intended to hold them together was the worship of one God through a new religious system that would incorporate a variety of practices ("statutes and ordinances") intended to make them unique. After they settled in Canaan, given its description as a land flowing with milk and honey and the promises that God was giving the people, it would not be surprising that outsiders would be attracted. A critical question would be, how were the Israelites supposed to handle these newcomers? Or, to put it another way, how would these "strangers" (NASB) affect the social fabric? This is the question at hand.

Most translations use either "stranger" or "foreigner" in Leviticus 19:33 for the Hebrew word גֵּר. In our translation analysis for Leviticus 19:10 we preferred "resident aliens" because of the focus on the nation after it settled. As such, the multiple uses of the term גֵּר in Leviticus that focus on the postsettlement situation must reflect non-Israelites who might come to Israel at some point in the future intending to settle. Here we see another aspect as God directs the Israelites on how *they* are to treat those same resident aliens. The Israelites are told that they must not do any wrong to them but "love them as yourself." This admonition produces challenges that are difficult to sort out.

Most of the discussion regarding resident aliens is within a context of specific guidelines that applied also to the native "Israelites." Leviticus 19:34 states that the resident alien was to be "as the native among you." Practically this would indicate an expectation that the resident alien would adapt to the Israelite culture. As we work through the last part of Leviticus, we will note areas where the resident aliens were differentiated in a variety of ways. However, largely, if they settled in Israel there would be many things of their own cultures that they would no longer be allowed to practice, especially certain religious practices, as noted in the passages cited above. Further, Leviticus 18:3 directs the Israelites at Sinai not to live like the Egyptians and the Canaanites.

A more difficult issue would be the question of the "aliens" who were currently living in the land, given that they were to be "under the ban" (חֵרֶם).

> ### *Herem* חֵרֶם
> While not used in this text, the Hebrew word חֵרֶם is germane because it applied to most of the tribes who were currently in the land. The term, however, is difficult to translate because the concept is complex. For that reason, we will use the term *herem* rather than any translation in this study. The NASB translation of *herem* as "under the ban" is one of the better translations, since it leaves open what is actually done. Because that could range from "to devote" to "to destroy utterly," with a variety of variants in between (Wood 1980c), it is possible that we are really looking at two roots that are homonyms (Lohfink 1986, 188–89). For further details see appendix 3, "*Herem*."

Levine (1989, 134) differentiates between the people who were currently living in the land and the future "resident aliens." He argues that the term גֵּר "never refers to the prior inhabitants of the land; those are identified by ethnological groupings, such as Canaanites and Amorites, or by other specific terms of reference." In other words, based on the terminology, the term "resident aliens" could never be applied to the current inhabitants of the land because prior to the conquest and settlement, the non-Israelites would not have been aliens living in Israel's land. Rather, at the time they were the inhabitants and the "dominant culture." However, even after the settlement, the situation is not as clear as one might expect. For example, Solomon is cited as forcing the remaining Amorites, Hittites, Perizzites, Hivites, and Jebusites (specific terms of reference) into forced labor (1 Kings 9:20–21), while Chronicles seems to use the term "resident aliens" (גֵּרִים) for them collectively (2 Chron. 2:16–18 [HB 15–17]). Thus, it really is an open question as to whether a Gibeonite who remained in the land after the conquest and who was submitted to forced labor by Joshua should be considered a resident alien. If not, then what term should be used?

> ### Gibeonites
> The question of the status of the Gibeonites seems very relevant, since the forced labor that Joshua submitted them to was to hew wood and draw water for "the altar of the Lord" (Josh. 9:27). It is then interesting that when Solomon became king, he went to Gibeon where there was a high place and at that time the location of the Tent of Meeting (2 Chron. 1:3).

In any regard, once the nation was settled in the land, this section was to apply. The key to the application of this section is that the Israelites were not to "do wrong" to any resident alien. Leviticus 19:34 amplifies this by saying that they were to be treated like the Israelites. In terms of evaluation, one must keep in mind that these guidelines would be applied locally. If our understanding is correct, there would have been enclaves—cities or towns or even small regions—that were predominantly non-Israelite ethnically (such as Jerusalem). However, in many cases the aliens would likely have been small groups or families, or individuals who settled in Israelite towns, which seems to be the primary focus of this command. While we will address these dispersed small groups later in Leviticus 25–27, as an alien minority in a foreign population they would be more likely to have been ignorant of Israelite customs, standards, and even prices (Hartley 1992, 322). Further, living in a small town, it would have been difficult for them

to break into the social network that the natives had intuitively formulated from birth. Levine (1989, 134) suggests that the phrase "not do him wrong" (לֹא תוֹנוּ אֹתוֹ) usually suggests economic exploitation. In that light it seems likely that the next two verses that address just measurements should be included with the present two verses highlighting that a basic measure of social justice would be economic justice—specifically, not taking advantage of the vulnerable. The admonition is that their measurements were to be just, or literally, righteous (צֶדֶק). It is in this light that twice in this section God reminds the nation that they had been oppressed in Egypt, and their response to that should be that they not oppress others in a similar plight.

> ### Just Measurements
> The measurements given here are samples of various measurements used in commerce. Our understanding of these is uncertain, although archaeologists have found weights with the amounts inscribed on them. As noted before, smaller weights were used on a balance scale (see the shekel excursus in the unit "Purifying Oneself Before a Holy God" [4:1–6:7 (HB 5:26)]). A dishonest merchant might have two sets of weights (forbidden in Deut. 19:36) that he could manipulate to increase the amount of silver or goods he was getting but decrease the amount of silver or goods he would be giving. Larger items were sold in terms of capacity, much as today we use pints, gallons, or bushels. Standards varied from country to country in the ANE (much like the difference between an Imperial gallon and a US gallon). The OT indicates that there might also be two standards at once in the same culture (such as a common and royal shekel). As F. B. Huey (1975, 922) expresses it, "there were no weights or measure sufficiently fixed in Biblical times to enable one to determine the exact metrical equivalents."

19:37. This last verse seems to tie Leviticus 18–19 together as a unit, serving as a counterpoint to the initial directive that the Israelites were not to do like they had seen done in Egypt and like they were going to see in Canaan, but rather do what has just been revealed, that is, to follow "all my statutes and all my ordinances." The phrase "observe . . . and do" would seem to be a hendiadys indicating not two acts, but as Levine (1989, 135) translates it, "take care to perform." This verse then serves as a transition to the next portion of this unit, which addresses what to do when someone violates any of the statutes or ordinances and threatens the social fabric of the community and thus the nation.

The Lord Provides Patches for Tears in the Social Fabric Produced by Specific Violations of the Covenant (20:1–27)

Like the two previous chapters, Leviticus 20 is a single speech that was likely given on the same occasion as the two previous chapters. The close relationship of 18 and 20 showing prohibitions and consequences suggest that they serve as an *inclusio* tying the three speeches together. In essence, Leviticus 20 provides three principles that address how the nation should respond to violations of the various directives in the other two chapters: sin is a serious matter, sin within God's covenant community must be addressed by the community, and those who persist in sin will experience God's judgment (Sklar 2014, 261). Because this final portion of the unit addresses family relations from the perspective of the judicial leaders, in essence it provides guidelines for patching various tears in the overall social fabric, especially the most serious tears for which the only solution is excision (Balentine 2002, 157). While Leviticus 20 addresses many of the same issues as 18 and 19, the order differs. Because the focus is on penalties, it would appear that in general the penalties are arranged by severity, from death to being "cut off" (i.e., to have one's genealogy come to an end), with the most severe being the most immediate (Sklar 2014,

254). This would suggest that while Leviticus 18–19 works outward from the head of the father's house to the entire culture, Leviticus 20 works down from the most serious issue from God's perspective, issues of idolatry. However, since the chapter's conclusion provides an *inclusio*, it emphasizes that "the primary concern was with the pagan religious practices that opened the door to all kinds of violations of God's order" (Ross 2002, 371).

20:1–2a. Once more the text begins with the *waw*, showing a continued sequence. Because the section seems to follow Leviticus 19, directly making 18–20 a unit, the *waw* is best translated as "then." The inclusion of the word "also" serves as a stylistic addition emphasizing the unity.

20:2b–6. The first issue addressed returns to the offering of offspring to Molech introduced in 18:21. To address the deeper spiritual issues that underlie idolatry, this section expands the earlier one-sentence prohibition with a stronger warning and directions on how it should be addressed.

First, the directive applied to anyone who lived in the land, whether they were from the "sons of Israel" or resident aliens. Coming immediately on the heels of the admonition to love the resident alien dwelling in the land, the text pointedly shows that hospitality for different cultures had limits. The most significant limit would be religious practices that violated God's position as the sovereign owner of the land and his covenant with the nation of Israel.

Second, in this case, the punishment was death by stoning because of the grave cultural consequences if left unaddressed. As Milgrom (2000, 1729) notes, the person who committed this act was guilty of two capital crimes: idolatry and murder. He does not mention that because of the covenant relationship with God as their suzerain, for an Israelite idolatry would effectively be treason, which is an extremely damaging tear in any social fabric.

Stoning

The standard method of execution in the OT was stoning. The reason stoning is mandated is never specifically given. James Moyer (1975) suggests that it was because of the abundance of stones in Palestine. However, Moses notes the possibility of Egyptians stoning them prior to the exodus (Exod. 8:26), which indicates that stoning had a broader cultural background. Moyer's further comment that it was "a convenient way to express anger or hatred" is perhaps more relevant in that respect. Radner further proposes that by crushing, stoning "represents a kind of *interior* disintegration of the created life, one that mirrors the effects of the sin itself in dismantling what God has put together" (2008, 220, emphasis original). Milgrom (2000, 1733) notes that the rabbinic tradition (apparently after the NT period), required that the criminal be thrown on stones and the public excluded, which would be a change from the earlier practice of casting stones (see John 8:7), with the public not only present but participating (as suggested here and made clearer in Leviticus 24:14, 16 where the congregation was directed to stone the blasphemer, and 24:23 where they did so). A common suggestion that stoning is a communal form of execution that required the entire community to participate, which also showed a larger scope in terms of the effects of the crime, seems to be the most pertinent explanation (Kleinig 2003, 424; Radner 2008, 220–21).

Third, the significance of this violation is such that God uses the first person to show that he would be personally involved—not just casually, but strongly in two different ways. He would set his face against the guilty individual.

TRANSLATION ANALYSIS: "I WILL SET MY FACE"

The sentence אֶתֵּן אֶת־פָּנַי בָּאִישׁ is one of two idioms that are deemed synonymous. Each consists of two parts. The first part in this instance is the declaration "I will give my face" (literal translation), which is a neutral phrase denoting giving attention. Its synonymous counterpart, וְשַׂמְתִּי אֲנִי אֶת־פָּנַי בָּאִישׁ, which is at the beginning of 20:5 in this section and literally means "I will set my face," is used more frequently. Because they seem synonymous, this is the usual translation. In both cases, the introductory phrase is followed by the term "man" or "person" with a preposition. When the preposition is בְּ, as in both of these cases, the concept is adversarial or "menacing" (Milgrom 2000, 1471).

In essence, he would look upon the matter with disfavor. According to Milgrom (2000, 1733), the rabbis understood this phrase as indicating "I will turn [*pôneh*] from all my other affairs and occupy myself (solely) with him." However, more significantly, God says he would "cut him off from among his people." As noted in the unit "The Role of the Priests" (6:8 [HB 6:1]–7:38), this seems to indicate death followed by separation from one's ancestors after death. Looking at the entire section, the community was directed to execute the individual. If they did not, then God would take the action (20:5). In either case, the cutting off follows the death.

The significance of the violation is highlighted even further when God warns the nation that if the community did not take action, he would, and this would involve not only the man but his family. The reason is that this sacrifice defiled the sanctuary and God's holy name.

This admonition would be most relevant in the culture of ancient Israel where most people lived in small communities and generally knew what was going on among their relatives and neighbors. We have learned that it is hard to keep a secret in a small town, and to not follow through to correct a clear wrong is tantamount to being an accessory to, or at least after, the fact.

While giving one's offspring to Molech may have been the most overt form of idolatry, consulting "mediums" (הָאֹבֹת) and "spiritists" (הַיִּדְּעֹנִים) warranted the same punishment. Both were considered "playing the harlot" or "spiritual prostitution" (זָנָה). However, consulting a medium or spiritist would be a more covert act, since it did not involve a sacrifice to an idol; and as in the case of Saul, who consulted a medium in 1 Samuel 28:7, it could be done secretly at night. Even so, it is interesting that while the woman Saul consulted was apparently not practicing because Saul had prohibited it, Saul's advisors knew who she was and where she could be found.

The key point here is that the consultation was forbidden not only because it was viewed as a form of idolatry and thus a form of spiritual prostitution, but it was looking to lies and liars to find spiritual truth. As a result, the action is viewed as being as bad as offering one's child to Molech, and the consequences are the same.

20:7–8. The function of these two verses is debated. Do they serve as a counterpoint to the preceding verses, or do they set up the subsequent material? Apparently, they do both, since they serve as a positive counter to both sections, stressing a continuing theme of how an Israelite was to live. One reminder that emerges from these verses is that it is not the washing of clothes or the body that sanctifies a person, but the Lord, and because of that the Israelites were expected to keep his statutes and practice them (see comment on Lev. 19:37). The shift to the second-person plural for these two verses emphasizes the corporate aspect of the admonition, highlighting the point noted in the introduction that holiness is primarily a corporate concept demonstrated by proper relationships. This type of pure unity can be built only on worship of the one true God.

20:9–21. This section is difficult. In terms of content, 20:9 seems totally out of place, and even taken by itself the admonition it contains is difficult. However, there are several grammatical factors that suggest this entire section addresses a single underlying concept, which led to our discussing this as a single unit. First, the text shifts back to the third-person singular to address the actions of an individual, before returning to the second-person plural in 20:22. Second, while English translations generally introduce each verse with the word "if," the Hebrew uses two different words. Leviticus 20:9 begins with the particle *ki* (כִּי), meaning "if" or "when." The rest of the verses of this section begin with the versatile *waw*. At first glance this might suggest separate issues. However, while the *waw* may be translated as "if," it would seem that in this context a better translation might be "and if," showing a sequence of actions that exemplify the common underlying problem introduced by the original *ki*. If that is the case, then what would be the common problem? We have suggested that the entire unit (Lev. 18–20) focuses on relationship tears that damage the social fabric of interrelated extended families. The first part of this chapter addressed spiritual tears. While this part of the chapter seems to address two social tears, the parent-child relationship and the marriage relationship as defined by sexual relations (as noted in Lev. 18), it seems to suggest that the second is a product of the first.

Using that as a general framework, we would note the following. If the stress of the entire unit is on relationships that form the social fabric, it is fitting that it begins with the parent-child relationship. In terms of society, this relationship is foundational for passing cultural values on to the next generation. However, in this context, that next generation person is not a child but a grown adult. He is initially addressed as "a man, a man" (אִישׁ אִישׁ), an identification we noted earlier in Leviticus 18:6 where the term introduced the section on illicit sexual (or marital) relationships. So, the initial condition is that a man grows up and then rejects the God-given culture of the nation of Israel and defies the values his parents tried to inculcate.

Most translations translate the verb as he "curses" (קָלַל) his parent, but it seems more complicated than that. The word basically means "to be little or slight" (Coppes 1980i, 800). This may reflect a verbalized curse, and in that context

Bailey (2005, 243) suggests that the issue is "adult children who show utter contempt for their parents and wish them serious harm by means of formal oaths taken in the name of the gods." On one hand, this meshes this issue with the preceding section regarding idolatry. However, since קָלַל is an antonym of "to honor," it seems that here it denotes doing the exact opposite of the fifth commandment, which can reflect actions as well as words. In this context it seems to reflect an adult who by action flaunts the cultural values and morals that his parents had exhibited and taught (which presumes that the values they presented were the values of both God and Israel). As such, the remainder of this section delineates community responses that Israel was to give to specific illicit sexual relations that would rip the social fabric. The sexual relationships addressed are the sexual relationships that Leviticus 18 forbids. Although essentially the same, the two lists are not identical (see the section on "Biblical Family Ties" in the introduction). While Leviticus 18 listed the invalid sexual relationships, here the penalties are prescribed. In most cases, given the impact that specific violations would produce on the welfare of the entire community, the death penalty is directed.

The last part of the list (20:17–21) gives several exceptions to the death penalty. First the phrase "cut off from among their people" as used here seems to carry a different connotation than we saw in the section "The Lord Gives Directions to the Priests for Shalom Offerings" (7:11–36) and earlier in this unit, where we concluded that it denoted a punishment following death after execution. In this case there is no specific declaration that the guilty must be put to death—the phrase is used by itself (although some commentators seem to take the view that capital punishment applies in all the cases in this section). While this may indicate that the punishment is actually banishment (Ross 2002, 375), it may also be a threat involving the afterlife following a death not by execution. Although from an eternal perspective this would seem to be essentially the same as noted earlier, it does omit the ignominy of public execution. The second phrase is "bear his guilt" (עֲוֹנוֹ יִשָּׂא). This phrase essentially means that the person involved (either one or both partners) is responsible for the consequences of the actions (Sklar 2014, 258). A final term that needs to be noted is the word that the NASB translates as "disgrace" in 20:17.

TRANSLATION ANALYSIS: חֶסֶד

The Hebrew noun חֶסֶד is a word that normally is understood to mean "kindness, loving-kindness, mercy" or something similar (Harris 1980c), which would be totally out of place in this context. Zobel (1986, 45) asserts that its etymology is unknown. Alternatively, *TWOT* (s.v. "חָסַד II" 1:307) proposes a second assumed root of חסד, which it defines as "be reproached, ashamed." This verb is found only in Proverbs 25:10 where it appears in the *piel* stem. The derived noun חֶסֶד is found here and Proverbs 14:34. Earlier we noted how the noun חַטָּאת appears to be derived from the *piel* stem of the verb חָטָא, which would seem to give it a "privative connotation" (i.e., the removal of some quality or attribute [GKC §52h]). It then seems possible that ancient Hebrew might have a verb חָסַד describing showing kindness as an action, which in the *piel* stem (and thus its derived noun form) indicated the opposite. In any case the consensus is that the context here demands a concept of shame, reproach, or disgrace.

It describes a specific sexual relationship of brother and sister, which appears to encompass both half-sisters (daughter of the father or mother) and full sisters (daughter of both; Lange 1960, 156). In this case, the idea of disgrace is descriptive of the reason that the two would be cut off, although the text places the guilt on the man. The third exception is the phrase "they will die childless." Since this pertains to a man who has sexual relation with an uncle's wife or his brother's wife, it seems to overlap levirate marriages.

Preserving the Social Fabric (18:1–20:27)

One view is that since the man married his brother's widow to provide seed, the offspring was not credited to the actual father but to the deceased brother. However, this would assume that a second born son was also accorded to the deceased, but that seems unlikely. Moreover, in the case of Boaz, Ruth 4:21 ascribes Obed as a son to Boaz rather than the deceased Mahlon. It is more likely that this reflects situations where the brother is still alive, which would not apply in the case of levirate marriage.

20:22–27. Kiuchi (2007, 378) fittingly describes the last section of this chapter as "a concluding statement regarding not just chs. 18–20, but chs. 11–20." These chapters all contain material that God had given through Moses in the days following the Nadab and Abihu disaster on the day of the tabernacle dedication, which would still have been fresh on the people's minds. It contains a promise—that the land was going to vomit the Canaanites out because of their abominations and Israel would be able to settle there. But it also contains a warning. To ensure that the land would not vomit the Israelites out the same way, they were to "keep" all of the "statutes" and "judgments" that God had just given (these are the same terms used in 18:5; see the translation analysis there). While these concepts have been addressed in our earlier studies of Leviticus 11–20, there are several items in this section that merit mention.

> *TRANSLATION ANALYSIS: "KEEP"*
> While often translated "keep," the verb שָׁמַר seems to carry a much stronger connotation. *TWOT* (s.v. "שָׁמַר I" 2:939) defines the term as "keep, guard, observe, give heed." They continue with the observation that the "basic idea of the root is 'to exercise great care over,'" which would suggest that "guard" or any translation that exhorted due diligence might be better.

The term that is translated "statutes" (חֹק) is the same term translated as "customs" when used in regard to the pagan practices of the Canaanites in 20:23. While the two contexts would seem to carry the same weight in terms of culture, in terms of validity the source of the statutes is what mattered. So a critical question is, what was the source of the statutes? Was it social custom developed over the years? Or perhaps they reflected traditions associated with the pagan gods—if so, how were those traditions substantiated? Or was it a Creator God who had demonstrated his authority by bringing the nation out of Egypt and who had burned the offerings with fire? Based on that authority demonstrated mightily a year earlier in all of the signs associated with the exodus, God reminds the Israelites that the customs of the people who currently occupied the land into which they were going, like poison, were destructive and needed to be avoided, regardless of how attractive they appeared. God, the owner of the land, "abhorred" (קוּץ) them. This verb "denotes the deep emotional reaction of the subject issuing in a desired repulsion (or destruction) of the object" (Coppes 1980h, 794), makes the description that land was "vomiting" the people out rather apropos.

Who Brought You Out of Egypt

Approximately a year earlier as the nation first stood at the foot of Sinai just a month after leaving Egypt, they heard God declare, "I am the Lord [YHWH] your God, who brought you out of the land of Egypt" (Exod. 20:2) the first time. This was followed immediately by the Decalogue, a series of ten apodictic declarations outlining the covenant that God was making with the newly established nation of Israel, suggesting a cause-and-effect relationship: "Because I brought you out, therefore you will have no other gods before me." A similar phrase is repeated some 138 times throughout the OT indicating that God was insisting that his authority was not only because he was their creator, but especially because he had delivered them.

But the land itself is described as "flowing with milk and honey." Hebrew has two words translated "land": אֲדָמָה translated as "ground or land" (Coppes 1980a), and אֶרֶץ translated as "earth or land" (Hamilton 1980a). In Leviticus, this is the only place where אֲדָמָה is used as opposed to sixty-five occasions for אֶרֶץ. While at times they have subtle distinctions, here they seem to be used interchangeably.

TRANSLATION ANALYSIS: "LAND"

Coppes (1980a, 10) suggests that the word אֲדָמָה "originally signified the red arable soil" and later came to refer to "any cultivated, plantable ground." In contrast Hamilton designates אֶרֶץ as "the earth" in a cosmological sense, or "'the land' in the sense of a specific territorial designation" (1980a, 74). However, in 20:24 modern translations consistently translate both Hebrew words as *land*, apparently with opposite connotations. The first English word "land," which refers to the territorial designation of Canaan, translates אֲדָמָה, while the second English word "land," which addresses the fertility of the ground, translates אֶרֶץ. This would suggest that the two Hebrew words are actually interchangeable.

The concept of "milk and honey" is a common phrase that essentially "describes Canaan as having agricultural and pastoral abundance" (Hess 2008, 764). It is interesting to note that later, as the Israelites suffer the consequences for their lack of trust after the spies had returned and reported that the land "certainly does flow with milk and honey" (Num. 13:27), they grouse about leaving Egypt, which they also describe with the same phrase (Num. 16:14).

A significant term in this section is the word translated "separate" (ESV, NASB, NRSV) or "set apart" (HCSB, NIV) in 20:24 (בָּדַל).

TRANSLATION ANALYSIS: "SEPARATE"

The verb בָּדַל, which means "to make a difference, divide, separate, sever" (McComiskey 1980b, 91) is used four times in 20:24–26. The NASB translates it as "separate" in 20:24 and 25. It is also translated "make a distinction" in 20:25, and "set apart" in 20:26. What is important is that it is God who separates. As far as the nation of Israel was concerned, they were not holy because they were set apart, but because they were set apart, they were to become or be holy.

The Israelites were told that they would be given the land because God had separated them from "the peoples." The plural used here would reflect both the people of Egypt and the people groups of Canaan. However, recognizing the wordplay of the Hebrew word "separate" (בָּדַל), which the NASB translates three different ways in 20:24–26, helps in understanding the structure. First, the people have been "separated" physically from the Egyptians. That is the history. Because of that "separation," the Israelites were in turn to make a "separation" between clean and unclean animals (Lev. 11–15), a personal present outcome that would affect both individual and communal lives. The reason they are to make that separation is because God "caused it [the unclean animals] to be 'separate' for you as uncleanness" (literal translation). Again, because of God's "separating" them "from the peoples" to belong to him, they were then to be or become holy (i.e., to have moral communal relationships, a future consequence) because that is God's character (see the discussion "Holy" in introduction). In other words, Israel was to realize and remember that their separation from the rest of the peoples was arbitrary on God's part, similar to the way that the designating of animals as clean or unclean was arbitrary (Lange 1960, 157).

The last verse in the chapter and in the unit seems to be a non sequitur, and many commentators treat it as an add-on or misplacement (Milgrom 2000, 1864–65). Rather, it would seem to be set here purposefully to address a critical point. While 20:6 gave the corporate response to the mediums and spiritists, it did not address how the nation was supposed to respond to the mediums and spiritists themselves. We have addressed aspects of the issue twice. In 19:31, the nation was warned not to consult them. In 20:2, the nation was warned that if they consult them, they would be cut off. Now, however, the question was what the nation should do with the mediums and spiritists themselves, and the answer was: they were to be stoned. As noted above, this is a spiritual issue and the mediums and spiritists might be considered analogically the beginning of an infection, which needs to be eradicated. Since this is more of a prophylactic response, it is set at the end of the section as a point of emphasis.

THEOLOGICAL FOCUS

The theological focus is clearly set forth in a phrase that is repeated eighteen times in the three chapters: a variation of the statement "I am the Lord [YHWH] your God." Because of who God is and what he has done, the people who are in a relationship to him have obligations. Because of the variety of issues addressed, this is most evident in Leviticus 19, where that phrase appears eleven times. This idea is reflected both directly and indirectly in the teaching of the NT. Indirectly, the interdependence of holiness and love exhibited in this chapter is evident in the NT, particularly in 1 Peter (Rooker 2000, 264). Since these issues affect God's created order, they are then relevant to any culture (Ross 2002, 369).

"I am the Lord your God!" Divine decree rather than inner desire will rule the lives (and the relationships) of God's people. Using others (spouses, neighbors, children, even animals, plants, and lands) for one's own purposes will lead to injury of oneself and others. God's decrees establish boundaries to prevent destructive depravities, perversions, and abominations that will damage persons, relationships, community, and all creation. Purposeful disobedience is a slow-working, deadly acid that can diffuse through the population, eating away at the threads that hold society together. The community is directed to "excise or expel" what has become hopelessly toxic before it is able to spread. God's people are not only to control their own house (Josh. 24:15). They are commanded to publicly correct and at times "cut off" all who rebel decisively against God's creation order.

PREACHING AND TEACHING STRATEGIES

Exegetical and Theological Synthesis

"You shall love your neighbor as yourself" (Lev. 19:18). "The one who loves another has fulfilled the law" (Rom. 13:8). These are verses we love to quote. These are verses we struggle to define. This may be because we seldom return to Leviticus to unpack how God defines love. By adding "I am the Lord [YHWH] your God," God makes clear that following his decrees and directives is how we will best love others. This flies in the face of our hands-off approach to loving others, characterized as granting everyone the freedom to discover what may be best for them. Is love "unconditional affirmation" of our bent toward self, or is love "intentional intervention" to bend one another back toward God?

This section directly addresses much of the relational pain endemic in our world today. Whether you choose to divide this section into three to five units or preach the principle as a single unit will depend upon your congregation and comfort with the challenging material. Either way, it will require discipline to keep the focus on the theme and minimize deciphering the minutiae. These chapters repeatedly challenge how we establish relational and sexual ethics by serving up countless examples of how humbly submitting to God's inscribed directives turns us from objectifying others for our profit and pleasure to intentionally loving others to create a holy, healthy community.

God defines loving our neighbor as living in community for our neighbor rather than for selfish profit and pleasure. This means reflecting God's sacrificial goodness in all our relationships. We are not to objectify others sexually, exclude them socially, take what is theirs, or endure others who regularly do so. Rather we are to value neighbors, honor strangers, and pursue living in holiness among all who are created in God's image! Simply said, God is crying out, "Be like me! Reflect me in the way you steward the blessings of intellect, power, justice, reason, and prosperity that I provide to you. Manifest my generosity (not the greed of the Evil One) by openly displaying impartiality, not prejudice. Allow others to glean your fields. Practice hospitality before strangers. I am the Lord your God! Be holy as I am holy. Reflect me in all that you do!"

Along with the do's come a few don'ts. God directs his people to find contentment in what he provides, rather than be lured beyond creation's boundaries by promises that the forbidden will deliver superior happiness. As they separated from unclean animals, they are to separate from unclean relational (and agriculture) practices. This secures biblical love rather than human lust and greed as the driver of relationships.

Preaching Idea

We are made holy by God by loving our neighbor, whom we love best by living holy lives before God.

Contemporary Connections

What does it mean?

God's divine character trumps human reason as society's guide for love and is the church's model for holiness. All people are made in God's image. Treating others as objects to pursue for our pleasure or profit is abhorrent to God! For believers, such actions profane God's name by reflecting to others that God is someone he is not. The Lord God's inscribed decrees, not the culture around us or the desires within us, must serve as our guide to protect us from destroying our friends, our families, our communities, and ourselves.

If we are to be holy, we should ask ourselves, "Am I promoting myself or am I reflecting my God in each interaction?" I am never free to selfishly scan a gathering of people to single out who might advance my career, bring delight into my life, or gratify my passions. Relational exploitation renders all parties subject to harm.

Culture may counter with the assertion that unconditional affirmation, not the promotion of God's (antiquated) decrees, will best build a loving community. Yet affirming the desires of one's heart as the standard for building community eventually leads to the exploitation of the weak, the poor, and the disenfranchised. In contrast, God calls his people to be holy (reflect him) before their neighbors. There is no more loving attitude that will purify our souls and protect our motives as we grow in relationship with all who are made in his image.

Is it true?

The preaching idea conveys two sides of a single coin. First, is it true that *we are made holy by God through loving our neighbor*? God commands his people, "Be holy because I am holy." If holiness can be summed up as actively imaging God rather than selfishly reflecting our will in all of our relationships with others and creation, then we are made holy by God as we put the interests of our neighbor as defined by God before our own as instructed by God. As Paul later teaches the Philippian believers, "do nothing out of selfish ambition or conceit [self-promotion], but in humility count others [even strangers and sojourners] more significant than yourselves" (Phil. 2:3 ESV).

How does one do that? This question calls us to flip the coin over to see if it is true that *we love our neighbor best by living holy lives before God*. If we actively image God in our relationships rather than choosing to defer to our own will, then others will experience the blessings of the sacrificial love of God.

Many may counter by lifting up unconditional affirmation as the foundation of love. Such thinking assumes the will and reasoning of each individual to be reliable, even sacred. We may imagine that reason will not lead us to sin, but desire packs sufficient power to bend our reasoning to accommodate our selfish desires. If God alone is perfect and holy, are we loving our neighbor if we are passive as they pursue desires that are contrary to God's divine degrees? It will usually be easier and less awkward to affirm than to intervene. However, love demands that we humbly intervene. Will we be labeled intolerant? Maybe. Yet if we are honest with ourselves, we must admit that choosing tolerance is often driven more by laziness or a desire to be accepted than by genuine love for our neighbor.

Now what?
Everyone wants to meaningfully relate to others. (Even those who may not want to, want to want to.) Loving others begins by removing the no vacancy signs in our lives. We are called to make room for others, to develop meaningful relationships built on trust and sacrifice. Are we ready to allow God to define not only who enters into our lives but how we engage with each person? It is intimidating. It is frightening. And it is the process God uses to sanctify his people.

Pursuing God-honoring, Christ-exalting relationships starts with humbly assessing whom I am pursuing and why am I pursuing them. Am I seeking another for my own gratification or advancement? It may be a seismic shift to truly move the center of my world off of myself and my interest and onto to others and their best interests.

Creativity in Presentation
The examples and illustrations you select will need to match the specifics of the text you elect to highlight. I have provided both humorous and sobering examples.

Who can resist a good story or even a graphic demonstration of purging! You can open this message with an illustration of God's warning that the land will vomit out the people if they "consume what is forbidden." If you do not have a personal example, a short video search should prove satisfactory! Such a graphic illustration will set the stage for how good intentions can go violently wrong.

Another angle may be to build an example from the familiar practice of posting selfies. Selfies can be hazardous (259 deaths between 2011 and 2017).[1] When our interest is divided between what we are doing and making sure others know what we are doing, we are in danger. Loving our neighbor is not intended to be an opportunity for virtue signaling. If one hand is used to love others while the other is kept free to promote the self, we may be growing more in vanity than in holiness. Those made in God's image are simply being selected to serve as objects we can use to promote our image before others.

Be sensitive, as creativity may appear as cruelty when you are expositing a text brimming with relational interactions. You may reach for a tragic news story centered on sexual exploitation. For example, in Amstetten, Austria, Josef Fritzl imprisoned his daughter Elizabeth for twenty-four years, sexually abusing her and leading to the birth of seven children. How could this happen in a free, "Christian" country? Where were the relational boundaries that should have prevented this tragedy? Where were the neighbors? How does a community develop if the powerful feel free to secretly exploit the weak for profit and pleasure?

The subprime lending crisis of 2008–2010 provides an economic example of the powerful exploiting those "alien" to home ownership. What appeared to be loving (let each borrower decide for him- or herself) was in fact

---

1   Agam Bansal, et al.., "Selfies: A Boon or Bane?" *J Family Med Prim Care.* 2018 Jul-Aug; 7(4): 828–831.

the powerful exploiting those unfamiliar with the dangers of subprime mortgages. Homes were foreclosed at such a rate that the housing market collapsed. What may have appeared as loving one's neighbor proved to be disastrous to entire communities. Where were the voices that should have intervened to protect the vulnerable?

We are made holy by God by loving our neighbor, whom we love best by living holy lives before God.

- We are not free to use others for our purposes.
  - Practices in which we defile others
  - Communal consequences of defiling others
- Be holy, because God is holy.
  - Reflect God's prosperity, power, justice, and reason
  - Live by faith in God's provision: breeds and seeds; relationships and worship
  - Honor the weak: aging and aliens; sojourners and widows
- Safeguard God's holiness before others.
  - Do not despise God through false worship or sexual relationships
  - Response to disobedience: how to love one's neighbor
    - Intentional intervention: cleansing individuals and community by identifying sin
    - Unconditional affirmation: damning individuals and community by affirming sin

DISCUSSION QUESTIONS

1. How important is desire to you in your determining what is right and wrong? What happens when your desire and God's inscribed decree fail to line up?

2. Why do we tend to think of holiness as being separated from others, rather than as being fully engaged with others?

3. How are the ways you are relating to the men and women around you distinct from what our culture is teaching? How are your actions declaring who God is?

4. Do you wince at the word "obedience"? Why do we favor being labeled as relevant, creative, or a great communicator rather than obedient?

5. Where in your life or profession are you being tempted to deceive the less informed?

6. How are you reducing your definition of obedience to what you are able or willing to do?

7. What is your experience with or attitude toward church discipline? How have you seen it practiced well? Poorly? What makes the difference?

8. Why is intentional sin addressed differently than unintentional sin? Why is it more poisonous?

9. How and where might you be tempted to despise (belittle, ignore, mock, demean, deny, grumble against or make light of) God's statutes, rules, and decrees?

10. Why does the world tend to define love as unconditional affirmation rather than sacrificial intervention? Why is the church being drawn to follow the same course?

Leviticus 21:1–22:33

EXEGETICAL IDEA
To avoid openly profaning his name before the people (and the nations), God required the priests to be held to the highest standard of holiness, specifically regarding their mourning over death, entering into the covenant of marriage, personal physiological limitations and defects, and their administration of the offerings of the people.

THEOLOGICAL FOCUS
The highest standards of holiness are required of the one who is to come into God's presence and serve as his representative to God's people.

PREACHING IDEA
As needy, imperfect intermediaries, we are called to perfectly represent a perfect God as the one who sanctifies.

PREACHING POINTERS
The Lord God had already severely limited the pool of potential priests through restrictive gender and genealogical constraints (a male descendant of Aaron). The number decreased further through binding restrictions on how and for whose death priests might mourn and whom they might and might not choose for a spouse. Would some become reluctant to make this sacrifice? Next, a list of prohibiting physiological constraints (most beyond their control) further diminished the pool of who might still be willing. Was anyone left? Then, Moses detailed God's restrictions on how priests must receive, process, and preserve the offerings of the people with integrity. Could the priesthood possibly maintain these costly and cumbersome relational, social, physiological, and administrative standards? If they failed to do so, they would profane the name of God! Would anyone in the line of Aaron be able to fill this role?

The same dilemma remains before church leaders today: "you are a chosen race, a royal priesthood, a holy nation, a people for his own possession, that you may proclaim the excellencies of him who called you out of darkness into his marvelous light" (1 Peter 2:9 ESV). How do church leaders proclaim the excellencies of God as unholy, imperfect, fallen, and wounded servants? How can a leader accurately image God's holy perfection to the nations? To deny the effect of sin is to profane his name. To rest in our fallenness is to celebrate cheap grace. To lower the standards of holiness to a level that is attainable is to turn everyone's eyes onto us and away from our need for a savior. When Paul outlines the standards for church leaders in 1 Timothy 3 and Titus 1, he is not offering a means to identify those already sanctified. He is calling out leaders who know their need for sanctification. God alone is the One who sanctifies. We are the ones who point to the One who sanctifies through Christ.

A HOLY PRIESTHOOD FOR A HOLY NATION
(21:1–22:33)

LITERARY STRUCTURE AND THEMES (21:1–22:33)

Just as Leviticus 18–20 comprises a topical unit, so do Leviticus 21 and 22. However, while 18–20 focused on human relationships among the Israelites as a God-centered community, Leviticus 21 and 22 address the priests. "The Role of the Priests" (Lev. 6–7) showed the role of the priests as leaders of corporate worship. Now, Leviticus 21–22 sets forth standards of individual holiness required of the spiritual leaders as they serve to reinforce the social fabric. While the entire nation was to serve a priestly function (see the section "Priests and Levites" in the introduction), the Levitical priesthood carried a greater responsibility in terms of guiding national worship. Similarly, just as the entire nation was to be holy before God, we will now see how the priests carried a greater responsibility in that regard. Although those responsibilities covered all aspects of life, this unit concentrates on several specific areas of life that were more crucial for a holy priesthood, including proper responses to death, standards of marriage, qualifications for service, maintaining cleanness, and managing the portions of the offerings allotted to them. In addition, the high priest was held to even more stringent guidelines in certain areas.

As is the case of most of the book of Leviticus, the material in these two chapters is presented as a series of speeches that the Lord addressed to Moses for further dissemination. Since the material largely affected the priests, most of the speeches were directed to Aaron and his sons, as will be noted in the exegesis. Interestingly at the same time, the entire nation was privy to the guidelines given to the priests, suggesting both transparency in terms of priestly expectations and corporate accountability, giving the people a role in helping the priests attain those standards.

Given the nature of the various topics, this material could readily be presented as a series of studies addressing specific areas of responsibility for leadership, as will be seen as we work through the passage. However, because of topical overlaps a single comprehensive study or sermon study may be more practical for a full congregation. Thus, for homiletical purposes, we have organized this material in terms of a single sermon addressing the responsibilities of leadership.

- ***The Lord Limits How Priests Might Mourn the Dead (21:1–6)***
- ***The Lord Warns Against Indirect Defilement of the Priest (21:7–9)***
- ***The Lord Limits How the High Priest Might Mourn the Dead (21:10–12)***
- ***The Lord Places Physical Constraints on Who Might Be a Priest (21:16–24)***
- ***The Lord Cautions the Priests Regarding Holy Gifts (22:1–16)***
- ***The Lord Cautions Regarding Acceptable Offerings (22:17–33)***

EXPOSITION (21:1–22:33)

In the previous unit, "Preserving the Social Fabric" (18:1–20:27), we saw how family relationships formed a social fabric for the nation and we noted general guidelines on how members of the community were to live together in a way that would avoid tearing that social fabric. We suggested that it was likely that that series

A Holy Priesthood for a Holy Nation (21:1–22:33)

of divine speeches was given to Israel on one occasion. Similarly, it seems that the material in this unit was provided very soon after the previous unit, as it addresses some of the same topics, noting how the guidelines differed for the priests (it is not clear if this just applied to the consecrated priests, i.e., the descendants of Aaron, or a larger group of Levites who performed some priestly functions) showing how the priests served to reinforce the social fabric through modeling holiness. And yet we will see that the differences were more in terms of degree rather than nature. For example, priests, like the lay people, were expected to marry and raise families. However, because of their differing role within the community, the priests had somewhat more stringent marital restrictions that affected not only the nature of their extended families but how they personally related to the rest of nation. Essentially, priestly community relationships seem somewhat more fragile because of their more stringent limits in terms of cleanness and holiness.

The Lord Limits How Priests Might Mourn the Dead (21:1–6)

21:1a. Following the familiar pattern, Leviticus 21, as a new section, begins with a *waw*, which should be translated as "then" in this narrative, showing the continued sequence of revelation. The chapter consists of two speeches that likely were given at the same time but are specified as separate speeches for topical reasons. The first speech covers two topics: which family members a priest might mourn following that member's death, and whom a priest might marry. Since both topics address family issues for priests, God directs Moses to convey this material directly to the priests (the sons of Aaron).

21:1b–5. The immediate topic is defilement in the case of death, although the term death is not used. Rather, the statement is literally "a person will not defile or make himself unclean to a *nephesh* among his people" (לֹא־יִטַּמָּא בְּעַמָּיו).

TRANSLATION ANALYSIS: NEPHESH

As noted in the introduction, the Hebrew term *nephesh* (נֶפֶשׁ) may be translated as "life" or "soul." It is the dead body that defiles (טָמֵא) any person (i.e., makes him or her unclean) when he or she handles the body. While the general premise that handling a dead body defiled was apparently tacitly understood (Noordtzij 1982, 215), it does not show up in the written record until Numbers 19:11–14. That passage also uses *nephesh*, but 19:13 and 14 add that the person has died, showing that the issue is death. That passage also notes that the tent in which the person died becomes unclean and that anyone who enters the tent becomes unclean. The Numbers passage also specifies the period of uncleanness as seven days, and that the unclean person is required to purify him- or herself twice—on the third and the seventh days following contamination.

However, an exception is made in the case of "relatives who are nearest to him." These nearest relatives are specifically defined as the priest's mother, father, son, daughter, and brother—that is, essentially his molecular family. Another individual included in this group is a sister who is unmarried—that is, she is of marriageable age, a *bethulah* (בְּתוּלָה), but does not have a husband.

TRANSLATION ANALYSIS: BETHULAH

While often understood to mean "virgin" (e.g., Waltke 1980a; BDB s.v. "בְּתוּלָה" 143), *bethulah* (בְּתוּלָה) is generally better translated as a "young woman [of a marriageable age]" (Bergman, Ringgren, and Tsevat 1977, 341; *DCH* s.v. "בְּתוּלָה" 2:289). However, as Hartley (1992, 342) notes, "It is then not a technical term for 'a virgin'; otherwise the clause 'who does not have a husband' would not be needed." Based on the use of the term in 21:7, Milgrom (2000, 1799) more strongly declares, "It cannot mean 'virgin' (the customary rendering); otherwise the next clause would be redundant, and the specifications for a bride (v. 7) would simply have read

A Holy Priesthood for a Holy Nation (21:1–22:33)

'he shall marry a *bĕtûlâ*' or would have followed the wording of v. 14." Kleinig (2003, 445) goes one step further to assert that the alternative word translated "virgin," "עַלְמָה, the term used in Isa. 7:14, in the OT always means 'virgin.'" In any case, as used here, the idea of "virgin" is stressed.

The rationale that only an unmarried sister is included is that once she marries, she would belong to another family (Levine 1989, 142; Sklar 2014, 264). As the text notes, the priest might defile himself only for a sister without a husband, since it was understood that if she were married her husband would "defile himself" for her. Commentators have struggled to explain why the priest's wife is not mentioned. If a sister who married was no longer considered a blood relation for this purpose, then it must follow that the wife whose relationship was a mirror image situation would have been considered a blood relative. As noted in the sidebar, this is the traditional rabbinic view. As Sklar (2014, 264) explains it: "But she was also 'bone of his bones and flesh of his flesh' (Gen. 2:23) . . . she was considered the priest's very closest relative, a point the law assumes to be understood."

Sister Without a Husband

The text indicates that a priest might defile himself in the case of the death of a sister who is not married, but omits the case of a wife. Commentators have struggled with this and have proposed a variety of explanations. Keil and Delitzsch (1956, 606) suggest that the wife is implicit in the phrase "kin that is near unto him." Kleinig (2003, 445) claims that the priest could mourn for his wife but could not prepare her for burial for she was not a "flesh relative." Milgrom (2000, 1798) notes that the rabbis disagreed regarding this; but generally, they concluded that a priest had a responsibility to "defile himself" for his wife with some arguing that the wife was included as a "flesh relative." While noting the disagreement, Milgrom's own

---

position is not clear. Levine (1989, 142–43) also maintains that a wife was considered a "flesh relative," noting a rabbinic tradition that drew from Genesis 2:24. This is the view held by many modern scholars (e.g., Ross 2002, 384; Sklar 2014, 264; and Wenham 1979, 290). The use of the term בַּעַל in 21:4 contributes to the difficulty. It can be translated as "lord, ruler, commander, husband, owner, or possessor" (*DCH* s.v. "בַּעַל I" 2:237), and the question is, how does it fit in this context? While a number of proposals have been made, the basic choice is either "lord" or "husband" (Milgrom 2000, 1800). The primary problem is the subsequent term, בְּעַמָּיו, which translates literally as "in (or among) his people." While it is not clear how a priest was a "lord" among his people, this seems to be the meaning at first glance and is the view taken by the ESV and NRSV. The alternative would seem to be that he was not to defile himself through people who were related by marriage, which is the view taken by the NIV and the HCSB (Ross 2002, 384). This seems to be the best understanding, drawing on the distinctions between the nuclear and extended families. For further discussion of the relationship see the material in "Biblical Family Ties" in the introduction.

Two issues are involved in the death of a "nearest relative." The first is the preparation of the body for burial. Regardless of how the body was prepared, the person who prepared the body would have handled it and by definition would have been unclean for seven days subsequently. For a priest, that would mean that he could not perform his priestly duties during that period. The second issue is displaying mourning. Leviticus 21:5 lists specific demonstrations of mourning that had been forbidden to the laymen (Lev. 19:27–28) but here are also forbidden to the priest, although expressed with slightly different terminology. The first practice listed is translated "make any baldness on their heads," which is similar

295

to the practice of laymen in Leviticus 19:27, which the NASB translates as "round off the side-growth of your heads."

TRANSLATION ANALYSIS: "MAKE ANY BALDNESS"

As noted earlier, the prohibitions in Leviticus 19:27 and 21:5 are very similar. The phrase translated "round off the side-growth of your heads" in 19:27 is תַקִּפוּ פְּאַת רֹאשְׁכֶם, which uses the verb נָקַף. This can mean "strike off" but in the *qal* and *hiphil* stem is understood to mean "go around" (BDB s.v. "נָקַף" 668; *DCH* s.v. "נָקַף" 5:753–54; *TWOT* s.v. "נָקַף" I" 2:599; Fisher 1980c). In this passage, the phrase used in the prohibition is יִקְרְחָה קָרְחָה בְּרֹאשָׁם, which uses the root קרח both as the main verb (*qal* imperfect) and a derived noun, literally saying "make bald baldness on the head." *TWOT* explains that the root "denotes the lack of hair on the human head," which can be a result of leprosy or other natural causes, but also as a result of shaving or plucking (see Neh. 13:25; Coppes 1980m). It is then interesting that Deuteronomy 14:1 uses the same verb as a general admonition against the general populace shaving their heads "for the dead." As noted in the unit "Preserving the Social Fabric" (18:1–20:27), this was apparently a practice of the Canaanite tribes surrounding Israel as it settled into the land.

Apparently, these were practices noted in other cultures. A number of commentators associate them with what is called the cult of the dead, which seems to be a form of ancestor worship. However, as noted in the unit "Preserving the Social Fabric" (18:1–20:27), the practices listed here and in Leviticus 19:27–28 do not seem to be associated with that practice but address what we might call excessive exhibitions associated with the loss of the loved one. If that is the case, this passage likely does not address an attempt to use the deceased relative as a means of determining the future, but rather challenges the Israelites to trust that God would ultimately provide a resurrection. This may provide background to David's response to the death of the child that he had illegitimately conceived with Bathsheba (2 Sam. 12:20–23).

21:6. The rationale for these restrictions was so that the priest might be holy—a point repeated twice for emphasis. As God's representatives, how the priests did their assigned job of presenting the offerings by fire reflected on the God they served, as did their overall lifestyles (see comments on 3:11). In this case, failing to exhibit decorum with respect to the dead was deemed to profane the name of God, who had created them and had given them life.

TRANSLATION ANALYSIS: "PROFANE"

The word translated "profane" (ESV, KJV, NASB, NRSV) is the *niphal* or passive form of the verb חָלַל, which means "to profane, defile, pollute, desecrate" (Wiseman 1980b, 289). We discussed the noun חֹל, a derivative of this verb, in the material on "Clean and Unclean" in the introduction. While lexicons translate the noun as "profane," we noted that the Hebrew *noun* did not carry the same negative connotations that the English noun "profane" carries, and suggested that a better translation of the noun was "common." However, it would appear that the *verb* "to profane" (חָלַל) does carry strong negative connotations. The verb is used thirteen times in these two chapters, noting a number of things that could be profaned by actions of the priest or individuals associated with the priest. Three times in this chapter it refers to the name of God (following four such uses in the previous unit, Lev. 18–20) indicating that violations of the various directives in this chapter not only defiled the person or thing addressed, but indirectly profaned or defiled the name of God. Profaning or defiling the name of God would seem to carry a sense of not just making it common, but would cause observers to disdain the God that the priest purported to represent. Perhaps

A Holy Priesthood for a Holy Nation (21:1–22:33)

an English analogy would be the colloquial expression "drag his name through the mud."

The Lord Warns Against Indirect Defilement of the Priest (21:7–9)

The second area of concern is difficult, since it presents two areas where a priest might be indirectly defiled as a result of actions by women in his life. Both address issues of sexual immorality on the part of the woman. The first case could be a result of premarital actions performed by the woman he married. The second case could be through a grown daughter's sexual immorality.

21:7–8. Two criteria are given to denote a woman that a priest could not marry. The primary criterion was that she was not to have been involved in sexual immorality. The term used here is זָנָה, which denotes a harlot or a woman who has committed fornication (Wood 1980b). This has often been viewed as containing "an implied connection with false worship in which sacred prostitution was prominent." However, another view is that it was just a matter of a sexual relationship with another man with a concern "that if the wife had been a prostitute and defiled by that or by other connections, then she could never be sure of the origin of her child" (Ross 2002, 385). Because the noun harlot (זָנָה) is joined to the adjective profaned (חָלָל) by a *waw*, some suggest a possible translation of "harlot or profaned" and understand the phrase to refer to two different categories. More likely it reflects how the woman was profaned, that is, by harlotry.

Harlot or Profaned?

At least four interpretations have been proposed for the adjective חֲלָלָה as used here with זָנָה. The first view notes a second root of חָלַל, which means "to wound or pierce," and suggests that in this context it means "a girl deflowered," but that would be redundant; second is a person devoted to prostitution; third is a view of a sacred prostitute; and the fourth suggests a hendiadys, a woman degraded by harlotry (Hartley 1992, 343). Most commentators seem to go with either the third or the fourth. The difference would be that the fourth would include a woman who had developed a reputation of sexual immorality, although not necessarily as a result of pagan cultic practices. Milgrom (2000, 1819) argues that these terms must denote two separate entities since the two terms are reversed in 21:14. However, while the terms are joined by a *waw* conjunction in 21:7, that is not the case in 21:14. Since the issue seems to be primarily a matter of reputation, it seems that the fourth would be the preferred understanding.

A second criterion was that the priest was not allowed to marry a divorcee. The Torah delineates divorce as a process initiated by the husband. According to Deuteronomy 24:1, if the wife found "no favor in his [her husband's] eyes because he has found some indecency in her" he could divorce her. The phrase in Deuteronomy translated "indecency" (עֶרְוַת דָּבָר) reads literally "the nakedness of a thing." Merrill (1994, 318) concludes that this "is to be understood as a euphemism that may or may not include adultery." As the Deuteronomy passage continues, it anticipates that the woman might remarry—however, not to a priest. It seems that the concept of indecency suggests a certain amount of latitude for the husband, as indicated by the debate among the Jews at the time of Jesus (Matt. 19:3–9; see also Blomberg 1992, 289–90). Given that the divorce was totally at the discretion of the husband, it is possible that the wife may have actually been innocent. Regardless, a divorced woman likely would be viewed with a question mark by the community, leaving her under a cloud of suspicion. In turn, that would also reflect on the priest and ultimately on God.

A Holy Priesthood for a Holy Nation (21:1–22:33)

Issue of Indecency

As presented in Matthew, Jesus seems to refer to the Deuteronomy command when he addresses divorce (Matt. 5:31–32; 19:7–9). In Matthew 19 the Pharisees bring their debate on the correct interpretation to Jesus. Craig Blomberg (1992, 289–90) summarizes their debate as follows: "Shammai, placing the emphasis on 'indecent,' took this to refer to sexual unfaithfulness; Hillel, placing the emphasis on 'anything,' allowed divorce even for as trivial an offense as a wife burning her husband's food (*m. Git.* 9:10)." While Merrill (1994, 318) notes that the phrase עֶרְוַת דָּבָר used in Deuteronomy reads literally "the nakedness of a thing," according to BDB the word עֶרְוַת can also refer to the pudenda, or the female sexual organs (BDB s.v. "עֶרְוָה" 788). Although adultery is not explicitly mentioned, the latter understanding of the term would seem to include adultery. However, the punishment for adultery was prescribed as stoning of both the man and the woman (Deut. 22:22), which could suggest that the betrayed husband of the adulterous wife had the option of divorce as opposed to mandatory capital punishment. Merrill goes on to suggest that while the remarriage of the woman was permitted, regardless of the cause, the divorce defiled her, which is why a priest could not marry her.

Regardless, the guideline was that the priest was not to marry either category of woman. Rather, he was to marry a woman with a good reputation, which would be viewed as honoring God and thus consecrating the priest. Again, the reason was that God, who sanctified, was holy.

21:9. The idea of indirect defilement is also seen in the case of a daughter of a priest who "was profaned by harlotry." Apparently, this would be a case where the daughter has reached sexual maturity but is not yet married and thus is still part of the household of the priest. Because her action then also profaned her father, she was

to be executed, which is perhaps analogous to the later command for stoning a rebellious son (Deut. 21:18–21). While the text states that she should be burned with fire, it is not clear if this was the method of execution, or what was to be done to the corpse. Milgrom (2000, 1811) argues for the first view, suggesting that this was the older punishment for adultery, citing Tamar (Gen. 38:24). Hartley (1992, 349) notes that most commentators take the latter view, suggesting that it was "part of the humiliating punishment, signifying that this daughter was totally removed from the face of the earth." This seems to be preferred as it "cleansed the camp of this defilement" (Ross 2002, 385).

The Lord Limits How the High Priest Might Mourn the Dead (21:10–12)

In the same speech, the Lord gives Moses a second set of instructions that apply only to the high priest. While the term "high priest" did not come about until later, three aspects spelled out here point to that position: he is "greater than his brothers" (הַגָּדוֹל מֵאֶחָיו), he is anointed, and he has been consecrated to "wear the garments." With the greater position, the high priest has greater responsibilities.

> *TRANSLATION ANALYSIS: "THE HIGH PRIEST"*
>
> The phrase הַגָּדוֹל מֵאֶחָיו, literally, "greater from his brothers," is a comparative construction that many translations render as "highest among his brothers," understanding "brothers" to mean fellow priests. For discussion on the anointing of the high priest, see comments on Leviticus 8:12. The reference to "the garments" refers to the specific garments that are described in Leviticus 8:7–9 (see comments there).

21:10. The high priest is prohibited from "uncovering his head" and "tearing his clothes," which seem to be demonstrations of mourning that directly affect evidences of his position. His head is anointed, and so he is not

A Holy Priesthood for a Holy Nation (21:1–22:33)

allowed to "dishevel" his hair (see comments on Lev. 8:12). His garments are specifically designed to indicate his position and are part of his ministry, so he is not allowed to tear them (Wenham 1979, 291).

21:11–12. Additionally, because of his position representing the nation before God, the high priest is not allowed to approach any dead person—even the closest relatives, including even the father and mother.

TRANSLATION ANALYSIS: "APPROACH"
The word translated "approach" is the very common verb בּוֹא, which basically means "to come" or "to go" (BDB s.v. "בּוֹא" 97; DCH s.v. "בּוֹא" 2:102) or variations of those verbs. In this case, it seems that the issue is coming close to the dead body that is to be avoided.

What is not addressed here is the question about his wife. It would appear that one must make the same inferences for her as in the case of a regular priest—she is to be treated the same as any other blood relation, which would suggest that he was not allowed to defile himself over her. One must also keep in mind that the career of a priest was ages twenty-five to fifty (Num. 4:4), which might suggest that the high priest (and perhaps even a regular priest) was expected to have retired prior to the death of his spouse, or she outlived him, as is often the case; in either case this aspect of the command would be a moot point.

Priestly Service
The only retirement mentioned in the OT is that of Levites, who are told in Numbers 8:24–25 that they would enter service at the age of twenty-five, and "at the age of fifty years they shall retire [literally 'return'] from service in the work and not work any more." See also the section on "Priests and Levites" in the introduction for more information on the number of priests.

Since the context is mourning, the statement that he might not go out of the sanctuary must refer to the mourning period and process as opposed to his entire ministerial career. Also, the distinction between unclean and defiled would be crucial in applying this command. While, as a human, the priest would become unclean on occasion just by living, he was to avoid actions that would defile or desanctify him with respect to his priestly responsibilities, as emphasized by the statement that "the consecration of the anointing oil of his God is upon him."

21:13–15. As in the case of a regular priest, the wife the high priest took was to be unmarried (בְּתוּלָה), an admonition repeated twice in this section. As noted earlier (see 21:3), while technically the word means a young woman of marriageable age, the context clearly suggests virginity. Also like a regular priest, the high priest was not allowed to marry a woman who was divorced, or who "was profaned by harlotry." However, while a regular priest was allowed to marry a widow, the high priest was not. Apparently, this was to ensure that the next high priest would be his son in accordance with God's directive regarding the high priest position (Exod. 29:29–30). As noted earlier (see Lev. 7:21), the phrase "of his own people" here would indicate that the wife was to be from a closer relationship than the nation of Israel, likely indicating that she was from the tribe of Levi (Sklar 2014, 266–67). Further, as in the case of a regular priest, he is sanctified by the Lord.

Not Marry a Widow
The prohibition against the high priest marrying a widow could reflect several aspects. On one hand, as in the case of marrying a nonvirgin, there would be a question of whether a son was actually his (Sklar 2014, 266–67). However, that question would really only be relevant for the first child following the marriage, and even then only within a few months after the marriage. Another factor is that a widow would likely already

have children, and thus there might be a conflict between a son fathered by her previous husband but raised by the high priest. If she did not have children, depending on the length of the marriage prior to her losing her husband, there might be a question regarding her fertility if she had been married several years without a child.

The Lord Places Physical Constraints on Who Might Be a Priest (21:16–24)

God reserves the right to determine who may or may not serve him in specific offices or ministries. For the nation of Israel, this was evident from the onset when at Mount Sinai God proclaimed that Aaron and his sons were "to serve as priests to me" (Exod. 28:1). At the same time, while God chooses his priests, those he chooses would be expected to meet specific criteria with respect to their having been chosen. While the previous material has focused on moral and spiritual qualifications that God demands that his priests meet, this section addresses physical qualifications. Although every priest was to be a male Levite, not every male Levite could be a priest (see the section "Priest and Levites" in the introduction). There were genealogical constraints; as

already seen, the priests had to be descendants of Aaron (Num. 16:8–11). There were marital constraints as we have just seen. Now, God gives physiological constraints—certain biological defects disqualified a male Levite from serving as a priest.

21:16–20. This new speech again begins with a *waw*, which should be translated "then." While the text states that the priest was to be without defect, the language suggests "nothing more than literal normality" as opposed to "perfect" (Kiuchi 2007, 397). Some of the disqualifying criteria are obvious in that the priestly requirements could be physically strenuous. The section lists twelve physical characteristics that disqualified a man from serving as a priest. These are called מוּם, which can be translated "defect" or "blemish" (Kaiser 1980c). While some of the Hebrew terms are obscure, most of the items listed are straightforward, citing physical characteristics that are readily apparent, such as blindness. They are of two types—birth defects and physical injuries—that deform the body (Levine 1989, 145). The defects specifically cited in Leviticus 21 as translated by the NASB are shown in chart 8.

Blindness	This may include loss of vision in one eye (Levine 1989, 145).
Lameness	Could be "cannot walk properly." Maybe lame in one leg (Levine 1989, 145).
Disfigured face	Uncertain. Hebrew חָרֻם II means "slit," or "mutilate" (Wood 1980d). Suggests a slit nose, or possibly cleft palate.
Deformed limb	Literally שָׂרַע means "extend" (*TWOT* s.v. "שָׂרַע" 2:884). Likely a birth defect.
Broken foot	Literal translation of שֶׁבֶר רָגֶל. Likely broken bone that did not heal properly.
Broken hand	Literal translation of שֶׁבֶר יָד. Likely broken bone that did not heal properly.
Hunchback	גִּבֵּן is a *hapax legomenon*, understood to be "humpbacked" (*TWOT* s.v. "גבן" 1:147). Note Harrison (1980, 211) who lists several possible physical issues.
Dwarf	דַּק means "thin, fine, or gaunt" (Wolf 1980b). As applied here, suggests dwarfism, which is a birth defect.

A Holy Priesthood for a Holy Nation (21:1–22:33)

Eye defect	תְּבַלֻּל is a *hapax legomenon*. Defined as "obscurity" (Kaiser 1980a, 112). Translated here as "defect." The following phrase "in his eye" shows it to be some type of eye defect, exact meaning unknown (Sklar 2014, 268).
Eczema	גָּרָב generally understood to be some type of skin problem associated with itching or scabbing (*TWOT* s.v. "גרב" 1:171).
Scabs	יַלֶּפֶת occurs only here and in Leviticus 22. It seems to refer to scabs or scales (*TWOT* s.v. "ילף" 1:381). The exact disease is not clear.
Crushed testicles	The construct structure indicates a problem with the testicles described as מְרוֹחַ, which is generally understood here to mean *crushed*. The only other use of the word is in Isaiah 38:21 where it describes treating a boil with a fig cake compress, which is understood as "to squeeze out" (Keil and Delitzsch 1956, 608). BDB (s.v. "מָרוֹחַ" 598) adds a second possibility from a different root of "enlarged," which may suggest a varicocele. Perhaps the best that can be said is as Hartley (1992, 344) states, "it describes abnormal testicles."

Chart 8. Disqualifying physical defects for priests.

21:21–23. After describing what disqualifies a man from serving as a priest, the text amplifies the issue. First, 21:21 gives the specific prohibition that the disqualified person may not offer "the Lord's offerings by fire." This is reiterated in the same verse as he shall not "offer the food of his God." As discussed in conjunction with Leviticus 3:11, this is not to imply that the sacrifice is being offered to God to eat. There we noted how the phrase reflected "sharing a meal" to strengthen the relationship between God, the priests, and the offeror and guests.

Should this disqualified person violate this directive, the Lord states that he would "profane [God's] sanctuaries." As we concluded earlier, throughout this section the verb translated "profane" (חָלַל) suggests actions that would cause observers to disdain the God that the priest represented.

What is interesting is that the term "sanctuary" (מִקְדָּשׁ) is used in the plural here. Kleinig (2003, 457) states, "The plural may refer to the various parts of the sacred precincts or, more likely, to the furnishings and objects in the sacred precinct around the altar for burnt offerings and in the outer room of the tabernacle." This seems to be a rather awkward use of the plural. Milgrom (2000, 1829) offers an alternative based on 1 Samuel 21:1–6, where David came to the priest Ahimelech at Nob and was given "consecrated bread" (לֶחֶם קֹדֶשׁ). Consecrated bread is explained in this text as the "bread of the presence," which was placed on the golden table in the Holy Place of the tabernacle, as directed in Exodus 25:30. However, since there is no indication that the tabernacle was ever set up at Nob, Milgrom infers the presence of "local sanctuaries" in premonarchial Israel. For evaluation of this premise, see the discussion "Celebratory" in the introduction.

Although the disqualified person might not offer the sacrifice, he was allowed to eat from the priestly share. More significantly, he was allowed to eat both the holy and the most holy portions. As we noted in Leviticus 6:16 (HB 9) the place where this food was to be eaten was the court of the tabernacle, described as "the Holy Place." Thus, while he was allowed to go into the tabernacle court, he just was not allowed to "go into the veil" or to approach the altar. As Sklar (2014, 268–69) describes it, while disqualified from this specific

A Holy Priesthood for a Holy Nation (21:1–22:33)

service, they were "not only allowed into the courtyard, but also welcomed as guests at this royal table."

21:24. This section concludes with the observation that Moses faithfully passed this information on to Aaron and his sons (the priests). However, it also notes that he did so before all of the sons of Israel. This provides both transparency and accountability. First, the people are aware of the higher standards that the priests are expected to live by. This allows the congregation to appreciate the role of the priests. But it also provides a degree of accountability, since the priests are aware that the people have this knowledge. Further, it shows that there was no "private professional knowledge" that the priests possessed (Hartley 1992, 350).

The Lord Cautions the Priests Regarding Holy Gifts (22:1–16)
Because the last verse in the previous speech reports that Moses shared the material with both the priests and the Israelites, it would appear that the next speech may not have immediately followed the previous one. However, it still addresses the responsibilities of the priests, emphasizing the high standards they were to uphold. This chapter consists of three speeches, each of which seems to cover a specific general topic. The first section collects a number of specific lifestyle issues the priest would need to follow to maintain his consecrated status. The remainder of this unit consists of two speeches that give standards that sacrificial animals would need to meet in order to be acceptable.

22:1–2. Subsequent to the previous warnings regarding qualifications for the priesthood, God gives Moses another message for Aaron and his successors regarding how they were to handle "the holy [things] of the sons of Israel." The Hebrew just has the abstract noun "holy." Again it is related to the previous material by a *waw*,

showing a chronological sequence and thus is translated "then."

TRANSLATION ANALYSIS: "HOLY"
The Hebrew term מִקׇּדְשֵׁי is a plural noun with a min (מִן) preposition in a construct relationship with the "sons of Israel." The basic meaning of the word קֹדֶשׁ is "holy," which we discuss in some detail in the introduction. There we pointed out that the primary function of "holy" (קֹדֶשׁ) is to describe an attribute of God, but with respect to the offering it is a derivative attribute that denoted something that had been dedicated to God (something like a gift to a king is to be a royal gift). In this context, the Hebrew would be translated literally as "be careful with the holies of the sons of Israel." English requires adding specification to explain the abstract concept by denoting what is holy. Consequently, translations add words such as "gifts" (NASB, NLT), "things" (ESV, KJV), "offerings" (HCSB, NIV), or "donations" (NRSV). The context here indicates that it refers to food, bringing to mind the gift offerings (מִנְחָה) in Leviticus 2 (see comments there). Still, there are several complexities. The construct relationship shows that it refers to food that belonged to the Israelites. (Yes, technically it had been given to them by God so in that respect it was God's to begin with.) It is also the object of the verb נָזַר, which means "to separate or consecrate." In the *niphal* stem followed by the *min* preposition, as here, the idea is "keep oneself away from" (McComiskey 1980d). Because the following verses focus on warning against being unclean when handling or eating, an obvious conclusion is that the priests are to avoid being unclean as they process the sacrifice or eat the portion assigned to them. However, other items also are viewed as dedicated to God, such as tithes. As such, it would seem that this admonition incorporates a proper handling of those gifts beyond just being clean. This suggests that incorporated in this warning are other aspects of the priestly duties, which include sharing the food with the priest's family

A Holy Priesthood for a Holy Nation (21:1–22:33)

(which would explain the subsequent verses), or distinguishing between produce that has been brought as an offering and that which has been brought for other purposes, such as the third-year tithe, which was to be given even to resident aliens (Deut. 26:12–13).

As mediators between the nation and God, the priests were responsible for gathering and appropriately allocating offerings or gifts that the Israelites brought to God. These include several offerings that have already been mentioned through the first parts of the book, such as portions of the gift (Lev. 2:10), the purification (Lev. 6:25–26, 29), the reparation (Lev. 7:6), and the shalom (Lev. 10:14) offerings. While the sacrifices had been given to God, portions were designated for the priests who performed the sacrifice, who were then able to share them with their family members. Subsequent revelation describes other gifts, including the firstfruits of oil, wine, and grain (Num. 18:8–13). Offerings that might not be sacrificed could include items promised as a result of a vow (Lev. 27:2–12). Additionally, all Israelites were required to bring tithes, which seem to have been viewed as an offering, although they were given directly to the priests as part of their inheritance. The priests in turn were required to tithe what they had received as an offering (Num. 18:24–30). Then there was the third-year tithe, which was to be deposited in the Israelite's town for distribution to Levites, aliens, orphans, and widows (Deut. 14:28–29). It would seem that the admonition to the priests (Aaron and his sons) was that they exercise care in their handling of the different products and not confuse what had been offered with common food (Hess 2008, 774). If they didn't, the result could be that they would defile the name of God to whom ultimately the gifts were given. As noted in our discussion of Leviticus 21:6, the idea was that improper handling or misappropriation would damage the reputation of the God that the priest purported to represent.

22:3–9. Perhaps the easiest way to err in this situation would be for the priest or other recipients to handle or eat the food while unclean. The warning here is that if any person approaches the holy items addressed while unclean, that person would be cut off from before God.

TRANSLATION ANALYSIS: "APPROACHES"
Unlike the case of Leviticus 21:11, the verb translated "approaches" here is the Hebrew verb קָרַב, which is defined as "to come near, approach." Coppes (1980k, 811) describes it as "the most near and intimate proximity," with a secondary meaning of actual contact. He then goes on to note a technical use associated with presenting an offering to God. The verb is used as a warning against a priest "approaching" what an Israelite had "dedicated" to God. While the immediate context is uncleanness, it seems that there is also a sense of possible misappropriation by the priest of what had been given to God. In this sense, we might note how the sons of Eli in 1 Samuel 2:12–17 misappropriated the sacrifices at Shiloh.

The text here recapitulates several items described in Leviticus 11–15 that produce uncleanness. A point easily overlooked is that it was anticipated that the priests would not be perfect. Even though some of the items that produced uncleanness were not issues of sin, some would be sinful and would violate God's directions. Still, once cleansed the person would be able to eat the holy gifts once more. This section closes with the reminder that if they followed these guidelines they would not sin and die, and that God was the one who sanctified them.

22:10–11. Throughout the description of the sacrifices, with the exception of the burnt offering, portions of the various offerings were given to the priest. In most cases this food was restricted to the priest and to his sons (e.g., the gift or grain offering in Lev. 2:3). However, on the day of the consecration of the tabernacle (Lev. 10), Aaron was told that while the portion of the gift offering remaining after the memorial section was burned belonged to him and his sons and had to be eaten in a holy place, in the case of shalom offerings (Lev. 7:33–34) the breast and the right thigh could be eaten in a clean place by him, his sons, and his daughters (and apparently by inference, his wife; Lev. 10:14). As we noted in the unit "The Role of the Priests" (6:8 [HB 6:1]–7:38), this may be associated with the fact that the offering was a shalom offering, which seemed to be open to the family and friends of the offeror. It would appear that this food is the subject of this section.

Specifically, the text reminds the priests that regarding their portion of that offering, while their families could eat of it, others could not. The first group excluded was "lay persons" or literally "strangers" (זָר), which is generally taken to mean someone outside the priest's family. The second excluded group was "guests" (תּוֹשָׁב).

TRANSLATION ANALYSIS: "GUESTS"
The term תּוֹשָׁב is a noun derived from the Hebrew verb יָשַׁב, which means "to sit, remain, or dwell" (Kaiser 1980b, 411). Kaiser translates the noun as "sojourner," as used by the KJV and the NASB. However, the English word "sojourner," which denotes one who makes a temporary stay or residence, is often used to translate the Hebrew גּוּר, which carries a number of different nuances. According to *TWOT* (Stigers 1980, 155) the term גּוּר denotes one "who did not enjoy the rights usually possessed by the resident." Usually this seems to describe one who is living in his own residence and has settled for the long haul in an alien population group. As used here, the תּוֹשָׁב appears to be a person who was residing with the priest and was thus dependent upon his hospitality. In this case, the person would not necessarily be an alien. As such, a better translation would be "guest."

They are generally viewed as individuals who were dwelling with the priest on a temporary basis. Even though they might be the guests of the priest and temporarily living in his household, as outsiders they were not allowed to partake of this food. Finally, "hired men" (שָׂכִיר) were not allowed to eat of the priest's portion. In contrast, a slave bought by the priest or born in the priest's house could eat of it. In essence, in this situation the slave would be considered part of the family (perhaps somewhat analogous to how Abraham viewed Eliezer; Gen. 15:2–3).

TRANSLATION ANALYSIS: "SLAVE"
The word often translated as "slave" in this verse is נֶפֶשׁ, which we have noted earlier normally is understood as "soul." Given the context, the expected word would be עֶבֶד (Harbin 2012, 56–57). The interesting point is that the priest has bought the person with his own money; literally the sentence might be translated: "if a priest acquired a soul with wealth, silver. . ." Given the purchase for money, this reflects true or chattel slavery, not temporary debt slavery. As such, the child born to that slave would also be considered a slave. However, that does raise a question regarding the apparent condoning of chattel slavery among the Israelites, for which we do not have a good answer. We will see later, however, that while the Torah tolerated chattel slavery, it restricted chattel slavery to non-Israelites (Lev. 25:44), usually individuals captured in war. They were subject to sale and had few rights, although the Torah did set forth more humane standards of treatment than elsewhere in the ANE (Baker 2009, 116–21).

22:12–13. In contrast, a daughter who had married a nonpriest would be ineligible to eat of the priest's portion of the shalom offering, identified here as the contribution (תְּרוּמָה), which Leviticus 7:34 specifies as the right thigh. If she loses her spouse, however, either through his death or divorce, and having no children, must return to her father's house, she may once again participate in these meals.

TRANSLATION ANALYSIS: "CONTRIBUTION" While the earlier verses discuss the "holy," in this case the text changes to the "offering" (KJV, NASB, NLT, NRSV) or "contribution" (ESV, HCSB, and NIV). This offering was described in 7:32, where we noted that it is also referred to as a "heave" offering.

22:14–16. One could conceive an occasion where a priest might have a complex group in his home including a slave, a guest, a daughter who is a widow, and another daughter who is married but is visiting. In that type of situation, which food is what could become confused. Whatever the reason, the person who has inadvertently eaten of the holy food would need to make reparations, which would also require restoration of what had been taken plus one fifth (Hartley 1992, 356; Sklar 2014, 272). In this case, the purpose is to avoid defiling the holy gifts that Israel gave. Who would bear iniquity should this happen is not clear. Willis (2009, 186) suggests three options: it could be the holy gift, the priest, or the person who inadvertently ate. It seems most likely to be the person who inadvertently ate. However, Willis's observation that regardless, "it is the Lord who sanctifies, so that the people will not assume that their own actions (the eating of sacred food) make them holy," is most pertinent.

The Lord Cautions Regarding Acceptable Offerings (22:17–33)

22:17–25. The last portion of the chapter consists of two speeches, both beginning with the introductory *waw*. The first speech notes that offerings could be brought by any Israelite or resident alien (see discussion on this at Lev. 17:7). Still, all had to meet the same criteria with regard to the animals being offered. However, this passage can be confusing with respect to what sacrifice is actually being offered: If it is a burnt offering, it is to be totally burned, but if it is a votive or freewill offering it is supposed to be shared with one's neighbors.

That seems to produce a case where two animals are actually being offered. The first is the animal given as a burnt offering, which we addressed in our discussion on Leviticus 1. As presented in Leviticus 1:3, the individual burnt offering was a voluntary offering that an individual might bring to God, although that text does not discuss what occasions might lead one to bring a burnt offering. Here, the text observes that it might be an occasion when the individual was fulfilling a vow, or it just might be a freewill offering. In the case of a vow, the burnt offering might be what the Israelite has promised God when he or she made the vow. Whatever the reason, it needed to be paid first (Deut. 23:21–23). Both votive offerings and freewill offerings were communal offerings that were to be performed with one's relatives and neighbors to celebrate what God had done. While the focus of the text in Leviticus 1 and 3 was the offering process, it did specify that the offering was to be without defect. Now the text spells out what that means.

Burnt Offering

The English translations of this verse can be confusing, since they generally follow the Hebrew word order, which places the votive and freewill offerings first followed by the burnt offering. The text seems best understood as indicating that the occasion is to fulfill a vow or just a freewill offering to celebrate God, but that as part of the occasion a burnt offering is also given to show consecration. As such, the actual votive or freewill offering is not being given as a burnt offering.

Vow

The purpose of a votive offering was to give thanks to God for fulfilling the worshipper's request. It seems that in most cases the promise or vow given involved something other than a burnt offering. For example, in Genesis 28:20–22, Jacob promised that he would serve God and always set aside a tithe. In 2 Samuel 15:7–8, Absalom promised that he would worship the Lord in Hebron. Hannah promised in 1 Samuel 1:11 that she would dedicate Samuel to the Lord. The most controversial case is Judges 11:31, where Jephthah promised that whatever came out of the doors of his house to greet him, וְהָיָה לַיהוָה וְהַעֲלִיתִהוּ עֹלָה. The problem here is the second *waw*, which as we have noted, can be translated a number of ways. Here it seems it is best understood as "or" giving the following translation: "it will be the Lord's *or* I will offer it as a burnt offering" (emphasis added; Marcus 1986, 14–27). In promising a burnt offering, Jephthah apparently anticipated that it would be an animal suitable for that offering. Without the implicit alternative, he would be left open to either sacrificing an unclean animal, or a human sacrifice. Neither case would be acceptable. However, understanding the translation as "or" provides various options. Whether animal or human, the offering could be utilized by the Levites on the Lord's behalf (such as the Gibeonites, who hauled water). If, as he made the oath, he even thought of the possibility of a human coming out, it seems likely that he would have thought in terms of one of his servants, whom he would dedicate to God. Clearly, he did not anticipate his daughter would be the one to meet him, and the resulting problem was "he had no son or daughter besides her" (Judg. 11:34). It is suggested that the outcome here is analogous to that of Hannah with her son Samuel. If in his daughter's case this service required that she remained a virgin (something for which the text is not explicit), it meant Jephthah did not have someone to care for him in his old age. It also explains why she bewailed her virginity rather than an anticipated early death (Judg. 11:37).

In Leviticus 22:23–24 Moses is given twelve specific defects that disqualify an animal as being an acceptable sacrifice. As noted earlier, they are very similar to the list of physical problems that might make a priest unclean (Lev. 21:17–20). Again, the terms are debated and we really don't know many of the specific issues (Sklar 2014, 273–74). In the overall context, it would appear that the issue was really a matter of priorities: the goal was to place God first and preserve the integrity of offering by not giving rejects (which some scholars suggest was the issue in regard to the acceptance of Abel's offering as opposed to Cain's).

22:26–33. The last section is a separate speech that is somewhat more difficult in that while it gives additional guidelines for proper sacrifices, the rationale is not clear. The first directive is that a newborn acceptable sacrificial animal (ox, sheep, or goat) must be allowed to live with its mother for seven days before it might be sacrificed, which is given as an apodictic command without explanation. Over the years various explanations have been proposed such as seven days was "the normal time for ritual transition from one state into another" (Kleinig 2003, 479). Milgrom (2000, 1883) notes five suggested rationales, and observes that the most common understanding views it as a humanitarian issue, but "a completely satisfying rationale has yet to be supplied." Ross (2002, 383) may be on the right track when he argues that beyond humanitarian reasons, this would ensure that the animal was viable, and thus indeed a live sacrifice.

Similarly, the second directive is that regardless of the animal, "you shall not kill both it and its young in one day." Again, there are a lot of suggestions such as saving the mother to build the flock or herd or avoiding an unknown pagan ritual. Milgrom's observation regarding the lack of a satisfying rationale may be equally pertinent here. However, it would seem that the context provides a hint. Leviticus 22:18 addressed a situation where an Israelite either fulfilled a vow that involved giving a burnt offering or gave a freewill offering as a burnt offering. We noted that since the votive and freewill offerings were communal, which involved giving part of the animal sacrifice to the priest and then cooking

A Holy Priesthood for a Holy Nation (21:1–22:33)

the rest for a community dinner, it would appear that while this section cautions against offering animals that had defects, the situation actually involved two sacrificial animals. If that was the case, it would seem that 22:28 prohibits using both the young animal (cited in 22:27) and its parent on that day. Perhaps because 22:28 addresses the mother of a newborn, the tradition has been that the reference here is to a female parent whether ox or sheep (Levine 1989, 152).

TRANSLATION ANALYSIS: "SHEEP"
Leviticus 22:27 uses two words as the alternative to oxen: כֶּבֶשׂ, which *TWOT* (s.v. "כֶּבֶשׂ" 1:429) translates as "lamb" or "sheep," and עֵז, which Allen (1980a) translates as "goat," "she-goat," or "kid." In contrast, 22:28 uses the single Hebrew word שֶׂה, which the NASB translates as "sheep." Hartley (1980d) explains that it can be either a sheep or a goat as a "member of the flock."

A third directive refers to the command in 7:15 that the meat of this offering was to be eaten on the day of the offering. This seems to reinforce the suggestion we made in the section "The Lord Gives Directions to the Priests for Shalom Offerings" (7:11–36) that a factor here would be the communal nature of the offering. Prohibiting leftovers would promote inviting more neighbors, thus enhancing the glory of God through a wider proclamation of what he had done, consequently strengthening the corporate faith and relationships.

The last item in this section is an overall exhortation for Israel to keep God's commandments. This is a strong hendiadys that literally reads "you shall guard my commandments and do them," thus emphasizing that "guarding" demands obedience. The alternative is that God's name will be defiled. In our comments on 21:6 we noted how "defiling" would cause observers to disdain God. The context there was death, suggesting profanation of the God who gave them life. As a summary for the two

chapters, here the context is more immediate and explicit: God is the One who sanctifies Israel, and then on a practical point, he reminds them that he brought them out of Egypt to be their God.

> ### Out of Egypt
> The first place that God used the expression "I brought you out of Egypt" was in Exodus 20:2 where it introduced the Ten Commandments, providing an implied cause-and-effect relationship: "Because I brought you out of Egypt, you need to make me your God and give me full allegiance." To paraphrase this somewhat crudely in today's parlance, "you owe me *big time*." The importance of this point is illustrated by the fact that throughout the OT, God makes this statement or a very close facsimile approximately 138 times.

THEOLOGICAL FOCUS

A significant factor in this unit is the repetition of two terms. The first is "profane" (חָלַל), which appears in this unit thirteen times, in a sense of defamation. Asserting something to be true about God through a word that is not true (or even inferred by action) profanes his name. Declaring a standard that is lower than perfect holiness profanes the name of God. While various actions could profane both people and objects, it was noted that ultimately the profanation touches God and besmirches his name. As leaders of the community, the priests had a great responsibility to ensure that God was not profaned because of how it affected the way others looked at him.

The second term that stands out is "sanctify" (קָדַשׁ), which in some ways is the mirror image of profaning (see chart 6 in the "Clean and Unclean" section of the introduction). On one hand, "YHWH is sanctified when Israel performs his commandments" (Milgrom 2000, 1888), which perhaps anticipates the words of Jesus as he taught the disciples to pray, "Hallowed be thy name." On the other hand, six times in these two chapters, God

307

stresses that he is the One who sanctifies the nation and the priests. This reminded the people that they could not assume that any of their own actions (such as eating holy food) would make them holy (Willis 2009, 186). These chapters draw specific attention to the physical, social, and relational wounds, scars, and imperfections one may cause and receive from living in a fallen world. All such imperfections render one unable to represent a perfect, holy God.

PREACHING AND TEACHING STRATEGIES

Exegetical and Theological Synthesis

This passage returns to some common themes in the book of Leviticus. How do unholy people commune with a holy God? How can unholy people proclaim the holiness of God? This is a much weightier question than we often allow it to be. God cannot become less than he is. A fallen people cannot become more than they are. A priest is needed to represent the people, a priest who is perfectly holy in every way to be in God's full presence and accurately image him to a sinful world. The ideal is becoming clear. The solution is not.

Initially, the idea is offensive to the ear. For whom is absolute holiness even a viable option? All are born outside this standard. Many either make early choices or become victims of the choices of others that disqualify them. Is this fair? Perfection lies beyond our imagination. So, we often respond by settling (even touting our comfort), serving God from a corrupted state. Persistent sins and imperfections may be worn as badges of honor by church leaders that allow them to better identify with the people. This is not warranted. We have Jesus, the perfect high priest, who identified with the people yet was without sin.

It is dangerous for pastors and elders, or ministers and priests, to create their own set of standards that can be met. Yes, Paul provides a baseline from which the church should select elders (1 Tim. 3; Titus 1), but what is the purpose of such criteria? Jesus sets the standard: "Be perfect, for I am perfect!" (cf. Lev. 19:2). Are we really expected to be perfect? No, not today. But one day, absolutely! As many have noted, God is not accepting us "as we are." If he did, we would be left in our fallen state forever. God is accepting us "in spite of the way we are," and by so doing he declares to the world the hope that he will not only redeem us to be his own but will fully restore (glorify) us into who we should be!

This frees us to long for perfection yet be content before God because he is the Lord who sanctifies. To be content with less than perfection is to profane the name of God. We are not content in ourselves. We are content in our God who will make us perfect. Perfection will not come to us in this lifetime. Yet believers are promised that Christ will transform our lowly bodies to be like his glorious body by the power that enables him to subject all things to himself (Phil. 3:21).

Preaching Idea

As needy, imperfect intermediaries, we are called to perfectly represent a perfect God as the One who sanctifies.

Contemporary Connections

What does it mean?

The Israelites have already witnessed in Leviticus 10 the lethal administrative failures of Aaron's sons who failed to perfectly represent the One who sanctifies. As qualifications rise for those who stand between God and the people, the pool of representatives dwindles. The sons of Aaron will not serve as the sanctified. They are forerunners to represent the One who does sanctify. How do those marred by sin (both the sin that is their own and the sin that comes at them from a fallen world) represent a perfect God to the world?

A Holy Priesthood for a Holy Nation (21:1–22:33)

We fear the word "perfection" and label its pursuit as a mental disorder. It is true that chasing perfection can provoke frustration, disappointment, envy, coveting, and discontentment. Yet God has created the means by which we can pursue perfection (that is unattainable) and be content as a servant of the One who perfects. For the servant of God, perfectionism is a future hope, not a mental disorder! It is a description of Christ our sinless Lord and Savior. He was and is and will remain absolutely holy. As his representatives and undershepherds, we image perfection to others when we keep the spotlight shining on him.

His representatives are called to live as stewards of his grace, who see their own need for sanctification and are prepared to live sacrificially for the One who sanctifies. This calls for behavioral, social, and relational constraints that will help but never fully eliminate one from misrepresenting the holiness of God and thus profaning his name. Living in a fallen world will create open wounds and lasting scars. But God is the One who has promised to sanctify our work, relationships, and lives as we humble ourselves before him.

Is it true?

Are we called to perfectly represent a perfect God? As soon as we answer "no," we are creating our own measure of how perfect one must be in one's conduct and relationships and administration of church practices and funds. Don't such high standards inevitably generate pride, frustration, and judgmentalism? No—not if we turn the spotlight for perfection onto Christ as our savior. This quickly frees us from such foolish pride by demonstrating our moment-by-moment need for grace and mercy and secures our hope in future glorification.

Might we be suggesting that no one is worthy to approach God? Most certainly. But no one has ever been free to come into the presence of a holy God apart from the justifying work of Christ. It is not about God accepting me just as I am. *Christ did not sacrifice God's perfect holiness on man's altar of unconditional love.* It is about God letting me see my fallenness, so that I may know he is accepting me in spite of who I am, so that I may become who he created me to be. He is the One who met the standard of holiness that he will one day place within all who believe (Phil. 3:21).

Now what?

The Israelites were far removed from Eden. In Eden, there was no sin and therefore there were no relational, physical, emotional, or social wounds that were the result of sin. Like the Israelites, we do not live in Eden—but one day all God's children will! In the new heavens and new earth, sin will be abolished. In that day, there will be no festering relational, physical, emotional, or social wounds or unhealed scars. All will be made right. All will be made perfect by the One who sanctifies.

As we await that day, how we respond to tragedy this day can carelessly profane the name of God. To despair of the pain in the present without confessing our hope of the future is to declare to those around us something about God that is not true. Yes, it is true that this world is fallen. Sin is wreaking havoc all around us. Yet God does not leave us without real-time hope. Christ has overcome the world (John 16:33). Though the world may intend so much that we see for evil, God is actively using it for our good and the good of those around us (Gen. 50:20). He is patiently opening our eyes to our sins, that we may fully see our need for redemption and restoration and publicly glorify the One who sanctifies!

Creativity in Presentation

Be aware! This passage will be among one of the more challenging in Leviticus. Declaring that we are far from perfect morally, physically,

A Holy Priesthood for a Holy Nation (21:1–22:33)

and socially can create a barrier between you and your congregation before you even begin! Here are a few ways to escape this pitfall. First, choose to focus on the body of believers as a whole rather than the individual. All can agree that the church is not perfect! And the church is the bride of Christ. We are called to glory in his perfection and long for the day when he will perfect the church that we may be with him forever.

Second, choose to focus on restoration rather than remodeling. You can use the picture of an old stately building that has been damaged either by weather, age, or neglect. All can agree that it is not now reflecting what it was created to be. It would be a disservice to the builder and the building to leave it forever in such a state. Someone needs to first recognize and confess that a restoration will bring glory to the builder (and the building). But this cannot be planned or completed by just anyone! The original architect and builder are the ones who are equipped to complete the job. If only they were available to us! They are, through God's Word and in the person of Christ.

You can also build on the AT&T slogan, "Just okay is not okay." In 2021, a series of commercials parroted the idea that one would not choose a surgeon (or other professional) who is "just okay" to complete an invasive surgery. Do we as believers want someone who is "just okay" to serve as our representative before a perfectly holy God? Clearly that is a dangerous proposition! That should be as apparent to us, and it was to the line of Aaron. Christ alone is sufficient to represent us.

Another example is to explain how lead absorbs radiation. Most have had an x-ray taken and will recall having most of their body "covered" by a lead apron to protect them from the penetrating effects of the radiation. Lead has the unique ability to absorb the radiation and deflect the energy, preventing us from being harmed. When we stand before a perfectly holy God, we need to be "covered" by

the righteousness of Christ. What else can absorb the judgment of sin and protect us from death? (Lead shields, by the way, never wear out!) No one wants a protective apron that is just okay. We want one that we are certain is effective, forever!

Show the congregation your physical imperfections, then ask: By what right am I allowed to represent God to you this morning?

As needy, imperfect intermediaries, we are called to perfectly represent a perfect God as the One who sanctifies.

- I am the Lord God who sanctifies (sets them apart)—an absolute standard!
  - Sanctifying life and work
  - Sanctifying for the banquet
  - Sanctifying through sacrifice
- What did this mean then? What does it mean always? What do we do now?
  - A scarred and sinful nation can become a nation of priests!
  - One must be perfect to be in God's presence.
    - All come imperfect and become imperfect, rendering us unable to be in God's presence.
    - Christ was/is perfect: he is transforming our lowly body to be like his glorious body!

DISCUSSION QUESTIONS

1. How do you process your physical, emotional, social, and spiritual imperfections?

2. God requires perfection to be in his presence. Why are we blessed because he requires nothing less?

3. Are there areas where you may be profaning yourself or the name of the Lord by embracing your deficiencies (profaning = declaring something is true about God that is not)?

A Holy Priesthood for a Holy Nation (21:1–22:33)

4. What imperfections in your life, which could bring despair, is God using for good to bring life to many (Gen. 50:20)?

5. Are there areas where you are glorying in your imperfections? How can you turn your glorying into longing for the perfection that will one day come?

Leviticus 23:1–24:9

EXEGETICAL IDEA
God established seven divine, recurring appointments for the people of Israel to meet regularly with him. The purpose of summoning everyone to these community celebrations (and priestly tasks) was to strengthen the social fabric of his people and keep their corporate focus on the worship of God.

THEOLOGICAL FOCUS
God commands corporate celebrations to gather his people before him, so that they may remember and rejoice in him as their Creator, redeemer, and provider.

PREACHING IDEA
We are summoned by God to stop and appear before him to affirm that he is our Creator, redeemer, and provider.

PREACHING POINTERS
Every agrarian community is dependent upon every individual doing an abundance of work. The animals need to be fed. The crops should be weeded. The fruit trees are ready to be pruned. There is so much to do! Will there be time to do it? The Lord God already claimed a day for worship (limiting the Israelites' work week to six days). He then established six annual feasts and daily maintenance tasks in the tabernacle! All of this would require time and expense. Worse yet, the feasts tended to be clumped around the busiest time of their year——when the harvest was coming in! Were these daily, weekly, and annual reminders really necessary? Did God not understand that his people were too busy in this fallen world to stop what they were doing for yet another holy gathering? Did God fail to realize that the work of his people would bring in the harvest so they would be free to continue worshipping him?

Is it our work or is it the blessing of God that will bring in the harvest? How we answer this question will in large part determine what holds our communities together. Do we believe we are blessed primarily through diligent work, wise decisions, and strategic planning, or by the ever-present hand of a gracious God? Our beliefs will determine whether we anticipate the coming celebrations with growing excitement or increasing dread. An easier question may be, which do we tend to minimize or even forget: God's blessing or our hard work? More often, we forget our God more than our own sacrifice. Once again, God knows us, his people. If our churches are to remain focused on worshipping our Creator and redeemer, we will need daily, weekly, and annual celebrations sewn into our social lives, reminding us of the source of our daily provision. Left to ourselves, we will fail to stop. We will quickly forget. We need a summons to recapture our attention.

STRENGTHENING THE SOCIAL FABRIC (23:1–24:9)

LITERARY STRUCTURE AND THEMES (23:1–24:9)

We noted in the unit "Life and Blood" (Lev. 17) that the last portion of Leviticus would focus less on the nation's relationship to God and more on proper human relationships, especially within the structure of a people chosen by God to represent him in this world. In Leviticus 18–22, we observed how the text addresses issues that would disrupt those relationships using a model of tears within the social fabric of the nation. Our next sections will cover Leviticus 23–25, although they do not follow chapter divisions. Collectively they continue to address human relationships within Israel's God-centered community but take different approaches. As a whole the three chapters are thematically related, presenting community activities designed to strengthen the social fabric by fostering celebrations that highlight how God worked in the nation both in terms of history and in terms of their agricultural economy, as well as corporate work projects intended to give the nation a sense of possession in terms of their worship practices. In the middle of this process, the second half of Leviticus 24 interrupts the divine directive sequence to report an actual disruptive event requiring divine guidance. That guidance reveals a third corporate strengthener when the community as a whole is required to administer appropriate discipline in the case of blasphemy, which for Israel as a covenant nation was also an act of treason. That event modeled how appropriate discipline might be necessary to prevent a personal snag from becoming a tear in Israel's social fabric. We will address that event and the implications of God's response in the next unit.

- ***The Lord Stresses the Importance of the Lord's Appointed Times (23:1–2)***
- ***The Lord Reiterates the Importance of the Sabbath (23:3)***
- ***The Lord Gives Directions for the Spring Appointed Times (23:4–22)***
- ***The Lord Gives Directions for the Autumn Appointed Times (23:23–43)***
- ***The Lord Directs the Nation to Use Its Corporate Production to Promote Corporate Worship (24:1–9)***

EXPOSITION (23:1–24:9)

Leviticus 17–22 illustrated personal actions that could tear the nation's social fabric by describing specific practices Israelites were to avoid. The current unit (Lev. 23:1–24:9) continues to develop the concept of social fabric through God-directed celebratory activities designed to reinforce the social fabric by bringing the people together through common positive practices designed to focus individual and corporate attention on God. While we have combined this material as one unit because of this common purpose, the text really describes two different types of corporate practices. The first type is called "appointed times" or something similar, depending on the translation. These are occasions where God has directed the people to take time from their routines and focus on him. They are the subject of Leviticus 23, which includes two types of appointed times: the weekly Sabbath day, and then six *annual* appointed times, popularly known as *festivals*. While this chapter addresses each of these seven appointed times, the chapter may be divided into three sections: the weekly Sabbath day, which seems to be the foundation of all the other appointed

Strengthening the Social Fabric (23:1–24:9)

times, and then three appointed times that occur in the spring of the year, followed by three that occur in the autumn. We use the terms "spring" and "autumn," but we need to remember that Israel's agricultural calendar was and is significantly different than the one most westerners are familiar with. While Israel's religious calendar begins with the spring equinox, the first celebrations (generally called spring celebrations) are associated with the beginning of the harvest rather than with the spring planting and new growth time we typically associate with Passover or Easter. The autumn festivals then wrap up a six-month-long harvest season. Because of associations with aspects of the harvest, some scholars have proposed that the original function of all of the festivals was agrarian and only later were they given a historical-theological function (Gerstenberger 1996, 338). As we will see, however, Leviticus 23 seems to generally anchor the festivals in historical occasions in the life of the nation (e.g., Passover and Succoth reflect aspects of the exodus) using specific agricultural motifs to highlight key concepts. The NT then ties those motifs theologically to aspects of salvation history, suggesting possible eschatological implications. While this unit will address each appointed time, they are discussed as a collection in the "Holy Days and Salvation History" section of the introduction.

Following Leviticus 23's anticipatory overview of the festival system the nation was to implement once it was settled in the land (which is amplified in other passages such as Numbers 28–29 and Deuteronomy 16), Leviticus 24:1–9 assigns two ongoing tasks to the congregation. As part of the worship system, they were to bring two harvest products (flour they manufactured from the wheat and oil they extracted from the olives) to the priests to use as resources for their task of representing the nation before God. This provision integrates the congregation as a whole into the priestly work of corporate worship.

The Lord Stresses the Importance of the Lord's Appointed Times (23:1–2)

23:1–2. The first two verses introduce the entire chapter, beginning with the standard introductory *waw*, which should be translated as "then" in this narrative, showing the continued sequence of revelation. This is followed by a declaration that the מוֹעֲדֵי יְהוָה or "appointed times of the Lord [YHWH]" that the Lord is about to delineate are to be treated as "holy convocations."

> *TRANSLATION ANALYSIS: "APPOINTED TIMES"*
>
> The phrase מוֹעֲדֵי יְהוָה combines the name YHWH with the word מוֹעֵד, which carries the basic idea of appointment, which may be a place or a time. This is the same word we have already seen some forty-two times in the book of Leviticus used in the term "the tent of meeting" (אֹהֶל מוֹעֵד), which emphasized the place (Lev. 1:1). There the noun denoted the location of the meeting. Here, the noun emphasizes who scheduled the meeting, and in this portion of Leviticus the focus is on the time of the appointment, hence the translation "appointed times" or "appointed festivals" (Lewis 1980d, 388–89). These are times that the Lord set up for the nation when the people were expected to show up for a meeting with God. As he develops the description of these appointed times and their tie *to* (לְ) the Lord, Milgrom (2001, 1962) rebuts Babylonian myth (the idea that "the gods built Marduk a temple") when he asserts that "God builds for himself (other gods being nonexistent), not in space but in time— the Sabbath." He goes on to claim: "Never in Scripture do we find that God sanctifies space. Although the world is his creation, he does not hallow it."

While collectively there are seven appointed times (the weekly Sabbath and six annual occasions), individually they are referred to by other terms such as "feast," but it is not clear what the significance of these other terms was. For the nation of Israel there were two key points. First,

314

the emphasis here is that the appointments that would be described in the rest of the chapter were from the Lord. As generally used in this chapter, the word for "appointment" (מוֹעֵד) is in construct or possessive relationship with the one who set the appointment, that is, the Lord. The sense of this structure is ambiguous in that while the appointments are intended *for* the worship of God, they are also designed and mandated *by* God (Milgrom 2001, 1955). As such, they are obligatory for the nation.

Second, these appointments were to be treated as "holy convocations" (מִקְרָאֵי קֹדֶשׁ). Here "holy" is used in a derivative sense as a reminder that the appointment was with the Lord, the Creator, the One who brought the nation out of Egypt. In other words, it was to have the highest priority. The term מִקְרָאֵי is generally translated either as "convocation" or "assembly," and most commentators seem to understand it in this sense. However, as Kleinig (2003, 487) and Kiuchi (2007, 415) point out, literally the phrase means a "proclamation" and in essence the mandate is to view the designated days as "extraordinary holy days." For example, in the case of both the Sabbath day and Yom Kippur, there was no assembly. Rather the Israelites observed the appointed time at home. As we will see in our discussion of the various celebrations, there were only three occasions during the year that required an actual assembly when "all Israel had to appear 'before the Lord'" (Mays 1963, 63).

The Lord Reiterates the Importance of the Sabbath (23:3)

23:3. The first appointed time is that of the Sabbath, which is defined here as a time of rest, and tied to the seventh day, although the concept of rest will also show up in the remaining appointed times.

TRANSLATION ANALYSIS: "SABBATH"
The relationship between the verb שָׁבַת meaning "to cease, desist, or rest" and the noun שַׁבָּת is unclear and disputed. The basic question is, did

the day derive its name from the idea that it was a day of rest, or was the verb a denominative derived from the noun (Haag 2004, 388–89, Hamilton 1980j). For the nation of Israel, the concept of Sabbath as presented in the book of Exodus is mandated in conjunction with the appearance of the "bread from heaven," which became known as "manna," a month after they left Egypt (Exod. 16:1). While the Israelites were told to gather each morning their daily provision, at the same time they were told that on the sixth day they were to gather twice as much (Exod. 16:18–26). Moses explained on the sixth day when the leaders asked about the double gathering, "This is what the Lord [YHWH] spoke: Tomorrow is a Sabbath observance, a holy Sabbath to the Lord [YHWH]" (Exod. 16:23). On the seventh day, he reiterated this when some Israelites tried to gather bread and told the Israelites to that no person was to "go out of his place." As a result, they "rested" (Exod. 16:29–30). The associated term שַׁבָּתוֹן is described as an abstract noun by Hamilton (1980j, 903), who defines it as "Sabbath observance." It is used by itself on a number of occasions to dictate rest on a non-Sabbath day (such as the Day of Atonement [Lev. 16:31; 23:32]; the Feast of Trumpets [Lev. 23:24]; and the first and last days of Sukkoth [Lev. 23:39]). It is also frequently used, as here, in construct to indicate intensification (Haag 2004, 396). This is often shown in translation as "a Sabbath of complete rest."

For the Israelites this command in Leviticus to observe a Sabbath day did not introduce something new. Even before the newly freed Israelites had reached Sinai a year earlier, they had been forced to observe the Sabbath on each seventh day when the manna did not appear (Exod. 16:25–30). Then, immediately after reaching Sinai, the people were admonished in the Decalogue to *remember* the Sabbath (Exod. 20:8). The word translated "remember" (זָכַר) carries variety of nuances, but all suggest prior awareness (McComiskey 1980c). While we have no evidence that a Sabbath day was observed prior to the exodus, the concept may well have reached back to creation, since the Decalogue tied the idea of the Sabbath to God's creation stating "in six days the Lord [YHWH] made the heavens and the earth, the sea and all that is in them, and rested on the seventh day; therefore the Lord [YHWH] blessed the Sabbath day and sanctified it" (Exod. 20:11; see also Gen. 2:3).

The Israelite Calendar and the Seven-Day Week

People around the world all use the same three basic measurements of time, which are based on astronomical data: day, month, and year. The day is the period when the earth completes one full rotation. A month is the period of time that it takes the moon to circle the earth. A year measures the amount of time it takes for the earth to go around the sun. These phenomena are so readily observed throughout the world we tend to take them for granted. However, because all three are cycles, different cultures use different starting points.

A day consists of a full cycle of daylight and darkness. While the total of the two remains constant, the proportions of that cycle that are of sunlight and darkness vary with location and season. For ease of observation, a new day might be considered to begin with sunrise or sunset. Historically, the nation of Israel used both (Finegan 1998, 8). Today we use an arbitrary starting point designated as midnight.

The lighted portion of the moon as seen from earth changes shape as it orbits the earth, going from completely dark to completely light and back, producing a period called a month. Historically most cultures, including Israel, began this cycle with the beginning of the lighted phase, called "the new moon." Because of the lack of synchronization between the lunar cycle and the annual solar cycle, today we use arbitrary, artificial months.

In the same way today, we use an arbitrary start date for a year. A year does have astronomical indicators, but they are not as readily identified

Figure 60. The new moon is the first sliver of light seen after sunset, as the moon moves away from its conjunction with the sun.

by a casual observer. Basically, the ancients noted either what constellations (various arbitrary star patterns) were visible, or where on the horizon the sun rose and set. They observed that different constellations were visible, not only by season but at the time of night. They also understood the seasonal variation of the length of the daylight and dark periods, although without clocks it would have been difficult to identify when a year or season began. Our ancestors also noted that the length of daylight correlated with the location of the rising or setting sun and discovered four anchor points, including the summer solstice (when sunrise and sunset were furthest north in the northern hemisphere) and the winter solstice (when sunrise and sunset were furthest south). The other two anchor points, interestingly, were the dates exactly in the middle of the solstices, the spring and fall equinoxes, when the length of daylight and darkness were essentially equal. (As I write this on the autumnal equinox, I note that at our latitude the day portion is approximately ten minutes longer than the night.[1]) Many ancient cultures built monuments that showed one of those anchor points. For example, the ancient Irish built Newgrange (apparently even before the pyramids), which was designed so that the dawn's first sunlight of the winter solstice shone down the corridor to the center of the edifice.

Figure 61. Newgrange, Ireland.

While many cultures used a solstice, most of the cultures in the ANE used one of the equinoxes as a starting point for the year, probably for agricultural purposes. Since this required careful observations of the constellations, it may explain one of the functions of the magi. Israel used both the spring and fall equinoxes (Finegan 1998, 76–80). According to Exodus 12:2, beginning with the exodus, Israel used the spring equinox for

---

[1] This correlates with data on the website www.weather.gov/cle/Seasons.

the religious calendar. Specifically, the first month (Abib or Nisan) began with the first new moon after the spring equinox. The Mishnah notes that this was also the new year for kings. The first of Tishri is known in the Pentateuch as the seventh month, but is named Ethanim in 1 Kings 8:1. In Leviticus 23:27, it is designated to be a "Sabbath" (שַׁבָּתוֹן) coupled with a special offering and indicated by the blowing of trumpets. Because of the trumpets, it later became celebrated as the Feast of Trumpets. Today the first of Tishri is known as Rosh Hashanah or New Year's Day.

While these measurements are based on astronomical data as noted in Genesis 1:14, the week is different. In essence the definition of a week as seven days is arbitrary (Mathews 2009, 194). While other cultures had some type of heptadic system, they were embedded in the month. For example, Cyrus Gordon (1982, 13) notes how the Babylonians noted the "seventh, fourteenth, twenty-first and twenty-eighth days of the month." However, these four dates were viewed as restrictive or unlucky. Interestingly, the most restrictive date was the nineteenth, which didn't even fit the heptadic pattern. Moreover, the cycles restarted with the new month, which left a few extra days at the end of each month, so it really wasn't a weekly system. Similar observations have been made regarding Sumer (Kramer 1963, 140) and Ugarit (Hallo 1977, 12). While those cultures forced their heptads of days into the lunar month, Israel did the opposite. As William Hallo expresses it, "The week was fundamental to the biblical calendar and immune to violation by any other consideration, least of all the phases of the moon. Even though these [lunar phases] consist of *ca.* seven and three-eighths days each, the biblical week is wholly independent of them" (1977, 11). The understanding of the biblical text is that the idea of a week derives from the creation process laid out in Genesis 1.

Because the Sabbath was blessed and made holy at the time of creation it has been suggested that it would have been a mandate for all humankind (Gane 2004a, 388). If so, this correlation was lost as a result of the fall (Ross 2002, 397). For the nation of Israel, at Sinai the celebration of the Sabbath as a divine appointment was emphasized. While prior to Sinai the idea that the Sabbath was to be a day of rest may have been inferential, here it is made explicit: by definition, following six days of work, the seventh is to be a day of rest. This seven-day sequence would become the foundation around which the rest of the calendar was to be built. As Kleinig (2003, 502) expresses it, "The Sabbath was the archetypal holy day. All other holy days were, as it were, derived

from it and extensions of it. Its position in the temporal order corresponded to the place of Holy of Holies in the spatial realm and the role of the daily sacrifice in the ritual order."

As given here, the nature of rest is left open. The command is that all work (כָּל־מְלָאכָה) is forbidden. Hartley notes that the term used here for "work" (מְלָאכָה) is more inclusive than עֲבֹדָה, which may also be translated "work," and thus is quite broad. Later in the chapter these two terms are combined (see 23:7). He expresses surprise that no specific laws are given that define work such as the rabbis developed later. However, he concludes, "God prefers to give his people principles to live by and let them fill in the details. This, of course, gives the law an enduring

Strengthening the Social Fabric (23:1–24:9)

quality that allows it to be applicable to a variety of cultural contexts amidst the changing times" (Hartley 1992, 375–76).

In terms of observing the Sabbath, two things were required of the nation. First, the people were to remain in "all [their] dwellings" (23:3). This was not a time to produce, but a time to personally, and perhaps as a family unit, focus on God. Further, this directive covered not only the Israelites but also their servants and their animals and was thus egalitarian. Second, the priests were to perform a Sabbath-day sacrifice of two lambs and their associated sacrifices (see Exod. 29:38–42) "in addition to" the standard corporate burnt offering. While Dennis Cole (2000, 473) suggests that this doubles the daily offering, the text seems to read as if it were a third sacrifice beyond the morning and evening lambs (Num. 28:9, 19). In either case, the extra lambs differentiated this day from the preceding six. The priests also replaced the loaves of the bread of presence with fresh loaves, and the older loaves were to be eaten (Lev. 24:5–9, see below). By following these practices, the nation kept the covenant with God strong by showing faithfulness (Ross 2002, 399).

The Lord Gives Directions for the Spring Appointed Times (23:4–22)

23:4. Leviticus 23:4 summarizes the rest of the chapter indicating that the Lord is about to give Moses the entire annual holy day calendar. As already noted, these were to be appointed times where the people turned their attention to God. One must also keep in mind that the instructions in this chapter are presented as having been given while the nation was at Sinai, beginning on the first day of the first month of the second year after leaving Egypt (the first of Nisan [Exod. 40:17–34]). It serves as a supplement to the short list of holy days that had been given in Exodus 34 as part of the covenant renewal following the golden calf incident.

Exodus's Short List

The short list in Exodus 34 does not include the Feast of Unleavened Bread. Rather it lists the Feast of Weeks, also designated as the firstfruits of the wheat harvest, and the Feast of Ingathering "at the turn of the [agricultural] year" (Exod. 34:22). The text goes on to state that on three occasions, "all your males are to appear before the Lord [YHWH] God, the God of Israel" (Exod. 34:23–24), apparently including the Feast of the Passover in the following verses with Unleavened Bread implied by the prohibition of leavened bread with Passover in Exodus 34:25.

While the entire holy day calendar is included here in the sequence the holy days were to be celebrated, when the calendar was given several of the holy days would not be celebrated for a number of years, that is, until after they were settled in the land and were actively farming. As such, some are presented here in capsule form, providing the name and purpose, but not giving the details of celebration until later. As we read in subsequent material, the adjustments made to the exodus program as a result of the judgment at Kadesh-barnea changed the actual institution of those postconquest holy days, which necessitated some changes in detail, while they remained the same conceptually. One example might be the celebration of the Passover in Numbers 9 where amplification provided an alternative for men who were unclean at the time, apparently because of the deaths of Nadab and Abihu.

Exodus Adjustments

I suggest in another context that the *toledot* of Terah (Gen. 11:27–25:11) through its highlighting of tensions between God's calling of Terah and Abraham "illustrates an intricate interweaving of God exercising sovereign control while allowing individuals within the account to exercise free will" (Harbin 2016a, 20). It is suggested that the exodus illustrates the same interweaving. For example, through God's sovereignty, the nation of

Israel was brought out, but individual Israelites had to make choices as to whether they would participate. Just as God seems to have originally called Terah to move to the land and father the nation, and when he failed to follow through Abraham received the call and the blessing, a similar disjunction occurs in Exodus. When the nation failed to follow through at Kadesh-barnea, it was the subsequent generation that now received the promise and subsequently moved into the land. In the process, through God's mercy on the disinherited generation, the actual entry to the land is deferred forty years and is moved from the relatively easy entry point north of Kadesh-barnea to the rigorous entry through the rift valley at Jericho.

Of the six annual festivals, the first three were in the spring and the last were in the autumn, but as observed earlier, all of the festivals represented aspects of the harvest season. This seasonal distinction is emphasized in 23:23, where the autumn festivals were given as a separate speech from God. Leviticus 23:4 ends with the declaration to the nation that "they" (the pronoun is plural) were to "proclaim [the appointed times] at the times appointed for them." Some have suggested that the dates were originally fluid, allowing the festivals to be celebrated based on the time of the actual harvests (Morgenstern 1926, 80–81). The variability of actual harvests from year to year and in different locations suggests this to have merit; however, the specificity of dates given throughout this chapter seems to indicate otherwise.

23:5. The first annual appointed time, both in terms of annual celebrations and as given to the nation, was the Lord's Passover.

TRANSLATION ANALYSIS: "PASSOVER"
The Hebrew word translated "Passover" is פֶּסַח, which is considered to derive from a root meaning "to pass or spring over" (Hamilton 1980g). Based on Isa. 31:5, some suggest that the verb in the key

passages regarding the event (Exod. 12:13, 23, 27) means "to defend, protect" (Ross 2002, 411). However, the context of exodus shows an interesting contrast between the actions of the Lord with respect to the Egyptians in contrast with the Israelites. For example, in Exodus 12:23, the text states that the Lord will "pass through" (here using the verb עָבַר, which primarily means "to pass over, by, through" [Van Groningen 1980b, 641]) the land "to smite the Egyptians," but "when he sees the blood on the lintel . . . the Lord will pass over [פֶּסַח] the door." It is true that he would provide protection to those inside of the door, but since the door is the object of the verb, the verb must mean "pass over" or "pass by."

The date of the appointed time is specific: the fourteenth day of the first month. Also, the text specifically notes that it was to be celebrated at twilight (literally "between the two evenings"). Interestingly, no further information regarding this festival is given in this passage, which is not surprising given that the entire audience would have experienced the original Passover approximately a year earlier, and according to the text would be celebrating its first anniversary in approximately a week (the account of the first Passover is in book of Exodus, which apparently Moses had already written by this time). The celebration of the first anniversary is recorded in Numbers 9:2–3.

TRANSLATION ANALYSIS: "TWILIGHT"
The phrase בֵּין הָעַרְבָּיִם uses the preposition בֵּין, which means "between or among" (*DCH* s.v. "בֵּין" 2:146), along with the dual form of the word עֶרֶב, which means "evening" or "night" (Allen 1980b). This is generally understood to mean twilight, although orthodox Jews take the view that it means "between midday and sunset." During the NT period, the sacrifices began at about 3 p.m. (Wenham 1979, 302).

23:6–14. This section on the Feast of Unleavened Bread contains two portions. Leviticus

Strengthening the Social Fabric (23:1–24:9)

23:6–8 ties the feast (it is called a חַג, "feast," instead of a מוֹעֵד, "appointed time") to Passover.

TRANSLATION ANALYSIS: "FEAST"

The Hebrew term חַג is a noun derived from the verb חָגַג, which is defined as "to celebrate, keep (hold) a (solemn) feast (holy day)" (Weber 1980b). The word "usually refers to the three main pilgrimage feasts" cited in Exodus 23:14–17: Passover-Unleavened Bread, Weeks or Firstfruits, and Booths or Tabernacles. These three are designated as times when all Israelite males were to "appear before the Lord God" (23:17).

Beginning with the Passover meal (at twilight on the fourteenth of Abib or Nisan), Israelites were not to eat leavened bread for the next seven days (Deut. 16:3), which seems to be the only restriction on their usual diet. The same verse in Deuteronomy calls the unleavened bread the "bread of affliction" to remind the nation that they "came out of the land of Egypt in haste." Because this was a week-long commemoration, the directions do not call for rest (as was the case of the archetypal appointed time Sabbath), but it does have a different work restriction, which seems to apply only to the first and seventh days. Those days are designated as the "appointed times" (or "convocations"), but they are not labeled Sabbaths. Still, on those days the Israelites were not to do "arduous work" (מְלֶאכֶת עֲבֹדָה) or perhaps better, their regular work. This would mean that regular chores might be done during those appointed times as opposed to the Sabbath rest (see also comments above on Lev. 23:3 regarding rest).

TRANSLATION ANALYSIS: "ARDUOUS WORK"

This combines the more general term מְלָאכָה (Bowling 1980c), which means "work" or "business" with the term עֲבֹדָה, which means "labor" or "service" (Kaiser 1980h). Perhaps because of the latter's relationship with עֶבֶד, which means "slave" or "servant" (Kaiser 1980h), the

combination is understood as arduous work such as might be done by a slave. Milgrom (2001, 1977) distinguishes between the idea of any enterprise and the physical labor attached to it. As such, some translators prefer "hard work" or something similar for the combination. Others suggest that the idea is ordinary occupations, understanding that the idea is to not do the work one would normally do (Péter-Contesse and Ellington 1992, 345). Kleinig (2003, 488) observes that most of the Israelites would have been farmers and seems to suggest that the more general term would restrict regular chores such as feeding animals (as in 23:3), while the stronger term might refer to the more arduous work such as plowing or harvesting (as in 23:7), which seems to be the best understanding.

While the Feast of Unleavened Bread was largely retrospective, reminding the nation of the exodus event as part of their past (Exod. 23:15), there was another element to it that looked to the future. In Leviticus 23:9 the Lord gives Moses another feature to the feast that would only apply when the nation entered the land and had begun farming. During this feast, the Israelites were told to bring "the sheaf [עֹמֶר] of the firstfruits of your harvest to the priest" (23:10). This was to be done on the "day after the Sabbath" (23:11), a phrase that is debated. While there are several interpretations, the question really comes down to whether the Sabbath cited is a regular Sabbath (here, specifically referring to the Saturday that followed Passover), or is it one of the appointment days of the feast (generally viewed as day 1, which was the fifteenth of Abib, but possibly day 8, the other day when arduous work was forbidden)? The view that identifies it as the fifteenth of Abib seems to predominate (Kleinig 2003, 175; Lange 1960, 175; Wenham 1979, 304), but there are problems with that. Ross (2002, 417) points out that "the more natural interpretation of the word Sabbath is that it refers to the actual Sabbath, meaning that the first sheaf was waved on Sunday, the day after

Strengthening the Social Fabric (23:1–24:9)

the Sabbath." Perhaps more significantly, while the term Sabbath is used in 23:11, the first day of the feast, the fifteenth of Abib, although called an appointed time, is not referred to as a Sabbath. Thus, it seems that the stronger view is to understand the Sabbath here as the first Saturday after Passover.

TRANSLATION ANALYSIS: "SHEAF"

The Hebrew word here is עֹמֶר, which is often transliterated as "omer." Literally it means "sheaf" (*TWOT* s.v. "עֹמֶר I" 2:679). The LXX uses the word δράγμα, which is defined as "as many stalks of corn as the reaper can grasp in his left hand, sheaf" (Lust, Eynikel, and Hauspie 2003, 161). Milgrom (2001, 1983) notes that later rabbis defined omer as a specific dry measure, "namely, one-tenth of an ephah of flour made from the grain." This could suggest that a sheaf of grain was the amount that produced an omer of flour. While Huey (1975, 917) states that an omer was exactly 2.087 qts. (2.299 L), other estimates (e.g., *ISBE* 4:2188) are that it contained about 7.5 pts. (or about 3.75 qts.). Either seems to be much more grain than produced by a sheaf, warranting a caution regarding interpreting OT weights and measures.

Coupled with the sheaf, the nation was to offer a one-year-old male lamb as a burnt offering (23:12) with requisite associated sacrifices (gift or grain offering, although in this case double the normal one-tenth ephah gift offering, and a drink offering) in addition to the regular daily sacrifices. The details for this sacrifice seem to be the same as given earlier for the respective sacrifices earlier in the book. The important thing the Israelites were to note was that until this offering had been made, they were not permitted to eat any product from the current harvest, whether as bread, roasted grain, or new growth. For that reason and the statement that this is "the sheaf of the firstfruits of your harvest," the feast is often called the Feast of Firstfruits. The theological significance for both

Passover and the Feast of Unleavened Bread is explored in the segment on "Holy Days and Salvation History" in the introduction, but is summarized in the "Theological Focus" at the end of this unit.

Gerstenberger (1996, 338), among others, has argued that originally the "festival days themselves were not precisely fixed," but were "celebrated locally when it [the harvest] was actually brought in." However, this presumes that the background was just a harvest cycle to which historical rationales were attached later. Milgrom (2001, 1983–89) cites rabbinic tradition that notes that only in the Jordan and Jezreel valleys would barley be ripe by mid-April to allow a fully ripe sheaf of barley to be presented. Rather, the sheaf would be barley that was "the color of ripe barley." He states that barley has three stages in ripening, which are reflected in the three ways 23:14 describes the grain being eaten. His list begins with *'abib* the first stage, which is also called "milky grain." This is a wet green stage. To be edible it must be "parched with fire" (*qālî*, translated "roasted grain"). The second stage is *karmel*, "fresh grain," which is waxy and yellow, and is translated here as "new growth." Finally, there is *dagan*, "fully dried kernels." These are edible after they are baked, producing a bread. With respect to the different ripening times throughout the land, the key seems to be a question of whether this firstfruits presentation is personal (i.e., given by each individual farmer or locale), or corporate (i.e., representing the entire nation). Apparently the latter was the intention, given that the specificity of the timing of the offering of the sheaf of the firstfruits (fifteenth of Abib) as opposed to being dependent upon the actual ripening of the grain. Thus, once the corporate first sheaf was presented and the corporate sacrifice given, the farmers could partake of their harvest as the grain in their region ripened and was harvested.

23:15–22. Beginning with the day after the Sabbath following Passover, the Israelites were to count fifty days to the third holy day. This day, which followed seven Sabbaths after the presentation of the first sheaf, is called by various names: Festival of Weeks (Exod. 34:22; Deut. 16:10) or Festival of the Harvest of the firstfruits of your labor (Exod. 23:16) or of the firstfruits of the wheat harvest (Exod. 34:22). After the exile it became known by a Greek name, Pentecost (2 Macc. 12:31–32; Acts 2:1).

Seven Weeks or Fifty Days

The period between the two dates equates to fifty days by what is known as inclusive reckoning or including both the first and last dates (Sklar 2014, 283). According to Péter-Contesse and Ellington (1992, 348) this was the Hebrew way of calculating time periods. It shows up in the Bible in a number of other cases, especially with respect to the three days Jesus was in the grave.

Given the various descriptions, it is not surprising that there is some confusion between the presentation of the first sheaf during the Festival of Unleavened Bread and the firstfruits during the Festival of Weeks, resulting in the term "firstfruits" being applied somewhat indiscriminately to both. For Israel, the sheaf in the former festival anticipated a bountiful harvest beginning with the barley, but also represented continuing trust in God's provision. Milgrom

(2001, 1980) observes that the period between the two harvests was a time "fraught with peril to the ripening grain lest it be devastated by the dreaded sirocco winds." In contrast, the firstfruits presentation during the Festival of Weeks was more celebratory, as indicating that they actually began the wheat harvest (Gane 2004a, 391).

Another point of confusion is the purpose of the fifty days. A common understanding is that the Festival of Weeks is associated with the end of the harvest period (Balentine 2002, 177; Harrison 1980, 220). As discussed in the "Holy Days and Salvation History" section of the introduction, completion of the harvest season actually is associated with the autumnal appointed times, and fits more closely with the final festival, that of Sukkoth. Another view is that the fifty days marks the beginning of the wheat harvest (Gane 2004a, 389). While this may be the rationale, the difficulties of matching the dates suggest something different, since the astronomical determination of the holy days could vary by about a month, which was coupled with two weather variables: the location in the country and whether the season began early or late. For the nation of Israel, there was then a tension between the calendar and the produce in the fields. Even so, the focus of the appointed times was to remind the nation that God is both sovereign and the One who supplies their every need.

Determining Holy Days on a Lunar Calendar

Ancient Israel used a lunar calendar to determine holy days; but agriculture, which was very seasonal, of necessity required a solar calendar. Correlating the two has always been a problem, since twelve lunar months are only 354 days, producing a discrepancy of eleven days compared to a solar year. To correct for this, several variables had to be considered to determine when to celebrate a holy day associated with a harvest that itself was variable. When God gave Moses the directions for the exodus and Passover, he told Moses that that month would mark the start of their calendar ("the beginning of months"; Exod. 12:2). That month was Abib, which later became known as Nisan, the term used today. For our purposes here, we will use Abib.

The Israelite calendar marks the start of a lunar month with the new moon (see below). It is likely that the Israelites before Moses knew that the month Abib was associated with the spring equinox, although we have no records that show how they accommodated the disjunctions between the lunar and solar years. It is enough to be aware that following the exodus, the first new moon following the spring equinox was nominally considered the beginning of the religious New Year. Thus, the first important date for the Israelites required that they verify when the spring equinox occurred. After the equinox, the first new moon began the month of Abib, and Passover was on the fourteenth of Abib, at the time of the full moon. Thus, essentially, Israelites marked the equinox, looked for the next new moon, then counted fourteen days for Passover. The next day, the fifteenth of Abib, would be the first day of the Feast of Unleavened Bread, and from there they calculated to the presentation of the first sheaf of the barley harvest. However, because of the solar-lunar disjunction, there were a number of variables that complicated the matter.

First, as shown in chart 9, line 1, astronomically the equinox could be March 19, 20, or 21 under the Gregorian calendar. If the new year began with the first new moon following the equinox, this would produce the earliest day of the Feast of Unleavened Bread (FUB) on 15 Nisan, as shown in line 3. Theoretically then, the latest date of the Feast of Unleavened Bread would be in line 5. This would produce the earliest and latest theoretical dates for Pentecost or the Festival of Weeks as shown in lines 6 and 7 respectively, giving a spread of about a month between the earliest and latest possible days.

		Early	**Middle**	**Late**
1	Equinox	March 19	March 20	March 21
2	Earliest New Moon	March 20	March 21	March 22
3	Earliest FUB (15 Nisan)	April 4	April 5	April 6
4	Latest New Moon	April 18	April 19	April 20
5	Latest FUB (15 Nisan)	May 3	May 4	May 5
6	Earliest Pentecost	May 24	May 25	May 26
7	Latest Pentecost	June 22	June 23	June 24

Chart 9. Variables for spring holy days.

According to the Torah Calendar website (http://torahcalendar.com), historically the determination of the equinox was accomplished by actual observation of the new moon with regard to the carefully determined point of the equinox sunset (beginning of a new day) on the western horizon from Jerusalem. The position of this point had been carefully calculated through observation through the years and affirmed by the Sanhedrin. To ensure spring-like conditions, according to Jewish tradition, the calendar was adjusted so that Passover (beginning 14 Abib) always falls after the equinox but not too far after it through the insertion of "leap months" (the addition of a second month of Adar [the month preceding Nisan or Abib]) as needed. Since the real issue was to produce proper timing for the Feast of the Unleavened Bread with the first sheaf, at times this produced the interesting situation where the calculated first of Nisan occurred prior to the actual equinox in some years. In the fourth century A.D., under the leadership of Hillel II the Sanhedrin developed a perpetual calendar that has a nineteen-year cycle with seven leap years (Posner 2021).

A second factor that might affect the offering of the first sheaf was the location in Israel the celebration took place. As noted, the fields in the Jezreel and Jordan Valleys ripened first and those in the highlands of Galilee later. This would be of great significance if the first sheaf represented the ripening of individual locations. However, since this appears to be a corporate practice, the single date for the location of the high priest served as the standard for the entire nation.

Even so, weather would be another factor that would affect when the crops might ripen, and thus when the first sheaf was ready. Clearly, one did not want the time for the first sheaf to be presented and have no first sheaf.

That focus is further demonstrated by two additional points in the text. In 23:16, the directive is that this offering is a new gift (or grain) offering (מִנְחָה חֲדָשָׁה), that is, a sacrifice from the newly harvested wheat. This is opposed to the situation with the barley, where the timing of the sheaf would anticipate the harvest by some time; therefore the grain offering associated with the yearling lamb (23:12 and 13) would be the old grain. This would be the first completely ripe grain from the new harvest. Second, at the Festival of Weeks, the Israelites were to bring two loaves of bread "baked with leaven" (23:17). This distinguished the grain offering at the Festival of Weeks from all other grain offerings, which were to be unleavened. As Lange (1960, 175) observes, this "shows that leaven does not, in and of itself signify the evil." Ross (2002, 424) observes that the requirement for baked loaves indicated that they not only were to give from what God gave, but from that which they produced from his gifts.

Coupled with the bread, the Israelites were to present seven yearling male lambs, a bull, and two rams as a corporate burnt offering, along with their associated grain and drink offerings. All of this is offered by fire as a "soothing aroma" (רֵיחַ נִיחֹחַ; see discussion on Lev. 1:9) to the Lord.

Strengthening the Social Fabric (23:1–24:9)

As was the case of the first and last days of the Feast of Unleavened Bread, that day of the Festival of Weeks was to be proclaimed a "holy convocation" (מִקְרָא־קֹדֶשׁ). Again, on that day the Israelites were to do no "arduous work" (מְלֶאכֶת עֲבֹדָה).

The last verse of this section, 23:22, seems somewhat out of place, since it does not address the feast. Instead, it repeats the command from Leviticus 19:9 that in the process of harvesting, the Israelites were not to reap "to the very corners of the field," but to leave that for the needy and the גֵּר (*resident alien*) that they might glean (see appendix 2 on gleaning). In contrast to Leviticus 19, this section omits gleaning grapes, but that was likely to have been expected, since this section specifically addresses the wheat harvest, which took place several weeks before the grapes were ripe. Although it anticipates the settlement in the land, which we now know was years in the future, it is still appropriate that it both reminds of the need to provide for gleaners, but only addresses the *Sitz im leben* of the wheat harvest. The verse then ends with the reminder that God was "the Lord [YHWH] your God."

The Lord Gives Directions for the Autumn Appointed Times (23:23–43)

The fall appointed times follow the Festival of Weeks in the month of Tishri after a gap of almost four and a half months. Then, the last three appointed times commence over a two-week period (the third, Sukkoth, lasts another week). Tishri is in the autumn of the year, which is the time normally associated with the finishing the last of the crops.

Autumn Harvests

King and Stager (2001, 87–92) note the Gezer Calendar, which lays out the agricultural year beginning with the olive harvest followed by the early rains (October–November) and the sowing of grain (see Gezer Calendar sidebar on Lev. 25:2).

Ross (2002, 428) picks up on this harvest imagery and suggests "judgment as an obvious association." The self-affliction nature of Yom Kippur seems to reinforce that. However, outside of a single statement in 23:39, which notes that Sukkoth is when the crops have been gathered, the text shows little reflection of this obvious tie-in to the completion of the harvest (unlike the two firstfruits rituals of the spring appointments). Instead, Sukkoth is celebratory, designed to remind the Israelites of when God brought the nation out of Egypt (23:43). And, as will be seen, the first of Tishri and Yom Kippur served entirely different purposes. Moreover, instead of anchoring those appointed times in the autumnal equinox, they build off the same spring equinox anchor as the spring appointed times. These suggest that the six should be considered a unit, which likely is indicative of an overall purpose, which we will discuss at the end of this unit.

23:23. As we have seen repeatedly, 23:23, which identifies the start of another oration from God to Moses, begins with the standard introductory *waw*, translated in this context "again." While it shows the continued sequence of revelation, this section presents a second set of three holy days, which complement the spring list.

23:24–25. In this case, God directs Moses to tell the people that the fourth divine appointment is to be observed on the first day of the seventh month.

Seventh Month

Following the Babylonian exile, the returning Israelites used adapted Babylonian names for the months, which is the style used today (Day 1939). Under this nomenclature, what is called the seventh month here became known as Tishri. However, Tishri also became the first month under the civilian calendar with the first of the month serving as Rosh Hashanah. Apparently under the older Hebrew calendar, it was either

---

326

Strengthening the Social Fabric (23:1–24:9)

called Ethanim (used in 1 Kings 8:2), or just the seventh month. The Pentateuch uses only the seventh month, which seems to reflect the early date of the Pentateuch.

According to Numbers 28:11, the first of each month, which began with the new moon, required a special burnt offering. That requirement is obscure and generally overlooked by scholars, although the practice is mentioned a number of times in the OT. While Numbers gives directions on special sacrifices to be performed each new moon, the only new moon listed in the calendar here is the new moon beginning the seventh month, which differs somewhat from the others.

New Moons

Like the Sabbath, the new moon required special sacrifices. However, they are not listed in Leviticus. Described some time later, Numbers 28:11–15 specifies that the new moon sacrifice was to consist of two bulls, one ram, and seven male yearling lambs, along with their grain and drink offerings. The grain offerings consisted of three-tenths of an ephah of fine flour mixed with oil for each bull, two-tenths mixed with oil for the ram, and a tenth mixed with oil for each lamb. The drink offering was to be half a hin of wine for each bull, a third of a hin for the ram, and a fourth of a hin for each lamb. Additionally, the nation was to sacrifice a male goat for a sin offering with its drink offering. Also, like the Sabbath, the new moon was not considered an appointed time (מוֹעֵד), nor a holy convocation (מִקְרָאֵי קֹדֶשׁ; Milgrom 2001, 2011). As such it is not listed in this calendar of holy days. The only directions with regard to the observance of the new moon are those given to the priests with respect to the special sacrifices noted above. Amos 8:5 indicates that the expectation was that it would be a day of rest, since the prophet condemns the people for complaining because they could not conduct business on that day. Interestingly, it shows up prominently in the conflict between David and Saul, in that David notes that with the

new moon, he was expected to dine with the king (1 Sam. 20:5–34), and his absence exposed Saul's increasing hatred. It is not clear why David's presence with the king was expected on the new moon, and the text suggests that David's excuse was a family sacrifice in Bethlehem. Several prophets condemn the people for failing to properly observe the festival (Isa. 1:13, 14; Hos. 2:11; Amos 8:5), and Ezekiel mentions several times that during the period of the new temple how the new moons and the Sabbaths would be properly observed (Ezek. 45:17; 46:1, 3, 6). While the Mishnah contains detailed directions on how to determine and announce the new moon (m. Roš Haš. 1:3–3:1), with the destruction of the temple and the loss of the sacrifices the practice apparently became irrelevant. Today, the festival is largely unknown.

Traditionally this day has been known as the Feast of Trumpets based on the idea of announcing it by a trumpet call (תְּרוּעָה) to describe how the nation was to deliver a reminder.

TRANSLATION ANALYSIS: "TRUMPET"
The Hebrew noun תְּרוּעָה is translated in the NASB as "blowing" with the inferred source "of trumpets." Most translations follow a similar pattern. *TWOT* defines the noun itself as meaning "alarm, signal, sound of trumpet" (White 1980a, 839). It observes that the primary meaning of the verb is "'to raise a noise' by shouting or with an instrument, especially a horn." This verb specifically denotes the "blowing" on the first of the seventh month. On the first of the rest of the months, the verb used is תָּקַע (Num. 10:10). Both terms seem to suggest a trumpet blast, but they differ in sound and in meaning. Rabbinic tradition suggests that the תָּקַע was a long blast, equivalent in length to three blasts of the תְּרוּעָה. In terms of meaning, Milgrom (2001, 2016–17) indicates that the תָּקַע was essentially a call for assembly for various purposes such as the coronation of Solomon, while the תְּרוּעָה was more of an alarm, a battle cry, or a cry for divine help.

Since that word does not necessarily denote a trumpet blast, Lange (1960, 172) and others describe it as a "memorial of joyful noise." However, apparently the practice was to announce each new month with a trumpet (Milgrom 2001, 2014), which would explain the association of the term and the date with trumpets. Today this date is known as Rosh Hashanah or the beginning of the new year, apparently based on Ezekiel 40:1 (Bailey 2005, 282), although Milgrom is adamant that "there exists not a single hint in all of Scripture that the first day of Tishri, the seventh month, was New Year's Day" (2001, 2013).

The text states the trumpet call (תְּרוּעָה) was to serve as a reminder, but it is not clear of what or for whom. Kleinig (2003, 491) suggests that it reminded the people of God. Rabbinic tradition suggests that this holy day marked the beginning of creation suggesting that they were reminded of God as the Creator (Radner 2008, 248). Milgrom (2001, 2017–19) notes other alternatives: a reminder of the kingdom of God, or to arouse the deity's attention. It would seem that since this introduced the seventh month, which included the last two divine appointments, there would be an association with those two significant events, both of which were characterized as a holy convocation (מִקְרָא־קֹדֶשׁ). Perhaps it is in that light that Gane (2004a, 402) observes that it would "also imply the solemn responsibility of repentance and reformation."

In addition to being reminded by the trumpet call (תְּרוּעָה) two other things were required of the Israelites on this date. As might be expected, 23:25 specifies that the priests were to provide the required corporate sacrifices. For the first of Tishri, that included an additional sacrifice as well as the standard new moon sacrifice and the requisite daily sacrifice (Num. 29:1–6). The only other guideline given here is that the Israelites were to have a rest (שַׁבָּתוֹן), although the day is not called a Sabbath. Instead, they were to avoid "arduous work," which we noted earlier may reflect work

such as might be done by a slave, or it might refer to ordinary occupations. The latter might explain the criticism of Amos 8:5 regarding selling grain on the new moon.

> ### First of Tishri Sacrifice
> After Moses commissioned Joshua to succeed him per God's directions, God provided supplementary directions on issues of worship beginning in Numbers 28. For our purposes, we would just note that in Numbers 29, he fleshes out the directions for the first of the seventh month "offering by fire" cited in Leviticus 23:25. According to Numbers 29:6, in addition to the perpetual daily corporate morning and evening burnt offering cited in Leviticus 6:8–13 (where we noted that this first mandate for this offering was actually made in Exodus 29), as well as the standard new moon offerings (see "New Moons" sidebar), the nation was to perform an additional sacrifice on this day consisting of one bull, one ram, and seven male yearling lambs, with the following grain offerings mixed with oil: three-tenths of a ephah for the bull, two-tenths for the ram, and one tenth for each lamb (Num. 29:2–4), along with a male goat for a sin offering.

Given the rather understated presentation of activities on this date, a key question would be, why were the Israelites commanded to do a trumpet call (תְּרוּעָה) on the new moon of Tishri, but a תָּקַע the other new moons during the year? It seems likely that a key factor is the last two divine appointments that were scheduled to commence in the following two weeks. The way this passage is structured would lead one to suspect that the three were somehow tied together, which we will address when we sum up the section.

23:26–32. While structured as a separate divine speech, the next pericope directly follows the seventh-month introduction. The directive declares that the tenth day of that month was to be the Day of Atonement. We have already

Strengthening the Social Fabric (23:1–24:9)

noted how Leviticus 16 gives specific procedures that were to be followed on this significant day. In our discussion in the unit "The Day of Atonement" (16:1–34) we noted how the guidelines there were for the priest, and this section focuses on the people. We also noted that this was not an occasion where the people were to gather at the central sanctuary to observe the activities. Rather, they were admonished simply to humble their souls and not do any work (Lev. 16:29). Here the guidelines reassert the responsibilities of the people and do not mention any of the activities the priests were going through for the nation (although subtly the text does note that the purpose of the day was to "make atonement on [their] behalf before the Lord [YHWH] [their] God"; Lev. 23:28).

The lack of further explanation seems to downplay the significance of the event; however, there are three points of emphasis. First, the Israelites were reminded of the directions when the day was first mentioned in Leviticus 16:29: they were to afflict their souls. Here the phrase is repeated three times, twice as a statement that they must do this, and once as a warning that any person who does not afflict him or herself shall be cut off from his or her people. As in Leviticus 16, the verb here is עָנָה, which means "to afflict, oppress or humble" (Coppes 1980g, 682). Again, while what that means is not specified, the understanding is that they were to fast (Péter-Contesse and Ellington 1992, 352–53). This is the only divine appointment that required affliction or humbling.

"Afflict Yourselves"

While the Feast of Unleavened Bread prohibited the use of leaven, it would appear that all other aspects of normal diet were permissible, which would make this the only one of the six divine appointments in this list that required that the Israelites עָנָה themselves. Rooker (2000, 223) concludes that this is the only fast day in the Mosaic law. He then cites the Mishnah tractate m. Yoma

8:1, which adds four activities from which Israelites were to abstain on this date: bathing, use of oil on the body, wearing shoes, and sexual intercourse.

The second point of emphasis is that it was to be a day of rest, an idea repeated five times. Twice they are told not to do any work (23:28, 31); once they are told that anyone who does work, God will destroy from among his people (23:30); and then in 23:32, they are told twice that they were to observe it as a Sabbath (תִּשְׁבְּתוּ שַׁבַּתְּכֶם and שַׁבַּת שַׁבָּתוֹן).

The use of the Hebrew particle אַךְ indicates a third point of emphasis. This term expresses "affirmative emphasis" (Scott 1980b, 39) and is often translated as "surely." Although many translations ignore the term, the NLT expresses it as an admonition, "Be careful to celebrate the Day of Atonement." Hartley (1992, 388) proposes that the use of this particle indicated the peculiarity of the sacrifice described in Leviticus 16 as well as the act of fasting, as opposed to the date. However, given the unusual nature of the date, the tenth of the month, perhaps the NASB's translation of "exactly" gives a better understanding. While the date is specific, there is no rationale given. It is not associated with any historical event like the Passover is. It is not an astronomical date that could be noted by careful observation of the heavens. Like the Sabbath, it is an arbitrary date with seemingly no connection to anything else in their culture. At the same time—unlike the Sabbath, which was based on the number seven for which there are strong indications of symbolic value, biblically, culturally, and regionally—there is no clear symbolic value for the tenth (Davis 1968, 115–24).

The last item to note regarding this event is the structure of the last verse, which specifies that the affliction was to begin with the evening of the ninth and continue to the evening of the tenth, lasting מֵעֶרֶב עַד־עֶרֶב.

TRANSLATION ANALYSIS: "FROM EVENING TO EVENING"

The phrase מֵעֶרֶב עַד־עֶרֶב is used only here and the meaning is debated. According to Allen (1980b, 353) the Hebrew word עֶרֶב means "evening, night" and he suggests that it derived from the expression "the setting of the sun." We noted in our translation analysis of Leviticus 6:8–13 [HB 1–6] in the unit "The Role of the Priests" that the evening sacrifice was to be performed "between the evenings" (בֵּין הָעַרְבָּיִם, citing Exod. 29:38–46), which is generally accepted as between approximately 3 p.m. and sunset. Beyond this, the overall picture of the OT is that the Israelites considered the day as beginning at sunrise (Cassuto 1961, 1:29; Levine 1989, 161; Milgrom 2001, 2021). While we do not know when sunset was standardized as the beginning of the day, it clearly was by the time of the Mishnah (Schorsch 1997). But the Mishnah is a collective work representing decades of discussion before it was completed about A.D. 170 (Neusner 1994, 40–53). Therefore, it would not be surprising if there were different practices, even in NT times (which we discuss in "Holy Days and Salvation History" in the introduction).

Hartley (1992, 388) observes, "Whether other festivals began in the evening in ancient Israel is debated." Milgrom (2001, 2021) argues that this specific delineation of the time frame shows it was not an ordinary day that went from sunrise to sunrise. Levine (1989, 161) claims the phrase "is not said of any other sacred occasion." He also notes that it is not certain that "in biblical times Sabbath and the festivals began on the prior evening, as became the custom in later Judaism" and concludes that they all began at dawn in "biblical times" (i.e., the OT period). If so, it appears that this verse came to determine the norm in rabbinic Judaism.

23:33–43. Five days later, the final divine appointment was to begin. It is called חַג הַסֻּכּוֹת,

specifically the Feast of Booths or Tabernacles, often just called Sukkoth. This was one of three national feasts delineated in Exodus 23 shortly after the people arrived at Sinai that were to be celebrated once they were settled in the land. Each of those three required that all males appear before the Lord as part of the divine appointment (Exod. 23:14–17). The first two were Passover-Unleavened Bread and Pentecost, both spring festivals. The third was Sukkoth, which in Exodus is called the Feast of the Ingathering and is described as "when you gather in the fruit of your labors from the field," pointing to it as a future event. As in the case of the Unleavened Bread, Sukkoth is termed a feast. Also, as in the case of the Unleavened Bread, the directions in this chapter contain two portions with the second portion adding more details to what is essentially a summary statement in the first portion. In the case of Unleavened Bread, the portions are divided by an introductory statement: "Then the Lord [YHWH] spoke to Moses, saying . . .". Here they are divided by a second summary statement (23:37 and 38), reminding the audience that all of what has been covered in this list are divine appointments ("appointments with YHWH" [מוֹעֲדֵי יְהוָה]) and "holy convocations" (מִקְרָאֵי קֹדֶשׁ). The first segment ties the event to the previous material, anchoring it as the fifteenth (the full moon) of the seventh month, that is, Tishri (just as the feast of Unleavened Bread was anchored in the fifteenth of the first month Abib or Nisan). For both, the feast lasted a week, and on the first and last days they were not to do any arduous work. Likewise for both, there was a seven-plus-one sequence, with Passover coming the day before the Unleavened Bread, and a day of rest following the celebration of Sukkoth (Gane 2004a, 402). Perhaps most significantly, both were living reminders of the exodus, intended to be passed on to future generations, and it is interesting that these two living reminders began and ended the sequence. In the case of Unleavened Bread, Deuteronomy 16:3 states that it was because they left Egypt in haste. In the case of Sukkoth it was so that they would remember that they lived in temporary shelters when they came out of Egypt (Lev. 23:43).

Seven-day Feasts

Both the Feast of Unleavened Bread and the Feast of Ingathering are described as lasting seven days. Leviticus 23:6 says of the former, "for seven days you shall eat unleavened bread," while Leviticus 23:39 states of the latter, "you shall celebrate the feast of the Lord for seven days." However, in the former case a holy convocation was to be held on both the first and the seventh days (23:6–7), and in the latter case the holy convocation and prohibition against arduous work was on the eighth day (23:36), the day after the seven days of celebration, indicating a change in tone at the conclusion of the feast.

These booths are one of two significant distinct features to Sukkoth that catch the focus of most studies. The mandate was that once they were settled in the land in the third week of the seventh month, they would build temporary shelters or booths in which all Israelites ("all the native-born in Israel") would live for a week to remind them of the time that God brought them out of Egypt. Leviticus 23:40 mandates that on the first day of the festival, they were to take the foliage of beautiful trees, palm branches and boughs of leafy trees and willows of the brook and rejoice and celebrate. Although the text does not specify that the booths were built of these items, it seems that by the return from exile that this was clearly understood to be the case (Péter-Contesse and Ellington 1992, 358). Nehemiah 8:15 records that following Ezra's teaching, a proclamation was made to "Go out to the hills, and bring branches from olive, wild olive, and myrtle trees, palms, and *other* leafy trees, to make booths, as it is written" (emphasis added).

Booths

Péter-Contesse and Ellington (1992, 358) observe that the text in Leviticus states that after they gather the branches, they were to rejoice before God, and they suggest that the items gathered were carried "in a joyous procession." While that may have been the case, the fact that the Israelites in Nehemiah returning from exile and under the teaching of Ezra, as well as other Levites, understood that the directive was to use the materials gathered to build is suggestive. It is important to remember that in Israel, this would be a mild time of the year, and that the booths were intended solely for a temporary shelter, such as a farmer might erect during harvest to avoid returning from outlying fields at night (Milgrom 2001, 2048–51).

Identification of the products cited in 23:40 is uncertain. If the פְּרִי עֵץ הָדָר is literally "fruit," the question is, What is the fruit? According to Milgrom (2001, 2041), four suggestions have been offered: citron (rabbinic 'etrog), olive, cone of a cedar, and fruit of any majestic tree. He and many commentators seem to agree with Keil and Delitzsch (1956, 618), who understand the phrase פְּרִי עֵץ הָדָר (literally "fruit of splendorous trees") to denote the shoots and branches of the tree. This seems to be the basic understanding of most modern translations, such as the NASB which translates it "foliage of beautiful trees." The other three items are generally agreed to be palm fronds, an unidentified leafy tree (the rabbis propose myrtle), and willows of the brook.

The second significant distinction of Sukkoth is the additional required sacrifices. Leviticus 23:37 merely sums up the requirement as "burnt offerings and gift offerings, sacrifices and drink offerings, a day's matter on its own day." The meaning of a "day's matter" is spelled out in Numbers 29:1–39. As Sklar (2014, 286) expresses it, the requirement was "extensive food offerings." In summation, day 1 required thirteen bulls, two rams, fourteen male yearling lambs, along with proper gift and drink offerings for each animal for burnt offerings and one male goat for a sin offering. Days 2–7 required the same sacrifice with one exception; each day decreased the number of bulls by one from the day before, arriving at seven bulls on day 7 (along with the rest of the sacrifice). Day 8 only required one bull.

The section ends with the reminder that the purpose of the booths was to remind future generations that God brought them out from Egypt. That fact had obligations, which is indicated by the last sentence of Leviticus 23:43: "I am the Lord [YHWH] your God."

NT Additions

During the Second Temple period, two additional items were added to the feast, which show up in the NT accounts. At the time of the morning sacrifice, the priests drew water from the pool of Siloam in a gold pitcher and poured it out as a libation (m. Sukkah 5:1). This seems to provide background to the announcement that Jesus made on the last day: "If anyone thirsts, let him come to me and drink. He who believes in me, just as the Scripture said, 'rivers of living water will flow from his innermost being'" (John 7:37–38). Further, in the evening, men and women would assemble in the court of women to rejoice over the morning ceremony. The court would be lit up with tall lampstands (m. Sukkah 5:2). This provides background for Jesus's further words in John 8:12, "I am the light of the world; the one who follows me will not walk in the darkness, but will have the light of life."

23:44. The chapter ends with the statement that Moses declared all of the appointed times of the Lord to Israel. Even so, this was largely information that they were to retain until they were in the land, where they could implement it. Passover, Unleavened Bread, Yom Kippur, and even the first of Tishri could be instituted immediately, but anything pertaining to agriculture required

regular agriculture, which would not be until they had settled in the land.

The Lord Directs the Nation to Use Its Corporate Production to Promote Corporate Worship (24:1–9)

A key aspect of Israel's corporate worship was the regular renewal of two symbols of Israel's relationship with God. As Balentine (2002, 186) expresses it, these verses serve as "a continuation of instruction in chapter 23 concerning the laity's responsibility for maintaining the public cult." Specifically, it addresses two symbols that were part of the Holy Place. The first symbol was the lamp inside the Holy Place. While the priest was required to check the lamps daily, renewing the wicks and replenishing the olive oil (Exod. 30:7–8), it was the responsibility of the people to provide the oil the priests used. The second symbol was the bread of presence, which was placed on a table inside the Holy Place (see discussion of Lev. 10). While the priest placed twelve new cakes of loaves out before the Lord weekly, it was the corporate responsibility of the nation to provide the flour that made the twelve loaves. Although the text only addresses the two clearly symbolic features, the requirements of community support are easily extrapolated to include other corporate requirements, such as wicks for the lamps.

24:1–4. When God gave Moses the directions recorded in Exodus for building the tabernacle, one of the furnishings was a lampstand. As described in the text, this gold object was designed to have six branches in addition to the main stand, thus holding seven lamps (Exod. 25:37). Likely these lamps were simple terra-cotta dishes of oil that held a wick. Each lamp would sit on a branch of the lampstand.

This passage gives two areas of responsibility for the lamps. Aaron and his successors were to tend the lamps regularly so that they were lit all night, that is, "from evening to morning" (Lev. 24:3; cf. Exod. 27:21).

Figure 62. Lampstand or menorah from second temple on Arch of Titus in Rome (this display records the looting of the temple in A.D. 70).

TRANSLATION ANALYSIS: "REGULARLY"
The word תָּמִיד, which is used twice in this passage, is translated "continually" in the NASB and several other translations. While continuity is the basic sense of the word (*DCH* s.v. "תָּמִיד" 8:641), *TWOT* notes that it is used adverbially "to denote constancy in cultic duties" (Kaiser 1980d). In this context, "regularly" seems a better translation (Ross 2002, 441).

Here, the Lord makes it clear that it was the responsibility of the people to bring the proper oil for the priests to maintain the lights. The direction is that the oil was to be "clear oil from beaten olives" (שֶׁמֶן זַיִת זָךְ כָּתִית), or as Péter-Contesse and Ellington (1992, 361–62) describe it, oil "which results from pounding the olives in a mortar and then straining the liquid."

Practically, the lampstand and lamps provided light for the dark holy place. While recognizing this basic purpose, one also needs to recall that only the priest entered the Holy Place—and then only twice daily, in the morning and evening when he brought incense and trimmed the wicks (Exod. 30:7–8). And yet the lamps were to be lit from evening to morning, the time when the people and the priests were asleep. This would suggest that there was also a symbolic value, although we are not told what it might be. Some suggestions include: it showed the presence of God in the camp (Milgrom 2001, 2094); drawing from Psalm 119:105, it represented the word of God (Hess 2008, 794); based on Revelation, it represented the Holy Spirit (Lange 1960, 181); anticipating John 8:12, it prefigured Jesus (Mathews 2009, 211); or drawing on Zechariah 4, it represented Israel as light to the nations (Harrison 1980, 222–23). A number of these suggestions come from later material and probably were not relevant to the original audience sitting at the foot of Mt. Sinai. Assuming symbolic significance to the lampstand and lamps, it seems likely that it was part of an overall picture tied into the three items in the Holy Place (lampstand, table of presence, and incense altar). We will address that after looking at the next section, the table of presence.

24:5–9. After declaring a second time that the priest was to "keep" the lampstand "before the Lord regularly," the text turns immediately to describing the bread of presence, here labeled cakes or loaves.

TRANSLATION ANALYSIS: "KEEP"
The verb עָרַךְ has multiple meanings, all related to preparation including "to set in order, set in array, prepare, order, ordain, handle, and furnish" but can also mean "to equal, direct, compare" (Allen 1980d, 695). It is suggested that the last could be "the result of arranging in order (for the purpose of comparison)." It is somewhat surprising that this verb is not used for the setting of the twelve cakes of bread on the table.

TRANSLATION ANALYSIS: "BREAD OF PRESENCE"
Here, the bread is merely described as "חַלּוֹת," which is generally understood to represent a plural form of "a special type of baked cake made of fine flour." Because the term is deemed

to derive from the verb חָלַל I, which means "to wound (fatally), bore through, or pierce," it is taken to have some "characteristic perforations" (Wiseman 1980a, 288). The amount of flour required, two-tenths of an ephah, determined the size of the cake. The term "bread of presence" comes from Exodus 25:30, where God tells Moses, "You shall set the bread of the presence on the table before me regularly." The phrase used there is לֶחֶם פָּנִים לְפָנַי, which literally may be translated as "bread before my face."

It was to be made of the same fine flour (סֹלֶת) prescribed for the stand-alone grain offering in Leviticus 2:1 (see units "Worshipping a Holy God" [1:1–3:17] and "The Role of the Priests" [6:8 (HB 6:1)–7:38]). Other ingredients are not specified, but it may be inferred that the flour was mixed with oil and salt, but no leavening.

> #### Other Ingredients
>
> The size of the bread was determined by how much flour was included, with other ingredients mixed proportionally. Leviticus 7:12 and Numbers 6:15 include oil in the breads they mention. Lange (1960, 180), and Kiuchi (2007, 187), among others, argue that the bread is leavened, apparently based on the supposition that the bread was intended to represent daily bread. Keil and Delitzsch (1956, 662) and Milgrom (2001, 2096) note reasons to reject this view, including the requirement set forth for the standard מִנְחָה to be unleavened, and unanimous Jewish tradition. Milgrom (2001, 2096) questions whether leavened bread would be edible after a week, implying that unleavened bread would be.

Frankincense was included in the layout on the table but was not part of the bread. The bread of presence actually is made up of twelve cakes, with each cake containing two tenths of an ephah of flour, which is estimated to be about five pounds (Sklar 2014, 288). According to the rabbis, this produced cakes of about ten handbreadths long, which were laid transversely on the table that was five-to-six handbreadths wide. The surplus was folded upward on each side (m. *Menaḥ.* 11:5). The directions were that they were to be placed in two מַעֲרָכוֹת, which is normally translated as "rows," but here is generally understood as "stacks" or something similar.

TRANSLATION ANALYSIS: "STACKS"

The term מַעֲרָכוֹת is defined as "row" (Allen 1980d, 695). In the OT, it most often means "to set in order, arrange." While one might expect two rows, given the size of the cakes, they most likely were stacked—two stacks of six.

The priest replaced the cakes each Sabbath with fresh cakes. The removed cakes were to be given to the priests (Aaron and his sons) who were then to eat them "in a holy place" (another reason for understanding that the bread was unleavened). In addition to the cakes, pure frankincense was placed "on each row."

TRANSLATION ANALYSIS: "BESIDE"

TWOT defines the preposition עַל as "above," but its discussion observes that it "is translated over thirty different ways in the OT, the most common being above, against, beside, concerning, on, over, upon" (Carr 1980b, 669). In this case, "beside" seems to be the best understanding, since on the Sabbath when the old bread is removed, the bread is given to the priests, but the frankincense is burned ("to the Lord [YHWH]," 23:7). According to the Mishnah (m. *Menaḥ.* 11:5, 7, 8), the frankincense was placed in two dishes (traditionally of gold) next to the two rows of bread.

When the old cakes were removed, the frankincense was burned. To facilitate this, Jewish tradition holds that the frankincense was placed in two gold containers next to each stack (Milgrom 2001, 2097–98).

In the excursus "The Ancient Near Eastern Context," in the section "The Lord Tells Israel How to Worship" (1:1–2), we

Strengthening the Social Fabric (23:1–24:9)

discussed that a number of scholars have observed how other cultures performed sacrifices to their gods and assumed that their gods "ate" the food. Unfortunately, there is a propensity among some scholars to attribute that belief to the Israelites also. This is another location where that tendency appears. Several observations have been made that indicate that not to be the case here. Milgrom (2001, 2099–101) notes that the fact that the food is provided weekly as opposed to daily suggests otherwise. Interestingly, he also calculates how much bread a typical human would require on a daily basis and then notes how even though these are large cakes, if one prorated them on a daily basis, they would be inadequate for a human—let alone God. Gane

(2004a, 422) echoes some of those arguments and also notes that only the frankincense as a token portion is given to God. It is important to note that the cakes are set before the Lord, and that only the frankincense, "a memorial portion," is offered by fire to the Lord.

In the excursus on the purpose of the tabernacle furnishings below, we discuss the context of the lampstand and the table in the Holy Place and the significance of that context. From that context, we propose that the purpose of the table of bread of presence represented the nation being before God (whose presence was located above the mercy seat in the Most Holy Place). As such, it is then suggested that lampstand was to represent the nation of Israel providing light to the nations.

Purpose of the Tabernacle Furnishings

While it may be presumed that the tabernacle furnishings carried symbolic meanings, we must exercise care in evaluating the symbolism. Symbols are problematic in that the originator of the symbol determines what the symbol means. If a specific interpretation is not given by the originator, then the receiver of the symbol must use logic and inference, building upon knowledge of the originator's culture, language, and even nature to determine what a symbol means. Sometimes, this seems readily determined, either from obvious affinities, or common understandings. Other times, it is much more difficult. In either case, unless the meaning is specifically given by the originator, any interpretation is somewhat tentative, although there is a mindset in our current culture that any person is free to interpret any symbol as he or she sees fit.

In terms of the tabernacle, there is a significant amount of symbolism involved. Here we can just address four items. First, three terms are used somewhat interchangeably, which leads to some confusion. While the term "tabernacle" refers to the entire structure including the courtyard (Exod. 27; 35; and 39:30–40), it is also used to refer to the inner tent (Exod. 26). This inner tent is also called the "tent of meeting" (אֹהֶל מוֹעֵד, see, e.g., Exod. 27:21; 29:4) but that term (tent of meeting) also seems to be applied to a separate tent that Moses used while the tabernacle was being built (Exod. 33:7). Additionally, the term "holy place" at times seems to refer to the entire tabernacle (Lev. 6) or to just the inner tent (Exod. 28:43; Lev. 16:17), or more technically, just the front portion of the inner tent (Exod. 26:33). This last reference notes that the inner tent is to be divided into two portions, the front portion designated the Holy Place, while the back portion is the

Most Holy Place or Holy of Holies. A veil separates the two, and technically, it was in the Most Holy Place where the high priest met with God, but only on the Day of Atonement. Figure 63 shows the layout of the inner tent as discussed in Exodus and Leviticus, and the approximate locations of the furniture items we will discuss below.

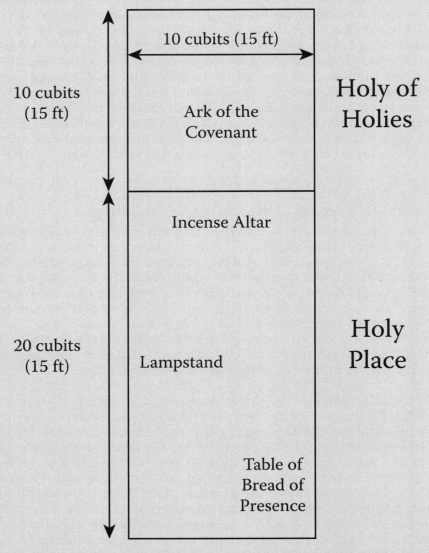

Figure 63. Diagram of the tent of meeting (or holy place) within the tabernacle.

The Most Holy Place contained the ark of the covenant. Above the wings of the two cherubim on top of the ark was the *kapporet* or mercy seat (Exod. 26:34; see the discussion at Lev. 16:2b–28). This was the place to which the shekinah descended when the tabernacle was inaugurated and where God met with the nation's representative on Yom Kippur (Exod. 25:21; Lev. 16:2). Since God is omnipresent, and his presence is addressed in a variety of contexts, we dare not say that there were situations where he was "more present" than others. It is clear that there were situations where the presence was more evident. In terms of the tabernacle, the mercy seat inside the Most Holy Place denoted the location where God would meet the priestly representative (Exod. 30:6).

If the Most Holy Place marked the location of the presence of the Lord, then the outer room, called the Holy Place, would be described as being "before the Lord [YHWH]" (לִפְנֵי יְהוָה). This phrase is repeated four times in the Leviticus 24:1–9 pericope. The Holy Place is described as having three items in it: the incense altar, the table of the bread of presence, and the lampstand with lamps. Each of these had a physical purpose, but it would appear that spiritual symbolism was involved with each, and that the three, being colocated, also had collective meanings.

The first item directed to be placed in the Holy Place was the altar of incense. Aaron was told that he was to burn incense every morning and evening when he trimmed the lamps (Exod. 30:7–8). The first mention of incense in the OT is associated with the directions for building the tabernacle (Exod. 25:6), although the directions indicate that the Israelites were already familiar with the material. J. Alexander Thompson claims that the earliest records show incense being used by the Egyptians, Babylonians, Assyrians, Arabians, and Canaanites (1975, 3:274). While an aspect of worship, the exact purpose of incense is never stated in the OT. Psalm 141:2 associates incense with prayer, and then in the NT, Revelation 5:8; 8:3 and 4 explicitly relate incense with "the prayers of the saints." Drawing from that, it would seem that the practice of the priest burning incense morning and evening represented daily corporate prayer to God.

It is generally accepted that the purpose of the twelve cakes was to represent the twelve tribes of Israel correlating with much of the priestly paraphernalia (see discussion regarding the priests under Lev. 8; see further Exod. 28). If so, then placing the twelve cakes of bread on the table represented the status of the nation of Israel before God. The replacement of the cakes weekly might then suggest a spiritual renewal through the Sabbath.

This leaves the lampstand and the lamps, which are more obscure. Numbers 8:1–4 notes that the purpose of the lamps was to give light "in the front of the lampstand." Harrison (1980, 222) sees a tie between this symbol and Zechariah's vision of a lampstand, which may be helpful. According to Leviticus 24:2, the nation of Israel was to bring oil "for the light" (לְמָאוֹר) so that the lamp could burn (i.e., provide light). This would seem to suggest that one of the functions of the people was to ensure that through the work they did before the Lord, the nation would provide light to a dark world. That may also explain two other interesting phrases in this paragraph. The first is that this was to be a "perpetual statute throughout [their] generations" (לְדֹרֹתֵיכֶם חֻקַּת עוֹלָם). In other words, it was something to be passed down through their descendants. The second is that through those efforts the lampstand was to be pure (הַטְּהֹרָה), which might allude to the concept we addressed in the section on cleanness in the introduction.

Collectively, it would seem that the purpose of the three elements was to represent the nation before God. It was to be a nation that had a constant presence before God, that regularly prayed to God, and that provided light to a dark world. This then might be construed as a symbolic mission statement for the nation, as a nation of priests.

THEOLOGICAL FOCUS

Through the performance of the various festivals, the nation developed a strong sense of God as their savior and provider. For the original audience, the Sabbath was grounded in creation, reminding the nation weekly that God was their Creator. The annual festivals began with Passover, which celebrated their deliverance from Egypt, followed immediately by the Feast of Unleavened Bread and then the Feast of Weeks, both of which celebrated God's provision of food for the people. The Feast of Trumpets reminded the people of the upcoming final celebrations of the year. While Yom Kippur was performed by the priests, the people fasted, trusting in their atonement. Every fifty years, it served a stronger purpose in that a shofar was sounded that "proclaimed a release through the land" inaugurating the Jubilee (Lev. 25:9, see unit below, "Preventing Social Unraveling, Part 1" [25:1–22]). The final festival was Sukkoth, which was a week-long celebration recognizing the completion of the harvest, which closed out with a rest on the final day. We joined the first nine verses with this unit because they reflect how the Israelites were to use gifts of God

(specifically the olives and wheat, their two primary crops) to provide the elements of worship through their work (the oil and bread).

In this section especially, we need to note a prophetic element. As developed in the "Holy Days and Salvation History" section of the introduction, the NT shows the spring divine appointments to be prophetic of the first coming of Christ: Passover is reflected in the crucifixion, with Christ as the Passover lamb; the first sheaf seems to be reflected in the resurrection; and the founding of the church on Pentecost reflects the Festival of Ingathering. From this we inferred that the fall festivals would also have a prophetic element, which logically would tie into the second coming, possibly initiated by the final trumpet, and concluded with the final and universal spiritual harvest with a final "affliction" of Israel in between (Kellogg 1978, 468–73). While this may provide a picture of how God works, it really does not answer the burning question we have of when it will be.

What was true for the original audience remains true today—our attention span is short (and getting shorter). We are easily drawn away from worship by life. Scheduled events not only require the community of believers to stop and refocus, but they also serve to teach children (and other new community members) the purposes behind gathering for worship. By requiring daily responsibilities for the leaders, a weekly summons to all individuals, and strategically placed annual celebrations for the full community, God has laid a complete foundation on which the community of believers are free to build their faith.

PREACHING AND TEACHING STRATEGIES

Exegetical and Theological Synthesis

The foundation for worship was the weekly Sabbath. This text systematically adds annual celebrations to expand this foundation to ensure that the people are not so caught up in their daily lives (the work of the harvest) that they forget the Lord of the harvest! When we are busy, we are quick to redirect our focus (and justify the change). What regains one's attention better than a summons? As anyone knows who has received an official summons to appear in court before a judge, it is nonnegotiable. It displaces every other event on your schedule. It is sobering. It is the final word. The recipient must appear at the indicated time on the stated day. No exceptions. No excuses. A failure to appear means that you are in contempt!

One may ask, "Are compulsory appearances really necessary? Couldn't God's people just come when they feel the need or when it is more convenient for them?" Obligatory events may seem legalistic and may appear to lack authenticity when our confidence is built in our own capacity to remain true to our savior. But are our feelings and assurance a good foundation to build on?

Believers are called to image to an unbelieving world their hope in God's eternal presence and their daily dependence on him. How are we doing? We may casually adopt phrases like "God showed up," verbally denying his constant presence and diminishing our endless need for his provision. As we fail to secure the major events of our lives in the workings of God, we will become filled with worry. Through his summons, God is calling us to stop and appear before him to redirect our focus from the worries and delights that distract us back onto the realities and provisions of serving our Creator. When we focus on worship, our worry transforms into wonder as we become excited over how God is at work in our world.

Preaching Idea
We are summoned by God to stop and to appear before him to affirm that he is our Creator, redeemer, and provider.

Contemporary Connections

What does it mean?
Should receiving a summons from God elicit joy and excitement, or fear and frustration? Do we believe we will be most blessed by living under his authority as our redeemer and provider, or do we think we could we develop a better life by setting our own schedule? This text gently reminds us that even when our hearts are in the right place, our confidence may lead us to stray into trusting our own abilities over God's provision.

By permanently connecting the key events of life in the community (the spring and fall harvests) to festivals designed to keep their eyes on their provider, God is bonding their hope to his benevolent hand. An alternative would have been for them to provide personal assurance that they will return for worship once the crop is in, celebrate the Sabbath day when their workload lightens, or relight the candles and set out the bread when their other important tasks were completed. In this alternative approach, individual tasks, efforts, and felt responsibilities replace God as the center point of their lives. We need a summons from God that packs the power to drown out the loud but less important callings in our lives.

Is it true?

Let's ask again: Should receiving a summons from God elicit joy and excitement, or fear and frustration? Is our faith innocent and childlike, or has it begun to grow a bit cynical and jaded? Imagine the anticipation of the children when they hear these feasts are coming—an extraordinary meal with family and friends! A week camping out in a booth! And then hear the sighs from the parents over the same feasts: Who has time to grind fine flour? Must we live in a booth every year? This may be a time when those around us are taught more by deeds than by words. Seeing adults cease their work to respond to a summons to appear before God makes a strong visual statement of what is important. It serves as an enduring reminder of who they believe is in charge.

We are challenged every day. When the family is in a hurry to get on the road, is there time to stop and pray for God's provision for their journey? When the week has been long and everyone is looking forward to a day of rest, will the day be marked by worship or sleep? Will annual gatherings (birthdays, Thanksgiving, Christmas) be days to step out of, or into, our belief that God is our Creator, redeemer, and provider? These questions are not designed to bind one in a legalistic life. They are simply reminders that without a summons, we may fail to appear where and when it is most important.

Now what?

Get out the calendar. Assess how your investment of time each day, week, and year declares about what you believe. What appears to be central in your life? Are you answering God's summons? Are you appearing before him because he is your Creator, redeemer, and provider? Or have you become a bit lax, believing that once your days and weeks are no longer crazy, then you can open the mail and answer his summons? Beware. That day may never come.

We are all susceptible to attention deficit disorder when it comes to worship. We need daily reminders, weekly calls, and annual celebrations to recapture our focus. Voluntary invitations may appear less invasive, but a summons comes with the authority to reorder our priorities.

The life of a Christian starts at the cross (Feast of Passover) and ends at the final ingathering of the church (Feast of Tabernacles). If we build our lives around self-image, politics, family values, success, or personal comfort, we may eventually fail to hear God's summons. Are we denying our dependence on our Creator and becoming dependent on others who promise to provide what we believe we need? If that happens, the center point of our worship has shifted off our God and found a new focus.

Creativity in Presentation

You will need to judge the sensitivity of your own congregation to determine what might be accepted as a stimulating challenge and what will be received as a harsh indictment. You could ask for a show of hands: "Who has received a court summons (even a jury summons)? What was your first thought?" Or consider holding up a (Christian) camp brochure that you received in the mail. Describe the events, all that would happen, and so on. Testify how you became excited about sending your children to camp until suddenly you read it more carefully—it is a family camp! You don't have time for this! Do camp hosts really believe you can step away from work for a week or even a weekend? Don't they understand the commitments and demands of pastoring a church?

If telling a joke on yourself is not your style, consider using this message to launch a real campout or cookout for your church. Suggest it as an annual event with a stated purpose to recapture everyone's minds and recalibrate their priorities. Send out invitations that look like a court summons.

For the courageous who know their congregations well, challenge them with what characterizes a Sunday in their household. Worship? Football games? Naps? Yardwork? How would their kids, neighbors, and friends answer this question for them? What is the main thing at Christmas? Easter? On birthdays? How is God the center of every celebration?

Finally, it may be valuable to hand out a festival page that (1) names each feast, (2) lists their OT source, (3) summarizes their focus, and (4) suggests a NT application. Chart 10 (below) is an example. You can invite small groups, families, or groups of friends to schedule a time(s) to gather and celebrate a particular feast to worship God as our Creator, redeemer, and provider.

Feast	OT Basis	Focus	New Covenant Application or Proclamation
SABBATH Weekly	Gen. 2:1–3	Creation	Acts 20:7: Lord's Day
PASSOVER Fourteenth of Abib (March/April)	Exod. 12:1–4	Salvation	1 Cor. 5:7: Christ our Passover lamb
UNLEAVENED FIRSTFRUITS Fifteenth to twenty-first of Abib	Exod. 12:5–6; Lev. 23:11	Faithful provision promise	1 Cor. 5:6–8: free from the old leaven; James 1:18: firstfruits
PENTECOST Fifty days after Firstfruits	Lev. 23:16–17	Harvest	Acts 1:4–5; 2:2, 8–11, 38: first harvest has come
TRUMPETS First of Tishri (September/October)	Num. 29:1–2	Position for redemption	Matt. 24:31: final call to gather
ATONEMENT Tenth of Tishri	Lev. 16	Time for redemption	Heb. 10:30: already but not yet
TABERNACLES Fifteenth to twenty-second of Tishri	Num. 29:12–13	Waiting	Zech. 14:16: rest and union with Christ

Chart 10. New Testament application of Israel's feasts.

We are summoned by God to stop and to appear before him, to affirm that he is our Creator, redeemer, and provider.

- Celebrating God's lovingkindness
  - Weekly: a Sabbath rest
  - Spring feasts
    - Passover and Unleavened Bread
    - Firstfruits and Pentecost
  - Autumn feasts
    - Feast of Trumpets
    - Day of Atonement
    - Feast of Tabernacles
- What did it mean to them then? What does it mean always? What do we do now?
  - As a kid, this is awesome! As an adult, this is burdensome!
  - Invasive refocusing of our priorities is required to keep the main thing the main thing.
  - "ADHD" reset in life begins with the weekly summons to worship

DISCUSSION QUESTIONS

1. What are your plans, hopes, desires, and ambitions founded on? Is this evident to those around you? What does this communicate to your friends, family, and coworkers?

2. Do you consider the Lord's Day a summons from God? Why or why not?

3. Why is it "work" for believers to worship God? Why is this good?

4. How are you imaging God's presence to your neighbor through your actions, attitudes, beliefs, and dreams?

5. Why are some feasts celebrated at home, others primarily celebrated by the high priest, and still others a call for all of God's people to come together as one body? How does each celebration strengthen the social fabric?

6. What is the main thing in your life? Are all your thoughts, visions, hopes, and emotions connected to the main thing? Are there any rabbit trails or bridges to nowhere that are consistently drawing you away from the main thing?

7. Do you think of yourself as a "kind of firstfruit" (James 1:18)? What might James be conveying to a church in the midst of persecution?

8. How are you preparing for the final ingathering of the harvest of believers?

Leviticus 24:10–23

EXEGETICAL IDEA
God's law had been given to Moses and read before the people, establishing how they as a people were to reflect him through their words and in their actions. When this law was violated, the people were expected to judge publicly and responsibly as directed by his Word in order to redeem the person and the community.

THEOLOGICAL FOCUS
God holds us accountable for both our words that bring spiritual harm (by inaccurately declaring something about his character or profaning his nature) and our actions that bring physical harm to others in the community—native and sojourners.

PREACHING IDEA
As image-bearers, we are responsible before God for all of our words and actions.

PREACHING POINTERS
The Israelites had received volumes of law for how they were to live before God and one another in community. When an unnamed man, in the heat of anger, spoke defaming words against the Lord God, it was a sobering moment for all present. They knew immediately this was a serious violation. His words could not be unheard. How was this man to give account for his careless words? What were the people to do? Who was to judge? How should they judge?

We are guilty of being careless with our words. We may blame our emotions or other people, or say, "That's just how I feel." Does this diminish our responsibility before God for every word that proceeds from our mouth? Are we accountable for the potential damage our words may cause to the souls of others? Jesus is very clear: "I tell you, on the day of judgment people will give account for every careless word they speak, for by your words you will be justified, and by your words you will be condemned" (Matt. 12:36–37 ESV). Words that escape from our mouths reveal deeper thoughts that we hold within our hearts (Matt. 12:34). So, this goes much deeper than a problem with our speech! We need someone to reach into our souls to fix our hearts. God is focused on redemption, not retribution. And it is ultimately our heart, not simply our tongue, that must be redeemed.

REPAIRING A SOCIAL SNAG (24:10–23)

LITERARY STRUCTURE AND THEMES (24:10–23)

The last portion of Leviticus 24 interrupts the overall structure of Leviticus as a series of divine speeches where God gives legal material. The interruption is the account of an actual event that threatened corporate unity. This historical narrative segment relates a situation where an individual committed a major violation of the Torah, specifically blasphemy. To clarify the proper response, the congregation as a whole looked to Moses, who went to God for guidance on how to address and nullify that disruption. God's response contains two parts. The first part gives specific directions for the immediate situation. The second part embeds those specific directions within a matrix of general provisions intended to guide future similar situations. The account culminates with the Israelites following God's directions.

Given the overall structure of the book, the two narrative sections (here and Lev. 10) appear anomalous. For that reason, some scholars see no relationship to previous material (Bailey 2005, 291). In contrast, many stress an overall narrative framework of the broader context of the Torah surrounding the book to explain the present location of this passage. That is, the portion of the Torah that relates the time of the stay at Sinai summarizes historically the revelations and specific actions that took place there. Consequently, it is maintained that the passage is placed here because the event took place shortly after Moses received the revelation regarding the lampstand and the bread. This then shows that Leviticus is "essentially a narrative work" (Wenham 1979, 308).

It is true that the book is framed by the narratives of Exodus 40 and Numbers 1, and

necessarily must be read in that context. Further, this particular narrative section relates an event that occurred as the overall material was being given, and records specific divine guidance that resulted from addressing the issue at hand but was deemed necessary for future guidance. However, that does not necessarily require that the specific incident happened as Moses was wrapping up the material recorded in the previous chapters. It could be that as Moses put the material from this period together, it was included here as exemplifying an aspect that reflected the material just presented.

Narrative Framework

We have already suggested that the entire book of Leviticus was given within the matter of a few weeks following the consecration of the tabernacle. Likely the segments were written shortly after given and thus added to the portions of Genesis and Exodus already given (Exod. 24:4). The Israelites then carried the composite work with them as they left Sinai a year, a month, and twenty days after the exodus (Num. 10:10). While a lot of that year-long period was spent constructing the tabernacle, it also would have been a teaching time. Likely the Israelites as a whole followed their daily routines while Moses received from God the material contained in the developing Torah, and then he taught them. While we do not have a good understanding of how that worked, several passages in Leviticus hint that periodically Moses would deliver to the people material that God gave him, perhaps at the end of a given day (e.g., see Lev. 8:4–5; 16:34; 21:24; 23:44). Sometimes the text reads like Moses merely turned around and shared what God had just told him to the people who were sitting or standing near him waiting for his declaration (as here in Lev. 24:23). That may not always be the case. While it appears that Moses generally compiled the written record after he announced it to the people (for example, in the sequence in Leviticus 7, which is summed up by 7:37–38), Exodus 24:7 may provide an alternative pattern where Moses first recorded what God told him and then read it to the people. In either case, comments showing compliance, as well as recording the responses of the people, would have been added later. This is especially evident within the two narrative sections. Given the amount of material included, it seems likely that the people discussed and debated the material daily during that year. It may well be that there were other issues that were addressed by the leaders and even Moses within the nation during this period but did not require special guidance or otherwise did not need to be recorded in this document. What we have may then be compared to the minutes of a long meeting. Under God's guidance, enough was recorded that the participants and future generations would understand what had been discussed and the results, while many details were omitted.

As we addressed the material in Leviticus 18:1–24:9, we modeled it as a social fabric showing the cohesiveness and fragility of community relationships. We include the word "snag" in the title of this unit because it seems that this portion of the chapter provides an example of the community taking preventive action when an individual commits a violation that has the potential to develop into an actual tear of the social fabric. Thus, there are two key themes. The first is that a community must be vigilant to discern activities that are destructive to the community as a whole. However, as we will see, the response to those activities needed to be derived from God's guidance, and care must be taken that the response is appropriate for the action, reflecting God's justice as well as his mercy and compassion.

- *A Man Commits Blasphemy While in a Fight (24:10–11)*
- *Israel Seeks God's Guidance (24:12)*
- *God Gives Direction on a Proper Response (24:13–22)*
- *Israel Follows God's Guidance (24:23)*

EXPOSITION (24:10–23)

Leviticus 18–22 addresses a number of issues crucial to corporate cohesion, which we have characterized as a social fabric. At this point, the text briefly examines an actual event that threatened that cohesion. It is a situation where an individual got into (perhaps instigated) a fight and in the process blasphemed God. The congregation united against this individual and asked Moses for guidance. Moses inquired of God, who gave broad guidelines on how to balance the corporate response so that it was appropriate for the act. The account ends with the congregation carrying out the God-given instructions.

Several issues arise in this case. First, the individual was of mixed ancestry, which raises issues regarding nonethnic Israelites. Second, we are not told the nature of the blasphemy committed by that individual, which leaves the situation open as a model. Third, the congregation realized immediately the nature of the act and apparently its significance with respect to corporate unity. However, fourth, while the act of blasphemy had been prohibited in the initial declaration of the Decalogue, directions on community response had not yet been given. Fifth, a key concern is that the community response needs to be appropriate to the transgression. And sixth, as appropriately understood, God's overall guidance seems to allow but limit retribution.

A Man Commits Blasphemy While in a Fight (24:10–11)

24:10–11. The use of the standard *waw* transition seems rather awkward in this passage. In the Hebrew it essentially serves as a structural marker. The translation of "now" used by several modern translations seems best in that it shows a change of subject but also seems to show the continuation of the material.

This segment relates the account of an unnamed man who had an Egyptian father and an Israelite mother. The way the three individuals are cited raises a number of questions and has led to much speculation.

Why is the man unnamed? Kiuchi (2007, 440) ties it to the use of "the Name" as opposed to YHWH or the title God, suggesting that "while the divine name was not to be pronounced, the culprit's name ought to be erased; thus it is not worth mentioning it." One does need to keep in mind that the original audience would have been very aware of the individual's identity and thus would not need to have his name mentioned. At the same time future generations really would not need to know the name. This might suggest that the identity was omitted in order to keep the focus on the issue.

Who was the father, and where was he? The fact that his father is described as an Egyptian is perhaps most significant. He is both unnamed and apparently absent. Milgrom (2001, 2107), apparently assuming that the parents were married, maintains that the father either remained in Egypt or that he had joined the mixed multitude referred to as rabble (Num. 11:4) or "riff-raff" (Winterbotham 1910, 106).

TRANSLATION ANALYSIS: "RABBLE"
While this reference is not part of the present text, Milgrom's identification is relevant to the current issue. The term "rabble" that many translations use for the collective noun אֲסַפְסֻף is derived from the verb אָסַף, which means "to gather, remove, or gather in (harvest)" (Feinberg 1980a, 60). The noun is used once in Numbers 11:4. There it is generally understood to refer to the "mixed multitude" that left Egypt with the Israelites, probably because

they are termed as "among them," with "them" seeming to refer back to "the people" in 11:2, and thus contrasted with the sons of Israel in 11:4 who also wept. While the word probably refers to non-Israelites in this context (Wenham 1979, 120), the Hebrew term seems somewhat neutral, and is translated that way by the KJV ("mixt multitude"); however, most modern translations adopt a more pejorative translation such as "rabble" (ESV, NASB, NIV, NRSV) or "contemptible people" (HCSB). This seems to be because of the earlier description in Numbers of the "people," apparently those on the outskirts of the camp, as "complainers," using a *hithpoel* participle of the verb אָנַן, which seems to occur only twice in the OT (BDB s.v. "אָנַן" 52).

Rabbinic tradition paints a different picture, supposing that the mother was not married to the father. There are a variety of stories, but the dominant themes suggest that either she had been deceived and thus committed adultery, or the Egyptian had killed her husband and had relations with the mother either through coercion or deception. A very interesting take in several versions is that the father of the man had been the Egyptian that Moses murdered some forty years earlier in Exodus 2:12 (Kadari 2021; Radner 2008, 258). While these proposals contain a lot of speculation, the consensus is that the man who pronounced the blasphemy did not have an Israelite father present to raise him, which may be suggestive in terms of his conflict with the native Israelite. At a minimum, Mathews (2009, 215) suggests that as a result he did not have the same respect for the Lord as the average Israelite.

The mother is named, albeit in a parenthetical thought at the end of 24:11. The question then is, why is she named? Traditionally, there have been a variety of explanations focusing either on the meaning of the woman's name or on her tribal identity.

The Mother's Name

The Midrashic tradition focuses on the mother's name, drawing explanations out of the meaning of the terms. Presented as the "daughter of Dibri," they concluded she was talkative (the Hebrew root דבר as a verb means "to speak"; as a noun it means a "word"). As a woman of words, tradition says she greeted everyone with "*Shalom* to you." As a result, some rabbis see this as leading her to engage in forbidden sexual relations (Kadari 2021). Douglas (1999, 207) takes this one step further, translating it as a "story told to children." In her take, she selects somewhat different meanings of key terms with the following result: "Once there was a man (with no name), son of Shelomith-Retribution, grandson of Dibri-Lawsuit, from the house of Dan-Judgement, and he pelted insults at the Name . . . and the Lord said 'He shall die, he pelted my Name, he shall be pelted to death.'"

The Tribal Identity

Both Levine (1989, 166) and Milgrom (2001, 210) emphasize the fact that she was a Danite and see this as an intentional slur. As Levine puts it, Dan was "associated with the northern cult at the temple of Dan, which the Jerusalemite priesthood considered illegitimate." His evaluation seems to derive from an assumption that Leviticus postdated the events cited in Judges 18 and 1 Kings 12, since that northern cult would have been several decades, if not a century or two, after the event in Leviticus.

Tikva Frymer-Kensky (2021) provides a pertinent explanation that seems to better fit the context, as well as the location and date of the event indicated by the text. She observes that identifying the absent father as an Egyptian helps justify applying the law to resident aliens as well as Israelites. The genealogy is "important in establishing him as an Israelite, perhaps because one's lineage was usually reckoned through the father's family." It would then seem that the identification of the mother and her father as Danites would suggest that they were camped with the tribe of Dan.

The action begins with the first word of 24:10, which states (and in the Hebrew the verb begins the sentence, which suggests emphasis) "[he] went out" (וַיֵּצֵא). The text does not say from where. It could be from his tent (Kleinig 2003, 522). It could be from a different part of the camp, specifically "the outskirts" where it was assumed non-Israelites were sequestered (Keil and Delitzsch 1956, 622). It then indicates that he went "among the sons of Israel," which again leaves room for a lot of speculation.

Went Out

The common assumption that the non-Israelites were excluded from the main camp of the Israelites seems to derive from Numbers 2:34, which states that the Israelites camped "everyone by his family according to his father's household." While it is not clear how the mixed multitude was handled, the overall picture of the OT is that they were eventually absorbed into the nation of Israel, in essence being adopted by various tribes, and at least in some cases early on. A case in point would be Caleb, the son of Jephunneh the Kenizzite (הַקְּנִזִּי). The Kenizzites (הַקְּנִזִּי) were one of the Canaanite tribes that Genesis 15:19 records would be given over to Abraham's descendants. And yet Caleb, who was at least half-Kenizzite, represented the tribe of Judah in the advance reconnaissance of the Promised Land in Numbers 32 that would take place just a few months after this event. In Numbers, he is honored for his faith and rewarded by being allowed to enter the Promised Land after the wandering. In Joshua 14 he receives Hebron as his portion of the conquest. Given that, it is likely that the unnamed man in Leviticus 24 had been "attached permanently to his mother's clan" (Milgrom 2001, 2107).

The pertinent issue, however, is that in the process, this unnamed man and a "man [of] the Israelites," also unnamed, got into a fight. The cause and nature of the fight are

Repairing a Social Snag (24:10–23)

not mentioned, nor are they really relevant. Rather, the issue was that in the process, the unnamed man "blasphemed the Name and cursed" (וַיִּקֹּב . . . אֶת־הַשֵּׁם וַיְקַלֵּל). There is a lot of conjecture as to what actually occurred. Two verbs are used here, both of which have wide fields of meaning, but neither of which technically means "blasphemy" (Hartley 1992, 408). Perhaps more difficult is the fact that "the Name" is used instead of a name or title of God, although 24:16 makes it clear that he "blasphemed the name of the Lord [YHWH]."

TRANSLATION ANALYSIS: "BLASPHEMY"
The two words used here, which denote cursing, are נקב and קָלַל. The clearer term is קָלַל, which we discussed with regard to Leviticus 20:9 in conjunction with a person cursing his parents. There we concluded that it appeared to denote utter contempt, and in the case of the parents expressed a desire that they incurred serious harm. The verb נָקַב is more difficult, since it is defined as "to pierce, bore; blaspheme; appoint" (Fisher 1980b, 595). Levine (1989, 166) suggests that the two together serve as a hendiadys, indicating a single act. In any case, it would seem that the understanding here was at least as strong as in the case of the cursing of one's parents.

Milgrom (2001, 2081, 2108) translates the phrase as he "pronounced the Name, cursing it," citing passages such as 2 Chronicles 28:15 where נָקַב means "to pronounce, designate" (although there the verb is in the *niphal* stem as opposed to the *qal* here). Likewise, Levine (1989, 166) cites Targum Onkelos, which renders the verb as "pronounced explicitly." Hess (2008, 797) notes that the use of "the Name" "as a circumlocution for God, so common in Orthodox Judaism, occurs only one other place in the Bible: Deuteronomy 28:58." Here, it likely merely shortens the fuller description of the act indicated by 24:16, which specifies "the name of the Lord

[YHWH]" (שֵׁם־יְהֹוָה). Bailey (2005, 292) seems hesitant in that regard, as he claims that according to tradition other individuals in the OT did pronounce the name without criticism and cites four examples in the Pentateuch: Eve (Gen. 4:1), Abraham (Gen. 15:2), Moses (Exod. 5:1), and Aaron (Exod. 32:5), "among others." If so, then it seems that the issue may not have been that he pronounced the name, but the manner or context in which he pronounced it. James Mays (1963, 66) concludes that the "sin seems rather to have been a belittling defamation of Israel's God, a rejection of reverence for his authority and his right over Israel." Given the overall situation and punishment, this may be the best understanding of what is involved.

At this point, the observers "brought him to Moses." They would have recalled that several months earlier in their stay at Sinai one of God's directives warned the Israelites that they were not to "curse [or revile—קָלַל] God" (Exod. 22:28 [HB 27]). However no specific directions had been given regarding an expected congregational response, which likely explains why they took the man to Moses. While they understood that what had been said was blasphemy, without a specific directive denoting the requisite punishment, likely no one was eager to take the initiative to throw the first stone.

Israel Seeks God's Guidance (24:12)
24:12. This verse marks a transition from the actual narration to a legal proclamation that not only addressed the particular issue but provided broader guidance, showing how punishment should be appropriate to the offense. While awaiting disposition of the matter, the accused was put under guard. While the NASB notes an alternate translation of "prison," since this was in the camp at Sinai without any permanent buildings, essentially he was kept in custody while Moses sought information from God.

TRANSLATION ANALYSIS: "UNDER GUARD"
This phrase uses the noun מִשְׁמָר (which means "guard," *TWOT* s.v. "מִשְׁמָר" 2:939–40) as the object of the preposition "in" (בְּ), following the *hiphil* form of the verb "to be," which might be translated literally as "they caused him to be in guard," or more properly "they put him in custody."

God Gives Direction on a Proper Response (24:13–22)

24:13–16. Following the narrative indicator of a *waw*, which is best translated as "then" in this case, the section begins with the clear statement that God gave a verbal directive to Moses. This response to Moses is in three parts. The three verses of the first part specify guidelines to be followed in this particular case. In the process, the act of blasphemy was shown to be among the most serious violations of the Torah for the nation of Israel, as one of a handful of capital offenses. The corporate response was first to take the person outside of the camp, likely to avoid "corpse contamination" (Rooker 2000, 297). Then the witnesses, those who had actually heard the blasphemy, were to "lay their hands on his head." Some argue that those who heard the blasphemy incurred guilt as well as the blasphemer. That does make some sense, since they would not be able to unhear what had been said. If that were the case, it is argued that this process would rid them of secondary guilt (Kleinig 2003, 527; Peter-Contesse and Ellington 1992, 368; Wenham 1979, 311). This raises a question as to whether there is such a thing as secondary guilt in a person who has witnessed someone committing a sin. Clearly, the memory of what had been observed would remain in the mind of the witnesses even after the retribution. More likely Kiuchi (2007, 440) is correct when he states that it was a form of attestation: "by laying their hands on the offender, the people testify before the Lord that they are witnesses to the blasphemy."

After this, "all the congregation" (כָּל־הָעֵדָה) was to stone him. We noted in our discussion of Leviticus 4:13–21 that Jewish commentators attributed the term "congregation" (עֵדָה) as a reference to the leadership, but that such a clear distinction could not be sustained. While here it seems clear that the term is intended to reflect more than just the witnesses, it is not clear whether it would encompass the entire population—which would involve a vast amount of stones. Even if the representative leadership is indicated, it seems that there would be a large number of stones, which may be a factor in requiring that the execution be conducted outside of the camp. In the later case of Achan, who was stoned after misappropriating goods from Jericho, the text notes that "all Israel" stoned Aachan, and they "raised over him a great heap of stones" (Josh. 7:25–26). That heap, which the book of Joshua characterizes as standing after the event, likely was a result of the execution process. On one hand this buried the victim on the spot. But it also produced a monument that could remind those who saw it of what happened and serve as a warning to others so that they did not commit the same act. This is indicated by God's declaration that the same punishment is applicable to anyone who "blasphemes the name of the Lord [YHWH]." Further, the warning was for all who were actively part of the community, including aliens. While resident aliens might not be required to follow the religious practices of the Israelites, they would be expected to remember that they were guests in Israel, and as such had to honor certain aspects of the culture and religion of their hosts. Not blaspheming the Israelite God would clearly be one such expectation.

24:17–21. Following the directions for the case at hand, the second part of God's response to Moses is a general, but somewhat complex, series of consequences that seem to

Repairing a Social Snag (24:10–23)

set forth a spectrum of corporate responses to physical harm done to either other humans or animals. Three levels of harm are listed.

The first is taking the life of any human being. Several observations should be noted here. First, the perpetrator is labeled a man (אִישׁ), a term that "connotes primarily the concept of man as an individual" (McComiskey 1980a, 38), while the victim is a man (אָדָם), which "refers to generic man as the image of God" (Coppes 1980a, 10). This use of the generic term also suggests that regardless of ethnic identity or gender (note Gen. 1:27 citing man [אָדָם] as both male and female) the recompense was to be the same—execution. A second point is the execution statement, which emphatically presents the punishment as death.

TRANSLATION ANALYSIS: "SURELY PUT TO DEATH"
The Hebrew phrase is מוֹת יוּמָת using a *qal* infinitive absolute and a *hophal* imperfect of the verb מוּת which means "to die." The infinitive absolute serves to emphasize the action. The *hophal* stem is a passive form of the *hiphil* that indicates causing action (GKC §53h, c). Thus, a literal translation might be, "dying, he shall be caused to be dead."

This is further emphasized by the inclusion of the particle כֹּל, which means "all." A third point is the use of the word *nephesh* (נֶפֶשׁ), which we discussed in the introduction as denoting the soul or that nonphysical aspect that humans and animals share that makes them alive. This is important because the same term is used in the next verse regarding animals.

TRANSLATION ANALYSIS: "ANY HUMAN BEING"
This translates the phrase כָּל־נֶפֶשׁ אָדָם. While the particle כֹּל basically means "all," because the word it modifies is נֶפֶשׁ, which is singular, it means "every" (Oswalt 1980d, 441). As such, the phrase might be translated "every soul of a man" or, in this context, standard English would suggest "any soul of a man." While this suggests that any death required the execution of the one who caused it, other passages provide a different punishment for accidental death (see Exod. 21:12–4).

The second level of harm is taking the life of an animal. The phrase used here is נֶפֶשׁ־בְּהֵמָה or "the *nephesh* of a beast." While *beast* (בְּהֵמָה) may refer to wild animals, it generally refers to domestic animals, usually large cattle and sheep (Martens 1980a). In this context it must refer to domestic animals, since the requirement is that the person who took the animal's life must make restitution (יְשַׁלְּמֶנָּה), which must refer to recompense to the owner of the animal. Here the recompense is in kind, *nephesh* for *nephesh*.

The third level of harm is physical injury to humans. There are two aspects to this in this passage. First, the term מוּם suggests an injury that disfigures a person. As Willis (2009, 203) describes it, "It renders the victim 'profane' and unfit to enter the sanctuary." Second, it precludes death as retribution in cases of physical injury.

TRANSLATION ANALYSIS: "INJURES"
According to *TWOT* (Kaiser 1980c, 488), the phrase יִתֵּן מוּם can be translated literally as "he gives a blemish." Conceptually, it is a term denoting a physical defect that would disqualify a priest from service (Lev. 21:17–20) or an animal from sacrifice (Lev. 22:20). While many translations use "injures" here, the terms "maims" (NRSV) or "permanent injury" (HCSB) seem more appropriate. Based on the Leviticus 21 qualifications for a priest, any of the three injuries cited in 24:20a could serve to disqualify a priest and thus may serve as conceptual guidance.

As Wenham (1979, 311) observes, "whereas the laws of Hammurabi regard property offenses and similar crimes as capital, the OT does not." Rather, retribution was intended to be appropriate to the act, described here as "just as he has done, so it shall be done to him," often referred to as *lex talionis*. Given the broader cultural context, this set equitable limits; however, even this seems harsh to modern western cultural values. A number of commentators suggest that in practice, monetary compensation was practiced and provided a "basis for determining just compensation" (Hartley 1992, 413; see also Ross 2002, 448; Wenham 1979, 312). This seems suggested by Exodus 21:22–25, which ties a similar *lex talionis* pattern to payment "as the judges decide." Additionally, there are other passages that actually disallow pity in certain cases, such as Deuteronomy 13:8, suggesting that pity may have been an option in many cases.

> ### Judges Decide
> Exodus 21:22–25 presents a situation where a pregnant woman is struck while a bystander to a fight and gives birth prematurely. As long as the child and mother live with no further injuries, the guilty party is required to pay a penalty as demanded by the woman's husband and as the judges agree. If there are further injuries, then the *lex talionis* material provides guidelines for compensation. One thing that must be remembered is that at the time of the stay at Sinai, when these passages were apparently written, money as we know it had not been invented, but silver and gold were used as media of exchange calculated by weight.

The heart of this section is actually 24:20a, which provides specifics: "fracture for fracture, eye for eye, tooth for tooth." Following this statement, the text restates the three levels of harm in reverse order. This type of structure is called a chiasm and could be outlined as follows:

A Taking the life of a human being (24:17)
B Taking the life of an animal (24:18)
C Injuring a human being (24:19)
D (*lex talionis*) (24:20a)
C' Injuring a human being (24:20b)
B' Taking the life of an animal (24:21a)
A' Taking the life of a human being (24:21b)

> ### Chiasm
> A chiasm is a literary structure that juxtaposes two series sharing a pivot term or phrase, with the second series being inverted. The title comes from the Greeks, who called it *chiasmos*. Bullinger (1968, 374) calls it "the most stately and dignified presentation of a subject." Bruce Waltke and Charles Yu (2007, 120) observe that it was a common pattern throughout ancient literature. As Bullinger notes, the practice has been recognized for some time, however Waltke and Yu cite John Welch as noting an increasing awareness of the practice in ancient literature. This awareness has shown up in recent OT studies, as the identification of chiasms of varying scope has exploded. In terms of OT studies, at times the identification of the chiasm seems somewhat forced, most noticeably when the study lacks an evaluation of the value of the chiasm with regard to the meaning of the passage.

As we have structured the chiasm, the beginning and end points are the killing of another human being. The difficulty in this case is defining the pivot. Sklar (2014, 292–93) combines what is presented here as levels C, D, C' as a single point and thus the pivot. Given the way C and C' reflect each other, it would seem that they are also reflective levels, which leaves D as the pivot at least for 24:19–20. But are they really just a single level? While, like Sklar, one could say that the pivot is a complex one incorporating both parts, that does not explain the repetition of 24:19 in 24:20b. We would suggest that here the pivot is a figure of speech called *enumeration* (Bullinger 1968, 436), where a series of examples is used to produce an overall concept in place of a technical term or concept, in this case describing a part of the body for an equivalent part. Essentially this would be what Kleinig (2003, 528) describes as "a legal principle that is couched in proverbial form." This would illustrate Waltke and Yu's (2007, 120) conclusion that "the pivot is the key to meaning (i.e., to the message)," providing a simple summation of the entire chiasm that would be readily recalled and expressed at appropriate times. Consequently, in the chiasm chart we have interpreted that figure with the Latin phrase *lex talionis*, which generally explicates the concept. While the specific items cited in 24:20a do seem to give specific examples of the verb "injures," it seems that this pivot balances more than just 24:19 and 20 but the entire pattern of 24:17–21. Overall, then, this complex passage envelops the death penalty that had just been given for the blasphemer as part of a broader legal principle that prescribes "the notion of equivalence in the administration of justice" (Kleinig 2003, 528). As such, it elevates the crime of blasphemy to the highest level within the nation of Israel. While not specified here, to allow blasphemy among God's people erodes the communal respect of God, and can eventually lead to destructive rips in the social fabric.

24:22. The third part of God's response addresses the issue of the blasphemer's ethnic identity. As noted earlier, the man's father was Egyptian. Should a non-Israelite be subject to Israelite law, especially on a matter of religion? Here God declares that for anyone who was part of the community, whether "native" (אֶזְרָח) or "resident alien" (גֵּר), to a degree the answer is yes. We noted earlier that while Leviticus 19:33–36 prescribes equal justice for the non-Israelites who settled in the midst of the Israelites, whom we have called resident aliens, there were restrictions in terms of how they could practice their religions. Not only could they not openly

worship their gods; in essence, they could not have their own legal systems. But while that meant that they were subject to the same judgments as the Israelites, they also enjoyed the same standards of fairness and justice. A key point in this case is that given the location of the nation at the time one may presume the man that had an Egyptian father had left Egypt with the Israelites. By this act of identifying with the Israelites he became responsible for adhering to the national guidelines. At the same time, for the Israelites the admonition that this declaration was from the Lord their God indicated that they were responsible for ensuring that resident aliens also had the same justice they expected, which is something that will be addressed in the final units (Harbin 2021b, 691–93).

Israel Follows God's Guidance (24:23)
24:23. The final verse in this unit and chapter merely reports that Moses told the Israelites what God had told him to tell them. They then followed directions and took the man outside the camp and stoned him for the capital crime of blasphemy.

THEOLOGICAL FOCUS
A normal human response to acts that cause physical injury is a desire for personal revenge, which generally leads to escalation. This passage primarily indicates that in contrast to the overall secular cultures of the area, response to injurious acts should be corporate and limited. In particular, capital punishment should be limited to cases that produce significant damage to society. In general, these would be cases of the taking of human life, because all humans are in the image of God. If humans, being in the image of God, hold such value, then arguing from the lesser to the greater, that same must be true regarding similar actions addressed to God. While God cannot be killed, inordinate disrespect of God can effectively remove him from society, thus removing the framework on which a strong society must be fabricated. In this regard, a key

point that tends to get overlooked is that the situation and structure of the passage place blasphemy against God as being on the same level as murder in terms of the consequences. This clearly places God at an even higher elevation than humans.

In regard to lesser assaults, Kleinig (2003, 529) argues that this passage does not describe "a primitive, barbaric form of punishment" but rather is "the basis for all civilized legal systems," since it sets limits on what may be done in terms of personal injury. One of the distinctions of the Israelite *lex talionis* practice is that it distinguishes sharply between injury to a domestic animal, such as an ox or sheep, and a human being. While the animals are valuable and possess a *nephesh*, the premise seems to be that they are not in the image of God, therefore the requisite response is compensation in terms of replacing the animal that was lost.

Gane (2004a, 427) notes how this practice shows a primary concern with justice for the victim in that it does mandate punishment. However, it balances that with a concern for the perpetrator in that it disallows execution for any act that produces physical harm except murder.

PREACHING AND TEACHING STRATEGIES

Exegetical and Theological Synthesis
Blasphemy a capital offense? Maybe premeditated murder or child sacrifice or a genocidal massacre, but the death penalty for blasphemy seems to be more than a bit over the top! Yet this is the moral standard applied to all—native and sojourner alike. Why would the Lord God first command such an action and then record its implementation for the coming generations to hear? Could it be that we are underestimating the power of destructive words to kill the soul of both the speaker and the recipients?

In this passage, we see that not only is this unnamed man held accountable for defaming the Lord, but all who heard his words are held accountable for administering the justice that God requires. This reminds us that the offense was not solely against God, but against all who heard. Careless words pack the power to sow seeds of doubt and unbelief, and even temper one's appropriate fear of God for all who hear them (and for others who repeat them). Words cannot be unheard. Will the hearing of such words be remembered for how they exposed the folly or released the reality of God's eternal judgment?

It is likely the words were said in a moment of anger. Does this lessen his guilt? Though we may make allowances for emotional outbursts, inebriation, and the rest, Scripture suggests such times may unmask what is hidden even to us in our hearts (Matt. 15:18). It is important to see that the people are not directed to act in haste. They are not motivated by their feelings or vengeance. This is far from a mob action. The community is expected to humbly yield to God's leading on justice. Don't ignore the wrong committed, whether verbal or physical. Don't exaggerate the offense. The *lex talionis* effectively eliminates revenge and overreach in favor or redeeming the offense and preserving the community.

Preaching Idea
As image-bearers, we are responsible before God for all of our words and actions.

Contemporary Connections

What does it mean?
What does it mean that image-bearers are responsible before God for all of their words and actions? We often tend to excuse rather than confess when the words that escape from our mouths are harmful either to us or those who hear them. While freedom of speech may be a constitutional right, it may also promote doubt,

Repairing a Social Snag (24:10–23)

unbelief, public defamation of God, and a loss of fear for his authority to judge all of creation. This is not a freedom for the believing community. Remaining silent during false declarations about God or others (whether intentional or carelessly uttered) will tempt all who hear to discount our Creator as the eternal judge of all humankind.

As image-bearers, we are responsible to accurately bear the image of our creator through our words and deeds. Speech is a gift to bless others and proclaim the true glories of our God. Speech is not a weapon to curse others and defame our redeemer. When we utter false declarations about God, we are doing the work of the serpent. God's will is to redeem both the speaker and the hearers from such idle words. Hearers are to recognize false declarations and humbly bring correction to a speaker. The motive is redemption, not retribution. The result is correction, not escalation. God alone remains the final judge in eternity for all people.

Is it true?

In a believing community, we are not free to embrace the Bill of Rights over Scripture as our standard for speech and behavior. Speech and reason were not given to us so we can promote ourselves. We remain bondservants of our Lord. Though we should not expect to be stoned to death for our words, we are not free from penalty either. Native and sojourner alike will be sentenced to eternal damnation by words that reveal stubborn darkness within our heart.

God's plan is to open our eyes that we may see what he sees, then redeem us as speakers and redeem the community as hearers. The community is compensated for the injury they receive either through words or deeds. For our words, they receive an apology and request for forgiveness from a contrite heart. If we injure another's leg, we plow their field. If we damage another's eye, we pick their grapes. The focus is set on redeeming the wrong both in the offender and in the offended so that the community will not be burdened by ongoing disobedience.

Now what?

The aim is to retake responsibility and assume the liability for all of our words and actions. Though we may be hesitant to hold ourselves accountable, and social media, professional standards, even friends, may be unwilling to hold us accountable, God holds us accountable. Speech is his gift to us. Words matter. They bless. They curse. They flow up from the heart. They penetrate to our soul. They lay bare the depths of our soul. They establish that we need a redeemer who will remove the heart of stone that declines to take responsibility for the pain we cause and replace it with a heart of flesh that will bless others by accurately imaging our Creator to the world through our speech.

Creativity in Presentation

You can expect this passage to raise some objections from your congregation. Each can be addressed with creativity and sensitivity. First, we live in a culture where speech is free and liability is limited, so freedom to express our careless words and uninformed opinions is considered more of a carefully guarded right than an eternal liability. There are ways to challenge the "sacred" belief that I have a right to "speak my mind."

You could opt for humorous examples of how spoken words though errant beliefs can become imbedded in our culture for generations. The rise of Popeye the sailor man emerged from a careless conclusion on the iron content of spinach. Spinach was reported to be rich in iron. It is not. It was a miscalculation that was undetected for years. During this time, the character Popeye was created as one whose strength was derived by eating spinach high in iron. A brief search will yield many such examples in health, medicine, fitness, and advertising.

You could choose a less humorous example such as the "War of the Worlds" radio broadcast on October 30, 1938. Thousands of people panicked, believing the broadcast on the radio was real. Were the writers and actors responsible for how they used their words? Depending on the nature of your congregation, you could use many political examples of careless words that led to great tragedies or wrong beliefs. You could share a personal story of when your words damaged someone else.

The point is to prepare your congregation by challenging the belief that "sticks and stone may break our bones, but words will never hurt us." Invite your congregation to consider the following questions: Is it a God-given right to speak our minds? Do I have a right to my personal opinion? Do I have a right to share every personal belief? If my opinions and beliefs are potentially lethal to the soul of another, will God hold me responsible? Then, read Matthew 12:36–37. How can we redeem our speech?

A second objection may surface by reading Leviticus 24:23, the stoning to death of the unnamed man by the people. You will have to determine the spiritual maturity of your congregation to decide how deeply to address the practice of stoning. I challenged my congregation to consider four portraits of this sobering event (the man being brought before God) and its effect on the community. First, a man defiantly cursing God to the end. Second, a man blaming others for his offense. Third, a man grieving that he is being held accountable by God for his sin. Fourth, a man broken and humbled for his lethal words, ready to forfeit his life to redeem the wrong. Where is God's grace in judgment evident in each portrait? Which of these is closest to your response when you sin against others? I had several congregational members testify how significant this was for them to work through.

As image-bearers, we are responsible before God for all of our words and actions.

- The power of words
  - Accountable for every word
  - Our careless words are a danger to others
- Sentenced by the Lord God
  - Understanding the offense and accepting a divine standard
  - Hearing the verdict and administering divine justice
- What did it mean to them then? What does it mean always? What do we do now?
  - Shocking and sobering to everyone in the community
  - All words matter, always!
    - Words we hear or say cannot be unheard or unsaid
    - Words can have lethal power
  - Listen to our own words—all words said, and those "spoken in silence" yet heard by God.

DISCUSSION QUESTIONS

1. Do you feel accountable before others as you share your thoughts, opinions, and teachings? How is God holding you responsible for the words you share before others?

2. Why are we quick to dismiss careless words shared in anger? What should such words reveal to us about our hearts? How should we respond?

3. Why are careless declarations about God considered a sin against our neighbor? How should this transform our speech?

4. God's standard is that a response to any offense is to be more redemptive than

punitive. How can we hold to this standard in our relationship with others?

5. Why is vengeance specifically forbidden? Why does vengeance belong to God alone?

6. What are specific ways we can redeem someone who is wounded by our careless words? By our actions? By our beliefs?

Leviticus 25:1–22

EXEGETICAL IDEA
God purposefully wove Sabbath and Jubilee years into the social fabric of his redeemed people so that they may live securely as stewards of the faith in the land that he had entrusted to them.

THEOLOGICAL FOCUS
God instructs his people in how to anchor their lives to him by corporately living out their belief in his faithfulness and imaging his gracious redemption to each other and the world, through their stewardship of his land and labor contracts with one another.

PREACHING IDEA
We declare our relationship to God and to the world through our relationships with others and our possessions.

PREACHING POINTERS
The people received the Sabbath and Jubilee commands from God through Moses when they were completely landless and dependent on daily manna. They were living for a promise that they were redeemed from bondage in Egypt to live one day in a land of milk and honey. But during Sabbath and Jubilee years it sounded like they would remain stewards of what belonged to God, never owners of the land they were preparing to possess. Would their life in the wilderness be more preparatory than temporary? A life of dependence sounded more like a permanent way of life under the Lord God that would continue as they entered the Promised Land. What was the purpose behind such binding laws? (The Scriptures record a consistent failure to observe the Sabbath and Jubilee years.) Why were the people hesitant to embrace these marks of permanent dependence on the Lord God?

It is easy as believers to reason ourselves away from all directives that reflect our dependence on God. God wants us to be fruitful, right? And he wants us to flaunt how he blesses us, right? And if we don't maximize our possessions, profits, and investments, then we will not be free to be generous with others! Through this vortex of unbelief, we effectively deny God his seat as the decisive factor in providence. Furthermore, we assume that seat as we are consumed by work, goals, planning, and prosperity. God draws us away from the toxic belief that we can be self-sustaining in this fallen world. He is repositioning us before him by directing how we are to relate to others and our possessions.

PREVENTING SOCIAL UNRAVELING, PART 1
(25:1–22)

LITERARY STRUCTURE AND THEMES (25:1–22)

Leviticus 25 returns to the divine directive sequence begun in Leviticus 23 (see unit "Strengthening the Social Fabric") that was interrupted by the incident of blasphemy in the last half of Leviticus 24. The structure of Leviticus 25 is somewhat complex, interweaving two different themes in two different ways. The first theme in 25:1–22 expands and embellishes the concept of appointed times spelled out in Leviticus 23 by extrapolating the seven-day Sabbath sequence into multiyear sequences of Sabbath years and Jubilees—every seven years and then every seven sevens of years (or fifties with Jubilees). It then contrasts the regular corporate work projects of providing oil and bread of presence (presented in Lev. 24) with periodic periods of rest for the land. These also serve to give rest to those who work the land. The remainder of Leviticus 25 explains how the Sabbath years and Jubilees not only provide rest for the land, but also produce a derivative theme of social resets through ensuring the heritage of family property and relieving debt. In this unit, we will explore the first theme of Sabbath years and Jubilees, noting how they were determined and provided social resets. In the unit "Preventing Social Unraveling, Part 2," we will evaluate this complex issue of social resets, noting how Israel was expected to sequentially work to alleviate issues of poverty. As will be seen, the two themes together were designed to prevent social unraveling in two ways. On the one hand, they served to prevent individuals or families from amassing extreme wealth by unscrupulous means. On the other hand, they served to

provide safety nets for individuals or families who experienced overwhelming setbacks. The promise given was that if the corporate body seriously worked together in this regard, the entire nation would prosper.

- ***The Lord Defines Sabbath Years (25:1–7)***
- ***The Lord Defines Jubilee (25:8–12)***
- ***The Lord Clarifies the Release of Property (25:13–19)***
- ***The Lord Encourages the Israelites to Trust Him (25:20–22)***

EXPOSITION (25:1–22)

The first twenty-two verses of Leviticus 25 broadly define Sabbath years and Jubilees. While not divine appointments in the same sense as the six-holy-day annual sequence listed in Leviticus 23, these two periods were important for maintaining the social fabric of the people of God. As stated in 25:19, if the nation took care to observe God's statutes and judgments, they would "live securely on the land."

Sabbath year describes the final year of a seven-year sequence where the nation of Israel was to work the land for six years, and then in the seventh year not work the land, that is, let the land rest. The text specifically states that "the *land* shall have a Sabbath to the Lord [YHWH]" (Lev. 25:2, emphasis added). It goes on to say that in the seventh year, the people were not to plant or harvest. The directive that the rest was for the land implies that other forms of work were permissible. This makes sense, since livestock still needed care, property still needed to be maintained, and people still needed to

359

eat. Still, it might be presumed that the daily workload would be less rigorous than normal. If given at Mount Sinai as the text presents, then the earliest anticipated first Sabbath year would have been probably at least a decade in the future, allowing for a time of conquest, settlement, and then the initial six years of farming. As such, amplifying details were to be expected at a later date, some of which are included in other texts. The present exegesis will cover just that which is recorded here.

After seven Sabbath years, a different pause was mandated called a Jubilee. While not called a Sabbath year, the directions do specify that like a Sabbath year, the land was not to be planted or harvested. Jubilee carries more significance because it carries powerful connotations with respect to the land that God was giving to the nation. Although they were to possess the land once they settled there, the gift was to be to the family, with the provision that the family was not to sell it to anyone else. While much could happen over a fifty-year period with regard to possession and use of the land, Jubilee provided a reset so that the original family again had possession and could use the land that God gave them. This was one of the provisions that God made for what we might call social justice, and the rest of the chapter amplifies those provisions in terms of alleviating poverty. However, that portion of the material will be covered in the next unit.

The Lord Defines Sabbath Years (25:1–7)

25:1. Leviticus 25 opens with an unexpected twist. While it begins with the familiar "Then the Lord [YHWH] spoke to Moses" it adds the locative phrase "at Mount Sinai" (בְּהַר סִינַי) using the בְּ preposition, which usually means "in" but also might mean "at" or "on" (as in most modern translations) among other meanings (BDB s.v. "בְּ" 800). This phrase is used only three other times in the book of Leviticus and only once prior to this (7:38; 26:46; and 27:34). The significance of its use here is not clear. If the intended

idea was "on," it would contrast the location of this section with that of the rest of the book, where God spoke to Moses while he was in the tabernacle courtyard at the foot of the mountain, as we noted in the unit "Worshipping a Holy God" (1:1–3:17). Although this could indicate that Moses went up on the mountain at this time, it is also possible that Leviticus 25–27 was given to him while he was on the mount earlier during the Sinai period and placed here when the book was written (cf. Exod. 23:10–13 with respect to the Sabbath year). Sklar (2014, 296) suggests that these last sections were placed here to provide a transition to the book of Numbers. If the intended idea was "at," it would suggest that this information was just part of the overall revelation given during the year the nation was camped at the foot of the mountain. That might suggest that the phrase here was a literary embellishment that, coupled with 26:46, served as an *inclusio* (Hartley 1992, 414). If intended as an *inclusio*, it would seem that the purpose was to emphasize the material. Given the later significance of the Sabbath year, where the length of the exile was predicated upon the nation's failure to give the land its rest (2 Chron. 36.21), this is perhaps the best understanding.

25:2–7. God directed Moses to inform Israel to observe this command when the nation had entered the land and had begun farming. Looking back long after the fact, we recognize that settling in the land would begin forty years later with the next generation, but the Israelites at Sinai apparently expected that the present generation would enter within a year. Regardless, once settled, the people were to begin counting when they planted their first crop after they entered the land, and then they were to follow a seven-year cycle.

> #### Sabbath Year Cycle
> Hoenig (1969, 222 n. 1) cites the Talmud as indicating that the Israelites began counting Sabbath years "fourteen years after Joshua's entrance into

the Land [*sic*]." Arakhin 12b claims there were seven years of conquest, and the first Sabbath year was celebrated seven years later. This would suggest that the nation really did not begin farming until the completion of the northern campaign and the subsequent division of the land by tribes (Josh. 13). While outside the subject at hand, that raises questions regarding the subsistence of the nation during that period, since Joshua 5:12 states that the manna ceased on the day they ate produce from the land after crossing the Jordan River. One possibility is that they were able to subsist on stores captured in various cities.

For the first six years of the cycle, they were to follow normal agricultural procedures, expressed in a three-step description of sowing, maintaining, and harvesting.

Gezer Calendar

The Gezer Calendar (fig. 64) is a limestone tablet discovered in 1908.

Figure 64. The Gezer Calendar.

Dated to the tenth century B.C., the same time frame of the Solomonic gates also excavated at Gezer, it is best understood as having been written in Paleo-Hebrew. The inscription describes the agricultural year and is deemed an educational exercise. William F. Albright translates it as

His two months are (olive) harvest, (S/O)
   His two months are planting (grain), (N/D)
      His two months are late planting; (J/F)

His month is hoeing up of flax (M)
   His month is harvest of barley, (A)
      His month is harvest and feasting; (M)

His two months are vine-tending, (J/J)
   His month is summer fruit. (A)

(ANET, 320; modern correlation added)

The calendar is currently on display at the Istanbul Archaeological Museum in Turkey.

This description follows a logical sequence rather than an actual chronological sequence, since some maintenance, such as the pruning of grape vines, is done during the winter dormant period, possibly even before sowing grain, and some would be done in the summer after the grain has been harvested.

Grapevine Pruning

According to the Washington State University extension program, there are two types of grape pruning: dormant pruning (which in the United States is late winter), and canopy pruning, which is done during the growing season (https://extension.wsu.edu/maritimefruit/grape-research/pruning-grapes-in-home-gardens-some-basic-guidelines). The latter is intended to take out unproductive shoots or thin out clusters that are too closely spaced. Figure 65 shows dormant pruned grapevines in January at Sataf Israel. Figure 66 shows some of the same grapevines growing in April.

Figure 65. Pruned grapevine at Sataf, Israel, in January.

Figure 66. Pruned grapevines at Sataf, Israel, in April.

The seventh year was to be a year of rest for the land. While there were practical aspects to this command, such as helping to reduce the amount of sodium in the soil (Levine 1989, 170), the main focus was that this was a "rest unto the Lord." As Milgrom (2001, 2153) observes, nothing regarding a practical consideration is mentioned, "Its requirement is justified theologically, not economically." Even so, the passage focuses on how this would affect the people.

First, they were not to sow, prune, or reap, the three key responsibilities for raising crops. Nothing is said regarding other forms of labor.

TRANSLATION ANALYSIS: "REAP"
The third of the three agricultural responsibilities is debated. The verb קָצַר is translated as "to reap, harvest" (Lewis 1980e, 809). This is understood by some commentators to mean that they were not allowed to eat from the aftergrowth, which presents problems when compared with 25:6, which tells the Israelites that they may have the "Sabbath *products* of the land" (וְהָיְתָה שַׁבַּת הָאָרֶץ לָכֶם). Literally the phrase reads "that of the Sabbath of the land will be to you." This is generally understood to say that they could have whatever voluntarily grew during the Sabbath year (Gerstenberger 1996, 375). In this case, Deuteronomy 23:25 may help clarify the matter, as it addresses the legitimacy of Israelites eating food from their neighbors' fields. It states that when walking through the field, they were free to "pluck the heads with their hands" (using the verb קָטַף), but they were not allowed to "wield a sickle," that is, reap or harvest it. Analogously, it then seems that going through one's own field one might pick or pluck food for the day, but not for preservation for the future.

Consequently, the rabbis disputed the implications. Milgrom (2001, 2158) notes that Rabbi Eliezer viewed the three prohibited labors as a merism for all labors, while Rabbi Yohanan maintained that those were the only labors prohibited. The specificity of the prohibition contrasts with the earlier, more encompassing prohibitions given for the Sabbath day, which stated specifically "You will not do any work" (כָּל־מְלָאכָה לֹא תַעֲשׂוּ) and it was to be "a Sabbath of complete rest" (שַׁבַּת שַׁבָּתוֹן). This suggests that the latter view is the correct one. This would indicate that while the land rested, people continued to perform nonagricultural labor.

Second, the text continues on to indicate that the people were permitted to use whatever grew voluntarily for food (see translation analysis of "reap" [קָצַר]). The first caveat to this permission was that they were not allowed to reap, which is understood to mean that while they were allowed to pick produce for daily provisions, they were not allowed to harvest to store for future use. The second caveat was that the "Sabbath products of the land" were available to *anyone*, that is, to whomever was willing to go out and procure them (given the first caveat), regardless of whose field the produce was growing in. This included all the men and their families, all slaves, both male and female, all hired workers, and all resident aliens. A third caveat was that animals were allowed to graze in the fields also.

Third, while not discussed in this passage, other passages note additional criteria that seem to fit within this seven-year cycle germane to the issue at hand. The key element seems to be the directive in Exodus that a Hebrew slave (עֶבֶד) would go out free in the seventh year (Exod. 21:2). Two factors in this directive generate discussion. The Exodus text states that this Hebrew slave will serve six years and go out free on the seventh. The question is whether the seventh year refers to the Sabbath year or to the seventh year of slavery, regardless of when it started. Another study concludes that based on Deuteronomy 15:1–18, the six years of service is a maximum, not a fixed figure (Harbin 2012, 53–74; see also appendix 4, "Slaves and Emancipation in Israel"). As such, the seventh year addressed in Exodus is the Sabbath year and all Hebrew slaves laboring under this guideline would be released in that year. A second question generated by this command involves the relationship of this freeing of a slave and the guidelines for the Jubilee. As will be discussed below, some scholars see Jubilee producing two emancipations in back-to-back years: one would be in the seventh Sabbath year (the forty-ninth year of the cycle) and then the following Year of Jubilee (the fiftieth year). However, as will be explained in the next section, this derives from a misconception regarding Jubilee.

A later Sabbath year provision modified the annual Feast of Booths (Lev. 23:34–44). As Moses was about to depart this world, he amplified directions for the Feast of Booths, one of the three divine appointments where the nation was to assemble before God "in the place that he chooses" (Exod. 23:14–17; Deut 16:1–16). When they gathered in the seventh year, the Torah was to be read orally before the entire nation including men, women, children, and resident aliens "so that they may hear and learn and fear the Lord [YHWH] your God, and be careful to observe all the words of this law" (Deut. 31:12). In a culture where likely many did not read, and few would have had copies of the Torah, periodic oral reviews of God's teaching were necessary, serving to remind the people collectively whence they came and why they were in the land. This suggests that the Sabbath year served as a time of spiritual renewal, despite the fact that no special rituals were dictated for corporate or even personal worship.

The Lord Defines Jubilee (25:8–12)

25:8. After introducing 25:8 with the versatile *waw*, which could be translated here as "and" (KJV) or "also" (NASB) or even ignored (several modern translations), the text switches abruptly to a directive to count forty-nine years. To emphasize this point, the concept is repeated here three times in different ways.

TRANSLATION ANALYSIS: "FORTY-NINE YEARS"
The directive begins that they were to count "seven Sabbaths of years" (שֶׁבַע שַׁבְּתֹת שָׁנִים). This is followed by the phrase "seven times seven years" (שֶׁבַע שָׁנִים שֶׁבַע פְּעָמִים literally "seven years seven times") emphasized by the subsequent phrases "seven Sabbaths of years" (שֶׁבַע שַׁבְּתֹת הַשָּׁנִים) with

the mathematical conclusion, "forty-nine years" (תֵּשַׁע וְאַרְבָּעִים שָׁנָה)

The object of that count was to denote a special event subsequent to that seventh Sabbath. With regard to the original audience, it would seem that despite the practical difficulties, the text is best understood as written thus requiring two full fallow years. The first would be the seventh Sabbath year, and the second would be Jubilee. At Sinai, the institution of both events would be a number of years in the future (Milgrom 2001, 2166; Ross 2002, 459). For a full analysis of the issues involved in defining Jubilee and how that conclusion was reached see appendix 5, "The Year of Jubilee." This special event was to have even more striking significance than the Sabbath year. While not named a Sabbath year, it was like a Sabbath year in that they were not to sow, maintain, or reap.

25:9–12. As noted in Leviticus 23:24–25, the seventh month was significant in the Israelite calendar in a variety of ways. While called the seventh month, it served to initiate the Year of Jubilee. It was announced with "a blowing" (תְּרוּעָה, with trumpets inferred) on the first of the month, in contrast to the announcement of other months by a תָּקַע (see translation analysis of תְּרוּעָה in section "The Lord Gives Directions for the Fall Appointed Times"). The year-long event of Jubilee was further differentiated from other years by giving the proclamation for its beginning on the tenth day of the seventh month instead of the first. This is emphasized with the phrase "on the Day of Atonement." Likewise, the horn cited here was specifically a ram's horn, although *TWOT* (Austel 1980d) suggests that the term is interchangeable with "trumpet" (יוֹבֵל).

Seven

Even a casual reading of the Old Testament shows an emphasis on the number 7, leading to a conclusion that it carries some symbolism. John Davis (1968, 119) points out, "nowhere in Scripture is any number given any specific theological or mystical meaning," although he concedes that "the only number used symbolically in the Scripture to any degree with *discernible significance* is the number seven" (emphasis original). Based on the wide use of that number throughout the Bible as well is in other contemporary cultures, he concludes that it conveys the idea of "completeness" or "perfection," which he attributes to its common usage. While its origin seems to be lost in history, if the biblical record is correct, it may well be that it is derived from the creation week, which is itself an arbitrary denotation as described in the excursus "Israelite Calendar and the Seven-Day Week" in the unit "Strengthening the Social Fabric" (23:1–24:9). As such, seven and multiples of seven served to mark the timing of God's divine appointments with the nation of Israel, reminding them that he was their Creator and their sovereign.

This proclamation on the Day of Atonement was to have three consequences. The first was that the year was to be sanctified (see the section "Holy" in the introduction). Second, a "release" was to be proclaimed throughout all of the land specifying that any person who had "sold" a portion of his land (i.e., he had leased it out because of debt) had the property released back to him.

TRANSLATION ANALYSIS: "RELEASE"

The noun דְּרוֹר, which is translated as "release" or "freedom," is characterized as "a technical expression referring to the release of Hebrew slaves and of property every 50 years in the Year of Jubilee" (Wolf 1980c, 198). As demonstrated in appendix 5 on the Jubilee, the release of the land marks the termination of a land lease that was set to expire in that year. This returned the *use* of the land back to the owner. As discussed in appendix 4, "Slaves and Emancipation in Israel," the release of slaves is more complicated because of the complexity of the Hebrew *'ebed*

Preventing Social Unraveling, Part 1 (25:1–22)

(עָבַד), which can describe a wide variety of types of service. It appears that in this case, it should be described as "bondservant," referring to one who agrees to a set period of service to work off debt. To complicate matters, debt servanthood more likely reflected smaller debts, which came under the Sabbath year criteria, and that release would have occurred in the seventh Sabbath year. This would mean that in the situation where the Sabbath year was the seventh in the Jubilee cycle there would not have been any debt slaves of this category. Of course, if the Jubilee was the same year as the seventh Sabbath year, this issue would be a moot point.

TRANSLATION ANALYSIS: "PROPERTY"
The noun אֲחֻזָּה (Wolf 1980a) seems to refer to something that is possessed. Most frequently it is used to describe land in Canaan that has been given to an Israelite although it is still owned by God. When used later in this chapter (25:46) to refer to non-Israelite inhabitants who were acquired to perform service (i.e., to be slaves) this might suggest that while the Israelites had possession of them, they did not own them.

The third consequence is problematic. The last phrase, וְאִישׁ אֶל־מִשְׁפַּחְתּוֹ תָּשֻׁבוּ, translates literally as "and a man will return to his own extended family" (see the section "Biblical Family Ties" in the introduction). Based on an understanding of Leviticus 25:39 as describing a person selling him- or herself into slavery (so Wenham 1979, 322: "the debtor sells himself into slavery"), this consequence is often understood as a release from slavery so that the person can return to his extended family. However, as will be seen below, Leviticus 25:39 refers to hired help. What the text seems to be saying is that because the land that the person has leased out is now returned to his use, the person no long needs to hire out and may return to his extended family (מִשְׁפָּחָה) and resume the normal agrarian life.

Following the description of the declaration of the Jubilee with its release, the text defines the

other major part of Jubilee. As in the case of the Sabbath, the people are told that they are not to sow nor reap (25:11). However, they are directed to eat the produce (תְּבוּאָה) from or "out of the field" (25:12), that is, whatever grows in the field voluntarily. This would apply to all people equally, including those who had just regained the use of their property.

The Lord Clarifies the Release of Property (25:13–19)

25:13. This verse repeats 25:10b to show that the subsequent material was to clarify the situation behind Jubilee, that is, how a person might end up not having the use of his property. It is important to realize that the use of the pronoun (as well as the noun) אֲחֻזָּתוֹ shows that in legal terms the property still belonged to the owner, despite the fact that for some years he did not have the use of the property. The discussion begins with the premise that an Israelite has sold some of his property.

25:14–19. The guidance given in these verses clarifies both what is involved in a sale of land and the rationale behind those guidelines. As will be emphasized in 25:23, the land belonged to God, even though the Israelites were given possession of it. As such, the first criterion of a sale was for the Israelites to show fairness. Neither the buyer nor the seller should intend to wrong the other, whether he is a friend or an associate (עֲמִית) or a brother, that is, a relative (אָח). In the buyer's case, wronging the other would be by offering too low of a price. In the seller's case, it would be by expecting too much. The question is, what is fair?

In terms of this transaction, the process is made clear: the person buying is only buying the crops the land will produce. In this light, it is then interesting that while the buyer is purchasing the crops, he is also assuming the responsibility of sowing, maintaining, and reaping the crops through each of the years he has possession of the land. What is not clear is how the price was calculated. While Leviticus 27:14–34 discusses valuation of the land in terms of consecration and redemption, what is involved here is the value of the crop. That would vary both in terms of location in the land and the year. Geographically, soil quality varied, as also did the annual rainfall. Further, the annual rainfall in a given location could vary greatly from year to year. As such, the buyer would be taking a risk, and apparently in the case of crop failure it was the buyer's loss (Milgrom 2001, 2178). However, if they turned out to be good years, the buyer might reap a windfall. Since neither result could be forecast, apparently there was an understood process that provided each community an understanding of at least ballpark figures for a given region (see appendix 6, "Land Measurement and Crop Value," for further discussion). In any case, apparently once the agreement was made, the buyer provided the requisite amount of precious metal to the seller and began to farm the land. Given the layout of a village and family structure, the seller likely remained in the village where he either continued to farm other pieces of land he owned and at this point still possessed, or performed some other form of work. These alternatives will be discussed in the next unit, when we look at the last portion of this chapter.

The Lord Encourages the Israelites to Trust Him (25:20–22)

25:20–22. This section finishes with an exhortation from God that the Israelites were to trust him. God begins by recognizing a probable point of doubt, one that is reflected in many of the questions scholars raise today with regard to whether the Sabbath year or Jubilee practices were realistic. In essence, for a farmer who normally lived from one year to the next based on that year's crops, the question was, how will we survive during Jubilee year—that is, the eighth year in that part of the cycle—if we are not even sure we can survive through the seventh year if we don't have any crops? God's answer covers

both. In the background is the information that they may eat anything that volunteers during the fallow year. But more importantly, God states that he would provide an adequate crop in the sixth year, the last year of their regular farming routine during the cycles, that would last not only through the Sabbath year (the seventh), but through Jubilee (the eighth), and during the growing season of the ninth year. It is then interesting that the surplus was given in advance, and the Israelites were to plan accordingly by putting aside and anticipating a year without a crop.

SUMMARY

The overriding principle of this entire portion of Leviticus is that if the whole community served God in truth and righteousness, the entire community would enjoy shalom. As 25:18 says, they could "live securely on the land." However, there is a suggestion here that there might be a disparity of outcomes based on individual family faithfulness, although the implication is that if they were faithful, they could expect that even those on the low end would be doing well, especially if compared to other cultures. However, as we will see in the next unit, there would be some who did not prosper for various reasons. One example of this might be seen in the book of Ruth. Elimelech, who became Ruth's father-in-law, left the land during a famine, which might suggest corporate unfaithfulness. In that account we read of how first he died, and then both sons married and then died in the foreign land. After this, Ruth, although a Moabitess, returned with Naomi, and then married Boaz, a relative of her father-in-law. We are not told what happened to Elimelech's land while they were in Moab. It seems likely that he sold the land, which gave him the resources to relocate. After Naomi's return it became clear that Boaz had the resources to serve as the kinsman-redeemer for Naomi, and Ruth. It is not clear how Boaz survived the famine.

One factor that tends to get overlooked is that God told the Israelites that if they were faithful, he would provide for them. On the one hand in this context, this would suggest that an Israelite farmer who helped his neighbor would prosper. But on the other hand, the help from the Israelite who was strong was intended to serve as a motivation for the one who was weak. Thus, corporate faithfulness would promote corporate bonding.

THEOLOGICAL FOCUS

One of the prevailing myths of our day is that our ancestors were naïve and attributed supernatural forces to many things they did not understand, and as a result developed the ideas of gods and religion (Harbin 1994, xi–xvi, 188–235). As seen in this passage, one of the struggles Israel faced as God set them up as a new nation was their struggle between their overwhelming sense of naturalism and their awareness of spiritual realities. Living on the land and working it, they were aware that things didn't just happen, but that there were physical cause-and-effect relationships throughout the world. They understood experientially that physical work was required to ensure they had enough to eat, hence the anticipated question in 25:20. They also understood innately and by revelation that God existed and was behind the scenes. But in general, their idea of God was too small. While they accepted his reality, they did not grasp his power, his holiness, and perhaps especially his love and grace. As a result, they were quick to seek alternatives that were more naturalistic, or supposed that spiritual beings were more human-like. Then, when God did do marvelous works, their corporate memory was too short to carry the lessons over into the next generation—or even maintain them long in their own generation. For this reason, we see the nesting of sevens in terms of the divine appointments: seven days, seventh month, seven years, seven Sabbath years, to provide periodic spiritual refreshers.

PREACHING AND TEACHING STRATEGIES

Exegetical and Theological Synthesis

The Sabbath principle emerges in Genesis 2:3: "God blessed the seventh day and made it holy, because on it God rested from all his work that he had done in creation" (ESV). It grows into a personal and corporate command in Exodus 20:10: "the seventh day is a Sabbath to the Lord your God. On it you shall not do any work, you, or your son, or your daughter, your male servant, or your female servant, or your livestock, or the sojourner who is within your gates" (ESV). Now it is woven deeply into the social fabric of how the people are to relate not only to their God, but to the land and one another. It was not presented as optional but essential, coming with warnings (Lev. 26:35) and consequences (2 Chron. 36:21).

Why then do we see such reluctance to observe Sabbath and Jubilee years? It could simply be rooted in greed—I want to keep all I have accumulated. Reason is easily manipulated by the desires of the heart. It could also be rooted in practicality. Biblical characters repeatedly choose practicality over obedience. Achan took forbidden items that seemed foolish to him to destroy (Josh. 7). King Saul spared what he believed was not necessary to sacrifice (1 Sam. 15). We are consistently slow to release what we have in the present—to trust that God as our provider will supply our needs for today, tomorrow, and eternity. Who do I believe is the decisive factor in preserving my future?

What should be clear is that God's people are always intended to live as stewards, not owners. The Sabbath and Jubilee years acknowledged that through poverty, famine, death, or even careless neglect, they may surrender the gift that had been entrusted to them. But by God's grace, the gift could be redeemed! They could once again be stewards of what God had given them! The Sabbath years should both alert and prepare the humbled and the proud for the coming Jubilee. The humbled will experience a renewed hope. The proud will be reminded that they are stewarding, for a season, what God has entrusted to someone else.

Preaching Idea

I declare my relationship to God to the world through my relationships to others and my possessions.

Contemporary Connections

What does it mean?

Beliefs are confirmed through behavior. What am I declaring about the depth and breadth of my relationship to God through the way I treat others and the way I hold onto my possessions? If we consider those around us a means to advance our job, improve our reputation, or increase our comfort, then we are at war with how God is calling us to live as his disciples. Our trust in a personalized formula for success and contentment reveals that we have limited faith in God's will for our lives. The mental move from steward to owner of what God entrusts to us fundamentally undermines God's plan for how we are to live in this world.

God knows that our tendency will be to rate our plan for daily life above his. Do our words about who we believe God is match our actions toward him? Is there tangible evidence that we believe our own words? Though we may call God omniscient, we may wonder if he knows. Though we know he is omnipresent, we may question whether he can see. Though he is omnipotent, we doubt his power. Though he is transcendent, we struggle over whether he cares. Though eternal, he seems to not be able to understand. When our hope in the future is centered on our planning rather than on the goodness of our God, we are failing to trust in the character of our Creator and are unable to image him accurately to the world.

Is it true?

Does one declare his or her relationship to God through his or her behavior toward others and their stuff? Culture directs us to use what we have worked so hard to accrue (possessions and personal contacts) to maximize our efficiency, profit, and production. Scripture directs us to use what God has entrusted to us (relationships and assets) to image him to a world that does not know him. How we relate to what we have portrays how we relate to the giver of every good gift.

It can seem easier if we have nothing (as the Israelites did when this directive was received) to reason that once we have accumulated much, then we will be generous toward others and free with our possessions. Will we? Such thoughts as delaying generous giving until we are secured, a reasoned greediness of personal items that others should leave alone, and so on, may serve as windows into our hearts, allowing us to see what God already sees. We are hesitant to live as stewards and sojourners before him. We love to call things our own—things God knows may one day own us!

Now what?

How does our relationship to others and our possessions practically impact our relationship to God and our world? Deuteronomy 6:20 tells you to prepare for your son or daughter to ask you the meaning of the testimonies and statutes and rules that the Lord God has commanded. (Why do we do what we do?) First Peter 3:15 tells you as a believer to be ready to give reason for the hope another may see in you as you suffer. What if no one—sons, daughters, friends, or strangers—is asking? Does this suggest that your behavior in this world may image the world in which you live more than it images the God whom you serve?

If we are to image our God, our relationship to those around us (and to our possessions) should be borne out of a desire to live in the

Promised Land, dependent on the care and in the company of our Creator forever.

Creativity in Presentation

Do you recall when "ecology" was the buzz-word that summarized environmentalism? Maybe not. Even so, you could project a picture of an ecology symbol from the 1960s and ask, "What is this?" Then, define ecology as "the relationships of organisms to one another and their physical surroundings." Some suggest that Sabbath years were simply an exercise in ecology. Ask, "What is the relationship of a believer (the organism) to others and the land (physical surrounding)? How does one decide? What is our purpose in relating to our surroundings?"

It may be intriguing to point out how the Sabbath year would place everyone on equal footing in the same way that collecting manna in the wilderness did. Invite people to consider what that would actually look like in their community. What would it be like to play Monopoly®, knowing that after a set period of time, money and properties that had exchanged hands would return to their original holder? How would this affect your attitude toward the game? The way you related to others in the game? Your purpose in playing the game?

Recall a natural disaster specific to your location. Retell anecdotal stories of people losing what they had, yet all pulling together to recover. How did this affect relationships? Was the fabric of the community strengthened? Present the Sabbath year as a planned natural disaster.

Finally, to help people appreciate the role and responsibility of a steward, you can use the example of ethics and laws pertaining to fiduciary responsibility. If one is stewarding funds or assets that belong to another, one cannot overrule the stated objectives and desires of the owner of the funds and assets. To do so is considered criminal, and just punishment can be expected.

I declare my relationship to God to the world through my relationships to others and my possessions.

- The one-in-seven principle
  - How it works
  - How it changes our relationship with the land, one another, and God
- The Jubilee: unjust suffering and unjust forgiveness
  - A plan of God: the release of debt
  - The depth of sin and the mercy of God
- The released proclaimed!

DISCUSSION QUESTIONS

1. Why do you think the Sabbath-year command was given to the people before they possessed land? Why do you think they "rarely if ever" observed the Sabbath year?

2. A year without planting or harvest (removing any economic advantage to possessing land) would make everyone socially equal. How do you believe this would affect the way everyone related to one another?

3. Why do we live and talk as owners of what we possess, when Scripture describes us as stewards?

4. How would living as a steward of your possessions change your relationship to others? How could it image God's character to others?

5. Where might you be elevating your plan and assessment above God's?

Leviticus 25:23–55

EXEGETICAL IDEA
God established (legislated) moral actions through detailed civil law to create a social reset—to confront the anticipated poverty and inequity that were expected to arise among the stewards of his land.

THEOLOGICAL FOCUS
As stewards, God's people are expected to attend to the social (and spiritual) health of the whole community by imaging his patience, grace, and mercy, in hopes of restoring each individual steward.

PREACHING IDEA
We are called to pursue those who are sinking into hardship and poverty in a redemptive way that images God's restorative patience, grace, and mercy to us.

PREACHING POINTERS
The people received these civil from God through Moses when they were completely landless. They heard that they would enjoy the power and provisions of the One who redeemed them from their bondage to Egypt. In the Promised Land, God would be the owner. He would provide for their needs. He would be their God! They would be his stewards. They would remain under his care. They would be a nation of priests to the world! Why then would there be a need for detailed civil law to confront poverty and inequity? How could it happen? *Why* would it happen? They might be quick to love the ill-fated and unfortunate, but were they expected to love the neighbor who squandered his resources and abused his possessions?

Wait! Are we accountable before God to invest in the lives of family and neighbors who are sinking into hardship and poverty? This is an invasive call to actively love family and neighbor through means that transform the way we live, the way we understand our lives, and the way we pursue our possessions. This call requires an outlay of time, emotion, and resources without a guarantee of return on investment. Will we be owners who amass fame and possessions for our name (and glory), or will we be progressively transformed into stewards who invest in others to glorify God's name?

PREVENTING SOCIAL UNRAVELING, PART 2 (25:23–55)

LITERARY STRUCTURE AND THEMES (25:23–55)

After broadly defining Sabbath years and Jubilees, the last part of Leviticus 25 goes into more detail regarding how a situation might arise that required the release mandated for Jubilee. Presented as a series of steps into poverty, it is contextualized within an agricultural society where the community is relatively small with significant interrelationships, thus building on the extended family ties we have already addressed. Overall, we see a broad theme of what we might call social justice, although it differs considerably from some of today's ideas. The major point of the material is that the steps designed to assist the person in need are limited in nature and designed to help the person in need get back on his feet. The crux of the process is the Jubilee, which provides a social reset by mandating that the *use* of the family heritage that had originally been given by God, but which had been leased out during extreme down times, is released back to the family. So, continuing the theme of Jubilee begun in the first part of the chapter, this unit explores several different ways to address various levels of poverty that would set the stage for Jubilee.

- *An Israelite Needs to Sell Land (25:23–34)*
- *An Israelite Needs Financial Aid (25:35–38)*
- *An Israelite Sells His Last Asset: His Labor (25:39–43)*
- *Alternative Servants for Israelites (25:44–46)*
- *God Gives Directions for the Redemption of a Poor Israelite from a Non-Israelite (25:47–55)*

EXPOSITION (25:23–55)

The last thirty-three verses of Leviticus 25 address ways that Israelites could help one of their countrymen survive a significant economic downturn. One perspective sees the various situations simply as different regulations regarding redemption (גְּאֻלָּה; Harley 1992, 446). A more common way divides this portion of the chapter into three sections that denote either different degrees or stages of poverty (Kleinig 2003, 544; Milgrom 2001, 2191–93; Sklar 2014, 303). Taking the latter view, we will focus on the stages of poverty in terms of how they affected the individual, but we will also explore the responsibility of the overall community in various processes of restoration.

Understanding the text as being given by God at Sinai leads to our beginning premise that it addresses a situation that was anticipated when the nation reached Canaan. Specifically, when the people got to the land and were settled, everyone would have land given to them by God that would be adequate for them to live on and raise their families. This is not to say that the playing field would be absolutely level, any more than saying that all people are created equal maintains that everyone is born with the same innate abilities and physical and cultural resources. In terms of the land distribution, the plots of land would be of different sizes, fertility, and have varying water resources (whether springs or annual rainfall). Further, there would be differing and unequal amenities, such as

Preventing Social Unraveling, Part 2 (25:23–55)

already existing houses and mature fruit trees and vines planted by the displaced Canaanites. Numbers 26:54 notes that the distribution would be by lots. As a statement coming from God, this would indicate providential guidance, not blind chance, in the distribution of resources (Harbin 2021a, 487–94). However, as we saw in Leviticus 18:24–30 and is repeated in a number of places, what the individual Israelites did once they received the land would be their responsibility. Many other passages such as Leviticus 25:17–22 that precede this section indicate that the included responsibilities were both physical and spiritual.

The first degree of poverty would require that individuals lease out some of their land to someone else in the village for a period of time, but no longer than to the next Jubilee (25:23–34). If the poverty deepened to what we call the second degree and he reached the point where his land assets were depleted, then the community was to sustain the person, but without "usurious interest." This sustenance could be monetary, characterized by "silver," or in kind, indicated by the idea of "food" (25:35–38). Apparently the second degree was viewed as short term that could devolve into the third degree of poverty, where a person with no other assets would sell his labor. This section includes an extensive discussion providing guidance on how that action would work, including significant limitations the nation was to observe.

An Israelite Needs to Sell Land (25:23–34)

25:23–24. After opening the chapter with directions on how to observe the Sabbath year and Jubilee, counting on God's promise of great provision, God now gives a stark command: they were not to "sell permanently" the land they were going to receive.

TRANSLATION ANALYSIS: "SELL PERMANENTLY"

The subject of this phrase is "the land" and the intent is that it may not be permanently

transferred to someone else. Here the verb מָכַר is defined as "to sell" (Kaiser 1980e). However, the object of the verb is a prepositional phrase with the noun צְמִיתֻת as the object of the preposition לְ. This noun, derived from the verb צָמַת, which means "to put an end to, cut off, destroy," is defined as "completion or finality" (Hartley 1980b). Thus, literally the phrase means "you will not sell to finality" or "permanently." In English, we would understand the concept of the permissible transaction as rent. However, since the transaction has an endpoint, the word "lease" would be better.

This is the foundation of the Jubilee concept. The reason that follows is important: the land was not theirs, but God's. His description of their status is interesting: while he was giving the land to them, they were still aliens and sojourners. The combination here serves to emphasize Israel's alienage—that is, while God made them a nation and was giving them land, it was not because of anything inherent in them. Consequently, they were told they needed to provide for redemption for the land that they possessed (see translation analysis for the term "property" in Leviticus 25:13).

TRANSLATION ANALYSIS: "ALIENS AND SOJOURNERS"

This phrase contains two related words. The first is גֵּרִים, the plural form of גֵּר, which is normally translated as "sojourner" (Stigers 1980). The second word is the plural form of תּוֹשָׁב, which is also generally translated as "sojourner" but is derived from the verb יָשַׁב, which means "to sit" or "to dwell" (Kaiser 1980b). It could carry the connotation of "squatter," although that implies illegality. Milgrom concludes that the two together form a hendiadys that emphasizes that whereas a גֵּר is an alien, this phrase emphasizes that the person has settled into the community (2001, 2187). The point is that it was someone who was not a blood relative (no matter how distant) with the people in whose region the person was dwelling. For the ANE, because national concepts were much more fluid, this generally referred to the locality in which they had settled. While they tended to be accepted at least on a provisional basis, they were still generally viewed as outsiders—for example, Uriah the Hittite or Ruth the Moabitess (Harbin 2021b, 691–93). Throughout this study we have generally used the term "resident alien" to show that while the non-Israelites were settled for the long term, they were not natives. Today we think in terms of citizenship. For Israel, while that might reflect certain expected civil rights, the concepts of government seemed much looser then and citizenship did not seem to be a formal process, again reflecting greater identification with locality than a broader governmental entity.

25:25–28. Redemption of the land was required in the case of poverty. The verb מוּך used here describes the result of a process—"to become poor" (*DCH* s.v. "מוּך" 5:173). Nothing is said about the cause of the poverty or the amount of debt. A distinction seems to be made between small debt, which could be repaid by the next Sabbath year, and larger debt, which would extend to Jubilee (Harbin 2012, 59–62). Once they settled in the land, most of the Israelites would live in villages, and consequently the lender would probably be another villager who not only lived nearby but was likely related. Their lifestyle is often termed *subsistence farming*, which produces an impression that they would barely make it through a year without starving, with nothing to carry over from one year to the next. While not wealthy, it would appear that in most years, the average farmer could anticipate an adequate food supply. Regarding Israel in the Iron Age, Oded Borowski (1987, 164) concludes, "All the aforementioned innovations resulted in a large surplus of foodstuffs. This situation led to the introduction of a new type of storage facility, the pillared storehouse." While "large surplus" might be a relative term, it would appear that a typical Israelite was not as close

to disaster as sometimes presumed. Otherwise, during a period like that of the judges where there was so much looting, there would have been regular widespread starvation that would have made the Great Hunger in Ireland in the 1800s look mild.

Even so, throughout life, incidents occur that require outside assistance. Often that assistance might come in the form of a loan; and even among relatives, collateral might be required. While a cloak may serve as collateral of a small debt (Exod. 22:26; Deut. 24:13), a larger debt might require something larger. Without banks or institutions with deep financial resources, the primary alternative for an individual with a larger need was to lease out some of the land that God had provided. Because this would be just a portion of what he farmed, this poor countryman would be further reduced in his circumstance, likely to the point that the family suffered significantly.

The Land God Provided

In an online article I (Harbin 2016b) discuss the structure of a typical Israelite community in the OT period, concluding that an individual family would live in a village where all of the farmland surrounding the village was owned by the villagers, and each villager likely had several plots of land varying in size, likely one to four acres each. In terms of this situation, it is likely that the Israelite who had become poor would lease one or more plots of land under the Jubilee structure.

As shown in appendix 5, "The Year of Jubilee," the result was that the person who leased the land really was only able to purchase the goods the land would produce during the years he possessed that plot. The text records three options for the owner to get the use of his land back. The first would be that the nearest *go'el* (גֹּאֵל), "kinsman-redeemer," would "repurchase" the land (i.e., buy out the lease). While this would keep it within the extended family, it is not clear who would then farm it the next year (Willis 2009, 211). The second option would be that if no kinsman stepped up, the poor farmer might accumulate the funds and buy out the lease himself. While we do not have records of any actual accounts that this may have occurred, apparently it could be out of the production of the rest of his plots. In either case, the amount of the repurchase would be the amount of the years remaining on the lease. Should neither solution develop, the third alternative would be that the individual would wait for the next Jubilee, at which time the use of the land would revert back to the legal owner, or his heir in what the text calls a "release" (Lev. 25:10).

> *TRANSLATION ANALYSIS:*
> *"KINSMAN-REDEEMER"*
> Often translated as "kinsman-redeemer," a גֹּאֵל would be a close relative who had several latent responsibilities, including redeeming the land of a relative who had sold it, freeing a relative who had sold himself into slavery, avenging the wrongful death of a relative, and marrying the widow of a close relative who did not have children (Harbin 2021b, 687–89; Harris 1980b).

25:29–31. Houses in walled cities were handled differently. Because those houses were not part of the original agricultural land distribution, the transaction was a sale not a lease. However, there was a one-year option for the individual who sold the house in the walled city to repurchase it. Otherwise, the sale was permanent. This did not apply to unwalled villages. In those situations, the house could be redeemed or it would revert in the Jubilee. It would appear that this might be a situation where an individual had run out of land to lease out as a result of an extremely large setback or a series of them, and as a last resort he sold the house in the village (which would be part of the land package that he owned but had already leased out). Apparently, this would be a last step before selling oneself into debt-slavery.

25:32–34. The cities of the Levites were another exception. This is the first (and only) mention of Levites in the book, and it hints at something that is not made clear to the reader until later. As the descendants of Jacob multiplied during their time in Egypt, it is likely that they dispersed throughout the region of Goshen, perhaps settling loosely in various locations by growing family units. But that probably was not a true tribal organization. Then, as they left Succoth where they had gathered after Passover, they were spread out more as a large crowd, although it is likely that through the trek to Sinai, clans and tribes gradually began to coalesce. Even so, it would not have been until the first census in Numbers 1 that the tribal organization was solidified, although at that point it was primarily for military purposes (Num. 1:2–3). That may also be the time where the "mixed multitude" (nonethnic Israelites) were more intentionally blended into the tribes, although apparently some may have already been adopted by various tribes, as noted in the discussion of Leviticus 24:10–11, specifically mentioning Caleb. Numbers 2:34 indicates that the nation reorganized the camp immediately after the census.

While there were hints, it appears that it was not until the second census, as the nation of Israel sat on the east bank of the Jordan River waiting to cross it (Num. 26:52–56), that settling the land by tribal territories was revealed. That may also have been when it was clarified that the Levites would not have a tribal territory (Deut. 18:1–2). It is true that at the first census, the Levites had been omitted from the count. But that census had been for military purposes, not land distribution, and the Levite responsibility was defined as spiritual intercession in the form of maintaining the tabernacle and sacrificial system (Num. 1:47–54). While that may have been a hint, the process of settlement had not yet been explained. Given the description of the camp around the tabernacle in Numbers 3, it is likely that the Levites anticipated having their own region surrounding a permanently located tabernacle (perhaps like Washington, DC, which was established as a separate entity so as to not be part of any state). In that regard, it was subsequent to the second census that they learned that they would have forty-eight cities spread throughout the land (Num. 35:6–8).

The brief guidelines given here that allowed a permanent right of redemption of houses that belonged to Levites in the cities of the Levites may also have been a hint. The passage in Numbers 35 also explains how the environs of the Levitical city would look, as it appears that individual Levites did not possess farmland like the members of the other tribes, including those non-Levites who lived in the Levitical cities. However, the pastureland described later (Num. 35:2–5) could not be sold, since it belonged to the community (Sklar 2014, 305).

Model of Israelite City

Elsewhere I (Harbin 2021a, 476–81) discuss how Richard Antoun (1972, 1–25) shows that many villages in the Middle East today resemble the same pattern as described of a typical village in OT Israel. Succinctly, a village could be described as a housing area surrounded by all of the farms of the village residents. The hatched area on Figure 67 indicates the scope of a typical "village," with the agricultural portion being the upper region on the map within the oval.

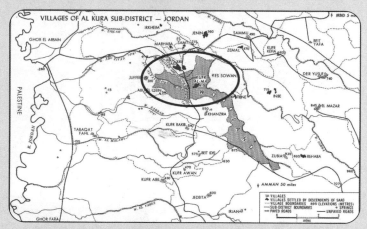

Figure 67. The village of Kfur al-Ma in Jordan in the late 1970s.

Most of the village area is described as woodland and pasture regions. Figure 68 is a larger scale diagram of the just the agricultural area. Even here, the actual housing area (what we might think of as the village) is only the portion within the dashed oval in the middle of the northern section. Antoun describes that housing area as a basin about a half mile in diameter. As can be seen in the figure, the agricultural area is broken up into a number of plots. Antoun's original diagram is color-coded, according to which extended families in the village of about two thousand people owned the fields.

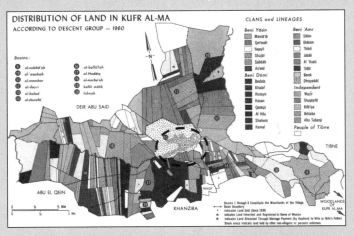

Figure 68. Agricultural area of Kfur al-Ma. The housing area is the slightly darker region inside the dashed oval.

In OT Israel, it appears that each family would have multiple plots, which may be in different portions of the overall field (Hopkins 1985, 237–45).

An Israelite Needs Financial Aid (25:35–38)

It seems that individuals were expected to support themselves and their families using the resources that God had given them. However, there might be times where that was not enough, at which point the community was expected to step in to provide a loan if that was in order.

25:35–38. Given our extremely leveraged economic system, one might wonder why a loan would be the second degree instead of the first. A key consideration is the fact that the Israelite economy was not primarily based on a monetary system, and the agricultural system built around a family farm stressed self-reliance. Thus, the first degree was to draw upon the capital assets (farm plots) that the individual possessed. As Sklar (2014, 305) put it, this law "assumes the person has no more property to sell and is still in debt." In that case, the community had various responsibilities. First, the community was to "sustain him" (וְהֶחֱזַקְתָּ בּוֹ) as they would a stranger or sojourner.

TRANSLATION ANALYSIS: "SUSTAIN HIM"
The phrase here might literally be understood as "give him strength," using the *hiphil* or causative form of the verb חָזַק (Weber 1980c). Sklar (2014, 305) prefers to translate it as "retain," with the idea that it describes someone who is "retained under the authority of another," in essence debt slavery. However, if used in the context of a

Preventing Social Unraveling, Part 2 (25:23–55)

loan, it might be understood as encouragement or giving strength.

This very brief admonition could be understood two ways. The comparison of the situation with that of a stranger or sojourner (the same terms God used to describe the Israelites in 25:23) could suggest providing work, which could be that of a hired hand. In that case, the community responsibility was to provide work. However, given the provisions for resident aliens described elsewhere, it could be that he and his family were allowed the opportunity to glean (see appendix 2, "Gleaning: A Case Study in Ruth"), which would mean that the community had the responsibility to allow the gleaning (Harbin 2021b, 694–95).

Alternatively, the admonition against interest suggests that a loan might be made. It could reflect a situation where the time frame involved might be short, such as when Jubilee was near, at which time the leased land would be returned. Or it may have bridged an ailment. In a case where the amount was small and the time frame of the expected return short, a loan might be more appropriate. In such a case, the community responsibility was to prevent "usurious interest." Leviticus 25:36 essentially makes this combination a hendiadys forbidding excessive interest, but 25:37 seems to distinguish the two terms by separating them with respect to the commodity. This might suggest the prohibition of two types of interest.

TRANSLATION ANALYSIS: "USURIOUS INTEREST"

While often just translated "interest," the phrase that itself really seems to denote "usurious interest" is נֶשֶׁךְ וְתַרְבִּית (so NASB). The first word, נֶשֶׁךְ, is a noun that means literally "bite" (Fisher 1980d). The second word, תַּרְבִּית, also means "interest," or "usury" (Yamauchi 1980d). In 25:37 נֶשֶׁךְ describes the use of silver, while תַּרְבִּית is tied to food items, which may indicate two different

methods of recompensing a loan. Levine (1989, 178) cites how the Mishnah understood the former to reflect "a demand for payment in excess of what was lent," which emphasized the monetary value of the loan, while the latter represented a "demand for more grain or foodstuffs than were provided to the borrower." The difference could be significant with fluctuation in commodity prices if, as Levine suggests, the farmer "went into debt at the time of planting [to buy seed corn] with the expectation of repaying the debt after the harvest." However, as noted elsewhere, "Most farmers through history saved some of their crop from one year to provide seed for the next year's crop. Buying 'seed corn' did not become a practice until the modern development of hybrids" (Harbin 2012, 59). Péter-Contesse and Ellington (1992, 391) suggest that נֶשֶׁךְ was interest paid regularly with the actual loan paid at the end, while תַּרְבִּית described a single larger sum repaid at the end of the loan. Despite the apparent sense of usurious interest here, as Milgrom (2001, 2209) observes, "What is clear from all biblical sources is that interest from an Israelite is prohibited."

While not addressed in this section, if the loan was a small loan, if it was not repaid by the Sabbath year it would then be forgiven (Harbin 2011, 685–99). This means all of these small loans would be either repaid or canceled out every seven years. Whether Jubilee was equivalent to the seventh Sabbath year or the year after it, the loan would be forgiven in conjunction with the Sabbath year, so there would be no debt to forgive in Jubilee. While Jubilee marked the end of the lease, the leased land would not have been planted in the Sabbath year whether it preceded or was equated with the Jubilee.

One thing that must be kept in mind is that it was anticipated that the nation would be very largely agricultural, where most farmers were expected to be essentially self-supporting in terms of food production. Even in that context, however, it would be expected that at times it was necessary to get resources from other people in the community. As noted in the unit "Purifying Oneself Before a Holy God" (4:1–6:7 [HB 5:26]), the predominant economic process was barter but could be supplemented by small amounts (measured by weight) of precious metals, usually silver. In either case, the repayment should match the loan with no extra fees punctuated at the end, with the strong reminder that God was the one who had brought them out of Egypt. Because of the mercy God had shown them, his people were expected to show mercy in the future.

Seed Corn Eaten

This might be a situation where one's seed corn had gone bad or through necessity had been eaten and the farmer had to buy new seed corn. Laura Ingalls Wilder describes an analogous situation in her autobiographic novel, *The Long Winter*. In Wilder's case, after brothers Royal and Almanzo Wilder moved into town anticipating blizzards, Almanzo built a wall inside the back room behind the feed store to hide the seed grain so it would not be sold (Wilder 1968, 162–68). After a long series of extreme blizzards, the situation became so bad that her father forced him to provide the seed corn to the family to get them through the winter (246–51). Although the idea of buying seed corn is mentioned frequently, the practice of buying seed corn is really relative modern. Throughout most of history, farmers saved their own seed for the next year's crops (Cummins and Ho 2005).

Whether through a short-term loan or through providing work, the second degree seemed to be a temporary fix. Should that be inadequate, the Israelite farmer had one more asset that he could use: his or his family's physical abilities. This would be a situation where the land had been leased and Jubilee was still a number of years off, and a loan would not resolve the long-term need. This would be the third degree of poverty, which involved the person "selling" his labor.

An Israelite Sells His Last Asset: His Labor (25:39–43)

25:39–40. This final degree or stage of poverty is where the individual reaches a situation where the only asset he had was his own physical labor. This degree reflects a situation where the person "sells himself"—or more properly, given the context, "sells his labor," much as in the case of the land where only the produce is sold. What is interesting is that this passage is directed to the person who buys the labor, setting forth limitations on what that person can do or expect.

> **TRANSLATION ANALYSIS: "SELLS HIMSELF"**
>
> The verb מָכַר, which means "to sell" (Kaiser 1980e) is in the *niphal* stem, followed by a prepositional phrase with the second-person pronoun (לָךְ). As such, it could be translated literally "is sold to you." However, because of the prohibitions on selling of slaves (Exod. 21:16; Deut. 24:7), it is generally translated as a reflexive, "sells himself to you" (for the reflexive use of the *niphal*, see GKC §51c).

First, the status of the individual is emphasized. As noted in appendix 4, "Slaves and Emancipation in Israel," the term *'ebed* is a broad term with a number of meanings, from high-level officials serving the king to the lowest level of chattel slaves. The structure here does not use the noun *'ebed* to describe the person (i.e., it does not say that "he is a [servant/slave/laborer]"). Rather, it combines three related terms from the basic verb meaning "to work" (עָבַד) to develop a statement that is very difficult to translate into English, something along the order of "you will not enslave him in the slavery of a slave." Rather, he is to be viewed as a "hired man" (שָׂכִיר) or a "sojourner" (תּוֹשָׁב). In this case, the difference seems to be that the

Preventing Social Unraveling, Part 2 (25:23–55)

first would be an Israelite, while the second would be a non-Israelite who lived in the land. Both would be individuals who were essentially free but who would work for pay.

25:40–41. Second, it is stated that the service (at this point using the verb עָבַד) would last until the Year of Jubilee. The conclusion is at that point, he would "go out from you." As was the case in 25:10, which proclaimed a release, the one who had sold his labor would return to his family and "to the property of his forefathers," which indicates that this service is of a similar nature as the land that had been leased out. Apparently, because it was associated with the use of the land, the man and his sons are a package deal, and they all are released (Milgrom 2001, 2224).

25:42–43. To emphasize their status, the text spells out prohibitions against selling them as slaves. As Israelites, they were servants or slaves (עֲבָדַי) of God who were brought out (in the sense that they descended from members of the exodus) from Egypt. Further, they are not to be treated with harshness or severity (פֶּרֶךְ).

Alternative Servants for Israelites (25:44–46)

25:44–46. This section is perhaps one of the hardest to reconcile with a modern understanding of human relations, especially for Christians. It seems to unequivocally authorize the Israelites to have slaves. There are several factors that must be considered.

First, the purpose of this section is to make a sharp distinction between the Israelites and non-Israelites who are dwelling in the land or from nations surrounding Israel. The previous verse contrasts Israelites who are servants from non-Israelites by declaring that the Israelites are not to be ruled "with severity." Sklar (2014, 309) asks the question: Does that then mean that non-Israelites may be treated with severity? He answers in the negative, saying "legal safeguards

[must be] applied," but he could be clearer in this regard.

Second, the scope of the Hebrew word עֶבֶד demands caution in translation, as noted above. On the one hand, the word does not necessarily denote slavery. On the other hand, the non-Israelites עֲבָדִים are described as a "possession" (אֲחֻזָּה), and it is noted that the Israelites could pass them on to their sons as possessions. This suggests property and chattel slavery. However, we have already noted in our discussion of 25:10 that the term does not indicate ownership, and for an Israelite that would mean that whatever possessions he had, he was to manage as assets for the one who possessed (having redeemed or bought) him.

Third, the language is suggestive that perhaps what is intended is not authorization. For example, the text of 25:44 may be translated as "And the male and female servants that will be to you from the nations." This could be understood as acquiescence. However, as Mathews (2009, 227) points out, "Slavery as an institution is not condemned outright in the Scriptures, but those same Scriptures teach that all men and women are created 'in the image of God' and so are to be treated with equity and integrity."

This section ends reiterating the warning that they were not to treat their fellow Israelites with harshness or severity (פֶּרֶךְ). This serves as a final reminder that they had a strong responsibility to their fellow Israelites as belonging to God in a special way.

God Gives Directions for the Redemption of a Poor Israelite from a Non-Israelite (25:47–55)

The last section of this chapter gives specifics in terms of the redemption of a poor Israelite who ended up selling his labor as described in the previous verses to a non-Israelite. What is not clear in this section is why a non-Israelite would be able to do this. While it might be that a non-Israelite, especially one who was from one of the earlier tribes in the land who had managed to remain after the conquest, might garner the assets to hire an Israelite as an עֶבֶד. But it seems that should such a situation transpire, it would be a significant embarrassment to the nation. Beyond that, this section is helpful in other regards, since it seems to give a procedure describing who has the *go'el* responsibility, which carries broader implications.

25:47. The situation described here reflects a case where an Israelite has become poor to the point of selling his labor, and the person who purchases it is a non-Israelite who is dwelling in the land but who has prospered (i.e., the Israelite becomes a servant or debt-slave to a resident alien).

25:48–49. Regardless of the circumstances, the Lord mandates that redemption rights (and responsibilities) begin immediately after "he has been sold." In terms of the Israelites, the first in line is one of the brothers of the man, followed by a brother of his father or mother, followed by a cousin. After this, any blood relative may take up the responsibility. Milgrom (2001, 2238) suggests that a son is not mentioned because if the father is impoverished it would be assumed that the son was likely also sold. Or it might be a situation where the son is still very young and thus does not have resources to redeem. He also suggests that an independent woman could be a kinsperson and redeem an Israelite based on the inheritance laws (p. 2237). Finally, the man might redeem himself if he is able to accrue the assets necessary, although there is no explanation of how that might happen.

25:50–53. The calculation of the redemption price was to be done the same way as the calculation of the redemption of land. It is based on the number of years of service that are being bought out.

25:54. If the man is not redeemed, then when the Jubilee Year arrives, he is released during that Jubilee Year. This would include his sons, which clarifies what Milgrom said regarding 25:48–49. While this seems to contradict the manumission during the Sabbath year, the suggestion seems to be that while a small loan is forgiven in the Sabbath year, this is a big ticket item involving multiple years. As such, the time of manumission or forgiveness parallels the practice for the sale of land—it expires in the Jubilee (Harbin 2012, 70–73).

25:55. The last verse of the chapter begins with the particle כִּי, which here shows the reason for the preceding material (Oswalt 1980c). The principle undergirding this entire process is that all the Israelites are the servants of God, and he is saying that he has first priority. The first portion of this verse stresses that they are servants (עֲבָדִים) but specifically that they are servants to God. They are his servants because he "brought them out of the land of Egypt" (a statement that God used first in Exodus 20:2 as the foundation for the entire Torah, beginning with the Ten Commandments, and repeated some 138 times through the Old Testament). Because of that, God is establishing his authority behind all of these guidelines. This verse also serves as a bridge to the next chapter.

SUMMARY

The previous unit noted that if the whole community served God in truth and righteousness, the entire community would enjoy shalom. But it cautioned that there would also be a disparity of outcomes. Some might be a consequence of individual family unfaithfulness. But it was also expected that untoward events might happen to anyone. As the nation of Israel settled in the land, members of local communities were expected to support each other. While the settlement process provided significant assets to each family, it was anticipated that at times, individuals and families might encounter situations where they had serious economic needs. It is interesting that regardless of the reason, the community was expected to support the impoverished. This section provides three specific actions that were to be implemented as necessary that would help the community as a whole prosper. First, an individual might lease out some of his land, which required that a neighbor or relative be willing to assume the responsibility of coming up with the assets to lease the property and then farm it for a period of years until Jubilee, when its use returned to the owner. Second, an individual might secure a loan, again, requiring a neighbor or relative to be willing to make the loan, recognizing that there was to be no interest, and that there was a chance the loan would need to be written off. Third, the individual might sell his labor for a period of time not to exceed the time until the next Jubilee. In all of these cases, provision is provided for early repayment, or redemption.

THEOLOGICAL FOCUS

Perhaps the primary theological point of this section is that God is not only sovereign but that he is the true owner of everything, whether it is the land people possess or the labor they produce. While he provides assets for his people to use, they are to use them fairly and to the benefit of their overall community. In this context, that is presented as a local community as opposed to a global one. The emphasis of this section is on the members of the community providing assistance to their neighbors in time of need.

God's call for his people to love their neighbors is a call to place a neighbor's needs before their personal desires. Granted, this would prove (and is) tricky to work out. Yet

no one will deny that it holds the power to transform a community by harnessing selfishness and nurturing benevolence. God has given a mandate to create a community of his chosen people that reflects him to the world. A nation of priests is expected to mediate the goodness of God to the world by mediating the gifts he has granted to them in their families and neighborhoods and sacrificially protecting them from unfair land and labor practices.

PREACHING AND TEACHING STRATEGIES

Exegetical and Theological Synthesis
After generations in bondage, excitement may be growing as the people anticipate the delight of cultivating their own land! Yet, are they foreseeing the need to cultivate their attitudes? Each family will receive an allotment of land, but each allocation will not be uniform in potential. All of God's people may be equal in value, but they will certainly not be identical in ability. The visionary will till the ground alongside the unimaginative. The skilled will plant a crop near the clumsy. The creative will harvest grain close to the wary. For these reasons, as the years go by, economic inequity will be expected to emerge (and grow). This is not inherently bad. Will inequity spawn a concern for the disadvantaged or an opportunistic desire to take advantage? God is pre-emptively arming his people for an upcoming war on their self-regarding souls.

Social inequities introduce the "weeds of greed and presumed superiority" that could choke out a love of neighbor in the community. God establishes civil law intended to harness their hearts by resetting the social community and encouraging his people to responsibly restore rather than take advantage of the disadvantaged. These civil laws create barriers that effectively dampen the overly entrepreneurial spirit and tamp down some of the familiar fires of capitalism: the lending practices of the rich (usury) and the monopolization of land ownership. While they avoid direct handouts, they make no clear distinction between the irresponsible and the responsible. They do make it clear that God will remain the owner of all land and labor. He is inviting his people to steward the land and labor as he would, so that other nations may see and ask for the reason for the spirit of care, redemption, and restoration that is evident among his people!

Preaching Idea

We are called to pursue family, friends, and neighbors who are sinking into hardship and poverty in a redemptive way that images God's restorative patience, grace, and mercy to us.

Contemporary Connections

What does it mean?

What does it mean to be called to pursue family, friends, and neighbors who are sinking into hardship and poverty in a redemptive way that images God's restorative patience, grace, and mercy to us? This is a big, broad, invasive calling! It means that believers are to see hardship in others' lives as an opportunity to image God's loving-kindness to others. It is also a call to restrain harsh judgment to engage in redemptive mercy.

It also means that we may need to rein in our capitalistic mindsets. God consistently calls us to live as aliens, exiles, and sojourners in this world (Lev. 25:33; Pss. 39:12; 119:19; Heb. 11:13; 1 Peter 2:11). A life with less permanence, stability, and order deters the steward's heart from challenging God's authority as the owner and hardening against one's neighbor as a brother or sister. It will be a battle to submit to God's law and to not justify creating a law unto ourselves.

Is it true?

Is it true that God is calling believers to selectively pursue family, friends, and neighbors who are sinking into hardship and poverty in a redemptive way that images God's restorative patience, grace, and mercy to us? The implications are great! While many may be quick to assist individuals in need (which is important), we may be slower to invest meaningfully in the lives of family members, friends, and neighbors who are economically struggling. The latter requires a significant investment of not only finances, but emotional and social capital as well. And without a Jubilee year, this may develop into an investment for the better part of our lifetime.

Is it reasonable to substitute activism against poverty and economic injustice in place of pursuing family, friends, and neighbors? While the former may be a larger goal, it produces the temptation for *slacktivism*—supporting a cause by performing a few simple measures but not engaging in a way devoted to a lasting change. In contrast, the latter allows for the relational, redemptive, and restorative components that change lives of both the provider and receiver.

Now what?

If it is true that God is calling believers to pursue family, friends, and neighbors in a redemptive way to image his restorative patience, grace, and mercy, what should we do? First, consider identity: Who may this be describing in my own life? One may find this a challenge to answer without immediately passing over names who are thought of as too hard, too grumpy, too foolish, or other undesirable traits. It may be good to recall that God did not pass over us, even though we hold some of the same traits!

Second, connect. Few economic hardships are solely economic. There will be relational, emotional, and behavioral aspects in the equation. Loving a person means knowing him or her sufficiently to begin to not only see these aspects but to learn how they became a part of this person's story.

And finally, commit. Imaging God's patience, grace, and mercy to another is not like picking out new shoes. They may turn out not to be the style we were looking for, and they may quickly prove to be painful to wear for long periods of time, but we can be certain that they are whom God has chosen to place in our closet.

Creativity in Presentation

It may be helpful (and provocative) to open by detailing one of the many studies on *slacktivism* undermining activism. Asking your congregation for the best ways to transform a community for the better will likely elicit thoughts built from social media. Research shows that those who publicly complete a small gesture to support a cause ("like" something, comment or repost an article, or send a small amount of money) are generally less likely to invest in the same cause in a meaningful way that will lead to societal change. Public reaction is not as helpful as personal conviction. The relational model of loving your neighbor in Leviticus is built on knowing your neighbor in order to invest into one another's lives.

Consider using the example of a game like Monopoly® that will be familiar to most of your congregation. Some may love it; others may avoid it. Everyone knows the objective of the game. What if every seventh round, rents were free? And what if every seventh round, properties were all returned to their original owner? How would the objective of the game change? How would the conversation around the game change? How would the attitudes of the players toward the game and toward one another change? Clearly, it would be a very different game. What game is God instructing us to "play" in our community to image him to our neighbors?

You may challenge your listeners to look at themselves as curators. Curators of a community cultural center have a specific responsibility to identify, preserve, and protect what belongs to the community. A good curator must ensure that what belongs to the community is not stolen or sold off to the highest bidder even in times of hardship and poverty. It is to be kept and displayed, so all may understand who they are in this community and recall their history. Should we be treating what God has entrusted to our care in this way? Are we guarding what is in our possession for the benefit of the full community of believers? Have we been given more to reestablish and restore the downtrodden? Are we imaging God's mercy through all that is at present in our possession?

We are called to pursue those who are sinking into hardship and poverty in a redemptive way that images God's restorative patience, grace, and mercy to us.

- Assessing one's heart: Whom are we imaging, ourselves or our God?
- Increasing levels of hardship, suffering, and poverty.
  - Liquidating assets to survive (selling inheritance)
  - Insolvent: cannot sustain food, clothing, shelter (embarrassing)
  - Servanthood: "sells" oneself to a "believer" (losing hope in God)
  - Enslavement: sold to a stranger (abandoning the faith)
- What did it mean to them then? What does it always mean? What do we do now?
  - Thoughts of independence are replaced by thoughts of preserving the community.
  - What we have is not our own. It is given to us by God to be stewarded in community.
  - Imaging God should transform our approach to our possessions.

DISCUSSION QUESTIONS

1. Why do you think that our public reactions and subsequent private follow-ups fail to line up?

2. What are the advantages to living as a sojourner on this earth? Why have all believers consistently been called to do so?

3. How do hardship and poverty entice the passions of the flesh in both the poor and the rich?

4. How do the moral actions and civil laws described in Leviticus 25 work toward redeeming a person rather than just addressing the hardship?

5. Why does God give us an enduring responsibility to care for those around us?

6. How are you imaging the restorative patience, grace, and mercy of God to those in your community?

Leviticus 26:1–46

EXEGETICAL IDEA
After God instructed his redeemed people to image his mercy as a nation by observing Sabbath and Jubilee years, he vowed that they belonged to him forever and were required to continuously walk in his presence under his law, to live in his protection, and to know his blessings (an opportunity to "reverse the curse" of Genesis 3).

THEOLOGICAL FOCUS
God is righteous and merciful. His character is revealed to his people and to the world not through his unconditional affirmation of a disobedient people, but by his sacrificial intervention to renew them from corporate disobedience into life-giving obedience.

PREACHING IDEA
We are loved by God through his sacrificial intervention to rescue us from the curse of following our own voice rather than his life-giving Word.

PREACHING POINTERS
God's people heard the Lord God summarize the legal contract he made between them. This was not new. They heard similar language before. What was unique was that the contract concluded with a detailed list of exciting consequences for walking in God's presence under his law and protection (which sounded like the Promised Land)—along with a more extensive list of horrifying penalties for turning away from his presence toward the idols and ideas of the nations around them! Why were these sevenfold progressive punishments necessary? They seem a bit extreme in light of the fact that the people anticipated leaving temptation behind as they crossed into the Promised Land. And more than that, they already pledged their obedience to God! Had he forgotten?

Sadly, they were the ones who had forgotten. God was preparing his people for the ongoing battle against their own wills. It would be a lifelong war. To remain under his protection, they must deny the voice inside that calls them to craft a law of their own. Would the Creator of the universe be their guiding star as they lived in freedom? Or would they follow another voice and agree to create a new, personalized star they could register as their own?

Their God is our God. Their battle against idolatry is—albeit in different ways—our battle against idolatry. If we elect to step onto the wide path that leads to destruction, what should our loving God do to turn us back?

ALTERNATIVE OUTCOMES FOR THE COMMUNITY OF GOD (26:1–46)

LITERARY STRUCTURE AND THEMES (26:1–46)

The last part of Leviticus 25 lists three stages of economic distress associated with the Year of Jubilee and then concludes with the reminder that the Israelites were given those admonitions and guidelines because they belonged to God. In terms of content, the chapter division seems to mark the introduction of a new topic, but the structure really continues the speech that God began in 25:1. A deeper examination suggests that Leviticus 26 really is a logical conclusion of the foundational principle of 25:55 that the people of Israel were God's servants. Often described as blessings and curses, it really describes consequences Israelites could expect depending on how they lived corporately, both in their interactions with God, and then in terms of their interactions with one another because of that divine relationship. Those consequences are of two types. There would be good consequences for proper behavior, that is, following God's guidance, and bad consequences for improper behavior, that is, defying God's guidance. The chapter ends with the promise that though the consequences through generations might be grave because of their misbehavior, God would not forget his covenant with them.

- **God Lays Out the Most Basic Components of His Covenant with Israel (26:1–2)**
- **God Cites the Positive Consequences of Faithful Behavior (26:3–13)**
- **God Warns of the Negative Consequences of Unfaithful Behavior (26:14–39)**
- **God Explains the Reason for His Hostility (26:40–43)**
- **God Reminds That He Will Always Remember and Be Faithful (26:44–46)**

> ### Blessings and Curses
>
> The concept of blessing and cursing is complex. Basically, it can be said that blessings have positive overtones, while curses have negative. We tend to think of them in physical terms: wealth, health, and personally favorable outcomes. However, biblically speaking, positive spiritual outcomes are more frequently the expectation. Both blessings and curses are ultimately from God. Although pronouncements of both can be expressed by a human mediator (Gen. 27), the efficacy of either is dependent on God's actuation of the human declaration. As such, they are not magical formulas (Sklar 2014, 313). Although it is recognized that Deuteronomy 11:26–28 uses the terms "blessing" and "curse" to describe the choices that Israel was going to have to make in the land, those choices are not labeled as "blessing" and "curse" here. Because today our English terms "bless" and "curse" carry overly materialistic weight, it was decided that in terms of the exegesis of this material the focus of the specifics would be on describing the outcomes as presented, generally avoiding those interpretative terms.

EXPOSITION (26:1–46)

The chapter division that separates Leviticus 25 and 26 obscures a very important point. Leviticus 25:55–26:1 really expresses a single cause-and-effect concept that echoes Exodus 20:2–5, where God told the Israelites that since he had

Alternative Outcomes for the Community of God (26:1–46)

brought them out of slavery in Egypt, *therefore* (implied) they were to have no other gods before him, nor were they to make any idols. Since the Israelites were God's servants, they were not to make any representations of other gods. The key difference is that while the Exodus passage introduces an outline of standards of relationship, Leviticus sketches alternative consequences to the community depending on how it lived out its primary relationship with God.

The chapter contains three parts. The first two verses summarize how Israel was to relate with God. Leviticus 26:3–13 lays out positive consequences resulting from faithful behavior and then ends with another reminder of how God brought them out of Egypt. Leviticus 26:13 also subtly reminds them of God's power, which could be turned against the Israelites should they prove to be unfaithful. Picking up that point, 26:14–39 describes how the same power that humbled the Egyptians would affect them by presenting five stages of negative consequences. The chapter then ends on a high note as it assures them that while God would discipline the nation, even severely if need be, the covenant relationship would not be broken.

God Lays Out the Most Basic Components of His Covenant with Israel (26:1–2)

26:1. The first component of Israel's covenant with God is that the nation was to avoid spiritual unfaithfulness, which is described as worship of false gods. In essence, the warning is that they were not to make physical representations that they would worship as God. The text here contains four different terms, which may have spelled out various types of images that the pagans worshipped. The varied terminology would have provided emphasis, as well as precluded loopholes. The first term is אֱלִילִם, which is translated as "idols." This term was addressed in Leviticus 19:4, where we noted that it means something worthless and said it probably refers to "anything physical that is intended to serve as a representation or substitute for the Lord God." It is connected to פֶּסֶל (which means "idol") with a *waw*, which is translated as "or." The term is derived from a verb meaning "to hew, hew into shape" (*TWOT* s.v. "פָּסַל 2:729"). This might suggest a distinction between something carved (e.g., from wood) as opposed to something molded (e.g., made from metal), but if the *waw* is translated "or," the prohibition includes both.

False Gods

The admonition not to makes idols is perhaps a reminder of the golden calf incident in Exodus 32:1–5. There, the people asked Aaron "to make us gods" (עֲשֵׂה־לָנוּ אֱלֹהִים), and after the calf was made, "they said, 'These are your gods'" (וַיֹּאמְרוּ אֵלֶּה אֱלֹהֶיךָ). The text in Exodus tends to be confusing regarding what Aaron did. First, the text uses the plural, gods (אֱלֹהִים), which is often translated as God, but it describes the result as a calf and uses singular pronouns. It then states that he took a graving tool (חֶרֶט)—a term otherwise used only in Isaiah 8:1, where it describes a tool that etches an inscription (Alden 1980c). The result in Exodus was a עֵגֶל מַסֵּכָה, which is translated as a "molten calf," literally a young bull or bull calf, which had been poured (the word מַסֵּכָה, which is derived from the verb נָסַךְ meaning "to pour," may mean a libation or a cast image [Wilson 1980]). It is possible that Aaron carved the golden image from a gold blank. However, given that the metal was brought to him as various gold rings, they would have had to be melted to produce the blank. We do not know how much gold they had, nor the size of the final product. While calf images have been found, they tend to be small, usually a few inches high. Regardless of the size, the best understanding might correlate the two terms used with the typical casting process, which involves preparing a mold by carving and then pouring the molten metal into it. If so, the terminology conflates the two steps in the process, carving the mold and then casting the gold image.

Alternative Outcomes for the Community of God (26:1–46)

In contrast, the next two terms suggest placement rather than manufacture. The מַצֵּבָה or "pillar," coming from the verb נָצַב meaning "to stand upright," appears to be a large stone that was stood upright and served as a cult object (Fisher 1980a). It seems to parallel the final term אֶבֶן מַשְׂכִּית, which is translated variously as a stone that is "figured," "carved," or "sculptured," but what that means is not really understood.

TRANSLATION ANALYSIS: "CARVED STONE"
This phrase consists of two words. The first, אֶבֶן, simply means "stone." The second, מַשְׂכִּית, describes it. It can mean "image, idol, figure, picture, imagination, opinion, thoughts, conceit, imagery" (Cohen 1980a, 876). It is thought to derive from a verbal root that may mean "to look" (*DCH* s.v. "שׂכה" 8:148). Some take this as representing a three-dimensional image before which one prostrates oneself. Others suggest a slab with a picture or relief on which one prostrates oneself.

According to Hartley (1992, 449–50), it means literally "a stone with a relief" and is to be understood as a stone formed into a figure before which one kneeled. Gane (2004a, 451–52), however, takes it as a stone slab laid on the ground on which a worshipper would kneel to make his supplication. In either case, using the item for worship (לְהִשְׁתַּחֲוֹת) was prohibited.

TRANSLATION ANALYSIS: "TO WORSHIP"
This verb, which means "to worship," historically was understood to be a *hithpael* of the verb שָׁחָה, which meant to bow down (BDB s.v. "שָׁחָה" 1005). More recently, it has been concluded that it was the rare *eshtaphal* stem of the verb חָוָה meaning "to prostrate oneself" or "to worship" (Yamauchi 1980b, 267). *DCH* (s.v. "שׁחה" 8:316) suggests either root is possible with either a *hithpael* or *histaphal* stem. In either case, the concept seems to be to bow down in worship.

All four forms of idolatrous worship are prohibited because of who God is: "for I am the Lord [YHWH] your God." The identity is YHWH, and the emphasis is that he is the God of Israel.

26:2. Contrasting what they were to avoid, there were two things that the Israelites were to do. The first was to keep God's Sabbaths, which was discussed in detail in the unit covering Leviticus 23–24. While the plural might address a pattern of observing every seventh day, more likely this includes every occasion noted as a Sabbath, that is, the Sabbath day, the Sabbath year, and any appointed time designated as a Sabbath. Second, they were to revere the sanctuary. At this point the sanctuary was the recently completed tabernacle (see Exod. 36:1–38:31, which addresses the construction of the tabernacle).

Given that the ark was located there, and the association of the ark with the הַכַּפֹּרֶת ("mercy seat"; see discussion of Lev. 16:2b–28) the verb "to revere" carries special significance, and in fact the more basic meaning of the Hebrew יָרֵא as "to fear" might be even more appropriate. Again, it is because of who God is.

TRANSLATION ANALYSIS: "REVERE"
The verb יָרֵא might best be translated "to revere" in this context. According to *TWOT* (Bowling 1980b 1:399), usage of the term falls into "five general categories: 1) the emotion of fear, 2) the intellectual anticipation of evil without emphasis upon the emotional reaction, 3) reverence or awe, 4) righteous behaviour or piety, and 5) formal religious worship." While the concepts of reverence or awe might be appropriate, the concept of both terms in English seems somewhat watered down from what might be expected given the consequences of the indiscretions that killed not only Nadab and Abihu, but later Uzzah (1 Chron. 13:7).

God Cites the Positive Consequences of Faithful Behavior (26:3–13)
While this section is often called "blessings," that word does not show up in this chapter.

Still, the term seems very appropriate in that some of the outcomes parallel the results of the sixth-year blessing in Leviticus 25:21. While there are a number of individual outcomes in this section, they seem to fit into four groups or categories.

26:3. Leviticus 26:3 sets the stage for the rest of this section by expressing the requirement for the positive items expressed in the following verses. Structurally, it contains three verbal clauses joined by two *waws*. The construction seems to suggest a single but complex contingency that sets the stage for the outcome should Israel comply. The first and second clauses both begin with the word "if" (אִם), suggesting two aspects of that contingency. The first aspect was that Israel must walk in God's statutes. The verb הָלַךְ ("to walk or go") reflects lifestyle, that is, their lives were to evidence God's statutes. The second aspect reflects an attitude: the Israelites must "guard or keep" (שָׁמַר) God's commandments. Here the issue is value, not a legalistic, begrudging keeping of the commandments just to avoid punishment. The last clause, which is not introduced by an "if," amplifies the second. The verb עָשָׂה, which means "to do," reflects outcome. As such, this verse really serves to emphasize that the following group of positive consequences depends upon a single contingency of a collective obedient lifestyle built on hearts that value God's guidelines. Since this declaration immediately follows 26:1–2, it would appear at a minimum 26:3 refers to the directives regarding idols and Sabbaths. However, given the double emphasis of the contingent "if," Willis (2009, 221) is probably correct when he states that "these verses envision all the preceding laws which had been given under the umbrella call for obedience."

So the thrust of the message is that the Israelites were to have a lifestyle that paid close attention to what God had told them to

do, and do it. If they did, they could expect the positive outcomes of the rest of this section.

26:4–5. The first positive outcome category was fertility resulting from the "rains in their seasons." The Israelite culture was going to be agricultural, and the promise was that the fields and orchards would be fertile. It began with the rains. Israel's agricultural calendar commenced following the autumnal equinox with what were called the early rains in the October–November time frame. These prepared the land for plowing. After the seed was sown, strong winter rains were expected from mid-December to mid-March. These saturated the soil and nourished the growing crops. The latter rains in March completed the winter crops and started the newly sown summer seed.

Grain usually was harvested in late spring, and in a good year the crop would be plentiful enough that the harvesting would go until the grapes were ripe. And if the grape harvest was strong, gathering would keep the farmer busy up to the time to start the cycle again. As the text states, there would be plenty of food, and they would "live securely" in their land. It is interesting that Milgrom (2001, 2294) expresses that "divine intervention [was] required *only* for abundant and timely rains" (emphasis added). In essence it did not require direct, miraculous intervention, but it did require divine supervision of the weather cycle, which today we are aware is a global phenomenon.

26:6–8. The second positive outcome category was peace in the land. Two kinds of peace are noted. The first was from harmful beasts. During that period predators still roamed the land, notably lions and bears. David remarked to Saul that while watching his father's sheep, "When a lion or a bear came. . . . Your servant has killed both the lion and the bear" (1 Sam. 17:34–36). This sounds as if it happened on multiple occasions.

Alternative Outcomes for the Community of God (26:1–46)

Additionally, the section says there would be peace in the land from foreign forces. Levine (1989, 183) suggests that the phrase "no sword will pass through" was a rare way of depicting freedom from the ravages of war. First, this was a promise specifically to the nation of Israel, not to the world of the time. Second, it is interesting that the text describes the preclusion of the sword from the land as a result of the Israelites being highly successful warriors; a handful could drive off much larger groups. In other words, they would have peace because potential invaders would know that Israel was strong, protected by God, and from experience they understood that if they attacked they would be handily defeated. This would seem to oppose a perspective of peace that believes that if they did not have arms, all would live in harmony and no one would be aggressive, threatening their neighbors. But it also seems to suggest that God would serve as a restrainer by reinforcing, or even introducing, that sense of respect and fear in the minds of their neighbors.

26:9. The third category of positive outcomes might be labeled posterity or population growth. God indicates that through this he would confirm his covenant with the Israelites as descendants of Abraham (Gen. 17:2). This is the first mention of the covenant in this chapter, although it will be cited another seven times before the end. We will focus on the concept in the section containing 26:44–46.

26:10. This verse seems to be out of place. It does not seem to be part of the third category of posterity, but it is not clearly a separate category. Since the verse opens with the statement that they would eat (second-person plural of the verb אָכַל) it is clear that the object is food, although that term must be added. Rather, it uses יָשָׁן, the word translated "old," three times in sequence.

TRANSLATION ANALYSIS: "OLD"
The root יָשֵׁן carries two concepts: "sleep" and "old." *DCH* (s.v. "יָשֵׁן" 4:334–35) maintains that they are two separate roots, while J. Schüpphaus (1990, 438–39) concludes that it is difficult to determine the etymology and observes that either understanding could explain the way it is used in the OT. Specifically, all agree that when the verbal form appears in the *niphal* (as here, although in company with two adjectival forms), the context indicates that "old" is the understanding. Given that, this verse might read literally, but awkwardly, as something like, "And you will eat the old, and the old will be [perhaps made] old because of the new you will bring out." Milgrom (2001, 2299) proposes that this is an idiom, but with two possible interpretations. The first is a comparison suggesting that they would eat the older before the old. The second is that the expression is essentially a hendiadys which means "very old." The second seems best, although either could fit here.

As Milgrom (2001, 2299) points out, the wording has long been considered idiomatic. The basic concept seems to be that the supply of food would be so abundant that when the new harvest came in, they would still be eating from the old. The final verb יָצָא, meaning here "to bring out," raises the question: "Brought out" in what sense?

It could suggest that the new would be so plentiful that they would need to dispose of the old to make room for it. Or, it could mean that the old would store so well that even when the new crop came in, the old food stuffs would still be good. Milgrom suggests that as the new comes in, the old would still be good in storage so that it would be given away. This understanding would supplement the discussion in Leviticus 25:22 about eating the old things during Jubilee. It also may be significant in terms of the responsibilities of the Levites in Numbers 18 and Deuteronomy 14 regarding third-year tithes and storage

Alternative Outcomes for the Community of God (26:1–46)

of food in Levitical cities (Harbin 2021b, 699–700).

The idea of abundant food would seem to place this material as an aspect of the first category of positive outcomes, but it follows the third category. It may be that the intent was that while their population would multiply, there would still be so much food that they could share it and use it even through the Sabbath-year/Jubilee two-year fallow period.

26:11–13. The fourth category of positive outcome is the presence of God. The phrase used in 26:11 literally states, "I will give my tabernacle among you." This is somewhat of a wordplay since they had just built and consecrated the tabernacle, and the entire book of Leviticus revolves around that edifice being in the middle of the camp. However, here the language goes to the root concept of the tent—it was the location of God's presence, and the point being made is that if the nation was corporately faithful in its rejection of idols, guarding the Sabbaths, and revering the sanctuary, God would remain in the camp. As Wenham (1979, 329) observes, if they did not, "Israel's sins could make it an empty shrine."

Leviticus 26:11 is somewhat of a hinge to this chapter in that the last phrase gives a hint to what will come in the last part of the chapter. If the people did not follow through, God would reject them. The word translated "reject" does not really address the actions God would take; that will come later. Rather, the verb גָּעַל means "to abhor, to loathe"; thus, it alludes to what would lead God to take those actions—their misdeeds would be extremely repulsive. It is interesting that in this case, God states that it would be his *nephesh* that abhorred Israel.

TRANSLATION ANALYSIS: "LOATHE"
Waltke (1980c, 169) describes גָּעַל as "an intense aversion which is expressed often in punitive or adverse action." Perhaps it is this that leads the NASB and the HCSB to translate it as "reject." Levine (1989, 183) indicates that when used with *nephesh* it serves to intensify the sense.

While this may just be an idiom, it could go deeper. In the "*Nephesh* (נֶפֶשׁ): Life and Soul" section in the introduction, we noted that in general the term reflects the nonphysical aspect of humans and animals that gives created beings life, probably referring to "conscious life." As the source of life, God is spirit (רוּחַ). While it is possible that an uncreated *nephesh* is an aspect of his being, it is more likely that this is an anthropomorphism used here to denote the core of his being. Its function then shows the depth of God's response that would lead to rejection, which is the last part of the chapter. However, it also serves to set up a comparison in 26:15, which shows the Israelites how their prospective rejection of the statutes and ordinances would be viewed by God—their disobedience would demonstrate that they abhorred what God had ordained.

Instead, God continues the promise using covenant language, "I will also walk in your midst and be your God, and you shall be my people." Beyond dwelling with the Israelites, God states that he would walk among them. This transcends God leading them as they had experienced to that point, but indicates a regular, close relationship. Hartley (1992, 463) notes that it suggests a situation where God would "watch over, care for, and bless every family." He also notes a tie with the patriarchs who walked with God: Enoch, Noah, and Abraham. But there, the idea was that the person had a lifestyle that pleased God. Here the idea is stronger. God is the subject, and this hints of the time in the garden before the fall. In this light, Milgrom (2001, 2302) cites the tradition that the garden of Eden was a sanctuary. All this suggests that the promise was that there would be tremendous intimate relationship between the people and God. Thus, Ross's (2002, 471) observation

392

that this prospective outcome really was the basis for the fulfillment of the rest is pertinent.

This section ends with a reminder of what God had done so far. Not only had he brought them out of Egypt, but he freed them from their slavery (a point touched on earlier in 25:55). Here he uses an interesting and powerful picture. Israel's slavery in Egypt is likened to a yoke that was used on work animals when plowing. If worn by humans, the heavy yoke would bend them over under the burden, so it serves as a figure representing the effects of slavery. But when God figuratively broke the bars that attached them to the slavery, they now could walk erect. As Sklar (2014, 317) explains, this upright walk is a fitting posture for servants of the King of kings.

God Warns of the Negative Consequences of Unfaithful Behavior (26:14–39)

After reminding the Israelites of what he had done to the Egyptians, God now presents the flip side—what will happen to the Israelites if *they* are unfaithful. Just as the word "blessing" was not used in the previous section, so the word "curse" is not used here. Again, the idea is not inappropriate, since the consequences listed are included in the list of curses in the parallel passage of Deuteronomy 28. There seem to be several reasons that the negative outcome section is much longer than the positive side. On one hand, that seemed to be the typical pattern in the ANE (Hartley 1992, 457–58). On the other hand, the positive outcomes are more general. Further, as Gane (2004a, 452) points out, "negative motivations need to be more substantial in order to serve as an effective deterrent."

26:14–15. The transition to the negative outcomes in 26:14–15 uses several strong descriptors to show the seriousness of what the nation would be doing. It begins in 26:14 with the versatile *waw*, coupled with an "if not" (אִם־לֹא) sequence. This clear contrast indicates that the

waw should be translated as "but." Thus, we see a sharp contrast with the "if" (אִם) of 26:3, showing an alternative contingency. Leviticus 26:15 is the first of four "and if" phrases (וְאִם) that will indicate steps of disobedience that would result in increasing divinely instituted consequence.

In these two verses, the "and if not" is followed by a sequence of explanations of what "if not" means. First, they would not "obey," using the verb that literally means "to hear" but carries the sense of "obey."

TRANSLATION ANALYSIS: "OBEY"
The English word "obey" translates the Hebrew word שָׁמַע, which means "to hear." Here, it would be "hear" in the sense of listen carefully, pay attention to, or more emphatically, obey (Austel 1980a).

This "if" clause explains that not obeying God involved not doing what was commanded. This is followed by another "if" clause, which clarifies that not doing the commands meant that they rejected the statutes; but this is followed by a third "if" clause, which maintains that it really showed that they abhorred God's judgments. In other words, it was not the disobedience that was the root issue but the Israelite resentment that God would tell them what to do that led to their not doing the commandments. The final phrase shows that the net result would be their breaking of the covenant that God had established with the nation, which they had agreed they would obey.

TRANSLATION ANALYSIS: "BREAK MY COVENANT"
This phrase is a prepositional phrase introduced by the לְ preposition, followed by the verb פָּרַר meaning "to break, destroy, frustrate, or invalidate" (Hamilton 1980i, 738), with the object being "my covenant" (Smick 1980). It is interesting that the term has the singular pronoun ("my") attached rather than the plural ("our"),

Alternative Outcomes for the Community of God (26:1–46)

which seems to point out that God had initiated the action.

26:16–17. Israel's anticipated disobedience would begin a series of consequences set forth by further "if" clauses. The pattern that emerges is a sequence of increasingly severe repercussions for continued rebellion on the part of Israel.

Corporate Rebellion

This entire section addresses the consequences of corporate rebellion as opposed to corporate obedience. The idea of corporate rebellion carries connotations of both quantity and degree—that is, the proportion of the population that rebelled and the overtness of the rebellion. Consequently, an area that bears consideration is: What might that mean? A case in point is the incident some time prior to this event, when Moses was on the mountain. Exodus 32:1 relates how "the people assembled about Aaron and said to him, 'Come, make us a god'" (see comment in the sidebar "False Gods" under Leviticus 26:1). And yet it was not all of the people. After Moses descended, some of the people helped him clean out the camp, which resulted in three thousand deaths among the disobedient. Clearly not everyone rebelled, but we have no idea how many did. That would suggest a spectrum of obedience in the community, with individuals falling out at different places on the spectrum (and likely constantly shifting somewhat as they wrestled with choices). If we could diagram the entire population in terms of the degree of obedience along that spectrum, likely the results would appear as a standard distribution curve with extreme outliers at either end and the majority somewhere in between. While we might hope and pray that everyone would walk with God and obey totally, we are reminded over and over that it will not be the case in this fallen world until the Messiah returns. In the interim, we will ponder as to what portion of a given culture—in this case, Israel—would carry the weight to determine whether

the culture is considered in rebellion or in obedience. Rather, all we can do individually is to look to our own hearts, to see where we might fit on that spectrum.

Leviticus 26:16 begins with God's response, a warning that as Israel turns from God, he would react by appointing a sudden terror (בֶּהָלָה), in terms of disease and invasion. The terms used here for "disease," שַׁחֶפֶת and קַדַּחַת, are medical terms for which we cannot identify specific diseases, just the general symptoms of wasting away and high fever (Levine 1989, 185). Externally, this would be coupled with invaders, and in their weakened state the Israelites would be unable to resist (Milgrom 2001, 2305).

TRANSLATION ANALYSIS: "CONSUMPTION" AND "FEVER"
Translated by the NASB and NRSV as "consumption" and "fever" and variously by other translations, שַׁחֶפֶת is defined as a "wasting disease" (*TWOT* s.v. "שַׁחֶפֶת" 2:916), while קַדַּחַת merely means "fever" (*TWOT* s.v. "קַדַּחַת" 2:785).

26:18–20. If Israel does not obey at this point, God states that he would punish them "seven times more." The phrase "seven times" is a round number used to express nonspecifically repeated punishments designed to break down the pride that prompts Israel to resist God (Wenham 1979, 331).

This stage also involves drought, vividly expressed as the sky being like iron and the earth like bronze. The fact that the same expression is in Deuteronomy 28:23, although the metals are reversed, and that similar expressions also appear in the treaties of Esarhaddon (Levine 1989, 186), suggests that this was a common idiom for which there were variations. Both iron and bronze are hard metals, and the gist of the expression would be that the rain would be held back (in this case, the sky would be like iron), and without rain the earth would harden, resisting cultivation (in this case, compared to bronze). As a result, it would be useless to labor to plant, since the fields would not grow crops and fruit trees would not bear. While some foodstuffs might be coaxed, most plants would struggle just to survive at best, and crops would wither and die. This would be the precursor to famine.

26:21–22. Leviticus 26:21 seems to incorporate another idiom using the noun קְרִי, meaning "opposition" or "hostility." Sherwood (2002, 85) suggests that perhaps the phrase תֵּלְכוּ עִמִּי קֶרִי (literally "walk with me in opposition") might be translated in idiomatic English as "if you take me on." This seems to suggest that instead of understanding and relenting, the people would press harder in their rebellion. In that case, once more using the seven-times expression, God states that he would increase the plague significantly.

This next increase would involve removing restraints on "beasts of the field" among the Israelites. This would seem to suggest that the wild animals such as lions and bears, and perhaps supposedly domesticated animals like dogs, would lose any inhibitions of attacking humans, especially children, and killing them. For the Israelites, being bereaved of children would be a double tragedy. Not only would the parents (especially the mothers) experience the actual bereavement with the loss of the child, but in that culture children were in essence their social security, that is, their provision for their old age. Wild beasts would also attack their cattle, and travelers (note the case of Samson; Judg. 14:5), causing people to avoid travel, leading to empty highways.

26:23–26. The fourth "and if" is very troubling. Once again, it is supposed that the Israelites would continue to respond with hostility. This time the Lord declares that at this stage he would return the hostility (the noun קְרִי [Coppes 1980] with the preposition בְּ attached) and he also would again strike them seven times for their sins. In this case, the Lord's act is to either cause or allow (the *hiphil* form of the verb בּוֹא meaning "to go in or enter" [Martens 1980b], 93) invasion (described as "a sword that will execute vengeance"). As a follow-on, when the people gather together in their cities for protection from the invasion, they would be struck with pestilence. The result would be conquest.

> **Gather Together in Your Cities**
> One common misconception regarding ancient cities is that the inhabitants all lived together inside the walls. While many did, the reality was that many lived outside of the city walls but would flee inside the walls during an attack. This would create crowded conditions, including lack of food and sanitation issues. Figure 69 shows the location of the gates of the city of Hazor (lower left) looking out to the north, but archaeologists report that many houses lie under the field beyond, which was outside of the gates.

Figure 69. The gates of Hazor and the lower city.

The "staff of bread" (מַטֵּה־לֶחֶם) is an interesting phrase that can be taken two ways. Some understand this as describing a pole on which bread baked in rings might be carried, and that may yet be seen in Middle Eastern cities. However, it also may be understood as a metaphor for the way that bread supports life, somewhat like a staff that provides support in walking (in Greek, this would be the difference between an objective and subjective genitive; Hebrew does not have genitives). The latter would seem to be preferred, since during a siege flour would be in short supply, thus "poles with bread" (if they used them) would be absent rather than broken. The idea is that what they depended on no longer supported them. Whereas prior to the invasion each homemaker would bake her bread in her own oven, due to the shortage of grain one oven would suffice for ten women to bake. Again, the people would be looking at famine, as they continually went hungry.

26:27–33. The final "and if" is the most severe, and the most troubling. It is introduced with a more emphatic וְאִם־בְּזֹאת, which might be translated "and if in all of this." The Israelite action may be characterized as continuing to refuse to listen to God and defiantly become increasingly hostile. In return God states that now, his return hostility will be wrathful, with the consequences ratcheted up another seven times. In their defiance, the Israelites would resort to eating the flesh of their own children rather than submit to God. Since they refused to give up their idolatry, God would destroy the various sites, the "high places," as well as remove incense altars—various locations where their idolatrous worship was practiced.

TRANSLATION ANALYSIS: "HIGH PLACES"
Translated "high place," a *bamah* (בָּמָה) is considered a technical name for a cultic platform, although there are several problems with the term (Martens 1980c). The etymology is uncertain. While a similar term appears in a number of Semitic languages, a clear background concept is not clear, although cognate terms indicating such concrete concepts as "back," "ridge," or "high place" are evident in related contexts (Schunck 1975, 139–43). The term *bamah* is most frequently used in conjunction with worship areas that tended to be placed on natural heights, but at times the word seems to reflect the tactical advantage of possessing the "high ground," Traditionally, it was assumed that

the idea of height derived from the location of the worship site, although a more recent counterargument reverses the relationship (Martens 1980c). The general understanding regarding a *bamah* in the OT is they were viewed negatively because they are largely associated with pagan worship. Clearly, many high places incorporated aspects of idolatry (2 Chron. 14:3; 33:19), which was prohibited and brought condemnation. However, there are a number of occasions where the use seems to denote a place to worship YHWH, such as Samuel performing a sacrifice on a "high place" in 1 Samuel 9:13–25. While this ambiguity makes this a tough issue to sort out in some cases, when used in the context of other aspects of idolatry it is clearly a prohibited practice.

TRANSLATION ANALYSIS: "IDOLS"
Translated as "idols," the word גִּלּוּל is a rare term that has a very uncertain etymology and does not appear outside of "Israelite-Jewish literature" (Preuss 1978, 2). *TWOT* (Kalland 1980) proposes that it derives from the root גלל, which purportedly lies behind concepts such as "to roll," "to commit," "to remove," among others. While the connection is not clear, given its pejorative usage some scholars connect it with גֵּל, which means "dung." That would produce a word that means "things of dung, dung idols" (Preuss 1978, 2; cf. Hartley 1992, 455). Given how it is used here and in Ezekiel to derogate idols, that would not be a poor interpretation.

TRANSLATION ANALYSIS: "CORPSE"
The word פֶּגֶר presents the idea of a human corpse in which the body has been allowed to lie there and begin to decay and smell—the word is never used to refer to the body of an animal (Hamilton 1980e). It is related to the verb פָּגַר, defined as "to be exhausted or faint." Since it is used only once in the *piel* (1 Sam. 30:10), it seems likely that this is a denominative usage (GKC §52h), that is, "become corpse-like." Given a Ugaritic correlation, some argue for an

Alternative Outcomes for the Community of God (26:1–46)

alternative translation of "stela" or "monument." However, in this context the result would not seem to make sense.

The key words are נִּלּוּל, which means "idols" or "dung," and פֶּגֶר, which means "corpse." Given the potential translations of those key words, the text might be seen as suggesting that God would be heaping the lifeless decaying bodies of the Israelite worshippers on top of lifeless decaying bodies of the dung heap idols that they were worshiping, and in essence entrusting their lives to. As Levine (1989, 188) notes, it is "a cruelly ironic statement." The sentence ends with the statement "my *nephesh* shall abhor you" (וְגָעֲלָה נַפְשִׁי אֶתְכֶם) connected to the rest of the sentence with the all-purpose *waw*. Generally, the *waw* is translated as "and," which might suggest a result; that is, God would "abhor" the nation as a result of what it had become. It would seem that the NASB catches the nuance by translating it as "for," suggesting that the abhorrence was because of the sin, not because of the outcome. If this comes across as exceedingly offensive, it may be that we do not find the sin being committed offensive enough.

Regardless of how it is understood, the bottom line is that the result would be dead Israelites lying before their dead idols. How the worshippers would die is not explained, but the next three verses suggest it would be by invading armies. God, through those armies, would make the cities ruins (חָרְבָּה). He, again through those armies, would make their sanctuaries desolate (שָׁמֵם). As a result, there would be no sacrifices, although the text may imply that if there were, they would not produce their "soothing aromas" (the רֵיחַ נִיחֹחַ of Leviticus 1; see commentary there). The desolation is characterized as so bad that even the conquerors who moved into the land would be appalled by it. Finally, those who survived all of this would be carried off into exile and scattered among the nations.

TRANSLATION ANALYSIS: "SCATTERED"

The word translated "scattered" is זָרָה, which can indicate "a scattering or dispersing for reasons of purification or chastisement" (Van Groningen 1980a, 251). The picture often given is of winnowing grain by blowing the chaff away. Ross (2002, 470) proposes that "the image indicates the wicked would be blown away like chaff (Ps. 1:4); but a remnant would remain faithful to the Lord and eventually see the restoration to the land." That idea would set up the next section, anticipating a remnant that would not only survive but repent and be restored.

Even there, God would draw out a sword after them, using the figure for the ravages of war. Milgrom (2001, 2322) makes an interesting observation in regard to this punishment. In ANE curses, "the punishing deity does not pursue his people in exile. He cannot, since it is the territory of another god." In that case, God is claiming authority over the entire world, including the alien nations. But while God indicates that he would make the land desolate, it would only be for a time.

26:34–39. These six verses make it clear that the last stage in this sequence of judgments is exile. However, this is not a separate "and if" phrase, but seems to be tied to making the land a desolation. The land will be made desolate because the inhabitants were removed. But more than that, the purpose of the exile is so that the land might enjoy its Sabbath years that were directed in 25:1–7.

TRANSLATION ANALYSIS: "ENJOY ITS SABBATH"

The verb used here is רָצָה, which means "to be pleased with or be favorable to" (White 1980e, 859). Commonly it is translated here as "enjoy," serving as an anthropomorphism to stress the value of the rest to the land and subsequently to those who lived on it.

Alternative Outcomes for the Community of God (26:1–46)

As such, this section demonstrates that Leviticus 25 and 26 are one unit, although we have broken them into three sections (or possibly four if one divides the positive and negative outcomes) for homiletic purposes. Because in this anticipated future the people had not given the land rest while they lived in it, God would remove them so that the land would have the rest God mandated. To emphasize this point, the statement that the land would enjoy its Sabbaths is repeated. However, the section also mentions "those who may be left" twice.

TRANSLATION ANALYSIS: "THOSE WHO MAY BE LEFT"

The phrase "those of you who may be left" translates the term נִשְׁאָרִים, which is followed by the prepositional phrase בָּכֶם ("in you all"). The word נִשְׁאָרִים is a *niphal* participle of the verb שָׁאַר, which means "to remain" (Cohen 1980c, 895). Normally one would expect this phrase to "refer to those who remained in the land after a devastating war" (Kleinig 2003, 556). However, it is clear here they will be in the hands of the enemies and that in those foreign locations they will experience despair, which might suggest that a better translation would be "survivors." Clements (2004, 274) suggests that in reference to the nation of Israel, the concept "arose that a surviving remnant would thus represent the believing minority."

Leviticus 26:36 and 38 indicate that those survivors would experience weakness or faintness in their hearts (מֹרֶךְ בִּלְבָבָם) while in those foreign lands, an experience that is described as excessive fear in a variety of ways. The result would be that even if they survived, they would perish in exile. Specifically, they would מָקַק, that is, decay or rot away because of their iniquities.

God Explains the Reason for His Hostility (26:40–43)

26:40–43. While 26:34 explains that a purpose of the exile would be to allow the land to enjoy its Sabbaths, this section indicates that a second, perhaps more significant purpose would be to soften the "uncircumcised hearts" of the Israelites so that they could confess their iniquity and that of their ancestors against God, which was why he responded to their hostility with hostility. When that happened, God would "remember" his covenant with Jacob, Isaac, and Abraham. This anthropomorphism is a special phrase that God uses with respect to himself and the covenant, which does not imply that it had been forgotten, but indicates a time for action to execute specifics of the promises (Hartley 1992, 469).

While it is generally agreed that this section marks an end to the downward spiral that began in 26:16, the structure of these four verses is problematic. The main difficulty is the use of the *waw*s at the beginning of 26:40 and 42, which would appear to be *waw* consecutives and might be expected to be translated just as "and" (GKC §112; Kleinig 2003, 566). However, the most common way the *waw* at the beginning of 26:40 is translated is "if" or "but if" for the first and "then" for the second. Kleinig objects that this makes the confession a condition for God's action. This introduces the possibility that the nation would never reach that point.

However, it would appear that the אוֹ־אָז ("or if") in 26:41 indicates that the key is the softening of their hearts that is the cause of the confession in 26:40. The interjection of the explanation of God's hostility might then be viewed as that which produced the softening so that the Israelites could confess.

TRANSLATION ANALYSIS: "OR IF"

The phrase אוֹ־אָז literally means "or if." Kleinig (2003, 567) notes that the function is uncertain and suggests a later addition to the text, maintaining that the difficulty is that there is no alternative. A better explanation would be to understand this as a different way of expressing the process of the corporate confession. Because their "uncircumcised heart" was softened, they were able to confess, something like how a specific mallet might be used to pound a steak to tenderize it.

This section concludes with two consequences: the land would make up for its Sabbaths, and the exiled inhabitants would make amends for their iniquities. Harrison (1980, 237) points out:

> Though God has afflicted his people with such a drastic punishment, they themselves must bear responsibility for it. . . . By disobeying the provisions of the covenant agreement, the vassal brings upon himself the maledictions which it contains.

God Reminds That He Will Always Remember and Be Faithful (26:44–46)

26:44–45. After this extensive delineation of the horrid consequences, the section ends with the consolation that God would never break his covenant. As such, although they might be in the foreign lands serving their enemies, they would never be rejected. While God might abhor the nation to the point that he sent it into exile (26:30), he would never abhor the nation to the point of destroying it. The evidence in this regard was the exodus, which the people who were receiving this promise had very recently experienced.

26:46. This last verse seems to be a conclusion, but there is another chapter to go. The question then is: If it is a conclusion, what does it conclude? Leviticus 25–26 (based on the *inclusio* with 25:1)? Leviticus 17–26 (the laws of holy living)? Leviticus 8–26 (based on a similar conclusion in 7:37–38)? Or the entire book? Given the overall content, Kiuchi (2007, 472) is correct when he states, "all the commandments in Leviticus are summarized in two stages, here and in 27:34." We will evaluate this in the next unit.

SUMMARY

Previously we noted the promise that if the nation as a whole observed God's guidelines, the entire community would enjoy shalom, but there could be a disparity of outcomes to the point that in this overall period of well-being, some might struggle significantly. However, the previous unit showed how the community as a whole could (and should) support those outliers and reintegrate them. Now, the text turns to the corporate alternatives that lay before the nation. If the nation as a whole obeyed, then positive outcomes were in store, essentially as a package. However, if the nation as a whole disobeyed, then negative outcomes were in store, although in this case, as an increasingly severe sequence of events. Much of the chapter focuses on those negative outcomes and stresses how their increase would be in correspondence with increased disobedience, culminating in exile.

But the final emphasis is that God would honor the covenant—and ultimately return the nation, the corporate whole, to the land that had been promised, and thus fulfill the covenants God had made with the nation's ancestors. The challenge would be for each generation to recognize the tension between individual responsibility and corporate outcome. The question for every Israelite would be to ask him- or herself whether his or her actions were a part of national faithfulness or unfaithfulness. As Mordecai put it to Esther several centuries later, national deliverance would come; the question is, would you have a part in it (Esther 4:14)?

THEOLOGICAL FOCUS

The key theological focus is that God is a God who is both righteous and merciful. Because he is righteous, he expected his people to live righteously and would judge them if they didn't. These judgments would culminate in national exile. However, because he is merciful, he promised that he would restore the nation when the nation returned to him in confession and repentance.

Alternative Outcomes for the Community of God (26:1–46)

God's people remain confident in their ability to live righteously. Receiving a conditional contract with its blessings and curses to direct their steps sounds fair and reasonable, even generous, to those confident in their ability to obey the law, control their passions, and live in submission to the will of their Lord. They have already declared to Moses in Exodus 24:7, "All that the Lord has spoken we will do, and we will be obedient!" (ESV). And after the conquest they will affirm once more to Joshua, "The Lord our God we will serve, and his voice we will obey!" (Josh. 24:24 ESV). As long as God does his part by annihilating the enemies coming at them, they trust in the capacity to ward off any enemies that may rise up from within them. They will live holy lives, love their God, and love their neighbor. They will seize this gracious opportunity to reverse the curse through obedience. How hard can this be? God's people have confidence, but their confidence is misplaced in the strength of their own will rather than in the covenant promise of the Lord God.

In many ways, Leviticus 26 serves as a summation of the storyline of Scripture. God makes a covenant with a people to live under his protection and blessing and proclaim his name to all the earth. They are confident that they will do it, denying the hold that sin has on them. They quickly turn away from God, believing they need to follow their own plan. God will intervene repeatedly through a variety of calamities to break their pride and turn them back, but he will never utterly destroy them because of his enduring covenant with their forefathers.

PREACHING AND TEACHING STRATEGIES

Exegetical and Theological Synthesis

For many reasons, Leviticus 26 is an easy text to blow by and a hard text to absorb. First, it applies consequences for disobedience corporately. God's people have already been instructed how to incorporate Sabbath and Jubilee years into their calendars to image his mercy and grace. One may be able to fool him- or herself into believing he or she will be that generous on a coming future date in a land of blessing to ensure that the blessing is experienced by all. But this new instruction pushes the bar between individual and corporate responsibility even further. If too many individuals step outside of God's law, turn away from his purposes, and bow down to foreign idols, the entire nation will be penalized. Where is divine precision? Where is individual responsibility? Will not two be in a field and one taken while the other is left (Matt 24:40)?

This is another opportunity for them, and us, to remember that what is seen in this life is not all there is. There will be a day, the day of judgment, when each will be judged with surgical precision according to what each has done. But that is not today. We live in the day of preparation for that coming day. Can God's people long for that day, yet have sufficient concern for their neighbor in this day to pray like Daniel, to intervene before God by humbly asking forgiveness for the sin of the nation (Dan. 9)?

Second, God's people often live with an overly developed confidence in our reason and conscience. This allows us to justify moving from being "under" God's Word to standing "beside" his Word. If we are under his Word, his Word fully instructs our thoughts and disciplines our will. If we are beside God's Word, God serves as our consultant, copilot, advisor, or similar, freeing us to entrust the final decision to our conscience. We become free to do what is right in our own mind.

Finally, God is boldly stating his intent to use nature, wild beasts, hostile nations, and any other means necessary to break our confidence and turn us back from the folly of listening to our own voice and following a law unto ourselves. Does God use evil for our good? In Leviticus 26, God is expressing his willingness to intervene because he loves us far beyond our ability to understand, even beyond our willingness to readily accept. That is a sacrificial love.

Preaching Idea

We are loved by God through his sacrificial intervention to rescue us from the curse of following our own voice rather than his life-giving Word.

Contemporary Connections

What does it mean?

What does it mean that we are loved through God's sacrificial intervention to rescue us from the curse of following our own voice instead of his life-giving Word? Primarily, it means we have a robust and dangerous habit of living out our confidence in our own voice, our own thoughts, and our own ways. We step off the witness stand to put God on the hot seat to defend his Word. This proves especially true in times of plenty. We use our own voice to select which words, his or ours, are superior and which are inferior. At times we may sound like we are in league with Jehoiakim in Jeremiah 36. As the words from God were read to him, he sliced off the scroll and burned it because he found it offensive. God intervened, sending the nation into exile.

But does God still sacrificially intervene to rescue us? Was God actually rescuing his people by sending them into exile? Yes. Otherwise, they would have all continued on the wide path of destruction and ceased to exist as a people. Did such violent calamities as exile lead to the sacrifice of his name? Yes. The other nations wondered how a god could do such a thing to his people (Deut. 29:24). Did God do this as an act of love? Yes. Doing what will lead one to cry out against you in anger, though it is required to save them from destruction, is an act of supreme, sacrificial love.

After watching my (Biehl) own son beaming with pride while riding his bike into the street in front of an oncoming car one too many times, I intervened, taking away his prized possession for a season so that he might be humbled, less confident in his own abilities, and more receptive to my life-preserving instruction. It proved to be a sacrificial intervention. He did not think of my "sovereign decision" as either loving or necessary, wondering why I had hurt him so badly. I believe I saved his life.

Is it true?

Is it true that God shows his love for us by sacrificially intervening to rescue us from the curse of following our own voice rather than abiding in his Word? Too often we are quick to follow our own voice. We fail repeatedly to discipline our passions and desires. This is the story of the fall of mankind. God told Adam and Eve all they could do and one thing they could not do. They heeded the advice of the serpent and stepped out from under God's "restrictive" law to stand beside his law. They determined that his law restrained who they could become and soon experienced the reality of all God had said. God would not abandon humankind. He promised a future sacrificial intervention to redeem his people—when the serpent would strike his heel as he crushed its head (Gen. 3:15).

Is it loving for a sovereign God to intervene with calamity upon a nation? We rarely have the necessary capacity to intervene when people are on the wide path that leads to destruction (Matt. 7:13). Have you ever said to someone (or thought), "I will do anything in my power to stop you from destroying yourself"? (This presumes, of course, that we are accurate judges of what one should and should not be doing.) As a father, I punished my children, when necessary, out of love. It was rarely welcomed. Often I lacked the power to do what was necessary for them to turn away from foolish behavior. This is never true of God. He always judges accurately. He remains completely sovereign, fully able to intervene sufficiently to change any circumstance.

So, what should God do if his children are skipping down the wide path that leads to destruction? If he provides unconditional affirmation, his children will die, though maybe with smiles on their faces. If he sacrificially intervenes,

Alternative Outcomes for the Community of God (26:1–46)

they may turn and repent and enter the narrow gate that leads to life (Matt 7:14). It would be unloving for him to refuse to intervene.

Now what?

We need to confess our misplaced confidence in our obedience—a confidence that too often leads us to judge God's Word. Are we ready for God to intervene into our carefully planned lives to turn us back from seeking our own will? Consider the outcome between holding a center point versus a boundary approach to how God is instructing us through his Word. If we are turned toward the center, seeking the heart of all he is calling us to be, we will continually walk deeper into God's will, becoming more like Christ. If we are habitually turned toward the boundary, questioning what we may be allowed to do, every step leads us away from the center and closer to denying his will in favor of our own. It may be time to look down at our feet. Which direction are they pointed? God expects his people to walk toward the center—to remain in his presence, under his law, and know the blessings he has prepared for us in eternity.

Creativity in Presentation

It may be helpful to start off with a clip from the movie *The Truman Show*. In the movie, Truman lives his life in a world created by the director as the world watches. When it is judged to be too confining, Truman seeks to escape his confinement as the audience cheers him on. The creator of his world sends a variety of calamities attempting to turn him back from seeking autonomy. In the end, Truman succeeds, stepping through a dark doorway out from under the arm of his protector to now live under his own control. Is this how we see the world? Are we in a battle to free ourselves from the limitations God and neighbor place upon us? In the movie, the creator of the world is a selfish, arrogant power-monger using Truman for his own purposes. Do we at times even subconsciously see God this way? Why? Oh, and by the way, what was

on the other side of that door that everyone was encouraging him to go through? What makes us think it was *good*?

You could share the common story of unknown origin that a shepherd will break the leg of a lamb that wanders off too often. (The problem is that this story appears not to be true; there is no evidence that this was ever a practice of shepherds.) The reason given is that it would create too much work for the shepherd! No shepherd would love a lamb sufficiently to intervene in a way that would lead to the sacrifice of carrying around the lamb for four to six weeks while its leg healed! It is only our God who would so sacrificially intervene because of his love for us!

Finally, to highlight our preoccupation with individuality, you could also put up an advertisement for the Star Registry. Someone is offering to name a star after you. Why would we do this? Does this make the star ours? Says who? Why do we need a personal star of our own? What does this reveal about us?

We are loved by God through his sacrificial intervention to rescue us from the curse of following our own voice rather than his life-giving Word.

- Are we living under, or alongside, God's words?
  - Blessing for the humble: those living under God's words
  - Breaking the proud: those walking alongside God's words (picking and choosing)
  - Redeeming the broken: restoring all who change direction
- What did it mean to them then? What does it mean always? What do we do now?
  - "This seems reasonable" would be a misplaced confidence in their ability to obey.
  - Since the garden, we tend to stand alongside, rather than live under,

God's Word and decide for ourselves if it is reasonable.

- ○ Where are we viewing God's law as inferior to our superior will? Are my feet pointing outward toward the boundary, or inward toward the center?

DISCUSSION QUESTIONS

1. Are you living under God's words or alongside God's words? How can you know?

2. Jehoiakim brazenly dismissed God's words. How should we approach such responses to God's words?

3. Where have you employed your wrath against someone because of your love for them?

4. Are you stepping toward trusting God or scoffing at his words? Denying yourself or proclaiming your will? Forgiving others or becoming bitter?

5. Are your feet pointed toward the center or toward the boundary? Is the cross fixed as the center point of your faith? How will this affect your next step?

Leviticus 27:1–34

EXEGETICAL IDEA
After God's people repeatedly witnessed the breadth of his power and goodness, they needed instruction in the foolhardiness of attempting to manipulate the Lord God by declaring rash and reckless personal or corporate vows.

THEOLOGICAL FOCUS
Vows are not a mechanism to manipulate God, but rather a means to humbly convey faithfulness to the Lord God who has been supremely faithful to his people.

PREACHING IDEA
My vow declares my devotion to God only if it is first carefully made and then faithfully kept.

PREACHING POINTERS
God's people gathered to hear a final speech. What more did God need to tell them? They knew they would soon step into the Promised Land. God promised to lead them, bless them, and protect them as he drove out the inhabitants before them. Some may have pondered, "Will God bless us all alike? Do I need to curry his favor to get my share? Are there mechanisms at my disposal to receive a larger share than my neighbor?" It would be easy to imagine gratefully giving to the Lord God when they had nothing—livestock or possessions—to give or withhold. But they speculated: What if the bull they promised to sacrifice matured into a prized bull? Could it be exchanged for one of lesser value? God should not care. One burnt carcass was the same as another, right (Mal. 1:14)? Wrong! Once again, God knew the thoughts and understood the hearts of his people. He warned them of the danger of declaring reckless vows made in haste both in times of hardship and exultation. Affection and gratitude might waver, but the vow must be faithfully kept..

Vows are not to be a declaration of how we feel, nor how we predict we will feel. They are a declaration of what we will do regardless of how we feel. They should not be a byproduct of emotion. They should not be proclaimed to manipulate or exploit. They are a means to harness our will that we will be faithful to a promise made, even if it requires great sacrifice. In our age, careless vows have become such a way of life that they are codified into law. We have no-fault divorce and prenuptial contracts. In many churches, parents take vows as they dedicate (or baptize) their children. Believers take vows when they become members. Why are so many vows so quickly (and thoughtlessly) broken? A vow kept testifies to faithfulness and self-sacrifice. A vow broken often exposes folly and our self-interest over the interests of others. Are our vows rash or reasonable? Is it time to listen more closely to our own words?

VOWS AND VALUES (27:1–34)

LITERARY STRUCTURE AND THEMES (27:1–34)

Chapter 27 of Leviticus is something of an enigma. Internally, it is structured like the other speeches from God in the book, where he gives Moses directions to pass on to the nation of Israel. It then concludes with a summary statement that fittingly closes the book. The problem is that it is immediately preceded by a similar summary statement (26:46), which many understand also seems to end the book. There are several different views on the matter (see the "Leviticus 27 Summary" excursus), but it would seem that the terminology of the summary statements provides some insight. As noted in the introduction, Leviticus presents itself as primarily recording various speeches that God gave to Moses at Mount Sinai punctuated with a couple of historical events from that period.

In the first twenty-four chapters, Mount Sinai is only mentioned in Leviticus 7:38, where it appears twice as it sums up the various offerings that are delineated in the first seven chapters, and thus provides a transition to the implementation of the sacrificial system in Leviticus 8. It does not appear again until the last three chapters, where it is cited three times. The first occasion is Leviticus 25:1, where it introduces a new section that builds on the social fabric material, blending guidelines regarding how the people were to be treated with guidelines on how the land was to be treated. Leviticus 25 and 26 focus on the people collectively, as shown by the predominant use of the second-person plural pronoun. The main thrust is that both the people and the land belonged to God and were to be treated with due respect. This culminates with the second Mount Sinai statement.

Leviticus 27 Summary

Both Leviticus 26:46 and 27:34 are summary verses that seem to transcend the chapters they close and thus provide closure to the book. If 26:46 actually serves to close the book, then one wonders how Leviticus 27 fits in. Many scholars view it as an appendix that is somewhat anticlimactic (Mathews 2009, 239). Four different reasons seem to have been given historically to explain Leviticus 27 (Kleinig 2003, 588–89; Milgrom 2001, 2407–9):

1. Some see a link between the promises that the Israelites would make in the form of vows and the promises that God had made to Israel in Leviticus 26.
2. It has been argued that these laws provided funding for the maintenance of the sanctuary.
3. Another view is that Leviticus 27 is added so that the book does not end on a negative note (i.e., the curses of Lev. 26).

Vows and Values (27:1–34)

4. Some argue that voluntary contributions provide a counterpart to the offerings presented in Leviticus 1–7.

Gane (2004a, 464) and others see Leviticus 25–27 as a unit, with Leviticus 27 as the logical conclusion:

> Leviticus 25–26 form a subunit framed by an *inclusio*: reference to Mount Sinai at the beginning of chapter 25 (v. 1) and again at the end of chapter 26 (v. 46). So, Leviticus 27 must come after this subunit rather than immediately following Leviticus 25. Placement of the dramatic climax in Leviticus 26 at the center of Leviticus 25–27 rather than at the very end of the book may disturb us, but it would be artistically satisfying from the viewpoint of ancient Hebrews, who often put their most weighty literary expressions at the centers of literary structures. Because Leviticus 27 is the real end of the book, it requires a concluding summary (27:34), echoing the earlier summary in 26:46.

If that is the case, an obvious question would be, how does it fit together? One key might be 25:2, which points to the future: "when you come into the land." The three chapters seem to interweave various personal and land issues that the nation would need to be concerned about as it settled the land, especially in subsequent generations. The Sabbath year appears as a first concern regarding land rest (25:2–7), which is extrapolated into the Jubilee year with regard to land possession and utilization (25:8–34). But that carries implications regarding economic well-being with subsequent poverty characterized as a result of land abuse (25:35–55). The consequences of proper use as opposed to misuse are then laid out in 26:1–45, summarized in 26:46, which refers to the above material as "statutes, ordinances, and teachings" (הַחֻקִּים וְהַמִּשְׁפָּטִים וְהַתּוֹרֹת). Leviticus 27 then picks up with warnings against false piety, which would be evidenced in careless vows that could jeopardize either the land or the people, followed by an admonition that they needed to remember that they did not own the land. Faithfully giving God, the owner, his share as a tithe served as a reminder of that fact (Kiuchi 2007, 494). The last chapter and the book then end with a final summary that ratchets the seriousness by emphasizing that all of the above are really commandments (הַמִּצְוֹת) to be followed by every individual.

Leviticus 27 then seems to shift to a primary focus on individuals, signaled by 27:2, which starts off with the phrase "when [or if] a man makes a difficult vow" (אִישׁ כִּי יַפְלִא נֶדֶר). This switch from the predominant use of the second-person pronoun to the generic term "man" (אִישׁ) suggests that while the subunit of Leviticus 25–26 addresses corporate responsibilities and consequences, Leviticus 27 addresses individual responses, stressing personal responsibilities. As Ross (2002, 487) notes, "most vows were made during times of God's blessing and curses, this chapter would provide necessary instruction to safeguard the people against foolish vows." The alternative consequences presented in Leviticus 26 then explicitly anticipate situations where individuals might respond both rashly and foolishly, which necessitates the final caution since individual responses collectively determine the corporate response.

Structurally, Leviticus 27 consists of three sections. The first section (Lev. 27:2–13), which is set off by כִּי (an "if" or "when" indicator), warns against rash vows, maintaining that if an individual makes a vow regarding a person, it must be followed through, although it does provide for redemption. The second section (Lev. 27:14–25), also set off by an "if/when" indicator, addresses the case of a rash vow involving land, whether a house or farmland. The final section, which begins with the restrictive particle אַךְ (translated as "however"), addresses situations that involved things that could not be vowed because they already belonged to God, including the firstborn animals, anything that was considered *herem* (see appendix 3), and tithes.

As such, Leviticus 27 circles back to the role of the individual within the nation, which is where the book began as noted in Leviticus 1:2, which starts "when [or if] any man of you brings an offering" (אָדָם כִּי־יַקְרִיב מִכֶּם קָרְבָּן). This would seem to explain the apparent dual ending to the book. Leviticus 26:46 concludes the corporate admonition described collectively as "statutes, ordinances, and teachings" (הַחֻקִּים וְהַמִּשְׁפָּטִים וְהַתּוֹרֹת), while individuals are to regard them personally as commandments (הַמִּצְוֹת). Kiuchi (2007, 494) concludes that the use of the term "commandments" in 27:34 suggests that Leviticus 27 "was intended as the concluding chapter from the outset." The thrust of both summaries serves to remind the nation that Leviticus (coupled with its preamble in Exodus 20–40) is the basic foundational document on which the nation was built, although, as may be seen throughout the Pentateuch, various adjustments or amendments would be made in response to circumstances. But those are issues for subsequent points of revelation and consideration of implications.

- ***Warnings Regarding Vowing Animate Objects (27:1–13)***
- ***Warnings Regarding Vowing Inanimate Objects (27:14–25)***
- ***Warnings Against Vowing Disallowed Items (27:26–33)***
- ***Conclusion (27:34)***

EXPOSITION (27:1–34)

This final chapter of Leviticus focuses on personal vows and dedications. Both are voluntary, and while different, they are related. In essence, the Hebrew vow was a promise to God, usually associated with a request. A dedication was something given to God as an act of worship. Often, the dedication was promised to God as part of the vow. Historically, the idea of vows to a deity has been widespread (Cartledge 1989, 417–21; Hankore 2013, 43–56; Kellogg 1978, 542–43), so much so that they seem somewhat instinctive to humans and even anecdotally are observed in individuals who claim to have no belief in God (note the cliché that there are no atheists in foxholes). Yet, as Wenham (1979, 337) notes, vows made in the heat of a moment may afterward seem foolish and unnecessary and are prone to be forgotten or modified. Perhaps it is for that reason that the Bible accepts but tends to discourage vows. Deuteronomy 23:22 emphasizes that to refrain from making a vow is not a sin. Ecclesiastes 5:5 reminds that it is better not to vow than to vow and not pay. But the Bible is emphatic that while vows are optional, once a vow is expressed and God fulfills the request, it is important that the requisite dedication is completed.

TRANSLATION ANALYSIS: יַפְלִא נֶדֶר

The noun נֶדֶר is derived from the verb נָדַר, which means "to make a vow" (Coppes 1980e, 557). While the noun is often used by itself, fifteen times it is the object of the verb form ("to vow a vow"). Here the noun is understood to be the object of the verb פָּלָא (Hartley 1992, 477), which

Vows and Values (27:1–34)

basically means "to do something wonderful or marvelous," or in the *hiphil* stem, as here, "to cause a wonderful thing to happen." The verb generally refers to acts of God, although when it is applied to humans, it is deemed to address an action that is "beyond one's capabilities" (Hamilton 1980f, 723). As used here, it could then be understood as a request for God to do a wonderful thing. Coupled with נֶדֶר the phrase essentially promises to express praise and gratitude to God in a specific manner when he has done the wonderful thing requested (Hankore 2013, 63). It is generally understood that the present context addresses a vow that, upon later examination, the person who made the promise finds that he or she is incapable of fulfilling.

Dedication

We use the English word "dedication" here as a collective description of whatever was promised to God as part of a vow, since a number of Hebrew words carry that connotation, several of which are used in this chapter. These words might be translated "dedicate" or something similar, but they all reflect something presented to God either as an act of worship or as an expression of gratitude following a vow. These include the following: When Aaron and his sons dedicated the gifts of the sons of Israel in Leviticus 22:2, the text uses the verb נָזַר, which means "to dedicate or consecrate" (BDB s.v. "נָזַר" 634; McComiskey 1980d, 567). When Hannah dedicated (so NASB) Samuel to God's service in 1 Samuel 1:28, she used the verb שָׁאַל, which literally means "to ask" (Cohen 1980b, 198) but in this context is understood as "lent" (so the ESV, KJV, NRSV) or "give" (so HCSB and NIV). When David dedicated gold and silver "to the Lord [YHWH]" in 2 Samuel 8:11, the text uses the verb קָדַשׁ in the *hiphil* stem, which would mean "to dedicate or consecrate" (McComiskey 1980e, 786). When Solomon dedicated the temple, the text in 1 Kings 8:63 used the verb חָנַךְ, which means "to dedicate" (Hamilton 1980b, 770). When God directed the dedication or devotion of the firstborn in Exodus 13:12, he

used the verb עָבַר (Van Groningen 1980b). Perhaps the most difficult is the verb חֵרֶם, which is understood to mean "devoted as given over to God," as seen in Numbers 18:14 where Aaron is told that every devoted thing in Israel would belong to him and his descendants as priests (Wood 1980c; see further discussion on 27:28 and in appendix 3). While often these gifts were the result of a vow, we must be aware that a person might dedicate something or someone to God as an act of worship that was not associated with a promise. Significant items that fit this description (i.e., items given for which we have no record of a promise having been made) might be the gold and silver that David had collected from his conquests, the temple that Solomon built and then dedicated to God, or the wall that Nehemiah built and then dedicated. In this chapter, the dominant term is קָדַשׁ.

Leviticus 26 emphasized the faithfulness of God, and Leviticus 27 primarily serves as a challenge to the nation that they also should be faithful. However, God recognized that it was possible that one would rashly make a vow that could not be kept. In that case, redemption was possible in some cases, although, as will be seen, it came with a cost.

Warnings Regarding Vowing Animate Objects (27:1–13)

27:1–2a. The chapter is introduced with the standard *waw* that indicates narrative sequence. As we have traced its usage through the book, a good translation is "then." In this case, many modern translations omit it, which seems to disassociate the chapter from the two preceding. Given the way the previous chapter ends, the NASB use of "again" seems appropriate.

27:2b–8. As noted before, the section begins with the phrase "if a man," which sets up a prospective situation where an individual has made a "difficult vow" in the NASB, or "special vow" in the ESV, NIV, and others (יַפְלִא נֶדֶר). A key to

Vows and Values (27:1–34)

remember here is that in terms of the vow, the assumption is that the person promised such and such (apodosis), *if* God did such and such (protasis). There is no indication throughout the OT that there were any limits to what an Israelite could promise, although later rabbis proposed some practical limitations. For example, the Mishnah discourages giving everything away (m. 'Arak. 8:4). Overall, the rabbis appear to define the practical limitation of retaining assets sufficient to fulfill one's community responsibilities, which they characterized as giving no more than one fifth of one's resources (Radner 2008, 282). While the structure of this larger unit (Lev. 25–27) might suggest that these vows could be individual responses by a person of strong faith in a situation where the nation was experiencing adverse circumstances, given the larger background of a fallen world and examples noted throughout Scripture, the concept of promising God seems to transcend a national context and thus is very applicable today.

The text here is difficult. Literally it reads, "A man if he makes a special vow according to your valuation [עֶרְכְּךָ] of a *nephesh* to the Lord," followed by a series of valuations. Several aspects need to be addressed.

The introduction is אִישׁ כִּי. The כִּי can be translated as either "when" or "if." As suggested in the translation analysis for Leviticus 1:2, here it may be understood as "when or if a person." While Leviticus 1:2 uses אָדָם, the text here uses אִישׁ (see the discussion of these two terms at Lev. 24:17–21). This seems to focus on "man as an individual" (McComiskey 1980a, 38) thus emphasizing the contrast with the corporate perspective of the two previous chapters, which is further indicated by the word order. As noted in other passages regarding vows, women are included in the concept (Milgrom 2001, 2368).

This is followed by the second aspect, the idea of the "special" (so ESV, HCSB, NIV, NLT) or "difficult" (NASB) vow (נֶדֶר יַפְלִא). This phrase indicates an unusual vow, and the question arises, is it the request or the promise that makes

this vow special or difficult? It may be that the individual is requesting supernormal divine intervention—in essence, a miracle. It may be that the individual is promising something that will be very difficult to fulfill. Based on the personal valuations that follow, the most common view among commentators is that it is the latter. Beyond that, Sklar (2014, 328) observes that "Israelites could use a vow to *dedicate* themselves or others *to the Lord* (v. 2), that is, to his service at the tabernacle (cf. 1 Sam. 1:11)" (emphasis original). This seems supported by Numbers 6:2, where the same phrase is used. In that passage, the structure suggests that the special vow may be termed a Nazirite vow.

The tie with the Nazirite vow may be supported by the last aspect, the phrase נְפָשֹׁת לַיהוָה, which may be translated as "persons belonging to the Lord [YHWH]," using the term *nephesh*. The plural used here would indicate that there was a standard valuation. As noted in the introduction, *nephesh* generally denotes the inner self. Here it seems to be a figure of speech reflecting the individual's anticipated response to the fulfillment of the vow, dedicating oneself or others to the Lord. The Numbers passage just describes a Nazirite vow as "to be separate to the Lord [YHWH]." While the term Nazirite is not used here, the ideas seem to correlate (see appendix 7, "Vows and Nazirites").

While either phrase is generally understood to involve service to God, what that means is unclear (Wenham 1979, 338). As Mathews (2009, 241) points out, "service of the Lord had its natural limitations since not all could help in the precincts of the Tent of Meeting. Only the priest and Levites could actually carry out the work of the Lord." This is one reason that many scholars suggest that in the present context the valuations seem to provide a way out for a person who realizes that he or she is unable to perform the service promised. But this still raises several questions. First, the subsequent valuations encompass every person from the age of one month and up. How might a one-month-old infant dedicate himself? Second, what type of service would a one-month-old infant perform? Third, the idea of a votive offering is given when the vow is completed. Since this includes Nazirite vows (see Num. 6:13), that indicates that vows are for a discrete period of time. How does that correlate with some OT vows that are described as lifelong vows? Further, how could a lifelong vow made by a person, even a parent, be binding on another individual (i.e., they are not self-dedications)?

The final aspect is the question of valuations. No purpose is given for the series of monetary valuations of humans based upon age and gender (see below) that immediately follow this statement. Mira Balberg (2013, 173) observes that "the dedication of a person is the only kind of dedication in this chapter which is *initially* described as a vow of 'value' (*neder be-'erkekha*), whereas regarding all other objects, the priest is said to assess their value *after* the person consecrates the object itself" (emphasis original). As such, she concludes that the issue is not substitution, but that the dedication was "meant as a gift of money to begin with—even though the money here stands, of course, as the monetary equivalent of a person" (p. 174).

That does not address the most significant case of a human dedication of a person as a result of a vow, that of Samuel. There, Hannah actually dedicated Samuel at the tabernacle in accordance with her vow (1 Sam. 1:26–29). It is possible that this was a specific exception to a rule because Samuel's family was from the tribe of Levi, and thus he was able to serve in the tabernacle. Or it may be that the intention of a gift of money was intended as an alternative, although that is not expressly stated.

In the subsequent sections of Leviticus 27, we will see that the remaining items promised did have actual values, which could be appraised by the priest. In the case of seeking release, that value would need to be provided with a 20 percent penalty. As we will see, there were also other criteria that applied to the various situations. The problem here is the assigning of monetary worth to humans.

How does one measure the worth of a person? A common assumption is that it measures "their capacity to do manual labor" and thus is tied to the slave market (Kleinig 2003, 591; Mathews 2009, 241; Noordtzij 1982, 273; Ross 2002, 492; Wenham 1979, 338). Similarly, Gane (2004a, 468) proposes that "this system of relative work has to do with the benefit that the sanctuary will receive if the vowed person belongs to it as a servant." But these also raise questions. Given that the valuations span from the age of one month to the end of life after more than sixty years, how would this valuation apply to work within both short-term and lifelong vows? What does this say about gender? What is actually being measured? Here one must ask again, what is the value of the labor of an infant?

	Valuation in Shekels	
Age	Male	Female
1 month to 5 years	5	3
5–20 years	20	10
20–60 years	50	30
Over 60	15	10

Chart 11. Valuation of persons in shekels.

In this regard, Balberg (2013, 178) argues that for the rabbis, these numbers "have nothing to do with the *actual* worth of the person; they only serve as a monetary expression of the very quality of being human" (emphasis original). As such, she concludes that "If one dedicates a fixed sum, one dedicates *a* person, but not *this* person" (p. 180). This still raises questions in terms of how the higher valuation represents a person in his or her prime of life as opposed to smaller valuations at either end of life. This may represent the ability to pay the valuation,

Vows and Values (27:1–34)

with smaller values for a younger parent who dedicates a child or an older adult who no longer works. In that sense, Philo (*Spec. Laws* 2.32–34) argued that these values are significant because of their equality in the sense that in any category, all persons have the same valuation, not varied by physical ability or appearances. But that still gives us problems in terms of differences, since the numbers seem arbitrary. Perhaps the best analysis of the issue is Kiuchi's (2007, 496) observation that the "prices are sanctuary prices made by God and unchangeable in relation to time and situation. As in other parts of Leviticus, it seems that, as far as human life on earth is concerned, more is expected of a man, as the head of a family, than of a woman, though the human souls are priceless regardless of gender." In any event, the value is arbitrarily set by God.

27:9–13. Expanding the premise that the entire chapter is related to promises made but for which there are second thoughts, the next category addresses animals that have been dedicated as a result of a vow. Two kinds of animals are noted. First, there are those that can be offered as sacrifices—the various animals covered in Leviticus 1 and 11. It would seem that in this case, the individual might promise to sacrifice a specific animal out of his or her herd or flock. Once it has been promised, substitutions cannot be made. It could be expected that upon second thought an Israelite might consider substituting an animal that was not quite as valuable for what he or she had originally promised. However, the Israelites were also not allowed to substitute a more valuable animal for what they had promised. Should the Israelite attempt a swap, both animals are then forfeit, that is, "become holy" (יִהְיֶה־קֹּדֶשׁ).

At the same time, Israelites were permitted to promise unclean animals. These were actually animals that the Israelites were not allowed to eat, which raises a very interesting situation. As delineated in Leviticus 11, this would include

donkeys, horses, and camels. While not allowed for food, all three were valuable work animals. It is interesting that handling them as work animals did not seem to have made the Israelites unclean. Not only that, but Israelites could bring the animal as an offering before the priest, and it could be used in work by the priests.

In the case of an unclean animal, the creature must be brought before the priest, who then valued it. As in the case of a person, the value was likely arbitrary, but unlike the case of a person the determination was made by the priest. While the animal could be used by the priests for work or sold by the priests, apparently at this point the Israelite bringing the animal had an option of continuing with the dedication or redeeming the animal. If redemption was chosen, the Israelite would pay the value but add the requisite 20 percent penalty.

Warnings Regarding Vowing Inanimate Objects (27:14–25)

27:14–15. This section marks with an "if" (כִּי) a transition from living dedications to nonliving, specifically houses and land. As described in Leviticus 25, there are several subcategories of each, addressing some properties that were permissible to be dedicated and some that were not. The first item is a house. According to Leviticus 25:29–31, two different rules of ownership applied to houses. Houses in rural villages reverted to an original owner at Jubilee, the same as the family heritage (אֲחֻזָּה), the land of the original heritage, while houses in a city could be permanently transferred. Since there is no distinction made here regarding location, Milgrom (2001, 2381) suggests that any house that had been dedicated (i.e., given to the use of the priests) would revert at the next Jubilee.

> *TRANSLATION ANALYSIS: "FAMILY HERITAGE"*
> The Hebrew word may also be spelled אֲחֻזָּה (Wolf 1980a). It basically means "possession," but here it would seem to refer specifically to the

Vows and Values (27:1–34)

extended family's portion of God's land gift. Leviticus anticipates the time after conquest when the Israelites would be settled in the land that had been promised to Abraham. After the initial distribution of land, Joshua 24:13 describes the nation as living on land that they had not labored for, in cities that they had not built, eating from vineyards and olive groves that they had not planted, and denotes it as an inheritance. As noted elsewhere (Harbin 2011, 689–91), this distribution was a one-time gift to the original settlers of the land following the exodus and wilderness wandering, which was to be passed on to future generations. The land promised to Abraham was much larger than the area conquered and settled in Joshua (Num. 34:1–12). Joshua's initial distribution provided for future growth to expand Israel to fulfill the entire promise (Deut. 19:8–9), a growth that never occurred because of continued disobedience. The land promised that was to be added later was not part of the original distribution by lots that is described in Joshua. Perhaps the land that Reuben, Gad, and half of Manasseh possessed could be considered part of that later distribution, since it lay outside of the land described in Numbers 34, but we have no record of how that land was divided.

Prior to Jubilee, the person who dedicated the house had the option of redeeming (גָּאַל) the house, which is understood to mean that the person who dedicated the house must pay to the sanctuary/priests the valuation that had been set on the house at the time of dedication along with the 20 percent penalty (Noordtzij 1982, 274). Gane (2004a, 465) observes that while redemption is not deemed a sin, nor is a sacrifice required, the penalty is the same as that for sacrilege (Lev. 5:16).

27:16. Farmland represented a different situation. As shown in our discussion of Leviticus 25, when Israel, which was receiving these directives at Sinai, came into the land and took

over, each family would receive farmland. Each farm would consist of several pieces of property dispersed around the village in which the family dwelt (Harbin 2021a, 476–85). This combined property and the house in which the family lived would be termed its אֲחֻזָּה or possession. Perhaps a better term would be "heritage property." As noted earlier, they were forbidden to sell that heritage property, but were permitted to "lease" (מָכַר, often translated as "sell"; see discussion on Lev. 25:23) parts of it with a termination of the lease in the next Jubilee. The material at hand indicates that a farmer could dedicate a piece of that heritage property to God, but as in the case of a lease the heritage property would revert to the farmer in the Jubilee. This likely meant that the harvests during the time of the dedication would go to the sanctuary, although it is not clear who would do the actual farming. Given our understanding that the family heritage property could not be sold, Wenham (1989, 340) suggests that the owner would continue to farm the land (the presumption is that the priest would not have the time nor resources to do the labor), but that the crop, or its monetary equivalent, would go to the sanctuary or the priests once it was harvested.

27:17–19. As in the case of a house that had been dedicated, the farm property could be redeemed (גָּאַל). Two types of farm property might be dedicated. The family heritage property, which God gave to the first settlers, is presented in these verses as the first case. As opposed to a house, which was valued by the priest, the land was valued by its size. Regardless of how productive or barren it was, the value was proportionate to a standard of fifty shekels for a field that required one homer of barley to sow it. In appendix 6, "Land Measurement and Crop Value," we estimate this area to be approximately an acre. Thus, if the field required only a half homer to sow it, its valuation was twenty-five shekels.

Vows and Values (27:1–34)

Appendix 6 determines a working average harvest of barley to be twenty-five homers per acre (the property that required one homer to sow). While historically commodity prices have been notoriously volatile, we used a working figure of fifteen shekels per homer based on the anecdotal evidence of 2 Kings 7:1. This suggested that the product of a typical field crop of barley might be worth approximately 375 shekels per acre. Of course, that is a theoretical value, since most of the farmers grew food for their own larders and it was unlikely any money would change hands on a routine basis. Still, should the Israelite dedicate this crop to God through the hands of the priests, it clearly would have significant economic implications on the farmer. Consequently, it would not be surprising if the individual had second thoughts when it came time to fulfill the vow. A typical case might be a vow made at the time of sowing, but then subsequent weather conditions resulted in a smaller than anticipated harvest.

Economic Implications

Based on Exodus 16:16 and 36, Milgrom (2001, 2096) proposes that a standard Israelite diet needed one tenth of an ephah of flour per day (an ephah equates to twenty-two liters; www.unit-converters.net); thus, an ephah would provide ten days of bread. According to Ezekiel 45:11, a homer is ten ephahs, which would mean that a homer would provide bread to feed one adult Israelite for one hundred days. Ignoring for the purposes of this calculation the differences between wheat and barley flour, this would suggest that a one-acre field with a yield of twenty-five homers could be expected to provide bread for a year for an Israelite family of six to seven adults. Since a farmer would have several plots of land around the village (Harbin 2021a, 476–85), as well as some livestock and also gardening space closer in, it would appear that the average Israelite could expect to be living above bare subsistence, but not substantially so.

The valuation of fifty shekels per acre then was, as in the case of a person, an arbitrary value assigned by God. Since this section addresses the family heritage property that could not be sold, the dedication was only valid to the next Jubilee. Leviticus 26:17–18 clarifies that if the land was dedicated or consecrated at the Year of Jubilee, the redemption price for an acre-sized plot was the full fifty shekels plus the 20 percent penalty. However, any time after that the redemption price would be prorated based on the number of years remaining to the next Jubilee. This would then work out to approximately a shekel a year for the time it was being redeemed. While this seems a rather low valuation, it should be noted that these crops were what the Israelites lived on, not what they sold. The point really is that while God would allow a person who made a vow that he was unable (or unwilling) to fulfill, there was still a cost, although apparently not an exorbitant one.

27:20–21. While there was a loophole for one who dedicated a portion of his family heritage property, there was another possible issue: if he "has sold the field to another man," although it is not clear what this phrase means in this context. While a complicated situation, the most likely explanation is that prior to dedicating the field the farmer sold (actually leased) the heritage property to someone else. As such, he was treating the land he had dedicated to God as his own (Gane, 2004a, 466; see Keil and Delitzsch 1956, 643–44, for a possible explanation of how this might work). The consequence of this act would be that when Jubilee came, the field would be forfeited to the sanctuary, that is, it would be treated as חֵרֶם (see appendix 3). In other words, it would be permanently and irrevocably dedicated to God, and would become heritage property to the priest.

27:22–24. The final category of land is farmland, which was not part of the heritage property, thus was "saleable" (Kiuchi 2007, 500). This

Vows and Values (27:1–34)

would seem to be land that lay within the territory of Israel described in Deuteronomy 19, but had not been distributed during the initial settlement. One way this might have happened might be that a farmer had managed to clear land not previously tilled, such as in Joshua 17:16. Another possibility might be later generations taking land from non-Israelites, similar to situations noted in Judges 18:27–29. Or it might refer to land that lay outside of the boundaries described in Deuteronomy 19 that was conquered later (such as described in 2 Sam. 8). In any case, the individual could dedicate this property to God. Another possibility is that it might be land that one had bought (or, more properly, leased) from another farmer's heritage property. In this case, all this farmer would own would be the crop that he harvested. However, one could even dedicate this, although the valuation would differ. Regardless, the value would be calculated by the priest, likely based on the anticipated production of the land rather than the fixed valuation of the heritage property, which had been set by God.

Another question for property in this category was whether the valuation was paid on the day the land was dedicated or on the Day of Atonement. Kleinig (2003, 587) argues for the Day of Atonement since that was the base day for the valuation. The text seems to read that the payment must be made on the day the assessment was made, which appears to be the view of most commentators. For example, Keil and Delitzsch (1956, 644) assert it must be "immediately, and all at once."

27:25. This verse seems rather awkward to modern readers, who are used to very rigid standards. However, prior to modern times, weights were more variable, as has been demonstrated through archaeology. As Huey puts it, "Hebrew standards of weight were not exact; variety exists even in weights with the same inscr[iption]" (1975, 918). This would have been an early attempt to impose standards in keeping with the

earlier admonition in Leviticus 19:35–36 (see also Deut. 25:13).

Warnings Against Vowing Disallowed Items (27:26–33)

The final portion of this chapter warns against the presumption of vowing things to God that God already owned. While in reality God owned everything, he most generously gave to the Israelites the land and its provisions to steward or manage. As stewards, while they did not have ownership, they had essentially full discretion regarding the use of what they had possession of, including the right (or responsibility) to give to others, and to dedicate things to God as an act of worship or thanksgiving. However, they could not dedicate things that had already been dedicated.

27:26–27. The first already dedicated category is that of the firstborn. Because the Israelite firstborn had been spared when God passed through Egypt during the tenth plague, every firstborn belonged to him. Consequently, they could not be dedicated in a vow. Animals of the flock (שֶׂה, sheep or goats) or oxen would be sacrificed. However, unclean animals were to be valuated and then either redeemed (with the penalty) or sold. Since there are some differences here with the details of Exodus 13:13 and 34:20, it is uncertain as to whether this passage replaces Exodus, or supplements it (Sklar 2014, 331). Since Exodus only addresses a donkey, it would seem that this is a supplement.

27:28–29. The second category addressed here is that of something that was *herem*. As discussed in appendix 3, *herem* is a more intense form of dedication or consecration than קָדַשׁ ("to sanctify or consecrate") that is used throughout this chapter. While this passage suggests that an individual could *herem* something from his own possessions, as used in the OT it tends to be a dedication by the community, normally at the direction of God. In any case, something or

414

Vows and Values (27:1–34)

someone who is *herem* is already dedicated or devoted to God and cannot be rededicated. In the case of an individual, this means that he or she may not be ransomed (פָּדָה) but must be put to death.

27:30–33. The final category that may not be dedicated to God is the tithe, since that was God's portion. By definition a tithe is 10 percent, and Deuteronomy 14:22 tells the Israelites that they were to tithe "all the produce from what they sow[ed], which [came] out of the field year by year." The Deuteronomy passage continues on to describe how they were to handle the tithe and adds some very interesting concepts regarding the use of portions of the tithe for Levites, widows, orphans, and resident aliens (Harbin 2021b, 695–700). While there are no directions to tithe the increase of the flocks, the Deuteronomy passage includes the firstborn of the herd and flock with the tithe, indicating that the two went together to teach the Israelites to love God (Deut. 14:23).

Conclusion (27:34)

27:34. The chapter ends with the summary statement emphasizing that the material that had been covered was given by Moses at Sinai. Kiuchi (2007, 503) observes that the only term used here is "commandment" (מִצְוֹת), which he argues is a "most comprehensive" term including the חֻקִּים (*rules*) and מִשְׁפָּטִים (*statutes*) listed at the end of Leviticus 26.

Following the conclusion of Leviticus, Numbers starts with a *waw*, noting that God then spoke to Moses, again in the tent of meeting, on the first of the second month of the second year following their leaving Egypt. Thus, Numbers really begins as a continuation of the revelation recorded in Leviticus. With that as a completion date, and Exodus 40:17 as a starting date, it would appear that the material in Leviticus was given during that one-month period following the erection of the tabernacle. Numbers begins with a census, which organized the twelve tribes for travel. Thus, it would seem that Leviticus provides the legal or governmental framework for the nation so that it was now primed to leave Sinai and head for the land that had been promised.

THEOLOGICAL FOCUS

The focus of the chapter is on vows or promises to God, usually as an addendum to a request. God is not one who can be bribed or manipulated, and as a result, vows are discouraged throughout the OT. As such, a person needs to be careful to avoid "foolish vows" (Ross 2002, 487). The premise behind the chapter is that if one makes a vow, one needs to be careful to fulfill it. Failure to do so reflects not only a lack of integrity, but Ecclesiastes 5:4–6 describes a person who fails to fulfill his or her vow as a fool and suggests that the failure angers God and can lead him to "destroy the work of your hands." One of the underlying premises of the two preceding chapters is an emphasis on God's faithfulness, which makes the emphasis of this chapter a powerful challenge to pursue personal integrity before God. Given all of this, the chapter serves to emphasize human faithfulness in his or her relationships with God.

A vow made is a vow taken seriously. Rescinding a vow, even a careless one, comes at a cost. There are different reasons one may make a vow that they later want to withdraw. One may simply be foolishness. People could fail to understand the impact of what they were saying. Also, a time of either great distress or euphoria can lead one to make a vow that may later be considered extreme when they return to a more sober state of mind. Finally, while one may be quick to give up one's right to possessions in time of fear and distress, the desire to retain those possessions may return in seasons of blessing. God is aware that many coming events would tempt his people to inappropriately put faith in a personal vow in the belief that they could force God's hand to bless them privately.

Neither personal nor corporate vows are ever to be used to gain prosperity.

PREACHING AND TEACHING STRATEGIES

Exegetical and Theological Synthesis
Vows to God often uncover the condition of the human heart. My mind can work something like this: I desire something to happen. It is out of my control. It is under God's control. I can make it happen by pressing God into action by adding a conditional vow to my prayer. By so doing, I have made my action rather than God's will the focal point of my prayer.

Why are such vows discouraged (not forbidden) across the OT? Vows, whether personal or corporate, are not to be a means to gain prosperity or force God's hand. Using them as such can lead us to believe we are sovereign over ourselves, even our world!

While vows, promises, and oaths are not strictly forbidden, their use is carefully constrained because people use them to manipulate others. In Matthew 5:33–37, Jesus forbids oaths that allowed for Jews to deceive Gentiles for commercial advantage. One could swear, but it was not binding unless they "swore by heaven." Jews would know this. Gentiles would not. It is like the child saying, "I had my fingers crossed so I don't have to keep my word." In Matthew 15:4–9, Jesus calls out the scribes and Pharisees for using personal vows to circumvent the commandments of God. In addition, rash vows to gain God's favor are clearly discouraged (Eccl. 5:3–5) because fulfilling them can be tragic (Judg. 11:30–31).

Yet, vows are not completely forbidden. Solemn vows remain a sign of devotion to the Lord if they are faithfully and sacrificially kept before God (Lev. 22:18–20; Pss. 56:11–13; 66:13–15). Believers in the early church in Jerusalem were using vows (Acts 21:23). Paul places the Thessalonian church under oath to read his letter to all the believers (1 Thess. 5:27). Marriage vows are frequently spoken of honorably. When our belief weakens or our desires wane, God's truth can still be shown to rule in our lives as we deny our will to fulfill a proper vow.

Preaching Idea
My vow declares my devotion to God only if it is first carefully made and then faithfully kept.

Contemporary Connections

What does it mean?
What does it mean that a vow declares devotion to God only if it is first carefully made and then faithfully kept? First, it means we have to carefully consider our words. Flippant vows or promises made in times of crisis or to make others love us may cause pain. Think of a promise you made that you know you can never keep. One may say to a child, "I will never let anyone hurt you" or "I will always be here to protect you." Is that true? Why would a parent say that? It is a careless vow that invites confusion, pain, and eventually unbelief. We are not God, nor are we free to speak for God. We must consider if a promise is made to advance our personal agenda or another's faith in us, or whether it is made out of our love for God and neighbor.

Second, it means that we are expected to keep the promises we make, even when unforeseen circumstances arise. Marriage vows are again a great example of promises that many believe they can annul, as life makes them less advantageous to our self-interests. Also, we may promise monetary gifts (stocks or bonds that mature) or make commitments to volunteer or sacrificially invest our time in certain relationships or organizations that may later feel unduly burdensome to fulfill. What is happening? Why are we having all of these second thoughts? As the impact of our vow is understood, our desire for our possessions or time may come into direct competition with our desire to serve God and our neighbor.

Vows and Values (27:1–34)

Is it true?

Is it true that my vow declares my devotion to God only if it is first carefully made and then faithfully kept? A vow that is not carefully made is often a vow that is made to force God into action or manipulate another person. I (Biehl) have made it a practice to present all couples with their marriage vows in writing long before their wedding so that they can carefully pray over them, even edit them if necessary, so they can be fully aware of what they are proclaiming before "God and these witnesses." This idea has broad implications for the church. Review your dedications, baptisms, membership classes, pledge practices, and the rest. Where might we be inviting our people to make careless vows that they are unwilling to bear?

Are promises pronounced in times of suffering or under emotional impulse always wrong? Does this idea effectively invalidate foxhole conversions and summer camp commitments to Christ? Certainly not! Yet it may help us recall that it is not the strength of our words, but the careful and quiet coming before the Lord to deny our will that exposes the depth of our devotion.

Now what?

Is it time to outlaw vows and prohibit oaths? No. It may be time to allow the Lord God to displace us as the primary purpose behind a vow. Vows are not to make us feel better about ourselves nor free us to believe we can press God into service on our behalf. Vows should humble us as we recognize and confess our total dependence on our creator. He may even use our rash words to reveal to us weaknesses in us that he already sees. Barbara Duguid (2013, 106) states the following in her book *Extravagant Grace*:

> Sometimes he [the Spirit of God] grants us fresh grace and power for obedience to show you what he can do in you, and sometimes he turns you over to yourself to discover

how weak, helpless, and sinful you still are in yourself. Either way, he is always actively at work in you for God's glory and your own good, and that of his body the church.

God is at work in us to humble us through the vows we make to him that he may replace our confidence in ourselves and our own will with a life-giving eternal confidence in him.

Creativity in Presentation

You could open by sharing a funny example of a rash vow that you blurted out when you were afraid, but later determined you had justifiable cause to recant. Or invite everyone to remember a vow they made in their youth that they failed to keep. It may be engaging to ask a more solemn question, "Do you recall a vow someone made to you but broke later on? Why would they make a vow, only to break it later?"

Many would enjoy the clip from *Lord of the Rings: Return of the King* when Pippin gets carried away in his emotions and makes a rash vow to Denethor despite being told repeatedly not to do so by Gandalf. Ask what led Pippin to blurt out such a foolish, restrictive promise.

For the older and/or "rerun" crowd, you can tell the story from the *Little House on the Prairie* episode called "The Award" (season 1, episode 12). Ma Ingalls makes a rash declaration preventing her daughter Mary from entering a writing contest. Mary enters anyway. The story is centered on the question of if and when one should renege on their hastily made statements.

You could also tell the familiar story of Martin Luther making the rash vow during a severe thunderstorm that he would become a monk if God would rescue him from the lightning. Luther lived and became a monk, which changed the course of Christianity. Does God then honor such hasty promises?

It would be valuable to incorporate specific examples of carefully made vows that were kept to God's glory. Consider the story of Benjamin Warfield. In 1876, he married Annie Pearce

Vows and Values (27:1–34)

Kinkead and left for Leipzig, Germany. On a walk, they were overtaken by a violent thunderstorm. Annie never fully recovered from the experience and progressively became an invalid. Warfield never left her side for more than two hours for the next thirty-nine years. Did his sacrificial faithfulness to his carefully made marriage vows before God and others reveal his devotion? Did God honor his faithfulness?

My vow declares my devotion to God only if it is first carefully made and then faithfully kept.

- Vows: Are they good or bad?
  - Vows that manipulate or deceive
  - Vows made rashly
- Vows to the Lord God
  - An offer of service to God
  - An offer of personal property: animal, house, land
  - An offer of what is already due to God: firstborn, tithe
- What did it mean to them then? What does it mean always? What do we do now?
  - What is the Lord's is the Lord's.
  - Be slow to offer and quick to keep a vow.

DISCUSSION QUESTIONS

1. What makes a vow a proper vow? Are there proper vows you have made that you are currently honoring?

2. Have you ever made a rash vow? Did you honor it if or when your desires began to change?

3. How can a rash vow inflict pain on others? How can you take a step to mitigate that pain?

4. When have you needed to call upon God's grace and strength to keep a proper vow?

5. (How) do vows before God help us discipline our will?

6. How can we help one another to honor our vows and thus image God's faithfulness?

APPENDIXES

APPENDIX 1: MOLECH

In Leviticus 18, the figure of Molech (מֹלֶךְ) appears in a significant sense. This figure is problematic and debated for several reasons. Given the context of an extended list of forbidden sexual relationships, an immediate question is, why is this verse located in this location? However, there are several questions that must be addressed. The two questions first address the identification of Molech, followed by the meaning of the expression "to offer [your offspring] to Molech" (לֹא־תִתֵּן לְהַעֲבִיר לַמֹּלֶךְ), which says, "you will not give to pass over to Molech."

The initial question is that of identification. Waltke (1975, 269) maintains that the term is used in the OT as a "divine name." Milgrom (2000, 1555–58) generally agrees with that, although he also sees the term being used as a title, since it generally appears with a definite article. In terms of origin, he lists seven different options that have been proposed, dismisses four, and then suggests that the remaining three are each partially correct. First, in terms of etymology the consonantal root of Molech (מלך) is the same as the Hebrew word for "king" (מלך), so the argument is that there was a kingly aspect associated with the role that Molech possessed, or that he was given royal honorifics. Second, he suggests a connection with a deity *mlk* or Malik who appears in names or other writings throughout the ANE (even as recently as the Qur'an [Sura 43:77]). There is also some association of this deity with a fire ritual. While references to this god appear widespread, the origin is disputed. Milgrom argues for a Mesopotamian source of a chthonic god (a god of the underworld) with the name Malik. Evidence for this god appears in the texts of Ugarit, Mari, and Ebla (Bermant and Weitzman 1979, 165–166; Olmo Lete 2004, 78–81; Waltke 1975, 269), but little is known about them. Finally, the traditional rabbinic view argued that whether the original term was *melek* or Malik, when the text was pointed, the vowels were changed to those of *bōshet*, the word for "shame" (like the term Ishbaal [1 Chron. 8:34] was changed to Ishbosheth [2 Sam. 2:10]). However, how the early rabbis euphemistically read the consonantal text aloud is not known. While there is evidence that the Canaanites did have a god called *mlk*, or Malik, who appears to be the figure that the Bible presents as Molech, we do not have much information regarding how he was worshipped or how popular he was in the Canaanite pantheon.

Since the 1920s, a number of tophets have been excavated in various Canaanite-Phoenician cities, most notably in Carthage, which began as a colony of Tyre-Sidon.

> *TRANSLATION ANALYSIS: "TOPHET"*
> The term "tophet" or "Topheth" originally referred to a location in "the valley of the son of Hinnom" outside of Jerusalem. Although not used in the Leviticus passage, it is described in Jeremiah 7:31 as a location the Judeans built "to burn their sons and their daughters in the fire." Jeremiah condemns the people of Judah for this and reports that God never intended for such a location or practice. Because the valley of Ben Hinnom later became identified as Gehenna, "Tophet" is used as a common noun as another name for hell. It is also used to identify a "place for child sacrifice" (Albright 1968, 237).

These cemeteries contain hundreds or thousands of urns (approximately twenty thousand in Carthage alone) that interred cremated infant remains. Many consider this to be significant archeological evidence that later Canaanites did practice child sacrifice, especially during

Appendix 1: Molech

the period of 900–700 B.C. although this conclusion is debated (DiBenedetto 2012, 7–32). However, because of a paucity of written texts, it is not clear what rituals were followed, or how much earlier this practice developed. The only Canaanite material we have from an earlier period is from Ugarit, a northern Canaanite city, which gives no indication of the practice. Gregorio del Olmo Lete (2004, 40) observes that archaeologically, the "'cemeteries' outside the city" as seen in Tyre, Carthage, and other Phoenician sites were a shift from family tombs in Ugarit, which was destroyed about 1200 B.C. This could allow for a much earlier practice without the communal evidence of an infant graveyard. In terms of Israel at Sinai, the practices of the southern Canaanites (the land Israel was preparing to invade) are an open question, even if the Canaanites in Ugarit did not generally practice infant sacrifice.

Given the lack of evidence, it is difficult to ascertain what specific practices were in place in southern Canaan at the time that Israel was at Sinai. Kleinig (2003, 433) seems to suggest that it was a given that Molech "required child sacrifice as the price for the fertility of a family and the prosperity of its land." However, that seems to derive primarily from his understanding that Leviticus specifically presents Molech worship as requiring child sacrifice. That is another factor with which scholars struggle, since the way Leviticus describes the issue is not that clear. As stated earlier, the text reads לֹא תִתֵּן לְהַעֲבִיר לַמֹּלֶךְ, which literally says, "you will not give to pass over to Molech." Because fire or burning is not mentioned here, a number of scholars suggest that what is being addressed is a practice of transferring or dedicating; that is, it involves giving the child to the Molech cult (the case of the young Samuel comes to mind as an illustration [1 Sam. 1:11]) for a variety of purposes, possibly including religious prostitution. They base this conclusion on the Hebrew verb "pass over" (עָבַר) as used in passages such as Numbers 27:7–8 (Noordtzij 1982, 187).

TRANSLATION ANALYSIS: "OFFER"

The term translated "offer" in Leviticus 18:21 is הַעֲבִיר, a *hiphil* infinitive construct of the verb עָבַר, which means "to pass over, by, through," among others. In Numbers 27:7–8, it is used twice to address the transfer on the inheritance of daughters of Zelophehad who had no sons, so his inheritance then was allowed to "pass over" or transfer to his daughters.

While it is not clear that עָבַר as used in Leviticus 18 specifically implies immolation, עָבַר is the term used in Deuteronomy 18:10 where the Israelites were told that they were not to make a son or daughter "pass through the fire." The issue is that Leviticus does not specify "to pass through fire." Given that other passages show that at this time the Canaanite occupants of the land did burn children in fire to their gods (Deut. 12:28–31), and that later kings were condemned because they made a son pass through the fire (e.g., Ahaz in 2 Kings 16:3), it seems the inference that this verse is addressing offering a child as a burnt offering is valid.

One last item that might be addressed in this summary is the action of King Josiah, a contemporary of Jeremiah, in 2 Kings 23:10. The text states that he defiled the Topheth so "that no man might make his son or his daughter pass through the fire for Molech." Here, we see the worship of Molech specifically identified with the practice of "passing" a child through the fire, which is generally understood to denote sacrifice.

Thus, it would appear that by the time God had delivered the Israelites from Egypt, the Canaanites had adopted the worship of Molech (as *mlk*), incorporating him into their pantheon. As such, it may be suggested that the adoption of this practice might be the completion of the "iniquity of the Amorite" that God mentioned in Genesis 15:16 as a prior condition for their removal from the land so that Abraham's descendants would be allowed to enter. If so, then Jeremiah's condemnation of the Topheth on the eve of Israel's exile probably was not coincidental.

APPENDIX 2: GLEANING—A CASE STUDY IN RUTH

Leviticus 19 introduces the concept of gleaning, which is an agricultural process where someone other than the farmer who sowed and harvested goes back through a field or orchard following the harvest to find produce that the harvesters had missed. To our largely nonagricultural western culture, this is a rather unknown process that carries significant weight in the Torah with respect to social justice issues.

While the produce gleaned would be just a fraction of that harvested, it could be a sizable amount. The only illustration we have of OT gleaning is Ruth in the grain fields, which is the image that comes to mind, but the OT gives guidelines not just for grain but for all other crops, mentioning vineyards (Lev. 19:10) and olive trees (Deut. 24:20).

An Ephah of Barley
When Ruth gleaned in Boaz's field, she finished the first day with an ephah of threshed barley, approximately two-thirds of a bushel (Ruth 2:17). As developed in the unit "Vows and Values" (27:1–34), at the estimated minimum daily requirement of approximately two liters of grain per day, this amount of grain would provide approximately ten days of bread for an adult Israelite. Another estimate is that this would have provided enough grain to last the two women several weeks, but that is based on a daily diet of a half of a liter of grain per day per person (Roop 2002, 51). Naomi seemed surprised at the quantity that Ruth brought home in one day, suggesting it was an unusual amount. In any case, this was one day's work, and the community harvest of each grain would take multiple days. While we do not know what a typical daily amount might have been, it is likely that her labor on subsequent days may have been somewhat smaller. The text notes that she then continued following the harvesters

through the entire barley and wheat harvests (Ruth 2:23). According to the Gezer Calendar, both the barley and wheat harvests lasted about a month (our April and May), which would suggest a total harvest period of perhaps six to eight weeks. Subsequent gleaning of other crops such as grapes and summer fruit could have augmented the yield. If she gleaned regularly over that period, a significant harvest for her and Naomi might be feasible. Modern reports of gleaning (including the writer's [Harbin] personal experience as part of charity operations) support this perception.

There seem to be two underlying principles governing the practice. The first is that the farmer was to work toward and anticipate intentional margin in terms of production to allow for gleaners. While difficult to implement in a subsistence culture, the basic premise was that if the people demonstrated trust in God, he would provide a surplus, which they were then expected to share. This may be indicated by the situation of Boaz, who apparently remained in the village and prospered, while Elimelech left because of the famine.

Microenvironments
One of the more interesting observations that Antoun (1972, 8) makes is that farmers within the same village might experience differential crop yields because of "micro-ecological differences in landscape and soil." Thus, it is possible that two farmers in the same village might have different experiences of agricultural success in the same season. This might also be a product of different degrees of blessing from God. In this light, one might note that while Boaz stayed in the land (an indication of trust), Elimelech fled to Moab (which might be an indication of lack of trust in God).

Appendix 2: Gleaning—A Case Study in Ruth

While agricultural gleaning is far removed from most people in the modern United States, the idea of developing intentional margin to provide for one's personal future and to share with others would be something that most could work toward. The second principle seems to be that the property owner simply provided an opportunity, and the gleaner was then required to work for the produce. A caveat of this practice is that the gleaners would have access to fields or orchards they did not own (i.e., they were able to use someone else's infrastructure).

Guidelines in Leviticus 19:9–10; 23:22; and Deuteronomy 24:19–22 give the greatest possible opportunity for would-be gleaners while safeguarding Israelite landowners. Succinctly, they are as follows.

1. When landowners harvested grain, they were not to reap to the corners. The grain left standing was intended for the gleaners, who are identified either as the needy and the resident aliens, or the widow, orphan, and resident aliens. While the KJV and NASB translate the Hebrew term פֵּאָה as "corner," the term would be better understood as "edge," which many modern translations use (Milgrom 2000, 1624). The text does not indicate how much of a field was to be left unharvested, but the Mishnah indicates that one-sixtieth of the harvest was considered the minimum, although it also suggests that provision depended on factors such as the size of the field, the number of the poor, and how generous the farmer was (m. Pe'ah 1:2).

2. If a harvester dropped a sheaf, he or she was to leave it behind. In this case, the produce would already have been harvested and bound together. The harvester likely would be carrying it to where it would be gathered for threshing or subsequent storage when the loss occurred. In that case, the sheaf was to be left on the ground.

3. Beyond grain fields, other crops were gleaned. Leviticus mentions vineyards. Deuteronomy notes olive groves. In the case of vineyards, the admonition was that any bunches of grapes that were missed or perhaps not yet ripe were to be left. In the case of olives, the harvesters would use sticks to knock the ripe olives off; they were not to shake the boughs (פְּאֵר) to get those they had missed (Keil and Delitzsch 1956, 600).

4. Given the scope of produce mentioned, it seems clear that the gleaning directive covered the entire harvest. Here the gleaner would have the same food preservation issues as the farmer.

"Reaping to the Corners"

When reading this phrase, we tend to think in terms of fenced fields, with these being where two sides came together. While portions of Israel enclosed their field portions (fig. 70), other portions seemed to have unfenced fields similar to what is seen in many areas of the Middle East today (fig. 71).

We suggest that for those fields the harvesters would likely leave a fringe of standing grain that would separate the portions of the fields owned by various farmers. A practical feature in this situation would be that during the harvest, it might lessen disagreement on where each farmer's portion ended if they didn't try to get all the way to the edge. Another practical feature would be a matter of safety. If the field were surrounded by a stone fence, a reaper swinging a sickle or scythe could work him- or herself into a corner and risk damaging the implement.

Appendix 2: Gleaning—A Case Study in Ruth

Figure 70. Fields near Bethlehem.

Figure 71. Fields in Ephraim.

Home

In terms of background, one should recall that Naomi and Ruth had a home "in the city" (Ruth 2:18), presumably, what we call "the town" of Bethlehem (Ruth 1:1). Based on the family inheritance laws, this home would not have a mortgage and there would be no utility expenses. As such, living expenses for a widow who remained in her husband's home would have been relatively minimal. A second example of a widow in a home, although outside of the actual Israelite culture, would be the case of the widow in 2 Kings 4. In this case, she did have debt and two children who were about to be taken by creditors, but she also had a house, although apparently no land. There Elisha performed a miracle that provided oil she could sell and dissolve the debt.

The produce the harvesters left behind provided an opportunity for the needy (see Lev. 19:10) to gather the residue for their own use. It is significant that the gleaning process provided an opportunity for a gleaner to gather food from land that she or he did not own, and for which she or he had not participated in the sowing and tending of the crops; but she or he was required to put in the labor to gather this produce, as well as to thresh it, and then take it home to process. Given the scope of the crops listed, it would seem then, based on the example of Ruth, that a gleaner would be able to follow the harvest, which began with the barley harvest (April–May) on into the fall with the grape and olive harvests (October–November).

APPENDIX 3: *ḤEREM*

While the concept of *ḥerem* (חֵרֶם) is difficult for several reasons, perhaps the key issue today is how the OT accounts tie it to the conquest of Canaan (primarily in Deuteronomy and Joshua). In that material, the term describes how Israel was to interact with the various Canaanite tribes they encountered in the land God had promised Israel—specifically, that they were required to *ḥerem* certain sites, which in many cases involved killing off the population and in some cases burning the city.

TRANSLATION ANALYSIS: "COMPLETELY DESTROY"

The Hebrew noun חֵרֶם, transliterated as *ḥerem,* is derived from the verb חָרַם *(ḥāram)*. Leon Wood (1980c, 325) defines the noun as "devoted thing, ban," and the verb as "to ban, devote, destroy utterly" (p. 324). Because of the complexity of the concept, for the purposes of this study we will use *ḥerem* as a loan word to encompass both forms.

Some understand this to be "the genocidal destruction of enemies . . . [where Moses and Joshua engaged] in campaigns of 'ethnic cleansing' as *ḥerem* ('acts of religious devotion')" (Cowles 2003, 16–17). While most of the *ḥerem* material lies outside of the current study, the fact that Leviticus provides much of the legal foundation of the nation and uses the term five times in Leviticus 27:28–29 requires a closer examination of the concept to clarify how this term that largely addresses a corporate response in warfare is relevant to the present topic of individual vows.

The origin of the term is obscure. Norbert Lohfink traces the word to a Semitic root *ḥrm* that reflects concepts of "to separate," "to forbid," or "to consecrate," although he also notes that in the Hebrew it seems to incorporate aspects of a second root *ḥrm*, which expresses meanings of "consecration" and "destruction" (1986, 188–89). Ross (2002, 494) concludes, "The basic idea of the Hebrew word is that the person or thing was devoted to God; it could either be sanctified for use in his service or utterly destroyed, but it was banned from possession or use by humans."

While the key seems to be the idea of devotion to God, this is not always clear. The first time the word occurs in the OT is in Exodus 22:19, which the NASB translates as "he who sacrifices to any god, other than to the LORD alone, shall be utterly destroyed [יָחֳרָם]." Most modern translations use similar terminology. Philip Stern (1991, 104) notes that the idea of "anti-idolatry" was "integral to the Israelite concept of חֵרֶם, and not incidental to it." This is a critical distinction when examining the use of the term in the later context of the conquest. There, only specific occupying tribes were to be subject to *ḥerem*, but the reason was not just their idolatry but how that idolatry had led to despicable practices.

Without using the term, this concept is introduced in the subsequent chapter of Exodus where God wraps up his initial proclamation given at Mount Sinai shortly after they had arrived from Egypt. Exodus 23:20–33, which describes the purpose and the goals of the upcoming Canaan campaign, is the final portion of the material that would be included in the initial book of the covenant cited in Exodus 24:4. It is also the final element of the initial covenant that the people affirmed in 24:3. In summary, God told the nation that he was sending an angel with them to lead them into the land, which is described as the land of the Amorites, the Hittites, the Perizzites, the Canaanites, the Hivites, and the Jebusites. These are five of the ten tribal groups cited in God's promise to Abraham in

Genesis 15:19–21, with the Hivites added. Five of the ten tribal groups cited in Genesis are not mentioned here, although one, the Girgashites, is included in later lists. The Israelites were told to listen to and obey that angelic leader, with a stress on the command not to worship or serve the gods of those tribes nor do the deeds that they were doing. This stress suggests that those prohibited deeds manifested the completion of the iniquity of those tribes, thus terminating the postponement from judgment that God described in Genesis 15:16.

As God prepared to vacate the land for the Israelites, he declared that he would כָּחַד those tribes (Exod. 23:23). Although translated "completely destroy" in the NASB (with similar terms in other modern translations), the word כָּחַד is defined as "to kick, conceal, cutoff, cut down, make desolate" (Oswalt 1980b, 436). This might suggest that the KJV translation of "cut them off" picks up on an ambiguity in the Hebrew, since the supplementary information in 23:28 states that God would send "hornets" that would "drive out the Hivites, the Canaanites, and the Hittites before you," suggesting possible eviction as opposed to extermination.

The Tribes of Canaan

The ten tribes mentioned in Genesis 15 were the Kenites, the Kenizzites, the Kadmonites, the Hittites, the Perizzites, the Rephaim, the Amorites, the Canaanites, the Girgashites, and the Jebusites. The text in Genesis describes the ten as living in a promised territory that stretched as far as the Euphrates. However, during the initial conquest and settlement under Joshua, that entire portion was not taken. The question is, what happened to the tribes listed in Genesis who are not mentioned in Exodus? There are several possibilities. Given that the land Joshua conquered did not go all the way to the Euphrates, some of those tribes may have dwelt in the northern portion not conquered. There are also indications that some of those tribes may have been absorbed. For example, there is evidence that at least some of the Kenizzites, notably Caleb's family, had managed to become connected with the Israelites while in Egypt (Harbin 2021a, 489). Judges also relates that there were Kenites who were relatives of Moses that settled in the southern part of Judah (Judg 1:16), but also in the region of Hazor, in the northern area (Judg. 4:11). The Jebusites remained in the land and still occupied Jerusalem at the time of David (2 Sam. 5). They appear to have been eventually absorbed. Given the way some of those tribes moved, it is possible that in the four hundred years between Abraham and Moses they may have left the land. Deuteronomy 2 indicates that at the time of the exodus, the Rephaim were in the Transjordan in the Bashan area, which is generally not considered part of the Promised Land.

After the forty years of wandering, Moses wrapped up his leadership responsibilities with the renewal of the covenant in the Arabah across from Jericho, which is recorded in Deuteronomy. In the process, he admonished the people regarding the anticipated Canaan campaign, citing the six nations addressed in Exodus 23, with the Girgashites added. In Deuteronomy 7:1–2, Moses anticipates that Israel would be victorious, but then tells the new generation of Israelites that when they defeated those seven nations, they were to הַחֲרֵם תַּחֲרִים combining the *hiphil* infinitive absolute of the verb חָרַם with the second-person *hiphil* imperfect to provide emphasis (GKC §113l–n). The criteria he specifies as incorporated in that action includes making no covenants, prohibiting intermarriage, and destroying their altars, sacred pillars, Asherim, and graven images (Deut. 7:3–5). Stern (1991, 97) observes "The law does not envision wholesale physical annihilation. The major clue to this is found in Deuteronomy 7:1, where the main verb is נָשַׁל, here equivalent to גֵּרֵשׁ, 'to expel.'"

Then in Deuteronomy 20, Moses provides overall instructions for how the Israelites were to conduct war in the future. The first part of the

Appendix 3: *Ḥerem*

chapter cites general guidelines, but beginning in Deuteronomy 20:16 an exception is made for the six nations that had been listed in Exodus 23. In their regard, Moses directs that the Israelites "shall not leave alive anything that breathes" (לֹא תְחַיֶּה כָּל־נְשָׁמָה) but were to "utterly destroy them" (NASB; כִּי־הַחֲרֵם תַּחֲרִימֵם). Moses goes on to explain that the reason was that their religion incorporated "detestable things," and this in essence served as a prophylactic to prevent an infestation of sin among the Israelites (Deut. 20:18).

It would appear that the command to "not leave alive anything that breathes" explained how they were to *ḥerem* those specific cities, since subsequent uses of the term generally include directions specifying what was to be done in each case. The first two cities within that region were Jericho and Ai. In the case of Jericho, *ḥerem* was applied to the city and every physical thing (Josh. 6:18) and living thing (6:21) in it, and the city was burned. In the case of Ai, after its conquest, *ḥerem* was applied to the inhabitants, but the cattle and spoil were given to the Israelites and the city was burned (Josh. 8:26–28). The standard practice, however, was to eliminate the humans (Josh. 10:28–40) because they would turn the Israelite descendants away from God. While this indicated a combined matter of national security as well as religious purity, they were allowed to appropriate the spoils and occupy the still-standing city.

It is then interesting that not every incident that involved eliminating idolaters was characterized as *ḥerem*. This is illustrated in the difficult case of Midian in Numbers 31. Following the seduction of Israel as a result of Balaam's counsel (Num. 25:1–18; 31:16), God directed Moses to "strike" (נָכָה, Num 25:17) the Midianites. Numbers 31 describes the strike, characterizing it as taking "vengeance" (נְקֹם נִקְמַת). In the process the Israelites killed all the males, females who had known a man intimately, and the five kings of Midian. They then burned their cities and camps and plundered the Midianite cattle, flocks, and goods. But the action is never characterized as *ḥerem*.

The above brief discussion illustrates the complexity of the term and some of the issues encountered when trying to nail down a clear definition encompassing all of the uses. When Joshua gave the Israelites their final directions on the day Jericho was destroyed, he told them that "the Lord has given you the city" but it was not theirs to take and use since הִיא וְכָל־אֲשֶׁר־בָּהּ לַיהוָה (literally, "it and all that is in it [are] to YHWH," Josh. 6:17). Thus, Ross's description of the basic meaning that "the person or thing was devoted to God" seems to be warranted, but the practical implications of how that worked are difficult. How is killing a person (even if he or she was an idolater) devoting that person to God? How is burning a city and leaving it as a barren mound a sacred act? Given the overall fierceness of the various specified actions, how does one explain that something might be preserved for use in God's service? Kellogg (1978, 555) proposes that the purpose was "the total nullification of their power for evil." This seems straightforward in the circumstances discussed thus far, which clearly present it as combat against idolatry, which may be viewed as spiritual warfare fought in a physical realm.

If the matter was actually a spiritual issue, and the purpose was to prevent any use for evil, that may explain the process of destruction, which in essence is removal from the physical realm. In the case of cities, it would involve burning, which was a means of purification, thus purifying the land. For humans, it would require execution. Since these are rather extreme measures, they were not to be instituted lightly. Rather, this required corporate agreement under the direct guidance of God.

But Leviticus 27:28 presents a situation where an individual might *ḥerem* something "out of all that he has, of man or animal or of the fields of his own property." How might an individual *ḥerem* another individual, or a personal possession? Sklar (2014, 331) maintains that it refers "to giving someone or something irrevocably to the Lord." Numbers 18:14 provides insight into this process, indicating that everything that was *herem* belonged to the priest and thus could be used in their service in the tabernacle. The contention is that this represented an extremely high sense of dedication, as shown by the statement that anything that was *herem* was "most holy" (קֹדֶשׁ־קָדָשִׁים) to the Lord. Stern (1991, 134) characterizes this extreme dedication "priestly חרם."

One of the difficulties of the Leviticus 27:28–29 passage is that it seems to provide conflicting admonitions with regard to persons. On one hand, 27:28 describes a person who is *herem* as being "most holy," and then 27:29 proclaims that a person who is *herem* "shall surely be put to death." Lohfink (1986, 186–87) suggests that the distinction is the use of the verb. Leviticus 27:28 uses the *hiphil*, while 27:29 uses the *hophal*. While that is the passive form of the *hiphil* stem, Lofink observes that the cases when חרם is used in the *hophal* "are associated with the semantic field of punishment." In other words, 27:29 would reflect the response of the community to an individual who was involved in something requiring capital punishment, such as gross idolatry.

The concept of *herem* is complicated. Perhaps the best way of looking at it is that it was a way that a theocratic government *under God's guidance* could address spiritual issues that threatened the survival of the community. They could be external, which in the case of Israel really only addressed the period of the conquest (later situations of national survival are really matters of God's judgment on a disobedient nation). They could also be internal, as in the case of an Israelite city that went into pagan idolatry (Deut. 13:12–17). While this doesn't explain the case of an individual, perhaps one could include it by extension, suggesting that the person who is designated for *herem* is a spiritual threat (Heiser 2015, 203–6). Overall, it would appear that given the damage that these cases could cause, one might use the analogy of either an amputation or cauterizing a wound—using extreme local damage to save the entirety (Walton and Walton 2017, 183–84).

APPENDIX 4: SLAVES AND EMANCIPATION IN ISRAEL

One of the cruelest manifestations of the breakdown of human relationships as a result of the fall of humankind in Genesis 3 is slavery. While the origin of the practice is lost to history, in essence it is a diabolical distortion of the basic principle underlying the creation of Eve in Genesis 2—the need of every human being for relationships and appropriate helpers. Humankind was originally designed to corporately manage the world (Harbin 2005, 64–66). That creation mandate was never revoked, but our management to date has been a horrendous history of *mis*management. Because of broken relationships and self-centeredness, the process of slavery substitutes possession for relationship and shackles for assistance. As a result, instead of a corporate cooperative management of God's kingdom, we find myriads of conflicting personal fiefdoms tearing each other down, as each person attempts to be king in his or her own way—a manifestation of the egocentric perception of the world we are born with as a result of the fall (see the section "*Nephesh* (נֶפֶשׁ): Life and Soul" in the introduction). The consequent competition for dominance results in the strong forcing others to serve them regardless of the others' willingness and with no regard to their well-being. As a result, while seen in a variety of forms, slavery has been a universal practice that has persisted down to modern times (Drescher 2009, 3–4; Heuman and Burnard 2011, 1–4). While private slavery has been largely legally abolished in the west, those same cultures are striving to install a political enslavement. This is a much more sophisticated and subtle form of slavery where citizens are beholden to their government, which "takes care of their needs, facilitates their pleasures, manages their most important affairs, directs their industry, regulates their successions, and divides their inheritances" (Alexis de Tocqueville, cited by McKenzie 2021, 211). Of course, tyrannical governments are not new—that was the background for the nation of Israel when the exodus brought them out of Egypt, out of slavery.

Given that the state of the world in which Israel was formed included slavery in every culture, it should not be surprising that even though they came out from slavery, the Israelites did not disavow it. More troubling is the fact that aspects of the Torah seem to suggest that God condoned the practice. And yet, a closer examination indicates that while God tolerated the practice as another evidence of the fallen state of human beings, like other cultural practices that eroded relationships with which Israel struggled such as divorce and polygamy, he never authorized it. Even after the ministry and resurrection of Jesus, the depravity of fallen humanity has continued to taint all societies in many ways, including those that attempted to follow Christian guidelines. Rodney Stark argues that "only one civilization ever rejected human bondage: Christianity. And it did it twice!" (Stark 2011, 247). The first time was at the end of the first millennium. However, as Spain and Portugal began to colonize the Americas, they saw a tremendous need for a large labor force. Observing that native tribes enslaved each other (Stark 2003, 293–95) the European powers attempted to follow that pattern but it proved impractical (Wood 2011, 67–69). As a result, beginning with Portugal and Spain, the Europeans plugged into and expanded the existing Islamic-African slave trade (Stark 2003, 305–18). However, Africa was not the only source for slaves. For example,

Appendix 4: Slaves and Emancipation in Israel

Oliver Cromwell was responsible for selling approximately 50,000 Irish into slavery in the Barbados and Virginia (O'Callaghan 2001, 9–25). While some individuals or groups recognized that forced service or slavery was inhumane and repudiated it, it was not until the eighteenth and nineteenth centuries that a critical mass of western European Christians was able to achieve enough social traction to begin to change this aspect of their cultures, and even there it was done only with a fight. This modern movement that primarily emerged in the United States and England out of conscience resulting from a Christian-based cultural consensus has produced a widespread rejection of slavery, to the point that many people in the modern western world are no longer aware of its dark history, even though aspects of the practice still remain globally (Stark 2003, 291–365). More subtly, a new philosophical system has developed that subordinates people to the state, essentially enslaving them to government (Dreher 2020, 7–19).

Regarding the practice in the OT, two observations are warranted. First, as noted in the units on Leviticus 25, the Hebrew noun translated as "slave" (עֶבֶד) is derived from the Hebrew verb עָבַד, which means both "to work" and "to serve" (Kaiser 1980h). Thus, the noun may have originally referred to one who worked. As used in the OT, the noun *'ebed* covers a spectrum of meanings ranging from voluntary service, which is even used of God and is a messianic title, to "chattel slavery" where the *'ebed* is considered property (Kaiser 1980h, 639–40), for which reason we will use the term *'ebed* for the subsequent discussion. While it is clear that chattel slavery existed in the nation of Israel, it did not seem to have been as prevalent as in other cultures such as Egypt or Rome. As such, we need to exercise great care to carefully differentiate the nuances of the term.

An עֶבֶד

A common use of the term *'ebed* (עֶבֶד) could denote a servant (both voluntary and mandatory). A

---

servant could be a position of high regard, such as Abraham's servant (Gen. 24:1–2) "who had charge of all that he owned" (NASB). Apparently, this was the case of Eliezer, considered at one point by Abraham to be his heir (Gen. 15:2). In this regard we should note that the term *'ebed* is also a messianic title, especially in Isaiah where it is "the most prominent personal, technical term to represent the OT teaching on the Messiah" (Kaiser 1980h, 639). Another sense of *'ebed* could be understood either as a debt slave or an indentured servant. While similar, there are subtle differences between the two. A debt slave is a person who is paying off an existing debt through labor but who really does not belong to the master (Chirichigno 1993, 145). Indentured servanthood is more of a situation where the person has agreed to work with the master for a period of time for some subsequent reward. In this light, Jacob's labor for his wives Leah and Rachel could be construed as indentured servanthood.

As we look at modern parallels, indentured servanthood was a fairly common practice in the eighteenth and nineteenth centuries, especially with respect to Irish immigrants in the middle Atlantic and northern states of the U.S., but some would argue also with the earliest (in 1619) Africans (McCartney 2003, 27; see also https://www.loc.gov/collections/thomas-jefferson-papers/articles-and-essays/virginia-records-timeline-1553-to-1743/1610-to-1619/; https://www.pbs.org/opb/historydetectives/feature/indentured-servants-in-the-us/). The concept of indentured servant has some very strong parallels with a number of contractual work relationships today where various liberties are given up for the period of the contract, especially in fields where the outcome of the work has high value. Some that come to mind include various professional athletes who are "owned" by their teams, entertainers who might be limited in the scope of their endeavors to one corporation, inventors whose work then belongs to the company, and even in some regards teachers whose research or publication does not

Appendix 4: Slaves and Emancipation in Israel

belong to them. The final category of *'ebed* is chattel slave. There are significant differences between a debt slave and a chattel slave. Since a debt slave is understood to be a person bound into service to pay off a debt, the expectation is that when the debt is paid the person goes free. A chattel slave is one who is arbitrarily attached for life, and in many ways is considered property.

These differences are especially evident when one compares the guidelines for the Jubilee and Sabbath years that are set forth in Exodus 21, Leviticus 25, and Deuteronomy 15. While largely outside of the current study, the Exodus and Deuteronomy passages are important for understanding the guidelines, giving directions regarding the release of individuals from specific roles of servitude that are part of the material at hand. Those three passages may be summarized as follows: Exodus 21 directs that a Hebrew *'ebed* could serve for six years but must be released in the seventh. Deuteronomy 15 indicates that seventh year is the Sabbath year. Leviticus 25 suggests an additional release as part of the Jubilee. While the release in the Sabbath year was from servitude associated with debt, Jubilee is more complex. In a prior study (Harbin 2012, 54–55, 57–61), I proposed that Jubilee involved a large financial need as opposed to small financial need for the Sabbath year. Further study suggests that debt is not the critical factor in the Jubilee. Primarily it completed a multiyear lease of land, the purchase of which was to provide financial assets for the landowner to meet a large need. Because it marked the termination of the lease, following Jubilee, the person who had leased out his land would now be able to work his own (i.e., his family's heritage) land for his own needs. A collateral aspect of Jubilee involved an individual who had leased out all parcels of his land to meet ongoing needs, and who had then gone to work for another Israelite as a result of continuing poverty. In this case, it released that debtor to return to working his own land, which was now returned as a result of the completion of the leases. During Jubilee he would be able to gather produce, but not harvest it.

The point is that the *'ebed* service that is the subject of the Exodus and Deuteronomy passages was not chattel slavery but debt slavery (Harbin 2012, 58). Specifically, it was a result of debt that could not be repaid and was then worked off through labor. A key premise of that conclusion is that the Israelite culture predominantly consisted of extended families that were largely self-sufficient. Given the structure of the nation as it settled the land, the Israelites lived within communities that were closely knit and interrelated. If an Israelite did have a need, perhaps to replace a tool, it was likely that the transaction was done through barter, or through the medium of precious metals, since actual money was not developed until the intertestamental period. Any debt that resulted would be relatively small, which could be repaid with the income of a few harvests. Within that cultural context, it is suggested that debt, while not unknown, was relatively infrequent, at least in the early time of the settlement (Harbin 2012, 59–61). Within the Torah, the Sabbath year concept suggests that the expectation was that repayment would be short-term—that is, no more than a few years—depending on the amount of the debt. An alternative, especially within a barter context, was that the individual might agree to work for or provide service to the lender to repay the loan. According to the Exodus and Deuteronomy passages, the expectation was that the debt would be repaid or worked off before the next Sabbath year, a maximum of six years. Given the cultural context, it would appear that the individual under these circumstances might still live in his or her home within the same community. However, the caveat was that should a Sabbath year come prior to the debt being repaid, the lender would forgive any debt still outstanding. If still more work was owed, the individual would be released and could return to his own work.

Debt Slavery

One of the more interesting instructions regarding debt slavery was an option where an individual might feel more secure continuing to work for someone else and conclude that the situation in which he was found was more attractive than trying to fend for himself. In that case he could go into permanent service, which really should be called voluntary servanthood (Exod. 21:5–7).

In contrast to the Sabbath year, Jubilee is presented as a consecrated year following seven Sabbath years, and in Leviticus 25:10 is called the "fiftieth year" (see appendix 5, "The Year of Jubilee," for further discussion). Although the land was to rest during Jubilee, that year was not labeled a Sabbath year. The Leviticus 25 description focuses on use of the land and land ownership. The text presents God revealing Leviticus to Moses while the nation was at Mount Sinai, anticipating that when the nation subsequently entered the land, all of the Israelite families would be provided with land that was to be a family heritage, described as their אֲחֻזָּה, that is, their possession or property. It would then be their responsibility to work the land and provide for their families and heirs. Since the actual owner of the land was God, the Israelites might best be described as designated stewards of specific estates. As such, they could not "sell" the land they would be farming. While there was a provision that allowed an Israelite who encountered financial difficulties to sell the land, the reality was that all he could sell legally was the use of the land for the period up to the next Jubilee—in other words, it was really a lease with the caveat that the land could be redeemed (i.e., the remaining debt be repaid) at any time prior to the end of the lease, that is, Jubilee. The sale price of the land was based on the number of crops that were expected prior to the next Jubilee (e.g., if it was fifteen years, the price would be fifteen times the typical crop value for that piece of land).

Elsewhere I (Harbin 2021a, 475–85) illustrate the social structure within a typical village settled by one or more extended families, centered on a compact residential area with houses built very close together. There I show how the housing cluster was surrounded by all of the agricultural land of the village, which was compositely called "the field." The field was divided into many plots that were assigned to the village farmers. Each farmer possessed several portions in various locations. Thus, the supposition is that a farmer who had encountered significant financial struggles had an option to sell one or more of his portions (which we might call *fields*) to someone else. Since this was just a lease for a period of years, when Jubilee came, the use of the land would revert to the owner or his family. In this case, there would be no debt forgiveness, since there would be no debt—the lender had already received his return in terms of the various crops he had harvested through the period of the lease.

In terms of selling one's labor, it would then seem that the understanding might be that when one sold one's labor, there would be an expectation that the labor would cease in the Year of Jubilee. However, unlike the land lease, labor probably had a constant wage. This might suggest that rather than paying off a debt, one was using one's labor to survive. In the situation where this law was to be implemented, each Israelite had family land that could not be sold. If the land had been leased out, when Jubilee came, the land would revert to the family. If the individual had sold his labor because he had already leased out his land, he would now have the use of land again, and in essence have a clean start.

It then seems while *emancipation* in Israel might be forgiveness of debt in the case of a small loan, it would be forgiven in the Sabbath year, not Jubilee. Since the year before Jubilee was a Sabbath year, there should have been no debt for an Israelite to repay. Thus, the release for the Year of Jubilee was the release of the land back to its owner, and the release of the owner who now had his land back from contracted labor—not the release of a slave from slavery.

APPENDIX 5: THE YEAR OF JUBILEE

Outside of one brief mention in the book of Numbers, the concept of Jubilee only appears in chapters 25 and 27 of Leviticus. This brief appearance has generated a number of questions. In terms of the name, there are questions regarding the origin and the actual meaning of the word. In terms of the description, the two primary issues are highly debated and often misunderstood.

There are misunderstandings of what the practice involves. There is significant debate as to when the Jubilee was supposed to take place. Further, in terms of the history of Israel, there is the question as to whether the practice was ever observed. This appendix will briefly address these questions.

The title "Jubilee" is generally understood as a transliteration of the Hebrew term יוֹבֵל (Lev. 25:10), which is translated as "trumpet" (Alexander 1980c), "ram" (*DCH* s.v. "יוֹבֵל I" 4:163), or "ram's horn or cornet" (BDB s.v. "יוֹבֵל" 385). This name of the event then is understood to derive from the declaration to proclaim it by blowing on a horn, as seen in Leviticus 25:9, even though the term used there is שׁוֹפָר, "a ram's horn." Because of uncertainties, most translations essentially transliterate the term, and as a result the term "Jubilee" has been assimilated into English. However, the English derivative "Jubilee" has merged with the verb "jubilate" (derived from the Latin *jubilare*), meaning "to utter sounds or make demonstrations of joy and exultation" (*WTNID* s.v. "jubilate"), producing the popular concept that a Jubilee was a time of celebration. This perception shows up even in commentaries, where the event is described in various terms such as "festival," which suggests a celebration or time of merrymaking (Ross 2002, 456). As will be seen below, while the perception of celebration is not necessarily wrong, the actual event seems to have been much more subdued than our concept of a festival.

The Levitical event opens with the sounding of "a ram's horn" in order to both "consecrate the fiftieth year" and to proclaim דְּרוֹר, which is translated as "release" or "freedom" (Wolf 1980c). The last part of Leviticus 25 discusses one aspect of this release as from a form of servitude generally interpreted as slavery (עֶבֶד, see appendix 4, "Slaves and Emancipation in Israel"). As a result, most English translations use the word "freedom" or "liberty." Consequently, throughout their history, Americans have resonated with 25:10, a portion of which was cast into the side of the Liberty Bell in Philadelphia—"Proclaim Liberty Throughout All the Land Unto All the Inhabitants thereof." Moreover, the concept of Jubilee was a key element of the American Civil War when slavery was abolished, and the word has been used in many contexts since (Harbin 2017).

However, as shown in the exegesis of Leviticus 25, the primary purpose of Jubilee was the termination of land leases. While this might be a time of celebration, there is no feast directed to be celebrated with the announcement. In fact, the announcement of Jubilee inaugurated a year of no planting or harvesting (like a Sabbath year, although the term Sabbath is not used), which might suggest a rather austere occasion—especially when, as seen below, it was a second year in a row when no harvest could be anticipated. As presented in the biblical text, when this material was delivered to the nation, no one owned any property. Everyone was a temporary nomad en route to a land where God had promised that he would give them land to farm. Because of corporate rebellion, it turned out that the actual settlement would not occur for another forty years, and the settlers would be the subsequent generation, as recorded in Joshua. However, God was already making it clear that when the land was given, it could not be sold. As shown elsewhere, once the people moved into the land, each family that was part of the conquest was given a portion of the agricultural land surrounding their village or town (called "the field") through a divinely directed distribution by lots. It would appear that the family's heritage portion consisted of several plots distributed through the overall field (Harbin 2021a, 487). We might consider the family's land as working capital, noting that God promised that should they be faithful, the land would be fruitful and support the family through the generations. While God warned that disobedience would bring consequences, he also indicated that there would be occasions when, for various other reasons, such as an injury or illness, an individual or family would experience hardships. In anticipation of that, the last portion of Leviticus 25 (see the unit "Preventing Social Unraveling, Part 2" [25:23–55]) provides a sequence of options that the individual and the community could use to ameliorate those situations. The strongest two and the most misunderstood were sale of part of the farm and selling oneself into servitude. In both cases, Jubilee rectified the issue, but how that was done is largely misunderstood.

Perhaps the primary misunderstanding involves the sale of the land. While Leviticus 25:14–16 makes it clear that the land could not be permanently sold, the text uses the word מָכַר, which involves a business transaction and as such can be and often is translated as "sell." As a result, there is a perception that Jubilee involved redistribution of land, and various modern writers have called for such a redistribution of modern capital assets or other forms of wealth (Sider 1997, 230–31). While Israelites did practice permanent sales (1 Kings 21:1–6; Mic. 2:2), when it involved the land that had been distributed by God it was in violation of the Torah and God's intentions. On multiple occasions the text stresses that the land really belonged to God.

Although the term "sale" was used, the buyer actually just purchased the *use* of the land. This is clearly indicated by the fact that the price was expressed in terms of the number of crops that the buyer was actually buying (Lev. 25:16). Thus, the proper concept was that the land was being leased, with the number of crops capped as the period of years remaining to the next Jubilee. Because ownership never changed, when Jubilee came, the *use* of the land reverted back to the owner, that is, it was "released" (דְּרוֹר). Since the buyer had bought a specific number of crops prior to Jubilee, which he had presumably been able to harvest, there were no further monetary obligations and thus no debt to be forgiven.

Similarly, while the translations appear to present slavery in Leviticus 25:39–43, this is the same word that is used for servant or indentured servitude. As explained in the exegesis, apparently this would be a situation where the individual sold his labor for a period of years. As suggested in appendix 4 regarding slavery, it is likely that this self-instituted servitude was for survival, not to retire a debt. Although the duration of the servitude is not as explicit, Leviticus 25:40 is explicit that the Israelite was to be considered as a hired hand, not a slave. Then, as expressed in Leviticus, when Jubilee came the period of servitude ended. Again, it was an occasion of "release" (דְּרוֹר), only this time from the service. Perhaps the key point to remember is that as the nation moved into the land, all of the people were apparently of comparable socioeconomic status, having just come out of slavery in Egypt. Thus, while it was possible (even probable given the humanness of the Israelites) that through a fifty-year cycle some families would do better economically, given the checks and balances of the system, if it were followed, there would not be an extreme disparity between the upper echelons and the lower.

Beyond this, there is a question regarding how Jubilee was calculated. Leviticus 25:8–10 specifies that the Israelites were to count seven Sabbath years (25:8 specifies forty-nine years),

Appendix 5: The Year of Jubilee

and then on the tenth day of the seventh month (the Day of Atonement) a ram's horn (שׁוֹפָר) was to proclaim "a Jubilee" (Lev. 25:10). The text clearly delineates that the "seven Sabbaths of years" were forty-nine (25:8). It then declares that the fiftieth year was to be the Jubilee (25:10–11). Since year forty-nine was a Sabbath year with no harvesting, and the Jubilee was a year with no harvesting, a straightforward reading of the text demands understanding that every fifty years the Israelites went for two years straight without a harvest.

It is difficult to understand how farmers of that period could survive a two-year period of not growing crops. Consequently, several alternative explanations of the Jubilee have been proposed. Suggestions to make the concept more palatable include: (1) both Jubilee and the Sabbath year were exilic ideals never really instituted (de Vaux 1965, 175–76); (2) Jubilee was not a full year, but a period of forty-nine days that corrected differences between the lunar and solar calendars (Hoenig 1969, 222–36); (3) the seventh Sabbath year and Jubilee overlapped by six months (Hartley 1992, 425); (4) Jubilee is identical with the seventh Sabbath year (Young 2006, 75–76). While the last suggestion seems the strongest since it is based upon inferences from talmudic evidence, a closer examination suggests that the inferences are somewhat weak.

as the tenth of the seventh month instead of the normal first of the month. Since that is the day Leviticus 25:9 identifies as the start of Jubilee, Young concludes that it must have been a Jubilee year. While this seems to be the rabbinic conclusion, it does not follow that Ezekiel was necessarily identifying the tenth as New Year's Day. In comparison, the Mishnah tractate Rosh Hashanah, which defines the four different New Years in the rabbinic calendar, uses a more specific phrase, identifying "on the first" (בְּאֶחָד), as opposed to "the head," as the autumnal or Tishri New Year's Day. The second reference, 2 Kings 22:3, tells of Josiah's discovery of the Torah in the temple. That event is dated to 623 B.C., but the inference that it was a Jubilee is based on a reference to b. Meg. 14a, which supposes that Josiah sent his advisors to Huldah because Jeremiah was away bringing the northern kingdom back, since the Jubilee could not be celebrated unless all twelve tribes were in the land. While Young notes this Gemara seems "highly imaginative," he suggests that the idea that it was an actual Jubilee may be valid (p. 74); however, this is an inference.

This supposition also overlooks a specific declaration in the Talmud that "four hundred years correspond to eight [cycles of] Jubilees" (b. Arak. 12a), which seems to explicitly label Jubilee as being the fiftieth year, which is likely what the original audience understood.

Historical Jubilees?

Rodger Young (2006, 71–83) primarily develops his argument that Jubilee was simultaneous with the seventh Sabbath year based on two references to Jubilee in the Talmud that seem to place actual celebrations of a Jubilee in 574 B.C. (inferred from Ezek. 40:1) and in 623 B.C. (inferred from 2 Kings 22:3). Ezekiel 40:1 dates the occasion of a vision that Ezekiel had as 574 B.C. The Talmud, b. 'Arak. 12a, suggests that it was a Jubilee year. The argument is that Ezekiel's phrase בְּרֹאשׁ הַשָּׁנָה ("in or at the head of the year") specifically refers to the first day of the year, which is then identified

Israelite Calendar

One of the difficulties regarding the Hebrew calendar is the nomenclature since there are two New Year's Days, and the months are often numbered rather than named (see the excursus "The Israelite Calendar and the Seven Day Week" in the "Strengthening the Social Fabric" [23:1–24:9]). We know that in the Pentateuch the year began in the month of Nisan, just after the spring equinox. The modern Hebrew calendar begins the civil year and the agricultural year with the month of Tishri, which is the seventh month after a Nisan New Year. Consequently, the first of Tishri

Appendix 5: The Year of Jubilee

is now called Rosh Hashanah, although we do not know when that practice began. In the OT, it is always called the seventh month, although we understand it to be the beginning of the agricultural year. Regardless of whether we use a Nisan (spring) or Tishri (fall) calendar, as seen on the Gezer Calendar, there seems to be some overlap with regard to the agricultural cycle as we try to match up to our solar calendar. Young (2006, 78) shows how the rabbis seemed to keep track of the years by noting which year of which Sabbath year of which Jubilee something happened.

The key is that Israel was told not to rely solely on human understanding, that is, a naturalistic worldview. As shown in the exegesis of Leviticus 25 addressing both the Sabbath year and the Jubilee, God told the Israelites that if they observed his statutes and judgments (25:18), then the crop in the sixth year (the last full agricultural year) would be enough for three years (25:21). Based on the seasons as we understand them, the agricultural cycle would seem to be as shown in chart 12, working with a Tishri beginning of the agricultural year:

Year 1	Fall and winter	sow	eat fresh produce/preserved grain
(Year 1 of jubilee cycle)	Late spring, summer, and early fall	harvest	eat fresh produce/preserved grain
Year 2	Fall and winter	sow	eat fresh produce/preserved grain
(Year 2 of jubilee cycle)	Late spring, summer, and early fall	harvest	eat fresh produce/preserved grain
Year 3	Fall and winter	sow	eat fresh produce/preserved grain
(Year 3 of jubilee cycle)	Late spring, summer, and early fall	harvest	eat fresh produce/preserved grain
Year 4	Fall and winter	sow	eat fresh produce/preserved grain
(Year 4 of jubilee cycle)	Late spring, summer, and early fall	harvest	eat fresh produce/preserved grain
Year 5	Fall and winter	sow	eat fresh produce/preserved grain
(Year 5 of jubilee cycle)	Late spring, summer, and early fall	harvest	eat fresh produce/preserved grain
Year 6	Fall and winter	sow	eat fresh produce/preserved grain
(Year 6 of jubilee cycle)	Late spring, summer, and early fall	harvest	eat fresh produce/preserved grain
Sabbath Year (year 7)	Fall and winter		eat volunteer/food/preserved grain
(Year 7 of jubilee cycle)	Late spring, summer, and early fall		eat volunteer/food/preserved grain
Year 1 of new cycle (year)	Fall and winter	sow	eat fresh produce/preserved grain
(Year 8 of jubilee cycle)	Late spring, summer, and early fall	harvest	eat fresh produce/preserved grain

Chart 12. Table showing process of a single Sabbath year cycle, modeling the first cycle in a Jubilee cycle.

Appendix 5: The Year of Jubilee

During a normal year, the Israelites would eat fresh food as it ripened, beginning in the late winter and early spring. They would harvest their grain and preserve it beginning in later spring to summer, finishing off the harvest season in the early fall. During a Sabbath year, the difference would be that while they could eat any volunteer produce on a daily basis, they could not sow new crops, which meant they had nothing to maintain them through the spring and summer, nor to harvest in the summer and fall. At the end of the Sabbath year, they could sow again and start the process over.

Year 1	Fall and winter	sow	eat fresh produce/preserved grain
(Year 43 of cycle)	Late spring, summer, and early fall	harvest	eat fresh produce/preserved grain
Year 2	Fall and winter	sow	eat fresh produce/preserved grain
(Year 44 of cycle)	Late spring, summer, and early fall	harvest	eat fresh produce/preserved grain
Year 3	Fall and winter	sow	eat fresh produce/preserved grain
(Year 45 of cycle)	Late spring, summer, and early fall	harvest	eat fresh produce/preserved grain
Year 4	Fall and winter	sow	eat fresh produce/preserved grain
(Year 46 of cycle)	Late spring, summer, and early fall	harvest	eat fresh produce/preserved grain
Year 5	Fall and winter	sow	eat fresh produce/preserved grain
(Year 47 of cycle)	Late spring, summer, and early fall	harvest	eat fresh produce/preserved grain
Year 6	Fall and winter	sow	eat fresh produce/preserved grain
(Year 48 of cycle)	Late spring, summer, and early fall	harvest	eat fresh produce/preserved grain
Sabbath Year (year 7)	Fall and winter		eat volunteer/food/preserved grain
(Year 49 of cycle)	Late spring, summer, and early fall		eat volunteer/food/preserved grain
Jubilee (year 8)	Fall and winter		eat volunteer/food/preserved grain
(Year 50 of cycle)	Late spring, summer, and early fall		eat volunteer/food/preserved grain
Year 1 of new cycle (year)	Fall and winter	sow	eat fresh produce/preserved grain
(Year 1 of cycle)	Late spring, summer, and early fall	harvest	eat fresh produce/preserved grain

Chart 13. Overview of seventh sabbatical cycle in Jubilee cycle with year 50 Jubilee.

439

Appendix 5: The Year of Jubilee

During a Jubilee, the difference in the procedure would seem to be as follows: While they would follow a normal Sabbath year cycle in year 7 of the seventh Sabbath cycle, in the fall of that seventh year they would not till the soil or plant. They would continue to live on the food that they had preserved during year 6 through that summer and early fall of year 7. However, now they would not sow in the beginning of year 8, and as a consequence they would have no harvest in year 8. In the fall and early winter of year 9, they would begin a normal season's soil preparation and sow. While Leviticus 25:22 refers to it as year 9, in actuality it would be the start of a new Sabbath year and Jubilee cycle.

While still living on the food preserved from the last harvest (year 6), they would be able to supplement it with fresh produce that voluntarily sprouted and produced. The key is that God had told them that he would provide enough in advance (in the year 6 harvest) that would last them until the spring of year 9 when they would begin harvesting their grain. Since the provision for the Sabbath years and Jubilee would be harvested in advance, it would seem that they should be able to see that God had provided enough for them to live on until the next regular year. However, given human nature, it is possible that some would be too extravagant, or for whatever reason refuse to believe that the food would last, and consequently violate the Sabbath year.

Despite the significant discussion of the concept in the last chapters of Leviticus, there is no reference in the rest of the OT that indicates that Jubilee was observed, although extrabiblical literature suggests it was. As noted, there are several references to Jubilee in the Talmud, predominantly in Arakhin, but they are difficult to follow and somewhat inconsistent. For example, b. 'Arak. 12b asserts that Israel counted seventeen Jubilee cycles from when they entered the land until the exile. Whether one takes an early date or a late date for the exodus, or a forty-nine-year Jubilee cycle or a fifty, these figures do not mesh. Consequently, while it would appear that the event was declared to the nation at Sinai, any actual observation of it is lost in the obscurity of tradition.

> ### Seventeenth Jubilee
> Young (2006, 80) calculates that if the seventeenth Jubilee was in 574 B.C. (using the Tishri new year), the first Jubilee would have been 1358 B.C., which would put the conquest at 1406 B.C. But in doing that, he begins the first Sabbath year/Jubilee cycle in 1406 B.C., overlooking the b. 'Arak. 12b notation that seems to require adding seven years for the conquest and seven years for the land distribution before the agricultural calendar started.

APPENDIX 6: LAND MEASUREMENT AND CROP VALUE

Leviticus 27:16–19 addresses valuation of land, which is based upon the size of the land, which is measured indirectly "according to its seed" (לְפִי זַרְעוֹ). The key term is "homer" in 27:6, which generates two questions. The first is whether the homer measures the amount of seed that will be harvested or the amount that would be sown. Although some modern scholars argue for the harvest figure (Wenham 1979, 339–40), the traditional understanding is that this is the amount of seed that could be sown (b. ʿArak. 14a). This is the understanding of most modern translations and commentaries. Milgrom (2001, 2380) observes that this is the commonsense approach. If that is the case, then the second question is: How much land would a homer of barley (the specified grain) sow?

Here we run into a number of issues with a number of estimates. *TWOT* (s.v. "חָמַר II" 1:299) derives the term "homer" from the verb חָמַר II, which means "to heap up." Ezekiel 45:10 indicates that a homer is ten ephahs; however, "estimates vary from about twenty-two liters (twenty dry quarts) to about forty-five liters (forty-one dry quarts)" (Scott 1980a, 38). Levine (1989, 196) estimates 3.6–6.5 bushels to a homer. Based on suspected equivalencies with other cultures, Roland de Vaux (1965, 199–203) calculates 3.1–5.7 bushels per homer. Herbert Danby (1933, 798) in his translation of the Mishnah gives 6.24 bushels.

Another approach views the term as originally a weight measurement with the word "homer" derived from חָמַר III, which means "donkey" (de Vaux 1965, 199; Livingston 1980c). This view concludes that a homer was basically a donkey load, or about 2 to 2.5 bushels. As shown in the sidebar, this would sow approximately an acre of land. Leviticus 27:16 sets a valuation of that as fifty shekels of silver.

Donkey Load

According to farmandanimals.com, a typical donkey could carry approximately one fourth of its weight (http://farmandanimals.com/how-to-care-for-a-donkey). Since a standard donkey weighs about 400–500 lbs. (https://www.livescience.com/54258-donkeys.html), this would make a donkey load about 100–125 lbs. The question then is, how much is that in terms of barley? Barley weighs approximately 48 lbs. per bushel (https://www.smallfarmcanada.ca). In terms of capacity, this would mean that a donkey load of barley would be approximately 2 to 2.5 bushels. The University of Missouri extension program indicates that the sowing rate of barley should be 2 to 2.5 bushels per acre (https://extension.missouri.edu/publications/g4312). Thus, a donkey load or homer of barley should sow about an acre to an acre and a quarter of land. For convenience, we will use an acre as an approximate area in our further discussion.

In terms of production, a good crop depends on the type of grain (Morris 1992, 347–48). For barley, a relatively average crop in the United States would be approximately sixty bushels (or about 24–30 homers) per acre, for a productivity of approximately thirty-fold, although there are several variables, such as the weather (https://www.sprowtlabs.com/blog/barley-growing-guide). As such, a good working number for a harvest might be twenty-five homers per acre. If a typical one-acre plot produced approximately twenty-five homers of barley, the question one then asks is, how did this correlate to the valuation? Again, this is complicated given the unknowns and the multicultural equivalencies used for evaluation.

Unfortunately, some of the published data do not take those into adequate consideration. For example, a number of scholars look to Mesopotamia for a model and claim that there "the standard price of barley was a shekel per homer" (Wenham 1979, 340). However, according to de Vaux (1965, 200), the following ratios have been established for the Neo-Babylonian period: 1 *kor* equals 30 *seah* and 180 *qa*. With that in mind, scholars then apply those ratios to the Laws of Eshunna (*ANET*, 161). While this is an Old Babylonian document, the ratios may be presumed to be valid for our purposes, neglecting any correspondence to modern measurement (Milgrom 2001, 2383–85; Nemet-Nejat 1998, 264). Since the first paragraph correlates approximately ten commodities to one shekel, the general conclusion is that these are market values, the first of which is barley, which equates 1 *kor* of barley (or 180 *qa*) to one shekel.

The problem is that the second paragraph of the same Laws of Eshunna correlates three of the above commodities to barley, and the ratios do not match. For example, in paragraph one, 1 *seah* (= 6 *qa*) and 2 *qa* or a total of 8 *qa* of sesame oil is correlated with one shekel. Since both barley and sesame oil are equated to one shekel, if this is a monetary value it would suggest that 180 *qa* of barley had the same value as 8 *qa* of sesame oil—or to reverse it, 1 *qa* of sesame oil is correlated to 22.5 *qa* of barley. But in paragraph two, 1 *qa* of sesame oil is correlated with 3 *seah* (or 18 *qa*) of barley. As such, the one shekel per homer value for barley in Mesopotamia is open to question, even more so when one realizes that commodity prices are very variable based on the quality of the harvest.

In terms of the OT, there are really no clear indications of land production. The closest seems to be 2 Kings 7:1, where Elisha predicts that following a severe famine (2 Kings 6:25) a handful of beans would sell for five shekels of silver, and that the next day, two measures (*seah*) of barley would sell for a shekel, which would equate to fifteen shekels per homer. Roger Omanson and John Ellington (2008, 848) point out, "Since it is not known what prices were before the siege and famine in Samaria, it is impossible to know whether these prices are back to normal, even lower than normal, or higher than normal." As such, we really don't know if the fifty shekels for redemption of the land was high or not.

Shekel's Worth of Beans

Second Kings 6:25 reads literally "a fourth of a *kab* of dove's dung [sold] for five shekels of silver." However, Omanson and Ellington (2008, 848) cite evidence that "pigeon dung" may have been a local expression for some kind of plant product such as wild onions or locust beans or carob beans. This view is accepted by the NIV and several commentators. They go on to note that the point was that Elisha's prophetic announcement indicated a drastic price drop.

Even so, Milgrom (2001, 2383) and others work with the presumption that this represents a normal crop and adopt this as a standard for a good season. At that rate, based on the working figures of the land measurement above of twenty-five homers of grain and an acre-sized plot, this would suggest that a good crop would be worth about 375 shekels. However, one must keep in mind that these farmers were producing primarily for personal consumption, not for commercial purposes.

One needs also to keep in mind that this is in terms of land production rather than land value. Few land transactions are mentioned in the OT, and those that are do not include the land size. Milgrom (2001, 2383) cites Jeremiah and David. He notes that Jeremiah "buys Hanamel's field for seventeen shekels," citing Jeremiah 32:9. However, the two preceding verses clearly indicate that this was a redemption, which indicates that it was a debt

Appendix 6: Land Measurement and Crop Value

settlement rather than a land purchase, as we addressed in Leviticus 25. In David's case, he bought a threshing floor and oxen for fifty shekels (2 Sam. 24:24). While a threshing floor itself would likely have been smaller than most plots of farmland, it also would have been nonproductive land in terms of crops, since it was tamped or compacted soil. As a result, we really do not have a good means to measure the costs.

David's Threshing Floor

Second Samuel specifies that David spent fifty shekels of silver on the threshing floor and the oxen of Araunah, while 1 Chronicles states that he bought the *site* for six hundred shekels of gold. Merrill (1985, 611) explains that the site was a larger parcel of land. Since the site became designated as the location of the temple that David's son would build, this seems to be a reasonable explanation.

In terms of the redemption, it is not clear if the fifty shekels valuation represented a total figure for the fifty-year period or for one year. Traditionally, the valuation-of-fifty-shekels-per-acre equivalent was the value for the entire period (m. 'Arak. 7:1). As such, the prorated annual value was approximately one shekel. Alternatively, if one takes the view that it represented just a year, then the valuation for a one-acre plot of land dedicated by an Israelite in the Year of Jubilee would have it valued at fifty times fifty shekels or 2,500 shekels. If the dedication stood, each year the Israelite would provide to the priests a crop that on the average might be valued as 375 shekels. However, should he decide to redeem the land, still in the Year of Jubilee, he would need to pay 2,500 shekels plus a 20 percent penalty. If instead he waited ten years to redeem the land, he would need to pay forty times fifty shekels, or 2,000 shekels, plus the 20 percent penalty. At the other end of the cycle, if he dedicated the land five years prior to Jubilee, the land would be valued at 250 shekels.

In either case, the arbitrary valuation set forth in Leviticus 27 would have been more than reasonable. In the case of a one-year valuation of fifty shekels, the payment would have been relatively low compared to the crops the Israelite could anticipate. It would have been extremely low if it were prorated to approximately one shekel per year.

APPENDIX 7: VOWS AND NAZIRITES

A vow (נֶדֶר) is essentially a promise made to God. Otto Kaiser maintains that in the OT they may be of two types: conditional promises or vows of abstinence (1998, 245–55). The first category contains an "if" request—that is, the one who vows asks God to do something based on a promise of something the person would do or dedicate if God fulfilled the request. The latter category is described as when "one dedicated oneself to Yahweh for a specific period of time." While the two may not necessarily be disparate (the abstinence may reflect a promise to give up something if God grants a specific request), Kaiser characterizes a Nazirite vow as a vow of abstinence focusing on what one abstains from during the period of the vow, which might be something like the modern practice of observing Lent.

A Vow

Some English translations use the word "vow" to refer to promises made to other humans such as when "Saul vowed, 'As the Lord lives, he [David] shall not be put to death" (1 Sam. 19:6). However, the Hebrew word there is שָׁבַע, which means "to swear" or take an oath (*TWOT* s.v. "שָׁבַע" 2:899).

Numbers 6:2–21 describes a Nazirite as an individual (male or female) who had made a "special vow" (יַפְלִא נֶדֶר) to God, specifically, "the vow of a Nazir" (נֶדֶר נָזִיר). The purpose of this vow was to "dedicate himself to the Lord" (לְהַזִּיר לַיהוָה). The verb נָזַר carries the basic meaning of "to separate" (McComiskey 1980d, 567). Depending on the context, it can indicate separation *from* something or separation *to* something. In Numbers 6:2–3 it is used twice in the same sentence to indicate that while the Nazirite separated him- or herself *to* God, he or she was to separate him- or herself *from* wine, strong drink,

or anything that came from the grapevine. Following this, two other criteria are included: not shaving one's head and not making oneself unclean by going near a dead person. These physical abstentions ("separated from" acts) are the most obvious features of a Nazirite; and as in abstinence for Lent, the primary function of the vow often gets lost in their observation.

However, the repetition of the phrase לַיהוָה in 6:5, 6, 8, and 12 emphasizes that biblically the focus should be on the separation *to* the Lord, with the separations *from* something merely superficial manifestations. But how one was to be separated *to* the Lord is never explained. A common assumption is that it is demonstrated by service in the sanctuary (Sklar 2014, 328) or, given priesthood limitations, to other unspecified service to God (Cole 2000, 121; Mathews 2009, 241; Wenham 1979, 338). Even so, this would suggest that the physical services should merely serve to demonstrate a spiritual quality.

As presented in Numbers 6, a Nazirite vow was for a set period of time, during which the person was to observe the three separation criteria. At the completion of that period, the individual was to perform a ritual following the guidelines shown in Numbers 6:13–20, indicating his or her completion of the vow. Other guidelines are included in the Numbers passage to cover a situation where the person had violated the criteria of separation, which apparently allowed a degree of reset following a failure. While the OT contains several examples of vows, none are labeled as Nazirite. However, there are four case studies that have been suggested as illustrating a form of Nazirite vow, which will be briefly reviewed here because of their relevance to the passage in Leviticus.

CASE 1: SAMUEL

Samuel is perhaps the clearest case of a vow with a conditional promise. In 1 Samuel 1:11, Hannah, Samuel's mother, made a vow and asked God for a son with the promise that she would "give him" to God all the days of his life, and a "razor shall never come on his head." The last phrase likely is a synecdoche of the part for the whole, indicating that Samuel would be under a Nazirite vow. This presents two problems. The first is that it is to be a lifetime vow, while the description of the Nazirite was for a limited period. The second is that Hannah is making the promise for her son, who was not even conceived yet. However, this is suggestive of the situation we find in Leviticus. Hannah used the verb נָתַן ("give") when she made her request in 1:11, but she then uses the verb שָׁאַל (translated as "lend") when she reports the fulfillment to Eli in 1:28. Although it does not use the word, both are suggestive of the situation in Leviticus 27:28 where a person might *herem* another person over whom he had authority. It is to be noted that after Samuel grew up, he married and had sons. One more observation here is that he served in the tabernacle, apparently because he was a Levite (1 Sam. 1; 1 Chron. 6). While he was called a judge, a prophet, and a man of God, he was never addressed as a priest. Even so, he performed sacrifices (1 Sam. 10:8), apparently with God's acceptance, although not actually in the tabernacle.

CASE 2: SAMSON

The case of Samson is tragic. As in the case of Samuel, Samson's mother, the wife of Manoah, was barren, but unlike the case of Samuel, apparently, she did not make a promise to God. Rather, Judges 13:3 reports that the angel of the Lord appeared to her and declared she was going to conceive and give birth to a son who was to "be a Nazirite to God from the womb" (Judg. 13:5). While his mother was to avoid wine and strong drink and unclean food, Samson was never to have his hair cut, again a synecdoche

representing all the criteria of a Nazirite. The purpose of Samson's separation was that Samson was to begin the deliverance of Israel from the Philistines. The story is well known, how he was given great strength whenever the "Spirit of the Lord [YHWH] came upon him." At the same time, Samson developed an attraction to Philistine women, which led to conflict between him and the Philistines. In the process, he gradually violated all three criteria of the Nazirite vow (Harbin 2005, 206). At the wedding feast in Timnah, he apparently drank wine. Subsequently he killed thirty Philistines in Ashkelon and stripped the bodies of their clothes. Finally, as is well known, he revealed to Delilah his Nazirite vow, and she cut his hair. This led to his capture, blindness, and ultimately to his death. This produces a baffling account of how God used Samson for the purpose for which he had been called, despite Samson's wanton behavior.

CASE 3: JEPHTHAH

Jephthah's case is also tragic and is probably the most difficult. Jephthah is described as the son of a harlot. While he was illegitimate, Gilead, his father, claimed him; but Gilead's legitimate sons drove him out and he developed a following of "worthless fellows." When Ammonites began incursions against Israel, the leaders of Gilead (the region) asked Jephthah to lead their forces against the Ammonites. Jephthah agreed, and as he went out to war, he made a vow (Judg. 11:30–31) that is problematic. While not specifically a Nazirite vow, the basic concept of making a vow is germane to the issue. As translated in the NASB the promise that he made if God gave him a victory was, "whatever comes out of the doors of my house to meet me when I return in peace from the sons of Ammon, it shall be the LORD'S, and I will offer it up as a burnt offering." As the story goes, he was met by his only child, his daughter. Because he was a man of his word, he felt obligated fulfill his promise, and his daughter agreed that this was the case.

Appendix 7: Vows and Nazirites

As such, the understanding is that Jephthah offered his daughter as a burnt offering. However, there are a number of problems with this understanding. The first and most telling is the translation. Jephthah's promise consisted of two parts. Part 1 stated that whatever came out would be the Lord's (וְהָיָה לַיהוה). Part 2 added that he would offer it as a burnt offering (הַעֲלִיתִהוּ עוֹלָה). They are joined by the ubiquitous conjunction *waw*, which we noted in our discussion of Leviticus 1:1 may be translated many ways, including "or." The only reason that it should be translated here as "and" would be if there was other evidence to solidly indicate that he did indeed offer his daughter as a burnt offering. But the account concludes ambiguously merely stating that he did "according to the vow." Even the questions of why she remained a virgin and why she mourned her virginity are ambiguous and subjective (Marcus 1986, 50–56). In addition to the reasons David Marcus cites that indicate she was not offered as a burnt offering, Lange (1960, 202) maintains that "no priest could have been found to offer it; nor could it possibly have received the Divine acceptance." In addition to those issues, since Leviticus 27:2 provides an alternative in the case of a vow that was too difficult, the option would have been for Jephthah to provide the valuation of ten shekels per Leviticus 2:5 and preserve his daughter. It would appear that in this case, the outcome was per the model of Samuel, and Jephthah's daughter was dedicated to service of God, although that still leaves a lot of questions.

CASE 4: PAUL

While not part of the OT, there is evidence that Paul made at least two Nazirite vows. The first is in Acts 18:18. On his way back to Jerusalem at the end of his second missionary journey, the text notes that Paul had his hair cut in Cenchrea, because "he was keeping a vow." The connection of cutting his hair because of a vow strongly suggests it was a Nazirite vow. The period of time involved would seem to have been at least part of the second journey, and given the conflicts he experienced at Philippi, Thessalonica, Athens, and Corinth, the vow may well have been for safety. While the text does not demonstrate that he performed the requisite sacrifices, the statement that he "went up and greeted the church," referring to Jerusalem, once he was back in Judea leaves that possibility open and following the Cenchrea statement makes it probable. This view is solidified following Paul's third journey. After Paul arrived in Jerusalem, in Acts 21:23–24, James suggested that he take four men who were under a vow and take them up to the temple and that all of them be purified, and then Paul should pay their expenses to get their hair cut. In other words, they were to fulfill the guidelines of Numbers 6 upon the completion of a vow.

While other OT texts talk of Nazirites (Amos 2:11–12) and vows (many examples), these illustrate how vows could be problematic. It is no wonder that so many passages in the wisdom literature and the prophets address keeping a vow that one made.

REFERENCES

Albright, William Foxwell. 1968. *Yahweh and the Gods of Canaan*. London: Athlone.

Albright, William F., and Thomas Oden Lambdin. 1970. "The Evidence of Language," In *The Cambridge Ancient History*, 3rd ed., edited by I. E. S. Edwards, C. J. Gadd, and N. G. L. Hammond. Cambridge: Cambridge University Press.

Alden, Robert L. 1980a. "אָהֵב." *TWOT* 1:14–15.

———. 1980b. "אוב." *TWOT* 1:16–17.

———. 1980c. "חרט I." *TWOT* 1:323.

Alexander, Ralph H. 1980a. "טָמֵא." *TWOT* 1:349–51.

———. 1980b. "טְרָף." *TWOT* 1:353.

———. 1980c. "יָבַל." *TWOT* 1:359–59.

———. 1980d. "יָרָה." *TWOT* 1:364–66.

Allen, Ronald B. 1980a. "ענז." *TWOT* 2:684.

———. 1980b. "עָרַב." *TWOT* 2:694.

———. 1980c. "עָרָה." *TWOT* 2:695.

———. 1980d. "עָרֵךְ." *TWOT* 2:695–97.

André, G. 1980. "זָרַק." *TDOT* 4:162–65.

Antoun, Richard T. 1972. *Arab Village: A Social Structural Study of a Transjordanian Peasant Community*. Bloomington: Indiana University Press.

Appel, Gersion. 2016. "Kosher Slaughter: An Introduction." *My Jewish Learning* (blog). https://www.myjewishlearning.com/article/kosher-slaughtering-an-introduction.

Ashley, Timothy R. 1993. *The Book of Numbers*. NICOT. Grand Rapids: Eerdmans.

Austel, Herman J. 1980a. "שָׁמַע." *TWOT* 2:938–39.

———. 1980b. "שָׁמַר." *TWOT* 2:939–40.

———. 1980c. "שׁפח." *TWOT* 2:946–47.

———. 1980d. "שָׁפַר." *TWOT* 2:951–52.

———. 1980e. "שָׁרַץ." *TWOT* 2:956–57.

———. 1980f. "שֵׁשׁ." *TWOT* 2:959.

Avner, Uzi. 1990. "Ancient Agricultural Settlement and Religion in the Uvda Valley in Southern Israel." *Biblical Archaeologist* 53, no. 3:125–41. DOI: 10.2307/3210113.

Bailey, Lloyd R. 2005. *Leviticus-Numbers*. SHBC 3. Macon, GA: Smyth & Helwys.

Baker, David L. 2009. *Tight Fists or Open Hands*. Grand Rapids: Eerdmans.

Baker, David W. 1996. *Leviticus*. Cornerstone Biblical Commentary. Carol Stream, IL: Tyndale House.

Balberg, Mira. 2013. "Pricing Persons: Consecration, Compensation, and Individuality in the Mishnah." *JQR* 103, no. 2:169–95. DOI: 10.1353/jqr.2013.0012.

Balentine, Samuel E. 2002. *Leviticus*. IB. Louisville: John Knox, 2002.

Bansal, Agam, et al. 2018. "Selfies: A Boon or Bane?" *J Family Med Prim Care*, Jul-Aug; 7(4): 828–831.

Barr, James. 1961. *The Semantics of Biblical Language*. Oxford: Oxford University Press.

Baumann, Bill B. 1960. "The Botanical Aspects of Ancient Egyptian Embalming and Burial." *Econ Bot* 14, no. 1:84–104. DOI: 10.1007/BF02859368.

Becker, Wayne M., Lewis J. Kleinsmith, and Jeff Hardin. 2000. *The World of the Cell*. 4th ed. San Francisco: Benjamin/Cummings.

Bergman, Jan, Helmer Ringgren, and M. Tsevat. 1977. "בְּתוּלָה." *TDOT* 2:338–43.

Berkhof, Louis. 1941. *Systematic Theology*. 4th ed. Grand Rapids: Eerdmans.

Bermant, Chaim, and Michael Weitzman. 1979. *Ebla: A Revelation in Archaeology*. New York: Times Books.

Blackman, Philip., ed. 1963. *Mishnayoth: Pointed Hebrew Text, English Translation, Introductions, Notes, Supplement, Appendix, Indexes, Addenda, Corrigenda*. 2nd ed. New York: Judaica Press.

Blomberg, Craig L. 1992. *Matthew*. NAC 22. Nashville: Broadman & Holman.

Borowski, Oded. 1987. *Agriculture in Iron Age Israel*. Winona Lake, IN: Eisenbrauns.

Botterweck, Johannes. 1975. "בְּהֵמָה." *TDOT* 2:6–20.

Bowling, Andrew. 1980a. "זָכַר." *TWOT* 1:241–43.

_____. 1980b. "יָרֵא." *TWOT* 1:399–401.

_____. 1980c. "לָאַךְ." *TWOT* 1:464–65.

_____. 1980d. "נוּף I." *TWOT* 2:565.

_____. 1980e. "נוּף II." *TWOT* 2:565.

_____. 1980f. "רוּם." *TWOT* 2:837–39.

Bratcher, Robert G., and Howard A. Hatton. 2000. *A Handbook on Deuteronomy*. UBS Handbook. New York: United Bible Societies.

Büchsel, Friedrich. 1965. "ἱλασμός." *TDNT* 3:316–17.

Budin, Stephanie Lynn. 2008. *The Myth of Sacred Prostitution in Antiquity*. Cambridge: Cambridge University Press.

Budziszewski, J. 2011. *What We Can't Not Know: A Guide*. Rev. ed. San Francisco: Ignatius Press.

Bukhari, Saleem 2002. "Hajj by the Numbers." *Saudi Aramco World* 53, no. 3:27.

Bullinger, E. W. 1968. *Figures of Speech Used in the Bible: Explained and Illustrated*. Grand Rapids: Baker.

Burnard, Travor. 2011. "The Atlantic Slave Trade." In *The Routledge History of Slavery*, edited by Gad Heuman and Trevor Burnard. New York: Routledge.

Caquot, André. 1978. "דְּבַשׁ." *TDOT* 3:128–31.

Carr, G. Lloyd. 1980a. "מִנְחָה." *TWOT* 1:514–15.

_____. 1980b. "עָלָה." *TWOT* 2:666–70.

_____. 1980c. "שָׁלֵם." *TWOT* 2:930–32.

Cartledge, Tony W. 1989. "Were Nazirite Vows Unconditional?" *CBQ* 51, no. 3:409–22.

Cassuto, Umberto. 1961. *A Commentary on the Book of Genesis: Part I: From Adam to Noah, Genesis 1–VI8*. Jerusalem: Magnes.

_____. 1987. *A Commentary on the Book of Exodus*. Jerusalem: Magnes.

Chirichigno, Gregory C. 1993. *Debt-Slavery in Israel and the Ancient Near East*. JSOTSup 141. Sheffield: JSOT Press.

Clements, R. E. 2004. "שָׁאַר." *TDOT* 14:272–86.

Clutton-Brock, Juliet. 2012. *Domesticates: A World View Through History*. East Lansing: Michigan State University Press.

Cohen, Gary G. 1980a. "שָׂכַה." *TWOT* 2:876.

_____. 1980b. "שָׁאַל." *TWOT* 2:891–92.

_____. 1980c. "שָׁאַר." *TWOT* 2:895.

Cole, R. Alan. 1973. *Exodus: An Introduction and Commentary*. TOTC 2. Downers Grove, IL: InterVarsity Press.

Cole, R. Dennis. 2000. *Numbers*. NAC 3b. Nashville: Broadman & Holman.

Coppes, Leonard J. 1980a. "אדם." *TWOT* 1:10–11.

_____. 1980b. "דָּרַשׁ." *TWOT* 1:198–99.

_____. 1980c. "נָגַע." *TWOT* 2:551–52.

_____. 1980d. "נָדַב." *TWOT* 2:554–55.

_____. 1980e. "נָדַר." *TWOT* 2:557–58.

_____. 1980f. "נוּחַ." *TWOT* 2:562–63.

_____. 1980g. "עָנָה III." *TWOT* 2:682–84.

_____. 1980h. "קוּץ." *TWOT* 2:794.

_____. 1980i. "קָלַל." *TWOT* 2:800–801.

_____. 1980j. "קֶמַח." *TWOT* 2:801.

_____. 1980k. "קָרַב I." *TWOT* 2:811–13.

_____. 1980l. "קָרַה." *TWOT* 2:813–14.

_____. 1980m. "קֶרַח." *TWOT* 2:815.

Cosgrove, Mark. 2018. *The Brain, the Mind, and the Person Within: The Enduring Mystery of the Soul*. Grand Rapids: Kregel.

Cowles, C. S. 2003. "The Case for Radical Discontinuity." In *Show Them No Mercy: 4 Views on God and Canaanite Genocide*, edited by Stanley N. Gundry, 13–44. Counterpoints. Grand Rapids: Zondervan.

Culver, Robert D. 1980. "שָׁפַט." *TWOT* 2:947–49.

Cummins, Joe, and Mae-Wan Ho. 2005. "Hybrid Seed." *Science in Society Archive*. https://www.i-sis.org.uk/hybridSeed.php.

Daane, James. 1985. "Sin and Sinner." *ZPEB* 5:444–47.

Danby, Herbert. 1933. *The Mishnah*. Oxford: Oxford University Press.

References

Davis, John J. 1968. *Biblical Numerology: A Basic Study of the Use of Numbers in the Bible*. Grand Rapids: Baker.

Day, Alfred Ely. 1939. "Calendar." *ISBE* 1:541–42.

Denton, Michael. 2016. *Evolution: Still a Theory in Crisis*. Rev. ed. Seattle: Discovery Institute Press.

de Vaux, Roland. 1965. *Ancient Israel: Its Life and Institutions*. New York: McGraw-Hill.

DiBenedetto, Katelyn. 2012. "Analyzing Tophets: Did the Phoenicians Practice Child Sacrifice?" Anthropology 5. https://scholarsarchive.library.albany.edu/honorscollege_anthro/5/.

Dommershausen, W. 1995. "כֹּהֵן." *TDOT* 7:66–75.

Dorman, Ted M. 2001. *A Faith for All Seasons*. 2nd ed. Nashville: Broadman & Holman.

Douglas, Mary. 1993. "The Forbidden Animals in Leviticus." *JSOT* 18, no. 59:3–23. DOI: 10.1177/0309089293018059.

———. 1996. "Sacred Contagion." In *Reading Leviticus: A Conversation with Mary Douglas*, edited by John F. A. Sawyer, 86–106. JSOTSup 227. Sheffield: Sheffield Academic.

———. 1999. *Leviticus as Literature*. Oxford: Oxford University Press.

———. 2002. *Purity and Danger: An Analysis of Concepts of Pollution and Taboo*. New York: Routledge.

Drescher, Seymour. 2009. *Abolition: A History of Slavery and Antislavery*. Cambridge: Cambridge University Press.

Dreher, Rod. 2020. *Live Not by Lies: A Manual for Christian Dissidents*. New York: Penguin Random House.

Driver, Godfrey Rolles. 1955a. "Birds in the Old Testament, I: Birds in Law." *PEQ* 87, no. 1:5–20. DOI: 10.1179/peq.1955.87.1.5.

———. 1955b. "Birds in the Old Testament, II: Birds in Life." *PEQ* 87, no. 2:129–40. DOI: 10.1179/peq.1955.87.2.129.

Drumwright, H. L. 1985. "Shekinah." *ZPEB* 5:388–91.

Duguid, Barbara R. 2013. *Extravagant Grace: God's Glory Displayed in Our Weakness*. Phillipsburg, NJ: P&R Publishing.

Durham, John I. 1987. *Exodus*. WBC 3. Waco, TX: Word.

Edersheim, Alfred. 1994. *The Temple: Its Ministry and Services*. Updated ed. Peabody, MA: Hendrickson.

Fabry, Heinz-Josef. 1997. "מִנְחָה." *TDOT* 8:407–21.

Feinberg, Charles L. 1975. "Priests and Levites." *ZPEB* 4:852–67.

———. 1980a. "אָסַף." *TWOT* 1:60–61.

———. 1980b. "צָנַף." *TWOT* 2:771.

Feinberg, John S. 1981. "Salvation in the Old Testament." In *Tradition and Testament: Essays in Honor of Charles Lee Feinberg*, edited by John S. Feinberg and Paul D. Feinberg, 39–77. Chicago: Moody Press.

Finegan, Jack. 1998. *Handbook of Biblical Chronology*. Rev. ed. Peabody, MA: Hendrickson.

Fisher, Milton C. 1980a. "נָצַב." *TWOT* 2:591–92.

———. 1980b. "נָקַב." *TWOT* 2:595–96.

———. 1980c. "נָקַף II." *TWOT* 2:599–600.

———. 1980d. "נָשַׁף." *TWOT* 2:604–5.

Flemming, Rebecca. 2019. "(The Wrong Kind of) Gonorrhea in Antiquity." In *The Hidden Affliction: Sexually Transmitted Infections and Infertility in History*, edited by Simon Szreter. Rochester, NY: University of Rochester Press. https://www.ncbi.nlm.nih.gov/books/NBK547155.

Frymer-Kensky, Tikva. 2021. "Shelomith 1: Bible." *JWA-S/HEJW*. https://jwa.org/encyclopedia/article/shelomith-1-bible.

Fuchs, Daniel. 1985. *Israel's Holy Days in Type and Prophecy*. New York: Chosen People Ministries.

Gane, Roy. 2004a. *Leviticus, Numbers*. NIVAC. Grand Rapids: Zondervan.

———. 2004b. *Ritual Dynamic Structure*. Gorgias Dissertations 14. Piscataway, NJ: Gorgias.

———. 2009. "Leviticus." *ZIBBCOT* 1:284–337.

Gentry, Peter J. 2013. "The Meaning of 'Holy' in the Old Testament." *BSac* 170, no. 680:400–417.

Gerstenberger, Erhard S. 1996. *Leviticus: A Commentary*. OTL. Louisville: Westminster John Knox.

Gilchrist, Paul R. 1980a. "יָכַח" *TWOT* 1:376–77.

———. 1980b. "יָצָא" *TWOT* 1:393–94.

Gladwell, Malcolm. 2002. *The Tipping Point: How Little Things Can Make a Big Difference*. Boston: Little, Brown, & Co.

Gordon, Cyrus H. 1982. "The Biblical Sabbath: Its Origin and Observance in the Ancient Near East." *Judaism* 31, no. 1:12–16.

Greenberg, James A. 2019. *A New Look at Atonement in Leviticus: The Meaning and Purpose of* Kipper *Revisited*. BBRSup 23. University Park, PA: Eisenbrauns.

Haag, E. 2004. "שָׁבַת" *TDOT* 14:387–97.

Hall, Elizabeth. 1989. "When Does Life Begin? An Embryologist Looks at the Abortion Debate." *Psychology Today* 23, no. 9:42–46.

Hallo, William H. 1977. "New Moons and Sabbaths: A Case-study in the Contrastive Approach." *HUCA* 48:1–18.

Hamilton, Victor P. 1980a. "אֶרֶץ" *TWOT* 1:74–75.

———. 1980b. "חָנַךְ II." *TWOT* 1:301–2.

———. 1980c. "מַעַל" *TWOT* 1:519–20.

———. 1980d. "מָשַׁח" *TWOT* 1:530–32.

———. 1980e. "פָּנַר" *TWOT* 2:715.

———. 1980f. "פָּלָא" *TWOT* 2:723.

———. 1980g. "פָּסַח" *TWOT* 2:728–29.

———. 1980h. "פָּרַע" *TWOT* 2:736–37.

———. 1980i. "פָּרַר I." *TWOT* 2:738.

———. 1980j. "שָׁבַת" *TWOT* 2:902–3.

———. 1980k. "שָׁגַג" *TWOT* 2:903–4.

———. 1980l. "שָׂרַף" *TWOT* 2:907–8.

———. 1980m. "שָׁחַט" *TWOT* 2:915–16.

Hankore, Daniel. 2013. "The Concept of 'Vow' in the Hebrew Scriptures." In *The Abduction of Dinah: Genesis 28:10–35:15 as a Votive Narrative*, 43–87. Cambridge: Clarke & Co.

Harbin, Michael A. 1982. "Language Was Created, Not Evolved." *CRSQ* 19:52–55.

———. 1994. *To Serve Other Gods: An Evangelical History of Religion*. Lanham, MD: University Press of America.

———. 2005. *The Promise and the Blessing: A Historical Survey of the Old and New Testaments*. Grand Rapids: Zondervan.

———. 2011. "Jubilee and Social Justice." *JETS* 54, no. 4:685–99.

———. 2012. "The Manumission of Slaves in Jubilee and Sabbath Years." *TynBul* 63, no. 1:53–74. DOI: 10.53751/001c.29326.

———. 2016a. "Sovereignty and Free Will in the Accounts of Terah and Abraham." *SBET* 34, no. 1:19–34.

———. 2016b. "A Typical Israelite Community in the OT Period." In *Associates for Biblical Research Newsletter*. https://biblearchaeology.org/research/chronological-categories/conquest-of-canaan/2648-a-typical-israelite-community-in-the-ot-period.

———. 2017. "Jubilee, Year of, IV: Christianity, Modern Europe and America." In *Encyclopedia of the Bible and Its Reception*, edited by Constance M. Furey, Joel Marcus LeMon, Brian Matz, Thomas Römer, Jens Schröter, Barry Dov Walfish, and Eric Ziolkowski, 14:858–859. Berlin: de Gruyter.

———. 2018. "Holiness: Moral Purity Between the Persons of the Trinity." *BSac* 175, no. 697:17–33.

———. 2021a. "Social Justice for Social Outliers in Ancient Israel, Part 1: Cultural Background." *JETS* 64, no. 3:471–94.

———. 2021b. "Social Justice and Social Outliers in Ancient Israel, Part 2: Provision for Widows, and Resident Aliens." *JETS* 64, no. 4:681–701.

Harris, R. Laird. 1980a. "בְּ" *TWOT* 1:87.

———. 1980b. "גָּאַל" *TWOT* 1:144–45.

———. 1980c. "חסד I." *TWOT* 1:305–7.

———. 1980d. "כָּסָה" *TWOT* 1:448–49.

———. 1980e. "עֹלָם" *TWOT* 2:671–72.

References

Harrison, R. K. 1980. *Leviticus, an Introduction and Commentary*. TOTC 3. Downers Grove, IL: InterVarsity Press.

Hartley, John E. 1980a. "צִיץ." *TWOT* 2:759–60.

———. 1980b. "צֶמַח." *TWOT* 2:770–71.

———. 1980c. "צָפַר." *TWOT* 2:775.

———. 1980d. "שֶׂה." *TWOT* 2:871–72.

———. 1992. *Leviticus*. WBC 4. Dallas: Word.

Heicksen, M. H. 1975. "Cooking." *ZPEB* 1:956–57.

Heiser, Michael S. 2015. *The Unseen Realm: Recovering the Supernatural Worldview of the Bible*. Bellingham, WA: Lexham Press.

Hendriksen, William. 1995. *Ephesians*. Grand Rapids: Baker.

Herodotus. 1952. *The History of Herodotus*. Great Books of the Western World 6. Chicago: Encyclopaedia Britannica.

Hess, Richard S. 2008. "Leviticus." In *The Expositor's Bible Commentary, Vol. 1 Genesis–Leviticus*, edited by Tremper Longman III and David E. Garland, 563–829. Grand Rapids: Zondervan.

Heuman, Gad, and Trevor Burnard. 2011. "Introduction." In *The Routledge History of Slavery*, edited by Gad Heuman and Trevor Burnard, 1–4. New York: Routledge.

Hill, Andrew E., and John H. Walton. 2009. *A Survey of the Old Testament*. 3rd ed. Grand Rapids: Zondervan.

Hoehner, Harold W. 1977. *Chronological Aspects of the Life of Christ*. Grand Rapids: Zondervan.

Hoenig, Sidney B. 1969. "Sabbatical Years and the Year of Jubilee." *JQR* 59, no. 3:222–36. DOI: 10.2307/1453647.

Homer. 1952. *The Odyssey*. Great Books of the Western World 4. Chicago: Encyclopaedia Britannica.

Hopkins, David C. 1985. *The Highlands of Canaan: Agricultural Life in the Early Iron Age*. Social World of Biblical Antiquity 3. Sheffield: Almond Press.

Houston, Walter. 1993. *Purity and Monotheism: Clean and Unclean Animals in Biblical Law*. JSOTSup 140. Sheffield: JSOT Press

Howard, David M., Jr. 1998. *Joshua*. NAC 5. Nashville: Broadman & Holman.

Huey, F. B., Jr. 1975. "Weights and Measures." *ZPEB* 5:913–22.

Hulse, E. V. 1975. "The Nature of Biblical 'Leprosy' and the Use of Alternative Medical Terms in Modern Translations of the Bible." *PEQ* 107:85–105. DOI: 10.1179/peq.1975.107.2.87.

J Family Med Prim Care. 2018 Jul-Aug; 7(4): 828–831.

Johnson, Phillip E. 1993. *Darwin on Trial*. 2nd ed. Downers Grove, IL: InterVarsity Press.

Joy, Alfred H. 1939. "Twilight." *ISBE* 5:3028.

Kadari, Tamar. 2021. "Shelomith 1: Midrash and Aggadah." *JWA-S/HEJW*. https://jwa.org/encyclopedia/article/shelomith-1-midrash-and-aggadah.

Kaiser, Otto. 1998. "נָדַר." *TDOT* 9:242–55.

Kaiser, Walter C. 1980a. "בָּלַל." *TWOT* 1:111–12.

———. 1980b. "יָשַׁב." *TWOT* 1:411–13.

———. 1980c. "מאס." *TWOT* 1:488.

———. 1980d. "מוד." *TWOT* 1:493.

———. 1980e. "מָכַר." *TWOT* 1:504–5.

———. 1980f. "מָלֵא." *TWOT* 1:505–6.

———. 1980g. "נָשָׂא." *TWOT* 2:600–602.

———. 1980h. "עָבַד." *TWOT* 2:639–41.

Kalland, Earl S. 1980. "גָּלַל." *TWOT* 1:162–65.

Keil, Carl Friedrich, and Franz Delitzsch. 1956. *Commentary on the Old Testament: Pentateuch*. Grand Rapids: Eerdmans

Kellerman, Diether. 1974. "אָשַׁם." *TDOT* 1:429–37.

Kellogg, Samuel H. 1978. *The Book of Leviticus*. 3rd ed. Minneapolis: Klock & Klock.

King, Philip J., and Lawrence E. Stager. 2001. *Life in Biblical Israel*. Library of Ancient Israel. Louisville: Westminster John Knox.

Kitchen, Kenneth A. 2003. *On The Reliability of the Old Testament*. Grand Rapids, Mich; Eerdmans.

Kiuchi, Nobuyoshi. 2003. *A Study of Ḥāṭā' and Ḥaṭṭā'ṭ in Leviticus 4–5*. FAT 2/2. Tübingen: Mohr Siebeck.

———. 2007. *Leviticus*. ApOTC 3. Downers Grove, IL: InterVarsity Press.

Kleinig, John W. 2003. *Leviticus*. Concordia Commentary. St. Louis: Concordia.

Koch, Klaus. 1980. "חָטָא." *TDOT* 4:309–19.

———. 1999. "עָוֹן." *TDOT* 10:546–62.

Kornfeld, W. 2003. "קדשׁ." *TDOT* 12:521–26.

Kramer, Samuel Noah. 1963. *The Sumerians: Their History, Culture, and Character*. Chicago: University of Chicago Press.

Kvavadze, Eliso, Ofer Bar-Yosuf, Anna Belfer-Cohen, Elisabetta Boaretto, Nino Jakeli, Zinovi Matskevich, and Tengiz Meshveliani. 2009. "30,000-Year-Old Wild Flax Fibers." *Science* 325, no. 5945:1359. DOI: 10.1126/science.1175404.

Lang, B. 1995. "כִּפֶּר." *TDOT* 7:289–303.

Lange, John Peter. 1960. *Leviticus: Or, the Third Book of Moses*, translated by Frederic Gardener. Grand Rapids: Zondervan.

Levine, Baruch A. 1989. *Leviticus = Va-Yikra: The Traditional Hebrew Text with the New JPS Translation*. JPS Torah Commentary. Philadelphia: Jewish Publication Society.

Lewis, Jack P. 1980a. "חָקַק." *TWOT* 1:316–18.

———. 1980b. "חָתַם." *TWOT* 1:334–35.

———. 1980c. "יָדַע." *TWOT* 1:366–67.

———. 1980d. "יָעַד." *TWOT* 1:387–89.

———. 1980e. "קָצַר II." *TWOT* 2:809–10.

Lilley, John P. 1975. "New Moon." *ZPEB* 4:417.

Livingston, G. Herbert. 1980a. "אָשֵׁם." *TWOT* 1:78–80.

———. 1980b. "חָטָא." *TWOT* 1:277–79.

———. 1980c. "חָמַר III." *TWOT* 1:299.

———. 1980d. "פָּשַׁע." *TWOT* 2:741–42.

Lohfink, Norbert. 1986. "חָרַם." *TDOT* 5:180–99.

Lust, Johan, Erik Eynikel, and Katrin Hauspie. 2003. *A Greek-English Lexicon of the Septuagint*. Rev. ed. Stuttgart: Deutsche Bibelgesellschaft.

Mader, Sylvia. 2001. *Biology*. 7th ed. Boston: McGraw-Hill.

Marcus, David. 1986. *Jephthah and His Vow*. Lubbock: Texas Tech Press.

Martens, Elmer A. 1980a. "בהם." *TWOT* 1:92–93.

———. 1980b. "בּוֹא." *TWOT* 1:93–95.

———. 1980c. "בָּמָה." *TWOT* 1:113.

———. 1980d. "בָּקַר." *TWOT* 1:124–26.

Mathews, Kenneth A. 2009. *Leviticus: Holy God, Holy People*. Preaching the Word. Wheaton, IL: Crossway, 2009.

Matthews, Victor Harold, and Don C. Benjamin. 1993. *Social World of Ancient Israel, 1250–587 BCE*. Peabody, MA: Hendrickson.

Mays, James Luther. 1963. *The Book of Leviticus; The Book of Numbers*. Layman's Bible Commentary 4. Richmond, VA: John Knox.

McCartney, Martha W. 2003. *A Study of the Africans and African Americans on Jamestown Island and at Green Spring, 1619–1803*. Williamsburg, VA: U.S. Department of the Interior.

McComiskey, Thomas E. 1980a. "אִישׁ." *TWOT* 1:38–39.

———. 1980b. "בָּדַל." *TWOT* 1:91–92.

———. 1980c. "זָכַר." *TWOT* 1:241–43.

———. 1980d. "נָזַר." *TWOT* 2:567–68.

———. 1980e. "קָדַשׁ." *TWOT* 2:786–89.

McKenzie, Robert Tracy. 2021. *We the Fallen People: The Founders and the Future of American Democracy*. Downers Grove, IL: InterVarsity Press.

McNutt, Paula M. 1990. *The Forging of Israel: Iron Technology, Symbolism, and Tradition in Ancient Society*. JSOTSup 108. Sheffield: Sheffield Academic.

Melo, Maria J. 2009. "History of Natural Dyes in the Ancient Mediterranean World." In *Handbook of Natural Colorants*, edited by Thomas Bechtold and Rita Mussak, 1–20. Hoboken, NJ: Wiley & Sons.

Merrill, Eugene. 1985. "1 Chronicles." In *The Bible Knowledge Commentary*, edited by John F. Walvoord and Roy B. Zuck, 589–617. Wheaton, IL: Victor Books.

———. 1994. *Deuteronomy*. NAC 4. Nashville: Broadman & Holman.

References

Milgrom, Jacob. 1991. *Leviticus 1–16: A New Translation with Introduction and Commentary.* AB 3. New York: Doubleday.

———. 2000. *Leviticus 17–22: A New Translation with Introduction and Commentary.* AB 3A. New York: Doubleday.

———. 2001. *Leviticus 23–27: A New Translation with Introduction and Commentary.* AB 3B. New York: Doubleday.

Milgrom, Jacob, David P. Wright, and Heinz-Josef Fabry. 1998. "נֵזֶר." *TDOT* 9:300–304.

Moorehead, William G. 1939. "Priest." *ISBE* 4:2439–41.

Morgenstern, Julian. 1926. "Additional Notes on 'The Three Calendars of Ancient Israel.'" *HUCA* 3:77–107.

Morris, Leon. 1992. *The Gospel According to Matthew.* PNTC. Grand Rapids: Eerdmans.

Moyer, James. C. 1975. "Stoning." *ZPEB* 5:524.

Muigai, Anne W. T., and Oliver Hanotte. 2013. "The Origin of African Sheep: Archaeological and Genetic Perspectives." *African Archaeological Review* 30, no. 1:39–50. DOI: 10.1007/s10437-013-9129-0.

Nadler, Sam. 2006. *Messiah in the Feasts of Israel.* Charlotte, NC: Word of Messiah Ministries.

Nemet-Nejat, Karen Rhea. 1998. *Daily Life in Ancient Mesopotamia.* Peabody, MA: Hendrickson.

Neusner, Jacob. 1994. *The Mishnah: An Introduction.* Northvale, NJ: Aronson.

Niehr, Herbert. 2006. "שָׁפַט." *TDOT* 15:411–31.

Noordtzij, A. 1982. *The Book of Leviticus,* translated by Raymond Toftman. Grand Rapids: Zondervan.

Norton, Michael. 2015. *Unlocking the Secrets of the Feasts: The Prophecies of the Feasts of Leviticus.* Nashville: WestBow.

Noss, John B. 1961. *Man's Religions.* 3rd ed. New York: Macmillan.

O'Callaghan, Sean. 2000. *To Hell or Barbados.* Kerry, Ireland: Brandon.

Olmo Lete, Gregorio del. 2004. *Canaanite Religion According to the Liturgical Texts of Ugarit.* Winona Lake, IN: Eisenbrauns.

Omanson, Roger L., and John E. Ellington. 2008. *A Handbook on 1–2 Kings.* UBS Handbook. New York: United Bible Societies.

Oppenheim, A. Leo. 1977. *Ancient Mesopotamia: Portrait of a Dead Civilization.* Rev. ed. Chicago: University of Chicago Press.

Oswalt, John N. 1980a. "בָּשַׂר." *TWOT* 1:135–36.

———. 1980b. "כָּחַד." *TWOT* 1:436.

———. 1980c "כִּי." *TWOT* 1:437–38.

———. 1980d. "כָּלַל." *TWOT* 1:441–42.

Otto, Rudolf. 1958. *The Idea of the Holy: An Inquiry into the Non-Rational Factor in the Idea of the Divine and Its Relation to the Rational.* 2nd ed. New York: Oxford University Press.

Parrinder, Geoffrey, ed. 1984. *World Religions from Ancient History to the Present.* New York: Facts on File.

Parry, John W. 1955. "The Story of Spices." *Econ Bot* 9:190–207. DOI: 10.1007/BF02898800.

Patterson, R. D. 1980a. "סֹלֶת." *TWOT* 2:628.

———. 1980b. "סָמַן" *TWOT* 2:628.

Payne, J. Barton. 1980. "רִיחַ." *TWOT* 2:836–37.

Péter-Contesse, René, and John Ellington. 1992. *A Handbook on Leviticus.* UBS Handbook. New York: United Bible Societies.

Philo. 1993. *The Special Laws.* In *The Works of Philo,* translated by C. D. Yonge. Peabody, MA: Hendrickson.

Posner, Menachem. 2021. "How Does the Spring Equinox Relate to the Timing of Passover?" Chabad.org. https://www.chabad.org/holidays/passover/pesach_cdo/aid/495531/jewish/How-Does-the-Spring-Equinox-Relate-to-the-Timing-of-Passover.htm.

Preuss, Horst Dietrich. 1978. "גִּלּוּלִים." *TDOT* 3:1–5.

Radner, Ephraim. 2008. *Leviticus.* Brazos Theological Commentary. Grand Rapids: Brazos.

Rainey, Anson. 1975. "Sacrifices and Offerings." *ZPEB* 5:194–211.

References

Raven, Peter H., Ray F. Evert, and Susan E. Eichhorn. 1999. *Biology of Plants*. 6th ed. New York: Freeman & Co.

Reeves, Michael. 2012. *Delighting in the Trinity: An Introduction to the Christian Faith*. Downers Grove, IL: InterVarsity Press.

Regt, L. J. de, and Ernst R. Wendland. 2016. *A Handbook on Numbers*. UBS Handbook. Miami: United Bible Societies.

Reuter, E. 2006. "שִׁפְחָה." *TDOT* 15:405–10.

Ringgren, Helmer. 2004. "שָׁאַר." *TDOT* 14:270–71.

Rooker, Mark F. 2000. *Leviticus*. NAC 3A. Nashville: Broadman & Holman.

Roop, Eugene F. 2002. *Ruth, Jonah, Esther*. Believers Church Commentary. Scottdale, PA: Herald Press.

Ross, Allen P. 2002. *Holiness to the Lord: A Guide to the Exposition of the Book of Leviticus*. Grand Rapids: Baker Academic.

Rubin, Barry, and Steffi Karen Rubin. 1998. *The Messianic Passover Haggadah*. Baltimore: Messianic Jewish Publishers.

Ryrie, Charles C. 1986. *Basic Theology*. Wheaton, IL: Victor Books.

Saggs, H. W. F. 1978. *The Encounter with the Divine in Mesopotamia and Israel*. London: Athlone.

Schnittjer, Gary Edward. 2006. *The Torah Story: An Apprenticeship on the Pentateuch*. Grand Rapids: Zondervan.

Schorsch, Ismar. 1997. "The Day Begins with Night." https://www.jtsa.edu/torah/the-day-begins-with-night.

Schultz, Carl. 1980a. "עָוָה." *TWOT* 1:650–52.

———. 1980b. "עוּף." *TWOT* 2:654–55.

———. 1980c. "עוּר." *TWOT* 2:656–57.

Schunk, K.-D. 1975. "בָּמָה." *TDOT* 2:139–45.

Schüpphaus, J. 1990. "יָשֵׁן." *TDOT* 6:438–41.

Schwartz, Glenn M. 2012. "Archaeology and Sacrifice." In *Sacred Killing: The Archaeology of Sacrifice in the Ancient Near East*, edited by Anne M. Porter and Glenn M. Schwartz, 1–32. Winona Lake, IN: Eisenbrauns.

Scott, Jack B. 1980a. "אֵיפָה." *TWOT* 1:38.

———. 1980b. "אַךְ." *TWOT* 1:39.

———. 1980c. "אָכַל." *TWOT* 1:39–40.

———. 1980d. "אלל." *TWOT* 1:46.

———. 1980e. "אָמָה." *TWOT* 1:49–50.

Seebass, Horst. 1998. "נֶפֶשׁ." *TDOT* 9:497–519.

Sevener, Harold A. n.d. *Passover Haggadah for Biblical Jews and Christians*. Orangeburg, NY: Chosen People Ministries.

Shepherd, Coulson. 1974. *Jewish Holy Days: Their Prophetic and Christian Significance*. 3rd ed. Neptune, NJ: Loizeaux.

Sherwood, Stephen K. 2002. *Leviticus, Numbers, Deuteronomy*. Berit Olam. Collegeville, MN: Liturgical Press.

Shutt, R. J. H. 1985. "Letter of Aristeas." In *The Old Testament Pseudepigrapha*, edited by James H. Charlesworth, 2 vols., 2:7–34. New York: Doubleday.

Sider, Ronald J. 1997. *Rich Christians in an Age of Hunger: Moving from Affluence to Generosity*. 20th anniversary revision. Nashville: Nelson.

Singer, Itamar. 2008. "Purple-Dyers in Lazpa." In *Anatolian Interfaces*, edited by Billie Jean Collins, Mary R. Bachvarova, and Ian C. Rutherford, 21–43. Oxford: Oxbow.

Sklar, Jay. 2014. *Leviticus: An Introduction and Commentary*. TOTC 3. Downers Grove, IL: InterVarsity Press.

Smick, Elmer B. 1980. "ברה." *TWOT* 1:128–30.

Stark, Rodney. 2003. *For The Glory of God: How Monotheism Led to Reformations, Science, Witch-hunts, and the End of Slavery*. Princeton, NJ: Princeton University Press.

———. 2011. *The Triumph of Christianity*. New York: Harper Collins.

Stein, Robert H. 1992. *Luke*. NAC 24. Nashville: Broadman & Holman.

Stern, Philip D. 1991. *The Biblical Ḥerem: A Window on Israel's Religious Experience*. BJS 211. Atlanta: Scholars Press.

Stigers, Harold G. 1980. "גּוּר." *TWOT* 1:155–56.

References

Strong, Augustus Hopkins. 1907. *Systematic Theology: A Compendium*. 3 vols. Old Tappan, NJ: Revell.

Stuart, Douglas K. 2006. *Exodus*. NAC 2. Nashville: Broadman & Holman.

Teeter, Emily. 2011. *Religion and Ritual in Ancient Egypt*. New York: Cambridge University Press.

Thompson, J. Alexander. 1975. "Incense." *ZPEB* 3:274–76.

Trutza, Peter. 1975. "Marriage." *ZPEB* 4:92–102.

Tucker, A. O. 1986. "Frankincense and Myrrh." *Econ Bot* 40:425–33. DOI: 10.1007/BF02859654.

Van Beek, Gus W. 1958. "Frankincense and Myrrh in Ancient South Arabia." *JAOS* 78, no. 3:141–52. DOI: 10.2307/595284.

_____. 1960. "Frankencense and Myrrh." *Biblical Archaeologist* 23, no. 3:69–95.

Van Dam, Cornelius. 1997. *The Urim and Thummim*. Winona Lake, IN: Eisenbrauns.

Van Groningen, Gerard. 1980a. "זָרה." *TWOT* 1:251.

_____. 1980b. "עָבַר." *TWOT* 2:641–44.

_____. 1980c. "עמם." *TWOT* 2:675–77.

Vos, Geerhardus. 1948. *Biblical Theology: Old and New Testaments*. Grand Rapids: Eerdmans.

Waltke, Bruce K. 1975. "Molech." *ZPEB* 4:269–70.

_____. 1980a. "בתל." *TWOT* 1:137–39.

_____. 1980b. "גָּלָה." *TWOT* 1:160–61.

_____. 1980c. "נָעַל." *TWOT* 1:169–70.

Waltke, Bruce K., with Charles Yu. 2007. *An Old Testament Theology: An Exegetical, Canonical, and Thematic Approach*. Grand Rapids: Zondervan.

Walton, John, and J. Harvey Walton. 2017. *The Lost World of the Israelite Conquest*. Downers Grove, IL: InterVarsity Press.

Weber, Carl Philip. 1980a. "וְ." *TWOT* 1:229–30.

_____. 1980b. "חָנֵג." *TWOT* 1:261–63.

_____. 1980c. "חָזַק." *TWOT* 1:276–77.

Wells, Bruce. 2009. "Exodus." *ZIBBCOT* 1:160–283.

Wenham, Gordon J. 1979. *The Book of Leviticus*. NICOT. Grand Rapids: Eerdmans.

_____. 1981. *Numbers: An Introduction and Commentary*. TOTC 4. Downers Grove, IL: InterVarsity Press.

White, William, Jr. 1975. "Birthright." *ZPEB* 1:617.

_____. 1980a. "רוּעַ." *TWOT* 2:839.

_____. 1980b. "רָחַן." *TWOT* 2:843.

_____. 1980c. "רָכַל." *TWOT* 2:848.

_____. 1980d. "רָנַן." *TWOT* 2:851.

_____. 1980e. "רָצָה." *TWOT* 2:859–60.

Wilder, Laura Ingalls. 1968. *The Long Winter*. New York: Scholastic Book Services.

Willis, Timothy M. 2009. *Leviticus*. AOTC. Nashville: Abingdon.

Wilson, John A. 1956. *The Culture of Ancient Egypt*. Chicago: University of Chicago Press.

Wilson, Marvin R. 1980. "נָסַךְ." *TWOT* 2:581–82.

Winterbotham, Rayner. 1910. *Numbers*. Pulpit Commentary 5. London: Funk & Wagnalls.

Wiseman, Donald J. 1980a. "חָלַל I." *TWOT* 1:288–89.

_____. 1980b. "חָלַל II." *TWOT* 2:289–90.

Wolf, Herbert. 1980a. "אָחַז." *TWOT* 1:32–33.

_____. 1980b. "דָּקַק." *TWOT* 1:194–95.

_____. 1980c. "דרר." *TWOT* 1:197–98.

Wolff, Hans Walter. 1974. *Anthropology of the Old Testament*. Philadelphia: Fortress.

Wolfson, Ben. 1998. "Kosher Slaughter." *Mishpahah* 364:16–17. http://grandin.com/ritual/kosher.slaughter.html.

Womack, Mari. 2005. *Symbols and Meaning: A Concise Introduction*. Walnut Creek, CA: AltaMira.

Wood, Betty. 2011. "The Origins of Slavery in the Americas, 1500–1700." In *The Routledge History of Slavery*, edited by Gad Heuman and Trevor Burnard (pp. 64–79). New York: Routledge.

Wood, Leon J. 1980a. "זוּב." *TWOT* 1:237.

_____. 1980b. "זָנָה." *TWOT* 1:246–47.

_____. 1980c. "חָרַם I." *TWOT* 1:324–25.

_____. 1980d. "חָרַם II." *TWOT* 1:325.

Yamauchi, Edwin M. 1973. "Cultic Prostitution: A Case Study in Cultural Diffusion." In *Orient and Occident: Essays Presented to Cyrus H. Gordon on the Occasion of His Sixty-Fifth Birthday*, edited by Harry A. Hoffner Jr., 213–22. AOAT 22. Neukirchen-Vluyn: Neukirchener Verlg; Kevelaer: Butzon & Bercker.

_____. 1980a. "חָגַר." *TWOT* 1:263.

_____. 1980b. "חָוָה III." *TWOT* 1:267–69.

_____. 1980c. "טָהֵר." *TWOT* 1:343–45.

_____. 1980d. "רָבַח." *TWOT* 2:828–29.

_____. Young, Rodger C. 2006. "The Talmud's Two Jubilees and Their Relevance to the Date of the Exodus." *WTJ* 68, no. 1:71–83.

Youngblood, Ronald F. 1980. "תָּעַב." *TWOT* 2:976–77.

Zamarripa, Maria. 2019. "What Is Semolina Flour? Everything You Need to Know." *Healthline.* https://www.healthline.com/nutrition/semolina.

Zertal, Adam. 2018. *A Nation Born: The Altar on Mount Ebal and the Birth of Israel.* Ofra: Lipkin.

Zobel, H.-J. 1986. "חֶסֶד." *TDOT* 5:44–64.